"Brent Strawn has long been recognized for his attention to exegetical detail, his keen interest in theological interpretation, and his profound concern for matters of Christian practice and belief. This collection of essays, carefully curated by Collin Cornell and Justin Walker, reveals the remarkable range of Strawn's work, as well as its depth. This volume will challenge scholars to expand their interpretive frameworks, to find fresh and creative ways of engaging Scripture following Strawn's lead. More importantly, these essays will inspire students and pastors to take up Scripture, to read it with critical eyes, and to encounter the incomparable God with hearts full of faith."

—**Joel M. LeMon**
Candler School of Theology, Emory University

"This excellent collection of articles showcases Strawn's deep exegetical insights. Strawn challenges us to ponder God's incomparability and encourages us to explore how the metaphoric language about God in the Hebrew Bible together fashions varied, often conflicting, yet always wondrous images of God. At the same time, this collection is deeply Christian in character, where many of the articles emphasize the canonical relationship between the Hebrew Bible and the New Testament."

—**Lena-Sofia Tiemeyer**
Örebro School of Theology, Sweden

THE INCOMPARABLE GOD

Readings in Biblical Theology

BRENT A. STRAWN

Edited by

COLLIN CORNELL *and* M. JUSTIN WALKER

WILLIAM B. EERDMANS PUBLISHING COMPANY
GRAND RAPIDS, MICHIGAN

Wm. B. Eerdmans Publishing Co.
4035 Park East Court SE, Grand Rapids, Michigan 49546
www.eerdmans.com

29 28 27 26 25 24 23   1 2 3 4 5 6 7

ISBN 978-0-8028-7949-3

Library of Congress Cataloging-in-Publication Data

A catalog record for this book is available from the Library of Congress.

For Walter Moberly—
master exegete and Christian theologian
and also faithful friend—
on the occasion of his retirement

There is no other God! This . . . is the unity of the Testaments.

—Kornelis H. Miskotte, *When the Gods Are Silent*

Contents

PART 3: PRACTICE

Author's Preface

M y thanks go first and foremost, of course, to my former students (T.) Collin
Cornell and M. Justin (T. R. M.) Walker for first imagining, next designing,
and then finally editing these essays for publication. I am deeply grateful for their
hard work and even more honored that they took time from their own busy lives
and vocations to perform this task for one of their old professors. In truth, Collin
and Justin transcended "former student status" years ago: they have long been
my trusted colleagues and, even more importantly, good friends. Indeed, I have
considered both of them my professional peers for many years now and in many
ways I deem them my superiors, both intellectually and pedagogically. That makes
my debt to them even more profound. I am also indebted to Andrew Knapp, a
longtime colleague and editor extraordinaire, for taking interest in this volume
and seeing it through so expertly with the wonderful press that is Eerdmans. Jenny
Hoffman and Kathy Noftsinger deserve special mention for their excellent work
on the manuscript. My research assistant Caleb Punt provided crucial assistance
at the very end of the project.

It is an exciting, but also humbling, thing to look over some of my past publications as they are gathered together—warts and all—along with six previously
unpublished contributions, into this collection.[1] Hindsight, as the old saying goes,
is 20/20 (or at least not horribly myopic), and such a review process thus brings
repeated interests, patterns, and emphases to light—even and perhaps especially
those that an author isn't aware of while "in the midst of." In their preface, Collin
and Justin have identified several of these repeated items and themes in my work

---

1. The previously published pieces have been only lightly revised, mostly in terms of format
and style. Even so, these versions are, I hope, improved over the originals, despite whatever
problems remain from their initial formulations.

that I found illuminating: news to me, as it were. I must admit that, in the throes of penning these various pieces—often under the crush of a deadline, or, rather *after* the crush of a missed deadline!—I don't recall having the idea of God's incomparability consistently in mind, but it is a trope that my editors have traced in intriguing and convincing ways.[2] While it wasn't always to the fore when I composed these various pieces, I must nevertheless also say that I have long been taken with the notion of God's incomparability as expressed in works by C. L. Labuschagne, Werner H. Schmidt, and Walter Brueggemann[3]—not to mention its presence in Hebrew names like Micah, which happens to be the name of my youngest child. I see now, thanks to Collin and Justin, that Micah's name is no accident!

If God's incomparability was something of a new and hidden treasure revealed by my editors, the other recurring trope identified by Collin and Justin—namely, Scripture's incomparability—*is* something I've been aware of in my writing, at least inchoately and sometimes more than that. What I haven't seen, however, prior to Collin and Justin, is how this trope, which I have tended to associate with the struggle (my own) to access Scripture's *totality*, is related equally also to incomparability, particularly divine incomparability. And so, to repeat myself, it is exciting, but also humbling, to look at this collection of essays now: *exciting*, because of the new insights gleaned from my friends' all-too-kind introduction; *humbling* because I have fallen immeasurably short in even approaching a capture of Scripture's, let alone God's, incomparability. And yet I guess that's the point: these things are, after all, incomparable—"uncapturable" by definition.

One thing that is very clear to me as I think back on more than twenty-five years of publishing is the influence of the individuals who have played significant roles in my life and who have deeply impacted my thinking, writing, and teaching. In its fullest form a list of those individuals would be very lengthy indeed, and would most certainly include the editors of the present volume. On the list also—and easily near its very top—would be Walter Moberly. Several of the pieces

2. Sometimes I did, as in my essay "'Mischmetaphors': (Re-)Presenting God in Unusual and Sophisticated Ways," in *Image as Theology: The Power of Art in Shaping Christian Thought, Devotion, and Imagination*, ed. C. A. Strine, Mark McInroy, and Alexis Torrance, Arts and the Sacred 6 (Turnhout: Brepols, 2021), 19–54, which is also slated for publication in a volume of my essays devoted to iconography: Brent A. Strawn, *The Visible Word: Essays in Iconography, the Hebrew Bible, and the History of Israelite Religion*, FAT (Tübingen: Mohr Siebeck, in press). A preliminary, student-facing version of this chapter appeared as: Izaak J. de Hulster and Brent A. Strawn, "Figuring YHWH in Unusual Ways."

3. E.g., C. J. Labuschagne, *The Incomparability of Yahweh in the Old Testament*, POS 5 (Leiden: Brill, 1966); Werner H. Schmidt, *The Faith of the Old Testament: A History*, trans. John Sturdy (Philadelphia: Westminster, 1983), esp. 177–81; and Walter Brueggemann, *Theology of the Old Testament: Testimony, Dispute, Advocacy* (Minneapolis: Fortress, 1997).

collected here, particularly two of the unpublished ones that were first presented to colloquia he hosted at Durham University, are clearly in "Moberly mode." One of these essays traffics a bit in J. R. R. Tolkien's Middle-earth, a world that Walter, like me, has loved from childhood: he even corresponded at one point with Tolkien about *The Silmarillion* and has the return letter from Tolkien to prove it. My dedication of these essays—indeed, the book as a whole—to Walter captures only a very small fraction of my great esteem for him.

A last and most important word of thanks goes to my *incomparable* wife, Holly, as ever and for ever.

bas
Epiphany 2022 | Durham, NC

Introduction

COLLIN CORNELL AND M. JUSTIN WALKER

The Rev. Dr. Brent A Strawn is nothing if not *rangy*: a scholar who is large, containing multitudes! The fact is apparent from any number of angles. His academic appointment spans Old Testament *and* Law (at Duke University). His books zigzag over immense intellectual terrain: *The Old Testament Is Dying* borrows metaphors from linguistics, samples recent sermons and hymnody, revisits Marcion and Tertullian, wrangles New Atheists and Joel Osteen, and exegetes Deuteronomy.[1] His journal articles and chapter publications ping across fields that are even more remote from one another: Herodotus, Käsemann, Ugaritic, Dead Sea Scrolls—their breadth is rare and daunting, even by scholarly standards.[2] And hence, too, is the

---

1. Brent A. Strawn, *The Old Testament Is Dying: A Diagnosis and Recommended Treatment*, Theological Explorations for the Church Catholic (Grand Rapids: Baker Academic, 2017).

2. See, for example, for Herodotus: "Herodotus' *Histories* 2.141 and the Deliverance of Jerusalem: On Parallels, Sources, and Histories of Ancient Israel," in *Israel's Prophets and Israel's Past: Essays on the Relationship of Prophetic Texts and Israelite History in Honor of John H. Hayes*, ed. Brad E. Kelle and Megan B. Moore, LHBOTS 466 (London and New York: T&T Clark, 2006), 210–38; for Käsemann: "Docetism, Käsemann, and Christology: Can Historical Criticism Help Christological Orthodoxy (and Other Theology) After All?" *JTI* 2 (2008): 161–80, now reprinted as chapter 12 of the present work; for Ugaritic: "*kwšrwt* in Psalm 68:7, Again: A (Small) Test Case in Relating Ugarit to the Hebrew Bible," *UF* 41 (2009): 631–48; "*wĕnil'ā(h)*, 'O Victorious One,'" in Ps 68,10," *UF* 34 (2002): 785–98; and a forthcoming handbook on Ugaritic (coauthored with Joel M. LeMon and Christopher B. Hays); for Dead Sea Scrolls: "David as One of the 'Perfect of (the) Way': On the Provenience of *David's Compositions* (and *11QPsa* as a Whole?)," *RevQ* 24/96 (2010): 607–26; and "Excerpted Manuscripts at Qumran: Their Significance for the Textual His-

challenge of identifying the theological nerve center of all that activity, the whence and wherefore from which such "Strawnian" industry arises. This is what we editors seek to do in this collection and in this brief introduction.

Our title makes an argument: that *the incomparable God* stands at the heart of Strawn's theological vision. Not that this has always or often been an explicit motif of his; indeed, patently it has not. But it does, at least as a heurism, connect a number of themes to which Strawn's writings return, time and again. This God, the God of Scripture, the God of Christian confession, is *one to whom none is like*. The psalmist's exclamation would make a fitting epigraph: "My Lord! There is no one like you among the gods! There is nothing that can compare to your works!" (Ps 86:8 CEB). We trace this divine unlikeness through several domains below. But first another and more general observation about divine incomparability—in Strawn's writings and in the psalmist's cry—is in order.

For them both, God is *addressee*. This is directly the case for the psalm. It is a prayer, calling out to God in petition and praise. Strawn's writings, including the chapters of this volume, are learned works of exegesis and biblical theology and not prayer proper or *eo ipso*. And yet, for all their scholarly rigor, Strawn's chapters maintain a lively sense of God's reality and nearness; of human responsiveness and relationality vis-à-vis God. This spirit comes most to the fore, perhaps, in the third section of this collection on "practice." But it can be felt earlier in the volume, especially in chapter six with its treatment of *lectio divina* (prayed reading), or in chapter ten's engagement with participation. At any rate: if not prayer proper, Strawn's writings, here and elsewhere, even at their most analytical and detailed, are oriented toward God and the life lived before God.

They also, like the psalm, keep their *human readership* in view. The speaker in Ps 86 who exclaims to God "there is no one like you" numbers himself among "all those who cry out to you" (v. 5b), and in its current, canonical presentation, this one psalmic instance of crying out to God provides a template for other, subsequent cryer-outers. The prayer-performance of the psalm models for others and after-comers. Strawn's exegeses and biblical-theological forays do likewise: they are offered for the church, the community of those who seek to speak of—and to—the Triune God of Christian confession. To be sure, they do not always flag this target audience. But even when they do not, these chapters render up examples for that readership all the same: (virtuoso) performances of biblical interpretation that demonstrate the viability, speak-ability, and pray-ability of the whole canon of Scripture.

---

tory of the Hebrew Bible and the Socio-Religious History of the Qumran Community and Its Literature," in *The Bible and the Dead Sea Scrolls*, vol. 2: *The Dead Sea Scrolls and the Qumran Community*, ed. James H. Charlesworth (Waco, TX: Baylor University Press, 2006), 107–67.

Incomparably Articulated

This leads to one of the main correlates of Strawn's vision of divine incomparability: the canonicity of the entire Christian Bible. The relationship of these two considerations might at first seem oblique. Divine incomparability is a theological claim (maybe even a theologically theological claim). Canonicity is a property of a certain body of literature: a working expectation of that literature that it is normative, formative, divinely pedagogical. Strawn's affirmation of the latter in connection with the Old and New Testaments complements (we propose) the "incomparable" portrait of God found in his biblical interpretation.

Strawn's canonical commitments are most explicitly discussed in his earlier book *The Old Testament Is Dying*, when he likens the Old Testament (and the broader Christian canon) to a language—especially a dying language—subject to dramatic reduction (pidginization) or mutation into an altogether different form (creolization). As Strawn demonstrates in that book, many Christians are largely unfamiliar with large parts of the Old Testament, and what little they do know is so fragmentary that other dominant "languages" or ideologies easily absorb and repurpose it (that is, they constitute language interference). Strawn therefore advocates for training and practice unto Old Testament "fluency," characterized not simply by knowledge of the canon's contents but by dexterous use of its rich "vocabulary" unto right(eous) ends—ultimately, to be a *poet*, as it were.

Strawn models the importance of canonicity in his own exegetical practice. For him, seeking biblical "fluency" means returning to the basics: reflecting on the regular and frequently used features of biblical discourse—for example, the metaphor of God as a parent (chapter 8), the oft-repeated articulation of Yhwh's character in the *Gnadenformel* (chapter 2), or the rhetoric of Deuteronomy (chapters 3 and 4). But Strawn's language school also covers rarer or more technical biblical vocabularies: the law (as in chapter 14) or the book of Job (chapter 9). Most importantly, Strawn reclaims what many assume to be the "bad words" in Old Testament lexicon: the imprecatory psalms (chapter 5), for example, the conquest traditions (chapter 11), and prophetic violence (chapter 6), among others. All these efforts are proof of concept for the canonicity, the ongoing instructiveness, of these biblical voices. In the case of such biblical "curse words" (even quite literally understood, as is the case with Elisha and the bears in chapter 6), Strawn's exegetical work showcases the usefulness and even needfulness of difficult texts. Whether in his analyses of more "mainstream" passages or his expeditions into irregular and vexatious units of biblical "speech," Strawn's readings insist on the profitability of *all* Scripture for teaching, reproof, and instruction (2 Tim 3:16).

But of what kind of God do all these diverse parts of biblical "language" speak? What manner of divine Subject do these linguistic constellations, in their various pathways and ellipses, orbit? One may think here of Irenaeus's "beautiful image of the king," constructed as a mosaic out of many individual scriptural jewels (*Against Heresies* 1.8). In this perspective, Strawn works as a conservator, dusting off the well-worn central tiles and restoring the darker, contrasting pieces that had fallen entirely out of frame. But to the most important point: *the whole canon musters a portrait of God.* And in its very prolixity, its complex visual contour, the divine image that the biblical canon produces is distinctive—even incomparable. If some pieces, even and especially irregular, challenging ones, are missing from the mosaic, the result is simpler, more familiar, and more assimilable—but seriously deficient. The psalmist's cry—"My Lord! There is no one like you among the gods!"—is far less convincing, no longer accurate. The God whom the Scriptures taken all together depict is truly one to whom none is like. Incomparable articulation across the range of Christian Scripture protects and precipitates divine incomparability. The incomparable word is in service to the incomparable God; the incomparable God is "made" of the incomparable word.

Incomparably Triune

Strawn is, as noted, a professor of Old Testament (and Law), and as such is hardly known as a theologian of the Trinity—a doctrine that many of his biblical colleagues in the guild would not countenance. We are thus glad to include in the present volume a little-known but important essay of his entitled "And These Three Are One" (chapter 7). Here Strawn strives against those christological interpretations of the Old Testament (and they are legion) that would limit the Old Testament's theological significance to its relationship to the Second Person of the Trinity; Brevard Childs's incautious (yet frequent) claims that the Old Testament *bears witness to Jesus Christ* serve as a stimulus and foil to Strawn's argument.

There are the standard literary and historical problems with a reduction of this kind: "The Old Testament," Strawn writes, "is about much more than just Christ—historically *and* literarily" (p. 176 below). But there are also theological problems, as he goes on to note—namely, that the Trinitarian persons mutually indwell and interpenetrate. Their operations are inseparable. Consequently, the Old Testament *can* and *does* bear witness to Christ but primarily (if not only) *in that* it refers to the Triune God. As per Augustine: "The Son does not do anything which the Father and the Holy Spirit do not also do" (*Epistle* 11.2).[3] Hence, the

---

3. Strawn cites from Lewis Ayres, "'Remember That You Are Catholic' (*serm.* 52.2): Augustine on the Unity of the Triune God," *JECS* 8 (2000): 39–82, here 46.

individual testimonies of the Old Testament need not be allocated primarily to one or another of the Trinitarian persons, as if to say, this angelophany is Christ, that stern narrative is God the Father, and the actions of that judge are the Spirit's power at work. Neither must one insist that Old Testament allusions to divine plurality directly adumbrate the divine hypostases of Christian confession (saying, e.g., that the three visitors in Gen 18 *are* the Triune persons). Strawn proposes instead a subtle and capacious Trinitarian approach, one commensurate with the doctrine of circumincession/perichoresis or reciprocal divine existence.

In this way, he seeks to do justice to the complexity of *the whole canon.* The Old Testament champions the unity of God, not least in the Shema (Deut 6:4). But the New Testament shows Jesus Christ as God's unique Son, and the Spirit appears as God's agent and power in both testaments. The early church slowly and painstakingly pieced these data together, discerning the profile of a single-yet-threefold God. The incomparable articulation of God in and through the two-testamented and internally variegated canon of Scripture led, historically, to Christian confessions of the Triune God. Strawn argues for a return to Scripture with these historic confessions in hand: a recursive hermeneutical move, but one that follows the trajectory of early Christianity, whose Trinitarian rule of faith was (in Robert Louis Wilken's words), "drawn from the Bible [and] reverberated back on the Bible as a key to its interpretation."[4] If, then, the canonicity of all Scripture yields a God like no other, one integral truth about that God in Christian faith and practice is God's three-in-one-ness. Some might call (and have called) the teaching of divine triunity a "metaphysical monstrosity." But if it does nothing else (and it does quite a lot more), the Triune understanding of God underlines and instantiates divine incomparability. Such triunity could, in this way, conceivably galvanize more recent, belated versions of the psalmist's exclamation: "There is no one like you among the gods!"

Incomparably Imaged

As early as his published dissertation, Strawn's interest in biblical metaphors for God focuses explicitly on incomparability. In his exhaustive study of lion imagery and metaphor in the Hebrew Bible and ancient Near East, he notes the importance of these data for understanding God's portrayal in Israel's texts: "The *theological* implications of leonine metaphor are thus underscored: this is a metaphor reserved, in

---

4. Robert Louis Wilken, *The Spirit of Early Christian Thought* (New Haven: Yale University Press, 2003), 66. Strawn quotes this sentence in his "YHWH, Chemosh, and the Rule of Faith," in *Divine Doppelgängers: YHWH's Ancient Look-alikes,* ed. Collin Cornell (University Park: Eisenbrauns/Penn State University Press, 2020), 138–58, here 153.

the main, for the Deity."[5] Still further, and in marked contrast to the Hebrew Bible's Canaanite context, he argues that "we know of no other Canaanite deity that is figured like a lion to the extent that Yahweh is."[6] Even as Strawn traces possible religio-historical or sociological lines of development behind this distinctive Yahwistic image, he recognizes the uncertainty of these hypotheses and holds out the possibility that Yahweh's leonine depiction may have been *sui generis*,[7] emerging from multiple (metaphorical) sources.[8] For Strawn, divine metaphors like that of the lion are more than a means of rendering God accessible or understandable. They equally also suggest the incomparable quality of the God of whom they speak.

There is a subtle irony here. As per the theme of this volume, Strawn's work variously demonstrates that the God of the Christian canon is without or beyond comparison. And yet, a major means by which Strawn indexes such incomparability is by recourse to biblical metaphors—figures of speech that, by definition, rely on comparison, bringing *this* together with *that*. By "picturing" God, the biblical authors bespeak (something of) God: the *this*. But they do not exhaust the *that*: the beyond-ness of God endures. Metaphors reveal God only in part, in part because they also obscure what remains "incomparable" between the comparanda. Strawn's exploration of biblical metaphors carefully threads this needle between the revealing and concealing capacities of metaphor—pressing the metaphor to "point out" God via the image while also pressing through the metaphor to "point beyond" the image toward God.[9]

Strawn's consideration of biblical metaphors addresses divine incomparability in one of two primary ways. The first method is more focused, exegeting the theological imagery of individual biblical texts. In these cases, it is not a single, governing metaphor for God that receives attention but the confluence of multiple divine metaphors. For example, in an essay on Deut 32 coauthored with Izaak de Hulster, Strawn itemizes the range of (mixed) metaphors used of God—a rock (v. 4), parent (v. 5), establisher (v. 6), and so forth. To help make sense of this dense, complex metaphor cluster, Strawn and de Hulster appeal to images of *Mischwesen*

---

5. Brent A. Strawn, *What Is Stronger Than a Lion? Leonine Image and Metaphor in the Hebrew Bible and the Ancient Near East*, OBO 212 (Fribourg: Academic, 2005), 250 (emphasis original).

6. Strawn, *What Is Stronger Than a Lion?* 251.

7. Strawn, *What Is Stronger Than a Lion?* 267.

8. Strawn, *What Is Stronger Than a Lion?* 270.

9. Strawn emphasizes the importance of imagery in the scriptural imagination, going as far to say that "Scripture itself lives on images," and this imagistic "life" has paramount theological import: "Imagery may, then, in the final analysis, be poetry's greatest contribution to theology." See Brent A. Strawn, "Imagery," in *Dictionary of the Old Testament: Wisdom, Poetry and Writings*, ed. Tremper Longman III and Peter Enns (Downers Grove, IL: IVP Academic, 2008), 312.

(mixed creatures) in ancient Near Eastern iconography. The unusual and complex forms of these hybrid beings in artistic representation resist categorization and so *"instantly embody and signal the presence of the divine."*[10] Most importantly, the iconographic *Mischwesen* help to reveal how the poem's metaphorical complex—a kind of "Mischmetaphor"—underscores God's incomparable nature: "In the final analysis, then, complex divine metaphors serve not only as ways to image/imagine the divine but as ways to chasten such imaging/imagining, especially if that imaging/imagining is confined to one particular image or one set of images (this chastening function is primary). In this way, Mischmetaphors appear to be literary enactments of the image-ban, even though they are ironically themselves *overfull* with images. Perhaps they also somehow enact the incomparability formula by showing that no one and no thing—not by itself at any rate—can be compared to Israel's God."[11] Strawn therefore takes literary images seriously as revelatory of God without making them more than what they are—(mere) images. Metaphors remain just that, instances of comparison and also somehow simultaneously *the failure of comparison*, which, taken together, bear witness to divine incomparability.

Strawn's second approach to biblical metaphors operates more thematically, examining important, recurring divine images across the biblical canon.[12] These

10. Izaak J. de Hulster and Brent A. Strawn, "Figuring YHWH in Unusual Ways: Deuteronomy 32 and Other Mixed Metaphors for God in the Old Testament," in *Iconographic Exegesis of the Hebrew Bible/Old Testament: An Introduction to Its Method and Practice*, ed. Izaak J. de Hulster, Brent A. Strawn, and Ryan P. Bonfiglio (Göttingen: Vandenhoeck & Ruprecht, 2015), 127, emphasis theirs. A fuller, solo-authored version of the argument appears in Brent A. Strawn, "'Mischmetaphors': (Re-)Presenting God in Unusual and Sophisticated Ways," in *Image as Theology: The Power of Art in Shaping Christian Thought, Devotion, and Imagination*, ed. C. A. Strine, Mark McInroy, and Alexis Torrance, Arts and the Sacred 6 (Turnhout: Brepols, 2021), 19–54, which will also appear in a volume of Strawn's iconographic essays: Brent A. Strawn, *The Visible Word: Essays in Iconography, the Hebrew Bible, and the History of Israelite Religion*, FAT (Tübingen: Mohr Siebeck, in press).

11. De Hulster and Strawn, "Figuring YHWH," 132. See, again, more fully, Strawn, "Mischmetaphors."

12. On God as a parent, see chapter 8 in this volume. On God as a lion, see Strawn, *What Is Stronger Than a Lion?*; Strawn, "Whence Leonine Yahweh? Iconography and the History of Israelite Religion," in *Images and Prophecy in the Ancient Eastern Mediterranean*, ed. Martti Nissinen and Charles A. Carter, FRLANT 233 (Göttingen: Vandenhoeck & Ruprecht, 2009), 51–85; Strawn, "Lion Hunting in the Psalms: Iconography and Images for God, the Self, and the Enemy," in de Hulster, Strawn, and Bonfiglio, *Iconographic Exegesis*, 245–62. On the image of God's arm, see "Yahweh's Outstretched Arm Revisited Iconographically," in *Iconography and Biblical Studies: Proceedings of the Iconography Sessions at the Joint EABS/SBL Conference, 22–26 July 2007, Vienna, Austria*, ed. Izaak J. de Hulster and Rüdiger Schmitt, AOAT 361 (Münster: Ugarit-Verlag, 2009), 163–211; Strawn, "'With a Strong Hand and an Outstretched Arm': On the Meaning(s) of the Exodus Tradition(s)," in de Hulster, Strawn, and Bonfiglio, *Iconographic Exegesis*, 103–16.

studies probe a given scriptural macro-metaphor, and in doing so, map out its outer theological edges and limitations. In his analysis of the *imago Dei*, for example (chapter 1), Strawn asks how humans "image" God in Genesis. The results are multifarious: "There is no one singular *imago Dei* but, rather, many *imagines* [plural of *imago*]."[13] Multiple humans "image God" in Genesis, especially Joseph. The point deserves underlining: the most explicit, canonical (and creational) "image" for God proves to have no outstanding, single exemplification. Even the humans who most approximate God's will in the world present but a partial and provisional picture of God, in need of filling out with yet other examples. If this is the case for the anthropological "image of God" par excellence in Scripture, how much more so for all the other literary images of God contained in the Bible! This is a God about whom no single individual comparison says it all, or says enough. Which is to say: this is an incomparable God.

In sum, the *ranginess* of our teacher is not only or simply temperamental, or an accident of his academic history (some nefarious "they" have "had to keep him broad for XYZ institutional reasons"). It is instead, we argue, the detritus of a theological discovery, or better yet, a doxological discovery: in praising God, we cherish each trace, each gift, each image. But we also always look for *further* divine traces, gifts, and images, because the greatness of this God "can't be grasped" (*ʾên ḥēqer*; Ps 145:3b CEB) and because God's commandment "is boundless" (*rəḥābâ . . . məʾōd*; Ps 119:96 CEB). Strawn's exegetical and even disciplinary restlessness issues from a conviction about the greatness of the Lord and of God's word.

Whether in person or via his writings, that conviction takes a pedagogical shape. Strawn wishes to induct others into the praise of God. Like the psalmist of Ps 86, and of so many other psalms, he speaks and writes praises to God, but also teaches others to praise God after him; he keeps his human readership in view. We are grateful to have received something of that education from him, and we offer this collection of essays in the same spirit, hoping to raise up nimble and fulsome exponents of the biblical canon.

---

13. See in this volume chapter 1, p. 15. On the *imago Dei*, see further Strawn, "The Image of God: Comparing the Old Testament with Other Ancient Near Eastern Cultures," in de Hulster, Strawn, and Bonfiglio, *Iconographic Exegesis*, 63–76; Strawn, "Comparative Approaches: History, Theory, and the Image of God," in *Method Matters: Essays on the Interpretation of the Hebrew Bible in Honor of David L. Petersen*, ed. Joel M. LeMon and Kent Harold Richards, RBS 56 (Atlanta: Society of Biblical Literature, 2009), 117–42.

Plan of the Work

We have drawn attention in this introduction to three "registers" of divine incomparability that we discern in Strawn's corpus. The God of Christian Scripture is like no other in terms of the sheer diversity of biblical stories, songs, musings, and so much else that discursively shroud him round about; God is incomparable and/because God is incomparably articulated. In Christian confession, this God is also incomparably Triune, a claim that itself responds to the unique exegetical pressures of the whole Christian Bible. Finally, much of Strawn's work has concentrated on images for God, artefactual and textual. He finds that biblical writers mix metaphors for God so prodigiously that their conglomerate divine portraiture has no ancient equal or counterpart; and that even the metaphors for God that the biblical authors foreground (such as humans-as-divine-image or God-as-parent) are somehow irreducibly plural and plastic. God is incomparably imaged, as well.

The following chapters from Strawn's publications are arranged into three major sections, each representing a different angle onto his theological vision of incomparability. The first section follows *an exegetical mode*, providing readings of specific biblical texts or themes. Chapter 1 examines the theological significance of the *imago Dei* motif within the book of Genesis, exploring the multiple *imagines* of God across the book's human actors. In chapter 2, Strawn conducts a reading of the famous *Gnadenformel* (Exod 34:6–7b) with special attention to its lyricism and the theological tension it expresses: even the "creedal God" is non-static and thus dynamic. Chapters 3 and 4 take up important rhetorical features of Deuteronomy. The first demonstrates the ethical and theological effect of Deuteronomy's repetitive discourse in forming obedient readers. The second draws attention to Deuteronomy's rhetorical conscription of its listeners as both "slaves" and "rebels." The book's first section concludes with two previously unpublished pieces. Chapter 5 focuses on the (in)famous Ps 137, tending to the beauty and movement of the poem before considering the function of what Strawn (perhaps surprisingly) finds to be poetically reticent. Chapter 6 discusses one of the Old Testament's most troubling and eccentric stories: Elisha and the bears in 2 Kgs 2. After critiquing some rather unimaginative analyses of secondary literature, Strawn asks whether the practice of prayed reading (*lectio divina*) might allow for a more empathetic and nuanced understanding of this tale.

The chapters in the book's second section gather Strawn's contributions to *biblical theology*. Each essay explores intersections between Old Testament exegesis and broader theological topics. Chapter 7 focuses on the implications of Trinitarian theology for Christological readings of the Old Testament. Chapter 8 examines a primary metaphor of the biblical canon—God as parent with Israel as child—and considers the limits and potentials along with the ethical implications of this imagery. Chapter 9 brings biblical theology to bear upon stratified and de-religionized construals of Israelite religion. Strawn draws attention to the book of Job as a work of extravagant and vivid theological imagination that complicates any and all flat accounts. Chapter 10 brings Old Testament scholarship into dialogue with Gregory of Nyssa, specifically his use of the life of Moses to articulate the soul's progress and participation in God; here again Strawn advocates a Trinitarian approach to biblical theology. Chapter 11, published here for the first time, approaches the problem of violence in the conquest narratives of Joshua through comparison with Tolkien's Middle-earth, in particular the at times parallel, at times divergent literary presentation of the Canaanites and Tolkien's Orcs. Chapter 12 revisits the work of the New Testament scholar Ernst Käsemann to show how constructive theology can draw positively on historical criticism.

The third and final section of the volume samples from Strawn's *pastoral and pedagogical work*. His canonical range is on display with sermons on Job (chapter 13), Deuteronomy (chapter 15), Leviticus (chapter 16, previously unpublished), and various texts that feature Pharaoh's different sides (chapter 14, previously unpublished), whether ambivalent (Genesis), oppressive (Exodus), or even repentant and restored (Isaiah and Ezekiel). These sermons draw upon New Testament examples to fill out Job's incomparable God (1 John 1:1–5), God's radical grace that welcomes all repentant pharaohs (Matt 20:15–16; Eph 6:10–18), or the priestly task incumbent upon all believers (Mark 1; 1 Peter 2). The volume concludes with two pedagogical pieces: the first gives a framework for teaching (and preaching) the Old Testament, with special attention to its urgency, integrity, honesty, and poetry (chapter 17). The second (chapter 18, previously unpublished) is an exhortation unto integration and holistic living, encouraging the biblical studies teacher and student to resist bifurcating faith from scholarship. Taken together, these essays, we hope, honor our teacher's exegetical finesse, theological agility, and pastoral charity—all of which attest and are in service to confirm and commend the God to whom none is like.

Abbreviations

AB	Anchor Bible
ABD	*Anchor Bible Dictionary*. Edited by David Noel Freedman. 6 vols. New York: Doubleday, 1992
ABRL	Anchor Bible Reference Library
ABS	Archaeology and Biblical Studies
ACCS	Ancient Christian Commentary on Scripture
ACCSOT	Ancient Christian Commentary on Scripture, Old Testament
AEL	*Ancient Egyptian Literature*. Miriam Lichtheim. 3 vols. Berkeley: University of California Press, 1971–1980
ADAIK	Abhandlungen des Deutschen Archäologischen Instituts Kairo
AnBib	Analecta Biblica
ANEP	*Ancient Near East in Pictures Relating to the Old Testament*. Edited by James B. Pritchard. 2nd ed. Princeton: Princeton University Press, 1994
ANET	*Ancient Near Eastern Texts Relating to the Old Testament*. Edited by James B. Pritchard. 3rd ed. Princeton: Princeton University Press, 1969
ANF	*The Ante-Nicene Fathers*
ANTC	Abingdon New Testament Commentaries
AOAT	Alter Orient und Altes Testament
AOTC	Abingdon Old Testament Commentaries
AYBC	Anchor Yale Bible Commentary
b. Ber.	Babylonian Talmud *Berakot*
BASOR	*Bulletin of the American Schools of Oriental Research*
BBB	Bonner biblische Beiträge
BBRSup	*Bulletin for Biblical Research Supplement Series*
BCOTWP	Baker Commentary on the Old Testament Wisdom and Psalms

BDB	Brown, Francis, S. R. Driver, and Charles A. Briggs. *A Hebrew and English Lexicon of the Old Testament*
BEvT	Beiträge zur evangelischen Theologie
BHQ	*Biblica Hebraica Quinta*
Bib	*Biblica*
BibInt	*Biblical Interpretation*
BibSem	The Biblical Seminar
BIS	Biblical Interpretation Series
BJRL	*Bulletin of the John Rylands University Library of Manchester*
BJS	Brown Judaic Studies
BR	*Biblical Research*
BRLJ	The Brill Reference Library of Judaism
BTB	*Biblical Theology Bulletin*
BWL	*Babylonian Wisdom Literature*. Wilfred G. Lambert. Oxford: Clarendon, 1960
BZAW	Beihefte zur Zeitschrift für die alttestamentliche Wissenschaft
BZNW	Beihefte zur Zeitschrift für die neutestamentliche Wissenschaft
CAD	*The Assyrian Dictionary of the Oriental Institute of the University of Chicago*. Chicago: The Oriental Institute of the University of Chicago, 1956–2006
CBET	Contributions to Biblical Exegesis and Theology
CBQ	*Catholic Biblical Quarterly*
CBQMS	Catholic Biblical Quarterly Monograph Series
CC	Continental Commentaries
CD	*Church Dogmatics*. Karl Barth. Edinburgh: T&T Clark, 1932–
CHANE	Culture and History of the Ancient Near East
ConBOT	Coniectanea Biblica: Old Testament Series
COS	*The Context of Scripture*. Edited by William H. Hallo and K. Lawson Younger. 4 vols. Leiden: Brill, 1997–2017
CurTM	*Currents in Theology & Mission*
CWS	Classics of Western Spirituality
DBI	*Dictionary of Biblical Interpretation*. Edited by John Hayes. 2 vols. Nashville: Abingdon, 1999
DBW	Dietrich Bonhoeffer Works
DCHR	Clines, David J. A., and David M. Stec, eds. *Dictionary of Classical Hebrew Revised*. 9 vols. Sheffield: Sheffield Phoenix Press, 2018–
ECC	Eerdmans Critical Commentary
FAT	Forschungen zum Alten Testament
FCI	Foundations of Contemporary Interpretation

FOTL	Forms of the Old Testament Literature
FRLANT	Forschungen zur Religion und Literatur des Alten und Neuen Testaments
HALOT	*The Hebrew and Aramaic Lexicon of the Old Testament.* Ludwig Koehler, Walter Baumgartner, and Johann J. Stamm. Translated and edited under the supervision of Mervyn E. J. Richardson. 4 vols. Leiden: Brill, 1994–1999
HBM	Hebrew Bible Monographs
HBS	Herders Biblische Studien
HdO	Handbuch der Orientalistik
HOTTP	*Preliminary and Interim Report on the Hebrew Old Testament Text Project,* 5 vols. New York: United Bible Societies, 1974–1980
HSS	Harvard Semitic Studies
HTR	*Harvard Theological Review*
ICC	International Critical Commentary
IEJ	*Israel Exploration Journal*
IliffRev	*Iliff Review*
Int	*Interpretation*
ISBL	Indiana Studies in Biblical Literature
JAAR	*Journal of the American Academy of Religion*
JAJSup	Journal of Ancient Judaism Supplements
JANER	*Journal of Ancient Near Eastern Religions*
JAOS	*Journal of the American Oriental Society*
JBL	*Journal of Biblical Literature*
JECS	*Journal of Early Christian Studies*
JETS	*Journal of the Evangelical Theological Society*
JHNES	The Johns Hopkins Near Eastern Studies
JP	*Journal for Preachers*
JPOS	*Journal of the Palestine Oriental Society*
JPS	Jewish Publication Society
JQR	*Jewish Quarterly Review*
JR	*Journal of Religion*
JSOT	*Journal for the Study of the Old Testament*
JSOTSup	Journal for the Study of the Old Testament Supplement Series
JTI	*Journal of Theological Interpretation*
JTISup	Journal of Theological Interpretation Supplement Series
JTS	*Journal of Theological Studies*
KTU	*Die keilalphabetischen Texte aus Ugarit.* Edited by Manfried Dietrich, Oswald Loretz, and Joaquín Sanmartín. Münster: Ugarit-Verlag,

	2013. 3rd enl. ed. of Manfried Dietrich, Oswald Loretz, and Joaquín Sanmartín, eds. *KTU: The Cuneiform Alphbetic Texts from Ugarit, Ras Ibn Hani, and Other Places*. Münster: Ugarit-Verlag, 1995 (= *CTU*)
LAE	*The Literature of Ancient Egypt: An Anthology of Stories, Instructions, Stelae, Autobiographies, and Poetry*. Edited by William Kelly Simpson. 3rd ed. New Haven: Yale University Press, 2003
LAI	Library of Ancient Israel
LHBOTS	The Library of Hebrew Bible/Old Testament Studies
MC	Mesopotamian Civilizations
MSU	Mitteilungen des Septuaginta-Unternehmens
NCB	New Cambridge Bible
NCBC	New Cambridge Bible Commentary
NEA	*Near Eastern Archaeology*
NIB	*New Interpreter's Bible*. 13 vols. Nashville: Abingdon, 1994–2004
NIDOTTE	*New International Dictionary of Old Testament Theology and Exegesis*. Edited by Willem A. VanGemeren. 5 vols. Grand Rapids: Zondervan, 1997
NRTh	*La nouvelle revue théologique*
NTS	*New Testament Studies*
NTSup	New Testament Studies Supplements
OBO	Orbis Biblicus et Orientalis
OBT	Overtures to Biblical Theology
OED	*Oxford English Dictionary*
OLA	Orientalia Lovaniensia Analecta
OLZ	*Orientalistische Literaturzeitung*
Or	*Orientalia*
OTL	Old Testament Library
OTT	Old Testament Theology
PdÄ	Probleme der Ägyptologie
POS	Pretoria Oriental Series
PSB	*Princeton Seminary Bulletin*
PTMS	Pittsburgh Theological Monograph Series
RBS	Resources for Biblical Study
RelSRev	*Religious Studies Review*
RevExp	*Review and Expositor*
RevQ	*Revue de Qumran*
RSPT	*Revue des sciences philosophiques et théologiques*
RSR	*Recherches de science religieuse*
SAA	State Archives of Assyria

SAACT	State Archives of Assyria Cuneiform Texts
SANT	Studien zum Alten und Neuen Testament
SBLDS	Society of Biblical Literature Dissertation Series
SBLMS	Society of Biblical Literature Monograph Series
SBLRBS	Society of Biblical Literature Resources for Biblical Study
SBLWAW	Society of Biblical Literature Writings from the Ancient World
SBT	Studies in Biblical Theology
SBTS	Sources for Biblical and Theological Study
SemeiaSt	Semeia Studies
SHBC	Smyth & Helwys Bible Commentary
SHCANE	Studies in the History and Culture of the Ancient Near East
SFSHJ	South Florida Studies in the History of Judaism
SH	Scripta Hierosolymitana
SJLA	Studies in Judaism in Late Antiquity
SJT	*Scottish Journal of Theology*
SR	*Studies in Religion*
SSN	Studia semitica neerlandica
StABH	Studies in American Biblical Hermeneutics
StBibLit	Studies in Biblical Literature
STDJ	Studies on the Texts of the Desert of Judah
ThTo	*Theology Today*
TJT	*Toronto Journal of Theology*
TLOT	*Theological Lexicon of the Old Testament*. Edited by Ernst Jenni and Claus Westermann. Translated by Mark E. Biddle. 3 vols. Peabody, MA: Hendrickson, 1997
TLZ	*Theologische Literaturzeitung*
TynBul	*Tyndale Bulletin*
UBL	Ugaritisch-biblische Literatur
UCOP	University of Cambridge Oriental Publications
UF	*Ugarit-Forschungen*
VC	*Vigiliae christianae*
VT	*Vetus Testamentum*
VTSup	Vetus Testamentum Supplement Series
WAW	Writings from the Ancient World
WBC	Word Biblical Commentary
WUNT	Wissenschaftliche Untersuchungen zum Neuen Testament
ZAW	*Zeitschrift für die alttestamentliche Wissenschaft*
ZKT	*Zeitschrift für katholische Theologie*
ZTK	*Zeitschrift für Theologie und Kirche*

PART 1

Readings

1

From *Imago* to *Imagines*:
The Image(s) of God in Genesis

The language of "the image of God" . . . [is] a relatively underdetermined place-holder for something that can only be more clearly defined by seeing how the canonical narrative develops, beyond Genesis, and indeed beyond the [Old Testament].[1]

T he image of God (Latin *imago Dei*) is a familiar, even fraught, biblical notion because it has served as something of an empty cipher that countless interpreters have sought to fill.[2] Despite a great deal of spilled ink, what, exactly, the *imago Dei* is remains no small mystery because the notion goes largely unde-

---

1. Richard S. Briggs, "Humans in the Image of God and Other Things Genesis Does Not Make Clear," *JTI* 4 (2010): 111–26 (112).

2. For important studies, see J. Richard Middleton, *The Liberating Image: The Imago Dei in Genesis 1* (Grand Rapids: Brazos, 2005); W. Randall Garr, *In His Own Image and Likeness: Humanity, Divinity, and Monotheism*, CHANE 15 (Leiden: Brill, 2003); and Gunnlaugur A. Jónsson, *The Image of God: Genesis 1:26–28 in a Century of Old Testament Research*, ConBOT 26 (Stockholm: Almqvist & Wiksell, 1988), whose main conclusion is that factors other than scholarship alone "have played an important role in the history of *imago Dei* studies" (218). Other helpful overviews include Claus Westermann, *Genesis 1–11: A Continental Commentary*, trans. John J. Scullion (Minneapolis: Fortress, 1994), 147–55; David J. A. Clines, "Humanity as the Image of God," in *On the Way to the Postmodern: Old Testament Essays, 1967–1998*, JSOTSup 292–93, 2 vols. (Sheffield: Sheffield Academic Press, 1998), 2:447–97 (originally published in *TynBul* 19 [1968]: 53–103); and Armand Puig I Tàrrech, ed., *Image de Déu*, Scripta Biblica 7 (Catalonia: Associació Bíblica de Catalunya, 2006). Most recently, see Ryan S. Petersen, *The Imago Dei as Human Identity: A Theological Interpretation*, JTISup 14 (Winona Lake, IN: Eisenbrauns, 2016).

veloped and underdeveloped in the Bible.[3] References to the *imago Dei* appear almost exclusively in Genesis—"almost" because interpreters often find traces of the concept elsewhere, including in the New Testament.[4] Be that as it may, the clearest and most important loci for the idea—if only because they are the originary texts—are four passages in the so-called Primeval History of Gen 1–11:[5]

1.   God said:

> Let us make humankind in our image (*bəṣalmēnû*),
> according to our likeness (*kidmûtēnû*),
> that they might rule over the fish of the sea,
> and over the birds of the air,
> and over the animals, and over all the earth,
> and over all the things that creep upon the earth.

So God created humankind in his image (*bəṣalmô*):

> in the divine image (*bəṣelem ʾĕlōhîm*), he created humankind—
> male and female, he created them. (Gen 1:26–27)

2.   This is the book of the genealogy of Adam:

On the day God created humankind

> he made him in the divine likeness (*bidmût ʾĕlōhîm*);
> male and female he created them.

---

3. Mark S. Smith, *The Genesis of Good and Evil: The Fall(out) and Original Sin in the Bible* (Louisville: Westminster John Knox, 2019), 52: a "somewhat abstract idea"; Andreas Schüle, *Theology from the Beginning: Essays on the Primeval History and Its Canonical Context*, FAT 113 (Tübingen: Mohr Siebeck, 2017), 13: "a *thick* but nonetheless *vague* symbol . . . provocatively fuzzy . . . highly suggestive and as such invit[ing] further interpretation" (his emphasis); Ellen F. Davis, *Opening Israel's Scriptures* (New York: Oxford University Press, 2019), 9: the "biblical phrasing is potent yet cryptic; in itself, it explains nothing, and perhaps for that very reason has proved to be endlessly intriguing." Andreas Wagner, *God's Body: The Anthropomorphic God in the Old Testament*, trans. Marion Salzmann (London: T&T Clark, 2019), 144, takes this lack of definition as proof that the concept is "not of central importance in the Old Testament." Cf. Westermann, *Genesis 1–11*, 148: "It has no . . . significance in the rest of the Old Testament." James Barr famously said "there is no answer to be found" for the question of the meaning of the *imago Dei* because "there is no reason to believe that this [biblical] writer had in his mind any definite idea about the content or the location of the image of God" ("The Image of God in the Book of Genesis—A Study of Terminology," *BJRL* 51 [1968]: 11–26). Surely Barr's is a counsel of despair.

4. Most especially 2 Cor 4:4 and Col 1:15 (of Christ; cf. Rom 8:29); see also 1 Cor 11:7; Jas 3:9; Wis 2:23; and Sir 17:3 (of humans; cf. Rom 8:29); and Wis 7:26 (of wisdom). I leave aside allusions to the notion (e.g., Ps 8) since these are by nature debatable. For Gen 1:26–27 in later Second Temple Literature, see Armin Lange and Matthias Weigold, *Biblical Quotations and Allusions in Second Temple Jewish Literature*, JAJSup 5 (Göttingen: Vandenhoeck & Ruprecht, 2011), 54–55.

5. They are also all typically associated with the Priestly source.

> He blessed them and named them "humanity"
> on the day he created them. (Gen 5:1–2)

3. Now when Adam was 130 years old,
   he fathered a son in his likeness (*bidmûtô*),
   according to his image (*kəṣalmô*).
   He named him Seth. (Gen 5:3)

4. The one who spills human blood
   a human will spill their blood,
   because in the divine image (*bəṣelem ʾĕlōhîm*)
   God made humankind. (Gen 9:6)[6]

The key Hebrew terms are *ṣelem* ("image") and *dəmût* ("likeness"),[7] and even a cursory investigation of these four texts conveys a decent amount of information, including:

a. *ṣelem* occurs more than *dəmût*: five times to three, respectively;

b. the literary form of texts (1) and (4) seems to be poetic, with texts (2) and (3)—or at least bits of them—also apparently on the high end of the poetry-prose spectrum;

c. it seems acceptable to speak of either "divine image" (*bəṣelem ʾĕlōhîm*, twice) or "divine likeness" (*bidmût ʾĕlōhîm*, once), which may suggest some synonymity between these compound terms if not also between *ṣelem* and *dəmût*;[8] and, finally,

---

6. Translations are my own, adhere closely to the Masoretic Text (MT), and intentionally tend toward the dynamic. For text-critical issues, see the commentaries and Abraham Tal, בראשית *Genesis, BHQ* 1 (Stuttgart: Deutsche Bibelgesellschaft, 2015), ad loc.

7. Translated in the Greek Septuagint and Latin Vulgate in intriguing ways that have often influenced subsequent interpretation: *ṣelem* by Greek εἰκών/*eikōn* ("image"; 1:26a, 27; 5:3b; 9:6) and Latin *imāgō* ("image"; 1:26a, 27; 5:3b; 9:6); *dĕmût* by Greek ὁμοίωσις/*homoiōsis* ("likeness") in 1:27b, εἰκών/*eikōn* in 5:1, and ἰδέα/*idea* ("appearance") in 5:3a; by Latin *similitūdō* ("likeness") in 1:26b; 5:1, 3a.

8. So, e.g., Konrad Schmid, *A Historical Theology of the Hebrew Bible*, trans. Peter Altmann (Grand Rapids: Eerdmans, 2019), 431. Barr, "Image," 24 thinks *dĕmût* functions "to define and limit" the meaning of "the more novel and the more ambiguous" *ṣelem*. See Tal, *Genesis*, 79*, for the tradition that treats the two terms as a unity; that perspective seems to be present in some early Versions (Symmachus, Theodotion, Syriac, Targum), with others (Samaritan Pentateuch, LXX, Aquila, Vulgate), however, consistently distinguishing the words. The Aramaic cognates *ṣlm'* and *dmwt'* appear together on an inscription from Tell Fekheriyeh, which many have taken as support that the two are somehow synonymous. See, e.g., Nahum M. Sarna, *Genesis*, JPS Torah Commentary (Philadelphia: Jewish Publication Society, 1989), 12. Cf., however, W. Randall Garr, "'Image' and 'Likeness' in the Inscription from Tell Fakhariyeh," *IEJ* 50 (2000): 227–34, who notes the distinct "rhetorical character" for these terms and the passages in which they appear, making them "pragmatically distinct," serving "different communicative functions" (233–34):

d. the reversal of the terms in text (3) compared to text (1) may function to *disassociate* Adam's likeness in his own offspring from the *imago Dei* in humanity.[9]

Indeed, text (3) seems quite different since it seems concerned with human (biological?) likeness. And yet, since it does employ the two key terms, many scholars think text (3) contributes something important to the proper interpretation of the *imago Dei*—namely, that it may have something to do with physical form.[10] Similarly, text (4) appears as part of a change in the diet of humanity after the flood and has a somewhat different effect than texts (1) and (2), having the force of law.[11]

Given how few and how brief—even *opaque*—these four texts are, it is not surprising that many different possibilities for the meaning of the image of God have been offered in the history of interpretation.[12] The *imago* has been a partic-

---

"'Likeness' introduces the section that focuses on the ruler's petitionary role; 'image' introduces the section that illustrates his commanding presence and authoritative status. . . . 'Likeness' is petitionary and directed at the deity; it is cultic and votive. 'Image' is majestic, absolute and commemorative; it is directed at the people" (231).

9. Cf. Barr, "Image," 25. This view is perhaps evident in Targum Onkelos, which does not render *baṣalmô* as it does in Gen 1:26, but uses an entirely different construction: "who resembled him" (*ddmy lyh*). Tal, *Genesis*, *91 deems this a theological change. Contrast Bill T. Arnold, *Genesis*, NCBC (Cambridge: Cambridge University Press, 2008), 85, who thinks text (3) "explain[s] how Adam actively continued God's creative work through fathering a child." For more on this text, see Jeffrey H. Tigay, "'He Begot a Son in His Likeness after His Image' (Genesis 5:3)," in *Tehillah le-Moshe: Biblical and Judaic Studies in Honor of Moshe Greenberg*, ed. Mordechai Cogan, Barry L. Eichler, and Jeffrey H. Tigay (Winona Lake, IN: Eisenbrauns, 1997), 139–47.

10. See the views discussed in Jónsson, *Image*, 54, 106, 112, etc. Texts like Exod 24:9–11 and Ezek 1:26–28 may also suggest some similarity between human and divine forms. On this matter, see already Maimonides in *Guide to the Perplexed* I,1; also Gerhard von Rad, *Genesis: A Commentary*, trans. John H. Marks, OTL (Philadelphia: Westminster, 1982), 58; and, more extensively, Wagner, *God's Body*; and Esther J. Hamori, *When Gods Were Men: The Embodied God in Biblical and Ancient Near Eastern Literature*, BZAW 384 (Berlin: de Gruyter, 2008). Cf. also Tigay, "He Begot." Related here is the idea that the image notion suggests some sort of divine parentage of the human being—that God "fathers" humanity as did Adam Seth—but see further below.

11. See Jónsson, *Image*, 59, 224–25n40; Jeffrey H. Tigay, "The Image of God and the Flood: Some New Developments," in ללמד וללמד: *Studies in Jewish Education and Judaica in Honor of Louis Newman*, ed. Alexander M. Shapiro and Burton I. Cohen (New York: Ktav, 1984), 174, 177; also James Barr, "Man and Nature: The Ecological Controversy and the Old Testament," *BJRL* 55 (1972): 9–32 (20): "Homicide was to be punished not because man [sic] had dominion over the animals, but because man [sic] was like God."

12. The main ones are humanity's physical form, the ability to walk upright, intelligence and reason, various spiritual characteristics, authority over the animal kingdom, and capacity to relate to God (Jónsson, *Image*, 2). Problems with associating the *imago* with, say, cognition

ularly generative topic in Christian theology.[13] In contrast, historical and comparative approaches to the subject have tended to set the notion in its literary and ancient Near Eastern contexts with more restricted results (see §1 below). While the constraints offered by the latter methodologies are instructive, it is clear that no study of the *imago* can be entirely confined to the four main texts if only because the *content* of these passages—limited as they are—nevertheless indicates that the "image of God" has two distinct referents: the divine (creator) and the human (creation), each of which is complex. The "image of God," that is, is *not*—not even in Genesis all by itself—a singular entity but, rather, a plural one. There is not just one *imago Dei* but *many images* of God. Indeed, if "image" is taken as a literary category, it is obvious that a large number of narrative and poetic representations of God are found in Genesis (see §2 below) with the same holding true for images of human beings as well (see §3 below). These various *imagines* (plural of *imago*)—of both referents, human and divine, and in their interrelationship(s) (see §4 below)—are taken up sequentially in what follows. First, however, the *imago Dei* should be put in its proper contexts.

1. The Image of God: Three Contextual Insights

Once the ancient Near Eastern material was discovered and deciphered, then compared to Israelite literature, wide speculation about the meaning of the *imago Dei* "found certain reasonable controls."[14] These controls, found in "numerous parallels from both Egypt and Mesopotamia," clarified that, in its cultural context, the *imago* was "related to royal language, in which a king or pharaoh is the 'image of

---

alone, are highlighted in works like George C. Hammond, *It Has Not Yet Appeared What We Shall Be: A Reconsideration of the Imago Dei in Light of Those with Severe Cognitive Disabilities* (Phillipsburg: P & R, 2017). As Jónsson's work demonstrates, "mental endowment" (*Image*, 33–43) is only one of *many* possible interpretations.

13. See, e.g., Geoffrey Wainwright, *Doxology: A Systematic Theology* (New York: Oxford University Press, 1980), 15–44; Jason S. Sexton, "The *Imago Dei* Once Again: Stanley Grenz's Journey toward a Theological Interpretation of Genesis 1:26–27," *JTI* 4 (2010): 187–206; and Ian A. McFarland, *The Divine Image: Envisioning the Invisible God* (Minneapolis: Fortress, 2005). The *imago* is also important within Judaism: see, e.g., Michael Wyschogrod, "The Impact of Dialogue with Christianity on the My Self-Understanding as a Jew," in *Die Hebräische Bibel und ihr zweifache Nachgeschichte: Festschrift für Rolf Rendtorff zum 65. Geburtstag*, ed. Erhard Blum, Christian Macholz, and Ekkehard W. Stegemann (Neukirchen-Vluyn: Neukirchener, 1990), 725–36 (736), who called Gen 1:26 "the single most powerful [statement] in the Bible." See further Tikva Frymer-Kensky et al., eds., *Christianity in Jewish Terms* (Boulder: Westview, 2000), 321–56.

14. Arnold, *Genesis*, 45.

(a) god.'"[15] That the concept derives from the royal domain is now the consensus view among investigators that are historically and comparatively driven; it is also the first of three important contextual insights about the image of God.

In truth, however, the comparative material is not uniform.[16] It clusters around two loci: the monarch as the image of a god and, in Mesopotamia, the monarch's use of his own image especially in statuary.[17] The first locus is manifest in the way the king could be described as, for example, "the image of [the god] Bel" (ṣalam Bēl) in Mesopotamia or, in Egypt, the way the pharaoh could be called "the likeness of [the god] Re" or even, via proper name: "the living image of [the god] Amun" (the meaning of *Tutankhamun*). The second locus is how kings set up images, particularly statues, of themselves as representations of the royal self in various places, including in devotional contexts or in conquered territories. In the case of occupied lands, the image of the king was to be carefully curated—alternatively, in instances of rebellion, the overlord's image was quickly defaced or destroyed. Wherever it was placed, however, the royal image served to "re-presence"[18] the monarch at a distance and/or in a particular role: sovereign, devotee, or both.

When applied to Genesis, this background suggests that humankind is the Divine Sovereign's stand-in within the created world, serving as God's viceroy, as it were, or, perhaps even more: as God's own "re-presence."[19] If correct, this line of

15. Arnold, *Genesis*, 45. Note that the verbs in Gen 1:28 that describe the roles of humankind, "subdue" (*k-b-š*) and "have dominion" (*r-d-h*; also in 1:26), are used elsewhere of royal activity (e.g., 2 Sam 8:11; 1 Kgs 4:21, 24; Ps 72:8); however, von Rad deems these commissioning verbs to belong, not "to the definition of God's image," but rather "its consequence" (*Genesis*, 59; cf. Jónsson, *Image*, 222).

16. For the ancient Near Eastern material that follows, see extensively, Middleton, *Liberating Image*, passim; also Brent A. Strawn, "Comparative Approaches: History, Theory, and the Image of God," in *Method Matters: Essays on the Interpretation of the Hebrew Bible in Honor of David L. Petersen*, ed. Joel M. LeMon and Kent Harold Richards, SBLRBS 56 (Atlanta: Society of Biblical Literature, 2009), 117–42; Strawn, "The Image of God: Comparing the Old Testament with Other Ancient Near Eastern Cultures," in *Iconographic Exegesis of the Hebrew Bible/Old Testament: An Introduction to Its Method and Practice*, ed. Izaak J. de Hulster, Brent A. Strawn, and Ryan P. Bonfiglio (Göttingen: Vandenhoeck & Ruprecht, 2015), 63–75; and Tigay, "Image," esp. 179nn8, 12.

17. There are also abundant references to images of deities proper—i.e., artistic depictions of the gods.

18. See Zainab Bahrani, *The Graven Image: Representation in Babylonia and Assyria* (Philadelphia: University of Pennsylvania Press, 2003), 121–48: "ṣalmu [the Akkadian cognate of Hebrew ṣelem] is better thought of as an ontological category rather than an aesthetic concept" (133); "ṣalmu is . . . a mode of presencing" (137); "the image repeats, rather than represents, the king" (144); "the image is no longer a representation but a being in its own right" (145). See also Irene J. Winter, *On Art in the Ancient Near East*, CHANE 34.1–2, 2 vols. (Leiden: Brill, 2010), 1:78–95.

19. Among other things, note, e.g., that in Gen 2:19, the human names the animals whereas

interpretation indicates that, in Genesis, the *imago* is, on the one hand, *royal*, and, on the other hand, *thoroughly democratized*. It is no longer the monarch alone who participates in or somehow actually is the divine image.[20] Instead, according to text (1) *all humans*—humanity as a whole—are (in) the image of God. This is theologically groundbreaking within the hierarchical polities of the ancient Near East (including ancient Israel),[21] since it dissolves any and all "classes" within the human species when it comes to God's image. There is no longer the singular king vs. all his subjects, the one monarch vs. the citizenry, royal vs. non-royal—so also there is no male vs. female (cf. Gal 3:28)[22] since humankind *en masse* and as such is (in) the image and likeness of God.[23]

A second contextual insight comes from those ancient Near Eastern texts that describe the creation of humans more generally. Unlike Genesis, the texts under consideration here do not employ the specific language of "image" and "likeness" but they occasionally suggest correspondence between the human and divine realms if not, in some instances, the divinity of humankind more generally, which is not unrelated.[24] The famous, but also enigmatic first line of the Babylonian flood story, *Atra-Ḥasis*, is a case in point: *i-nu-ma i-lu a-wi-lum*. This is often translated "when the gods *like* men . . . ," but there is no comparative particle in the text that

---

in Gen 1, it is God who names things. See Victor Avigdor Hurowitz, "The Divinity of Humankind in the Bible and the Ancient Near East: A New Mesopotamian Parallel," in *Mishneh Todah: Studies in Deuteronomy and Its Cultural Environment in Honor of Jeffrey H. Tigay*, ed. Nili Sacher Fox, David A. Glatt-Gilad, and Michael J. Williams (Winona Lake, IN: Eisenbrauns, 2009), 273.

20. Sarna, *Genesis*, 12 and 353n22; Samuel Loewenstamm, *Comparative Studies in Biblical and Ancient Oriental Literatures*, AOAT 204 (Neukirchen-Vluyn: Neukirchener, 1980), 48–50.

21. See Schmid, *Historical Theology*, 431–32; J. Gordon McConville, *Being Human in God's World: An Old Testament Theology of Humanity* (Grand Rapids: Baker Academic, 2016), 29.

22. Brevard S. Childs, *Old Testament Theology in a Canonical Context* (Philadelphia: Fortress, 1985), 189: "Surely this is a witness of absolute [gender] equality." See further Maryanne Cline Horowitz, "The Image of God in Man—Is Woman Included?" *HTR* 72 (1979): 175–206; Wagner, *God's Body*, 151–52, 155; and Paul Niskanen, "The Poetics of Adam: The Creation of אדם in the Image of אלהים," *JBL* 128 (2009): 417–36; but cf. Phyllis Bird, "'Male and Female He Created Them': Gen 1:27b in the Context of the Priestly Account of Creation," *HTR* 74 (1981): 129–59.

23. Note Benno Jacob, *The First Book of the Bible, Genesis: Augmented Edition*, trans. and ed. Ernest I. Jacob and Walter Jacob (Brooklyn: Ktav, 2007 [1974]), 10: the image in the first human couple together "is the opposite of racism and emphasizes the unity of [hu]mankind."

24. See Hurowitz, "Divinity," 265. At least one Egyptian text, *Instruction for Merikare*, also speaks of all humankind as the image of god: "mankind—god's cattle. . . . They are his images, who came from his body" (*AEL* 1:106). For more on the Egyptian materials, see Middleton, *Liberating Image*, 99–111. An important study that drew attention to the Egyptian evidence is Siegfried Herrmann, "Die Naturlehre des Schöpfungsberichtes: Erwägungen zur Vorgeschichte von Genesis 1," *TLZ* 86 (1961): 413–24. See further below on the question of divinization.

would signal a simile.[25] Instead, the words for "gods" (*ilū*, plural) and "humans" (*awilūm*, here a collective singular) are "immediately juxtaposed as though they were one."[26] If so, "when the gods were human" is a possible translation, but so is "when humans were gods."[27]

An even more apt parallel for the *imago* in Genesis is found in an omen series called *šumma kataduggû*, which begins, "When the great gods put the soul in humankind for Enlilship and established *kataduggû*-omens to guide them. . . ."[28] The key term here is "Enlilship" (*illilūtu*) which is "specifically a divine characteristic and in all cases is possessed by gods and goddesses."[29] This text indicates, therefore, that humans' "soul" or "spirit" (*zaqīqu*)[30] is given to them so that they have "executive power, [the] highest rank (of gods and goddesses)."[31] In this view, humanity "is not just a supreme leader but is divine," indeed "of the highest divinity."[32]

The two insights mentioned thus far are mostly concerned with the historical and cultural background of the image concept. Unfortunately, studies in this vein have sometimes paid little attention to how they impact the interpretation of the biblical *imago Dei*; even when they do, the discussion is often restricted to text (1). A third important contextual insight, therefore, comes from those studies that have been more concerned with the biblical image *in its present literary context*. Especially since the Scriptural texts make no explicit mention of the cultural background (notwithstanding the importance of the same), these studies have

---

25. See W. G. Lambert and A. R. Millard, *Atra-Ḥasis: The Babylonian Story of the Flood* (Winona Lake, IN: Eisenbrauns, 1999), 42–43 (emphasis added). They argue that the word *awilum* "has the locative *-um* with the meaning of the comparative *-iš*" (146). Cf. Benjamin R. Foster, *Before the Muses: An Anthology of Akkadian Literature* (Bethesda: CDL, 2005), 229n1: "The line is a metaphor," though he adds that "this does not mean that the gods were actually human beings; rather, they had to work as humans do."

26. Hurowitz, "Divinity," 266n12.

27. According to Hurowitz, "at the beginning of the myth, the gods are manly, whereas at the time of its creation humanity is made godly" ("Divinity," 266n12). A very different interpretation is found in Thorkild Jacobsen, "*Inuma Ilu awīlum*," in *Essays on the Ancient Near East in Memory of Jacob Joel Finkelstein*, ed. Maria de Jong Ellis (Hamden, CT: Archon Books, 1977), 113–17, who renders the line: "When (the god) Ilu was the boss."

28. *enūma ilāni rabiūtum ša amēlūti zaqīqša ana illilūti iškunū u kataduggâša ana reteddîša ukinnū*, text and translation (slightly modified) from Hurowitz, "Divinity," 269–70.

29. Hurowitz, "Divinity," 270.

30. According to Hurowitz, *zaqīqu* "seems to mean some sort of intelligence distinguishing humanity from animals and permitting humans to utter comprehensible sounds rather than mere noises" and "probably designates thoughts articulated verbally in the mind that are then expressed orally as speech" ("Divinity," 271).

31. *CAD* 8, 85.

32. Hurowitz, "Divinity," 270, 272.

suggested that the *imago* may best be understood as an open-ended, even processual conception. Put differently: if the image of God notion is somewhat unclear in Genesis (which it is), despite the helpful ancient Near Eastern background (which, while helpful, may not be determinative), perhaps the meaning of the *imago* is answered only in the unfolding of the book.[33] The image, that is, may not be an essential(ized) category but a functional one. *Imago* is what *imago* does. Human beings *will be* (in/as) the image of God—or show themselves to be (in/as) the image of God—if they *actually image* God. Image, according to this view, is a verb as much as it is a noun, an action more than a state of being, and is unfinished, not yet complete, with Genesis telling the story of if and how human beings do (and/or do not) turn out to image the Deity.[34] This line of interpretation is not only opened up by text (1) and its lack of specificity, it may even be present in the way text (1) is formulated: some interpreters argue that the preposition "in" (*bə-*) in "in our image (*bəṣalmēnû*)" is perhaps better translated by "as": "Let us make humankind *as* our image. . . ."[35] Be that as it may, Briggs nicely captures the gist of the third contextual insight: "Genesis uses the phrase 'image of God' to set us reading the canonical narrative with certain questions in mind, or, as one might say, 'the image of God' serves as a hermeneutical lens through which to read the OT's subsequent narratives."[36] The *imago* is an "anthropological question."[37]

It seems worthwhile to attempt to combine the three insights won by previous scholarship; even so, in their individuality, each evidences a range of potential

---

33. See Briggs, "Humans in the Image of God," 111–26, esp. 123–24.

34. Cf. von Rad, *Genesis*, 59: "The text speaks less of the nature of God's image than of its purpose. There is less said about the gift itself than about the task." So also Schüle, *Theology*, 27–44; McConville, *Being Human*, esp. 29–45; Yochanan Muffs, *The Personhood of God: Biblical Theology, Human Faith and the Divine Image* (Woodstock, VT: Jewish Lights, 2005), 174–75: "As image, his is an unrealized potential. Only by becoming human under the guidance of the law does man [sic] actualize this potential"; and Leon R. Kass, *The Beginning of Wisdom: Reading Genesis* (Chicago: University of Chicago, 2003), 38–40. In Kass's opinion, the open-ended nature of the text indicates that the first chapter of Genesis "begins the moral education of the reader" (40). A similar sentiment may be present in the *šumma kataduggû* text: "To the extent that *zaqīqu* [the human "spirit"] is not a physical characteristic, humanity's divine quality is not physically embodied or expressed but is manifest by his spirit and behavior" (Hurowitz, "Divinity," 273–74). Similarly, Tigay, "Image," 172–73, notes that the king Tukulti-Ninurta's status as the image of the god Enlil appears to depend on his attentiveness to his subjects and his understanding.

35. E.g., Davis, *Opening*, 9, 13n1; similarly, Gordon J. Wenham, *Genesis 1–15*, WBC 1 (Waco, TX: Word, 1987), 29 who thinks "according to [with *kĕ-*] our likeness" is "an explanatory gloss indicating the precise sense of 'in [*bĕ-*] our image.'" For an analysis of such arguments, see Clines, "Humanity," 2:470–75.

36. Briggs, "Humans," 123.

37. Briggs, "Humans," 124.

meaning(s) for the image of God. And so, again, what the *imago* is, precisely, remains a live and lively question, as does another: how do (or perhaps better: will) humans manifest that image? The latter question depends on the former one in a primal way—the issue is not simply what the *image* of God means, but *how is God imaged* in the first place? What is God like, how is God understood? Only by answering these types of questions can one determine if (and how) human beings properly "image" God. But only so much can be gathered about God's own image from the four classic texts in Gen 1–11. Any investigation of the divine referent of the *imago*—the divine *self*-image, as it were—must look to the entirety of Genesis, if not also well beyond it. As Leon R. Kass puts it: "To see how man [sic] might be godlike, we look at the text to see what God is like."[38]

2. Imagines Dei, *Part 1: God's Own Image(s) in Genesis*

Taking his own advice, Kass notes that Genesis 1 "introduces us to God's *activities and powers:* (1) God speaks, commands, names, blesses, and hallows; (2) God makes, and makes freely; (3) God looks at and beholds the world; (4) God is concerned with the goodness or perfection of things; (5) God addresses solicitously other living creatures and provides for their sustenance. In short: God exercises speech and reason, freedom in doing and making, and the powers of contemplation, judgment, and care."[39]

All well and good—and quite correct, too. Two things seem missing, however. The first is the *nonviolent nature* of God's activities and powers and how those may come to be in the *imago Dei* in humanity.[40] In comparative perspective, the *imago* may well evoke a Divine Sovereign who has placed a "presence" of the royal self in subjugated territory,[41] but what is decidedly absent from Gen 1 is any indication that the territory in question was subjugated in the first place.[42] Instead, the land

38. Kass, *Beginning of Wisdom*, 37. Similarly, von Rad, *Genesis*, 59: "If one wants to determine the content of this statement more closely, one must ask how ancient Israel thought in details of this Elohim," though he immediately goes beyond Genesis by mentioning the divine predicates "wise" (2 Sam 14:17, 20) and "good" (1 Sam 29:9).

39. Kass, *Beginning of Wisdom*, 37–38.

40. See Jerome F. D. Creach, *Violence in Scripture*, Interpretation (Louisville: Westminster John Knox, 2013), 26: "To bear God's image—means *not* to act imperialistically and coercively." More extensively, see Middleton, *Liberating Image*.

41. So John T. Strong, "Shattering the Image of God: A Response to Theodore Hiebert's Interpretation of the Story of the Tower of Babel," *JBL* 127 (2008): 625–34, esp. 631.

42. To be sure, scholars have argued that a divine combat myth lies behind Gen 1, but for compelling critiques of such a perspective, see Middleton, *Liberating Image*, 235–69; Garr, *In His Own Image*, 191–211; and Jon D. Levenson, *Creation and the Persistence of Evil: The Jewish*

in question is *created*—apparently generously and peacefully—and then *blessed*, even *sanctified* by God. The image the Deity sets in creation is, of course, nothing less than humankind, which is subsequently—and correlatively, it would seem—tasked with proper care of the earth in the next chapter (Gen 2:15);[43] but already in Gen 1, the human *imago* is given a diet that is altogether commensurate with the nonviolent ways of God: vegetables, not meat from slaughter, is what humans are to eat (1:29; see also 2:16). The same is true for all other animals as well; there is no such thing as a carnivore yet! The first (implied) mention of animal slaughter is Gen 4:4, outside of Eden, but it is for liturgical, not dietary reasons: when Abel brings a sacrifice of his flock to God.[44] There is no mention of animal consumption proper until Gen 9, in conjunction with text (4), the last of the image texts in Genesis. From Gen 9:3 forward, the non-violent *imago* is no longer replicated in humankind—at least in alimentary ways. Before that, however, human "dominion" over the animal kingdom does *not* include its death or destruction.[45]

Now, in truth, humanity proves itself incapable of imaging the nonviolent God long before its diet is changed in Gen 9. The most egregious transgression, given its sheer novelty, is Cain's murder of his brother Abel in Gen 4. Here, in the first human family according to Genesis, in the very first story outside the garden of Eden,

---

Drama of Divine Omnipotence, rev. ed. (Princeton: Princeton University Press, 1994), esp. 122, 127. If a combat myth is present, it is *at best* only hinted at, as distant background, and would probably only have been activated for those with rather extensive *extra*-textual knowledge. For contrasting opinions, see C. L. Crouch, "Made in the Image of God: The Creation of אדם, the Commissioning of the King and the *Chaoskampf* of YHWH," *JANER* 16 (2016): 1–21; and Jeffrey M. Leonard, *Creation Rediscovered: Finding New Meaning in an Ancient Story* (Peabody, MA: Hendrickson, 2020).

43. The second creation account in Gen 2:4(b)–3:24 is traditionally attributed to the J (non-P) source. Even so, for the resonance of Gen 2–3 with ancient Near Eastern image practices, see Schüle, *Theology*, 7–25, also 27–44; and, especially, Catherine L. McDowell, *The Image of God in the Garden of Eden: The Creation of Humankind in Genesis 2:5–3:24 in Light of the* mīs pî pīt pî *and* wpt-r *Rituals of Mesopotamia and Ancient Egypt*, Siphrut 15 (Winona Lake, IN: Eisenbrauns, 2015).

44. Some interpreters think Gen 3:21 implies animal killing, but this is unnecessary. See Brent A. Strawn, "Must Animals Die? Genesis 3:21, *Enūma Eliš* IV, and the Power of Divine Utterance," *VT* 72 (2022): 122–50.

45. Davis, *Opening*, 11, notes how the blessing of God comes *before* the verbs speaking of human rule and so "the human exercise of skilled mastery [how Davis translates "to have dominion"] must be intended to reinforce that prior blessing, not to annul it." Care for the nonhuman world may be set in contrast to the royal image in comparative perspective since ancient Near Eastern monarchs were often presented in excessively violent ways vis-à-vis animals, especially in the royal hunt. See Strawn, "Comparative Approaches," esp. 132–35; Strawn, "Image," esp. 70–72: "The non-violent *imago* reflects the non-violent *Deus*" (72).

among the very first brothers, is a case of fratricide. Here is also the first mention of "sin" (*ḥaṭṭāʾt*) in the Bible. Things go downhill quickly thereafter, which is not surprising since the murderous Cain is presented as the progenitor of urbanism and culture (4:17–22). One of Cain's descendants, Lamech, is remembered for his "doctrine of inordinate retaliation": murdering someone who merely wounded him (4:23–24). And so it is that, just a bit later, Genesis speaks of the great wickedness of humankind on the earth, how "every inclination of the thoughts of its heart was only evil always" (6:5), and how the planet "was full of violence" (6:11). Kass, evidently, is not the only one to have overlooked the nonviolent aspects of the divine image in Genesis! Humanity shows itself quick to fail in this aspect of divine imaging, and to be guilty of repeat offense on the matter. Before all that, however, "in the beginning," the human image of God is *primordially nonviolent* toward animals (1:29; 2:16; 9:4) *and* also, ideally, toward humans (9:5–6; cf. 4:10).[46]

The second thing missing from Kass's list is actually plural: the *many ways God is imaged* beyond the first chapter of the Bible and beyond its first book. As Yochanan Muffs has noted: "The image of God in the Bible is not a monolith; the divine persona is refracted through a wide range of personal prisms. [For example,] Isaiah sees God as a city sophisticate; Ezekiel as a country bumpkin.... Each prophet, in his own style, captures different aspects of the divine person."[47]

The same holds true for the different accounts found within Genesis itself and the various traditions that make up the book (however those are parsed out). Even if the Pentateuchal sources are reduced to three—"the Picasso called D . . . the Rembrandt called J . . . the Blake called P"[48]—the range of presentation, replete with distinct emphases, is remarkable and impossible to reduce, let alone capture, especially in a brief essay like the present one.

Painting in broad brushstrokes, therefore, one might say that the presentation of God in the Bible is tragic, with the Lord "constantly torn between His love for Israel and His profound exasperation with them."[49] More specifically with regard to Genesis, one could—following Muffs—see God as naïvely optimistic in Gen 1 (e.g., 1:31: "God looked at everything . . . and it was very good") only to watch God turn deeply pessimistic in the Flood Narrative (e.g., 6:7: "I am sorry I made

---

46. There are further exhibits of divine nonviolence: God does not execute capital punishment on the first human couple, despite their transgression (Gen 2:17), neither does God take Cain's life (4:15). In both of these cases, the Deity spares the offenders, proving both patient and merciful.

47. Muffs, *Personhood of God*, 97.

48. Muffs, *Personhood of God*, 98; Muffs leaves out mention of an E source.

49. Muffs, *Personhood of God*, 99.

them").[50] What transpires after the flood—in which God realizes that, despite that desperate measure, "the inclination of the human heart" was still "evil from youth" (8:21)—might be seen as a transformation of initial divine optimism and subsequent divine pessimism "into what one may call divine realism. God now realizes that He cannot expect perfection from man [sic] and that human corruption is something He will have to make peace with. Man [sic] is not totally good, nor is he totally bad; he is simply human. God concludes that the appropriate reaction to man's sinfulness is not an outburst of punitive anger . . . but rather forbearance and educational discipline in harmony with man's less-than-perfect nature."[51]

Perhaps so, though this interpretation is not airtight (none are). With reference to the matters at hand, if the *imago* is a moving target, something to be realized (or not) in the course of Genesis (and in human life/lives), divine realism about humanity may be present from the very beginning, not simply or only a hard lesson God derives from the flood. The *imago*, that is, may be an "anthropological question" or "hermeneutical lens" (see above). Regardless, Muffs seems more right than wrong when he asserts that "in the first chapters of Genesis, God emerges before us as a moral personality who grows and learns through tragedy and experimentation to become a model for man. The crucial message is that even God makes mistakes and actually learns from them."[52] This summation is a far cry from the impassible God of the later philosophers but seems on point for the biblical portrayal of God writ large, not just in the opening chapters of Genesis. Indeed, a number of scholars have tracked how God is presented across the entire Old Testament, not just in Genesis, with the results bearing noteworthy similarity to Muffs's accounting.

W. Lee Humphreys, for instance, has concluded that God is very much a moving target in Genesis. This is to say once again that, in terms of literary presentation, there is no one singular *imago Dei* but, rather, many *imagines*. Humpheys identifies no less than twelve divine images, which he maps onto particular blocks of text:

God as:	Chapters in Genesis:
Sovereign Designer	1, 12–14, 15, 16–17, 23–24
Struggling Parent	2–3, 4, 12–14, 15, 16–17
Disciplining Father	2–3, 4
Destroyer-Sustainer	5–9, 18–19, 22
Jealous	10–11
Patron	12–14, 16–17, 23–24, 25, 26, 27, 28–30, 31, 32–36, 37–41

50. Muffs, *Personhood of God*, 99–100.
51. Muffs, *Personhood of God*, 100.
52. Muffs, *Personhood of God*, 100.

Patron Challenged	15, 32–36
Judge	18–19, 31
Deliverer	20–21, 25, 28–30
Savage	22
Opponent	32–36
Providential Designer	42–50[53]

It is easy enough to quibble with some of Humphreys's categories and/or the texts he has associated with each;[54] the point, regardless, is that the depiction of God in Genesis is on the move, in no small measure because—and this is crucial—the human images of God are on the move.[55] As an example, in his treatment of God's character as a parent "engaging a child with a mind of its own," Humphreys writes: "*Yahweh's parental engagement with his human creations entails a continued becoming on his part as well as theirs.* . . . God the parent is a God becoming."[56] Or, again, more generally this time: "[Various divine reactions in Genesis] suggest that God himself, especially in relation to a creation that is not as fully under his control or as ordered a whole as first depicted, is more complex and in process of becoming than our first construction of him suggests."[57] Hence: "*The movement [of God's character] is from type to full-fledged character to agent, as we move from God the sovereign designer in Genesis 1 to the complex, multi-faceted, and changing figure in the bulk of Genesis 2–36, to God as an agent silently shaping events in the stories other characters tell of him in the latter segments of Genesis.*"[58]

53. W. Lee Humphreys, *The Character of God in the Book of Genesis: A Narrative Appraisal* (Louisville: Westminster John Knox, 2001), 234–35; further passim, esp. 237–56.

54. Cf., e.g., Jack Miles, *God: A Biography* (New York: Alfred A. Knopf, 1995), who catalogues twenty-four categories across the entire Hebrew Bible, but only four for Genesis: creator, destroyer, creator/destroyer, and friend of the family (25–84). The metaphorical nature of categories like Miles's and Humphreys's should not be missed; these categories are not always explicitly flagged as such in the narratives proper.

55. Humphreys, *Character*, 252: "Once God enters into real relationship with the humans he creates in Gen 2, he enters a dynamic story-world that is often marked by tensions and conflicts with other characters who are dynamic as well. For God to engage these other characters entails the real possibilities of dynamic change and development in his own being."

56. Humphreys, *Character*, 61 (his emphasis); see also 244, which adds that the process of becoming reveals that God is "at points . . . torn by inner conflict"; and 252: "The character God is on a learning curve." Contrary to Humphreys and others (e.g., C. L. Crouch, "Genesis 1:26–27 as a Statement of Humanity's Divine Parentage," *JTS* 61 [2010]: 1–15), it may be doubted that there is any divine parental metaphor prior to Exod 4:22; still further, there is no explicit identification of God as a *male* parent prior to Deut 1:31 (see 32:5, 18 for divine father and mother metaphors). See chapter 8 of the present work.

57. Humphreys, *Character*, 239.

58. Humphreys, *Character*, 241 (his emphasis); further, 242–43 and passim.

These citations show that Humphreys thinks that "the character God" recedes in the course of Genesis—a recession or "removal" that might be seen as a disappearance, gradual or otherwise, from the human scene.[59] He is not alone, with Richard Elliott Friedman tracking the mystery of God's disappearance in Scripture, and Jack Miles asking, at the conclusion of his own literary reading, "does God lose interest?"[60] In Miles's own words: "The Lord God's life in the Tanakh begins in activity and speech and ends in passivity and silence. . . . Why does this work take the form of a long decrescendo to silence? Why does it, so to speak, begin with its climax and decline from there?"[61]

Humphreys's analysis of Genesis paints it as nothing less than a microcosm of what Friedman and Miles see across the whole Hebrew Bible: "After Genesis 36, God rarely acts and speaks no more, with the single brief exception of his final meeting with Jacob at Beer-sheba where God joins him in the descent into Egypt [46:1–4]. It is now [after this point] largely in the words of other characters that we meet God. He becomes a God constituted through their words. And while they speak of him in ways that recall his sovereign mastery in Genesis 1, we must temper their constructions with our realization of their own partiality and with our own experience of God in Genesis 2–36."[62] But what does this "becoming" or "decrescendo" of the divine *imago* (and *imagines*) mean and what might it have to do with the human *imago/imagines* of God?

3. Imagines Dei, Part 2: God's Human (Non-)Image(s) in Genesis

Perhaps it means that God has "no life unconnected to his human creature."[63] Or perhaps it is some sort of desperate bid for divine omniscience, achieved at the cost of solitude, or an attempt to grasp divine sovereignty at the cost of silence.[64] Whatever the case, does it mean that humans, now, are to be gods or at least

---

59. Humphreys, *Character*, 237, 240, 246, and 271n1. Humphreys's identification of this literary movement is correct (e.g., 254), but his interpretation of *why* it is present (i.e., why God would self-remove) is unconvincing to my mind. I hold the same judgment for Miles. See further below.

60. See Richard Elliott Friedman, *The Disappearance of God: A Divine Mystery* (Boston: Little, Brown, 1995); Miles, *God: A Biography*, 397–408. The idea precedes both Friedman and Miles; see, e.g., Erich Fromm, *You Shall Be as Gods: A Radical Interpretation of the Old Testament and Its Tradition* (New York: Henry Holt, 1991 [1966]).

61. Miles, *God: A Biography*, 402. Miles goes on to posit both Job (404: "God's most perfect image") and Nehemiah (406: "the perfect reflection, the comprehensive self-image, the quasi incarnation") as images of God.

62. Humphreys, *Character*, 248.

63. Miles, *God: A Biography*, 402.

64. See Miles, *God: A Biography*, 402–3; and Humphreys, *Character*, 246, respectively.

god-like after God's slow retreat? That is, after all, one way to understand the *imago*, especially in comparative perspective: that humans rule in God's stead (see §1 above)—though in varying ways, alternatively beneficent or malevolent,[65] humans understand and enact such rule in Genesis.

But there is another option. God's "subsiding," if that is in fact what it is, might be viewed more positively. Instead of God receding out of weakness or passivity, or whatever, the attenuation of God's direct communication, self-characterization, and activity in Genesis (and the Bible writ large) might be seen as nothing less than the continuation of the primal divine generosity evident in Gen 1 that made room for other subjects beyond the divine self.[66] J. Gerald Janzen has argued that "the word that initiates the creative process" in Gen 1 is *there*, as in "Let *there* be light," because that is the word that makes room for *everything* else.[67] The creation of humankind in the divine image is just one more, even if somehow climactic, instance of God creating space: *there-ness*. And if the *imago* is a matter of function and proper ethic, not a given of dignified essence, then the rest of Genesis and God's tempered direction makes room for humans to answer the anthropological question evoked by the *imago*: Will they image God or not?

The answer humans give is decidedly mixed.[68] As already noted, Gen 4 is quick to showcase the presence of sin that eventuates in murder with things devolving quickly thereafter.[69] And yet, the relationship of real integrity—the dynamism within God summoned in part by the dynamism of the created world, especially the dynamic human *imagines*—means that both the divine image and the human *imago Dei* constantly interact and adjust.[70] When humans fail to image God rightly, there is usually a calling to account, which is often accompanied by a new strategy, as it were, in the divine plan. This is the familiar cycle of disobedience–punishment–grace identified by many scholars in the Primeval History, but the

---

65. For the latter, see Donald E. Gowan, *When Man Becomes God: Humanism and Hybris in the Old Testament*, PTMS 6 (Eugene, OR: Pickwick, 1975).

66. Cf. Steven A. Rogers, "The Parent-Child Relationship as an Archetype for the Relationship Between God and Humanity in Genesis," *Pastoral Psychology* 50 (202): 377–85; see Brent A. Strawn, "'Israel, My Child': The Ethics of a Biblical Metaphor," in *The Child in the Bible*, ed. Marcia Bunge, Terence E. Fretheim, and Beverly R. Gaventa (Grand Rapids: Eerdmans, 2008), 137–38, for discussion (reprinted as chapter 8 in the present volume).

67. J. Gerald Janzen, *When Prayer Takes Place: Forays into a Biblical World*, ed. Brent A. Strawn and Patrick D. Miller (Eugene, OR: Cascade, 2012), 51, see also 46, and further, 51–52.

68. See Briggs, "Humans," 119–24.

69. It is common to find such problems even earlier, particularly in Gen 3. For a recent treatment of this material, see Smith, *Genesis*. See also below.

70. More generally, see Terence E. Fretheim, *God and World in the Old Testament: A Relational Theology of Creation* (Nashville: Abingdon, 2005).

pattern of divine-human interactivity continues on, and apace, in the ancestral stories, particularly around the problems of progeny and blessing. To be sure, this interactive story and vibrant process of (non-)imaging is not all dreary; there are real high points: the righteousness of Noah, for example, who walked with God (Gen 6:9), and God's remembrance of Noah and all the animals on the ark (Gen 8:1). Or, again, there is the obedience of Abraham, quite mixed at the start and at several points along the way, but decisive, though devastating, in the end (Gen 22:12). And then there is Joseph.

Genesis ends with an extended block of material devoted to Jacob's favorite son (chaps. 37–50). What is significant for present purposes is how Joseph "in his commanding authority and effective control seems in many ways to assume God's place in the last segments of the Genesis story";[71] put differently, Joseph may be a final and remarkably successful instance of the *imago*. This is perhaps clearest in the two important theological statements Joseph makes with reference to his brothers' act of selling him into slavery:

> Now, don't worry, and don't be angry at yourselves that you sold me here be-cause God sent me before you in order to save lives. . . . God sent me before you to establish a remnant for you on the earth and to save you in a great deliv-erance. So, *you* did not send me here: it was God! He has made me a father to Pharaoh, lord of all his house, and master of the entire land of Egypt. . . . God has made me lord of all Egypt. (Gen 45:5, 7–8, 9)

> Don't be afraid! Am I in God's place? You planned evil against me; God planned it for good in order to do as is the case right now: to save many people. So, don't be afraid! I will take care of you and your little ones. (Gen 50:19–21a)

Both statements are made *by Joseph*, not by the narrator and not by God, but they are striking nevertheless in what they say about God and how they paint Joseph as a privileged interpreter of God's acts, even God's intentions. With refer-ence to the *imago*, does this index a closeness between Joseph and God, signaled already by the earlier notice that "the LORD was with Joseph" (Gen 39:2)—a fact that was evident even to others who weren't native Yhwh-worshippers (Gen 39:3; cf. 41:38–39)—and slightly later, where, even in prison, Yhwh is again said to be "with Joseph" showing him steadfast love (*ḥesed*) and giving him favor in the sight of his jailor (39:21, 23)? It would seem so, and, from the other side of the equation, it should be observed how frequently Joseph is found mentioning God, depicted

---

71. Humphreys, *Character*, 256; see also 249.

as concerned with God's ways, and fond of giving credit to the Lord (Gen 39:9; 40:8; 41:16, 25, 28, 32, 51–52; 42:18, 23; 43:29; 48:9; 50:24).

This is not to say that Joseph is perfect. Readers often wonder about Joseph, especially early on, when he is presented at odds with his brothers (Gen 37:2, 4–5, 8, 11) and worthy of rebuke by his father (Gen 37:10). But that is Joseph at the start, premature—failing, or so it would seem, to properly image God. Joseph at the end, mature, is a very different *imago* in at least two ways, beyond the closeness between him and God that has already been mentioned.

First and most importantly, Joseph not only understands what has happened to him to be God's doing, he explicitly states that it is for the purpose of *saving life*. The life that is saved, furthermore, is not limited only to his immediate family circle. Joseph includes his clan within the deliverance, to be sure (Gen 45:7; 50:21), but Joseph is equally clear that the preservation of life is larger still: somewhat nondescript, perhaps, in Gen 45:5 ("lives") but explicated clearly as "many people" (*'am-rāb*) in Gen 50:20, including, therefore, the Egyptians.[72] Indeed, according to the narrator, Joseph's agricultural strategy was highly effective, not only for Egypt but for "the whole world" (Gen 41:57).[73]

Second, Joseph's key theological assertions are made in the context of *forgiving his brothers*. Matthew Schlimm has observed that Joseph functions here as an "anti-Cain": he is "a brother who has all the power and all the reasons to harm his brothers but instead turns away from anger, and, despite the inherent difficulties, offers forgiveness."[74] Schlimm continues: "There is thus a chiastic interplay between Gen 4:7 and the book of Genesis as a whole, moving from fratricide to forgiveness."[75] In terms of the *imago*, Joseph models the nonviolent primordial image in a way that Cain does not, and this is not to mention how Joseph also images God's habits of mercy vis-à-vis Cain (Gen 4:15) and others (e.g., Gen 3:21; 8:21). It is worth noting that, in the second forgiveness scene, the brothers speak to Joseph as if he were God by the strategic use of prayer language, especially the unusual rhetorical particle *'ānnā'* (Gen 50:17), which is otherwise used only in direct prayer to God (Exod 32:31; 2 Kgs 20:3; Isa 38:3; Jonah 1:14; 4:2; Pss 116:4, 16; 118:25; Dan 9:4; Neh 1:5, 11). Not surprisingly, Joseph—positive *imago Dei* that he

---

72. See Jacob, *Genesis*, 342; and Claus Westermann, *Genesis 37–50: A Continental Commentary*, trans. John J. Scullion (Minneapolis: Fortress, 2002), 205.

73. Westermann, *Genesis 37–50*, 251, who thinks the outlook of the Joseph story is "universal" and that it "served a critical function in a period of strong nationalistic aspirations," pointing "to the creator who is concerned for all his creatures."

74. Matthew Richard Schlimm, *From Fratricide to Forgiveness: The Language and Ethics of Anger in Genesis*, Siphrut 7 (Winona Lake, IN: Eisenbrauns, 2011), 178.

75. Schlimm, *From Fratricide to Forgiveness*, 179.

is—recognizes what his brothers are doing, but also knows that, at best, he is only an *image* of God, not God. Hence his response: "Am I in God's place?" (Gen 50:19). While Joseph appropriately and humbly eschews identifying with God, he nevertheless replies to the brothers' "prayer" by offering them what God so often gives in response to the prayers of Israel: an oracle of salvation—"Don't be afraid!"—not once but twice (Gen 50:19, 21a), following that with a promise to provide for his brothers and their toddlers (*ṭappəkem*). In this way, the narrator concludes, Joseph comforted his brothers and spoke tenderly to them (Gen 50:21b).

So, although Joseph is definitely *not* God, he certainly acts *like* God. Or, put differently, Joseph *images* God. It comes as no surprise, therefore, that later Christian interpreters often understood Joseph to be a type of Christ, another image of the invisible God (Col 1:15; cf. Heb 1:3).[76]

4. Limits to the Imago, the Imagines, and Divine-Human Imaging

That Joseph acts *like* God harkens back to text (1) at the beginning of Genesis, where humans are made not only "in [*bə-*] the divine image" but also "according to" or "like [*kə-*] the likeness" of God. Being or acting like God, whether for good, as in the case of Joseph (et al.), or ill, as in the case of Cain (et al.), are case studies in whether or not humanity can and will *image* God.[77] But one last aspect of being "like God" must be mentioned: the limits Genesis places on imaging and the divine-human relationship.

In the Eden narrative, the possibility to be "like God" (*kē'lōhîm*) is part of the first challenge posed to humankind (Gen 3:5).[78] This story is too profound to engage here properly; it is enough to observe that the desire to be "like God," at first just a possibility presented by the serpent, turns out to be an actual reality, recognized by none other than God. At the end of Gen 3, the Deity remarks: "Look! Humanity has become like one of us (*kə'aḥad mimmennû*) knowing good and evil . . ." (Gen 3:22a).

---

76. Gary A. Anderson, "Joseph and the Passion of Our Lord," in *The Art of Reading Scripture*, ed. Ellen F. Davis and Richard B. Hays (Grand Rapids: Eerdmans, 2003), 198–215. Anderson's essay is useful in highlighting the many ways the ancestors' characters are "tied to the very identity of God" and how their individual roles are bequeathed "to a much larger sodality, the nation Israel" (198–99). See also, more extensively, Jon D. Levenson, *The Death and Resurrection of the Beloved Son: The Transformation of Child Sacrifice in Judaism and Christianity* (New Haven: Yale University Press, 1993).

77. See Briggs, "Humans," 123.

78. For a classic interpretation of the temptation to be *sicut Deus* ("like God"), see Dietrich Bonhoeffer, *Creation and Fall: A Theological Exposition of Genesis 1–3*, trans. Douglas Stephen Bax, ed. John W. de Gruchy, DBW 3 (Minneapolis: Fortress, 1997), 111–14.

Note: the humans have *already become* like us! The text makes immediately clear that this newfound divine-likeness on the part of humanity, which evidently surpasses the likeness in the *imago*, constitutes some kind of threat to the divine world. It is something that the Deity must properly contain, which is accomplished by denying humans access to the tree of life (Gen 3:22b). Human beings may have become divine, at least to some degree, by their actions in the garden, but they are denied immortality. They are, at best, little godlings with limited lifespans (Gen 6:3) to do good or ill with their remarkable God-like capacities.

The notion of divinization (Greek *theōsis*) becomes an important part of mystical religious experience, especially within Christianity, in later periods, but here in Gen 3 the idea is something that causes concern. Some sort of boundary has been transgressed, and the problem has precisely to do with being (too much) "like God." Said differently, the divine-human (inter)relationship has limits. Divinization, at least in this part of Genesis, is a real theological problem that the book seeks to redress. If not *sui generis*, the problem of divinization may have become known to ancient Israelites via the ways various kings and heroes from well-known ancient Near Eastern epics were thought to be divine.[79]

79. Note, e.g., that in various versions of the Etana legend, the hero's name is differently written: in the Old Version, simply Etana, in the Middle Assyrian Version, [m]Etana (with the masculine determinative), and, in the Late Version, [d]Etana (with the divine determinative: "divine Etana"). See J. V. Kinnier Wilson, *The Legend of Etana: A New Edition* (Chicago: Bolchazy-Carducci, 1985). The divinity of Gilgamesh, whose name is often written with the divine determinative and who is said to receive cult, is attested already in the Early Dynastic god list from Šuruppak (mid-third millennium BCE) and continues on into Neo-Assyrian lists. See A. R. George, *The Babylonian Gilgamesh Epic: Introduction, Critical Edition and Cuneiform Texts* (Oxford: Oxford University Press, 2003), 1:70–90, 119–35. The divinization of Mesopotamian and Levantine kings is debated, though it seems likely especially in early periods. See, inter alia, Loewenstamm, *Comparative Studies*, 48; Jacob Klein, "Sumerian Kingship and the Gods," in *Text, Artifact, and Image: Revealing Ancient Israelite Religion*, ed. Gary Beckman and Theodore J. Lewis, BJS 346 (Providence, RI: Brown Judaic Studies, 2006), 115–31; and Peter Machinist, "Kingship and Divinity in Imperial Assyria," in Beckman and Lewis, *Text, Artifact, and Image*, 152–88. Naram-Sin is apparently "the first attested ancient Mesopotamian ruler to have used the divine determinative before his name" (Winter, *On Art*, 1:87; citing Walter Farber, "Die Vergöttlichung Naram-Sins," *Or* 52 [1983]: 67–72). Note also Michael C. Astour, "*Rdmn*/Rhadamanthys and the Motif of Selective Immortality," in *"Und Mose schrieb dieses Lied auf": Studien zum Alten Testament und zum Alten Orient: Festschrift für Oswald Loretz zur Vollendung seines 70. Lebensjohres mit Beiträgen von Freuden, Schülern und Kollegen*, ed. Manfried Dietrich and Ingo Kottsieper, AOAT 250 (Münster: Ugarit-Verlag, 1998), 55–89. For the Egyptian material, see Labib Habachi, *Features of the Deification of Ramesses II*, ADAIK 5 (Glückstadt: J. J. Augustin, 1969); and Racheli Shalomi-Hen, *The Writing of Gods: The Evolution of Divine Classifiers in the Old Kingdom*, Göttinger Orientforschungen IV/Reihe Ägypten 38 (Wiesbaden: Harrassowitz, 2006), 159–60.

Patrick Miller has noted that all three of the passages in the Primeval History where God uses "we-language" (Gen 1:26; 3:22; and 11:7) are places where the human and divine worlds come into close contact.[80] Many reasons for the so-called divine plural ("Let us . . .") have been offered in the history of interpretation, but Miller thinks the plural is present because these texts deal "with the divine world as such and not simply the god Yahweh."[81] At the end of Gen 3, the relationship between the divine and human worlds is very close—uncomfortably so. And so, while it is apparently humanly "possible to overstep the bounds and seek to blend the two [realms] into one," Gen 3:22 and 11:7 resist that. A similar scenario, but without "we-language," is found in the highly enigmatic story in Gen 6:1–4, which David Clines has called "a satanic parody of the idea of the image of God in man."[82] In this instance, the "breakdown" between the divine and human arenas "is from the reverse direction."[83] At issue in each of these four stories is "the nature of humanity, its sphere of life and its powers, and to what extent human nature and human domain overlap with divine nature"; in each case, "limits upon the *ĕlōhîm*-like creature are . . . enforced."[84] Still other passages depict human characters overstepping their creaturely bounds, misappropriating divine responsibilities. Cain is once again a paradigmatic example as he inappropriately plays the role of "brother's keeper" (though he actually disavows it); it is God alone who properly—and safely—keeps humanity (see Ps 121:4; cf. Ps 4:8).[85]

5. A Final Image

In point of fact, limits for the human *imago* seem present already in text (1) which states that humans are *not* God but only (and at best) *in* God's *image* and *after* God's *likeness*—which is to say "*similar . . . but not identical.*"[86] The many different

80. Patrick D. Miller, *Genesis 1–11: Studies in Structure and Theme*, JSOTSup 8 (Sheffield: University of Sheffield, 1978), 25. See also Lyle Eslinger, "The Enigmatic Plurals Like 'One of Us' (Genesis I 26, III 22, and XI 7) in Hyperchronic Perspective," *VT* 56 (2006): 171–84.

81. Miller, *Genesis 1–11*, 25.

82. David J. A. Clines, "The Significance of the 'Sons of God' Episode (Genesis 6:1–4) in the Context of the 'Primeval History' (Genesis 1–11)," *JSOT* 4 (1979): 33–46 (37).

83. Miller, *Genesis 1–11*, 26.

84. Miller, *Genesis 1–11*, 26.

85. See Paul A. Riemann, "Am I My Brother's Keeper?" *Int* 24 (1970): 482–91.

86. Wagner, *God's Body*, 153 (his emphasis). Von Rad, *Genesis*, 58, thought the divine plurals functioned to prevent "one from referring God's image too directly to God the Lord. God . . . conceals himself in this multiplicity." For a fascinating fictional treatment of how pronounced divine-human similarity is inescapably still distinct, see C. S. Lewis, *Perelandra: A Novel* (New York: Scribner, 1944), 176–77.

instantiations of the human *imago*, the many *imagines* in Genesis and beyond, reveal that there are countless ways that humans properly image God and/or fail to do so in comparison with God's own *imagines*. The biblical material in Genesis and beyond contributes much by way of rounding out the latter, especially in God's relentless pursuit of humankind, despite its many schemes.

On this point, one last image is worth pondering. In Genesis, God is frequently portrayed as *Lord of the womb*. In Gen 20, after Abraham has pawned off Sarah as his sister for a second time, we learn that "the LORD had shut up entirely every womb in the house of Abimelech on account of Sarah, Abraham's wife" (v. 18). Only after Abraham prays does God heal Abimelech, his wife, and his maidservants "so they could bear children again" (v. 17). In Gen 25:23, God knows the contents of Rebekah's womb: that she is carrying twins. In Gen 29:31a, when Yhwh sees that Leah was unloved, he opens her womb, and later does the same for her sister, Rachel, who is said to be infertile (29:31b). Before that turn of events, however, Jacob, apparently exasperated by the two sisters' rivalry, blurts out to Rachel's request for children: "Am I in the place of God, who has kept from you the fruit of the womb?" (Gen 30:2). The first part is identical to Joseph's response to his brothers in Gen 50:19: "Am I in God's place?" No, just as was the case with Joseph, Jacob is most certainly *not* God. Therefore only God can give Rachel what she wishes—something that God does very quickly thereafter (Gen 30:22). That divine action confirms, in retrospect, that Rachel's infertility, which is *divinely rectified*, may also have been *divinely caused* (see 1 Sam 1:5–6). A bit earlier, in the previous generation,

> Isaac prayed to the LORD for his wife because she was infertile. The LORD granted his prayer, and his wife Rebekah conceived. (Gen 25:21)

The Hebrew word for "infertile" is *'āqārâ*. Besides the mentions in Gen 25:21, of Rebekah, and Gen 29:31, of Rachel—both of whose inability to conceive is reversed by God—there is only one other instance of *'āqārâ* in Genesis, at the very end of the Primeval History:

> Now Sarai was infertile. She had no children. (11:30)

In light of Genesis as a whole, one might wonder if Sarai's infertility is yet another instance of God's control of the womb, its closing and also its opening. Genesis goes on to report, after all, that "the LORD visited Sarah just as he said, and the LORD did for Sarah just as he promised: Sarah conceived and gave birth . . ." (Gen 21:1–2a; cf. also Pss 113:9; 127:3). If so, what Gen 11:30 may signal—in a subtle and yet not-so-subtle way—is nothing short of the *calling of Sarai*, prior even to the more famous calling of her husband, a calling that, in Sarai's case, occurs within and precisely because of her infertility. If so, the mystery of divine election does not wait until Abram in Gen 12, but is present already in the mysterious workings of God amid humanity—in this specific case, amid one family, one elderly couple, one woman and her womb—and how God uses that to set the world aright with humanity as *imago Dei*. What an image!

2

Yhwh's Poesie: The *Gnadenformel*, the Book of Exodus, and Beyond

LORD our God, you answered them.
    To them you were a God who forgives
    but also the one who avenged their wrong deeds. (Ps 99:8 CEB)

Yhwh utters many words in the book of Exodus, even more in the Torah as a whole. Much of this divine speech is *reported*—that is, mediated through Moses—and the majority of it is thoroughly *prosaic*, even legal. Peppered here and there, however, like spice to flavor a dish, are snatches of poetry from Yhwh's own mouth. The purpose of the present study is to look at perhaps the most important instance of Yhwh's poesie in Exodus, namely Exod 34:6b–7. This text, the so-called *Gnadenformel* (German for "grace formula"), is a statement about Yhwh's nature that is itself peppered throughout the Old Testament, such that, according to some scholars, it attained creedal or quasi-creedal status in ancient Israel.[1] In what follows, I will argue that the *Gnadenformel*, understood as poetic utterance, bears within itself a lyric tension between the (far more) merciful and (far less) punitive sides of Yhwh's character. The first section of the essay establishes Exod 34:6b–7 as poetry so as to assess its poetics (§1). The next section notes divine poetry elsewhere in the Bible, especially in Exodus, and comments on the significance of the Exodus poems, and particularly the *Gnadenformel*, for their literary

My thanks go to J. Blake Couey and Elaine T. James for their assistance and also to the editors for comments on an earlier draft.

    1. See, inter alia, Thomas B. Dozeman, "Inner-biblical Interpretation of Yahweh's Gracious and Compassionate Character," *JBL* 108 (1989): 207–23; and Walter Brueggemann, *Theology of the Old Testament: Testimony, Dispute, Advocacy* (Minneapolis: Fortress, 1997), 215–24, esp. 216.

contexts (§2). The essay concludes with a brief reflection on what Yhwh's poetry in Exodus (and elsewhere) might suggest about the nature of the Torah, if not Scripture as a whole (§3).

1. The Poetics of the Gnadenformel (*Exodus 34:6b–7*)

Before assessing Exod 34:6–7 as poetry, the text must be laid out and translated. For present purposes, v. 6a can be set aside as a narrative introduction to the *Gnadenformel* proper, which begins immediately thereafter. Neither of the great codices of the Hebrew Bible (Aleppo and Leningradensis) lines out 34:6b–7 as poetry, but that is not unusual since most poetic sections of the Hebrew Bible are not stichometrically presented. "Finding poetry," then, will depend on other factors internal to the content itself, not (solely) on the (re)presentation of the texts as we find them in ancient manuscripts or now-standard editions.[2]

In prose format, the text may be provisionally translated as follows:

34:6bThen Yhwh called out:

> "Yhwh: A God merciful and gracious, patient and abounding in faithfulness and truth! 7One who keeps faithfulness to thousands. One who forgives iniquity, transgression, and sin and does not leave (such wrongdoing) unpunished. One who repays the iniquity of parents upon children and grandchildren unto the third, even the fourth generation."

Other translations are possible, and I will revisit some of the phrasing offered here in what follows; but even this provisional translation evidences features of the text that are more indicative of poetry than prose—or, at least, nearer the poetic side of the poetry-prose continuum.[3] These include parataxis, repetition, assonance/consonance, anaphora, rhythm, and parallelism. These elements become even clearer in a poetically lined version:

(1)

a	*wayyiqrā' yhwh:*	Then Yhwh called out:
b	*yhwh 'ēl raḥûm wəḥannûn*	"Yhwh: A God merciful and gracious,

---

2. See J. Blake Couey, *Reading the Poetry of First Isaiah: The Most Perfect Model of the Prophetic Poetry* (Oxford: Oxford University Press, 2015), 22–27; F. W. Dobbs-Allsopp, *On Biblical Poetry* (Oxford: Oxford University Press, 2015), 29–42.

3. On which see James L. Kugel, *The Idea of Biblical Poetry: Parallelism and Its History* (New Haven: Yale University Press, 1981), 59–95.

c	*'erek 'appayim*	patient
d	*wərab-ḥesed we'ĕmet*	and abounding in faithfulness and truth!
e	*nōṣēr ḥesed lā'ălāpîm*	One who keeps faithfulness to thousands.
f	*nōśē' 'āwōn wāpeša' wəḥaṭṭā'â*	One who forgives iniquity, transgression, and sin
g	*wənaqqēh lō' yənaqqeh*	and does not leave (such wrongdoing) unpunished.
h	*pōqēd 'āwōn 'ābôt*	One who repays the iniquity of parents
i	*'al-bānîm wə'al-bənê bānîm*	upon children and grandchildren
j	*'al-šillēšîm wə'al-ribbē'îm*	unto the third, even the fourth generation."

A number of features indicate the poetic nature of the text. First, the text manifests a good deal of repetition: key words are repeated, including *yhwh* (a, b), *ḥesed* ("faithfulness," d, e), *'āwôn* ("iniquity," f, h), √*nqh* ("leave unpunished," g [2×]), *bānîm* ("children," i [3×]); as are the particles *wə-* ("and," b, d, f [2×], g, i, j) and *'al* ("upon," i [2×], j [2×]). Perhaps most striking in terms of repetition is the three-fold use of the same grammatical form (*qal* active participle, *qōṭēl* form) at the beginning of lines e, f, and h ("One who . . ."), two of which also begin with the same consonant (*n*) and contain a sibilant as the second consonant (*nōṣēr*, "one who keeps," in e, and *nōśē'*, "one who forgives," in f). The lines thus share parallel structures reinforced by assonance.[4] Consonance and assonance are also present in repeated endings: the dual (*-ayim*, c) and masculine plural (*-îm*; e, i [2×], j), which are near-rhymes, if not actual rhymes. The same holds true for the heavy use of the *a* vowel, which occurs in every line; the use of the labial consonants *b* and *p* throughout; the long /ū/ sound that binds *raḥûm wəḥannûn* together (b); and so on and so forth. Finally, despite the not infrequent use of *waw* (b, d, f–g, i–j), several parts of the unit are conjoined asyndetically/paratactically—that is, *without* a conjunction—or, put differently, these parts are serially arranged: *yhwh yhwh* (a–b); *'erek 'appayim* ("patient," c); *'al-bānîm . . . 'al-šillēšîm* ("upon children . . . unto the third," i–j); and *nōṣēr* ("one who keeps," e), *nōśē'* ("one who forgives," f), *pōqēd* ("one who repays," h). Each of the latter three participles have

---

4. Other grammatical and phonological repetitions include the repeated syndetic (b, d, f–g, i–j) and prepositional constructions (i–j); the two segholate (*qeṭel*) noun forms, *ḥesed* ("faithfulness") and *'ĕmet* ("truth") in d; the two adjectival *qaṭṭûl* forms *raḥûm* ("merciful") and *ḥannûn* ("gracious") in b; and the emphatic infinitive + verb construction *wənaqqēh lō' yənaqqeh* ("and does not leave unpunished") in line g.

extended adjuncts, of course, but their morphology and close concatenation are reminiscent of dense doxological poetry like that found in Second Isaiah (e.g., Isa 41:13–14; 44:24b–28; 48:17).

These elements are present, at least in the Hebrew text as it currently stands, regardless of the precise lineation used, and their presence already suggests a poetic composition. Even so, the lineation offered above should not go unexamined. At least four items call for careful investigation, and since all poetry, including Hebrew poetry, depends on the line,[5] assessing each of these four will help to determine the nature of the *Gnadenforrmel* as poetic discourse even as it will also facilitate a close(r) engagement with the poetics of the text itself.

The Lineation of Lines a–b

There are two main alternatives to consider for lines a–b:

(2)

wayyiqrā᾽ yhwh	Then Yhwh called out:
yhwh ᾽ēl raḥûm wəhannûn	"Yhwh: A God merciful and gracious"

or

(3)

wayyiqrā᾽	Then he called out:
yhwh yhwh	"Yhwh, Yhwh:
᾽ēl raḥûm wəhannûn	A God merciful and gracious."

In (2), the first instance of *yhwh* functions as the subject of the verb *wayyiqrā᾽* ("he called out"), with the second *yhwh* serving as the first word of the reported speech. In (3), *both* instances of *yhwh* belong to the divine speech and are best understood as an emphatic repetition of the divine name: "Yhwh, Yhwh!"

Deciding between (2) and (3) is no easy matter. Yhwh's name is also used in Exod 34:6a as the subject of the verb *wayyaʿăbōr* ("he [Yhwh] crossed over"), and so, syntactically, it does not need to be repeated here, where it would be technically superfluous.[6] This observation would seem to support option (3). Also

---

5. See Couey, *Reading the Poetry*, 21–54; Dobbs-Allsopp, *On Biblical Poetry*, 14–94.

6. The repetition of *yhwh* following "and he called out," coupled with the explicit mention of Moses as subject of the verbs in v. 8, should leave little doubt that Yhwh is the one who speaks vv. 6b–7. Despite these factors, Targum Neofiti and (apparently) the Septuagint (LXX) under-

favoring (3) is the disjunctive accent *səgōltā* found with *wayyiqrā'* in the Hebrew text, which serves to separate it from the first instance of *yhwh*; that first instance, in turn, has a conjunctive accent (*mûnāḥ*), which connects it to the second *yhwh*.[7] On the other hand, perhaps in favor of (2), is the specific conjunction of the verb *qārā'* ("to call out") with the divine name: elsewhere, this combination means "to invoke."[8] If that is the case here, the second *yhwh* would be the subject of the entire formulation, producing yet another possible lineation-with-translation:

(4)

wayyiqrā' yhwh yhwh	Then Yhwh invoked (the name) "Yhwh":
'ēl raḥûm wəhannûn	"A God merciful and gracious . . ."

though this lineation could also be understood along the lines of (3):

(4*)

wayyiqrā' yhwh yhwh	Then he called out: "Yhwh, Yhwh:
'ēl raḥûm wəhannûn	A God merciful and gracious . . ."

While the disjunctive accent on *wayyiqrā'* appears to argue against (4) or (4*), the accent over the second *yhwh* (*zāqēp parvum*) might support either, insofar as it separates, even if only slightly, the second *yhwh* from the *'ēl raḥûm wəhannûn* ("A God merciful and gracious") that follows. Of course, that may simply mark *yhwh yhwh* as separate from *'ēl raḥûm wəhannûn*, which would work for (3), (4), and (4*).

To be sure, the punctuation of the Hebrew text (no less than its vocalization) is not foolproof, but the same judgment holds true for every other evaluative instrument as well.[9] Meter, for instance, is now widely believed to not be operative in Hebrew poetry. But even the harshest critics of metrical approaches to Hebrew poetry often still end up counting various elements, even if that is only for descriptive purposes.[10] But what, exactly, should one count: words, syllables, stresses, or

---

stood Moses, not Yhwh, to have spoken the *Gnadenformel*. The Samaritan tradition supports Yhwh as speaker.

7. For the importance of punctuation in ancient manuscripts for poetic analysis, see Couey, *Reading the Poetry*, 28.

8. See Gerhard von Rad, *Old Testament Theology*, trans. D. M. G. Stalker, 2 vols. (San Francisco: Harper & Row, 1962), 1:183; cf. William H. C. Propp, *Exodus 19–40: A New Translation with Introduction and Commentary*, AB 2A (New York: Doubleday, 2006), 610.

9. Cf. Couey, *Reading the Poetry*, 26, 47, 54.

10. See Couey, *Reading the Poetry*, 22, 28, 40–49.

all of the above?[11] Still further, what, if anything, constitutes an "acceptable" or "regular" structure ("meter") or at what point does "free rhythm" become so free as to no longer be properly considered verse? Finally, should the lines "balance" somehow, or be otherwise regular(ized) in some way? Consider, again, (2) and (3), this time with word + syllable and stress counts:

(2)

wayyiqrāʾ yhwh:	[2+3; 2]
yhwh ʾēl raḥûm wəhannûn	[4+8; 4]

(3)

(*wayyiqrāʾ*)	[∅][12]
yhwh yhwh	[2+4; 2]
ʾēl raḥûm wəhannûn	[3+6; 3]

Since we are not entirely certain what would have been acceptable prosody in terms of quantitative evaluation (if such ever existed), it is difficult, if not impossible, to know if (2) or (3) is superior. Furthermore, it is entirely possible that a poem (or poet) might break with form for any number of reasons, which would effectively obviate any "metrical" analysis—or at least the attempt to deploy it prescriptively. These important caveats entered, it remains the case, in terms of balance or symmetry, that the second line in (2) seems overloaded, with twice as many words, syllables, and stresses as the first line. Although (3) is better on this point, (4) or (4*) seems best of all.[13]

Whatever the precise case, it seems fair to say—both from the perspective of balance/symmetry and on the basis of the Hebrew punctuation and syntactical considerations—that the lineation of lines a–b is susceptible to more than one analysis.[14] Among other things, *yhwh yhwh* may be polyvalent, with one or both

---

11. See, inter alia, Oswald Loretz and Ingo Kottsieper, *Colometry in Ugaritic and Biblical Poetry: Introduction, Illustrations and Topical Bibliography*, UBL 5 (Altenberge: CIS-Verlag, 1987).

12. In this understanding, *wayyiqrāʾ* is the narrative introduction to the poetry and thus "extra-metrical."

13. If so, this has bearing on *wayyiqrāʾ*: might it have been considered part of the poetry—a kind of frozen introduction? The pleasing rhythm of (4), especially when understood as per (4*), would permit as much.

14. Lineation is, of course, not determined by any one single consideration like balance or parallelism but by a host of factors. See Couey, *Reading the Poetry*, 21–54; Dobbs-Allsopp, *On Biblical Poetry*, 14–94.

instances functioning with the verb, even as one or both could be taken as that which is invoked (the divine name itself) or with the following definition of the Deity as *ʾēl raḥûm wəḥannûn*. These apparently unresolvable questions about lines a–b should not be taken as indicating that they are *not* poetry, but simple prose. Quite to the contrary, the polyvalence at work in these lines seems sufficient by itself to suggest that Exod 34:6b–7 is poetic utterance.

ʾēl raḥûm wəḥannûn in Context

The second factor that needs discussion is the relationship of *ʾēl raḥûm wəḥannûn* ("A God merciful and gracious") to what follows. If the force of *wayyiqrāʾ yhwh yhwh* is to invoke the divine name "Yhwh," a name (or entity) that is immediately glossed as *ʾēl raḥûm wəḥannûn*, then the next, paratactically conjoined line offers further definition of Yhwh as *ʾerek ʾappayim* ("patient"). This two-fold, asyndetic definition of Yhwh is followed immediately by a clause with the conjunction: *wərab-ḥesed weʾĕmet* ("and abounding in faithfulness and truth"). An important question at this point, to put it in contemporary terms, is whether this long description of Yhwh is a case of the "Oxford comma." Is Yhwh thrice-defined: (i) a gracious-and-merciful God, (ii) patient, and (iii) abounding in faithfulness and truth? Or is the last mentioned item further definition of the second, such that there are only two groups of qualities mentioned here—namely, Yhwh as (i) gracious-and-merciful and (ii) patient-and-abounding-in-faithfulness-and-truth? The repetition of the conjunction *waw* ("and") in *wəḥannûn* and *wərab* suggests the latter is the case, resulting in a nice balance:

raḥûm	*wəḥannûn*
ʾerek ʾappayim	*wərab-ḥesed weʾĕmet*

In this understanding we seem to have a total of four qualities,[15] with *ḥesed weʾĕmet* functioning as one (hendiatically): "true faithfulness," "loyal truth," or the like.[16] This suggestion is strengthened by the phonological and grammatical binding that is evident in the repetition of these two *qeṭel* forms in close succession (along with *ʾerek* in line c). Whatever the case, the semantic overlap between these

---

15. In point of fact, Exod 34:6b–7 is the locus of the famous Thirteen Attributes of God in Judaism, for which see Benno Jacob, *The Second Book of the Bible: Exodus*, trans. W. Jacob (Hoboken, NJ: Ktav, 1992), 985.

16. Cf. Ruth Scoralick, *Gottes Güte und Gottes Zorn: Die Gottesprädikationen in Exodus 34,6f und ihre intertextuellen Beziehungen zum Zwölfprophetenbuch*, HBS 33 (Freiburg: Herder, 2002), 37–38.

four qualities is a clear case of heaping up terms—a certain poetic density—so as to underscore the benevolence of Yhwh, if not also to merge or mix the four qualities such that each is somehow defined with reference to the others.

wənaqqēh lōʾ yənaqqeh in Context

The third item that requires discussion is the relationship of *wənaqqēh lōʾyənaqqeh* ("and does not leave unpunished") to the surrounding material. This phrase (in boldface) clearly interrupts the series of three participles (underlined):

e <u>*nōṣēr*...</u> ("One who keeps...")
f <u>*nōśēʾ*...</u> ("One who forgives...")
g **wənaqqēh lōʾ yənaqqeh**
h <u>*pōqēd*...</u> ("One who repays...")

In some ways, the issue here is not unlike the preceding one: Is *wənaqqēh lōʾ yənaqqeh* subordinate to *nōśēʾ ʿāwōn wāpešaʿ wəhaṭṭāʾâ* ("one who forgives iniquity, transgression, and sin")—a kind of parenthetical aside or further definition—or is it to be considered in line with the other participles, such that one has a string of four (more) qualities of Yhwh? Are there, that is, three qualities here—

Keeper (*nōṣēr*)
Forgiver (*nōśēʾ*)—but not leaving unpunished (*wənaqqēh lōʾyənaqqeh*)
Repayer (*pōqēd*)

—or four?

Keeper (*nōṣēr*)
Forgiver (*nōśēʾ*)
Requiter (*wənaqqēh lōʾ yənaqqeh*)
Repayer (*pōqēd*)

In favor of the four-fold understanding is that the preceding lines also manifested a string of four qualities:

Gracious
Merciful
Patient
Abounding

33

Perhaps also in favor of a four-element listing is that "Requiter" makes this second string of divine descriptions divide evenly between two more benevolent ("Keeper," "Forgiver") and two more judgmental ("Requiter," "Repayer") qualities. Perhaps arguing against it, however, is that *wənaqqēh lō' yənaqqeh* is itself not a participial construction, coupled with the fact that it seems to depend syntactically on the preceding line for the objects of its verbal action (*'āwōn wāpeša' wəḥaṭṭā'â*, "iniquity, transgression, and sin") not to mention its semantic content, even if that is antithetically flexed: *forgiver* of x, y, and z, *but not acquitting* the same. Then again, as in the case of *'erek 'appayim wərab-ḥesed we'ĕmet* discussed above, perhaps one should not be too quick to judge the *waw*-constructions as dependent solely on their immediately preceding lines. It remains possible, that is, given the sparseness that marks poetry, which so often leaves syntactical relations un(der)specified, that the phrase "and does not leave unpunished" is janus-faced: it may well be an indication of one way Yhwh keeps *ḥesed* ("faithfulness") to thousands (line e) even as it simultaneously segues into the following description of Yhwh as *pōqēd 'āwōn 'ābôt* ("one who repays the iniquity of parents"). Here too, then, as with *yhwh yhwh* earlier, we have an element in the *Gnadenformel* that appears to do double-duty, working both backward and forward, and which manifests a kind of polyvalence within the play of what increasingly appears to be poetic utterance.[17]

Lines i–j in Context

The same may hold true for the fourth issue that requires discussion—namely, the relationship of the final two lines with what precedes them. The lineation offered in (1) above made lines i–j subordinate to line h:

h   *pōqēd 'āwōn 'ābôt*
i   *'al-bānîm wə'al-bənê bānîm*
j   *'al-šillēšîm wə'al-ribbē'îm*

which is perfectly sensible and how most translations understand the syntax:

17. To be sure, a confluence of numerous factors is required to determine the presence of poetry (see above and further below, esp. note 21). For other treatments that consider Exod 34:6b–7 to be poetic, see, inter alia, William Johnstone, *Exodus 20–40*, SHBC (Macon, GA: Smyth & Helwys, 2014), 406–8; and Duane A. Garrett, *A Commentary on Exodus* (Grand Rapids: Kregel Academic, 2014), 639–42, 652–53, 721. Contrary opinions exist: John I. Durham, *Exodus*, WBC 3 (Waco, TX: Word, 1987), 450, lines out the *Gnadenformel* "not to indicate any poetic form, but to give this recital something of the sonorous impact it has in Hebrew." But such impact may itself be proof of poetry!

h   One who repays the iniquity of parents
i   upon children and grandchildren
j   unto the third, even the fourth generation.

Two observations caution against a hard and fast conclusion, however, or at least an inflexible understanding of the lines. The first is to recall that line h is the third in a sequence of participles describing Yhwh. Lines i–j, that is, may relate somehow to the entire string of participles, or, to be more precise, the last two (*nōṣēr*, "Keeper"; and *nōśē'*, "Forgiver"), not just the third in the sequence (*pōqēd*, "Repayer"). The second observation is that a similarly extended poetic relationship was posited for *wənaqqēh lōʾ yənaqqeh* in line g. That line, too, may not relate exclusively to the preceding line f ("one who forgives..."), but might also operate with reference to line e ("one who keeps...") even as it anticipates line h ("one who repays...").

If a same situation obtains for lines i–j, they would modify not only line h but also line f. A diagram demonstrates this relationship clearly:

e	*nōṣēr ḥesed lāʾǎlāpîm*	One who keeps faithfulness to thousands.
f	*nōśē' ʾāwōn wāpešaʿ wəḥaṭṭāʾâ*	One who forgives iniquity, transgression, and sin
(i)	(*ʾal-bānîm wəʾal-bənê bānîm*)	(of[18] children and grandchildren)
(j)	(*ʾal-šillēšîm wəʾal-ribbēʿîm*)	(unto the third, even the fourth generation,)
g	*wənaqqēh lōʾ yənaqqeh*	and does not leave (such wrongdoing) unpunished.
h	*pōqēd ʾāwōn ʾābôt*	One who repays the iniquity of parents
i	*ʾal-bānîm wəʾal-bənê bānîm*	upon children and grandchildren
j	*ʾal-šillēšîm wəʾal-ribbēʿîm*	unto the third, even the fourth generation.

If this is correct, the double-duty of lines i–j produces several effects: the first is to draw an additional distinction between lines e and f. Beyond the obvious lexical

18. Taking *'al* here as "with regard to, concerning" (see *HALOT* 2:826; BDB 754); hence: "of." The polyvalence of Hebrew prepositions frequently requires that they be translated in various ways, even when they appear in close succession (cf. lines i–j: "upon... unto"), which can lead to the need for reanalysis. For reanalysis in Hebrew poetry, see, inter alia, Edward L. Greenstein, "How Does Parallelism Mean?" in *A Sense of Text: The Art of Language in the Study of Biblical Literature*, ed. L. Nemoy (Winona Lake, IN: Eisenbrauns, 1983), 41–70.

differences between the two lines, there is now the additional difference between "thousands" (*'ălāpîm*)[19] in line e and the more restricted number of generations (*'al-bānîm . . . wə'al-ribbē'îm*) in line f (via lines i–j). Even so, understanding lines i–j in this way means that each participle in the sequence now has its own associated temporal phrase:

nōṣēr . . . lā'ălāpîm	Keeper . . . to thousands
nōśē' . . . ('al-bānîm . . . wə'al-ribbē'îm)	Forgiver . . . (unto the third, even the fourth generation)
pōqēd . . . 'al-bānîm . . . wə'al-ribbē'îm	Repayer . . . unto the third, even the fourth generation

A second effect is that line g (*wənaqqēh lō' yənaqqeh*, "and does not leave unpunished") is highlighted even more than it already was. Even if line g is not subordinate to line f, it is nevertheless distinctive—a point signaled by its different, non-participial construction, and now further underscored insofar as it occurs between two constructions that concern forgiveness for and punishment upon children and grandchildren. But the third, and by far the most important, effect is that lines i–j now extend Yhwh's forgiving action (line f) as far into the future as Yhwh's repaying action (line h). It is not only Yhwh's punishment that reaches to the third and fourth generation: so also now does Yhwh's forgiveness.

An analogue from a much later poetic text lends support to this understanding of how lines i–j relate to lines f and h. According to some scholars, the phrase "on earth as it is in heaven" (*hōs en ouranō kai epi gēs*) in the Lord's Prayer (Matt 6:9–13; cf. Luke 11:2–4) applies to each of the three preceding requests, not simply the final petition:[20]

> Our Father in heaven,
>> hallowed be your name (on earth as it is in heaven).
>> Your kingdom come (on earth as it is in heaven).
>> Your will be done, on earth as it is in heaven. (Matt 6:9b–10)

---

19. *'ălāpîm* probably refers to generations—either "the thousandth generation" or "thousands of generations." Cf. Propp, *Exodus 19–40*, 173: "We should understand *'ălāpîm* as an expression of infinity."

20. See Alan Hugh McNeile, *The Gospel according to St. Matthew: The Greek Text with Introduction, Notes, and Indices* (London: Macmillan, 1915), 79; and Frederick Dale Bruner, *Matthew: A Commentary*, vol. 1: *The Christbook: Matthew 1–12*, rev. ed. (Grand Rapids: Eerdmans, 2004), 304.

Summary

To sum up to this point: Exod 34:6b–7 gives ample evidence of sophisticated artistry and a concentration of poetic elements, all of which support its assessment as high diction—in a word, poetry.[21] If this is correct, then several things follow. Paramount among these would be that the poetic nature of the *Gnadenformel* suggests that it is less linear in terms of logic than typically construed and also less straightforward in terms of syntactical relationships (at least in English translation). Indeed, no less than three different parts of this unit appear to serve more than one function within the utterance (*yhwh yhwh*, *wənaqqēh lōʾ yənaqqeh*, and *ʿal-bānîm ... wəʿal-ribbēʿîm*). Furthermore, it has long been clear in almost any reading (even rather prosaic ones) that divine benevolence outweighs divine judgment in the *Gnadenformel*: Yhwh forgives three things (line f: *ʿāwōn wāpešaʿ wəḥaṭṭāʾâ*), but only punishes one (line h: *ʿāwōn*) and shows *ḥesed* to "thousands" (line e) but extends punishment to (merely) the fourth generation (lines i–j). But the effect of the double-duty parts *wənaqqēh lōʾ yənaqqeh* and *ʿal-bānîm ... wəʿal-ribbēʿîm* is to make the divine benevolence *even more extensive* than typically recognized. Yhwh's commitment to not leave wrongdoing unpunished (line g) is not only an *anticipation* of Yhwh's repayment of wrongdoing (line h) but equally also an *instantiation of how Yhwh keeps ḥesed* (line e). Additionally, it is not only Yhwh's repayment of iniquity (line h), *but also his forgiveness* of iniquity, transgression, and sin (line f)

---

21. It is instructive at this point to compare the *Gnadenformel* with Exod 20:5b–6 (the second commandment), where similar language is also found: "Because I, Yhwh your God, am a jealous God: One who repays the iniquity of parents upon children unto the third, even the fourth generation of those who hate me [*pōqēd ʿāwōn ʾābōt ʿal-bānîm ʿal-šillēšîm wəʿal-ribbēʿîm ləśōnʾāy*], but one who shows faithfulness to thousands of those who love me and keep my commandments [*wəʿōśeh ḥesed lāʾălāpîm ləʾōhăbay ûləšōmrê miṣwōtāy*]." Could Exod 20:5b–6 also be poetry? One immediately notes the balance offered by the two participial phrases ("One who repays ... one who shows ..."), but those would be inordinately long poetic lines without further division. Other details, such as the syndetic construction *pōqēd ... wəʿōśeh* ("One who repays ... *but* one who shows ...") in Exod 20 vs. the paratactic one in Exod 34; the frequency of prose particles in Exod 20 and their absence in Exod 34; and the difficulties in understanding the poetic relationship between the "lines" of Exod 20 (even if one employs a generous understanding of "synthetic" parallelism or "seconding/intensification" categories) are all indicators that, despite the semantic similarity to the *Gnadenformel*, Exod 20:5b–6 is decidedly *not* poetic. The comparison also helps to underscore the poetic nature of the *Gnadenformel*. For further observations on Exod 20 vis-à-vis Exod 34, see Nahum M. Sarna, *Exodus* שמות*: The Traditional Hebrew Text with the New JPS Translation* (Philadelphia: Jewish Publication Society, 1991), 216; W. Johnstone, *Exodus 20–40*, 400, 405; Jacob, *Exodus*, 982–85; and Thomas B. Dozeman, *Exodus*, ECC (Grand Rapids: Eerdmans, 2009), 736–39.

that extends to children and grandchildren—even to the third and fourth generations (lines i–j). In brief, analyzing the *Gnadenformel* as poetry produces a far more dynamic understanding of the presentation of the divine character: Yhwh's character turns out to be flexible and porous—not unlike so much poetry—and ultimately not simply or predominantly benevolent, but *superabundantly if not almost exclusively* benevolent. This proves extremely important when Exod 34:6b–7 is considered within its larger literary context (see §2 below).

Before offering such a reading of the *Gnadenformel* in context, the provisional translation offered initially may be revisited, this time with an eye on trying to make the poetic aspects of the unit more readily apparent in a rendering that is freer:

> Then he shouted: "Yhwh! Yhwh!
> A God merciful and gracious,
> A God patient and abounding in faithfulness and truth!
> Keeper of faithfulness to thousands!
>> (One who does not leave wrongdoing unpunished.)
> Forgiver of iniquity, transgression, and sin!
>> (For children, even grandchildren
>> to the third, even the fourth generation!)
> One who does not leave wrongdoing unpunished!
> Repayer of parental guilt
>> to children, even grandchildren
>> to the third, even the fourth generation!"

2. Yhwh's Poetry Elsewhere and in the Context of Exodus 32–34

With the poetry and poetics of the *Gnadenformel* established to sufficient degree, we may now turn to larger, contextual considerations. Yhwh's utterance of this poetic unit occurs within a book that is full of divine speech, most of which is *not* poetry. In Exodus, that is, Yhwh does not always or often speak in poetry, but sometimes can and sometimes does. This raises questions: Where else does Yhwh prove the poet? And why would Yhwh speak in poetry in such places and, especially, here in Exod 34:6b–7?

There is not space in the present chapter to explore every instance of divine poetic utterance in the Hebrew Bible. The Latter Prophets represent extended poetic speeches by the Deity (mediated by the prophetic figures themselves), but God speaks poetically elsewhere as well, as in Job 38–41. In these cases, poetry may be mostly a matter of course—part and parcel of the underlying literary genre (prophecy or wisdom, respectively). The most instructive comparables to the *Gnadenformel*, therefore, are those places where Yhwh utters poetry that is embedded within larger prose contexts.[22] These, too, are not unknown in the prophets (e.g., Jeremiah, Ezekiel), but are best traced in the narrative works of the Old Testament.

But even with this generic restriction, there is not space to explore divine poetry within the Torah alone, let alone the entire Primary History (or beyond). That point granted, a fruitful way of proceeding is to investigate those instances of divine speech within narrative contexts in which God's discourse takes poetic form. Texts such as Gen 1:28b; Gen 3:14–19; 8:22; 9:5–6; 12:3; 16:10–12; and 25:23 are among those in the opening book of the Bible that have often been identified and lined out as poetry in English translations. But other passages in the Torah also represent Yhwh's poetic flair, though these poetic snatches remain just that: scattered bits of poetry amidst a sea of prose. Even so, two poetic moments within Exodus are particularly significant:[23]

(1) The first is the revelation of the divine name *'ehyeh 'ăšer 'ehyeh* ("I am who I am" or the like) in Exod 3:14. This name, which seems poetic enough on its own, is immediately recast by the Deity (*'ĕlōhîm*, "God") as "the LORD" (*yhwh*). After this (re)definition comes a conclusion that is a perfect poetic couplet:

zeh-šəmî lə'ōlām	This is my name forever,
wəzeh zikrî lədōr dōr	and this is my memorial for all time. (Exod 3:15b)

(2) The second is the divine speech in Exod 19:3–6, which begins with an introduction that is, just like 3:15b, a textbook example of "synonymous" parallelism:

kōh tō'mar ləbêt ya'ăqōb	Thus you will speak to the house of Jacob,
wətaggêd libnê yiśrā'ēl	and declare to the children of Israel. (Exod 19:3b)

---

22. On inset poetry generally, see James W. Watts, *Psalm and Story: Inset Hymns in Hebrew Narrative*, JSOTSup 139 (Sheffield: JSOT Press, 1992); and Steven Weitzman, *Song and Story in Biblical Narrative: The History of a Literary Convention in Ancient Israel* (Bloomington: Indiana University Press, 1997).

23. For more on poetic texts in Exodus, see James Muilenburg, "The Form and Structure of the Covenantal Formulations," *VT* 9 (1959): 347–65, esp. 352–53, who deems all of Exod 19:3–6 poetic; and Garrett, *Exodus*, passim, who finds no less than eight poems in Exodus: 5:21; 6:2–8; 15:1–18; 15:25–26; 19:3–6; 24:15–18; 29:42–46; and 34:6–7. Not all of Garrett's corpus are divine speech, and some of these texts are non-controversial (15:1–18). In several instances, however, Garrett fails to provide adequate justification that the texts in his corpus are, in fact, poetry, and there is oftentimes good evidence against such a determination (e.g., the presence of prose particles). Finally, some texts that could be poetic (e.g., 32:18) are not identified by Garrett as such.

Both of these poetic snippets are un(der)developed, to be sure, and shift quickly enough back into prose discourse, but both are intriguing as they represent Yhwh with a poetic penchant, sliding into high diction at what appear to be singularly important moments: the revelation of God's own name (Exod 3:14–15) and the introduction to the Sinaitic covenant (Exod 19:1–6). In the case of Exod 3, the couplet that concludes the exchange about Yhwh's name underscores the poetic nature of the name itself—in this case its given-ness (*yhwh*) coupled with its opacity (*'ehyeh 'ăšer 'ehyeh*).[24] The poetic conclusion in Exod 3:15b instantiates both aspects, semantically signaling that God's name is secure (*lə'ōlām, lədōr dōr*) even while playing with non-identical equivalences (*šēm, zēker*) and omitting any finite verb, including the copula, which would otherwise lock the name down or determine it in some axiomatic "equation." God's name is given, therefore, but not in any final sort of way. In the case of Exod 19, so much of what follows in the Sinai pericope is *far* from poetic—much appears downright pedantic given the legalese of it all. But, despite that, Yhwh's covenant begins with poetic balance and style, suggesting that the law to follow, similarly, should be considered beautiful—perhaps due to its own symmetries and balance (cf. Hebrew *mišpāṭ*)—and so the law deserves to be artfully introduced by means of poetry.[25]

This leads back to a consideration of Exod 34:6b–7 in its wider literary context. Why should Yhwh speak poetically precisely at this point and what does the poetry do in this particular setting? Tradition-historical or compositional-critical perspectives might suggest that the *Gnadenformel* is an ancient cultic fragment that has been simply inserted here, or, alternatively, that it is a text of more recent vintage that was composed for just this literary context. Either approach would explain, diachronically, why the poetic *Gnadenformel* appears literarily distinct from its more prosaic context. Neither, however, would explain its poetic function in context. A wider consideration of Exod 32–34, coupled with the insights provided by the interaction of the poetic bits of 3:14–15 and 19:3 with their surrounding prose contexts, proves far more interesting and instructive than tradition-historical or composition-critical perspectives.

Exodus 32 famously recounts the incident of the golden calf (vv. 1–6). The complete obliteration of Israel is only prevented by Moses's intercession with Yhwh (vv. 7–14), though the aftermath remains nothing short of deathly (vv. 15–35). Yhwh's anger seems mostly assuaged at the end of chapter 32, but Yhwh is adamant that he will accompany the Israelites no further (Exod 33:1–6). This leads

---

24. For reflections on Yhwh's presence in the divine name, which nevertheless remains elusive and intangible, see von Rad, *Old Testament Theology*, 180–83.

25. For more poetry that celebrates the perfections of God's law, see Pss 1, 19, and 119.

to a second important intercession by Moses and Yhwh's apparent concession to accompany Moses (Exod 33:12–14). But Moses isn't satisfied and so continues to press for God's continuing presence with Israel as a whole, and Yhwh eventually concedes (vv. 15–17). After this comes the exchange about Moses seeing Yhwh's "glory" (v. 18), but Yhwh states that only his "goodness," not his face, may be seen (vv. 19–23). At last we come to chapter 34, and Moses ascends Sinai once more with two new tablets (vv. 1–4). This is the moment when Yhwh appears, invokes the name, and speaks the *Gnadenformel* (vv. 5–7). Moses's response is obeisance and worship and a third intercessory request that Yhwh accompany the people and forgive their sin (vv. 8–9). After this comes the account of the so-called cultic Decalogue (vv. 10–28), but it is quite striking that Yhwh does not reply directly or explicitly to Moses's most recent request, and, up to v. 10 at least, it is possible to take Yhwh's words as having to do *solely* with Moses (the first instance of a second-person plural verb referring to all Israel is found in v. 13).

The poetry and poetics of the *Gnadenformel* fit this larger literary context in two primary ways. First, as virtually all commentators note, what is needed after the stupendous breach of covenant found in Exod 32 is nothing less than a full pardon, total forgiveness. As detailed in the preceding analysis (§1), the poetics of the *Gnadenformel* indicate that Yhwh's character is fully capable of such clemency, and in far more extensive and developed ways (thanks to the poetry) than is typically recognized. Yhwh's character is not just benevolent in this regard but *superabundantly* benevolent. Yhwh's capacity for faithfulness and forgiveness matches, but then surpasses—exponentially!—his ability to punish. And yet, the *Gnadenformel* continues to acknowledge Yhwh's punitive capacities; indeed, the poetics of the *Gnadenformel* make Yhwh's punishment part of the way Yhwh keeps ḥesed.[26] The *Gnadenformel*, that is, bears within itself what could be called a lyric tension—replete with lyric cohesion—between Yhwh's (far more) merciful and (far less) punitive sides.[27] *Both* sides of Yhwh *must* be acknowledged within the context of Exod 32–34: the former since the breach brought about in the calf debacle is too fundamental, the cut too deep, to think it could be repaired easily or quickly. Hence, barring a superabundance of divine mercy, there will simply be no more story of Israel to tell—at least no more story of *Israel-with-Yhwh*. But the punishing side of Yhwh must also be admitted because, again, the covenant wound is deep, and the judgment experienced

---

26. Cf. George V. Pixley, *On Exodus: A Liberation Perspective*, trans. R. R. Barr (Maryknoll, NY: Orbis, 1987), 157–58.

27. For a similar dynamic in Second Isaiah, see Katie M. Heffelfinger, *I Am Large, I Contain Multitudes: Lyric Cohesion and Conflict in Second Isaiah*, BIS 105 (Leiden: Brill, 2011). For her comments on the *Gnadenformel*, see Heffelfinger, *I Am Large*, 225.

by Israel in its aftermath was both costly and deathly—so much so that it cannot be forgotten or ignored.[28] Both sides of the divine nature *must* be acknowledged, then—and for both Yhwh and Israel alike—and both sides *are* acknowledged in the *Gnadenformel*: they cohere. But it is equally evident by means of explicit semantic content and via the poetics that Yhwh's benevolence outpaces his punitive sensibilities. The coherence is not equal, therefore, but decidedly unbalanced: (poetic) tension is at work. Among other things, the tension between these two sides protects Yhwh: he remains free to punish even if his mercy far outweighs his wrath, and he remains free to forgive even if wrath is part of his nature. In this way, the *Gnadenformel* addresses the crisis of the covenant moving forward—for both Yhwh and Israel alike—but it does not limit Yhwh to only one mode of being or relating vis-à-vis Israel. Yhwh can and will punish should the need arise; Yhwh can and will forgive, and is overwhelmingly predisposed to doing so.[29]

Second, the poetics of the *Gnadenformel* may explain why Yhwh does not reply explicitly to Moses's last intercession in Exod 34:8–9. In one sense, Yhwh's silence here may be compared to Yhwh's exchange with Jeremiah in his "confessions." Yhwh answers one of the prophet's laments in Jer 12:5–6 and does so again in 15:19–21. After this, however, Yhwh speaks no more, even though Jeremiah's laments continue (e.g., Jer 20:7–18). The reason for Yhwh's silence may well be due to the last line of his final response in Jer 15:20 ("because I am with you, to save you and to deliver you"), which echoes the divine promise of presence and deliverance given at the time of Jeremiah's call in Jer 1:8 ("because I am with you to deliver you").[30] There is, in a very real sense, nothing further Yhwh *can* say or that Yhwh *needs* to say. God's initial promise of divine accompaniment and protection remains in place. Jeremiah will have to go on with just that much: no more, certainly, but certainly no less.

Analogously, the *Gnadenformel* within Exod 32–34 may, in Yhwh's perspective, suffice such that he need not say anything further in response to Moses's third request (Exod 34:9).[31] After the *Gnadenformel*, what more needs to be said?

---

28. Cf. Propp, *Exodus 19–40*, 611; Umberto Cassuto, *A Commentary on the Book of Exodus*, trans. I. Abrahams, repr. ed. (Skokie, IL: Varda, 2005), 438; and, analogously, Heffelfinger, *I Am Large*.

29. Cf. Brueggemann, *Theology*, 217–18; Donald E. Gowan, *Theology in Exodus: Biblical Theology in the Form of a Commentary* (Louisville: Westminster John Knox, 1994), 236; and Mark J. Boda, *A Severe Mercy: Sin and Its Remedy in the Old Testament*, Siphrut 1 (Winona Lake, IN: Eisenbrauns, 2009), 523.

30. See Brent A. Strawn, "Jeremiah's In/Effective Plea: Another Look at נער in Jeremiah I 6," *VT* 55 (2005): 366–77.

31. The lack of explicit responsiveness to Moses might underscore the lyric nature of the *Gnadenformel*. Jonathan Culler has suggested that the "fundamental characteristic of lyric . . .

Moses's further intercession thereafter misses the point. The poetry makes (super)abundantly clear that Yhwh is precisely what Moses continues (somewhat pedantically) to request: a forgiver of guilt and sin—to far off generations!—even if Moses employs the verb √*slḥ* ("to forgive") while Yhwh prefers √*nś'* ("to forgive").[32] Moses, it would seem, has missed the larger point(s) of the poetry with this additional, but completely unnecessary, intercession. Of course, Moses would not be the first person to inadequately grasp a poem! But, before we are too hard on Moses, it should be admitted that there is no indication in the larger context that he is a poor interpreter of Yhwh. To the contrary, Moses seems to know just what to say to Yhwh and exactly when to say it. Still further, rather stunning commendations of Moses bracket the *Gnadenformel* in the unit about Moses speaking with Yhwh "face-to-face" (Exod 33:7–11) and in the unit describing Moses's "shining" face (Exod 34:29–35). Far from being a poor interpreter of poetry, that is, Moses might be an excellent one, sensing within the lyric play that Yhwh's opacity remains firmly in place (cf. "my back" vs. "my face" in Exod 33:23) and that Yhwh's punishing side remains a lively (and deathly) option—even to far off generations![33] And so, in light of the cohesion and conflict of Yhwh's bipolar nature, Moses feels the need to implore yet once more that the triumph of mercy be decisive in this particular case. If, that is, Yhwh, by means of the poetry, is somehow hedging the divine bets to some degree, retaining divine freedom, even definitively, Moses nevertheless prays one more time that Yhwh's mercy and grace triumph decisively (Exod 34:9).[34] Given the superabundance of mercy in the divine character as pronounced in the *Gnadenformel*, such a prayer has a very good chance of success indeed.[35]

---

is not the description and interpretation of a past event but the performance of an event in the lyric present, a time of enunciation" ("Lyric, History, and Genre," in *The Lyric Theory Reader: A Critical Anthology*, ed. Virginia Jackson and Yopie Prins [Baltimore: Johns Hopkins University Press, 2014], 63–77 [68]).

32. For √*slḥ*, see Walter Brueggemann, "The Travail of Pardon: Reflections on *slḥ*," in *A God So Near: Essays on Old Testament Theology in Honor of Patrick D. Miller*, ed. Brent A. Strawn and Nancy R. Bowen (Winona Lake, IN: Eisenbrauns, 2003), 283–97. For √*nś'*, which may connote Yhwh's *own* carrying of the sin, see Jacob, *Exodus*, 984; and Gary A. Anderson, *Sin: A History* (New Haven: Yale University Press, 2009), 15–26.

33. For another instance of this sort of lyric tension in the space of a single verse, see Ps 99:8 (used as the epigraph above): "Yhwh, our God, you answered them; you were a Forgiving God [*'ēl nōśē'*] to them and a Requiter [*wanōqēm*] for their wrongdoings."

34. Another, related possibility, as Justin Walker has pointed out to me (personal communication), is that Moses may be *resisting* Yhwh's poetry at this point, hoping to return to something more prosaic and more certain *à la*, say, Exod 33:17.

35. According to b. Ber. 7a, God prays the same thing to himself (!) every day: "May it be My

3. Yhwh's Poetry and/as Scripture

More could be said on the matters discussed above. But that is to be expected whenever the subject is poetry, which does not answer every question but instead seems to invite any and all questions. I wish to conclude, then, not by recapitulating what has been argued here, or strengthening those points further, but by asking a question. Is what one finds in the *Gnadenformel* and in its relationship to its larger literary context, as well as what one sees in traces of Yhwh's *poesie* elsewhere in the Torah (and beyond), instructive for how to best understand the divine address in Scripture? By means of the poetry of Exodus, we see that the *divine nature* is both revealed and concealed (Exod 3:14–15), and is (at least) bivalent, even if *divine mercy overwhelms divine wrath* (Exod 34:6b–7). Then, too, there is *divine instruction*: so extensive, so detailed, so overwrought, but introduced with a snippet of perfect poetry as if to frame it all in high artistic style (Exod 19:3a). Perhaps in lyrical moments such as these, we see a microcosm of the Torah writ large—if not Scripture itself, in its entirety: it is something on the move, something in profound tension and yet still cohesive, something in (and at) play, something somehow fundamentally and at root, in ipse, *poetic*. It is not unusual, after all, for the spice that is peppered here and there in a dish to turn out to be that which makes it tasty, delicious, and altogether memorable.

---

will that My mercy may suppress My anger, and that My mercy may prevail over My [other] attributes, so that I may deal with My children in the attribute of mercy and, on their behalf, stop short of the limit of strict justice." I owe this reference to Kimberley C. Patton, *The Religion of the Gods: Ritual, Paradox, and Reflexivity* (Oxford: Oxford University Press, 2009), 265–73.

3

Keep/Observe/Do—Carefully—Today!
The Rhetoric of Repetition in Deuteronomy

In art, too, repetition is a sign of maturity, of assurance and strength.[1]

"Repetition" is and remains a religious category.[2]

I n the scholarly literature on Deuteronomy, statements about the book's style are among those most frequently encountered. That style, or what might better be called Deuteronomy's rhetoric, is typically said to be hortatory, proclamatory, even "preachy."[3] It is also said to be prolix, redundant, even monotonous—especially in its repetition of certain key words and formulae.[4]

It is a true and distinct honor and privilege to dedicate this chapter to my late professor Patrick D. Miller, who first led me into the (Hebrew) rhetoric of Deuteronomy and who, I am happy to say, never restrained himself from participating in and seconding its proclamatory aspects! There is no doubt in my mind that these two elements, Miller's teaching and preaching (perhaps it would be better to speak of his teaching/preaching or preaching/teaching), have had a decisive impact on my own occupational and vocational pursuits.

1. Bruce F. Kawin, *Telling It Again and Again: Repetition in Literature and Film* (Boulder: University Press of Colorado, 1989), 181.

2. Søren Kierkegaard, *Fear and Trembling; Repetition*, trans. and ed. Howard V. Hong and Edna H. Hong, Kierkegaard's Writings 6 (Princeton: Princeton University Press, 1983), 326.

3. See, e.g., Moshe Weinfeld, *Deuteronomy and the Deuteronomic School* (Winona Lake, IN: Eisenbrauns, 1992), 1.

4. See, e.g., Ernst Sellin and Georg Fohrer, *Introduction to the Old Testament*, trans. David E. Green (Nashville: Abingdon, 1968), 167. John William Wevers has tracked the same tendency in LXX Deuteronomy (*Text History of the Greek Deuteronomy*, MSU 13 [Göttingen: Vandenhoeck and Ruprecht, 1978], 86).

Unfortunately, beyond identifying exhortation and repetition as two main components of Deuteronomy's rhetoric, scholars usually have little more to say. Instead, these elements, whether they are spoken of approvingly or disparagingly, have been used most often by scholars to track the influence of Deuteronomy in other portions of the canon, most notably, in the Deuteronomistic History.[5] With regard to repetition specifically, previous scholarship has typically employed it in source-critical and/or tradition-historical pursuits, finding in it proof of development, the existence of literary seams, redaction, and the like.[6]

But much more can be said about repetition and exhortation—especially when they are found together, as they are in Deuteronomy—especially with regard to their *rhetorical effect* and *theological function*. The present chapter draws upon various treatments of repetition in literature, film, and discourse analysis[7] to

---

5. See, e.g., Martin Noth, *The Deuteronomistic History*, 2nd ed., JSOTSup 15 (Sheffield: JSOT Press, 1991), 18. For listings of terms and phrases that occur in Deuteronomy and other books, especially those in DtrH, see Weinfeld, *Deuteronomy and the Deuteronomic School*, 320–65; S. R. Driver, *A Critical and Exegetical Commentary on Deuteronomy*, 3rd ed., ICC (Edinburgh: T&T Clark, 1902), lxxviii–lxxxiv, xci–xciv; and Driver, *An Introduction to the Literature of the Old Testament* (New York: Meridian Books, 1960), 99–102.

6. See, e.g., A. D. H. Mayes, *Deuteronomy*, NCB (Grand Rapids: Eerdmans, 1981), 34–35; Rolf Rendtorff, *The Old Testament: An Introduction*, trans. John Bowden (Philadelphia: Fortress, 1986), 150; and Thomas B. Dozeman, *God on the Mountain: A Study of Redaction, Theology and Canon in Exodus 19–24*, SBLMS 37 (Atlanta: Scholars Press, 1989), 148 and n. 11—both of the latter on Wellhausen's assessment and historical (diachronic) use of repetition. To some extent, Dozeman follows in this diachronic tradition, though with significant nuance. The same holds true of Bernard Levinson's important work, *Deuteronomy and the Hermeneutics of Legal Innovation* (New York: Oxford University Press, 1997), though it should be noted that he takes issue with both classical diachronic approaches to the problem of repetition as well as synchronic approaches that treat the phenomenon "as deliberate rhetorical emphasis" (27).

7. Especially Kawin's work, *Telling It Again and Again*; but also J. Hillis Miller's work, *Fiction and Repetition: Seven English Novels* (Cambridge: Harvard University Press, 1982); and other theoretical works on repetition from a discourse perspective. For the latter, see especially Barbara Johnstone, ed., *Repetition in Discourse: Interdisciplinary Perspectives*, Advances in Discourse Processes 47–48 (Norwood, NJ: Ablex, 1994); Barbara Johnstone, "An Introduction," *Text* 7 (1987): 205–14; Neal R. Norrick, "Functions of Repetition in Conversation," *Text* 7 (1987): 245–64; Deborah Tannen, "Repetition in Conversation as Spontaneous Formulaicity," *Text* 7 (1987): 215–43; and Tannen, "Repetition in Conversation: Toward a Poetics of Talk," *Language* 63 (1987): 574–605. To my knowledge, the extensive theoretical work on repetition has not been applied to Deuteronomy, though one should note Dozeman, *God on the Mountain*, 145–75, who discusses Kawin's and Miller's work with reference to the problem of repetition in Exod 19–24 (and beyond). Even so, Dozeman interacts primarily with Miller, citing Kawin only in passing. Levinson, *Deuteronomy*, 156–57 has discussed Kierkegaard's *Repetition* with reference to Deuteronomy but, again, only briefly and in a less direct fashion than that undertaken here. Finally, Timothy A. Lenchak,

argue that repetition in Deuteronomy functions to leave the reader—or, perhaps better, the hearer—of the book with a few key items in mind. These include, above all, characteristic Deuteronomic *verbs*, "keep/observe" ($\sqrt{šmr}$), "do" ($\sqrt{'śh}$), and "listen/hear/obey" ($\sqrt{šm'}$); and the typical *objects of those verbs*: "law" (*tôrâ*), "commandment(s)" (*miṣwôt / miṣwâ*), and the ubiquitous "statutes and ordinances" (*ḥuqqîm ûmišpāṭîm*). When the reader/hearer is done with Deuteronomy these are what remain—in ear, mind, and heart. This *rhetorical effect* produces, in turn, an *ethical and theological result*: one who *really does do* the law, does it quite carefully at that, and does it, furthermore, within the primary timeframes of the book: "now, today, always" (*hayyôm, hayyôm hazzeh, kol-hayyāmîm*).

1. Repetition in Deuteronomy and Beyond: A Functional Typology

Statements about repetition in Deuteronomy abound but are not uniform. Although positive assessments are made occasionally,[8] more frequently the statement appears to be negative. Consider the following:

> The language and style . . . of all the sermons in Deuteronomy, appear at first sight to be framed in a somewhat conventional way, and the continual repetition of phrases seems almost monotonous.[9]

> [The speeches'] characteristic features are not only the style, which is broad, often overloaded and seemingly prolix (and the easy Hebrew!), but also [the] paraenesis, i.e., constantly repeated admonitions to observe the commandments, often bound up with the promise of blessings on life in the promised land.[10]

Whatever the exact intent of these citations, it is the negative assessment that seems to dominate scholarly treatments of Deuteronomic repetition. Perhaps

---

"Choose Life!": A Rhetorical-Critical Investigation of Deuteronomy 28,69–30,20, AnBib 129 (Rome: Pontifical Biblical Institute, 1993), 130–35, treats some discourse works on repetition, but cites neither Kawin nor Miller.

8. See, e.g., Driver, *Deuteronomy*, lxxxvii–lxxxviii, who writes that the discourse is "never (in the bad sense of the term [!]) rhetorical, always maintains its freshness, and is never monotonous or prolix." Cf. Driver, *Deuteronomy*, lxxxiv; Driver, *Introduction*, 102; and James Muilenburg, "A Study in Hebrew Rhetoric: Repetition and Style," in *Congress Volume: Copenhagen, 1953*, ed. George W. Anderson, VTSup 1 (Leiden: Brill, 1953), 97–111 (100).

9. Gerhard von Rad, *Deuteronomy: A Commentary*, trans. Dorothea Barton, OTL (Philadelphia: Westminster, 1966), 20.

10. Rendtorff, *Old Testament*, 151–52.

this is because, as J. P. Fokkelman has recently reiterated, repetition is in bad company today.[11] We learn from an early age to avoid it: it is an indication of poor style, bad writing, and so forth. Negative assessments of repetition also enjoy a long history in classical rhetoric[12] and in still earlier work.[13] Fokkelman rightly observes, however, that this situation is in marked contrast to the practices of the biblical text. That contrast, furthermore, poses a problem insofar as "we run the risk of misunderstanding and misjudging forms of [biblical] repetition."[14] It is noteworthy in this regard, for example, to observe that even recent treatments of repetition in biblical texts typically place special emphasis, not on repetition proper, but on variation-within-repetition.[15] Hermeneutical significance is found especially there—on *variation* and *difference*—even though the subject at issue, repetition, is dominated by *similarity*.[16] It is also significant that most treatments

11. See J. P. Fokkelman, *Reading Biblical Narrative: An Introductory Guide* (Louisville: Westminster John Knox, 1999), 112.

12. Too much repetition, in particular, was a bad thing. Note, e.g., *homoiologia* (tedious or redundant style) and *pleonasmus* (needless repetition)—not to mention *tautologia*. These terms belong to repetition at the clause/phrase/idea level (see Richard A. Lanham, *A Handlist of Rhetorical Terms: A Guide for Students of English Literature* [Berkeley: University of California Press, 1969], 125). Note further that one of the categories of good style, *dignitas*, is marked by "embellishment by a *variety* of figures tastefully used" (Lanham, *Handlist of Rhetorical Terms*, 116 [emphasis mine]).

13. Note, e.g., the following lines from the Middle Kingdom Egyptian work, *The Complaints of Khakheperre-sonb*: "Had I unknown phrases, / Sayings that are strange, / Novel, untried words, / Free of repetition; / Not transmitted sayings, / Spoken by the ancestors!" (*AEL* 1:146).

14. Fokkelman, *Reading Biblical Narrative*, 112–13; citation from 113. So also Robert Alter, *The Art of Biblical Narrative* (New York: Basic Books, 1981), 88, who states that the "extraordinary prominence of verbatim repetition" in the Bible is a barrier to modern readers to whom it appears "primitive" (cf. 96).

15. This is true, I believe, of both Alter, *Art of Biblical Narrative*, 88–113 ("The Techniques of Repetition"), see especially 91, 96–97 (where he contrasts prose repetition with poetic parallelism), 104, 112; and Meir Sternberg, *The Poetics of Biblical Narrative: Ideological Literature and the Drama of Reading* (Bloomington: Indiana University Press, 1987), 364–440. See also Dozeman, *God on the Mountain*, 148; and David M. Gunn and Danna Nolan Fewell, *Narrative in the Hebrew Bible*, Oxford Bible Series (Oxford: Oxford University Press, 1993), 148, 155. An exception to this judgment is Muilenburg, "Study in Hebrew Rhetoric," who emphasizes *both* (the "intimate relation between old and new" in repetition; 98), but who also devotes his primary attention to "actual repetition" (99).

16. At the very least, one must grant that similarity is *as important* as difference to the concept of repetition. Interestingly, the recent emphasis on difference within repetition corresponds, in part, to the two types of repetition that Miller lays out: that of repetition based on *similarity* (mimesis, which implies the existence of an archetype of sorts) and that of repetition based on *difference* (ungrounded doubling, which implies no archetype). See Miller, *Fiction and*

of repetition in the field of biblical studies deal only with the phenomenon in *narrative*. Treatments of repetition within the legal material are rare and, when present, typically concerned with other, more diachronic issues.[17]

But it must be said in response to negative assessments of repetition that it has not always been so. Despite their generally negative view of repetition, some of the classical rhetoricians considered it a highly useful device, especially in suasive speech. And, regardless of the canons of classical rhetoric, Hebrew literature abounds in repetition in both prose and poetry.[18] Indeed, some scholars have argued that repetition is built into the very structure of the Hebrew language itself—not only in its syntax, but even its morphology (consider the limitations of the tri-consonantal root).[19] One might well wonder, then, if contemporary distastes for repetition are not only anachronistic with reference to the Old Testament, but also if they have little to do with rhetoric *qua* rhetoric and more with favoring modern, predominantly literate culture (and literacy) over pre-modern, predominantly oral culture (and orality).[20] In any event, whatever the origins of scholarly estimations of Deuteronomy's repetition and whatever its possible oral traditions or origins may be, there can be no doubt that Deuteronomy is a

---

Repetition, 1–21, esp. 5–6. If this is accurate, most theorists have tended to favor the latter type. One wonders if this emphasis on difference is theoretically related to the importance of difference in structuralism. Whatever the case, *both* sameness *and* difference are important. "A cultural account that looks at difference needs to acknowledge sameness; one that understands discourse as linearity needs to accede to cyclicity and repetitiveness" (Greg Urban, "Repetition and Cultural Replication: Three Examples from Shokleng," in Johnstone, *Repetition in Discourse*, 2:145–61 [160]).

17. See the work of Guy Lasserre, *Synopse des lois du Pentateuque*, VTSup 59 (Leiden: Brill, 1994), esp. 116–50, which lists a number of parallels to the Deuteronomic law code, but which is not concerned with the kind of close (micro-level) and intra-Deuteronomic repetition that is my primary concern here. A good treatment of repetition in legal material with an eye toward persuasion can be found in the work of James W. Watts, *Reading Law: The Rhetorical Shaping of the Pentateuch*, BibSem 59 (Sheffield: Sheffield Academic Press, 1999), esp. 61–88.

18. If one includes repetition not only of key words, but also of motifs, themes, sequences of action, and so forth, the amount of repetition in the Old Testament multiplies exponentially. For these and other types of repetition see Alter, *Art of Biblical Narrative*, 95–96; Miller, *Fiction and Repetition*, 1–2.

19. See Israel Eitan, "La répétition de la racine en Hébreu," *JPOS* 1 (1921): 171–86; cf. Alter, *Art of Biblical Narrative*, 92; Muilenburg, "Study in Hebrew Rhetoric," 101. Such a phenomenon is, of course, not restricted to Hebrew. See Barbara Johnstone et al., "Repetition in Discourse: A Dialogue," in Johnstone, *Repetition in Discourse*, 1:11.

20. According to Sternberg, a literate culture can forego repetition more easily than an oral one given the former's various media possibilities (*Poetics of Biblical Narrative*, 368–69; also 374, 387–88, 406). Still, as the works cited in this chapter amply attest, even highly literate cultures (and media) abound in repetition.

literary text,[21] and is, simultaneously, shot full of repetition. But this begs the question for, as Sternberg has pointed out, the use of repetition in literary texts is not required nor expected.[22] Why, then, is there so much repetition—verbatim and near-verbatim—in Deuteronomy, a literary text that could easily avoid such? Perhaps a better question, and a more answerable one, is *what is the function(s)* of this repetitive rhetoric?

There can be no singular response to this question. The functions of repetition are legion and polyvalent.[23] Context is everything: each instance of repetition must be evaluated on its own.[24] To complicate matters, there has been no shortage of treatments of repetition. According to J. Hillis Miller,

> The history of Western ideas of repetition begins, like our culture generally, with the Bible on the one hand and with Homer, the Pre-Socratics, and Plato on the other. The long centuries of Biblical hermeneutics whereby the New Testament was seen in one way or another as repeating the Old are still supposed in the use of Biblical types in *Henry Esmond* or *Adam Bede*. The modern history of ideas about repetition goes by way of Vico to Hegel and the German Romantics, to Kierkegaard's *Repetition*, to Marx (in *The Eighteenth Brumaire*), to Nietzsche's concept of the eternal return, to Freud's notion of the compulsion to repeat, to the Joyce of *Finnegans Wake*, on down to such diverse present-day theorists of repetition as Jacques Lacan or Gilles Deleuze, Mircea Eliade or Jacques Derrida.[25]

There is not space here to fully engage this history of scholarship. Still, among the theorists that Miller includes in his own study of repetition is Bruce F. Kawin, whose typology of repetition is both insightful and generative when applied to Deuteronomy.

---

21. See, e.g., the work of Jean-Pierre Sonnet, *The Book within the Book: Writing in Deuteronomy*, BIS 14 (Leiden: Brill, 1997); and Sonnet, "Le Deutéronome et la modernité du livre," *NRTh* 118 (1996): 481–96.

22. See note 20; note, additionally, that there are other legal *corpora* that do not evidence the same type of repetition.

23. See, e.g., Sternberg, *Poetics of Biblical Narrative*, 375–87, 438–39; Muilenburg, "Study in Hebrew Rhetoric," 99; and Johnstone et al., "Repetition in Discourse," 6–19, esp. 10–11 on the function of repetition always remaining open. See further the works in the annotated bibliography (275 items) in Johnstone, *Repetition in Discourse*, 2:176–98.

24. Sternberg, *Poetics of Biblical Narrative*, 387–88, 437.

25. Miller, *Fiction and Repetition*, 5; see also 233–34n3.

Kawin's Typology of Repetition

"Life takes its tone and character from repetition," begins Kawin, but immediately notes the contemporary tendency to neglect and devalue repetition. Things that are capable of being repeated are thought of as "lower" or "more boring." In contrast, "the ultimate romantic experience of our culture is First Love" and we try to do everything at least "once."[26] But even extraordinary events are often deemed such because "they approximately repeat earlier experiences, or because they fulfill earlier expectations long rehearsed in fantasy; so that in both instances an event may have an air of familiarity about it even as it is occurring."[27] Kawin argues that novelty is, in fact, exhaustible; the search for it leads ultimately to boredom. Repetition, on the contrary, has the ability to move us "as time moves, in the present—the only existing tense."[28]

Kawin is careful to draw a distinction between repetition and repetitiousness. Repetition is "when a word, percept, or experience is repeated *with equal or greater force* at each occurrence." Repetitiousness is "when a word, percept, or experience is repeated *with less impact* at each recurrence; repeated *to no particular end*, out of a *failure of invention* or *sloppiness of thought*."[29] It is the unfortunate inability to distinguish between these two that has led to misconceptions of repetition. Even so, there is a shadow-side of repetition, one that is not unrelated to repetitiousness, that is frequently encountered, especially in the first type of repetition Kawin discusses: destructive repetition.

1. *Destructive repetition.* To this first category in Kawin's typology belongs repetition that has either "gone flat or has actually had a destructive effect on its material."[30] For Kawin, Sigmund Freud's conception of "repetition compulsion" provides an excellent example of this phenomenon. Freud uses this concept to speak of the repetition of certain, usually negative, patterns of behavior and the unavoidable nature of that repetition.[31] This compulsion to repeat pathologies is,

---

26. Kawin, *Telling It Again and Again*, 1.
27. Kawin, *Telling It Again and Again*, 2.
28. Kawin, *Telling It Again and Again*, 3.
29. Kawin, *Telling It Again and Again*, 4 (emphases mine).
30. Kawin, *Telling It Again and Again*, 10.
31. See Sigmund Freud, *Beyond the Pleasure Principle*, trans. and ed. James Strachey (New York: Norton, 1961); and Freud, "Further Recommendations in the Technique of Psycho-Analysis: Recollection, Repetition and Working Through," in *Collected Papers*, trans. Joan Riviere (New York: Basic Books, 1959), 2:366–76. Note also Gregory Zilboorg's introduction to Freud, *Beyond the Pleasure Principle*, xxxiii.

in fact, what facilitates the therapeutic process of transference between patient and therapist.[32] This repetitive process is largely *unconscious*, but not necessarily neurotic. Even so, Freud calls the compulsion to repeat "the manifestation of the power of the repressed."[33]

Why do people repeat in this way? At least one answer is that people attempt to *master* various situations through repetition. As an example, Freud cites children at play.[34] It is a small step to apply this insight to adults who are often prone to choose familiar over unfamiliar modes of action, even if those produce suffering and hardship.

From Freud's work and other examples, Kawin concludes that a type of destructive repetition exists. Perhaps the most innocuous form of destructive repetition is *habit*: "Repetition without insight or excitement creates routine, takes the life out of living, and *cannot cause us pain*."[35] But at what price is this peace—if it is that? Happily, in contrast to destructive repetition, Kawin believes that there are two *positive* or *constructive* types that differ mainly in how they employ memory.

2. *Emphasizing, echoing, building*. The first type of positive repetition is "involved with the concepts of past and future, and believing in the integrity of memory, builds repetitions one on the other toward some total effect; this 'repetition with remembering' takes place in cumulative or 'building time.'"[36] This emphatic, "outright" repetition "aims to make us remember something."[37] Repetition is used in this way in poetry, for instance, where it lends a source of lyrical strength to the work. Kawin claims that the Old Testament itself offers "some of the finest and most familiar examples of the beauty and strength of repetition."[38] This kind of repetition is not repetitious, according to Kawin, "because each rediscovery is preceded by a conclusion that, closing the matter for us, frees us to experience each repetition as something new."[39] It is thus critical to the function and apprehension of this type of repetition that it takes place *in time*. It is "a sequence that begins the viewer in it again as it begins again."[40] It can thus function in expressive and

32. Freud, *Beyond the Pleasure Principle*, 19, 22, 42. Cf. Kawin, *Telling It Again and Again*, 16.

33. Freud, *Beyond the Pleasure Principle*, 21.

34. Freud, *Beyond the Pleasure Principle*, 16, 42; Kawin, *Telling It Again and Again*, 16.

35. Kawin, *Telling It Again and Again*, 20 (emphasis his).

36. Kawin, *Telling It Again and Again*, 33; cf. 34 and Frank McConnell's remarks in the foreword to *Telling It Again and Again*, xiv.

37. Kawin, *Telling It Again and Again*, 35.

38. Kawin, *Telling It Again and Again*, 38; see 38–43 for a treatment of Old Testament texts, esp. and interestingly, Ecclesiastes.

39. Kawin, *Telling It Again and Again*, 41. Cf. Johnstone et al., "Repetition in Discourse," 10.

40. Kawin, *Telling It Again and Again*, 47.

didactic ways, especially because it *"makes intense and solid through persistence.* Repeated enough, a word or idea or phrase or image or name will come to dominate us to such an extent that our only defenses are to concede its importance or turn off the stimulus completely."[41]

3. *The continuous present (transcendence).* The second type of positive repetition considers "the present the only artistically approachable tense, [and] deals with each instant and subject as a new thing, to such an extent that the sympathetic reader is aware less of repetition than of continuity; this 'repetition without remembering' takes place in 'continuing time.'"[42]

Kawin treats the notion of continuing time, or repetition that takes one out of time, under the rubric of transcendence. Drawing most notably on Gertrude Stein and Søren Kierkegaard (among others), Kawin argues that repetition can be understood as transcendent because it transports one to a moment that is fully *present*, fully *now*, and by definition, therefore, outside of time-consciousness and time itself. Beginning over and over again feels *atemporal*. Of course, it only *feels* that way and is not really that way unless one can forget—forget that one has already been here before. This is what Kawin means by stating that this type of repetition can only take place *without* voluntary memory. One cannot voluntarily remember that one has done this or that before, been here or there before. That would be to place one's self in *building* time (see above), not *continuing* time. But *in*voluntary memory is another matter: "When the impression literally repeats, we are in its time. Involuntary memory is a time-warp that not only returns the past to us, but returns us to the past, makes us who we were when we lived in that time."[43] So, as "long as we do not falsify our past with possession and fear and remembering, we can in the instants of its *repetition* live both in the ordinary 'now' and in the 'then made now'—transcending our life in space by discovering our freedom in time."[44] In this space, then, there is only "now" and variations of "now," or what Kawin and others have called "the continuous present." And, as should be obvious from the above, in contrast to the first type of positive repetition, this second type of positive repetition deals largely with exact repetition or the nearest the artist can get to that: near-repetition.[45]

---

41. Kawin, *Telling It Again and Again*, 49–50 (emphasis his). George Orwell's *Nineteen Eighty-Four: A Novel* (New York: Harcourt, Brace and World, 1949) comes to mind.

42. Kawin, *Telling It Again and Again*, 33; cf. McConnell's remarks in the foreword (xiv).

43. Kawin, *Telling It Again and Again*, 84.

44. Kawin, *Telling It Again and Again*, 85.

45. Many theorists argue that exact repetition is impossible or nearly so. On near-repetition see Kawin, *Telling It Again and Again*, 7; Sternberg, *Poetics of Biblical Narrative*, 390; Fokkelman, *Reading Biblical Narrative*, 112–22, esp. 121–22.

The power that repetition has to negate time is due in part to the fact that repetition is "minimum syntax: a word relating to and acting on itself. . . . The word, and then the word." In this sense, repetition "takes the word further, into its inherent preverbal timelessness."[46] Repetition's quality of being the exact same thing all over again "makes us doubt that this thing was ever not here, or that there was any time in which it could have not been here, any time other than this time."[47] But, again, this effect is contingent on the person(s) involved being *truly involved*; the repetition must be *felt*, must be *real*: "It is further true that nothing actually felt, nothing real in its moment is boring. Sexual intercourse, for example, loses neither its attractiveness nor its reality through being repeated; its felt intensity is entirely independent of previous experience. Why, since it is the same every time, does it not become boring? The answer is, because it is interesting to us: it proceeds from our basic needs, it is urgent and pleasant and present. It is outside time, and therefore outside futility."[48]

Repetition in Deuteronomy

Before proceeding to an analysis of Deuteronomic repetition in light of Kawin's typology, it is necessary to step back and repeat (!) that Deuteronomy is replete with repetition. The notion of repetition is already present in the *title* of the book—at least as that has been brought into English via the Septuagint, even if that is a misinterpretation of the Hebrew of Deut 17:18.[49] Further, the *structure* of the book itself is repetitive; the book employs repetition on the *macro-structural level(s)*. There are, for example, two introductions (1:1–4:40; 4:44–11:32), two sections of blessings and curses (27:11–13; 28:3–6, 16–19 and the remaining curses in chapter 28), and two poems of Moses (32:1–43; chapter 33).[50] Missing from this listing is the repetition of covenant/covenant-making in Moab (29:1 [28:69])[51]; the repetitions of speeches by Moses; the repeated superscriptions that mark those speeches; and the material that follows the Decalogue, whether it be in chapters 5–11 or in the central law code (12–28), which is a working out, or repeti-

---

46. Kawin, *Telling It Again and Again*, 176.

47. Kawin, *Telling It Again and Again*, 104; cf. 3.

48. Kawin, *Telling It Again and Again*, 2; see also x, 151.

49. LXX: *to deuteronomion touto*, "this second law"; MT: *'et-mišnê hattôrâ hazzō't*, "a copy of this Torah."

50. See Moshe Weinfeld, "Deuteronomy, Book of," *ABD* 2:171; Weinfeld, *Deuteronomy 1–11*, AB 5 (New York: Doubleday, 1991), 9.

51. In references where the English and Hebrew versification differ, the English versification will be provided first, followed by the Hebrew versification in square brackets.

tion of sorts, of the Decalogue or the great/first commandment.[52] Of course, the Decalogue itself is a repetition—within the final form of the Pentateuch—of the version given in Exod 20:1–17.

The last item is yet another example that Deuteronomy's repetition extends beyond itself, crossing over and beyond the book's literary boundaries. This is especially true in the legal material where Deuteronomy picks up on and reiterates legislation from elsewhere in the Pentateuch, particularly the book of the covenant (Exod 20:22–23:19). In this sense, the book's Greek title, whatever the demerits of its origin may be, is well chosen. But Deuteronomy's repetition works forward, as well as backward, as the book not only repeats earlier legislation but also makes its rhetoric known and felt in subsequent portions of the Old Testament.

These considerations demonstrate that Deuteronomy also knows of repetition on the *micro-structural level(s)*. Smaller units—laws, sentences, clauses, words—are also repeated. And repeated. And repeated. Extensively. The primary concern of this chapter, however, is not with the exact details of all this repetition,[53] but the method and meaning of it. In answering this question, it is instructive to ask to which one (or more), if any, of Kawin's types does Deuteronomy's repetition belong.

2. The Emphasis of/on Emphasis: The Rhetoric of Deuteronomy's Repetition

In my judgment, Deuteronomy's repetition falls, not under Kawin's first category of negative, destructive, or compulsive repetition, but among his two positive types: those of emphasis and transcendence. This decision against compulsion and in

---

52. See Georg Braulik, "The Sequence of the Laws in Deuteronomy 12–26 and in the Decalogue," in *A Song of Power and the Power of Song: Essays on the Book of Deuteronomy*, ed. Duane L. Christensen, SBTS 3 (Winona Lake, IN: Eisenbrauns, 1993), 313–35; Braulik, "Zur Abfolge der Gesetze in Deuteronomium 16,18–21,23: Weitere Beobachtungen," *Bib* 69 (1988): 63–92; Stephen A. Kaufman, "The Structure of the Deuteronomic Law," *Maarav* 1/2 (1978–1979): 105–58; Norbert Lohfink, *Das Hauptgebot: eine Untersuchung literarischer Einleitungsfragen zu Dtn 5–11*, AnBib 20 (Rome: Pontifical Biblical Institute, 1963); and Dennis T. Olson, *Deuteronomy and the Death of Moses: A Theological Reading*, OBT (Minneapolis: Fortress, 1994), 49–125. Olson also argues that Deut 5 is a type of "blueprint" for the rest of the book (see *Deuteronomy and the Death of Moses*, 40–48), which, accordingly, would be a repetition and elaboration of that blueprint.

53. The raw data has been collected in the works of Moshe Weinfeld, John W. Wevers, and Norbert Lohfink. For the MT, see Weinfeld, *Deuteronomy and the Deuteronomic School*, 320–65; and Lohfink, *Das Hauptgebot*, 295–312. For the LXX, see Wevers, *Text History of the Greek Deuteronomy*, 86–99 (I thank Julie A. Duncan for drawing my attention to the listing in Wevers). Virtually every commentary on Deuteronomy or introduction to the Old Testament also provides at least a few examples of this type of micro-structural repetition.

favor of emphasis and transcendence is not arbitrary; it is *textual*. As Kawin points out, "one of the principal characteristics of useless repetition is that it locks a work or a life into an unfulfillable compulsive cycle."[54] But Moses is at pains in Deuteronomy to indicate that this material *is* fulfillable (see, e.g., 30:11–14, 19b–20). The specific content of Deuteronomic repetition; its connection to persuasion, didacticism, and memory; and textual enactments of that repetition are all additional factors that support a positive—emphatic and transcendent—understanding of Deuteronomy's repetitive rhetoric. Each of these items are treated below with special attention to the *ethics* of the rhetoric—*what it does* and *how it does* it.

The Content of Repetition in Deuteronomy

The *content* of Deuteronomy's repetition is arguably the most important item to consider in evaluating its overall effect. That content, in brief, seeks to inculcate life. The famous "choose life!" passage (30:19b) comes to mind, as do the many other texts dealing with life[55] and long life, especially in the land.[56] Still other texts promise prosperity (√*rbh*), blessing (*bərākâ* / √*brk*), or general goodness (√*yṭb*).[57] Equally important are the *numerous motivation clauses* that serve to underscore and motivate Israel's keeping of the law.[58] Rifat Sonsino has estimated that the percentage of motivated regulations in Deuteronomy is as high as 50 percent.[59] Patrick D. Miller puts it well, then, when he writes: "That the exercise of power was by persuasion and rhetoric is seen in the covenant document par excellence, Deuteronomy. It set up a structure for existence—social, political, economic, and religious—that depended upon the willingness of the people to accede to the demands of the covenant, a willingness that was elicited in large part by preaching, testimony, self-understanding, and self-indictment through song and instruction taught and learned by the people."[60]

The content of Deuteronomy's repetition, therefore, is not only explicitly concerned with life, prosperity, and blessing, but the very repetitive rhetorical strategy of

---

54. Kawin, *Telling It Again and Again*, 12.

55. E.g., *ləmaʿan* + √*hyh* (in order to/so that + live): 4:1; 5:33; 8:1; 16:20; 30:6, 19; cf. 6:24; 30:16.

56. E.g., √*rk* + *yāmîm* (to prolong + days), frequently with *ləmaʿan* (in order to/so that): 4:40; 5:16, 33; 6:2; 11:9, 21; 22:7; 25:15; 30:20; 32:47; cf. 4:26; 17:20; 30:18.

57. For an extensive listing, see Weinfeld, *Deuteronomy and the Deuteronomic School*, 345–50.

58. E.g., *ʾăšer* / *lə* / *ləmaʿan* + *ṭôb* / √*yṭb* (so that/to/in order to + good/to be good): 4:40; 5:16, 29, 33; 6:3, 18; 12:25, 28; 19:13; 22:7.

59. Rifat Sonsino, *Motive Clauses in Hebrew Law: Biblical Forms and Near Eastern Parallels*, SBLDS 45 (Chico, CA: Scholars Press, 1980), 221.

60. Patrick D. Miller, *The Religion of Ancient Israel*, LAI (Louisville: Westminster John Knox, 2000), 5; cf. Miller, *Deuteronomy*, Interpretation (Louisville: John Knox, 1990), 12.

the book motivates one to enact these laws, statutes, and ordinances by means of valid and persuasive reasoning. Indeed, these two things are often interconnected: many of the life-in-the-land passages, for example, belong to the motivational clauses.

Still further, it is often the case that other repetitions, beyond those dealing explicitly with life or blessing, are equally positive. So it is that one encounters repeated references to the God who "brought out" ($\sqrt{ys'}$)[61] or "ransomed" ($\sqrt{pdh}$)[62] Israel from Egypt/the house of bondage, which is certainly among the great deeds "that Yahweh did" for Israel.[63] And God is not finished. Repeatedly it is asserted that God "swore" ($\sqrt{sb'}$)[64] or "promised" ($\sqrt{dbr}$)[65] to give ($\sqrt{ntn}$)[66] the land and, now, "is giving" (*nōtēn*)[67] the land to Israel. More generally, the LORD is repeatedly said to be an agent of blessing.[68]

The extent of this repetition is impressive and is but the beginning of a partial listing. In the face of such rhetoric, it is not surprising to find the injunction for Israel to "do what is right (and good) in the sight of the LORD (your God)" repeated five times.[69] Indeed, nowhere is repetition more pronounced in Deuteronomy than with reference to *obedience*. Note the following collocations:[70]

- $\sqrt{smr}$ + $\sqrt{'sh}$ or $\sqrt{smr}$ + *la'ăśôt* (keep + do): 4:6; 5:1, 32; 6:3, 25; 7:11, 12; 8:1; 11:22, 32; 12:1, 32[13:1]; 13:18[19]; 15:5; 16:12; 17:10, 19; 19:9; 23:23[24]; 24:8; 26:16; 28:1, 13, 15, 58; 29:9[8]; 31:12; 32:46.
- $\sqrt{smr}$ + *miṣwâ* (*miṣwôt*) / *ḥuqqîm* / *'ēdôt* / *mišpāṭîm* (keep + commandment[s], statutes, decrees, or ordinances): 4:2, 6, 40; 5:1, 10; 6:2, 17; 7:9, 11, 12; 8:1, 2, 6, 11; 10:13; 11:1, 32; 12:1; 13:4[5]; 16:12; 26:16, 17; 28:9, 13, 15, 45; 30:10, 16 (cf. 5:12).

---

61. See 4:20, 37; 5:6, 15; 6:12, 21, 23; 7:8, 19; 8:14; 9:26, 28–29; 13:5[6], 10[11]; 16:1; 20:1; 26:8; 29:25[24].

62. See 7:8; 9:26; 13:5[6]; 15:15; 21:8; 24:18.

63. $\sqrt{'sh}$ + *YHWH*: 1:30; 3:21; 4:3, 34; 7:18; 11:4, 7; 29:2[1], 24[23]; 31:4.

64. See 1:8, 35; 6:10, 18, 23; 7:8, 12, 13; 8:1; 10:11; 11:9, 21; 19:8; 26:3, 15; 28:11; 30:20; 31:7, 20, 21, 23; 34:4.

65. See 1:21; 19:8; 27:3.

66. In addition to the texts cited in the two previous notes, see 1:36; 2:12, 19, 36; 3:18; 4:38; 8:10; 9:23; 12:1, 15; 26:9; 28:52.

67. See 1:20, 25; 2:29; 4:1, 21, 40; 5:16, 31; 9:6; 11:17, 31; 12:9; 15:4, 7; 16:20; 17:14; 18:9; 19:1, 2, 10, 14; 21:1, 23; 24:4; 25:15, 19; 26:1, 2; 27:2, 3; 28:8; 32:49, 52.

68. See 1:11; 2:7; 7:13; 12:7; 14:24, 29; 15:4, 6, 10, 14, 18; 16:10, 15; 23:20[21]; 24:19; 28:8, 12; 30:16.

69. 6:18; 12:25, 28; 13:18[19]; 21:9; contrast 17:2; 31:29.

70. These follow Weinfeld, *Deuteronomy and the Deuteronomic School*, 336–37 (see further 332–39) though at times my presentation of the total number and location of the occurrences differs. If the present listing reflects an improvement, it is due to the advantages of computer software, in this case BibleWorks for Windows (Version 4.0; Big Fork, Montana: Hermeneutika Bible Research Software, 1999).

- √*šmr* + *kol hammiṣwâ* / *kol miṣwôtay* / *miṣwôtâw* (keep [often with √*śh* (do)] + the entire commandment or all my/his commandments): 5:29; 6:25; 11:8, 22; 13:18[19]; 15:5; 19:9; 26:18; 27:1; 28:1, 15; cf. 30:8 (√*śh* without √*šmr*).

- √*šmr* / √*śh* *'et-kol-dibrê hattôrâ hazzō't* (*hakkətubîm bassēper hazzeh*) (keep or do + all the words of this Torah [that are written in this book]): 17:19; 28:58; 29:29[28]; 31:12; 32:46.

- √*šm'* + *'el miṣwôt yhwh* (listen + to the commandments of the LORD): 11:27, 28; 28:13; cf. 11:13.

- √*šm'* + *bəqôlô* / *bəqôl yhwh* (listen + his voice or the voice of the LORD): 13:4[5], 18[19]; 15:5; 26:14, 17; 27:10; 28:1, 2; 30:8, 10.

To be sure, these formulations are not identical—each is distinct and should not be simplistically identified with the others—but they are sufficiently similar to muddle their precise differences in a listener's/reader's mind. That is, can a listener/reader—whether novice or experienced—describe in detail the subtle nuances between

- *kî-tišmōr 'et-kol hammiṣwâ hazzō't la'áśōtāh 'ăšer 'ānōkî məṣawwəkā hayyôm*, "if you carefully keep the entirety of this commandment, which I am commanding you today" (19:9); and
- *kî-tišma' 'el-miṣwôt yhwh 'ĕlōhēkā 'ăšer 'ānōkî məṣawwəkā hayyôm*, "if you listen to the commandments of the LORD your God, which I am commanding you today" (28:13)?

This *muddling effect* is made even worse (or better, as the case may be) by other, closely similar, collocations not presented here. But the corollary of this muddling effect is, paradoxically, a *sharpening* one: it is a heaping up, a getting-at-by-all-possible-means. This effect, in short, actually functions to underscore a singular point: "keep/observe/do!" In fact, keep/observe/do *carefully*,[71] *exactly* as God commanded![72]

The verbal emphasis is thus quite clear. But the identification of *what*, exactly and carefully, one is to keep/observe/do is equally as repetitive and similarly confusing. Consider the following collocations:[73]

---

71. √*šmr* (*niphal* or *hiphil*) + *bənepeš* / *lənepeš* / *lākā* / *lākem* (watch + you/yourself): 4:9, 15, 23; 6:12; 8:11; 11:16; 12:13, 19, 30; 15:9; cf. 23:9[10]; 24:8 (both of the latter without pronoun or *nepeš*).

72. E.g., *ka'ăšer* / *kə* + √*ṣwh yhwh* (just as/as + the LORD commanded): 1:3, 19; 2:37; 5:32; 34:9; cf. 5:33.

73. See Weinfeld, *Deuteronomy and the Deuteronomic School*, 339–40.

- *ḥuqqîm + mišpāṭîm* (statutes + ordinances): 4:1, 5, 8, 14, 45 (with *ʿēdôt*, decrees); 5:1; 6:20 (with *ʿēdôt*); 11:32; 12:1; 26:16.
- *miṣwôt + ḥuqqîm / ḥuqqôt or ḥuqqîm / ḥuqqôt + miṣwôt* (commandments + statutes or statutes + commandments): 4:40; 6:2, 17 (with *ʿēdôt* intervening); 10:13; 27:10; 28:15, 45; 30:10.
- *ḥuqqîm miṣwôt ûmišpāṭîm or ḥuqqôt mišpāṭîm ûmiṣwôt or miṣwôt mišpāṭîm wǝḥuqqôt* (statutes, commandments, and ordinances; or statutes, ordinances, and commandments; or commandments, ordinances, and statutes): 8:11; 11:1; 26:17; 30:16.
- *hammiṣwâ / hammiṣwôt + ḥuqqîm ûmišpāṭîm* (the commandment[s] + statutes and ordinances): 5:31; 6:1; 7:11.

As if these were not enough, there are still more formulations—those that take Yhwh or Yhwh's way(s) as the verbal object, for instance—that are not included in this listing.[74] Keeping all of these items straight is no less difficult or confusing than was the case with the verbs themselves. And yet, the point is the same. The rhetorical issue is not precise collocation or whether each specific formulation means something in contrast to its near-identical siblings. Instead, it is a case of *heaping up* in the textual environment (whether oral or written), which leaves the reader/hearer without escape from these terms. One *must* obey/observe/enact—and must do that *carefully*.[75] This much is clear from the repetition. And now it is equally clear *what* one must obey: it has to do with the statutes and ordinances, the commandments and the laws, the Torah and the testimonies, Yhwh and Yhwh's ways. And, of course, Deuteronomy's repetitive rhetoric is also quite clear on what one is *not* to do/obey,[76] as well as the precise manner in which one is to perform this mandated obedience and disobedience. Finally, it is highly pertinent in light of Kawin's emphasis on the continuing present to note that Deuteronomy also repeats itself on the *when* of this obedience. There is a constant emphasis on "today" (*hayyôm hazzeh / hayyôm*) or "always" (*kol-hayyāmîm*).[77]

---

74. See Weinfeld, *Deuteronomy and the Deuteronomic School*, 332–33.

75. Or, *à la* Kawin, turn the stimulus off completely (see note 41 above). Deuteronomy's motivation clauses, however, would obviate this move even while its possibility is granted.

76. See, e.g., Kawin, *Telling It Again and Again*, 320, 339–41.

77. See Kawin, *Telling It Again and Again*, 356–57. *Yôm* occurs 167 times in Deuteronomy. Though not all of these are directly connected to parenesis, and instead describe specific periods of time, duration, or the like, the vast majority of instances are in service to the hortatory statements of Moses. For the background and function of the "today" passages in Deuteronomy, see Weinfeld, *Deuteronomy and the Deuteronomic School*, 174; Robert Polzin, "Deuteronomy," in *The Literary Guide to the Bible*, ed. Robert Alter and Frank Kermode (Cambridge: Belknap,

Also important are the specific *subjects* of the majority of these verbal formulations. The subjects are invariably *the second person*—sometimes imperative[78]—whether singular or plural: "you." Second-person address lends to the commandments "a sense of immediacy and urgency lacking in the hypothetical formulation of (usually) third-person casuistic laws. . . . Hearers and readers are likely to feel directly addressed and therefore obliged to respond."[79] Without engaging the vexed question of the switch in grammatical number (*Numeruswechsel*) in Deuteronomy, it can be stated simply that this effect is felt whether the addressee is designated in the singular or plural.

In sum, the content of Deuteronomic repetition—in verbal emphasis, object, and addressee—is clearly of the emphatic variety. Repeated formulations with attention to the present and "always" may also relate this repetition to Kawin's transcendent type. But before a final decision can be made on this point, there are other aspects of Deuteronomy's repetition that must be considered.

Repetition, Persuasion, and Didacticism

Repetition is highly effective in *suasive* discourse, be it oral or literary.[80] Despite some distaste for repetition, the classical rhetoricians also realized its importance and effectiveness. Quintilian, for instance, wrote: "Our aim must be not to put him [the judge] in a position to understand our argument, but to force him to understand it. Consequently we shall frequently repeat anything which we think the

---

1987), 92–101, here 92–93; and E. Theodore Mullen Jr., *Narrative History and Ethnic Boundaries: The Deuteronomistic Historian and the Creation of Israelite National Identity*, SemeiaSt (Atlanta: Scholars, 1993), 75.

78. Somewhat surprisingly, the frequency of imperatives in Deuteronomy is low. According to my search, there are only 112 imperatives in the book. Of course, if one counted negative commands, the number would increase. L. J. de Regt, *A Parametric Model for Syntactic Studies of a Textual Corpus, Demonstrated on the Hebrew of Deuteronomy 1–30*, SSN 24 (Assen: Van Gorcum, 1988), 95, 114–15, argues that clauses in which legislative rules are formulated and in which imperatives occur, do not appear together, and "seem to be mutually exclusive" (95). This is further evidence that the vision of Deuteronomy is "persuasively taught rather than forcefully dictated" (Olson, *Deuteronomy and the Death of Moses*, 4).

79. Watts, *Reading Law*, 64. Sonsino identified direct address as one of the legal forms found only in biblical law (*Motive Clauses*, 36–38).

80. It is not necessary to pick between oral or written environments at this point. Note Watts, *Reading Law*, 61n1: "The distinction between hearers and readers, which has been so fruitful for studies of orality and literacy, is blurred by the practice of reading aloud for aural reception" (see also Watts, *Reading Law*, 65). Regardless of environment, then, Deuteronomy's repetition is suasive. For more on Deuteronomy and oratory, see Weinfeld, *Deuteronomy and the Deuteronomic School*, 3, 8, 171–73, 176–77; Alter, *Art of Biblical Narrative*, 89–90; and von Rad, *Deuteronomy*, 29.

judge has failed to take in as he should."[81] To this end, repetition was frequently utilized by classical rhetoricians, especially in the conclusion (*epilogos* or *peroratio*) of their arguments.[82] It also figures into discussions of arrangement (*taxis*, *dispositio*) and style (*lexis*, *elocutio*).[83] More recent studies of rhetoric, both oral and written, continue to note the effectiveness of repetition within persuasive intent.[84]

The motivated nature of Deuteronomic law is again pertinent here since at least one function of the motive clauses is to strengthen the persuasive appeal of the legal material. Moreover, "the motivations attached to laws point out *the didactic intent* in their formulation, wishing to instruct hearers/readers not only in specific regulations but also in the law's foundations in Israel's communal experiences and religious ideas."[85] It is not only the motive clauses that do this; the exhortations found throughout the material also make didactic purposes explicit. Moreover, many theorists have pointed to didacticism as a primary function of repetition.[86]

In short, Deuteronomy seeks to *teach* and *persuade*.[87] This is widely known and frequently said about Deuteronomy's rhetoric, but it is equally true of the

---

81. Quintilian, *Institutio Oratoria* 8.2.22–24 (cited in Watts, *Reading Law*, 70 and n. 38).

82. See, e.g., Aristotle, *On Rhetoric* 3.19 (1419b); however, he criticizes earlier rhetorical handbooks for too much repetition in the *proemium* (entrance or *exordium*). In conclusions, repetition functions as a type of recapitulation, a refreshing of the memory. In this light, Deuteronomy's repetition functions as a constant refreshing of the memory (see further below).

83. Note, e.g., the repetition of letters, syllables, or sounds (e.g., alliteration, assonance, *parechesis*, *parimion*) that was frequently lauded by ancient rhetoricians. On these terms, as well as those relating to repetition at the word and clause/phrase/idea levels, see Lanham, *Handlist of Rhetorical Terms*, 124–25.

84. See, e.g., James W. Cox, *Preaching: A Comprehensive Approach to the Design and Delivery of Sermons* (San Francisco: Harper & Row, 1985), 231; and Raymond S. Ross, *Understanding Persuasion*, 3rd ed. (Englewood Cliffs, NJ: Prentice Hall, 1990), 161–63. Kenneth Burke, *The Philosophy of Literary Form: Studies in Symbolic Action*, 3rd ed. (Berkeley: University of California Press, 1973), 217, has noted "the power of endless repetition" in more ominous ways ("to a disturbing degree") in Hitler's *Mein Kampf*.

85. Watts, *Reading Law*, 67 (emphasis mine).

86. See, e.g., Martha S. Bean and G. Genevieve Patthey-Chavez, "Repetition in Instructional Discourse: A Means for Joint Cognition," in Johnstone, *Repetition in Discourse*, 1:207–20; Russell S. Tomlin, "Repetition in Second Language Acquisition," in Johnstone, *Repetition in Discourse*, 1:172–94; and Tannen, "Repetition in Conversation as Spontaneous Formulaicity," 215–17.

87. One need not take these insights and the obvious similarities to wisdom traditions and put them to work in hypotheses about the origin of Deuteronomy, though obviously Weinfeld has attempted to do that in systematic fashion (*Deuteronomy and the Deuteronomic School*; for particular phraseological links, see 362–63). It is interesting, however, to consider connections between didacticism and the presentation of the learner as a *child* in wisdom literature. Deuteronomy also knows of repetition to children (see, e.g., 6:7, 20–25) but, more generally, one wonders if the repetitive didacticism of Moses in Deuteronomy makes Israel/the reader out to

book's *repetition* for the purpose of repetition is "to point, to direct a hearer back to something and say, 'Pay attention to this again. This is still salient; this still has potential meaning; let's make use of it in some way.'"[88] Repetition is thus hermeneutically helpful and instructive.[89]

Here too, then, Deuteronomy's repetition largely falls under Kawin's second, emphatic type. After all, Deuteronomy repeats the Sinai-Horeb event and its legislation throughout chapters 5–28 (especially) and undertakes yet another, different type of repetition in the Moab covenant (chapters 29–30; see especially 29:1[28:69]).[90] Still more to the point, Moses makes clear that the Sinai-Horeb event is not just "back then" but is present; the cutting of the covenant is "with us, those of us here today, all of us who are alive" (5:3). In this nexus, elements of emphatic repetition (beginning the viewer in it again as it starts again) and transcendent repetition (the continuous present and the ubiquitous "today") combine.

Repetition and Memory

While repetition, by today's standards, might make for *boring* literature, it is equally true that repetition makes for *highly effective* literature. At least part of that is due to repetition's connection to memory. At this point the oral vs. written question might be more significant as there have been a number of studies that

---

be childlike, if only because "in the instruction of the young . . . iteration proved an effective device for stamping the mind with the things that must be remembered" (Muilenburg, "Study in Hebrew Rhetoric," 100). For further studies on the use of repetition in speech with children, especially in language acquisition, see Johnstone, "An Introduction," 205–14.

88. Johnstone et al., "Repetition in Discourse," 13. Cf. James E. Porter and Patricia A. Sullivan, "Repetition and the Rhetoric of Visual Design," in Johnstone, *Repetition in Discourse*, 1:27–28; and Watts, *Reading Law*, 61, 70–71, 88, esp. 71.

89. See Miller, *Fiction and Repetition*, 1–2; Sternberg, *Poetics of Biblical Narrative*, 368; Gunn and Fewell, *Narrative in the Hebrew Bible*, 148; Wolfgang Iser, *The Act of Reading: A Theory of Aesthetic Response* (Baltimore: Johns Hopkins University Press, 1978), 94 (cf. also 209); and Norrick, "Functions of Repetition in Conversation," 257. It must be admitted that repetition is not foolproof in controlling meaning control. See Steven Cushing, "'Air Cal Three Thirty Six, Go Around Three Thirty Six, Go Around': Linguistic Repetition in Air-Ground Communication," in Johnstone, *Repetition in Discourse*, 2:62.

90. The Moab covenant may be related to repetitions that repeat archetypal actions performed "in the beginning of time." See Kawin, *Telling It Again and Again*, 91, 94, and Mircea Eliade, *The Myth of the Eternal Return*, trans. Willard R. Trask (Princeton: Princeton University Press, 1965). Note also Dennis T. Olson, "How Does Deuteronomy Do Theology? Literary Juxtaposition and Paradox in the New Moab Covenant in Deuteronomy 29–32," in *A God So Near: Essays on Old Testament Theology in Honor of Patrick D. Miller*, ed. Brent A. Strawn and Nancy R. Bowen (Winona Lake, IN: Eisenbrauns, 2003), 201–213.

demonstrate that repetition works especially well when it is originally (or) primarily *oral* in presentation. Simply put, people remember what they have heard and heard often.[91]

Even so, the function of repetition as mnemonic device is not restricted to its use in oral contexts. The issue is also related to the nature of repetition and/as suasive rhetoric. Whatever the case, it is clear that Deuteronomy places a special—and repeated!—emphasis on *memory*.[92] An interesting example of the effect of Deuteronomy's repetition on memory is found in some of the Dead Sea Scrolls. Julie A. Duncan has shown that the excerpted biblical manuscripts that include passages from Deuteronomy often have alternative, slightly expanded readings. Apparently, these are the result of a scribe copying by memory and being influenced by other, closely similar passages.[93] This example shows that the muddling effect of Deuteronomy's repetition is quite real and that, especially due to instances of near-

---

91. E.g., Aristotle, *On Rhetoric*, 3.12.2 (1413b): "*Asyndeta* and constant repetition are rightly criticized in writing but not in speaking, and the orators use them; for they lend themselves to oral delivery" (the translation is from Aristotle, *On Rhetoric: A Theory of Civic Discourse*, trans. George A. Kennedy [New York: Oxford University Press, 1991], 255). Cf., more recently, Alter, *Art of Biblical Narrative*, 90. Many more works could be summoned in support of these sentiments. See, e.g., Walter J. Ong, *Orality and Literacy: The Technologizing of the Word* (London: Routledge, 1982), esp. 33–36, 39–41; Birger Gerhardsson, *Memory and Manuscript: Oral Tradition and Written Transmission in Rabbinic Judaism and Early Christianity* with *Tradition and Transmission in Early Christianity* (Grand Rapids: Eerdmans and Livonia: Dove, 1998), 122–70, esp. 148–56, 163–70; Susan Niditch, *Oral World and Written Word: Ancient Israelite Literature*, LAI (Louisville: Westminster John Knox, 1996), 10–11, 13–14; Johnstone et al., "Repetition in Discourse," 8; and, more generally, William M. Schniedewind, "Orality and Literacy in Ancient Israel," *RelSRev* 26 (2000): 327–32. Note also Watts, *Reading Law*, 70 (see also 61, 71, 88) who thinks that in a public recitation, repetition would largely provide "thematic unity, emphasis and mnemonic effect." Variation, on the other hand, would have served to maintain audience interest. This may be correct, but it is the repetition that would primarily indicate *what* the people are to remember. One additional item that should be mentioned in connection with orality is the importance of intonation and performance in oral environments. See, e.g., JoEllen M. Simpson, "Regularized Intonation in Conversational Repetition," in Johnstone, *Repetition in Discourse*, 2:48.

92. Note √*zkr*, "remember" (5:15; 7:18; 8:2, 18; 9:7, 27; 15:15; 16:3; 12; 24:9, 18, 22; 25:17, 32:7) and *lō'* or *pen* + √*škḥ*, "do not/lest you forget" (4:9, 23; 6:12; 8:11, 14, 19; 9:7; 25:19; 26:13; 31:21; 32:18). For a study of the memory motif in Deuteronomy, see Edward P. Blair, "An Appeal to Remembrance: The Memory Motif in Deuteronomy," *Int* 15 (1961): 41–47, esp. 45 on the objects of remembrance in Deuteronomy. Notably, Blair highlights the ability of memory to actualize.

93. See Julie A. Duncan, "Considerations of 4QDt^j in Light of the 'All Souls Deuteronomy' and Cave 4 Phylactery Texts," in *The Madrid Qumran Congress: Proceedings of the International Congress on the Dead Sea Scrolls, Madrid 18–21 March, 1991*, ed. Julio Trebolle Barrera and Luis Vegas Montaner, STDJ 11, 2 vols. (Leiden: Brill, 1992), 1:199–215; and Duncan, "Excerpted Texts of Deuteronomy at Qumran," *RevQ* 18 (1997): 43–62. It is noteworthy that 11QTemple removes

repetition, it complicates memory while simultaneously producing a sharpened focus on concepts that are closely similar and frequently repeated.

Textual Enactments of Deuteronomy's Repetition

Repetitions of Deuteronomy's own repetitive rhetoric elsewhere in the Old Testament are extensive. These might be termed *textual enactments* of Deuteronomic rhetoric. A particularly fascinating example of this enactment and its positive outcome is found in 2 Kgs 23:25, a text describing Josiah, the ultimate Deuteronomic king:

> Before him, there was no one like him: a king who turned to the LORD with all his heart, and with all his soul, and with all his might [*bəkol-ləbābô ûbəkol-napšô ûbəkol-mə'ōdô*], according to all the law of Moses [*kəkōl tôrat mōšeh*]. And no one like him arose after him.

Not only does Josiah repeat and enact Deuteronomy's repeated phrase "with all the heart and with all the soul (and with all the might) [*bəkol-lēb ûbəkol-nepeš (ûbəkol-mə'ōd)*]" (4:29; 6:5; 10:12; 11:13; 13:3[4]; 26:16; 30:2, 6, 10), he does this *exactly* (cf. *kəkōl tôrat mōšeh*), in the full phrase as set forth in the Shema (6:5: *bəkol-ləbābəkā ûbəkol-napšəkā ûbəkol-mə'ōdekā*). Textual enactments such as Josiah's show that Deuteronomy's repetitive rhetoric is effective, doable, and, in this case, beneficial.

These enactments are also another example of *the deep connection between the psyche—that is, human behavior—and the structures of repetition.* Repetition is deeply connected to what we do and even why we do it. This finds support in the work of Freud, more negatively, and in the work of Kierkegaard, more positively.[94] Although Kierkegaard knew of negative repetition, he also spoke of the positive variety, a kind that demonstrated that repetition was a religious category—an element of the eternal and timeless. Even Freud, despite repetition compulsion, knew of enjoyable and pleasurable repetition, especially in children.[95] But the connection between repetition and behavior should not be construed only in an individualistic or intrapsychic fashion. E. Theodore Mullen Jr., among others, has argued that Deuteronomy is comprised of community-constitutive discourse.[96] This business

---

many of the repetitions of Deuteronomy (see Emanuel Tov, "*Deut.* 12 and *11QTemple* LII–LIII: A Contrastive Analysis," *RevQ* 15 [1991]: 169–73).

94. See Kierkegaard, *Repetition*, 131–33, 149, esp. 131 and 132.

95. See Freud, *Beyond the Pleasure Principle*, 42. See also Johnstone et al., "Repetition in Discourse," 6–7.

96. Mullen, *Narrative History and Ethnic Boundaries*, 55–85. Note esp. Mullen's important

of community creation, constitution, and maintenance is furthered, in the case of Deuteronomy, by its extensive and excessive repetition. And, *à la* Freud, Deuteronomy's rhetoric also knows of repetition that has to do with joy and enjoyment.[97]

3. Dis/orientation and Surrender: The Aesthetics of Repetition in Deuteronomy

One final and important element remains to be treated: *the aesthetics of repetition* in Deuteronomy. Aesthetics are a main consideration in Kawin's typology because "successful repetition depends both on the inherent interest of the recurring unit and on its context."[98] Much of what has already been said above applies to any discussion of the aesthetics of Deuteronomic repetition. Even so, two particular aesthetics should be lifted up.

The *first aesthetic*, touched on above under the rubric of *muddling*, is this: the similar and repeated language, themes, passages, words, and the like in Deuteronomy have a *disorienting* effect, causing one to feel as if one is "Lost in Deuteronomy."[99] But, while it is probably true that it is repetition at the microstructural level(s) in Deuteronomy that is most disorienting in its tendency toward near-verbatim repetition, even macro-structural repetition can bring the reader back and forth in Deuteronomy, not permitting a simplistic linear flow or "plot" progression. This disorienting effect would be greatest, no doubt, in an oral/aural environment for a first-time hearer, but the same holds true, in my judgment, for a first-time (and perhaps even a multiple-time) reader. How could either of these audiences differentiate or even recall significant differences between 6:6–9 and 11:18–20 after just one, initial reading/hearing? This disorientation diminishes as one moves through Deuteronomy, if only because the laws frequently become more specific and thus more distinguishable.[100] Yet, simultaneously and concurrently, the opposite effect (the *sharpening* element discussed earlier) is taking

---

observation that the Israel that is created in Moses's speeches is one that does not yet exist. Part of Deuteronomy's function, then, is "to supply the defining characteristics to that people that will then be applied to the latter groups who accept this as a part of their ethnic history and authoritative account of their temporal and spatial origins" (58). Cf. further 75, 79, and, more recently, Walter Brueggemann, *Deuteronomy*, AOTC (Nashville: Abingdon, 2001), 18.

97. See, e.g., √*śmḥ*, "rejoice": 12:7, 12, 18; 14:26; 16:11, 14, 15; 26:11; 27:7.

98. Kawin, *Telling It Again and Again*, 4–5; see also Johnstone et al., "Repetition in Discourse," 9.

99. Cf. Weinfeld, *Deuteronomy and the Deuteronomic School*, 173: "The deuteronomic orator often employs rhetorical phrases . . . and he repeats these phrases again and again as if to hypnotize his audience." Note also Johnstone et al., "Repetition in Discourse," 17 on repetition functioning as *disintensification*.

100. See von Rad, *Deuteronomy*, 19–20, though the connection of even the later laws and

place: the disorientation caused by repetition at the macro-structural level(s) is countered by an orientation caused by the high instance of repetition (especially) at the micro-structural level(s).[101] Again, there is a massive amount of this latter type of repetition in Deuteronomy, but it is imperative to remember that not all of it occurs with equal frequency. The clear preponderance of repetition favors the verbs, words, and phrases mentioned above: hear, keep, do; Torah, statutes, ordinances; and so forth. Moreover, even some of the macro-structural repetition is in service to this type of orientation. This is especially true of the repetitions that bring the reader/hearer back to the ten commandments or to the most important word (the Shema).[102]

The *second aesthetic* has less to do with Deuteronomy itself; instead, as aesthetic implies, it has to do with *our own involvement and assessment* of this repetition. Kawin's work underscores the importance of this involvement at every turn: the positive effects of repetition are only experienced if they are *truly experienced*, if they are *really felt* and this, of course, means if *we* truly experience them, if *we* really feel them.[103]

On the one hand, this is, or should be, a most obvious point in the contemporary climate of hermeneutics and biblical studies. *We*, after all, are the ones interpreting these texts, interacting with them and affecting them in the process. But the obviousness of that enterprise does not make this insight any easier to swallow, for it would indicate, as Sandra Schneiders has rightly pointed out, that the process of "entering into the world projected by the text is not first and foremost an exercise of discursive rationality, but a process of aesthetic involvement"—even aesthetic surrender.[104] That is, we must surrender to the aesthetics

---

their structure to the earlier materials (especially the Decalogue), and thus that repetition of a sort, must not be forgotten.

101. Cf. the dynamic discussed in Watts, *Reading Law*, 71; and note Tannen, "Repetition in Conversation as Spontaneous Formulaicity," 223, who notes that altered forms of set expressions can actually be enhanced by connection to other set expressions.

102. For the first/great commandment, see S. Dean McBride Jr., "The Yoke of the Kingdom: An Exposition of Deuteronomy 6:4–5," *Int* 27 (1973): 273–306; and Patrick D. Miller, "The Most Important Word: The Yoke of the Kingdom," *IliffRev* 41 (1984): 17–29, esp. 18–19 on repetition underscoring its importance.

103. See, e.g., Kawin, *Telling It Again and Again*, 33, 151, 172–73; as well as the two essays by Tannen ("Repetition in Conversation" and "Repetition in Conversation as Spontaneous Formulaicity") and the literature cited there.

104. Sandra M. Schneiders, *The Revelatory Text: Interpreting the New Testament as Sacred Scripture*, 2nd ed. (Collegeville, MN: Liturgical Press, 1999), 172; see further 172–78. Schneiders rightly points out that this type of engagement is not uncritical. One may decide, after surrendering for the duration, that the text or some of its parts are to be rejected or, at the very least, that the dialogue between interpreter and text "not only permits but demands development

of the text, at least for the duration of the experience, if we are ever to understand it aright. In the case of Deuteronomy, this would entail giving ourselves over to its repetitive rhetoric with the possibility, perhaps even the likelihood, that we would emerge on the other side transformed by that rhetoric—suddenly attuned to the suasive mood, the content of the actions enjoined, and the objects of the verbal commands, not to mention to the One who commands. Repetition's connection to this second aesthetic requires us to carry the point yet one step further: Could it be that our negative assessments of Deuteronomy's repetitive rhetoric have more to say about *us* than they do about the book and its rhetoric?

4. Conclusion: The Theological Result(s) of Repetition in Deuteronomy

In closing, it must be granted that instances of repetition that are less connected to the overall rhetorical force of Deuteronomy do exist. But it is the *ethical* repetition that is most pronounced. This observation indicates that, in contrast to previous scholarly perspectives, it is the suasive nature of Deuteronomic repetition that is most important and that cannot be overlooked or neglected, whatever else one might think of it or do with it. Indeed, this suasive intent is the primary purpose of the repetition and its *raison d'être*.

Several points must be made in conclusion:

1. The rhetoric of repetition in Deuteronomy suggests that the importance and meaning of repetition is found not only in difference, but also in similarity, in emphasis, even in muddled redundancy.

2. In the main, Deuteronomic repetition seems to fit the Kawinian category of emphasis. But its tendency to begin again and again, and its enactment, especially in the present and continuous timeframes of the book, indicate that it also belongs to Kawin's category of transcendence. There is, however, one notable difference: for Kawin transcendent repetition must take place without memory. Deuteronomy, by contrast, is quite emphatic—and repetitive!—that one *must* remember and not forget. This does not necessarily mean that Deuteronomic repetition is not transcendent, for Kawin speaks of yet another category that blurs the distinction between emphasis and transcendence. To this category belong those works that describe "eternity in an hour"—that is, "works that exist on the margins of both time-systems, whose characters move both in time and in eternity."[105] It may very well be that Deuteronomy belongs in this tertiary, hybrid category. This would certainly help to explain the book's ability to function at

---

of both" parties involved (175). It is not, then, in the final analysis, "blind submission to what the text says" (177).

105. Kawin, *Telling It Again and Again*, 72.

many different times and places, including within the canon of Scripture, both "today" and "always."

3. But the pragmatic question must still be addressed: does Deuteronomy's repetitive rhetoric really work? Greg Urban has written that "for something to be replicable and hence capable of forming part of socially circulating discourse, and, therefore, also part of culture, it is helpful and perhaps essential that it be built around a structure of internal repetition. . . . The repetition picks out what it is about the discourse that is *replicable*."[106]

According to this, there *is* much in Deuteronomy that is (and was) replicable. Moreover, Scripture is quite clear that, despite possible doubts to the contrary, Deuteronomy's repetition was effective. The Old Testament knows of positive, textual enactments of Deuteronomy's rhetoric and these come from disparate time periods. The specifics of that effect, therefore—especially its *first* instance—are not the primary issue. Scholars have discussed at least three audiences for the book of Deuteronomy (the literary, the Josianic/monarchic, and the exilic) and it is more significant to ask whether and how these various audiences would have experienced this effect. There can be little doubt from texts like Deut 17:18–20; 31:9–13; 2 Kgs 22:11–23:25; and Neh 7:73–8:12 that Deuteronomy (or something like it) was to be read/heard (and was read/heard) periodically and was to make (and did make) a significant impact in vastly different contexts and periods.[107] At this point, the importance of the septennial reading of Deuteronomy prescribed in 31:9–13 cannot be overstated.[108]

The rhetorical impact of Deuteronomic repetition is felt whether the book is read or heard. It is that rhetorical force, not its specific or original delivery that is of primary import. Indeed, the repetition itself fosters the impetus and motivation to return to the words and study them again. After all, the fact that one must keep/observe/do—carefully—all this Torah/these words/commandments/statutes and ordinances, and so forth, means that one must go back and learn these latter in great detail.[109] To come full circle, the intimate familiarity with Deuteronomy

---

106. Urban, "Repetition and Cultural Replication," 2:160.

107. See, recently, Daniel J. Harrington, *Invitation to the Apocrypha* (Grand Rapids: Eerdmans, 1999), 11–13, 23, 25, who has highlighted the impact of Deuteronomy on the book (and character) of Tobit.

108. Note William L. Holladay's application of the septennial reading in his treatment of Jeremiah (*Jeremiah 1: A Commentary on the Book of the Prophet Jeremiah Chapters 1–25*, ed. Paul D. Hanson, Hermeneia [Philadelphia: Fortress, 1986], 1–2). For more recent times and contexts, appeal might be made to the eleven *parashot* and thirty-one *sedarim* in Deuteronomy, which, though they divide the text into smaller parts, nevertheless expose the reader/listener to large sections of the book at a time.

109. On going back to the beginning and starting over again, see Watts, *Reading Law*, 83;

that comes from such repetitive (!) study actually works against the rhetorical effect produced in an initial hearing or reading. It diminishes, that is, the "Lost in Deuteronomy" feeling. When one knows Deuteronomy well, one is not lost at all. But this only serves to underscore that the rhetoric of Deuteronomy accomplishes its task remarkably well. It wants us to keep its words—to do them and do them carefully—and by the time we have *superseded* that rhetoric we have, in all actuality, *succumbed* to it. In so doing, we have been transformed into the people of God that Deuteronomy so desperately seeks.[110] So, again, any inability we may have with respect to Deuteronomy's repetition may very well go beyond our inability to appreciate that repetition and include our inability to enact it as well.

4. Of course, it must be admitted that not everything is so easy, not even in the face of an overwhelming, pervasive, and persuasive repetitive rhetoric like that of Deuteronomy. This, too, is signaled in repetition; there is something about repetition that evidences a difficulty in the subject matter. So Kawin, quoting Ecclesiasties: "'Man cannot utter it,' but he can utter around it. He can, through repetition, 'make it manifest.'"[111] Repetition helps the speaker/writer talk around an issue that is unclear and uncertain, that is hard to say and hard to say right. Perhaps the repetition around obedience in Deuteronomy is similar: it is hard to get obedience said right and even harder to get it done right. Perhaps the rhetoric of repetition in Deuteronomy, then, despite urging this obedience upon all of us who take the book up, nevertheless understands and acknowledges the difficulties involved in this, *even within the very rhetoric that urges it upon us.*

Perhaps related to the difficulty repetition attempts to counter is the observation that repetition sometimes functions as a means to gain or regain control.[112] Was the Israelite audience who heard Deuteronomy out of control? *Which* Isra-

---

Johnstone et al., "Repetition in Discourse," 7, 18; and Rebecca S. Gault, "Education by the Use of Ghosts: Strategies of Repetition in *Effi Briest*," in Johnstone, *Repetition in Discourse*, 1:139–51.

110. See Watts, *Reading Law*, 57: "Deuteronomy obliges Israel not only to legal obedience but also repetition of the book's own rhetoric of persuasion through reenactment, both by individuals (6.2–25; 17.18–20) and by the nation as a whole (11.29; 27.12; cf. 31.10–13)"; and Miller, *Deuteronomy*, 10: "Thus the Book of Deuteronomy is to be understood backwards; its significance is its summarizing and closing of the foundational period. Deuteronomy signals that the period is over. That very fact, however, means that the book is also to be understood from the future. Its impact is not fully comprehended apart from reading the books that follow and sensing sharply that the word of the LORD in Deuteronomy *is always set for future generations*. The intentionality of the book prohibits its ever being viewed as over and done, an enterprise belonging only to the past. No other book of the Old Testament is so straightforward and self-conscious about *its character as a guide for the future*" (emphasis mine).

111. Kawin, *Telling It Again and Again*, 7–8. See also Dozeman, *God on the Mountain*, 173–75; and, further, Kawin, *Telling It Again and Again*, 50–51, 61–62.

112. See above on Freud and Johnstone et al., "Repetition in Discourse," 19.

elite audience? An out-of-control scenario certainly makes sense with the presentation of the Josianic reform in Kings,[113] but it may also make sense of the narrative audience, insofar as Moses is about to die and lose control of Israel. Deuteronomy is his last opportunity to get some words in edgewise. And this, again—always again!—reminds us of why repetition is there in the first place: to remind us, over and over and over again, to keep/observe/do, carefully, today! I close with the words of Patrick D. Miller: "From the beginning, its [Deuteronomy's] words have claimed that its readers' lives depend upon careful attention to them. So read on, carefully."[114] The present chapter would add only that the book's words—*repeated* words—urge one additional item: to not only read on, but also to *live* on, carefully.[115]

---

113. Cf. Kawin, *Telling It Again and Again*, 122 (a quote from Stein): "The excitingness of pure being had withdrawn from them [the words]; they were just rather stale literary words. Now the poet has to work in the excitingness of pure being; he has to get back that intensity into the language." If repetition is a part of getting that intensity back into the language, one wonders what had become stale in the Josianic or exilic periods that Deuteronomy's rhetoric sought to address.

114. Miller, *Deuteronomy*, 17.

115. An early version of this chapter was drafted at the Mount Calvary Monastery and Retreat House in Santa Barbara, California. I am deeply thankful to Carlos Estrada for making that trip possible. I am also grateful to Bill T. Arnold, Nancy R. Bowen, Henry W. Rietz, Brad D. Strawn, and Christine Roy Yoder for reading and commenting on an earlier draft of this chapter.

4

Slaves and Rebels: Inscription, Identity, and Time in the Rhetoric of Deuteronomy

Those who composed [Deuteronomy] in this form did not consider themselves to be guilty of some pious fraud and were not using a literary artifice either. Moses' voice, as it was heard in their imaginations in the late royal era, went forth to this declining period, taking account of its specific troubles and grappling with the disorder of its religious and social life. Over a distance of many centuries past it was possible once again to stand at the foot of Mount Sinai and hear God's will. Thus Israel introduced her divine history into the present! Perhaps we may express it better by saying that history itself intruded again and again into Israel.[1]

Moses shifts back and forth between that day at Horeb and this day in Moab; so too the Deuteronomist, by breaking frame throughout the book, subtly—almost subliminally—forces us to shuttle back and forth between the narrated past and the narrator's present. Both Moses and the narrator shift temporal gears in the process of teaching.[2]

I thank the editors and conveners of the Wheaton conference at which this chapter was originally presented for their kind invitation and assistance, and I am grateful to the other participants for a very collegial and enjoyable exchange. I am indebted to Bill T. Arnold for his feedback, encouragement, and bibliographical suggestions, and am particularly grateful to Aubrey E. Buster for her close reading of an earlier draft, which helped me reformulate several important aspects of the argument.

1. Gerhard von Rad, "How to Read the Old Testament," in *God at Work in Israel*, trans. John H. Marks (Nashville: Abingdon, 1980), 14.

2. Robert Polzin, "Deuteronomy," in *The Literary Guide to the Bible*, ed. Robert Alter and Frank Kermode (Cambridge: Belknap, 1987), 92–101, here 94. Cf. Polzin, *Moses and the Deuteronomist: Deuteronomy, Joshua, Judges*, ISBL (Bloomington: Indiana University Press, 1993), 32.

1. Two Key Texts

The inspiration for the present chapter (as well as its title) is taken from two passages in the book of Deuteronomy that situate the Israelites in two modes. The first text is Deut 6:21, which discusses *Israel's Egyptian servitude*:

> Tell your children: "We were Pharaoh's slaves in Egypt, but Yhwh brought us out from Egypt with a strong hand."[3]

The second text is Deut 9:7, which mentions *Israel's seemingly incessant rebellion*:

> From the day that you left the land of Egypt, until you arrived at this place, you've been rebels against Yhwh.

These two verses have more than a few things in common, including some repeated words and several syntactical details, but perhaps the most striking commonality is the use of a masculine plural substantive fronted before a *qal* suffix-conjugation verb form of √*hyh* in order to describe the Israelites in two very different states and within two distinct temporal frames: "*Slaves* we were" (*ʿăbādîm hāyînû*) vs. "*Rebels* you've been" (*mamrîm hĕyîtem*).

The present chapter argues that Deuteronomic rhetoric can be aptly summarized by this twinned presentation of the audience as "slaves" and "rebels," insofar as this presentation functions to constantly (re)situate its readers (or hearers)[4] into these two roles and their correlate temporal frames. This (re)situation has great significance for the construction of the audience's identity, as signaled already in the two verbal subjects employed in 6:21 and 9:7 ("we" and "you," respectively), even as it also affords insight into the *telos* of this rhetoric. To put matters in words borrowed from Gerhard von Rad, used as the first epigraph above, while the rhetoric of Deuteronomy is no "pious fraud," it is nevertheless nothing if not high artistry and thus an *artifact*—that is, a rhetorical construction[5]—and thus an

---

3. Translations are my own, and have been made as fluid as possible, with an eye on the CEB.

4. For present purposes, no significant difference obtains between these two forms of reception, though they are obviously distinct. Hereafter, I prefer to speak more generally of "audience."

5. So, if nothing else, Deuteronomy's rhetoric is marked by what is known in the classical study of rhetoric as "arrangement" (*dispositio, taxis*). See Richard A. Lanham, *A Handlist of Rhetorical Terms: A Guide for Students of English Literature* (Berkeley: University of California Press, 1969), 165–66, 171–74. For rhetoric in Deuteronomy proper, see, inter alia, Moshe Weinfeld, *Deuteronomy and the Deuteronomic School* (Winona Lake, IN: Eisenbrauns, 1992), 320–65; Timothy A. Lenchak, *"Choose Life!" A Rhetorical-Critical Investigation of Deuteronomy 28,69–*

artifice in the best sense of the term.[6] Similarly, Deuteronomy's rhetoric definitely makes it "possible once again to stand at the foot of Mount Sinai and hear God's will," and to do so "over a distance of many centuries," but that distance should not be restricted only to "the late royal era." Instead, it is better to cite Robert Polzin's opinion, used as the second epigraph above, that Deuteronomy "forces us to shuttle back and forth between the narrated past and the narrator's present." Of course, von Rad, too, speaks of Deuteronomy consistently intersecting with the present; even so, that intersection is not solely nor primarily a matter of "divine *history*" being introduced or somehow intruding (so von Rad), as much as it is a case of "divine *presence*" doing that work in Israel—a divine presence that is facilitated, in the end, not by history per se or as such, but *by rhetoric*,[7] which means that this intersection is ever mobile, always (re)applicable, and ultimately *trans*-historical. In what follows, these points are argued more fully through attention to inscription, identity, and time in Deuteronomy's rhetoric, though all three of these elements are interrelated, even inextricably so. The chapter concludes with a consideration of the several functions and effects of this rhetoric.

2. Inscription: "We" and "You"

Perhaps the easiest way to describe what transpires in Deut 6:21 and 9:7 is to term both verses instances of (literary) "inscription."[8] By this term I simply mean that, via

---

30,20, AnBib 129 (Rome: Pontifical Biblical Institute, 1993), 63–66; Jerry Hwang, *The Rhetoric of Remembrance: An Investigation of the "Fathers" in Deuteronomy*, Siphrut 8 (Winona Lake, IN: Eisenbrauns, 2012); Shin Wook Hur, "The Rhetoric of the Deuteronomic Code: Its Structures and Devices" (PhD diss., Emory University, 2013); and see chapter 3 of the present work. See also Jack R. Lundbom, *Deuteronomy: A Commentary* (Grand Rapids: Eerdmans, 2013), and the earlier work by the same author: *Jeremiah: A Study in Ancient Hebrew Rhetoric*, 2nd ed. (Winona Lake, IN: Eisenbrauns, 1997), esp. xix–xliii; and his volume of collected essays: *Biblical Rhetoric and Rhetorical Criticism*, HBM 45 (Sheffield: Sheffield Phoenix, 2013), esp. chs. 1, 11–13.

6. Both "artifice" and "artifact" trace back to Latin and have to do with making with skill. See *OED*, s.v. "artifice" and "artefact" (2nd ed.; online). Cf. Polzin, "Deuteronomy," 93: "We are dealing with an unusually sophisticated and artfully constructed work of the first millennium B.C.E."

7. This should not be taken as a suggestion that history and rhetoric are completely discrete, which of course is not the case. See, inter alia, V. Philips Long, *The Art of Biblical History*, FCI 5 (Grand Rapids: Zondervan, 1994), 58–87; and Hayden White, *The Content of the Form: Narrative Discourse and Historical Representation* (Baltimore: Johns Hopkins University Press, 1987).

8. Not entirely unrelated is the notion of interpellation, though critics use that term in slightly different ways, often with strong connections to ideology and its manifestation. If interpellation applies in this case, it would be in a somewhat "weaker" form: "The constitutive process where individuals acknowledge and respond to ideologies [or, in this case theologies], thereby recognizing themselves as subjects" (https://lucian.uchicago.edu/blogs/mediatheory

the rhetorical presentation, the audience is *written into* the story, made to be (and feel) a part of it. That is to say that the members of the audience are inscribed directly as "Pharaoh's slaves in Egypt" (6:21) and "rebels against Yhwh" (9:7), and this is true whether or not they agree to the inscription and whether or not such an identification is accurate or otherwise feasible. Both of these points deserve further discussion.

First, the audience is not given space—at least within the rhetoric as we now have it—to respond to this literary inscription, whether affirmatively or negatively. There are instances elsewhere in the Bible where the literary audience responds positively (see, e.g., Exod 19:8; cf. also Josh 24:21–22, 24; Neh 8), but that does not take place in these two specific passages—nor, indeed, almost anywhere else in Deuteronomy proper.[9] The audience is simply identified as "slaves" and "rebels"; that is who they are, whether they like it or not.

Second, the literary *fabula*[10] of both Deuteronomy and the Torah writ large (see, esp. Num 14:26–35 and 26:63–65)[11] suggests that this inscription is simply not

---

9. Deuteronomy 26:17; 27:15–26 might be considered here. See also below for the important case of 32:31. Whatever the case, another way to put the matter at hand is to say that, if the audience of Deuteronomy does have a choice, it is not unlike the choice offered the youth in Proverbs or the individual in Ps 1: yes, there may be two ways, but no one in their right mind (after succumbing to the rhetoric) would pick the foolish or wicked way. In this light, Deuteronomy's rhetoric begins to approach that of wisdom canons. See, in this regard, Weinfeld, *Deuteronomy and the Deuteronomic School*; Stephen A. Geller, "Fiery Wisdom: The Deuteronomic Tradition," in *Sacred Enigmas: Literary Religion in the Hebrew Bible* (London: Routledge, 1996), 30–61; and Georg Braulik, "Wisdom, Divine Presence and Law," in *The Theology of Deuteronomy: Collected Essays of Georg Braulik*, trans. Ulrika Lindblad (North Richland Hills, TX: BIBAL Press, 1994), 1–25.

10. I mean by this term simply "the narrated world," following Norbert Lohfink, "Reading Deuteronomy 5 as Narrative," in *A God So Near: Essays on Old Testament Theology in Honor of Patrick D. Miller*, ed. Brent A. Strawn and Nancy R. Bowen (Winona Lake, IN: Eisenbrauns, 2003), 261–81. Cf. the distinction drawn in Russian Formalism between plot and story: plot (*syuzhet*) refers "to the order and manner in which events are actually presented in the narrative," and story (*fabula*) refers "to the chronological sequence of events" (J. A. Cuddon and C. E. Preston, *The Penguin Dictionary of Literary Terms and Literary Theory*, 4th ed. [London: Penguin, 1998], 328). In this article, my use of *fabula* is closer to "plot," not "story," following Lohfink as well as Mieke Bal, *Narratology: Introduction to the Theory of Narrative*, 3rd ed. (Toronto: University of Toronto Press, 2009), who defines *fabula* as "the sequence of events as they 'occur' in the imaginative world." See Bal, *Narratology*, 5–12 and passim for Bal's differentiation between narrative, text, story, and fabula.

11. See Dennis T. Olson, *The Death of the Old and the Birth of the New: The Framework of the Book of Numbers and the Pentateuch*, BJS 71 (Chico, CA: Scholars Press, 1985).

74

accurate in terms of historical/temporal sequence.[12] In Deuteronomy, the literary audience that hears Moses's address is comprised extensively, if not exclusively, of those who were neither actual slaves in Egypt nor rebels in the wilderness—at least not as major participants in the foundational redemptive act, nor as agents in the paradigmatic moments of rebellion (the golden calf and spy incidents). Rather, it is precisely those who were *not* disobedient (either because they were not yet born or were minors) who have survived the wilderness wanderings and who now stand poised to take possession of Canaan.[13] This generational change is specified early in Deuteronomy in its recapitulation of the spy debacle in Deut 1:34–40, and signaled again slightly later with the chronological reference (thirty-eight years) and the notification of the death of "every one of the previous generation, those of fighting age, from the camp . . . just as Yhwh had sworn about them" in Deut 2:14 (cf. 2:15–16).[14] Assuming something like a forty-year generation,[15] this means that many if not most (or even all) of those listening at Moab were not born in Egypt but represent the second generation from there—the notable exceptions, which in this instance proverbially prove the rule, being Caleb and Joshua (see 1:36 and 1:38; 3:28; 31:3, 7, respectively).

These considerations indicate that Deuteronomic inscription is somewhat "out of order." Perhaps the clearest example of the issue at hand is Deut 5:3, especially given its over-the-top syntactical emphasis:

12. So similarly Hwang, *Rhetoric of Remembrance*, 6.

13. For more on Deuteronomy's *Generationswechsel* (generational changing), see Hwang, *Rhetoric of Remembrance*, passim, and Bill T. Arnold, "Reexamining the 'Fathers' in Deuteronomy's Framework" in *Torah and Tradition: Papers Read at the Sixteenth Joint Meeting of the Society for Old Testament Study and the Oudtestamentisch Werkgezelschap, Edinburgh 2015*, ed. Klaas Spronk and Hans Barstad, Oudtestamentische Studiën 70 (Leiden: Brill, 2017), 10–41, both of whom argue that the rhetorical blending of generations is an intentional rhetorical device. Arnold believes "this intentional ambiguity" functions to create "deliberate solidarity . . . among Israel's generations. . . . This intentional indeterminateness draws Israelite readers into solidarity with each generation of ancestors" (19). Arnold speaks of "trans-generational Israel" (18–19), "transgenerational solidarity" (39–40), "rhetorical generation-blending" (39), and the "rhetorical conflation of Israel's generations" (28). Bernd Biberger, *Unsere Väter und Wir: Unterteilung von Geschichtsdarstellungen in Generationen und das Verhältnis der Generationen im Alten Testament*, BBB 145 (Berlin: Philo, 2003), 332–61, has catalogued no fewer than five generational groups: (1) the patriarchal generation; (2) the exodus generation; (3) the wilderness generation; (4) the generation in the plains of Moab; and (5) future generations.

14. Note also the mention of "forty years" in the wilderness in Deut 2:7; 8:2, 4; 29:5.

15. See, inter alia, the data on average life expectancy in Hans Walter Wolff, *Anthropology of the Old Testament*, trans. Margaret Kohl, repr. ed. (Mifflintown, PA: Sigler, 1996), 119–20; and Philip J. King and Lawrence E. Stager, *Life in Biblical Israel*, LAI (Louisville: Westminster John Knox, 2001), 37, 58.

Yhwh did not make this covenant with our ancestors, but with us, those of us here now, all of us who are alive (*kî 'ittānû 'ănaḥnû 'ēlleh pōh hayyôm kullānû ḥayyîm*).

Once again, according to the literary *fabula* of Deuteronomy and the sweep of the Pentateuchal narrative from Exodus until this point, this is simply not true—at least not entirely. Even if this statement is true with respect to the "ancestors" Abraham, Isaac, and Jacob,[16] it would not hold true for all who are alive in the plains of Moab. Their more immediate ancestors *were* present at the covenant-making on Horeb; conversely, many of the "us here now, all of us who are alive" *were not*.

Rather than considering Deut 5:3 some sort of slip—whether one that was somehow accidental, related to composition/redaction, or downright duplicitous ("pious fraud")—it is better to recognize it as another instance of literary inscription, a device that characterizes Deuteronomy's rhetoric and that is robustly employed throughout the book. Indeed, the very first unit of Deuteronomy after the opening superscription manifests this very same kind of inscription. Immediately after we learn that Moses was willing (or began) to explain this Torah (*hô'îl mōšeh bē'ēr 'et-hattôrâ hazzō't*, 1:5), a statement that is followed by a recitative *lē'mōr* ("saying" or "as follows"), Moses speaks:

Yhwh our God spoke *to us* (*'ēlênû*) at Horeb: "You've stayed at this mountain long enough (*rab-lākem šebet*)." (1:6)

The very same problems of the addressed audience vis-à-vis the literary *fabula* obtain here, just as they did in the other texts cited thus far (along with the many others that might be added). That is, many if not most of the members of the audience addressed in the plains of Moab were *not* present at Horeb because, according to the *fabula*, they were not yet alive. But no matter: they are inscribed as if they were.

The presence of this type of literary inscription at the very outset of Deuteronomy signals its importance in the book's rhetoric. Therefore it is not surprising

---

16. Much depends on the definition of "ancestors" here: does it refer only to the great patriarchs and matriarchs of old? If so, Deut 5:3 would be correct: Horeb represents a new thing not experienced by them. But if it refers more generally to the previous generation(s), then it is patently *in*accurate (see below). The precise referent of the "fathers" in Deuteronomy has occasioned much discussion, esp. after Thomas Römer, *Israels Väter: Untersuchungen zur Väterthematik im Deuteronomium und in der deuteronomistischen Tradition*, OBO 99 (Göttingen: Vandenhoeck & Ruprecht, 1990). Here is not the place to engage Römer's "insertion theory," for which see Norbert Lohfink, *Die Väter Israels im Deuteronomium*, OBO 111 (Göttingen: Vandenhoeck & Ruprecht, 1991); Hwang, *Rhetoric of Remembrance*; and esp. Arnold, "Reexamining."

to find inscription used throughout much of what follows, whether that be in 5:3 or 6:21 or 9:7, and whether that inscription is accomplished by means of the first-person common plural or second-person (singular and/or plural) forms.[17] Stated most simply, inscription is a hallmark of Deuteronomic rhetoric, perhaps even *the* hallmark of that rhetoric. The pervasiveness of this technique and its presence from the very start of the book in the transition from Deut 1:5 to 1:6 suggests that one of the primary ways Torah is expounded (*bēʾēr*) in Deuteronomy is not only by means of storytelling (as opposed to some sort of formal legal explication) but by *storytelling that inscribes the audience into the very story being told*—once again, whether they like it or not, and whether or not the inscription "fits" the temporal sequence of events. The main point, regardless of agreement or accuracy, is, once again, to inscribe the audience directly into the story that Moses tells. That story revolves around two primary nodes: redemption from slavery and rebellion against the Lord.

3. *"We Were Slaves" (Deut 6:21)*

The first of the two key texts mentioned above exemplifies the workings of Deuteronomic inscription even as it showcases how central this rhetorical move is for the way the book of Deuteronomy works. In Deut 6:20–25, a hypothetical (or inevitable) scenario[18] is raised in which children inquire about the "laws, regulations, and case laws" (*hāʿēdōt wǝhahuqqîm wǝhammišpāṭîm*). In a move that is entirely familiar from the shift from 1:5 to 1:6, the parental answer that is commended has virtually nothing to do with legal explication proper but, instead, with inscription into the story of the exodus:

> Tell your children: "We were Pharaoh's slaves in Egypt, but Yhwh brought us out from Egypt with a strong hand. Before our own eyes, Yhwh performed great and terrible signs and wonders against Egypt, against Pharaoh and his dynasty. But

17. For the alteration in second-person forms (plural and singular)—the famous *Numeruswechsel*—see further below.

18. Note 6:20a: *kî-yišʾālǝkā binkā māhār*, "If [or: when] your child asks you, in the future . . ." Bill T. Arnold and John H. Choi, *A Guide to Biblical Hebrew Syntax* (Cambridge: Cambridge University Press, 2003), 151, note that "the distinction between temporal and conditional [instances of כִּי] is somewhat vague, especially when dealing with future temporal statements," and illustrate the conundrum with reference to Deut 6:20. See further Anneli Aejmelaeus, "Function and Interpretation of *kî* in Biblical Hebrew," *JBL* 105 (1986): 193–209, esp. 197, who writes, again with reference to Deut 6:20: "In several cases, the interpreter may freely choose either interpretation [temporal or conditional] according to one's own consideration of the wider context."

he brought us out from there in order to bring us in—to give us the land that he promised our ancestors. Yhwh commanded us to perform all these regulations by fearing Yhwh our God, for our good always, to preserve us alive, just as we are right now. Furthermore, we will be righteous if we carefully perform all this commandment before Yhwh our God, exactly as he commanded us." (6:21–25)

The parent's answer precisely imitates the rhetorical movement found in Deut 1:5–6 (and elsewhere). Hence, inscribing future generations into the story is not simply a rhetorical device that can be *identified* in a particular passage and *subsequently described*; in Deuteronomy, this type of inscription is also—and far more importantly—*applied prescriptively, even mandated*.

Deuteronomy 6:20–25 is an important passage in still other ways, insofar as verse 20 casts light on *why* rhetorical inscription is necessary in the first place, or, put differently, how such inscription addresses a specific rhetorical situation.[19] The clue is found in how the children who will ask this question about the legislation carefully differentiate themselves from their parents:

What is the meaning of the laws, regulations, and case laws that Yhwh our God commanded *you*? (6:20b)

The exact meaning of this question, which is verbless in Hebrew, is somewhat uncertain. Perhaps the child is simply asking about the *content*: *what are* the laws, regulations, and case laws? However, it seems more likely—precisely because of the pronominal distinction that, though it acknowledges Yhwh as *our* God, nevertheless makes clear that the legislation itself and the command to obey it apply only to the parents (*'etkem*: "you," second masculine plural)—that the child is asking not simply about the content of this legislation but about its *meaning for* and/or *pertinence to* the child. This latter option is confirmed by both the details and rhetoric of the parental answer.

Before addressing those details and that rhetoric, it should be noted that the versions reflect variants in the pronouns used in 6:20b, with some having the child say "commanded *us*" (*'ōtānû*: first common plural).[20] If the latter reading is

19. For more on the rhetorical situation, see below, and, more generally, Chaïm Perelman and L. Olbrechts-Tyteca, *The New Rhetoric: A Treatise on Argumentation*, trans. John Wilkinson and Purcell Weaver (Notre Dame: University of Notre Dame Press, 1969), esp. 17–26, 35–40, 59–62, 495–502.

20. *'etkem* ("you," pl.) is found in SamP, LXX^mss, Syr, and Targ; *'ōtānû* ("us") is reflected in LXX and Vulg. Carmel McCarthy, *Biblia Hebraica Quinta: Deuteronomy* (Stuttgart: Deutsche Bibelgesellschaft, 2007), 24 (hereafter *BHQ*) thinks the latter is a case of harmonization of syn-

correct, there would be no difference between the child's and the parent's reception of the laws after all. However, the difference in the pronouns as reflected in MT seems most likely to be original (*"our* God," "commanded *you"*), the versional evidence constituting what is the easier reading and therefore the likely result of harmonization. "Commanded *you"* is not only the more difficult reading, it is also the most interesting one, since it draws a clear distinction between what God commanded the previous generation ("you," plural) and everything thereafter, since the prior generation does not include the child, apparently (if only) because the child was not there.[21] The generational, temporal, and historical differential evoked by the child's shrewd use of pronouns is quite legitimate and accurate— as far as such things go—but in this specific case none of that goes very far at all since the distinction is granted neither legitimacy nor accuracy because the parental answer to what seems to be an entirely sensible question functions to collapse all distance—generational, temporal, and historical—by means of literary inscription. The child says "you," but the parent responds with an onslaught of "we"-language. The child says "you" once, but the parent uses some form of "we" or "us" no fewer than fifteen times in a *tour de force* of literary inscription. This "we"-language is not restricted to the parents themselves (the speaking subjects in vv. 21–25) but necessarily includes the child for several reasons, one of which

---

tax, though she seems to posit the same for the reading in MT[L]. This confusion is clarified in McCarthy's textual commentary where she notes that John Wevers, who edited the Göttingen Septuagint of Deuteronomy, has changed his mind on the original reading of LXX, which he now deems was *hēmōn hymin*, "our [God commanded] *you*," because the distinction in pronouns seems intentional and because he deems the temptation to level the pronouns to have been too powerful to resist (*BHQ*, 72*). A similar but reversed case of such leveling is found in the case of *'ĕlōhênû*, "our God," since, according to J. Hempel in *BHS*, *'ĕlōhêkā* ("your [sg.] God") is reflected in Cairo and LXX*L*[min], with *'ĕlōhêkem* ("your [pl.] God") reflected in LXX[min] OL.

21. I.e., at Sinai; but, as per the preceding discussion, the very same situation likely obtained for the child's parents! This is to consider only generations 2.0 and 3.0 (or generations 1.5 and 2.0). It is even truer for future generations further down the line. This is the force of von Rad's remarks used as the first epigraph in this chapter, and, further, von Rad's comment in his *Studies in Deuteronomy*, trans. David Stalker, SBT (London: SCM, 1953), 70: "This Israel which is addressed by Moses is, of course, *completely different* from the one that stood at the foot of Mount Horeb. It knows Palestine with all its religious temptations, it has a king and a graded civil service; economically its life is no longer the patriarchal, but it has entered upon the stage of an economy based on currency, with all its perilous consequences; it knows the prophets, and has indeed already had unpleasant experiences with these men; and so on. . . . This Israel *has in actual fact no longer any points of comparison* with the Israel that in the past stood at Horeb; [it is] separated from the events at Horeb by a very long and extremely incriminating history . . . six centuries wasted in sin and constant apostasy" (my emphasis). See further *Studies in Deuteronomy*, 71–73.

is the first-person common plural subject[22] and another of which is the climax of the parental response in verses 24b–25 (especially *ləḥayyōtēnû kəhayyôm hazzeh*). The child has asked a question—perhaps innocently, but perhaps frustrated by the imposition of so many *ḥuqqîm ûmišpāṭîm*—and, in reply, gets overwhelmingly and inescapably narrated into the story of Israel. In the process, the parents play the part of "little Moseses," rhetorically inscribing their children into the story, with the children becoming the "little Israelites" so inscribed.[23]

It bears repeating that 6:20–25 not only exemplifies the Deuteronomic rhetoric of inscription, it *legislates* the same. What Moses provides throughout the book is not simply a model, then, it is a *mandate*—one that can be and will need to be enacted for all generations: "*whenever* your child asks you in the future." Still further, as noted above, the child's question reflects a likely rhetorical situation that calls for (or calls forth) this particular rhetorical move—namely, the problem younger generations face when they encounter (often with some measure of dissatisfaction) religious systems for themselves. It is at exactly this significant and tenuous moment in the transgenerational communication of religious values that Deuteronomy commends and commands inscription: narrating the next generation into the story of Israel with its God—a story that begins, fundamentally and paradigmatically, with "we were slaves."

22. Note that the pronouns in 6:20a are second masculine singular (*binkā, yišʾāləkā*), as is the verbal form in 6:21a (*wəʾāmartā*), suggesting, as it were, a *singular* parent interacting with a *singular* child. Given this, the instructed response of "we" does not imagine a mother-father pairing talking to a child but a singular parent addressing a child, with the two of them together subsequently comprising the "we" of the discourse in vv. 21–25.

23. For Moses as the model teacher, see Olson, *Deuteronomy and the Death of Moses*, 11; David G. Firth, "Passing On the Faith in Deuteronomy," in *Interpreting Deuteronomy: Issues and Approaches*, ed. David G. Firth and Philip S. Johnston (Downers Grove, IL: IVP Academic, 2012), 157–76, here 164. For more on Deuteronomy, children, and instruction in the faith, see Firth, "Passing On the Faith," passim; Mark A. Awabdy, "Teaching Children in the Instruction of Amenemope and Deuteronomy," *VT* 65 (2015): 1–8, who speaks of how Deuteronomy uses "the common human desire for formative parental teaching and filial obedience in order to contextualize Israel's exodus experience in quotidian life" (8); and esp. Patrick D. Miller, "That the Children May Know: Children in Deuteronomy," in *The Child in the Bible*, ed. Marcia J. Bunge, Terence E. Fretheim, and Beverly Roberts Gaventa (Grand Rapids: Eerdmans, 2008), 45–62. For research supporting the importance of parents and parental instruction in children's faith in contemporary North America, see Kenda Creasy Dean, *Almost Christian: What the Faith of Our Teenagers Is Telling the American Church* (Oxford: Oxford University Press, 2010), 109–30; and Christian Smith with Melinda Lundquist Denton, *Soul Searching: The Religious and Spiritual Lives of American Teenagers* (Oxford: Oxford University Press, 2005), 54–61.

4. "You've Been Rebels" (Deut 9:7)

While the story begins with slavery and the exodus from Egypt, it certainly does not end there, because there is the second key text to consider, Deut 9:7, which also evidences literary inscription but to very different effect. To allude to a much later legal discussion (see Matt 22:34–40), if this second inscription is not quite equal to the first and greatest one (Deut 6:21), it is at least "like it," such that one might say that "on these two hang" all instances of Deuteronomic inscription. This is to say that the second inscription—the one concerning Israel's rebelliousness—is also basic to and pervasive in Deuteronomy's rhetoric, even if it remains somewhat secondary to the first inscription, which concerns Israel's deliverance from Egyptian servitude.[24]

Deuteronomy 9:7 appears as the introduction to the golden calf incident, which belongs, in turn, to the third in a series of "do not say/think" passages in Deut 7–9. These passages are united by the thrice-repeated use of the phrase "speaking" ($\sqrt{'}mr$) + "in your heart" (bilbābəkā) in 7:17; 8:17; and 9:4. In each case, what Israel says in its heart concerns possible estimations of its life-situation or life-status that are expressly forbidden.[25] Coming hard upon the heels of the positive reformulation of the first commandment in the Shema, as these three passages do, and taking their place amid the larger oration on the Great Commandment in chs. 6–11,[26] these three passages comprise vignettes—sermon illustrations, as it were—that deal with possible rivals to Israel's sole allegiance to Yhwh, each of which must be vigorously resisted. But if these rivals are false gods, as suggested by the larger literary context, they are very subtle ones: the kind that haunt the human heart (hence $\sqrt{'}mr$ + bilbābəkā!), not necessarily an Iron Age cult site.

In the first vignette, Israel is tempted to trust in *military might*, or, perhaps more precisely, to despair in its absence (7:17–24); in the second, the temptation is *wealth or self-sufficiency* (8:17–20); in the third, *morality or false piety* (9:4–10:11).[27] In each case the struggle is with estimations of Israel's "self," especially vis-à-vis the facts "on the ground," at least from Yhwh's perspective. So it is that these three rivals to Israel's sole allegiance could be termed the struggle with the *untrusting, overconfident*, and *immodest* self.[28]

---

24. If nothing else, the secondary nature of this second inscription is due to the Pentateuchal *fabula*: Israel was in slavery first and rebelled thereafter.

25. See Olson, *Deuteronomy and the Death of Moses*, 52–58.

26. On which, see Norbert Lohfink, *Das Hauptgebot*.

27. Olson, *Deuteronomy and the Death of Moses*, 52, names these "gods of death" as militarism, materialism, and moralism.

28. See Brent A. Strawn, "Deuteronomy," in *Theological Bible Commentary*, ed. Gail R. O'Day

Once again, Deut 9:7 appears in the third and final vignette, which forbids Israel from overestimating its own righteousness vis-à-vis the disinherited nations. Here Deuteronomy finally mentions the golden calf debacle. Norbert Lohfink has made a compelling case that it is precisely for rhetorical effect that Deuteronomy does not mention this incident earlier.[29] Deuteronomy 1:6 begins with the departure from Horeb, and the *fabula* moves forward in time from that point, through the spy incident and the victories in the Transjordan (1:19–3:29) until Moses's flashback to the fireworks at Horeb (4:1–24), which is replete with an accompanying sermon that focuses on the second commandment (4:25–40). After a short interlude (4:41–49), Moses returns to Horeb with a recapitulation of the Decalogue (5:1–22) and remarks about his intercessory role thereafter (5:23–33). All of this is in concert with the *fabula* as known from Exod 19:1–20:21. Perhaps the legislation of Exodus 20:22–31:18 could be located "between the lines" of Deut 5:23–33; what is certain, regardless, is that the events of Exod 32–34 are held in reserve. It is altogether possible, that is, that the golden calf story could have been mentioned earlier, at some point in chapter 6, with its focus on the first commandment, or even in chapter 4, with its attention to the second commandment.[30] Instead, it is saved until chapter 9. It fits perfectly well there, to be sure, within the extended sermon on the first commandment found in chapters 6–11, but it seems to have been held back until this moment for rhetorical reasons: in brief, it comprises definitive proof countering Israel's final temptation to immodesty and overestimation of its own self-righteousness. The most pertinent verses follow:

> Once Yhwh your God drives them [i.e., the nations] out before you, do not say in your heart: "It's because of my righteousness that Yhwh has brought me to possess this land." Rather, it's because of the wickedness of these nations that Yhwh is removing them before you! It is not because of your righteousness or the uprightness of your heart that you are entering to take possession of their land, but because of the wickedness of these nations that Yhwh your God is removing them before you in order that Yhwh might prove what he promised to your ancestors: to Abraham, Isaac, and Jacob. So, know that it is not because of your righteousness that Yhwh your God is giving you this good land to pos-

---

and David L. Petersen (Louisville: Westminster John Knox, 2009), 63–76, here 70; also Strawn, "Deuteronomy," in *The Wesley Study Bible: NRSV* (Nashville: Abingdon, 2009), 226–29.

29. See Lohfink, "Reading Deuteronomy 5," esp. 263–65, 277–78.

30. I leave aside here the issue of the combination or division of what the Reformed Christian tradition numbers as the first (no other gods) and second (no idols) commandments. In my judgment, even if they are numbered separately, these prohibitions are closely related and best interpreted together. This may be reflected in the way they overlap in Deut 4, 6, and 9.

sess—because you are a stubborn people! Remember—do not forget!—how you made Yhwh your God furious in the wilderness. From the day that you left the land of Egypt, until you arrived at this place, you've been rebels against Yhwh. (Deut 9:4–7)

The passage continues with specifics about the golden calf incident as proof par excellence that Israel is not more righteous than the nations but, in fact, just as wicked as they are. For present purposes, however, the point is simply that the dynamics of literary inscription are clearly at work in 9:7 and function in the very same way(s) that the inscription of 6:21 does. Once again, the audience is not granted space to dispute the inscription. They are simply identified as rebels—and persistent and intractable ones at that. This point is underscored still further in what might be seen as the negative climax of this second paradigmatic inscription, at least as found in chapter 9:

> Also at Taberah, and at Massah, and at Kibroth-hattaavah you've been the kind of people who make Yhwh furious (*maqṣipîm hĕyîtem 'et-yhwh*). And, when Yhwh sent you from Kadesh-barnea, saying, "Go up and take possession of the land that I have given to you," you rebelled (√*mrh*) against Yhwh your God's command. You did not trust in him and you did not listen to his voice. You've been rebels against Yhwh (*mamrîm hĕyîtem 'im-yhwh*) from the day <he>[31] knew you. (Deut 9:22–24)

This second inscription, which might be termed the rebel- or *mamrîm*-type, is similar to the first inscription (the slave- or *'ebed*-type of inscription) in several ways: (1) not only is the audience not given permission to respond (approvingly or disapprovingly), as already noted, but (2) this second type of inscription is also *contra-fabula*. This is to say that the same problems that obtained for the literary audience's identification as Pharaoh's slaves in Egypt also obtain for that self-same audience being identified as those who rebelled at Horeb or at Kadesh-barnea. The guilt of most, if not all, of those hearing Moses in Moab is at best by association only, since they are generation 2.0 (or 1.5, at the very least). If this Moab audience were *truly* guilty, they would be dead in the wilderness. The precious few—make

---

31. Here there is another text-critical issue with MT (*da'tî*), Syr, and Targ reading "I (Moses) knew you," but SamP, σ', and θ' reflecting *da'tô*: "he (i.e., YHWH) knew you." The latter is to be preferred, with LXX and Vulg offering something of a middle position (see *BHQ*, 32) and MT probably reflecting a theological smoothing. For discussion, see *BHQ*, 78*; *HOTTP* 1:279. Covenantal connotations of √*yd'* are likely operative here (for which, see *TLOT* 2:515–18; *NIDOTTE* 2:411–13).

that two—people who are not dead from generation 1.0 are precisely those who were *not* rebels, namely, Caleb and Joshua.[32] Finally, (3) the *mamrîm*-inscription, like the *'ebed*-inscription found in Deut 6:20–25, affords insight into the rhetorical situation lying behind or perhaps before it—that is, why such rhetoric is required and needed in the first place. In the case of Deut 9:4–10:11, it is not a frustrated question from the next generation in the middle of a confirmation class; it is, instead, the settled self-righteous estimation of the elect lording it over those who are *not*—not elect and thus (presumably) not righteous. In the *'ebed*-inscription, the child's question imposed distance between the next generation and the faith community—at least to some degree—and so the inscription narrated the child into the story of the faith community that undergirds its religious system and motivates adherence to the same. In the *mamrîm*-inscription, the immodest and inaccurate estimation of the faith community imposes distance between it and all others, simultaneously aligning it unrealistically close(r) to the Deity. It is thus the burden of this second type of inscription to disabuse the faith community of all such false (self-righteous) estimations. While the wickedness of the nations cannot be denied, the gap between Israel and them is not large; conversely, the distance between Israel and Yhwh remains significant because who Israel is and what Israel does, at least according to the *mamrîm*-inscription, is to be ($\sqrt{hyh}$) rebels/rebellious ($\sqrt{mrh}$) and to make Yhwh furious ($\sqrt{qṣp}$)—incessantly. The palpable difference in rhetorical situations explains the very different content of this second type of literary inscription: in this case, Israel is no longer comprised of "slaves" who receive the benefits of Yhwh's redeeming activity; they are now nothing more than "rebels" entirely deserving of Yhwh's judgment.

5. The Song of Moses

These, then, are the two types of literary inscription in Deuteronomy's rhetoric: the *'ebed*-type and the *mamrîm*-type. The preceding discussion has already touched on how these two relate to matters of *identity* (slaves vs. rebels) and *time* ("in Egypt"; "from then until now"), but these call for additional discussion. Before turning to these topics, one particularly important instance of the *mamrîm-*

---

32. To be sure, one should not ignore issues of corporate responsibility, identity, or punishment at this point. See, e.g., H. Wheeler Robinson, *Corporate Personality in Ancient Israel* (Philadelphia: Fortress, 1964); Joel S. Kaminsky, *Corporate Responsibility in the Hebrew Bible*, JSOTSup 196 (Sheffield: Sheffield Academic, 1995); and Jurrien Mol, *Collective and Individual Responsibility: A Description of Corporate Personality in Ezekiel 18 and 20*, SSN 53 (Leiden: Brill, 2009). Even so, Deut 7:10 and 24:16 loom large here in promising individual retribution (contrast 5:9!); even more important is the larger literary *fabula*.

inscription deserves mention.[33] It is found in Deut 32:15. There, in the middle of a section describing Israel's rebellion in the third person, the Song of Moses (*Haʾăzînû*) suddenly inscribes the audience directly into the story by means of second-person address before it returns to third-person discourse:

(a)   Jacob ate until he was stuffed;

(b)   Jeshurun got fat, then rebellious.

(c)   *It was you who got fat, thick, stubborn!* (*šāmantā ʿābîtā kāśîtā*)

(d)   He gave up on the God who made him,

(e)   thought the Rock of his salvation was worthless.

(Deut 32:15)[34]

The lineation offered here shows how v. 15c intrudes upon the poetry and syntax of the verse. Without it, the discourse remains in the third person, recounting the failures of Jacob/Jeshurun in two nicely balanced bicola.[35] Verse 15c manifests similar colometry,[36] but its second-person forms are completely unexpected and out of place within the third-person context,[37] rendering verse 15d understandable only if it is taken as a direct resumption of verse 15b. Such factors make it tempting to excise verse 15c altogether as a secondary addition,[38] if it were not for the text-critical data supporting it[39] and, even more to the point at hand, the fact that literary inscription is a hallmark of Deuteronomic rhetoric and thus not unexpected, even here. So, whether or not verse 15c was originally part of some

33. For another instance of inscription in ch. 32, this one akin to the *ʿebed*-type, see below.

34. See *BHS* and *BHQ* for the many text-critical issues that plague this verse. In addition to CEB, see also NRSV; contrast NJPS.

35. Bicola a–b: 3+3 words and stresses, 8+9 syllables; bicola d–e: 3+3 words and stresses, 8+9 syllables. All such counts are of mixed utility, of course, and should not be depended upon overmuch. For the approach more generally, see Oswald Loretz and Ingo Kottsieper, *Colometry in Ugaritic and Biblical Poetry: Introduction, Illustrations and Topical Bibliography*, UBL 5 (Altenberge: CIS-Verlag, 1987).

36. Three words plus three stresses, nine syllables.

37. Cf., e.g., LXX, S, T[O] (singular), as well as T[JNF] (plural), which read third-person forms in v. 15c, in a clear case of harmonizing with the surrounding context (see *BHQ*, 94, 144*). The singular forms are supported by SamP and, in the first instance, by 4QPhyl[n], σ′, and θ′.

38. À la *Wiederaufnahme* (repetitive resumption) or *Ringkomposition*, for which, see, e.g., Shemaryahu Talmon, "The Textual Study of the Bible—A New Outlook," in *Qumran and the History of the Biblical Text*, ed. Frank Moore Cross and Shemaryahu Talmon (Cambridge: Harvard University Press, 1975), 321–400, esp. 363–64 and 395n174; and Bernard M. Levinson, *Deuteronomy and the Hermeneutics of Legal Innovation* (New York: Oxford University Press, 1997), 17–20.

39. That is, v. 15c is not missing from the versions, though note MT, which lost the first three words of v. 15 (colon a), apparently through haplography (see *BHQ*, 94, 144*).

Urform of the Song of Moses is of little significance. Even if it is somehow a Deuteronomic plus—an addition to some early/earlier form of the poem as received into Deut 32—it would be a plus that is completely at home in Deuteronomy's rhetoric of inscription.

6. Identity: "Slaves" and "Rebels"

Much of what has been said in the preceding section demonstrates how Deuteronomy's rhetoric of inscription bears directly on the construction of the audience's identity. In a word—or, better, in two words—this rhetoric figures Israel as either "slaves" or "rebels," or rather *both*. As noted above, the audience is given no space to accept or reject this identification: the inscription simply makes them either one of these two subjects alternatively, if not both simultaneously. Of course, we might presume that the audience's reception of this inscription matters in crucial ways. If the audience accepts the inscription, that would make the rhetoric somehow more active or effective; alternatively, if the audience rejects the inscription, all bets are off. But, again, in terms of rhetorical effect (see further below), the inscription figures the audience as, or in, one or both of these categories quite apart from their say in the matter. Inscription and identity are therefore indelibly linked. The former leads directly to the latter; the latter is entirely contingent on the former.

As observed above, these two "existential categories"—that of redeemed slave and/or obstinate rebel—are found throughout Deuteronomy, not just in the two key texts 6:21 and 9:7. The book repeatedly circles back, in one way or another, to these two possibilities and, in doing so, underscores how each is in some way *fundamental* and/or *paradigmatic* for Israel. The following delineation of these two identities is brief but representative.

7. Israel's Identification as (Former) Slaves Rescued from Egypt: The 'ebed-Inscription

In the warp and woof of the *fabula*—in both Deuteronomy and in Exodus–Deuteronomy—Egyptian slavery stands at the head of all other elements of Israel's relationship with God, the only possible exception being the (still earlier) promises to the ancestors (see Deut 1:8, 11, 21, 35; 4:1, 31, 37; 6:3, 10, 18, 23; 7:8, 12, 13; 8:1, 18; 9:5; 10:11, 15; 11:9, 21; 12:1; 13:17; 19:8; 26:3, 15; 27:3; 28:11; 29:13; 30:20; 31:7, 20; cf. 26:7; 29:25).[40] In this way, Egyptian servitude and the release therefrom are *fun-*

---

40. The importance of the ancestors makes Deut 5:3 that much more unexpected. Similarly striking in this perspective are 8:1, 16; 30:5, 9 (texts that have the audience somehow surpassing

damental. It is *paradigmatic* insofar as it is constantly and consistently referenced throughout Deuteronomy, often at crucial junctures, including its deployment as motivation for obedience to key legislation. A few examples suffice:[41]

(a) I am Yhwh your God who brought you out of the land of Egypt, out of the house of slavery [*bêt 'ăbādîm*]. (5:6)

(b) Remember that you were a slave [*'ebed hāyîtā*] in the land of Egypt, but Yhwh your God brought you out of there with a strong hand and an outstretched arm. That's why Yhwh your God commanded you to keep the Sabbath day. (5:15)

(c) Tell your children: "We were Pharaoh's slaves [*'ăbādîm hāyînû*] in Egypt, but Yhwh brought us out from Egypt with a strong hand." (6:21)

(d) Remember that you were a slave [*'ebed hāyîtā*] in the land of Egypt, but Yhwh your God rescued you. That's why I am commanding you to do this thing right now. (15:15)

(e) Remember that you were a slave [*'ebed hāyîtā*] in Egypt, so be careful to perform these regulations. (16:12)

(f) Remember that you were a slave [*'ebed hāyîtā*] in Egypt, but Yhwh your God rescued you from there. That's why I am commanding you to do this thing. (24:18)

(g) Remember that you were a slave [*'ebed hāyîtā*] in the land of Egypt. That's why I am commanding you to do this thing. (24:22)

---

the ancestors), as well as 13:6; 28:36, 64; 32:17 (the invocation of the ancestors in judgment passages). Of course, the precise valence of these passages depends in no small measure on the specific referent of "ancestors" (for which see note 16 above). For those who hold to a redactional theory like Römer's and its relationship to a certain understanding of the composition and formation of the Pentateuch, Deuteronomy's origin story began with Egyptian slavery and thus the exodus and did not include the ancestors as known from Genesis.

41. In addition to the texts that follow, see also, inter alia, 1:30; 4:20, 34, 37; 6:12, 22; 7:8, 18; 8:14; 9:12; 11:3; 13:5, 10; 16:1, 3, 6; 20:1; 23:4; 24:9; 25:17; 26:8; 29:2, 16; 34:11; cf. 4:45–46; 29:25. This is but a partial listing compiled by tracing the presence of *miṣrayim* in Deuteronomy. In any event, the pervasive import of the servitude in and deliverance from Egypt is no doubt what makes the sentiment expressed in 1:27 appear so shocking and unfaithful. It is also what lends power to the different expressions in 9:12 and 9:26, even as it underscores the severity of 28:27, 60, 68 (cf. 7:15).

Outside of example (a), the passages conjoin √hyh with *'ebed*, always in the singular, save for the one plural instance found in the parent's reply in 6:21 (example [c]; see above). However, example (a) deserves to be mentioned, since the reference to Egyptian slavery at the very start of the Decalogue more than suffices to indicate the importance of that experience and its place within Yhwh's relationship to Israel as well as its role in motivating Israel's obedient response to Yhwh's covenant. The function of the *'ebed*-inscription in the prologue to the Decalogue is quite similar in this regard to the way the mention of Egyptian slavery functions in the fourth commandment. It should also be recalled that Deuteronomy uniquely formulates its version thereof (example [b]) by mentioning the oppression under Pharaoh and not God's rest on the seventh day of creation (contrast Exod 20:11).

Although they do not employ the language of slavery proper (√*'bd*), two additional verses should also be included here since they evoke the same situation (life in Egypt) and with the same verbal construction, only this time with *gēr*-language:[42]

(h) Love the immigrant because you were immigrants [*gērîm hĕyîtem*] in the land of Egypt. (10:19)

(i) Do not detest any Edomite because they are your kin. Do not detest any Egyptian because you were an immigrant [*gēr hāyîtā*] in their land. (23:7[8])

More texts could be cited, but examples (a)–(i) demonstrate that the story of Egyptian servitude (and sojourn) pervades Deuteronomy, crisscrossing the various parts of the book and comprising a consistent and repeated element in its rhetorical program.[43] This is to say that, once inscribed into this story, the audience is never allowed to forget it. Or, perhaps it would be better or more accurate to put the matter in reverse: given the importance of this story, the audience is not allowed to escape it, but is thoroughly and repeatedly inscribed into it.

---

42. For more on the *gēr* in Deuteronomy, see Mark A. Awabdy, *Immigrants and Innovative Law: Deuteronomy's Theological and Social Vision for the* רֵג, FAT 2.67 (Tübingen: Mohr Siebeck, 2014), who draws a careful distinction between *gēr*-Egypt and *'ebed*-Egypt traditions (see Awabdy, *Immigrants and Innovative Law*, 127–64).

43. On the rhetorical function of repetition in Deuteronomy, see chapter 3 of the present work. For an extended recent study of (poetic) repetition, see Knut Martin Heim, *Poetic Imagination in Proverbs: Variant Repetitions and the Nature of Poetry*, BBRSup 4 (Winona Lake, IN: Eisenbrauns, 2013).

8. Israel's Identification as (Constant) Rebels: The mamrîm-Inscription

While this second inscription is not as pervasive as the *'ebed*-inscription, it is important nevertheless. Three of the key passages from chapter 9 have already been discussed above:

> (a) From the day that you left the land of Egypt, until you arrived at this place, you've been rebels [*mamrîm hĕyîtem*] against Yhwh. (9:7)

> (b) Also at Taberah, and at Massah, and at Kibroth-hattaavah you've been the kind of people who make Yhwh furious [*maqṣipîm hĕyîtem*]. (9:22)

> (c) You've been rebels [*mamrîm hĕyîtem*] against Yhwh from the day <he> knew you. (9:24)

To these three, a fourth should be added:

> (d) Because I know your rebelliousness and stubbornness. If you've been rebels [*mamrîm hĕyitem*] against Yhwh while I'm still alive and with you here and now, then how much more after my death! (31:27)

The syntax of these four verses is remarkably similar—a *hiphil* masculine plural participle conjoined with the *qal* suffix-conjugation of √*hyh*. This construction is also quite similar to that found in the √*hyh* + *'ebed/gēr* passages outlined above. However, a signal difference between the two types of inscriptions is that, when the *'ebed*-inscription is constructed with a second-person form of √*hyh*, the verbal form is singular, whereas the *mamrîm*-inscription is consistently plural. This difference is related to the famous problem of *Numeruswechsel* in Deuteronomy and may simply be another example of the same. Either way, like the *Numeruswechsel*, it is best treated as a stylistic device: the singular emphasizing the responsibility of each individual Israelite, the plural emphasizing the collective responsibility of the people as a whole.[44] If so, then the *'ebed*-inscription would be primarily a point of attention for an *individual* Israelite, each of whom is specifically and

---

44. See, e.g., Lundbom, *Deuteronomy*, 9–10; cf. Jeffrey H. Tigay, *Deuteronomy*, JPS Torah Commentary (Philadelphia: Jewish Publication Society, 1996), 62, and further, Moshe Weinfeld, *Deuteronomy 1–11*, AB 5 (New York: Doubleday, 1991), 15–16. The most extensive work is Christopher T. Begg, "Contributions to the Elucidation of the Composition of Deuteronomy with Special Attention to the Significance of the *Numeruswechsel*" (PhD diss., Louvain, 1987).

personally inscribed into the story of Israel's rescue from Egypt.[45] The *mamrîm*-inscription would be different, however, and would focus the audience's attention on their *collective* guilt as rebels, since this is how they are so inscribed: as a people-group, as a whole.

Although it may not be coextensive with the *'ebed*-inscription, there is sufficient mention of rebellion and disobedience outside of the three instances in chapter 9 and the fourth mention in 31:27 to demonstrate that the *mamrîm*-inscription, too, is *fundamental* and *paradigmatic*. The early positioning and significance of the spy disaster (1:19–46) have already been mentioned. The specific language of disobedience is varied here (e.g., √*'bh* + *lō'*, √*šm'* + *lō'*, √*'mn* + *'ayin*), but it is significant that √*mrh* is found in 1:26 and 1:43. As noted earlier, the foundational failure in the golden calf episode is held in reserve until chapter 9, but the persistent rhetoric of obedience, remembering, not forgetting, and being on constant guard implies the very real potential of future failure—and in these specific ways.[46] This possibility is also suggested by the syntactically similar construction found in 7:26a,[47] but it comes to its fullest fruition (or deepest nadir) in chapter 28, especially in the transition evident from the hypothetical "*if* you will not obey" (*'im-lō' tišma'*) of verse 15 to the certain "*because* you did not obey" (*kî-lō' šama'tā*) in verses 45 and 62 and the firm "*because* you did not serve" (*taḥat 'ăšer lō'-'ābadtā*) in verse 47. Here, in Deut 28, one finds a dense concatenation of second-person *waw*-consecutive suffix-conjugation forms of √*hyh*—seven of the nine such forms that appear in the book (78 percent).[48] The first is a *positive* instance in the event of *obedience*:

> Yhwh will make you the head of things, not the tail. You will always be at the top of things [*wəhāyîtā raq ləma'lâ*]; you will not be at the bottom because you will obey the commandments of Yhwh your God that I am commanding you right now by carefully doing them. (28:13)

---

45. Despite the plural "we"-constructions in 6:21–25, this receives further support from the introductory frame of 6:20–25, since it is the singular child (*binkā*) that is so inscribed (see above).

46. See, among many others, J. G. Millar, "Living at the Place of Decision: Time and Place in the Framework of Deuteronomy," in J. G. McConville and J. G. Millar, *Time and Place in Deuteronomy*, JSOTSup 179 (Sheffield: Sheffield Academic, 1994), 15.

47. "Do not bring any detestable thing into your house or you will be *ḥērem* (*wəhāyîtā ḥērem*) like it!"

48. The other two instances are 7:26 (see preceding note) and 16:15: *wəhāyîtā 'ak śāmēăḥ*, "then you will surely rejoice." Note that all nine instances are singular.

But this bright potential future quickly fades from view after the sea change wrought in the curse section of Deut 28 (vv. 15–68). The rest of the instances are *negative* and concern the dread results of *disobedience*:

Yhwh will hand you over to your enemies, defeated. You will go out against them by one direction, but you will run for your life away from them in seven different directions! You will be a terrifying example [*wəhāyîtā ləzaʿăwâ*] to every kingdom on earth. (28:25)

You will grope around [*wəhāyîtā məmaššēš*] at high noon just like blind people grope around in darkness. Your plans will not succeed. Instead, you will be constantly oppressed and taken advantage of [*wəhāyîtā ʾak ʿāšûq wəgāzûl*] without any one to help. (28:29 [2×])

The produce of your land and all your hard work will be consumed by people you do not know. You will be nothing but oppressed and mistreated [*wəhāyîtā raq ʿāšûq wərāṣûṣ*] constantly. (28:33)

You will go insane [*wəhāyîtā məšuggāʿ*] by what your eyes see. (28:34)

You will become something horrible [*wəhāyîtā ləšammâ*], fit only for use in proverbs and in insults by all the peoples where Yhwh drives you. (28:37)

In this expansive curse section, every blessing in the blessing section is systematically refuted, leaving no doubt that *Israel's undoing* is *Yhwh's direct doing*, precisely because of Israel's inevitable disobedience (vv. 45, 47, 62).[49] The *coup de grâce* is the final verse of this unit (and of the central section of the book):[50]

Finally, Yhwh will take you back to Egypt in ships, by the route I promised you would never see again. There you will try to sell yourselves to your enemies as slaves—male and female [*laʿăbādîm wəlišpāḥôt*]—but no one will buy you. (28:68)

---

49. See Strawn, "Deuteronomy," 73.

50. I understand Deut 28:69 as a superscription for what follows, not a subscription to what precedes. The debate here is a lively one. See recently Lundbom, *Biblical Rhetoric and Rhetorical Criticism*, 102–20.

There is no specific use of √*hyh* here, but this, too, is an instance of *mamrîm*-inscription, and a vision of its most horrific future.[51] It is stunning though not surprising (rhetorically ironic, at the very least) that the end-result of being *mamrîm* is a precise reversal of the '*ebed*-inscription; the audience is no longer a people *freed from Egypt* but a people *returned to Egypt*, with their slavery now self-imposed in order to eke out some sort of existence (*wəhitmakkartem*). However, despite this worst-case scenario, even these measures are completely ineffectual (*wə'ên qōneh*). This change of status—from '*ăbādîm* to *mamrîm* to '*ăbādîm*—is figured in terms of the past versus the future and the future versus the past, and so leads directly into the next topic to be discussed: time. But before turning to that matter, it should be noted that the *mamrîm*-inscription is found in Deuteronomy even after the brutal ending promised in chapter 28. The striking instance in Deut 32:15c, for example, has already been mentioned above, as has 31:27, but other texts, too, might be included (see, e.g., 29:22–30:5; 31:16–22), all of which offer further proof that this second type of inscription is also well attested across the book of Deuteronomy and is a generative rhetorical device.

9. Time: "Were," "Are/Have Been," and "Will Be"

The two main types of Deuteronomy's rhetoric of inscription map not only onto two primary identities but also onto two different temporal frames:

- The '*ebed*-inscription is almost exclusively a *past-tense phenomenon*: you (or we) *were* slaves to Pharaoh, but are no longer because of God's act of *hôṣē'* (i.e., deliverance). Yhwh's exodus-activity marks the decisive point that restricts the time of being '*ăbādîm* to the past. Israel was a slave once, but *is* such *no longer*, though Israel must never forget that former state of being.
- The *mamrîm*-inscription is a *past-tense phenomenon with continuing effects up to the current moment*. The addition of a temporal complement in texts like 9:7 (*ləmin-hayyôm 'ăšer- yāṣā'tā . . . 'ad-bō'ăkem 'ad-hammāqôm hazzeh*, "from the day that you left . . . until you arrived at this place") or 9:24 (*miyyôm da'tô 'etkem*, "from the day <he> knew you")[52] signals that the action of being *mamrîm* is

---

51. Deuteronomy 28:62 deserves mention here. This verse employs *hĕyîtem* in a contrast with the multitude of Israelites prior to the devastation wrought by destruction: "Instead of being as many as the stars of the sky [*taḥat 'ăšer hĕyîtem kəkôkəbê haššāmayim lārōb*], only a few of you will survive because you did not obey Yhwh your God's voice."

52. For the emendation, reading *da'tô* for *da'tî*, see note 31 above.

something that happened in the past but continues into the contemporary moment of rhetorical exchange. In this way, Israel has been rebellious and still is.

Thus far the inscription corresponds to simple past (*were*) and present perfect (*have been and still are*), but the *future* is also at play in this rhetoric:

- There is only one instance of *ʿebed*-language that threatens a *future* existence as slaves, though that is unique and rather distinctive (28:68; see discussion above); in terms of its semantic content and rhetorical force (future judgment), it actually belongs with the next category.[53]
- Since Israel's past rebelliousness continues up to the present, it has a *possible if not likely future afterlife*. This is the burden of Moses's constant exhortation *not* to disobey, *not* to forget, *not* to go astray. However, chapters 28 and 31 (among others) indicate that such a disobedient future is both imminent and (or so it would seem) inevitable. In chapter 28, the use of the *waw*-consecutive on the suffix-conjugation of √*hyh* signals the *futurity* of the disobedience (28:25, 29 [2×], 33, 34, 37; see above), while the negated suffix-conjugations constructed with *kî* in verses 45 and 62 or with *taḥat ʾăšer* in verse 47 indicate the *certainty* of the same.[54] The syntax and semantic content of 31:16–21, 27 follow suit.

However, the future is not a time solely for failure or for an inescapable recapitulation of life as *mamrîm*. Indeed, the force of so much Deuteronomic rhetoric to *avoid* disobedience, amnesia, and sin envisions a possible future that is *not* marked by the same; otherwise the rhetoric would be unnecessary and altogether futile. But this is to anticipate the next section of the present study, which attends to the several functions and effects of the book's literary inscription. Here too a final temporal frame in Deuteronomic rhetoric must be considered that has not yet been sufficiently treated: namely, the place of the *present tense*.

10. The Functions/Effects of Deuteronomy's Rhetoric of Inscription

In this final section, I wish to highlight three primary functions or effects of Deuteronomy's rhetoric of inscription. Each can be captured by a single word: involvement, trans-historicism, and "bothness."

---

53. Cf. Deut 17:16 for a somewhat similar syntactical construction, though the statement there is negated and the action it describes is expressly forbidden.

54. Note that *taḥat ʾăšer* also occurs in v. 62. Elsewhere in Deuteronomy this construction appears only in 21:14; 22:29.

Involvement

The first major function or effect of Deuteronomy's rhetoric of inscription is to *involve its audience*. By means of literary inscription, the audience is written directly into the story in both positive and negative ways: as slaves who have been rescued and as rebels who are recalcitrant and heading for doom. The rhetoric grants no pause, no stay in its onslaught consistently and constantly to involve the audience in this way and in these modes. The only way to escape would be to shut down the stimulus altogether and walk away from Deuteronomy completely. But according to the logic of Deuteronomy, to do that would be to no longer be Israel.[55]

Inasmuch as the rhetoric of the entire book consistently situates the audience between these two poles—as slaves and as rebels—the audience is incessantly pressed with the existential moment of decision.[56] This is indeed the whole point of the rhetoric: Which pole will dominate and be the way forward? Will Israel remember its prior servitude and be motivated by its redemption to unswerving fealty to its redeeming Lord? Or will the predilection toward rebellion triumph, with all ending in ruin? Deuteronomic inscription presses this dilemma relentlessly and intensely upon the audience. Like it or not, "accurate" or otherwise, these are the two identities the audience manifests. For this reason, the present moment of existential decision, the pervasive Deuteronomic "now/today," is the ultimate temporal frame manifested in the book, created, sustained, and maintained by its rhetorical art.[57]

Trans-historicism

This existential quality of "always being in the moment of decision" creates a *trans-historical effect*, constantly taking the members of the audience out of their own historical situation (whatever, wherever, or whenever that might be) and *re*-situating them in the plains of Moab, *re*configuring them as slaves and rebels, and *repeatedly* calling them to choose life rather than death.[58] Insofar as this *re*-

---

55. Cf. Strawn, "Keep/Observe/Do—Carefully—Today! The Rhetoric of Repetition in Deuteronomy," chapter 3 of the present work.

56. See Millar, "Living at the Place of Decision," 15–88.

57. *yôm* occurs 167 times in Deuteronomy, and while not all instances of the word are directly related to the book's hortatory rhetoric, the majority are. See Strawn, "Keep/Observe/Do," 47, 59, and 59n77 above; Weinfeld, *Deuteronomy and the Deuteronomic School*, 356–57; and cf. von Rad, *Studies*, 70: "'This day' appears throughout the Deuteronomic utterances, highlighting the existential quality of this divine *praedicatio impii*." Note also Hwang, *Rhetoric of Remembrance*, 6–7.

58. See Strawn, "Keep/Observe/Do," 52–54 above, for other non-time-constrained aspects

situation, reconfiguration, and *repetition* is temporal—"we were slaves," "you've been rebels," etc. (see above)—the proper adjective to describe Deuteronomy's rhetoric is not "timeless,"[59] as if the rhetoric were somehow or fundamentally *unrelated* to matters of time and history, but rather "trans-historical"; it is thoroughly related to the audience's life within time and history and yet, simultaneously, is somehow and nevertheless *above* the same.

It is instructive to compare the trans-historical quality of Deuteronomic rhetoric to the eighth principle of Judaism and what Jon Levenson has called "the literary simultaneity of Scripture."[60] The eighth principle, as known in "Ani Ma'amin," states, "I believe with perfect faith that the entire Torah presently in our possession is the one given to Moses our master (may he rest in peace)."[61] This is a paraphrase of one of the thirteen principles of Maimonides (1138–1204 CE), which reads, in part: "That the Torah is from heaven . . . that is: that we believe that the entire Torah presently in our possession is the one given to Moses our master (may he rest in peace), [and] that it is all from the mouth of God, that is, that it was all given to him from the Lord (may he be blessed) in the manner that is metaphorically called 'speaking.'"[62] According to Levenson, this principle has to do with the ultimate "unity and divinity of the Torah."[63] Moving in reverse order, this means that the *divine* origin of the Torah must not be expunged, and that all parts of the Torah—its most exalted verses and its most mundane—come from

---

of repetition within Deuteronomy's rhetoric. See also Millar, "Living at the Place of Decision," 15: "The effect is to gather up *every significant moment in Israel's past experience in the present dilemma at Moab*" (my emphasis); and 88: "Yesterday, Today, and Tomorrow, wherever the nation finds itself—in the land or outside it—a simple decision faces Israel: to live for Yahweh or not—to move further into the land with Yahweh or to go back to Egypt. There can be no standing still." Cf. von Rad, *Studies,* 70–71: "Six centuries . . . *are cancelled out and Israel is set once more* at Horeb to hear Jahweh's word of salvation. . . . It is the tremendous 'here and now' in the divine election that lies at the back of Deuteronomy's attempt to *re-comprehend* the Israel that was now in the grip of an inner disintegration as the holy people of God" (my emphases). Hwang, *Rhetoric of Remembrance,* 8, speaks of how Deuteronomy "recreate[s] imaginatively the experiences of Moab for future generations."

59. Contra Hwang, *Rhetoric of Remembrance,* 233, who speaks of the "fathers" as a "timeless symbol" in Deuteronomy. However, Hwang is quite right in his understanding of the rhetorical flexibility of Deuteronomic rhetoric on this subject (and others).

60. Jon D. Levenson, "The Eighth Principle of Judaism and the Literary Simultaneity of Scripture," in Levenson, *The Hebrew Bible, the Old Testament, and Historical Criticism: Jews and Christians in Biblical Studies* (Louisville: Westminster John Knox, 1993), 62–81 (the essay was originally published in 1988).

61. Levenson, "Eighth Principle," 63.

62. Levenson, "Eighth Principle," 63.

63. Levenson, "Eighth Principle," 65.

the mouth of God.[64] Levenson defines the *unity* of the Torah as "the simultaneity, self-referentiality, and mutual implication of *all* its parts."[65]

Levenson notes that such a disposition toward the Torah's divine and unified nature is at variance with (at least some) modern critical approaches to the Bible as practiced widely for the past few centuries. This is especially true for the second point, regarding whether the Bible can be treated (even if only in some final, ultimate fashion) as a unity rather than as an agglutinative pastiche that must be surgically filleted so as to arrive at the right literary-compositional-historical stratification and, correlatively, the right interpretation (presumably). Levenson cites Menahem Haran's apt summary: "The postulate of [premodern or pre-critical] exegesis is that Scripture, being the word of God and not subject to change, is not bound to time and place, whereas the [modern] critical method regards Scripture as a human manifestation (to be sure, a most brilliant one) of a culture confined to its own bounds of time and space—the culture of the ancient Near East."[66] According to Levenson, the price to be paid for many of modern historicizing approaches "is the dismemberment—the decomposition—of the synchronic literary reality that was the Bible and the displacement of authority from the text as a whole onto those aspects of it *with which the interpreter is already in sympathy.*"[67]

This is not the place to discuss all the aspects of Levenson's argument, specifically, or the idea of literary simultaneity, more generally,[68] but at least two points of comparison with Deuteronomic rhetoric deserve mention.

64. Levenson, "Eighth Principle," 64.

65. Levenson, "Eighth Principle," 75 (his emphasis).

66. Menahem Haran, "Midrashic and Literal Exegesis and the Critical Method in Biblical Research," in *Studies in Bible*, ed. Sara Japhet, SH 31 (Jerusalem: Magnes, 1986), 19–48, here 36–37; also cited in Levenson, "Eighth Principle," 69–70. The additions of "premodern or pre-critical" and "modern" to Haran's citation are my own, not Levenson's, due to the larger argument Levenson is making. Perhaps "traditional or confessional" versus "non-confessional" would work just as well. Haran himself goes on to speak of "classical exegesis" versus the "secular essence" of modern criticism ("Midrashic," 37). In my judgment, the dichotomy—however construed—is a false one, and the poles need not be construed antithetically or as completely discrete sets. Cf., among others, David C. Steinmetz, "The Superiority of Pre-Critical Exegesis," in *The Theological Interpretation of Scripture: Classic and Contemporary Readings*, ed. Stephen E. Fowl (Malden, MA: Blackwell, 1997), 26–38; and Michael C. Legaspi, *The Death of Scripture and the Rise of Biblical Studies* (Oxford: Oxford University Press, 2010). See also further below.

67. Levenson, "Eighth Principle," 72–73 (my emphasis).

68. For example, when, exactly, "was" the Bible "the synchronic literary reality" of which Levenson speaks (see previous note)? As Levenson notes elsewhere, "the juxtaposition of these various sorts of literature [now found in the Old Testament] in the same book [i.e., within the covers of one Bible] is a matter of *literary* context; it becomes a fact of *history* per se only

The first is that, on the one hand, Deuteronomy's rhetoric of inscription may be seen as an instance or manifestation of Levenson's notion of literary simultaneity. If so, in the case of Deuteronomy one is not simply fideistically believing (*'ănî ma'ămîn*) the Torah (or *sēper hattôrâ*!) to be literarily simultaneous; the Torah *is* in fact literarily simultaneous *precisely by means* of Deuteronomy's own rhetoric. That Deuteronomy manifests such simultaneity, inscribing the same on its audience, suggests that simultaneity might be found elsewhere in Scripture and that it may even (and as a result) be a reasonable understanding of Scripture's rhetoric writ large, and thus a matter worthy of belief (or disposition) regarding how Scripture as a whole functions—exactly as per the eighth principle.

Even so—and this is the proverbial "on the other hand"—Deuteronomy's literary simultaneity, regardless of its pre- or post-critical nature, is (to reverse Haran's language) *not* above alteration (contra Haran's "not subject to change") and also *not* unmoored from circumstance and location (contra Haran's "not bound to time and place"). To the contrary, Deuteronomy's rhetoric—and its rhetorical situation(s)—live, move, and have their being in *changed times* and in *altered circumstances*—in repetition that always comes replete with its two aspects of sameness and difference.[69] Deuteronomy's rhetoric is thus *thoroughly* bound to time and space; the audience receiving Deuteronomy is inscribed into the twin poles of slavery and rebellion, into the existential locations of Egypt, Horeb/Sinai, and Kadesh—not to mention other points along the way. This is not timelessness, like some proverb that could be applied anywhere at any time. Take Prov 6:6, for example:

> Go to the ant, you lazy person;
> observe its ways and grow wise. (CEB)

This is a far cry indeed from "we were slaves *to Pharaoh in Egypt*" (Deut 6:21) and "you've been rebels until you arrived *at this place* [i.e., the plains of Moab]" (9:7). In contrast to wisdom literature, which can instruct an audience from twenty-first-

---

very late in the period of the Second Temple—long after the original historical contexts of the Pentateuchal literature and perhaps also the proverb collections [for example] had vanished" ("Why Jews Are Not Interested in Biblical Theology," in Levenson, *Hebrew Bible, the Old Testament, and Historical Criticism*, 37; his emphasis [this essay was originally published in 1987]). But Levenson's formulation in "Eighth Principle" suggests a point (or points) in time in which this literary juxtaposition was also (or became) something real: a reality from which modern biblical scholarship subsequently prescinded. When did that happen and how? And how do we know about that, and how can we access it, assuming that we can and should?

69. See above and, further, Strawn, "Keep/Observe/Do," chapter 3 of the present work.

century Georgia as directly as one from Iron Age Judah, Deuteronomy re-places and re-situates its audience by inscribing them into the past, but always so as to force the existential decision today (*trans*-historicism).[70] Thus, while Deuteronomy can be seen as an instance of literary simultaneity, it is a rather particular and peculiar sort thereof. And while not entirely "confined to its own bounds of time and space—the culture of the ancient Near East" (Haran), it is equally at home there, even as it is always equally at home *beyond* there; and so, ultimately, it is not "confined" there at all or in the least. Here, again, Deuteronomy may offer an instructive model for how Scripture as a whole functions.

This leads directly to the second point, which is to note, as Levenson himself has, that an appropriate method of interpretation that takes seriously the literary simultaneity of the text—or, in the present case, that takes seriously Deuteronomy's trans-historicism—need not *deny* historical investigation even though it would almost certainly *relativize* it.[71] Speaking concretely about biblical scholarship—specifically Pentateuchal criticism—Levenson writes: "The efforts to take the text apart would not cease; they are informative and . . . not without precedent in the premodern tradition of biblical interpretation. They would, however, be dialectically checked by a continual awareness of the need to put the text back together in a way that makes it available in the present and in its entirety—not merely in the past and [not merely] in the form of historically contextualized fragments."[72] Once again, Deuteronomy serves as a parade example of the kind of constructive move Levenson advocates, offering this example *from within the pages of Scripture itself.* So despite, or perhaps better, in spite of the seemingly endless attempts to analyze compositional strata within Deuteronomy, find its earliest form, and so on, the rhetoric of the book consistently resists such attempts to fix its primary semantic value in this or that location, period, or century.[73] Deuteronomy's rhetoric traffics in the "back then," to be sure, but primarily and

70. Cf. Polzin, "Deuteronomy," 92: "The *temporal perspectives* of both audiences *merge in the book* through the phrases 'that day' and 'this day.' Moses' 'that (future) day' becomes 'this (present) day' of the narrator"; 92–93: an important "temporal aspect of the book's composition is Moses' and the narrator's practice of shuttling back and forth *between 'that day' of the speaker's past and 'this day' of his here-and-now*"; and 93: "Both Moses and the narrator use 'that day' to *help them put into context this day's recitation* of the law" (emphases added).

71. See Levenson, "Eighth Principle," 79.

72. Levenson, "Eighth Principle," 79.

73. Cf., somewhat similarly, J. G. McConville's understanding that "the silence of Deuteronomy on the identity of the place [where God will set the divine name] . . . encapsulates (not to say enshrines) the *non-significance of individual places*" ("Time, Place and the Deuteronomic Altar-Law," in McConville and Millar, *Time and Place in Deuteronomy*, 89–139, here 139 [my emphasis]).

ultimately so as to address the audience in the eternal "now,"[74] which is an eternal now-*cum*-then. Among other things, this explains why scholars have successfully located multiple audiences within Deuteronomy and have appropriately placed the book (or some of its parts) in different eras. Within the rhetoric of inscription, *all* such audiences and eras are correct! This is an impossible scenario for a thin historicism to conceive, but, per Luke 1:37 (similarly Matt 19:26 // Mark 10:27 // Luke 18:27), nothing is impossible for God, and, in Deuteronomy, Moses says much the same thing (e.g., Deut 30:11–14).[75] Put differently, Deuteronomy's rhetoric summons all people and times to itself (cf. John 12:32), inscribing them yet again—always again!—into the roles of slaves and rebels, pressing on them to decide, here and now, today.

This rhetoric is not *non*historical, and certainly not *a*historical, for the reasons expressed above, but it is definitely *trans-* or *supra-*historical. And yet, if this is correct, then it may not be going too far to say that, in some important ways, Deuteronomy's rhetoric *does* approach the nonhistorical, for the reasons expressed above. It is not constrained or confined by the limits of history, and certainly not ultimately. Deuteronomy is not (only) about *then*, it is (equally if not more so) about *now*. Once again, Deuteronomy is about *both then and now*, along with *what yet will be*, but the clear accent in terms of literary effect is on *now*. Whatever the case, the trans-historical nature of Deuteronomy's rhetoric—its point and purpose—need not pose a threat to those who care deeply about matters of history and historicity, facticity or verity,[76] though it puts all those commitments in considerable and relativized perspective, indicating, among other things, that Scripture's truthfulness is not reducible (solely) to matters of "history" or "fact," however those are defined. So, while one might still care deeply about such matters, whether in Deuteronomy or elsewhere in Scripture, one must not care about them too much, and certainly not ultimately. This is the lesson that the

74. I am conscious of the echo here of Paul Tillich's *The Eternal Now* (New York: Scribner's, 1963), esp. 122–32, though I am thinking more of Bruce F. Kawin's sense of the transcendent aspects of repetition (the continuous present) in his *Telling It Again and Again: Repetition in Literature and Film* (Boulder: University Press of Colorado, 1989). For application to Deuteronomy, see Strawn, "Keep/Observe/Do," chapter 3 of the present work, esp. 51–54. See also notes 56–59 and 70 above.

75. The whole Moab covenant might be considered at this point, on which see Olson, *Deuteronomy and the Death of Moses*, 126–58; and Olson, "How Does Deuteronomy Do Theology? Literary Juxtaposition and Paradox in the New Moab Covenant in Deuteronomy 29–32," in *A God So Near: Essays on Old Testament Theology in Honor of Patrick D. Miller*, ed. Brent A. Strawn and Nancy R. Bowen (Winona Lake, IN: Eisenbrauns, 2003), 201–13.

76. It is worth observing that such people are found on both poles of the confessional/nonconfessional spectrum.

trans-historicism of Deuteronomy's powerful theological rhetoric (or its powerful rhetorical theology) teaches and manifests. That theological rhetoric/rhetorical theology can be encapsulated rather pithily by another, much later text:

> I tell you, now is the time of God's favor, now is the day of salvation.
> (2 Cor 6:2 NIV)[77]

And, Deuteronomy would be quick to add, now is also "the time of God's judgment, now is the day of decision."

"Bothness"

Finally, *bothness* indicates that Deuteronomy's rhetoric of inscription will not permit the audience to identify with *only one* of the two poles: either that of slaves or that of rebels. Instead, the audience is *both* of these and so must hear what it means to be both—both in the past and for the possible future, but above all and especially in and for the present. If given the choice, most modern readers are probably wont to identify with only the "positive" pole—in Deuteronomy's case, that of rescued and redeemed slaves—letting the "negative" part about being rebels go. This applies whether that is due to supersessionist tendencies[78] or simply to old-fashioned Freudian projection, or both.[79] The reverse is also possible, though I suspect that overidentification with the pole representing judgment is far less common, at least in many Christian circles in affluent North America.

Regardless, in Deuteronomy the point is that you cannot pick just one pole: you must read (and be!) both—both "good" parts and "bad" parts are part and parcel of the rhetoric. Furthermore, the "bad" parts prove to be as good for the soul as the "good" parts. That is how Deuteronomy's inscription works: *writing the audience into the story's most noble and most ignoble moments for salutary ends.*

The benefits of accepting such inscription, of learning how to read in Deuteronomy's way, are exemplified in a stunning way in chapter 32, in the second of the two striking instances of inscription that are found in that famous poem. The first

---

77. Note that this text from 2 Corinthians cites Isa 49:8, which is, in turn, replete with exodus motifs.

78. See the trenchant insights of Levenson, "Eighth Principle," and passim in *Hebrew Bible, the Old Testament, and Historical Criticism.*

79. Cf. Levenson's remark ("Eighth Principle," 72–73; cited above at note 67) on how such "dismemberment" and "decomposition" of Scripture "as a whole" results in a "displacement of authority from the text . . . onto those aspects of it *with which the interpreter is already in sympathy*" (my emphasis).

instance, found in verse 15c, was discussed at some length above. In that verse, the poem writes the members of the audience directly into the story line, if by chance they somehow did not realize this song of torah was really about them: "*It was you* who got fat, thick, stubborn!" The audience is *acted upon* in verse 15c, as is always the case with Deuteronomic inscription; their permission is not sought, they are not asked if they agree with, let alone appreciate, the identification. By means of this rhetoric they are simply told, "This is a story about you."

The second instance of inscription is found in verse 31, where, just when it seems that all is lost after the apostasy that has led to divine judgment and total devastation (vv. 5–6, 15–30), suddenly and unexpectedly Israel *writes itself* into the poem:[80]

> But no! Their rock is not like our Rock!
> Our enemies are completely foolish.[81]

This proves to be the turning point in the poem. Hereafter, all is most assuredly *not* lost, and things change decisively with Yhwh doing an about-face vis-à-vis the enemies who were previously the divine instrument of punishment. Hereafter, Yhwh chooses instead to "acquit" (√*dyn*) and "have compassion" (√*nḥm*) on helpless Israel.

In this second case of inscription in chapter 32, Israel is not inscribed into the song *passively* as an *object acted upon*, but *re-inscribes itself as an active subject*, *re-inserting* itself into the stanza, and to stunning effect. The first inscription, in verse 15, was for *judgment*: "You grew fat!" This is a case of *mamrîm*-inscription. This second self-inscription, in verse 31, is for *hope*, if not for *doxology*: "Our God is incomparable!" And this second inscription works: the hope pays off and God attends to Israel, saving it once again.[82]

It is essential that the hope undergirding this second instance of (re-)inscrip-

80. What follows is indebted to Brent A. Strawn, *The Old Testament Is Dying: A Diagnosis and Recommended Treatment*, Theological Explorations for the Church Catholic (Grand Rapids: Baker Academic, 2015), 205–11.

81. The last colon is in some doubt. J. Hempel (in *BHS*, 347) suggests inserting *kullām* ("all of them") after *wêʾōyəbênû*, *metri causa*, which is always a dubious reason, especially in the absence of text-critical support. Perhaps something is simply gapped from the first colon. However, the real question concerns *pəlîlîm*. The translation above follows LXX's *anoētoi* (so also NRSV), which may actually be ignorant of the Hebrew lexeme (see *BHQ*, 96, *149–50). Other solutions are possible, of course, for which see the commentaries.

82. For other examples of how Deut 32 worked, as attested in texts like 2 Macc 7; 4 Macc 18; and Rev 15, see Strawn, *The Old Testament Is Dying*, 209–11.

tion, in verse 31, is entirely predicated on the *'ebed*-type inscription—it depends on knowing that God is a saving and redeeming God who has cared for Israel in the past and still does so (cf. the dynamics in Deut 6:20–25: "for our good always, to preserve us alive, just as we are right now"). The self-inscription of the audience in verse 31 is only possible because the audience has learned what inscription is about and how it works, and because—in this crucial moment at least, if not also at last—the audience accepts all of that, applying the tools of Deuteronomy's rhetorical trade just in time, exactly when it is needed most.

What Deuteronomy shows in this verse and throughout its rhetoric of inscription, therefore, is how the "good" and "bad" parts of Scripture go together; both are equally important, and both are equally precious. No less than in the case of existential involvement or trans-historicism, in this way Deuteronomy offers us a model for reading Scripture—*all* of Scripture—every nook and cranny, whether we like it or not, whether we want to or not, and reading ourselves therein. We must read all of Scripture this way, deeming each part important, holding each part precious, because, in the end, it is we, all of us here alive today, who are both slaves and rebels.

5

The Art of Poetry in Psalm 137:
Movement, Reticence, Cursing

O Lord God of vengeance,
O God of vengeance, show yourself. (Ps 94:1; BCP)

Woe to you, Chorazin! Woe to you, Bethsaida!
(Matt 11:21 // Luke 10:13; NRSV)

Those who confuse the longing of love with a plan of action will
never understand Psalm 137.[1]

There is widespread, virtually unanimous agreement that Ps 137 is a beautiful
poem—parts of it, anyway. A positive valuation of the psalm is mostly true
for verses 1–6, which have inspired numerous renditions of the poem, especially
in song.[2] But there is equally widespread, virtually unanimous agreement that

In addition to the editors, I thank Tod Linafelt, Brittany Kim, Michael Mears Bruner, and Jonathan Parker for helpful comments and/or critique of an earlier version of this chapter, which
was first presented at the annual meeting of the Society of Biblical Literature in San Diego,
California in November 2019.

1. Erich Zenger, *A God of Vengeance? Understanding the Psalms of Divine Wrath* (Louisville:
Westminster John Knox, 1996), 50.

2. See, inter alia, Joel M. LeMon, "Rereading a Difficult Text: Violence against Children and
Girls in the Reception History of Psalm 137," in *Reading for Faith and Learning: Essays on Scripture, Community, and Libraries in Honor of M. Patrick Graham*, ed. John B. Weaver and Douglas L.
Gragg (Abilene: Abilene Christian University Press, 2017), 75–93; LeMon, "Saying Amen to Violent Psalms: Patterns of Prayer, Belief, and Action in the Psalter," in *Soundings in the Theology
of Psalms: Perspectives and Methods in Contemporary Scholarship*, ed. Rolf A. Jacobson (Min-

Ps 137 is an extremely troubling poem.[3] This second evaluation is especially true for estimations of verses 7–9, which are notorious for culminating in a commendation on the one who seizes and smashes the little ones of Babylon against a rock (v. 9: *šeyyōʾḥēz wənippēṣ ʾet-ʿōlālayik ʾel-hassālaʿ*). These two judgments regarding these two parts of the psalm are at sharp odds with one another—if not, in fact, mutually exclusive.[4] And so it is that one finds that the first six verses have been the subject of musical compositions, lectionary readings, and so on and so forth, but musical renditions that include verses 7–9 are decidedly far fewer, and it is only recently that the Revised Common Lectionary (in contrast to some of its predecessors) saw fit to include the whole of Ps 137 in its three-year cycle—though even now the psalm is listed but once and only then as an alternative text (to Lam 1:1–6 + 3:19–26) on an obscure Sunday in "Ordinary Time." So it is that one might wonder, especially given conflicted estimations of the psalm, if this poem is ever selected for use or reading at all. Then, too, one might wonder if anyone is even in church on the Seventeenth Sunday after Pentecost![5]

---

neapolis: Fortress, 2011), 93–111; also Susan Gillingham, "The Reception of Psalm 137 in Jewish and Christian Tradition," in *Jewish and Christian Approaches to the Psalms: Conflict and Convergence*, ed. Susan Gillingham (Oxford: Oxford University Press, 2013), 64–82; Jonathan Magonet, "Psalm 137: Unlikely Liturgy or Partisan Poem? A Response to Sue Gillingham," in Gillingham, *Jewish and Christian Approaches to the Psalms*, 83–88; James L. Kugel, *In Potiphar's House: The Interpretive Life of Biblical Texts*, 2nd ed. (Cambridge: Harvard University Press, 1994), 173–213; Siegfried Risse, "'Wohl dem, der deine kleinen Kinder packt und sie am Felsen zerschmettert': zur Auglegungsgeschichte von Ps 137,9," *BibInt* 14 (2006): 364–84; and, more extensively, David W. Stowe, *Song of Exile: The Enduring Mystery of Psalm 137* (Oxford: Oxford University Press, 2016). Additional information from the history of interpretation may be found in J. M. Neale and R. F. Littledale, *A Commentary on the Psalms from Primitive and Mediaeval Writers*, 2nd ed. (London: Joseph Masters, 1883), 4:300–308; Quentin F. Wesselschmidt, *Psalms 51–150*, ACCSOT 8 (Downers Grove, IL: InterVarsity, 2007), 378–80; Avrohom Chaim Feuer, *Tehillim: A New Translation with a Commentary, Anthologized from Talmuidc, Midrashic and Rabbinic Sources* (New York: Mesorah, 2013), 2:1619–25; and William G. Braude, *The Midrash on Psalms* (New Haven: Yale University Press, 1959), 2:331–39.

3. In addition to works cited in the previous note, see also, e.g., Hans-Joachim Kraus, *Psalms 60–150: A Continental Commentary*, trans. Hilton C. Oswald (Minneapolis: Fortress, 1993), 504. More generally, see Nancy L. deClaissé-Walford, "The Theology of the Imprecatory Psalms," in Jacobson, *Soundings in the Theology of Psalms*, 77–92, esp. 79 and the literature cited there.

4. This "felt" contrast (as opposed to a "true" or clearly evident "literary" one) may be what led John Ahn to posit that the Psalm was comprised of two distinct laments ("Psalm 137: Complex Communal Laments," *JBL* 127 [2008]: 267–89), a suggestion that I find unconvincing (see further below). Far better is Magonet's thematic observation: "Given the explicit violence in the first two sections, the third with its measure for measure conclusion, though shocking, should not be seen as inconsistent with what has gone before" ("Psalm 137," 84).

5. See Magonet, "Psalm 137," 83n1 for Jewish liturgical uses of Ps 137, which are restricted to

The present chapter pursues two aspects of the poetics of Ps 137—that is, how the psalm *works*—with special attention to the deeply problematic and thus frequently neglected or underappreciated imprecatory section of the poem.[6] The first aspect is that of *poetic movement*: the movement of the poem generally and the movement of verses 7–9 specifically (see §1). The poem gives every indication of being a unity and, if so, the psalm is heading to its brutal conclusion right from its opening line. Beyond this point, attention to the movement within verses 7–9, most especially the movement within verses 8–9, casts significant light on the emotions captured there, perhaps making those more understandable or "empathizable" even if they remain unpalatable to many (likely not all) readers. The latter movement might be described as dependent upon or otherwise akin to the

---

two: (1) the prelude to the evening service on the Ninth of Av, which commemorates the destruction of the Temple in 586 BCE and 70 CE; and (2) before reciting Grace after Meals during weekdays: "Even the pleasure of a meal should be diminished by recalling and mourning the destruction of Jerusalem and the Temple," though Magonet is uncertain if anyone "actually reads it aloud or simply glosses over it" (83n1). On Shabbat and festivals Ps 126 is read instead at mealtimes. See also Jon D. Levenson, "The Horrifying Closing of Psalm 137, or, The Limitations of Ethical Reading," in *Opportunity for No Little Instruction: Biblical Essays in Honor of Daniel J. Harrington, SJ, and Richard J. Clifford, SJ*, ed. Christopher G. Frechette, Christopher R. Matthews, and Thomas D. Stegman, SJ (New York: Paulist, 2014), 18–40, esp. 19–21; and Athalya Brenner, "'On the Rivers of Babylon' (Psalm 137), or between Victim and Perpetrator," in *Sanctified Aggression: Legacies of Biblical and Post Biblical Vocabularies of Violence*, ed. Jonneke Bekkenkamp and Yvonne Sherwood, JSOTSup 400 (London: T&T Clark, 2003), 76–91, who argues on the basis of 150 years of Jewish prayerbooks that "*whenever it* [Psalm 137] *is recited only the first six verses are recited. The offending vv. 7–9 are removed from the relevant prayers and services*" (86; her emphasis).

6. Treatments of the psalm's poetry as such are, oddly enough, fairly rare; those that exist aren't always appreciative. James L. Kugel, for instance, finds Psalm 137 to be "one of the 'prosiest' psalms in the Bible" (*The Great Poems of the Bible: A Reader's Companion with New Translations* [New York: Free, 1999], 235). Contrast Ernest R. Wendland, *Lovely, Lively Lyrics: Selected Studies in Biblical Hebrew Verse* (Dallas: SIL International, 2013), 123–24, who thinks otherwise (and more highly) of Ps 137 qua poetry. Other positive assessments of the psalm's poetry may be found in Shimon Bar-Efrat, "Love of Zion: A Literary Interpretation of Psalm 137," in *Tehillah le-Moshe: Biblical and Judaic Studies in Honor of Moshe Greenberg*, ed. Mordechai Cogan, Barry L. Eichler, and Jeffrey H. Tigay (Winona Lake, IN: Eisenbrauns, 1997), 3–11; and Levenson, "Horrifying Closing," esp. 19, who speaks of "the exquisite literary effects of the Hebrew diction" and "the highly intricate structures" in the poem. Finally, the essay by Rodney S. Sadler Jr., "Singing a Subversive Song: Psalm 137 and 'Colored Pompey,'" in *The Oxford Handbook of the Psalms*, ed. William P. Brown (Oxford: Oxford University Press, 2014), 447–58, esp. 453–56, also contains a number of very insightful poetic observations, though his ultimate point about the rhetorical deployment of the poetry seems to falter on the assumption that the Babylonians knew Aramaic decently well but not enough Hebrew to tell what was being said about them in the poem. It is hard to know if either was the case for the average Babylonian soldier. Cf. 2 Kgs 18:26 // Isa 36:11.

legal notion of *lex talionis*—a conception that itself may, or may not, be palatable to modern sensibilities, but which seems manifest in the psalm regardless.[7]

The second poetic aspect concerns *poetic reticence* and how that is manifested in Psalm 137, once again and most especially in verses 7–9 (see §2). Poetry of all sorts is marked to some degree by studied reticence. As Mary Kinzie has written: "All good poetry fends something off. What a poet keeps out of a poem is as necessary to its success as what the poet lets into it. In a complementary way, what the poet lets into the poem is a choice from among a number of poetic ideas that are (if not exactly banished) displaced into a background. Here they not only serve to throw the chosen elements into higher relief but also form the support against which the active elements can lean."[8]

This is to say that a poet—*any and every* poet, according to Kinzie—has at hand a seemingly infinite number of ways to put things. The poet must *resist*, therefore, all of these other options so as to choose the one option that is deemed best and that is subsequently employed in the poem. For Samuel Taylor Coleridge (1772–1834) such an endeavor marked the distinction between the *best words* (prose) and the *best words in the best order* (poetry).[9] For Mark Twain (1835–1910), it marked the difference between the right word and the almost right word, which he memorably likened to the difference between lightning and the lightning bug.[10] The one option selected by the poet—ideally: the best word in the best order (per Coleridge), lightning as opposed to the lightning bug (per Twain)—still does not "say it all" simply because any one poem (let alone word) *cannot* say it all. But what the selected thing says is nevertheless "good enough" and "on target" for the poetic task at hand as that is constructed by the poet. In any event, this notion of poetic reticence or "fending off" may be seen as a kind of resistance that is related

---

7. See, e.g., the "new" atheist writer Christopher Hitchens, *God Is Not Great: How Religion Poisons Everything* (New York: Twelve, 2007), 100, who speaks of "the notorious verses forfeiting 'life for life, eye for eye, tooth for tooth.'"

8. Mary Kinzie, *A Poet's Guide to Poetry*, 2nd ed. (Chicago: University of Chicago, 2013), 46. Kinzie credits Donald Davie with this notion of "fending off." See his *Purity of Diction in English Verse* (London: Routledge & Kegan Paul, 1952). See also Terry Eagleton, *How to Read a Poem* (Malden, MA: Blackwell, 2007), 144.

9. The full citation is as follows: "I wish our clever young poets would remember my homely definitions of prose and poetry; that is, prose,—words in their best order; poetry,—the best words in their best order" (from Coleridge's *Table Talk*, cited in John Bartlett, *Familiar Quotations*, 10th ed. [New York: Blue Ribbon Books, 1919], 505).

10. Cited in George Bainton, *The Art of Authorship: Literary Reminiscences, Methods of Work, and Advice to Young Beginners* (New York: D. Appleton and Company, 1890), 87–88.

to the nature of poetry as difficult literature: dense and economical, spare and terse, deep and concise.[11]

In the end, I will argue that, while negative judgments about Ps 137 (especially vv. 7–9) are almost always oriented around what appears to be its very *explicit* content (especially in v. 9b), the facts of poetry per Kinzie are that Ps 137, no less than any other poem, *resists* alternative ways of putting things, offering something that is, upon closer inspection, rather reticent and therefore *far less* explicit than what might otherwise have been the case. Seen in this way, verse 9 is far from obscene and much more understandable—again, "empathizable" even if (again) not quite palatable. Indeed, to press the point still further, Ps 137 might even be *admirable* in what turns out to be its reticent way of putting things. Such a judgment depends, of course, on empathetic attunement to the poetics of the psalm, but may be prompted—or at least illustrated—by reading Ps 137 in the context of different, far less reticent exemplars, something I offer by way of conclusion (§3).

1. Poetic Movement in Psalm 137 (Especially Verses 7–9)

Notwithstanding a few notable opinions to the contrary,[12] there is little to no evidence, redactional or otherwise, that suggests Ps 137 is anything other than a unified composition.[13] The poem's integrity, along with its correlate and inherent

11. Cf. James Longenbach, *The Resistance to Poetry* (Chicago: University of Chicago Press, 2004).

12. E.g., Ahn, "Psalm 137." Similarly unconvincing to my mind is the much earlier opinion of Charles Augustus Briggs and Emilie Grace Briggs, *A Critical and Exegetical Commentary on the Book of Psalms*, 2 vols., ICC (Edinburgh: T&T Clark, 1906–1907), 2:485–87, who speak repeatedly of a "glossator" or of "late gl[osses]," especially around the mention of *bābel* in verses 1 and 8. The Briggses unfortunately provide no support for taking these elements as secondary, except, or so it seems, via the notorious (and dubious) appeal to *metri causa* (e.g., 486: "at the expense of the measure"; 487: "no place for it in measure . . . at cost of measure"). To be sure, poetic balance does seem to be one important aspect of Hebrew poetics, but it is certainly not the only one, and poets are notorious for breaking form if and as they wish. It appears that the Briggses are motivated to conduct their metrical surgery on the basis of their belief that Ps 137 is largely or only (originally) about Edom, not Babylon, though this, too, proves unconvincing mostly because it is, in the final analysis, entirely speculative.

13. So, e.g., David Noel Freedman, "The Structure of Psalm 137," in *Near Eastern Studies in Honor of William Foxwell Albright*, ed. Hans Goedicke (Baltimore: Johns Hopkins University Press, 1971), 187–205: "The poem is complete as it stands, and . . . we have it as it was composed without significant subsequent alteration. If in fact the end product is the work of a later editor, we can only marvel at his skill in erasing all the usual signs of such activity" (188). This judgment is in some tension with Freedman's statement that the poem has "abrupt shifts in content and tone" (Freedman, 188). Bar-Efrat, "Love of Zion," 10, rightfully states that even though the dif-

flow,[14] means that any attempt to bifurcate Ps 137—even if only at the level of litur-gical or devotional use—is misguided and violates the literary unity of the work. At least two aspects of the poetic movement of the psalm deserve attention.

The Movement from Verses 1–6 to Verses 7–9

If the poem is indeed an integral whole, that means that the poem (and the poet) is moving toward verses 7–9 from the get go, with the end of the poem in mind from the very start.[15] To be sure, compositions can unfold differently than origi-nally expected as one writes (or as one reads) them—that is, of course, what takes place in the case of "surprise endings." Perhaps something like that happened along the way to the poet of Ps 137, but there is much to suggest that the poem is comprised of interlocking parts with a discernible flow that, again, suggests an integrity to the poem from start to finish with obvious ramifications for its interpretation.

The psalm can be divided into three parts or "stanzas": verses 1–3, verses 4–6, and verses 7–9.[16] Verses 1–3 set the stage by placing the psalmist and company "by the rivers of Babylon," where they wept when they remembered Zion (v. 1), espe-cially in the face of cruel mockery on the part of their tormenters (v. 3). Verse 4 picks up on these captors' request for "a song of Zion" by asking the famous ques-tion: "How could we sing the LORD's song in a foreign land?" This leads directly

---

ferent parts of the psalm "differ to some degree in character and atmosphere . . . they are firmly tied together by common elements."

14. For poetic movement or flow in the psalms, see, inter alia, Dennis Sylva, *Psalms and the Transformation of Stress: Poetic-Communal Interpretation and the Family*, Louvain Theological and Pastoral Monographs 16 (Louvain: Peeters and Grand Rapids: Eerdmans, 1994), 15–29. More generally, see Helen Vendler, *Poets Thinking: Pope, Whitman, Dickinson, Yeats* (Cambridge: Har-vard University Press, 2004).

15. Cf. Freedman, "Structure," 199: "Vs. 7 introduces the final section of the poem (vss. 7–9), which corresponds to the opening unit (vss. 1–3). There is a logical connection between this verse and the preceding block of material, as the poet proceeds from his oath of loyalty to Yahweh to the demand that Yahweh vindicate his justice by dealing in the same measure with those who had invaded Judah and destroyed Jerusalem." For the *inclusio* provided by "Babylon" in vv. 1 and 8, see further below.

16. Such a division is reflected in several English versions (e.g., NRSV, CEB). Other divisions are possible and are frequently encountered in the literature. For example: Wendland, *Lovely, Lively Lyrics*, 122–23, has three strophes but divides them differently (vv. 1–4, 5–6, 7–9); Freed-man, "Structure," 188, identified five units (vv. 1–2, 3, 4–6, 7, 8–9); J. P. Fokkelman, *The Psalms in Form: The Hebrew Psalter in Its Poetic Shape* (Leiden: Deo, 2002), 142, also has five (vv. 1–2, 3–4, 5–6, 7, 8–9); NJPSV/TNK has only two (vv. 1–6; vv. 7–9).

to the psalmist (remaining in first-person discourse, but shifting from the plural to the singular) uttering a self-imprecation if Jerusalem is forgotten (vv. 5–6). Finally, verses 7–9 reveal the specific Zion/Jerusalem that is being remembered (cf. v. 1) and that must never be forgotten (v. 5) and cherished above all else (v. 6): it is *destroyed* Jerusalem—the one "ripped" or "torn down" (*'ārû 'ārû*) by Edom (at least verbally, v. 7),[17] which leads, finally, to the devastating comments about Babylon (vv. 8–9). The flow of the poem thus seems clear enough, then, even if the final verse strikes some readers as unexpected in force.

> Mention of a foreign locale, following the destruction of 587 BCE
> leads to (→) the sardonic request for a song about the destroyed
> capital city
> leads to (→) acute articulation of grief over that destroyed city
> leads to (→) a prayer (v. 7) and hope (vv. 8–9) that those
> responsible for the destruction be recompensed.

This flow is quite natural, downright sensible—with all due respect to the shock verse 9 often occasions to modern readers' sensibilities.[18]

The coherence of the three parts of the psalm is signaled, not only by this flow, but also by the repetition of key terms. Chart 1 collates some of the more significant correspondences, but even this presentation is only a beginning since other recurrent elements could be cataloged,[19] particularly the frequent mention of musical motifs (see chart 2). It is noteworthy that no music is found in the third part of the poem (vv. 7–9) but that is perhaps to be expected, especially given the association of music in verse 3 (and perhaps also v. 6) with joy—"joy," too, goes unmentioned in the third and final part (cf. vv. 3, 6).

---

17. So also, rightly, Levenson, "Horrifying Closing," 25–26.

18. To be sure, the relationship of Babylon's activity to Edom's goes unspecified. Perhaps it might be seen as an instance of *specification*; if so, Edom's articulation "rip down" becomes identified as Babylon's "your deed." See further below.

19. Including such details as: similarities of sound, repetition of prepositions or particles (e.g., *'al, 'im, 'ēt/'et*), syntagms (hypotheticals with *'im*, negatives with *lō'*), and so forth. See, e.g., J. P. Fokkelman, *85 Psalms and Job 4–14*, vol. 2 of *Major Poems of the Hebrew Bible at the Interface of Prosody and Structural Analysis* (Assen: Van Gorcum, 2000), 301–2, for a number of useful poetic observations. For a "maximalist" presentation of such poetic details in Hebrew poetry more generally, see Dennis Pardee, *Ugaritic and Hebrew Poetic Parallelism: A Trial Cut ('nt I and Proverbs 2)*, VTSup39 (Leiden: Brill, 1988); as well as Joel M. LeMon, "The Power of Parallelism in KTU² 1.119: Another 'Trial Cut,'" *UF* 37 (2005): 375–94.

CHART 1: REPETITIONS IN PSALM 137[20]

	vv. 1–3	vv. 4–6	vv. 7–9
Babylon (*bābel*)	v. 1	(note *'admat nēkar*, "foreign land," in v. 4)	v. 8, with direct address to Babylon continuing into v. 9 (note also "Edom" in v. 7)
Zion (*ṣîyōn*)	vv. 1, 3	Ø (but note "Jerusalem" in vv. 5–6)	Ø (but note "Jerusalem" v. 7)
Remember (√*zkr*)	v. 1	v. 6 (note also the desire to "not forget" in v. 5)	v. 7
Sing (*šîr*, verb)	v. 3	v. 4	Ø
Song (*šîr*, noun)	v. 3	v. 4	Ø
Joy (*śimḥâ*)	v. 3	v. 6	Ø
LORD (*Yhwh*)	Ø	v. 4	v. 7
Jerusalem (*yərûšālaim*)	Ø (but note "Zion" in vv. 1, 3)	vv. 5–6	v. 7
Edom (*'ĕdōm*)	Ø (but note "Babylon" in v. 1)	Ø (but note "foreign land" in v. 4)	v. 7 (note also "Babylon" in v. 8)

CHART 2: MUSICAL MOTIFS IN PSALM 137

	vv. 1–3	vv. 4–6	vv. 7–9
Music	harps (*kinnōrôtênû*, v. 2), words of song (*dibrê-šîr*, v. 3), sing (*šîrû*, v. 3), song of Zion (*miššîr ṣîyōn*, v. 3)	sing (*nāšîr*, v. 4), song of Yhwh (*šîr-Yhwh*, v. 4)[21]	Ø

---

20. This presentation only includes terms that appear in two or more of the three parts of the psalm with the exception of the correspondences "Zion/Jerusalem," a common poetic word pair, and the "Babylon/foreign land/Edom" complex. These latter are treated as closely related and thus included.

21. Note also the withering of the right hand (v. 5) and the tongue clinging to the palate (v. 6). Not all agree that these phrases connote musical dexterity and singing ability. Patrick D. Miller, "The Hermeneutics of Imprecation," in *The Way of the Lord: Essays in Old Testament Theology*, FAT 39 (Tübingen: Mohr Siebeck, 2004), 193–202 (196), for example, raises the intriguing possibility that they may evoke, not a loss of musical/singing ability, but rather evidence of a stroke (though the latter would presumably also produce the former). Cf. Gary Rendsburg and Susan Rendsburg, "Physiological and Philological Notes to Psalm 137," *JQR* 83 (1993): 385–99. See also Israel Eitan, "An Identification of *tiškaḥ yəmīnī*, Ps 137:5," *JBL* 47 (1928): 193–95; Ahn, "Psalm 137," 284.

When the musical motifs are taken into consideration along with the repetition of certain key terms, every verse in each of the three sections of the poem finds a complement of some sort in at least one of the other sections. The only exception is verse 9; however, since this verse continues the direct address to Babylon begun in verse 8, it might be considered as of a piece with that verse and thus not exceptional after all.[22] It is obvious, regardless, that verse 9 has correspondence within its own unit, not only with regard to semantic content (i.e., the direct address to Babylon) but also and more specifically by means of the repetition of 'ašrê in verses 8 and 9.[23]

The main issues at work in the psalm are the first three elements in chart 1—each of which is mentioned, in one way or another, in all three parts of the poem: foreign land(s), Zion/Jerusalem, and memory. These three issues interrelate and it is not hard to link them causally since that is what the poem itself does: *foreign entities* have played a role in destroying *Zion/Jerusalem*, involving a dislocation of those who *remember* that city, who cannot forget its destruction, who therefore pray that God *remembers* the same, and who also offer a commendation on the one who recompenses these reprehensible acts.

Once again, this poetic movement or flow is perfectly sensible, perhaps even "logical." And so, again, there is no reason not to think that the poem is heading to the final section (vv. 7–9) from its inception. This, surely, is the effect of the *inclusio* created by the mention of Babylon in verse 1, at the start of the psalm, and again, at the end, in verse 8 (with the address to Babylon continuing into v. 9).[24] If this reading of the poetic movement is correct, the first two sections serve to involve the reader affectively in the pathos of the poem and the poet's plight. These sections function, as it were, as a kind of "set up" for the climactic concluding verses of the poem which come only in the last and final section. Patrick D. Miller has captured this point nicely: "In Ps 137, we are drawn to the lament over human and communal suffering, the depiction of oppression, of persons

22. Versification is, after all, late and secondary. Note again, e.g., Fokkelman, *Psalms in Form*, 142, who treats vv. 8–9 together as the fifth and final strophe in the psalm.

23. Here too, other items could be added: only vv. 8–9 employ the relative prefix *še-*, for instance, which is used no less than three times. Freedman, "Structure," 201, also notes that both vv. 1–2 and vv. 8–9 "are materially longer than the standard units making up the body" and that "the opening and closing sections fall into a different pattern [than the body does], each consisting of a pair of matching lines modifying a pivotal phrase or clause." (See the visual layout in Fokkelman, *Psalms in Form*, 142.) Earlier in his essay, after noting "the exact repetition of 'ašrê še- in vss. 8, 9," Freedman states that these verses complement and correspond to vss. 1, 2 ("Structure," 191).

24. Cf. Freedman, "Structure," 188 (cf. 201), who also notes this *inclusio* between verses 1 and 8. See also the previous note and further below.

exiled and tormented, of the loss of everything dear and meaningful."[25] Miller goes on to note how this dynamic leads to a profound interpretive question once we reach the psalm's end: "What the rest of the psalm does, at a minimum, is to ask if the clash or contradiction we experience in reading the psalm is the result of a [too] sentimental appropriation of the first part so that we do not really know the depth of the psalmist's torment. To find the psalm as a whole both intelligible and meaningful *requires* that our romantic and sentimental appropriation of the first part be abandoned. These words have their power and truthfulness *only within the devastating experience to which they point.*"[26]

Miller's acknowledgment that the beginning of the poem, especially its affective elements aspects, is captivating—in his words, "we are drawn to the lament"—and is precisely what leads to the question of (in)sufficient readerly empathy at the end. That is to say, if it isn't hard to empathize with the psalmist's grief in verses 1–6, why should it be difficult to empathize with verses 7–9, especially as these verses, too, are yet another and integrally related articulation of the psalmist's grief, indeed the poem's grand finale? Miller's work implies that it *shouldn't* be any harder to empathize with verses 7–9 than with verses 1–6, and several other interpreters concur—at least on the general point that Ps 137 requires a certain kind of readerly disposition for full appreciation.[27] That verses 7–9 are equally also part of the psalmist's *grief*, not irrational hate or cursing for cursing's sake,[28] receives further support from the second movement that can be traced in the psalm.

25. Miller, "Hermeneutics of Imprecation," 198. Cf. Miller, 200: the rage at the end of the poem "already boils under the surface of the first part of the psalm."

26. Miller, "Hermeneutics of Imprecation," 198 (emphases added).

27. See, e.g., Leslie C. Allen, *Psalms 101–150*, rev. ed., WBC 21 (Nashville: Nelson, 2002), 309: "The citizen of a European country who has experienced its invasion and destruction or a victim of the Holocaust would be the best expositor of such a psalm." Cf. Konrad Schaeffer, *Psalms*, Berit Olam (Collegeville, MN: Liturgical Press, 2001), xliii: "Perhaps such outbursts [as are present in the imprecatory psalms] will be understood and valued first by those who have experienced or are enduring oppression and abuse"; and xliv: "Who is justified in praying like this? A victim of rape or assault, who is weary of awaiting a proper outcome of the clogged legal procedures. An Israeli taxpayer who is exasperated at the frustrated peace promises. A Palestinian refugee weary of war, resentful of displacement. A nun or social worker in the highlands of Chiapas who faces the tensions between military occupation and the struggle for basic human rights of the indigenous peoples." Similarly Walter Brueggemann, *The Message of the Psalms: A Theological Commentary* (Minneapolis: Augsburg, 1984), 77: "Perhaps this psalm will be understood and valued among us only if we experience some concrete brutalization." See more generally the poignant reflections of Miroslav Volf, *Exclusion and Embrace: A Theological Exploration of Identity, Otherness, and Reconciliation*, rev. ed. (Nashville: Abingdon, 2019). See also at note 54 below.

28. Imprecation in the Psalms specifically, or the Bible more broadly, is never simple or simplis-

The Movement within Verses 7–9, Especially Verses 8–9

Aspects of this second movement are already found in chart 1; two deserve special attention and further discussion.

First, the final section of the psalm moves from Edom and the part it played on "the day of Jerusalem" (v. 7a) to Babylon and the deed it did "to us" (v. 8b). This movement can be seen as in parallel, generally, but also as a matter of specification, more particularly—and this both across and within verse 7 and verse 8.

	Verse 7		Verse 8
Parallel (→):	Edom	→	Babylon
	↓		↓
Specification (↓):	Jerusalem's day	→	the deed done
	↓		↓
	strip/tear down to foundations	→	to us

The parallel specification is by locale. Edom is to be remembered by Yhwh due to "the day of Jerusalem," which is then specified as a matter of the Edomites

---

tic. Part of the problems facing the interpretation and reception of Ps 137 or any other imprecatory text is precisely due to ignorance of this fact or an inability to adequately deal with it. For useful entrées into the issues, see Zenger, *God of Vengeance?*; Miller, "Hermeneutics of Imprecation"; Brent A. Strawn, "Imprecation," in *Dictionary of the Old Testament: Wisdom, Poetry and Writings*, ed. Tremper Longman III and Peter Enns (Downers Grove, IL: IVP Academic, 2008), 314–20; Strawn, "Sanctified and Commercially Successful Curses: On Gangsta Rap and the Canonization of the Imprecatory Psalms," *ThTo* 69 (2013): 403–17; Strawn, "Who's Afraid of the Old Testament? Tough Texts for Rough Times," in *The Oxford Handbook of the Bible in Orthodox Christianity*, ed. Eugen J. Pentiuc (Oxford: Oxford University Press, 2022), 539–55; and Strawn, "On (Not) Bashing Babies," *JP* 43.4 (Pentecost 2020): 34–38. Larger treatments include Daniel Michael Nehrbass, *Praying Curses: The Therapeutic and Preaching Value of the Imprecatory Psalms* (Eugene, OR: Pickwick, 2013); Kit Barker, *Imprecation as Divine Discourse: Speech Act Theory, Dual Authorship, and Theological Interpretation*, JTISup 16 (Winona Lake, IN: Eisenbrauns, 2016); and Trevor Laurence, "Cursing with God: The Imprecatory Psalms and the Ethics of Christian Prayer" (PhD diss., Exeter University, 2020). More generally, see Anne Marie Kitz, *Cursed Are You! The Phenomenology of Cursing in Cuneiform and Hebrew Texts* (Winona Lake, IN: Eisenbrauns, 2014), and note also Dominick D. Hankle, "The Therapeutic Implications of the Imprecatory Psalms in the Christian Counseling Setting," *Journal of Psychology and Theology* 38 (2010): 275–80; Thomas L. Mowbray, "The Function in Ministry of Psalms Dealing with Anger: The Angry Psalmist," *Journal of Pastoral Counseling* 21 (1986): 34–39; Christopher G. Frechette, "Destroying the Internalized Perpetrator: A Healing Function of the Violent Language against Enemies in the Psalms," in *Trauma and Traumatization in Individual and Collective Dimensions: Insights from Biblical Studies and Beyond*, ed. Eve-Marie Becker, Jan Dochhorn, and Else Kragelund Holt, SANT 2 (Göttingen: Vandenhoeck & Ruprecht, 2014), 71–84.

saying that the city should be ripped or torn down to its foundations (v. 7). Next, Babylon is to be recompensed, which is further specified as a matter of the deed that it did—still more specifically—"to us" (v. 8).

Edom and Babylon are distinct terms, groups, locales—presented in parallel—but there is specification, if not also intensification, across these verses not just within them.[29] That is to say that what is done to Jerusalem is done also "to us." The nondescript "day of Jerusalem" and the verbal cry (of spectators?) to "rip down" becomes "your [Babylon's] deed that you did to us."

Second, the movement within verses 8–9 is also one of specification and intensification, though it is a movement that is delayed or interrupted temporarily by an extra-long line:

> [8]Daughter Babylon, the devastator[30]—
> happy is the one who pays you back
> > your deed that you did to us;
> [9]happy is the one who seizes and smashes
> > your children against the rock.

It is the last part of verse 8, "your deed that you did to us" (*'et-gəmûlēk šeggāmalt lānû*), that has appeared extraneous to many scholars, leading some to propose that it is a gloss that should be deleted.[31] But while this clause certainly interrupts or delays the completion of the twin *'ašrê*-statements,[32] it nevertheless specifies and intensifies what precedes: the more generic notion that Babylon has done something that deserves recompense (*šeyəšallem-lāk*) becomes "your deed that you did to us"—a phrase that, by means of the cognate accusative with the verb $\sqrt{gml}$, nicely underscores the perfect payback evoked by *šillam*, the *piel* of $\sqrt{šlm}$.[33]

---

29. Cf. Walter Brueggemann and William H. Bellinger Jr., *Psalms* NCBC (Cambridge: Cambridge University Press, 2014), 575, who deem the entire psalm "an arresting example of a structure of intensification."

30. Or: "devastated one" (*haššədûdâ*). The interpretive issues here are several. See the standard commentaries for discussions. Brenner, "On the Rivers," 77n9 and 83n39, understands the formulation to be "formally passive but functionally active," which she deems a feature of Late Biblical Hebrew.

31. So, e.g., H. Bardtke in *BHS*; Briggs and Briggs, *Psalms*, 2:487. Note the response by Allen, *Psalms 101–150*, 302n8b.

32. The repetition found in vv. 8b and 9a (*'ašrê . . . 'ašrê*) is not properly an instance of staircase parallelism, but also not identical to what Wilfred G. E. Watson describes as an "aba-monocolon" structure (see *Classical Hebrew Poetry: A Guide to Its Techniques*, 2nd ed., JSOTSup 26 [Sheffield: Sheffield Academic, 2001], 150, 276). Whatever the case, it does serve to bind vv. 8–9 closely together and in more than one way.

33. Erich Zenger in Frank-Lothar Hossfeld and Erich Zenger, *Psalms 3: A Commentary on*

But there is still more to say because this "additional" part not only delays the second *'ašrê*-statement, it also ends up forming a perfect complement to the final clause, "your children against the rock" (*'et-'ōlālayik 'el-hassāla'*), so much so that, at the end of verse 9, reanalysis of the poetry suggests that the first part of verse 8 (*bat-bābel haššədûdâ*) functions as an introduction of sorts, which stands somewhat outside of what ends up being a rather tightly presented piece of poetic matching:[34]

> V. 8a *bat-bābel haššədûdâ:*
> V. 8b *'ašrê šeyəšallem-lāk*
> V. 8c *'et-gəmûlēk šeggāmalt lānû*
> V. 9a *'ašrê šeyyō'ḥēz wənippēṣ*
> V. 9b *'et-'ōlālayik 'el-hassāla'*

The effect, both syntactically and semantically, is a slow, inexorable clarification of the type of payback that Babylon deserves: it turns out to be of the most exactingly precise kind. That is signaled already in the use of *yəšallem-lāk*, of course, but is also conveyed by the use of √*gml* with cognate accusative: a double-use of that root which seems quite emphatic. It is further underscored by the double-use of *'ašrê*, the second of which in verse 9a is followed by the relative *še-* and the *yod* of the prefix-conjugation third masculine singular, just as was the case in verse 8b, after which points the verbal roots diverge. Instead of *šillam* it is now *'āḥaz* conjoined, quickly, with *wənippēṣ*. But seize and smash *what*? The answer comes, finally and only, at the very end of verse 9: *'et-'ōlālayik*, "your children," further specified with an adverbial (locative) adjunct, *'el-hassāla'*, "against the rock."[35]

Analyzed in this way, the movement of the final two verses suggests that their climactic and culminating moment—the part that many readers find so disturb-

---

Psalms 101–150, ed. Klaus Baltzer, trans. Linda M. Maloney, Hermeneia (Minneapolis: Fortress, 2011), 519, speaks of the *piel* of √*šlm* as "a *terminus technicus* for the idea of retaliation." Bar-Efrat, "Love of Zion," 9, draws attention to how √*šlm* is also present in the geographical name (GN) Jerusalem, perhaps hinting "that the city will repay those who do her evil." The latter goes too far; it may be, rather and more simply, that what has happened to *Yərûšālaim* deserves recompense (√*šlm*).

34. Treating the mention of daughter Babylon as somehow "extrametrical" (as problematic as that term is), may help with this particular analysis. Such a treatment makes sense given the vocative nature of this part, yielding a monocolon (v. 8a) followed by bicolon (vv. 8b–9b). The other alternative, followed by many interpreters, is to excise *'et-gəmûlēk šeggāmalt lānû* (v. 8c), perhaps *metri causa* (equally problematic!), so as to produce one bicolon.

35. See Bill T. Arnold and John H. Choi, *A Guide to Biblical Hebrew Syntax*, 2nd ed. (Cambridge: Cambridge University Press, 2018), 112–14 (§4.1.2) for "terminative," "estimative," and "spatial" uses of *'el*.

ing—is nothing other than an instance of exact recompense, of precise payback, a doing unto Babylon what Babylon has done unto Judah. The seizing and smashing of (*'et*) "your children" is, in this vein, a specification of the recompense of (*'et*) "your deed which you did to us."

If this is correct, the psalm offers a remarkably poetic case of poetic justice, an instance of *lex talionis* or, perhaps better, *talion* in *poesy*. Several scholars have said something similar, making a connection to talionic law, if only because the language of recompense and payback is obvious in verse 8. So, for example, A. A. Anderson writes that "The author of Ps. 137 longs essentially for the application of the *lex talionis*, or the legal principle of 'eye for eye, tooth for tooth' (cf. Exod. 21:24)."[36] Or again, according to Erich Zenger: "The whole psalm is shaped by legal categories and ideas of right and justice. Contrary to first impressions, it is based on neither feelings of hatred nor irrational vengeance. The very first part of the psalm [vv. 5–6], with its gesture of swearing formulated in terms of the *lex talionis* (the law of retaliation), evokes the fundamental order of justice established and protected by Yhwh, to which those praying also submit themselves. This is still more the case with the especially difficult verses 8–9.[37]

36. A. A. Anderson, *The Book of Psalms*, NCB (Grand Rapids: Eerdmans, 1972), 2:900. In addition to Exod 21:24, see also Lev 24:19–20 and Deut 19:21.

37. Zenger, *God of Vengeance?* 49; cf. Zenger in Hossfeld and Zenger, *Psalms 3*, 520, 523. See also Wendland, *Lovely, Lively Lyrics*, 130–31; and Brueggemann and Bellinger, *Psalms*, 575, who speak of the "'blessing' of the law of retaliation" and the "hope for divine justice with blessing on those who do unto Babylon what Babylon has done to Jerusalem." Similarly Freedman, "Structure," 203: "The destruction of Babylon will conform to the standard of divine retribution: payment will be in kind and in equal measure. As Babylon did to others, so it shall be done to her. A vivid example of such retribution, which at the same time illustrates prevailing practice all over the ancient world, including the Babylonians themselves, suffices to complete the case. The appalling procedure is fully attested." At this point Freedman cites Jer 51:49; and 2 Kgs 8:12; Isa 13:16; and Hos 14:1; and Nah 3:10 (Freedman, 203nn22–23); cf. also Jer 51:55–56 (also verses 48, 53), which is mentioned in Freedman, 203n21.

Others think the matter is not *lex talionis* proper but nevertheless still closely related to other texts in the Bible. So, for example, John Goldingay, *Psalms 90–150*, vol. 3 of *Psalms*, BCOTWP (Grand Rapids: Baker Academic, 2008), 610:

> The psalm's words are also not surprising because all they are doing is expressing confidence that Yhwh will fulfill the promises made by the prophets. It is not devising from scratch the most vicious image it can think of to express the warped nature of its mind but taking up Yhwh's own image. There is some appropriateness to it: Yhwh had declared the intention to do this to Judah's children and had used Babylon as the means of doing so; again, it is an image [used elsewhere] (Jer. 13:14; 51:20–23). . . . Thus the psalm develops no new ideas for the way Babylon might be punished. Every word in this chilling declaration takes up Yhwh's promises . . . and envisages them being fulfilled. Then justice will have been done.

Zenger isn't the only interpreter to draw attention to the cursing that takes place in the first part of the psalm—as already noted earlier, verses 5–6 contain a self-imprecation, wherein the psalmist asks for a withered hand and an ineffective tongue should the poet forget Jerusalem.[38] The imprecations relating to the Edomites and Babylonians are constructed differently, of course: with the Edomites via the verb √zkr, "remember," and with the Babylonians, somewhat ironically, with a commendation utilizing 'ašrê. Be that as it may, it is important to note that the poet curses the self, first and foremost, before cursing anyone else;[39] still further, the ultimate curse of enemies comes through a blessing pronounced on some other person or entity. I will return to these points momentarily (§2).

In Zenger's understanding, the key rhetorical move in the imprecatory psalms is made when the enemies are portrayed as *God's* enemies, not merely or simply the psalmists' alone. This makes the matter at hand something that is profoundly theological and therefore not solely or thinly personal.[40] The use of *lex talionis* in such a context makes good sense. This type of law effectively limits personal retaliation so that punishment does not exceed the crime. The talionic principle, far from being barbaric, is therefore a matter of justice—justice of the most exacting and accurate kind: no more, no less.[41] In this way the justice that is served is properly constrained so that it does not become unjust.

Goldingay calls this sort of intertextual reading with the prophets a "scriptural perspective" (612) and goes on to assert that "the psalm is simply asking for the implementation of those declarations of intent" (612–13). While Goldingay's comments are illuminating, one may reasonably wonder if the psalmist knew these prophetic texts.

Perhaps the two options—*lex talionis* and intertextual connections with the prophets—are, in the end, two sides of the same coin: that of poetic justice. See, e.g., Patrick D. Miller, *Sin and Judgment in the Prophets: A Stylistic and Theological Analysis*, SBLMS 27 (Chico, CA: Scholars, 1982); cf. Martha C. Nussbaum, *Poetic Justice: The Literary Imagination and Public Life* (Boston: Beacon, 1995). Note, finally, Bar-Efrat, "Love of Zion," 7, who finds traces of talion in the self-curse in vv. 5–6. Slightly later, Bar-Efrat asserts that "v. 9 is an example of v. 8, the wished-for retribution" (Bar-Efrat, "Love of Zion," 9).

38. For the hand as "withered" (*škḥ* II, so most English translations [ET]) as opposed to "forgetful" (*škḥ* I), see *HALOT* 4:1490–91. Several scholars dispute the need for *škḥ* II (e.g., Goldingay, *Psalms 90–150*, 606). Bar-Efrat, "Love of Zion," 7, finds traces of talion in the self-curse in vv. 5–6.

39. See Carol A. Miles, "'Singing the Songs of Zion' and Other Sermons from the Margins of the Canon," *Koinonia* 6 (1994): 151–73; also Magonet, "Psalm 137," 84, who deems this part "as violent and destructive in its way as the threat in the closing section."

40. For more on this, see Ellen F. Davis, *Getting Involved with God: Rediscovering the Old Testament* (Cambridge, MA: Cowley, 2001), 27; and Strawn, "Who's Afraid?" on Ps 139.

41. Calum Carmichael, *The Spirit of Biblical Law* (Athens: University of Georgia Press, 1996), 108, calls this the "kindly interpretation" of the formula, an interpretation that sees it as putting "a check on the limitless vengeance to which the society in question supposedly resorted." Kindly

Nahum Sarna has argued, compellingly in my view, that talion law was just in yet still another way: by ensuring equity among the rich and poor.[42] In the absence of talion, the rich could simply pay for damages in a way that the poor could not: out of their financial largesse. The law of talion, however, mandates that *all* must pay *in kind*, adding a layer of socio-economic equality that goes beyond (or beneath) the specific offense and its punishment.[43] The rich could not, that is, get away with physical harm and simply compensate the victim. No, instead: eye for eye, tooth for tooth, life for life, whether rich or poor.

In sum and in context, the prayer for precise payback—the talionic principle—in Ps 137 means that the wished-for punishment in this poem is not vindictive or some sort of unhelpful revenge fantasy.[44] It is, instead, a prayer for justice that *precisely* suits the crime.[45] This point granted, the crime in question appears

---

or not (one may query if "kindness" is the correct metric), this interpretation is most likely and widely held—its accuracy, furthermore, does not depend on any (dubious) supposition that the general society was interested in "limitless vengeance." For more on talion law see, inter alia, Trevor Thompson, "Punishment and Restitution," in *The Oxford Encyclopedia of the Bible and Law*, ed. Brent A. Strawn et al. (Oxford: Oxford University Press, 2015), 2:183–93, esp. 183–84; David Daube, *Studies in Biblical Law* (Cambridge: Cambridge University Press, 1947), 102–53; Zainab Bahrani, *The Graven Image: Representation in Babylonia and Assyria* (Philadelphia: University of Pennsylvania Press, 2003), 165–71, esp. 170; and Jonathan Burnside, *God, Justice, and Society: Aspects of Law and Legality in the Bible* (Oxford: Oxford University Press, 2011), 275–82, who sees "not one talionic formula, but two, both of which have proportionality as their goal.... Even the literal application of the *lex talionis* radically insists on the need for restraint" (282). For still more on this topic, esp. the way talion law functions to restrict escalation of violence, see Amy-Jill Levine and Marc Zvi Brettler, *The Bible with and without Jesus: How Jews and Christians Read the Same Stories Differently* (New York: HarperOne, 2020), esp. 202, 208–9, 211.

42. Nahum M. Sarna, *Exploring Exodus: The Origins of Biblical Israel* (New York: Schocken, 1996), 182–85. Cf. Levine and Bretter, *Bible with and without Jesus*, 209, though they end up arguing for a monetary compensation understanding of *lex talionis* (see 211). Sarna's treatment effectively counters such an interpretation.

43. The Babylonian Empire could pay out the notes, presumably, for damages filed or for restitution later. But that doesn't suffice when the issue is not only the destruction of God's city and its tumultuous aftermath, but also *one's own child* (and vice versa!). In any event, the statement frequently attributed to M. K. Gandhi—"an eye for an eye will leave the whole world blind"—while rhetorically powerful, is, in the end, not accurate. It is only those who blind others who will be blinded in turn.

44. On which see Judith Hermann, *Trauma and Recovery* (New York: Basic Books, 1997), 189–90, who points out that "though the traumatized person imagines that revenge will bring relief, repetitive revenge fantasies actually increase ... torment." I have explored the imprecatory psalms, especially Ps 137, and Hermann's work more fully in Brent A. Strawn, *Honest to God Preaching: Talking Sin, Suffering, and Violence*, Working Preacher Books 7 (Minneapolis: Fortress, 2021), 99–138.

45. See Magonet, "Psalm 137," esp. 83, on how a hallmark of Jewish exegesis of Ps 137 is that

somewhat un(der)determined: the Edomites are said to have uttered five words (one repeated) while the Babylonians are accused of having done (√*gml*) something. What, exactly, is to be "paid back" (√*šlm*) here and with talionic precision? Upon further analysis and closer inspection, however, the talionic principle at work in verses 8–9, especially when considered within the flow of verses 7–9, suggests that the poet does in fact reveal what Babylon's initially non-descript deed was, at least in part—but the poet reveals this slowly, inexorably, *painfully*. To be more specific, given the poetic movement and the evocation of talion in the psalm, it is very difficult to escape the impression that "your deed that you did to us" (v. 8c) that must be paid back precisely (v. 8b), has everything to do with the seizing and dashing of children (v. 9). The horrific act of infanticide/pedicide is known from war practices described elsewhere in the Hebrew Bible and the ancient Near East.[46] But few, if any, scholars have drawn the conclusion—evident, in my judgment, when the poetic movement and talionic aspects are considered

---

it sees "the punishment exacted on the Babylonians ... as an exact counterpart to the gruesome behavior of the Babylonians during the conquest of Jerusalem and so fitted the expectations of a just, measure for measure requital at the hands of God." According to Meir Lob Ben Yehiel Michal (Malbim; 1809–1879 CE), the "same measure" nature of the punishment of Babylon means that "her suffering will be, in a sense, self-inflicted" (see Feuer, *Tehillim*, 2:1625).

46. See note 37 above, to which one might add 2 Kgs 25:7 and Hos 10:14. Bar-Efrat, "Love of Zion," 9n17 adds Homer, *Iliad* 22.63–64, while Brenner, "On the Rivers," 85, challenges the accuracy of these texts as reflecting actual ancient Near Eastern war practice. Note Goldingay, *Psalms 90–150*, 609: "The words are chilling, but hardly surprising. They are a recurrent OT image for what happens in war. ... Indeed, a nation may make a point of killing its enemies' children, because they are its future. ... Yet we should not press the psalm's metaphorical language. None of the passages that refer to smashing children are simple reports of someone's action: all come in the words of prophets, apart from this psalm that appeals to the words of prophets." It is instructive to compare Stowe, *Song of Exile*, 131: "The modern sense that babies are the most innocent of bystanders and therefore off-limits to warfare is a relatively recent moral innovation. For most readers over the past 2,500 years, verse nine would not have stood out as violating some sort of taboo"; with Wendland, *Lovely, Lively Lyrics*, 131: readers "should note the fact that such imprecatory language always features conventionalized hyperbolic sayings that cannot be interpreted literally; rather, the literary style is highly figurative and operates functionally in a very specific manner." Wendland sees the supplicant of Ps 137 "pleading with God to uphold his honor and that of his covenant people by exercising penal justice in vengeance upon the wicked. ... by utilizing the most vivid, emotively cathartic, *and spiritually healing* terms that are available in his precative vocabulary and the religious corpus from which it springs" (Wendland, 131, emphasis added). Cf. also Gary A. Anderson, "King David and the Psalms of Imprecation," in *The Harp of Prophecy: Early Christian Interpretation of the Psalms*, ed. Brian E. Daley and Paul R. Kolbet (Notre Dame: University of Notre Dame Press, 2015), 29–45, who states: "Surprisingly, the barbarity of these [imprecatory] psalms did not prove to be such a problem for premodern readers" (30).

together—that the precise payback that is prayed for here is directly connected to the psalm's climactic sentiment regarding the brutalization of children.[47] What the psalmist hopes for, with emphatic grammar, is a strictly corresponding retribution ($\sqrt{šlm}$ + $\sqrt{gml}$ with *gəmûlēk*); the poet then moves directly to the line about children, which suggests that the seizing and smashing in question is, in fact, *exactly* what Babylon did to the poet's *own child*.

As further support of this interpretation, it might be noted that it helps to make sense of an otherwise odd detail in the poetry: the definite article on the word for "rock." Why, we might ask, does the poet write "*the* rock" (*hassāla'*)? Why not simply "a rock" (*sela'*) or perhaps "rocks" (*səlā'îm*) given the plural *'ōlālîm*? Generally speaking, Hebrew poetry does not require the definite article, and often eschews it,[48] but perhaps the particular circumstances of this particular poem *do* require it. Instead of *hassāla'* being an instance of what some grammarians might call an indefinite use of the definite article (oxymoronic to say the least),[49] the definite article here might be exactly that—*definite*. The poet may be thinking, that is, of one very specific, definite rock: *the* rock, *that* rock, the one where the psalmist's own child was seized and smashed. That is the rock that the psalmist just can't get out of her head.[50]

If this interpretation of the poetic movement coupled with the principle of talionic retribution at work in the psalm is accurate, it should be observed that the

---

47. Cf. Ahn, "Psalm 137," 287–89, who notes that "the events of 587 entailed not only a collective experience of the destruction of the temple and the city but also the painful personal loss of children" (287), though he does not marshal evidence from Ps 137 proper to support this point as I am doing here.

48. It is admittedly not uncommon in late poetry and is found in Ps 137:7b (2×) and 8a. It is absent in v. 2 (*'ărābîm*) where it could have conceivably been used.

49. See, e.g., Ronald J. Williams and John C. Beckman, *Williams' Hebrew Syntax*, 3rd ed. (Toronto: University of Toronto Press, 2007), 36–37 (§84).

50. Recall, in this connection, that Ps 137 is usually considered one of the few psalms that can be dated with some degree of certainty (at least in terms of *terminus a quo*), which suggests a historical specificity for the poem more generally (cf. Wendland, *Lovely, Lively Lyrics*, 127: "the most situationally marked, setting-specific psalm of the Psalter"). Whatever the case, the poetry *permits* an interpretation like that offered above, even if it does not *require* it. Zenger's statement, that "the children of daughter Babylon . . . are to be smashed against the stone pavements of the capital city" is odd—it must be a rhetorical flourish, otherwise it is in error (*God of Vengeance*, 50). But see note 33 above. Other interpreters have attempted to relate *sela'* to Edom (see, e.g., Adele Berlin, "Psalms and the Literature of Exile," in *The Book of Psalms: Composition and Reception*, ed. Peter W. Flint and Patrick D. Miller, VTSup 99 [Leiden: Brill, 2005], 65–86 [69 with n. 10]), but this makes little sense in the current form of the psalm—Babylon's babies will be smashed against Edom?—and thus depends on surgery to Ps 137 (*viz.*, attributing vv. 7–9 in their entirety to Edom, not Babylon; thus Brenner, "On the Rivers," 83). This is completely unnecessary and also textually unwarranted.

poetry is nevertheless somewhat understated—or, at the very least, not nearly as explicit as it might have been. The poet did not, that is, add at the end of verse 9: "just like you did to us," though in many ways the poet already said as much at the end of verse 8 and that lingers in the poetic air, as it were, as one moves from verse 8 to verse 9.[51] The poem's understatement would help to explain why so many interpreters seem to have missed the poetic point, as it were, focusing only on the "shocking" final verse without more careful attention to verses 7–9, especially vv. 8–9 and the movement of the poem at this point(s). The presence of poetic understatement here in Ps 137 leads directly to a discussion of poetic reticence. Before turning to that topic directly, it should be underscored that while the understanding of poetic movement presented here may not justify the sentiment expressed in the psalm, it nevertheless makes it "empathizable," even if it remains still unpalatable to many.[52] Sympathetic readers, that is, might conceivably empathize with someone bereft of children—worse: someone who has had a child murdered—just as well as, if not better than, they might empathize with those who have suffered military defeat, forced migration, and humiliating mockery.[53] In this way, the end of Ps 137 functions in the same way as the beginning of the poem: both parts—indeed the whole psalm—summon the reader's empathy, though they may also test the limits of the same. About such limits, the words of the nineteenth-century preacher Charles Spurgeon (1834–1892) continue to ring true: "Let those find fault with [Psalm 137] who have never seen their temple burned, their city ruined, their wives ravished, and their children slain; they might not, perhaps, be so velvet-mouthed if they had suffered after this fashion."[54]

---

51. In the visual representation found in Fokkelman, *Psalms in Form*, 142 (and present in the text, regardless), the extra-long line in v. 8 shows that v. 8c is gapped in v. 9. Should v. 8c be understood somehow as operating also in v. 9 and thus be supplied by the reader? If so, the effect is: "happy the-one-who-seizes and-dashes your-little-ones against-the-rock (the deed that you did to us!)."

52. Cf. Schaeffer, *Psalms*, xliii–xliv: "Even if a person finds such poetry unacceptable, he or she can still respect the emotional heat which ignites such protest and understand it as a witness to the intensity of the struggle against evil, oppression, and dehumanization which can become so familiar that it arouses no more than passing interest."

53. Contra Robert Alter, *The Hebrew Bible* (New York: Norton, 2019), 3:314: "No moral justification can be offered for this notorious concluding line." He ends by saying that "fortunately, [the captors] do not understand the Hebrew in which it [the curse] is pronounced."

54. Charles H. Spurgeon, *The Treasury of David: Spurgeon's Classic Work on the Psalms* (Grand Rapids: Kregel, 2004), 627. See also Magonet, "Psalm 137," 88, who cites Claude G. Montefiore: "Doubtless the Psalmist had seen and heard of many deeds of heartless cruelty, which partly palliate the cruelty of his own heart's desire." Schaeffer, *Psalms*, xli–xlii, is even more pointed: "Along with the discomfort which the reader may feel in the face of violence in the Bible, it

One final point: as analyzed above, the empathy summoned in verses 7–9 (especially vv. 8–9) vis-à-vis that evoked by verses 1–6 may be yet one more instance of poetic dynamism, even specification. In this way the most brutal strike, generated by Babylon's own murderous acts, concludes the arc of readerly sympathy begun already in verse 1 with its mention of weeping over lost Zion. Once again, later readers may (or may not) be moved by a destroyed city which they may (or may not) have witnessed or ever seen—but a murdered child? Only the most callous of readers could pass over that without being shaken to their core. Alas, many readers these days seem unfortunately quite callous.[55] One suspects, however, that the poet knew what she was doing: the last, most brutal detail of the poem is held back until the very end.[56] Not only does the final detail culminate the flow and clarify what kind of talionic retribution is called for, it also confronts the reader with the traumatic memory of the psalmist—and the traumatic memory of her traumatized community as well—because the poet's use of Babylon in verses 8–9

---

is good to investigate, within oneself, whether the discomfort is born of a sincere fidelity to the Gospel which commands believers to love their enemies or whether it is rather a subtle, unconscious tactic of appropriation of a dominant ideology which accepts and legitimizes the present politic and feels uncomfortable when someone appears to shake it up." Bar-Efrat, "Love of Zion," 11, presses the point even further: "We know that acts of revenge and atrocities are not only perpetrated but frequently justified and glorified in our time, even in 'civilized' societies." One worries, therefore, about psychological dynamics like projection in some modern offense at biblical violence. For some general reflections on this point, see Brent A. Strawn, "Projecting on Joshua: You Can't Worship Both God and Glock," in *God and Guns: The Bible against American Gun Culture*, ed. Christopher B. Hays and C. L. Crouch (Louisville: Westminster John Knox, 2021), 13–38.

55. This has been empirically demonstrated in a Stanford study that showed a 40 percent decline in empathy among young people in the two decades prior to the study's publication. The decline is due in part, it seems, to individuals' (esp. young people) difficulties in balancing online interactions with those that take place "in real life." See S. H. Konrath, E. H. O'Brien, and C. Hsing, "Changes in Dispositional Empathy in American College Students over Time: A Meta-analysis," *Personality and Social Psychology Review* 15 (2011): 180–98; S. Turkle, *Reclaiming Conversation: The Power of Talk in a Digital Age* (New York: Penguin, 2015), 171–72. Maryanne Wolf, *Reader, Come Home: The Reading Brain in a Digital World* (New York: Harper, 2018), has mounted a convincing argument that "reading at the deepest levels may provide one part of the antidote to the noted trend away from empathy" (50, further 42–53). Cf. more generally, Wayne C. Booth, *The Company We Keep: An Ethics of Fiction* (Berkeley: University of California Press, 1989). While Wolf and Booth speak mostly about novels, one can hardly imagine a deeper reading than that prompted (and required) by poetry.

56. Cf. Levenson, "Horrifying Closing," 35, who comes to a similar conclusion: "It seems likely that the poet wanted to end with the most potent expression of his rage that he could find," but Levenson then parts company with the present chapter when he writes, "deliberately leaving a bitter taste in his readers' mouths."

and 1 forms an *inclusio* requiring a re-reading of the different "parts" of the psalm that results, ultimately, in the realization that these parts belong together, as one devastatingly broken piece.[57]

This slow, painful revelation on the part of the poet of Ps 137 may be related to the insight of another poet, Emily Dickinson, who said "Tell all the Truth but tell it slant— / Success in Circuit lies" because "The Truth must dazzle gradually."[58] Perhaps telling "the Truth" obliquely is even more necessary when the truth in question doesn't dazzle so much as trouble because in this particular case it is truly horrifying. Such is the nature of traumatic experience and, correlatively, with the slow unveiling of trauma—the urgent but oh-so-difficult speaking of trauma that is so often profoundly unspeakable.[59]

2. Poetic Reticence in Psalm 137 (Especially Verses 7–9)

What has been said thus far has touched on reticence more than once, but the emphasis to this point has been primarily on how readerly empathy is cultivated and curated by the movement of the poem writ large, within verses 7–9 specifically, and within verses 8–9 still more specifically. In what follows, I turn from *poetic movement* to *poetic reticence* to see how it might contribute to a better understanding of Ps 137. If paying attention to poetic movement affects readerly empathy, then an appreciation of poetic reticence may deepen readerly comprehension.

To return to Kinzie's remarks cited earlier, we might begin by asking, "What does the poet of Ps 137 fend off here? What has this poet kept out of this poem—especially from verses 7–9?"[60] The answer, as surprising as it might at first appear given the shock of verse 9, would seem to be "quite a lot."[61]

We may begin with the role of the Deity. God isn't mentioned in the psalm until verse 4 and only then indirectly in the reference to "the LORD's song" (*'et-šîr-Yhwh*).

---

57. This last paragraph is indebted to discussions with Justin Walker, who has my thanks for prompting my thinking and sharing his observations about the Babylon *inclusio* and the effect of v. 9's final positioning.

58. Emily Dickinson, "Tell all the Truth but tell it slant (1129)," in *The Complete Poems of Emily Dickinson*, ed. Thomas H. Johnson (Boston: Back Bay, 1976), 506–7.

59. See further Strawn, *Honest to God Preaching*, 104–20, which depends on Hermann, *Trauma and Recovery*. Cf. the oblique nature of Jesus's (imprecatory?) comments on the way to the cross in Luke 23:28–31.

60. Kinzie, *A Poet's Guide*, 46 (cited above; see note 8).

61. Cf. Schaefer, *Psalms*, 323: Ps 137 contains "an overflow of feeling in a *restrained* composition" (emphasis added). Note Alter's brief comment that "the painful noun of destruction [in v. 7] is suppressed, as though it stuck in the throat of the poet" (*Hebrew Bible*, 3:314). The phrase "the day of Jerusalem" (*yôm yərûšālāim*) might also be somewhat reticent.

The next two verses address Jerusalem, which further delays any mention of the Deity until verse 7. There, finally, God appears as the recipient of direct address: "Remember, O LORD, against the Edomites" (NRSV). It is only at this point, and perhaps only in this verse about the Edomites, that the poem becomes what could be properly termed *prayer*.[62] Immediately after this verse, the Deity again fades from view. The most brutal strike, against Babylon in verses 8–9, *contains no mention of God whatsoever*. Moreover, insofar as those verses are addressed directly to Babylon, they are decidedly *not* prayer to the Lord.

Even when God is invoked in verse 7, the situation is un(der)determined. An imperative addresses God: "Remember, O LORD," but this verse about the Edomites is remarkably reticent when it comes to expressing many details.[63] Note, first, the use of the rather nondescript syntagma: $\sqrt{zkr}$ + *lə*-, "remember to." The use of this combination elsewhere in the Hebrew Bible makes clear that it is far from unambiguously negative or adversarial;[64] indeed, positive uses of $\sqrt{zkr}$ coupled with *lə*- outnumber negative uses.[65] One usually has to add something, at least in English translation but also often in the original Hebrew, to clarify the connotation intended by $\sqrt{zkr}$ + *lə*-, be it benevolent or otherwise.[66] To be sure, given the apostrophe to Jerusalem in verses 4–6, the destructive acts spoken about by Edom—and their doubled presentation (*ʿārû ʿārû*)—are likely sufficient to suggest that the hoped-for divine remembering of the Edomites is to their detriment. Such is the understanding of most English translations: "Remember, O LORD, *against* ..." (so NRSV, NJPSV, NAB, RSV; cf. CEB, NIV).

But none of that is operative in verses 8–9 about Babylon. Yhwh is nowhere to be seen. To be sure, there is a double-use of *ʾašrê* in what Walter Brueggemann and William Bellinger call a "scalding beatitude,"[67] but *ʾašrê* need not invoke the Deity.

---

62. Similarly, Zenger, *God of Vengeance?* 49.

63. Cf. Goldingay, *Psalms 90–150*, 613: "In the case of the psalm's actual prayer, concerning Edom, the words are extraordinarily mild compared with the promises of the prophets about Edom." He goes on to note the lack of judgment on Edom: "It thus rather looks as if Yhwh no more implemented warnings about casting off Edom than warnings about casting off Judah."

64. See, e.g., Exod 32:13; Lev 26:45; Num 10:9; Deut 9:27; 2 Chr 6:42; Neh 13:14, 22.

65. Neither $\sqrt{zkr}$ + *ʿal* nor $\sqrt{zkr}$ + *ʾel* is used in biblical Hebrew with negative sense, though the number of instances is admittedly very small.

66. E.g., Neh 5:19 and 13:31 add *laṭôbâ*; Ps 25:7 adds *ləmaʿan ṭûbəkā*; see also Ps 135:23 and Jer 2:2. Contrast Neh 13:29; Ps 79:8; and Ezek 18:22; 33:16, which add negative elements in the context.

67. Brueggeman and Bellinger, *Psalms*, 575. Cf. Schaefer, *Psalms*, 323: "cruel beatitudes"; Wendland, *Lovely, Lively Lyrics*, 130–31, deems the double beatitude sarcastic and "a (mock) blessing." Kraus, *Psalms 60–150*, 504, thinks vv. 8–9 are "loaded with ironic felicitations against the avenger."

People can be "happy," that is, without a heavy theological layering, even in ancient Israel.[68] The idea of being "blessed" (another popular English translation of *ʾašrê*), as William P. Brown has pointed out, is better associated with the root √*brk*; in contrast, "the designation *ʾašrê* [itself] need not directly presuppose divine agency."[69] With Kinzie we may say something has been fended off here and at this point; things might have been put differently. Consider, for example, a somewhat comparable situation in Ps 1 and Ps 146 with regard to the way of the wicked.

Ps 1:6b: *wəderek rəšāʿîm tōʾbēd*   "but the way of the wicked will perish"
Ps 146:9b: *wəderek rəšāʿîm yəʿawwēt*   "but the way of the wicked he [Yhwh] brings to ruin."[70]

The two verses are quite similar, even more so when it is recalled that both begin with Yhwh as the subject of an active participle: "Yhwh knows the way of the righteous" (*yôdēʿ[a]ʿ Yhwh derek ṣaddîqîm*) in Ps 1 and God "protects immigrants" (*Yhwh šōmēr ʾet-gērîm*) in Ps 146. But Ps 1 fends something off, something that the poet of Ps 146 did not see fit to avoid: namely, the active role of the Deity in the downfall of the wicked. The poet of the first psalm could have followed suit, even with the same verbal root (√*ʾbd*), by simply flexing it in the *piel* or *hiphil* in order to achieve a sense

---

68. Cf. further Brenner, "On the Rivers," 78, also 90–91, for *ʾašrê*, which she translates (in part depending on Rashi) as "praised/praiseworthy." It does not, in her opinion, depict the avengers themselves as "happy" or as "actually enjoying" the retribution (91). To be sure, one should beware any interpretation of anything in antiquity, especially in Israel, as a-theological; the pervasiveness of God and the gods was ubiquitous in the ancient world. Justin Walker has thus rightly pointed out (private communication) that *ʾašrê* seems frequently correlated with divine benefits and presence, especially divine deliverance, but not—and this is important—with divine retribution (cf. Magonet, "Psalm 137," 85). That is to say that even if God "sneaks in" somehow behind *ʾašrê* it is not necessarily with reference to the retributive act proper. Instead, the accent of *ʾašrê* here may be less on *lex talionis* than on *ius talionis*, the legal principle (not specific punishment), and therefore on the divine "rightness" of this instance of Torah justice implementation. For *ius talionis*, see Bernard S. Jackson, *Essays in Jewish and Comparative Legal History*, SJLA 10 (Leiden: Brill, 1975), 75–107.

69. William P. Brown, "Happiness and Its Discontents in the Psalms," in *The Bible and the Pursuit of Happiness: What the Old and New Testaments Teach Us about the Good Life*, ed. Brent A. Strawn (New York: Oxford University Press, 2012), 95–115 (99). The missing divine agency is bipartite: God is not necessary to make one happy (the divine agent of blessedness, as it were); neither, to my knowledge, is the Deity ever said to be *ʾašrê* in the Hebrew Bible. This latter point means that the blessing of v. 9 is *not* predicated of God as the implied actor, contra Ahn ("Psalm 137"), among others, who asserts the opposite without proof.

70. NRSV here seems dependent on LXX (*aphaniē*). Cf. NJPSV: "makes . . . tortuous"; CEB: "makes . . . twist and turn!"

entirely akin to Ps 146. But the poet didn't do that; Ps 1 has kept the Deity out of the destruction of the wicked way in a manner that Ps 146 does not. That is noteworthy.

Returning to Ps 137, one sees that it would have been easy enough to substitute the second *'ašrê* statement for something like "may *the Lord* seize and smash" (*Yhwh ye'ǝḥōz wǝnippēṣ*) or "let *me* seize and smash" (*'ōḥāzâ wǝnippaṣtî*) or (impersonally, perhaps with passive sense) "let *them* seize and smash" (*yō'ḥāzû wǝnippaṣû*). But that is *not* what is present in the psalm, which instead maintains poetic balance with the two *'ašrê*-statements bracketing the internal verse 8c:

'ašrê šeyǝšallem-lak [*'et-gǝmûlēk šeggāmalt lānû*] *'ašrê šeyyō'ḥēz wǝnippēṣ*

One effect of this phrasing is the movement traced in §1 above. Another is that it keeps the Deity out of verse 9—not unlike the situation in Ps 1:6b. Once again, things might have been otherwise, the poem could have been written differently. The simple replacement of the second *'ašrê* with *bārûk* would have involved (or at least invoked) the Deity in a still-somewhat-reticent-but-far-more-obvious way, but no, that is *not* what the poet did. The poet of Ps 137 has fended some things off—a Very Large Thing in this particular case.

Seen in this light, Zenger's understanding of the logic of the imprecatory psalms isn't exactly right. Speaking of Ps 137 he wrote: "The psalm does not ask for power to carry out punishment against the enemies by one's own initiative but leaves it to God."[71] The first part of that sentence seems accurate, but the bit about leaving things to God is not nearly so clear. The Lord is mentioned in verse 7, to be sure, but as already

71. Zenger in Hossfeld and Zenger, *Psalms 3*, 523; similarly Zenger, *God of Vengeance?*, 48. (The sentiment is widely found in secondary literature, esp. that concerned with reclaiming the imprecatory psalms in some fashion for the contemporary life of faith.) Goldingay is also only partly right when he writes:

> Ezekiel 25:12–14 declares that Yhwh would bring recompense on Edom for its action against Judah and would do so through Israel itself (cf. Obad. 17–21; Jer. 49:7–22 lacks the reference to Israel's own action). The psalmist asks Yhwh to act in accordance with that commitment but apparently does not look forward to taking action in person. . . . Typically the plea is quite unspecific in the action it looks for; it is concerned to get Yhwh to act but content to leave it to Yhwh to determine what the action should be. . . . Who is to be responsible for this destruction? Ultimately it is Yhwh; the human agent is unnamed. The psalm does again imply that it is not the suppliants who expect to undertake it. They believe that the destroyers are privileged, people of good fortune, but Babylon's destruction is not the suppliants' own task. Their task is simply to trust Yhwh to fulfill the promises they have been given. (*Psalms 90–150*, 608–9)

The problems with Goldingay's reading are that (a) the poem does not mention any divine promises, so it is difficult to know if any were operative for the poet; and (b) the art of reticence indicates that Yhwh may in fact *not* be the agent responsible for destruction. The psalm, at any rate, certainly does not say that Yhwh will destroy anything—it most certainly resists that. So noted, it is Babylon itself (*bat-bābel*) that is directly addressed in verse 8. At best one might say the Lord overhears this part of the poem, after being invited into the room in verse 8, as it were; but in verses 8–9, the psalm is no longer a prayer, at least not a prayer addressed directly to God as is verse 7, or as in so many other poems in the Psalter.[72]

And why should that be the case? Of course it is difficult to say, one cannot know for certain. Poets have their reasons, after all, and those (authorial) reasons may or may not matter much in subsequent reading(s) of their poems. It is enough to note that the poet *could* have said things differently—more directly, for one thing, more theologically, for another—but the poet did not. That is a significant fact that must be considered in any assessment of Ps 137, whether one likes it or dislikes it—or, rather, whenever one likes the first six verses but hates the last three. While the reasons behind the poem's reticence remain elusive, one should note that, at least in the case of Babylon—but perhaps also even with the Edomites[73]—imprecation of the religious variety, with a god or gods mentioned in the curse and thus active in its implementation, is technically not present in Ps 137.[74] Throughout the ancient Near East, *non*-religious imprecations carried significantly less weight. Invoking a god or gods by name in a curse significantly upped the rhetorical ante: perhaps the gods didn't or wouldn't support the curse in question; in such cases, perhaps the curse could even rebound upon the one who uttered it. Without any mention of the gods, cursing was considerably less fraught—the ancient equivalent, maybe, of letting off steam.[75]

---

also, and as a result, interpretations of the psalm must similarly resist attributing to the psalm (or God) sentiments that are simply not present therein.

72. The Targum's rendering of Ps 137 offers further proof that the Hebrew original is somehow underwrought on this matter as it specifies divine agents, making the speaker of v. 7 "Michael the prince of Jerusalem," and the speaker of vv. 8–9 "Gabriel the prince of Zion." See David M. Stec, *The Targum of Psalms: Translated with Critical Introduction, Apparatus, and Notes*, Aramaic Bible 16 (Collegeville, MN: Liturgical Press, 2004), 231, for these and other innovative aspects of the targumic rendition. According to Gillingham, "this raises this cry of vengeance to a supernatural level. The curse on the enemy comes not only from the people but from angelic beings as well" ("Psalm 137," 67). In *Midrash Tehillim*, God, too, is involved in the weeping of the exiles and in their self-curse (see Braude, *Midrash on Psalms*, 2:334–35). For other ways God may be involved in (as) the praying of Ps 137, see Kit Barker, "Divine Illocutions in Psalm 137: A Critique of Nicholas Wolterstorff's 'Second Hermeneutic,'" *TynBul* 60 (2009): 1–14; and, further, Barker, *Imprecation as Divine Discourse*, esp. 158–79.

73. Once again, while Yhwh is mentioned in the verse about the Edomites, any "curse" proper is understated, if not altogether absent. See at notes 63–66 above.

74. The point is quite striking given the presence of the oath language earlier in the psalm, if not also the evocation of *lex talionis*. Such would lead one to expect a full-blown imprecation that includes mention of the Deity in v. 9, but that is precisely what the poet withholds. Cf. Goldingay, *Psalms 90–150*, 608: "The only curse in the psalm is the self-curse in vv. 5–6."

75. See Strawn, "Imprecation," 315–16, 317. For a thoughtful exploration of such dynamics,

3. Psalm 137's Reticence in Context

The reticence operative in Ps 137:7–9, and most especially in verses 8–9, can be cast into even sharper relief by additional counter-examples beyond the one from Ps 146:9 vis-à-vis Ps 1:6. After all, the active, even violent judgment of God is not infrequently encountered in the Psalms, even if that is not all of one piece.[76] Psalm 110 is just one instance, but an instructive one:

> The Lord is at your right hand;
>> he will shatter kings on the day of his wrath.
> He will execute judgment among the nations,
>> filling them with corpses;
> he will shatter heads
>> over the wide earth.
> He will drink from the stream by the path;
>> therefore he will lift up his head. (Ps 110:5–7 NRSV; cf. Ps 68:21 [22])

The poet of Ps 110, per Kinzie's axiom, presumably also fended some things off, left some things out, but one might well wonder (maybe even shudder) about what those things might have been! Psalm 110 is far more graphic than Ps 137, which tells us something about both poems.

Turning to extrabiblical material, one could consider the many and gruesome imprecations in various treaty texts that have been recovered from the ancient Near East. So, for example, consider the following passage from the seventh-century Neo-Assyrian treaty between Esarhaddon and Baal, the king of Tyre:

> [May Ninlil, who dwells in Nineveh, bind the flaming sword
>> to your side].
> [May] Ishtar, [who dwells in Arbela, not show] you [mercy
>> (and compassion].
> May Gula, the [great] woman physician, [put sickness (and) weari-
>> ness in] your [hearts], (and) an unhealing wound in your body.
> Bathe [in blood and pus as if in water].

see Melissa Mohr, *Holy Sh*t: A Brief History of Swearing* (Oxford: Oxford University Press, 2013), who writes: "Swearing is an important safety valve, allowing people to express negative emotions without resorting to physical violence. . . . Take away swearwords, and we are left with fists and guns."

76. I refer readers to Joel M. LeMon's forthcoming monograph on violence in the Psalms in light of ancient Near Eastern iconography.

> May the Pleiades, the heroic gods, establish your [devastation] with
>   their [fierce] weapons.
> May the deities Bethel and Anath-Bethel
> [hand you over] to the paws of a man-eating lion.
> May the great gods of heaven and earth, the gods of Assyria,
> the gods of Akkad, (and) the gods of Eber-nari, curse you with an
>   indissoluble curse.
> May Baal Shamaim, Baal Malage (and) Baal Saphon,
> let loose an evil wind against your ships, to undo their moorings,
> and tear out their mooring pole.
> May a strong wave sink them in the sea
> and a violent flood [rise] against you.
> May Melqart (and) Eshmun deliver your land to destruction
> (and) your people to deportation; may they [uproot] you from
>   your land,
> the food from your mouth, the cloak from your body,
> and the oil for your anointing may they take away.
> May Astarte break your bow in the thick of battle
> and make you sit beneath your enemy;
> may a foreign enemy divide your belongings.[77]

The genre here is different, of course, with treaties typically more legal and prosaic than a psalm, but regardless of that important distinction, "happy is the one who pays you back for what you did to us; happy is the one who seizes and smashes your children against the rock" sounds and feels quite different than the treaty— and not only because of the sheer scale and extent of the latter, also because of the content. And because of who expressed that content: the psalm was apparently spoken by an exiled and bereaved parent, while the treaty was uttered by the great Esarhaddon, son of Sennacherib, king of Assyria, and imposed on his vassal. Esarhaddon, it seems, felt little compulsion to leave *anything* out. So it is that Esarhaddon invokes the gods: *lots* of gods, *extensively*. In comparison, the poet of Ps 137 looks remarkably tight-lipped.

   In the end, then, attention to poetic movement and poetic reticence combine

---

77. Kenneth A. Kitchen and Paul J. N. Lawrence, "No. 93 Esarhaddon of Assyria and Baal, King of Tyre," in *Treaty, Law and Covenant in the Ancient Near East* (Wiesbaden: Harrassowitz, 2012), 1:957–62 (961–62). The text may also be found in *ANET*, 533–34 (E. Reiner); and Simo Parpola and Kazuko Watanabe, *Neo-Assyrian Treaties and Loyalty Oaths*, SAA 2, repr. ed. (Winona Lake, IN: Eisenbrauns, 2014), 24–27.

to increase our empathy with the poet responsible for Ps 137 and to offer us a better understanding of this psalmist's predicament and subsequent sentiment. At the very least, taking careful note of how the poem moves coupled with some awareness of what the psalmist appears to have fended off and left out means that so many cavalier and inexact characterizations of what transpires in Ps 137 must be soberly assessed and, to choose a verb not at random, strongly *resisted*.[78]

78. As examples of inaccurate assessments, consider Ahn, "Psalm 137": "The unfathomable plea to kill innocent children" (286), but there is, in fact, no such plea; "Yahweh . . . who is called upon (not only to remember but moreover) to do likewise. It is this retributive act and image of God dashing innocent children against the rock that immediately troubles us" (288), but God is not called upon to do such an act and neither is God imaged nor imagined as doing any such thing in this psalm. Levenson, "Horrifying Closing," 23, makes a similar mistake when he mentions "the deed for which the verse [v. 9] calls," but there is no "call" whatsoever in v. 9. Ahn's appeal to the antecedent of Yhwh's presence in v. 7 or to the relative pronoun in Pss 135:8, 10; 136:23 is simply not convincing (as also noted by Levenson, "Horrifying Closing," 32). By way of contrast, numerous resources can be found in the work of scholars like Miller, Davis, Nehrbass, Barker, Laurence, and others that allow us to deal appreciatively with the imprecatory psalms in meaningful and substantive ways. (So also, to his credit, Levenson, "Horrifying Closing.") For a profound reflection on retribution more generally, see Laura Blumfeld, *Revenge: A Story of Hope* (New York: Simon & Schuster, 2002). The subtitle is determinative. See also, recently, Timothy Troutner, "Bring Back the Imprecatory Psalms," *Church Life Journal*, August 11, 2021, https://churchlifejournal.nd.edu/articles/a-church-in-crisis-needs-the-imprecatory-psalms/, who speaks of the utility of these texts in the face of sex abuse scandals in the church.

6

Revisiting Elisha and the Bears: Can Modern Christians Read—That Is, *Pray*— the "Worst Texts" of the Old Testament?

The answer to the question: How am I to pray something that is still so incomprehensible to me? is: How are you to understand *what you have not yet prayed*? Rather than our own prayer being the standard for the psalm, it is rather the psalm that is the proper standard for our prayer.[1]

At the base of the problem ... is the privilege ... modern interpreters assert for themselves not only against their own contemporaries, but also, and more revealingly, against the very material that they are seeking to understand.[2]

My inner Origen is twitching.[3]

The Old Testament causes many people problems and not without good reason—or, rather, good *reasons* (plural). One such reason is that a decent

---

A version of this chapter was presented at Durham University in February 2021 for a group of doctoral students and faculty convened by Walter Moberly. I am thankful for the helpful feedback I received at that time.

1. Dietrich Bonhoeffer, "Lecture on Christ in the Psalms," in *Theological Education at Finkenwalde: 1935–1937*, trans. Douglas W. Stott, ed. H. Gaylon Barker and Mark S. Brocker, DBW 14 (Minneapolis: Fortress, 2013), 386–93 (387; emphasis original).

2. Jon D. Levenson, *The Hebrew Bible, the Old Testament, and Historical Criticism: Jews and Christians in Biblical Studies* (Louisville: Westminster John Knox, 1993), 114.

3. Walter Moberly, private communication (email on February 24, 2021).

number of texts cause a decent number of nice persons of faith (or no faith) real concern—"scandalize" would likely be the better verb—again for a number of reasons, most of which these days come down to violence, judgment, God's wrath, or some biblical instantiation of "premodern" ethics of one sort or the other. The list of these problematic texts is long, if not quite literally legion, but among the greatest hits—or, rather, among the worst of the lot—is 2 Kgs 2:23–25, the story of Elisha and the bears.[4] Given its brevity, I translate it in full here:

> Then he [Elisha], went up from there to Bethel. Now, he was going up on the road, but[5] some young boys came out from the city and mocked him. They said to him: "Go on up, Baldy! Go on up, Baldy!" He turned back behind him, saw them, and cursed them in Yhwh's name. And two she-bears[6] came out from the forest and ripped some of them to pieces: forty-two youths. He went from there to Mount Carmel, and from there he returned to Samaria.[7]

Short, yes, but brutal; this unit indubitably belongs on the list of troublemaking texts. Indeed, writes Choon-Leong Seow, "no other passage in the Elisha cycle has offended the moral sensibilities of readers more than the episode of the prophet's deadly curse of the youngsters for what seems like mischievous behavior."[8] Here is a dubious distinction if ever there was one, or perhaps better a well-deserved backhanded compliment!

But perhaps there is more to Elisha and the bears than meets the eye or that

---

4. Herbert Chanan Brichto, *Toward a Grammar of Biblical Poetics: Tales of the Prophets* (New York: Oxford University Press, 1992), 196: "possibly . . . the most embarrassing tale in the Bible."

5. Note the marked word order suggesting that the *waw* is likely adversative ("but") not conjunctive ("and"). Another option is that the young boys themselves are somehow being emphasized. See further below.

6. Note that *dubbîm* has a masculine plural ending, but the accompanying verbs are feminine plural, revealing the gender of the bears to be female.

7. Verse 25 is, in some ways, irrelevant to the story of the bears proper, but all of vv. 23–25 is separated off by means of *pǝtûḥôt* in the MT and so I include it here. For the use of this kind of sense divider, see, inter alia, Emanuel Tov, *Textual Criticism of the Hebrew Bible*, 3rd ed. (Minneapolis: Fortress, 2012), 48–49; and Ernst Würthwein, *The Text of the Old Testament: An Introduction to the Biblia Hebraica*, 3rd ed., rev. and exp. by Alexander Achilles Fischer (Grand Rapids: Eerdmans, 2014), 31–32.

8. Choon-Leong Seow, "The First and Second Books of Kings: Introduction, Commentary, and Reflections," in *The New Interpreter's Bible*, ed. Leander E. Keck et al. (Nashville: Abingdon, 1999), 3:179. Cf. Terence E. Fretheim, *First and Second Kings*, Westminster Bible Companion (Louisville: Westminster John Knox, 1999), 139: the story "seems designed to make a point by pushing the edges of reason and good sense."

offends the sensibilities. In what follows, I will first overview some typical assessments of this passage as found in some commentaries on Kings (§1). This overview is not exhaustive by any means but representative nevertheless. What is most striking about the treatments I collect is their almost total *in*ability to assess this text in anything but the most negative way. I will next summarize some of the main tenets of *lectio divina* according to Mariano Magrassi's stunning book on the subject (§2).[9] This summary must also be brief because the subject is a vast one, and Magrassi's book is equally rich. For now, and speaking generally, *lectio divina* may be defined as a type of spiritual reading of Scripture that focuses on the text as (among other things) a word of personal address to the reader, eventuating in their benefit and salutary transformation.[10] This passage about Elisha, the boys, and the bears would seem to pose a particularly difficult case for that kind of reading, especially in light of the assessments in §1. But, inspired by Magrassi's approach that seeks to include the best of exegetical method within the practice of *lectio*, the next section of the chapter (§3) attends to some of the textual details that seem crucial, not just for interpretation of this unit, but also, in terms of *lectio*, for proper meditation, prayer, and contemplation (*meditatio, oratio, contemplatio*) on and of it.[11] The goal here is not to "solve" the problems presented by (or in) this passage by finding some secret key by which to baptize it; the goal, instead, is to see how the exegetical details might contribute to the *spiritual reading* of this text, which is to say the process of *praying* this text. For Christians, the latter practice is far more important than a simple "reading for information." In the penultimate section, I will return to the commentary literature for insights that might provide a more excellent way than the ones reviewed earlier (§4). Walter Brueggemann's commentary on Kings is a particularly noteworthy example of such,[12] instantiating—or so it seems to me—many of the insights present in Magrassi's work. In this part of the chapter, and throughout, I hope to demonstrate that, yes, it is indeed possible for modern Christians to read (that is, *pray*) the worst texts of the Old Testament, including even the story of Elisha and the bears, and I attempt

9. Mariano Magrassi, *Praying the Bible: An Introduction to* Lectio Divina (Collegeville, MN: Liturgical Press, 1998).

10. According to Eugene H. Peterson, "Spiritual Reading (*Lectio Divina*)," in *Dictionary of Christian Spirituality*, ed. Glen G. Scorgie et al. (Grand Rapids: Zondervan, 2011), 768: "The term *spiritual* in 'spiritual reading' has to do with the way we read the biblical text, not just the text that we are reading. Spiritual means that we read with our spirits participating in the spirit of the text."

11. See Peterson, "Spiritual Reading," 768, for these four elements taken from Guigo the Second (twelfth century CE).

12. Walter Brueggemann, *1 & 2 Kings*, SHBC (Macon, GA: Smyth & Helwys, 2000).

that very thing before I close with some conclusions. The present probe may be instructive, therefore, with any and all other texts that occasion concern or alarm. The praying of "easier" texts should, by way of comparison but also as a matter of course, be similarly productive.

1. Review of Negative (Modern) Opinions

According to Marvin Sweeney, "interpreters treat [2 Kings 2] vv. 23–24 as a typical example of a prophetic legend that relates a miraculous act by Elisha or as a grandmother's tale that promotes respect for elders."[13] While perhaps a bit insensitive to grandmothers who often know exactly what they are talking about (!), Sweeney's remark seems fairly accurate in terms of the commentary literature on 2 Kings 2.[14] In light of the widespread similarity of modern scholars' generally negative or dismissive takes on the passage, it will suffice to cite just a few works with only brief remarks.[15]

James A. Montgomery and Henry Snyder Gehman's volume in the highly technical and respected International Critical Commentary series is one example of what Sweeney had in mind with his reference to a grandmother's tale.[16] Montgomery and Gehman speak of the "awful penalty on the little boys who mocked the prophet. The story reads like a *Bubenmärchen* [fairy tale] to frighten the young into respect for their reverend elders."[17] Apart from this remark, however, Montgomery and Gehman are rather tight-lipped about the episode.

---

13. Marvin A. Sweeney, *I & II Kings: A Commentary*, OTL (Louisville: Westminster John Knox, 2007), 275. Cf. Robert L. Cohn, *2 Kings*, Berit Olam (Collegeville, MN: Liturgical Press, 2000), 17: "Whether or not the bad boys of Beth-el got what was coming to them, the tale engenders in the reader a healthy respect for the authority of Elijah's successor."

14. Sweeney himself knows the text is about more than this: "Certainly, the mauling of forty-two boys for their taunts against the prophet points to him as a powerful man with whom no one should trifle. But respect for elders hardly exhausts the literary function of this brief narrative" (*I & II Kings*, 275). Even so, Sweeney's evaluation of "its specific function in the immediate literary context" is ultimately a bit flat: "It is placed here to validate Elisha's role as Elijah's prophetic successor by demonstrating that Elijah's powers have passed to Elisha" (Sweeney, 275; so similarly many others, e.g., Fretheim, *First and Second Kings*, 138). That is certainly correct but hardly tells us all we'd like to know.

15. In what follows I focus mostly on mid-range commentaries as these are the ones that purportedly address interpretive matters in more holistic and helpful fashion, esp. for religious practitioners. Technical commentaries, therefore, are not discussed extensively with a few notable exceptions. Perhaps surprisingly (perhaps not), these latter types, despite the fact that they are typically longer, are usually even more devoid of theological "help" when it comes to Elisha and the bears than are more concise treatments.

16. See Sweeney, *I & II Kings*, 275n20.

17. James A. Montgomery, *A Critical and Exegetical Commentary on the Books of Kings*, ed.

The same cannot be said of John Gray in the second edition of his well-known Old Testament Library commentary on Kings. His opening remarks are worth quoting in full: "This is in every respect a puerile tale, and serves as gauge of the moral level of the . . . communities from which the strictly hagiographical matter in the Elisha cycle emanated. . . . There is no serious point in this incident, and it does not reflect much to the credit of the prophet. It is difficult to regard it otherwise than as, at the best, the memory of some catastrophe which happened to coincide with Elisha's visit to Bethel and was turned to account by the local . . . community to awe their children."[18] Both the general sentiment and the specific terms employed make clear Gray's opinion of this story. "At best" it is a "memory of some catastrophe," which perhaps wasn't originally about the prophet at all—it just "happened to coincide" with his visit, after all—but was put to hegemonic purposes by primitive, unruly (if not immoral) people so as to scare their kids. That said, Gray doesn't let Elisha (or the narrator, at least) off the hook completely: the story *is* a smear on the prophet's credibility, Gray asserts, and he goes on to state that "the supposition that Elisha invoked the name of Yhwh to curse the boys, with such terrible consequences, is derogatory to the great public figure, and borders on blasphemy."[19] The exact relationship between the curse itself and the "terrible consequences" that follow it will be examined in greater detail below. Here it is enough to note that Gray finds the whole matter extremely distasteful for an important prophet like Elisha, and, if that weren't bad enough, he thinks it comes very close to *religious transgression*: blasphemy. Unfortunately, Gray does not clarify the nature of this blasphemy charge. Is it because he thinks Elisha is using Yhwh's name tritely, in some sort of violation of the Second Commandment? That is an intriguing possibility, though what follows the curse—*if* it is directly connected—may suggest that it isn't blasphemy at all; it appears, instead, to have *worked*.

For present purposes, the commentary by Gina Hens-Piazza is most interesting. A key passage is worth citing in full: "Taken by itself, this is a strange and disturbing

---

Henry Snyder Gehman, ICC (Edinburgh: T&T Clark, 1951), 355; they go on to speak of "the unfortunate children" (356). Cf. Richard D. Nelson, *First and Second Kings*, Interpretation (Louisville: John Knox, 1987), 157: "Perhaps the reader was once told bogeyman stories like verses 23–24: Be good or Elisha will get you!" See further Burke O. Long, *2 Kings*, FOTL 10 (Grand Rapids: Eerdmans, 1991), 35.

18. John Gray, *I & II Kings: A Commentary*, 2nd rev. ed., OTL (Philadelphia: Westminster, 1970), 479.

19. Gray, *I & II Kings*, 480. It is not clear to me why Gray calls the invocation-for-purpose-of-cursing a "supposition" when the text indicates as much quite plainly. Perhaps this is just a turn of phrase; alternatively, Gray may want to impute the curse → mauling connection to the author(s) of the text and/or the communities behind it rather than grant that it "really" happened somehow or was intended by Elisha.

story....The curse that results in such a harsh punishment is utterly disproportionate to the misbehavior.... Shouting an insult to the Lord's prophet approaches hurling an insult at the Lord. Such behavior warrants immediate chastisement. However, the outcome of the prophet's pronouncement is still difficult to endorse.... The prophet's condemnation of the youth promotes a violence that we cannot ignore or simply explain away in order to absolve Elisha. Overexuberance in one's early ministry unaccompanied by self-criticism can do more harm than good."[20] Several things are worth observing here. First and foremost, it is a question of great significance to wonder if this "strange and disturbing story" can (or should) be "taken by itself." What, precisely, does "taken by itself" *mean*? Is it even (or ever) possible to take a story "by itself," devoid of other things like, say, literary context and readerly dispositions, to name only two rather obvious and important items? It is also not clear—at least not from Hens-Piazza's exegesis—if the punishment is, in fact, disproportionate to the misbehavior.[21] She asserts this inequity but does not argue for it, neither does she demonstrate it. Before we can agree, we would need to know more about the specifics of the punishment and of the misbehavior—and, most important of all, of their interconnection.[22] Now, Hens-Piazza's assumption of a close relationship between the prophet and the Lord, such that insulting one "approaches" insulting the other, seems likely correct to me; still further, such a connection would, or so she reasonably asserts, warrant the "immediate chastisement" of which she speaks. But this remark by Hens-Piazza is something of an aside, or is at least penultimate, since her ultimate judgment is that the story is "difficult to endorse." Unfortunately, what "endorsement" might mean or entail is left unspecified.

Similarly vague in Hens-Piazza's treatment is how the prophet's condemnation of the youths "promotes . . . violence," or—even if it did do such a thing (granting for the moment that it *does* or *can* or *might*)—why such promotion could *not* be ignored or explained away. In point of fact and in direct contradiction to Hens-Piazza's assertion otherwise, it seems most readers of the Bible are perfectly happy to ignore this passage (and many others like it) with regularity if not impunity, which refutes that part, at least, of her claim, even if the part about explaining it away lingers a while longer.

What, next, of Hens-Piazza's comment about "absolving" Elisha? Here, as is common in so much commentary literature, the relationship between the

---

20. Gina Hens-Piazza, *1–2 Kings*, AOTC (Nashville: Abingdon, 2006), 237.

21. Cf. Cohn, *2 Kings*, 17: "Their repeated taunt . . . hardly seems enough to warrant Elisha's curse"; and David Marcus, *From Balaam to Jonah: Anti-prophetic Satire in the Hebrew Bible*, BJS 301 (Atlanta: Scholars, 1995), 43: "seemingly out of all proportion to the provocation" (see also Marcus, 51, 65).

22. These details are not discussed by Hens-Piazza in her commentary.

prophet's curse and the action of the she-bears is *simply assumed* even though it is *not* explicitly stated by the text itself (see §3 below). As a result of this assumption, Hens-Piazza appears to hold Elisha personally responsible for the punishment, but we should pause at exactly this point because that is generally *not* how curses worked in the ancient world—and certainly not curses uttered in the name of a deity.[23] Curses without mention of any gods were apparently equivalent to "blowing off steam."[24] Curses that invoked the name of a god were a good bit more serious and were not to be done lightly (see, e.g., the second commandment) as the deity in question may not appreciate having his or her name being so "used." The curse could, in such cases, redound against the utterer, leaving the intended object untouched, but the oath-taker him- or herself seriously damaged. Another important point is that the (high) gods were rarely if ever beholden to do what a human being said, even if the human used a god's name.[25] Still further, if the imprecatory action did come about—especially in the case of supernatural activity (surely a well-timed bear-mauling must count as such if anything ever could)— then that action was ultimately *the Deity's doing*, not the speaker's. All of that is to say that, if there is any "absolving" to be done in this text, it will need to be an absolution *of Yhwh*, not his servant Elisha.

What is perhaps most striking about Hens-Piazza's interpretation, however, is the attitude of superiority it strikes, not only vis-à-vis the text, but also vis-à-vis the prophet.[26] Elisha is apparently "overexuberant" without an appropriate dose of "self-criticism." Again, in her own words: "When [Elisha] responds to [the children], it is the Lord whose power he manifests. At the same time, he appears as a rather unrestrained defender of the Lord. In his assessment, boys who would mock a prophet of the Lord have no respect for the Lord. The prophet's pronouncement results in a very disquieting punishment. The man, who was shrouded with fear and uncertainty, has begun the long and arduous journey of discerning the Lord's will. Like most beginners in ministry, he has much to learn

23. For what follows, see Strawn, "Imprecation," in *Dictionary of the Old Testament: Wisdom, Poetry and Writings*, ed. Tremper Longman III and Peter Enns (Downers Grove, IL: IVP Academic, 2008), 314–20, and the literature cited there. A more recent and thorough treatment may be found in Anne Marie Kitz, *Cursed Are You! The Phenomenology of Cursing in Cuneiform and Hebrew Texts* (Winona Lake, IN: Eisenbrauns, 2014).

24. See Strawn, "Imprecation," 315–17.

25. See, e.g., J. J. M. Roberts, "Divine Freedom and Cultic Manipulation in Israel and Mesopotamia," in Roberts, *The Bible and the Ancient Near East: Collected Essays* (Winona Lake, IN: Eisenbrauns, 2002), 72–82.

26. Hens-Piazza is not alone; see, e.g., B. Long, *2 Kings*, 33: "Elisha is . . . a bad-tempered wizard who strikes immediately at those who belittle him."

before he will be recognized as an accomplished agent of that plan."[27] The exegesis here does not seem entirely airtight. Where in 2 Kgs 2:23–25 do we hear of Elisha's "assessment" of the boys? The text says only that he turned ($\sqrt{pnh}$) and looked at ($\sqrt{r'h}$) the boys; it gives no indication of Elisha's interior thought processes or if he deemed mockery of himself equivalent to disrespecting Yhwh.[28] We also have no clear sense of the relationship between the pronouncement and the punishment, despite Hens-Piazza's use of the verb "results," which suggests close if not immediate causation. It is the final two sentences of the citation above, however, that go furthest beyond the text itself. Indeed, these two sentences are no longer attempts at understanding the passage in question—not, at least in the etymological sense of that word as "standing under" the text—but rather stand in judgment *over* it. Elisha is painted as a mere "beginner in ministry" with a "long and arduous journey" ahead of him.[29] Hopefully, in the end, he will be able to discern the Lord's will! The clear implication, however, is that, here, in this specific instance with the youths, he does not. Poor Elisha, he should have known better! Maybe he will learn some things by the end of his ministry. At this point, alas, he is still early in the process—full of "growing edges"—and so (once again, and not surprisingly) is plagued by "overexuberance" without sufficient "self-criticism." No wonder he did "more harm than good"! If only Elisha had had a biblical scholar there to help him along. Hens-Piazza herself, perhaps, or maybe Gray? Things might have been different for him, not to mention for those poor young boys!

Now, I do not mean by my line of argument (or my perhaps too-sharp prose) to imply that literary characters do not develop; they most surely do, or at least they *can*. I wish merely to make the point that Hens-Piazza's ultimate judgment on this text is just that: a judgment—and a judgment that is, upon closer inspection, based far less on the details of the text than on her own assessment of the text and how it sounds to us nowadays. Hens-Piazza is not especially guilty at this juncture; she is, after all, hardly alone in this opinion. Gray, Montgomery and Gehman, and many, many others—whether professional biblical scholars or lay readers—line up with her and agree wholeheartedly.[30] And yet, despite

---

27. Hens-Piazza, *1–2 Kings*, 239.

28. Hebrew narrative is typically spare on such matters. See generally Robert Alter, *The Art of Biblical Narrative*, rev. ed. (New York: Basic Books, 2011), 143–62. Cf. Long, *2 Kings*, 33, who rightly speaks of 2 Kgs 2:23–25's "compact expressivity."

29. Note Cohn, *2 Kings*, 17, who writes of "the fledgling prophet." Cf. also Marcus, *From Balaam to Jonah*, 43–65, who attempts an interpretation of 2 Kgs 2:23–25 as anti-Elisha satire. Marcus's overall case is unconvincing in my judgment, despite the presence of some literary features in the account that are also well attested in satire.

30. E.g., Seow, "First and Second Books of Kings," 178–79: "The incident . . . is not so savory. . . .

her protestations against "explaining" this text away, it seems that Hens-Piazza's painting of Elisha's curse as a "rookie mistake" is in fact nothing less than a way to make this difficult story palatable to contemporary sensibilities by chastening if not censoring it altogether. Even that doesn't "absolve Elisha"—not completely, at any rate—but it is definitely on the road toward such a goal, and it is hard not to see that move as, at root, apologetic in some way. But, as I've already noted, there is no necessary nor immediate act-consequence relationship in the ancient world between a curse and its enactment. The Lord didn't *need* to nor did the Lord *have* to send the bears just because Elisha said so. Indeed, Elisha himself didn't say anything about any bears![31] All Elisha did, according to the text, was to curse the youths *bǝ-šēm Yhwh*, which could be (little more than?) the ancient equivalent of saying something like "Goddammit" or "Goddamn you."[32] Still further, the text doesn't say that it is *Yhwh* who sent these bears, even though most interpreters assume that to be the case.[33] If that assumption is correct, then in the case of 2 Kgs 2, it isn't Elisha, "shrouded with fear and uncertainty," who must travel "the long and arduous journey of discerning the Lord's will"—presumably a kinder, less violent version. No, it would be *Yhwh himself* who must make that journey. Then again, the text seems remarkably tight-lipped about who sent (or *didn't*, as the case may be) the two she-bears in the first place.

2. *The Practice of* Lectio Divina

So far, then, we have observed two important items: (1) readers have a hard time with Elisha and the bears; and (2) interpreters' problems with this text and their (non-)"solutions" to the same often come at the expense of close attention to the details of the account itself. The latter item—interpretive problems and solutions—seems to emerge, not entirely from the text itself, but from assumptions

---

Elisha's harsh reaction to the seemingly innocuous taunt seems horribly out of proportion.... Elisha's response seems vindictive, petty, and morally unjustifiable"; and Volkmar Fritz, *1 & 2 Kings: A Continental Commentary*, trans. Anselm Hagedorn (Minneapolis: Augsburg Fortress, 2003), 239: the curse "is effectively out of proportion."

31. Kitz, *Cursed Are You!* 191, is revealing at this point: "Elisha's pronounced malediction can be *reconstructed* according to the form that emphasizes the permissive will of the importuned deity: 'May Yahweh let two bears slaughter you' or 'Let two bears slaughter you'" (emphasis added). There is absolutely no certainty that the reconstructed portions she posits are accurate in the case of 2 Kgs 2:24 since they are, of course, *entirely absent* from this particular instance of cursing. If anything, that is, the text as it stands tells *against* Kitz's speculative reconstruction.

32. An intriguing treatment of curse language may be found in Mohr, *Holy Sh*t.*

33. E.g., Kitz, *Cursed Are You!* 191: "*Presumably* Yahweh discharges the two female bears who eliminate some of the offensive instigators" (emphasis added).

about it, from contemporary sensibilities about various matters, and/or from filling in those places (gaps) where the text is unclear. If that is correct, it is cause to be concerned about, maybe even distrustful of, any number of prior interpretations. But the first item—about reading in general—mustn't be neglected at this point because it isn't just professional exegesis that hangs on attention to detail(s). According to Magrassi, the art of "sacred reading" known as *lectio divina* also depends heavily on fine points of the text. "Serious study," he writes, is "a genuine tool of spiritual research," and "can be of greatest service to *lectio divina*. Jerome insisted on this by his words and the example of his life, in which learning and contemplation were so harmoniously allied. Criticism is at the service of fervent piety. Meditation, that most faithful companion, is always found alongside knowledge of Hebrew."[34] Well, one at least hopes that is the case! But one may also worry about that, too, not least in light of the previous discussion. I will consider some details of the Hebrew text momentarily (§3), but first some orientation to *lectio divina* is in order—especially in concert with exegesis, which is exactly how Magrassi would have it.

Lectio divina, "prayed reading,"[35] is an ancient practice that has enjoyed a resurgence of popularity in some spirituality circles of late, especially in connection with spiritual direction. A host of works exist that introduce or discuss the subject,[36] but what follows centers on Magrassi's *Praying the Bible* (1998), not only because it is something of a contemporary classic on the subject, but also because it is less concerned with specific steps by which one "does" *lectio divina* (e.g., setting a context with candles, quiet, incense, etc.) than it is with showing the venerable nature of the practice, its dependence on crucial readerly dispositions, and its beneficial outcomes.[37]

Already on the first page of *Praying the Bible*, in an anonymously authored "To the Reader," the main problems facing a contemporary reception of difficult

34. Magrassi, *Praying the Bible*, 72.

35. Magrassi, *Praying the Bible*, 18.

36. See, inter alia, Carl McColman, *The Big Book of Christian Mysticism: The Essential Guide to Contemplative Spirituality* (Charlottesville, VA: Hampton Roads, 2010), 187–97; Peterson, "Spiritual Reading," 768–69; and Peterson, *Eat This Book: A Conversation in the Art of Spiritual Reading* (Grand Rapids: Eerdmans, 2006), esp. 81–117. It is worth noting, and is rather telling, that neither *The Oxford Dictionary of the Christian Church*, 3rd ed., ed. F. L. Cross and E. A. Livingstone (Oxford: Oxford University Press, 1997), nor the *Dictionary of Biblical Interpretation*, ed. John H. Hayes (Nashville: Abingdon, 1999), contains entries on "Lectio divina" or "spiritual reading." For a spiritual reading of the entire Bible, see Jean Corbon, *Path to Freedom: Christian Experiences and the Bible* (Cincinnati: St. Anthony Messenger, 2004). I thank Stephen B. Chapman for bringing this volume to my attention.

37. Subsequent citations of Magrassi, *Praying the Bible*, will be parenthetical in the body.

texts like 2 Kgs 2:23–25 are frankly acknowledged. "Today's advances in biblical studies have become increasingly known even to non-specialists," this preface reads, which "enable us to adhere to the literal sense, careful to situate the sacred texts in their original historical-religious context" (vii). But "the very fact that we have these things makes our situation ambiguous. Either we become enclosed in our self-sufficiency or we open ourselves to communion. . . . [Magrassi's] book can be appreciated only by one who feels the limits of our present knowledge and the urgent need to incorporate it into a broader spiritual synthesis" (vii).

Lectio divina shouldn't be imagined as somehow perfect or foolproof in this endeavor; even so, its goal is to create a "'biblical person' from the spiritual and mental fibers impregnated with words, images, and reminiscences of the sacred text" (viii). *Lectio* accomplishes this act of creation because it is a "personal continuation of liturgical hearing of the Word" and a highly regular one at that: "For the Fathers and monks there is no Christian life or Christian prayer that is not nourished daily—and in a certain sense exclusively—on Sacred Scripture" (viii).

Magrassi's book proceeds to develop these insights and many others. He begins with the relationship of *lectio divina* to Christian worship. "Only the presence of Christ prevents the Word from becoming a purely historical document," he writes (3). The ecclesial hearing of Scripture is thus primary but that "does not mean that everything is reduced to liturgy" (4). Indeed, the liturgy "will always give us no more than biblical fragments" and the Lectionary, too, "does not give us the whole Bible" (5).[38] So, while the monks were "practically living concordances . . . we, unfortunately, are far from this!" (5). The solution is to supplement the short readings of the liturgy with "a longer, private reading," by which "the 'short reading' regains its full meaning" (6).

But it isn't just *how much* Scripture is read—a matter of breadth; instead, it is first and foremost *how* it is read—a matter of depth. "Vital hearing requires loving, calm, reflective, personal poring over the text," Magrassi asserts (6). Here is where *lectio divina* offers a way to go deeper and to "personalize" the text beyond the confines of but still in concert with Christian worship: "It is not enough to eat; we must assimilate, or as the ancients would say, "ruminate." Thus *lectio sacra* is the natural complement of ecclesial proclamation. There the soul digs deeper and deeper into the riches of an inexhaustible text" (7). This "going deeper becomes personalization," in part due to "a harmonious blend of . . . two elements. . . . God speaks not only to his people; he also addresses me personally" (7). Magrassi illus-

---

38. For an interesting remark on the "unreadability" of the lectionary, see Jonathan Z. Smith, *On Teaching Religion: Essays by Jonathan Z. Smith*, ed. Christopher I. Lehrich (Oxford: Oxford University Press, 2013), 34–35.

trates this point with reference to the revelations of St. Gertrude. When God spoke to St. Gertrude, the words she heard were "the same words he spoke in the liturgy," and when St. Gertrude wrote these experiences down, "her language is that of the Scripture texts from the day's liturgy" (8). Scripture is thus the Word of God that addresses us *and that also* becomes the words we say back to God in prayer.[39]

Magrassi is fully aware of the fact that contemporary readings of Scripture are often quite deficient, and in more than one way. By connecting contemporary Christian readers to the great spiritual reading practices of the past, he hopes "to inject new life into the more-or-less scientific dryness of our reading. For the latter is no longer able to transform itself into prayer and become direct nourishment for our spiritual life" (13). This transformation and subsequent nourishment mustn't be confused with simply adopting ancient allegorical interpretations. That would be like building "a Gothic church in the twentieth century" (13). But we do need to adopt the "faith vision and spiritual attitudes [of the ancients] in the presence of the Word" (13). Certain "chief values" must be reclaimed, Magrassi writes—namely,

> a living and coherent faith in the transcendence of God's Word; a sense of Scripture's infinite fruitfulness and inexhaustible riches; a deep admiration for the biblical world where beauty is a reflection of God's face and truth a foretaste of the vision toward which he is leading us; a profound sense of the unity of Scripture, so that everything is seen as a single, vast parabola, one great sacrament of the Christian realities; above all, a way to read it as a Word that is present and puts me in dialogue with the God who is living and present; an ease in translating reading into prayer and using it to shed light on questions of existence in order to model my life on it. . . . And if we do not reach their [ancient interpreters'] level of fervor, we will at least avoid turning our present aridity into theory. We will no longer believe that a little historical criticism plus the deliberate cautions of our methods are enough to enter into the mystery of a Word that is divine Act. (13)

Despite the pointedness of the last sentence, *lectio divina* is not anti-intellectual or anti-exegetical. Magrassi cites Paul Delatte approvingly: "*Lectio divina* is the organized totality of those progressive intellectual methods by which we make the things of God familiar to us and accustom ourselves to the contemplation of the in-

---

39. Magrassi speaks of the liturgy as the place where Scripture is understood *allegorically* and *anagogically*, whereas it is in personal reading that the *anthropological* dimension is especially pronounced (*Praying the Bible*, 8–9). For similar dynamics within the biblical Psalter, see Patrick D. Miller, *The Lord of the Psalms* (Louisville: Westminster John Knox, 2013).

visible."[40] Spiritual reading is not, therefore, some sort of *replacement exercise* but a *further, supplementary* one—or, better, a *synthetic* or *integrative* one—though the proper order of things is important: "The work of the attentive faculty must be placed alongside that of the intellect, and above them the light of faith which transforms both and allows the soul to enter the divine world" (19). One needs, that is, love and knowledge, knowledge and love—but faith above all else.

Faith is hard these days, Magrassi admits, and yet it remains indispensable: "If systematic application of scientific categories to the Bible—from literary genres to *Formgeschichte*—can yield valuable results, it can also weaken that living sense of the Word's transcendence. Of what use would be all our scientific tools if they destroyed the basic values? That would not be a step forward but a step backward. In the presence of divine realities (such as the Word) what counts most is faith. It alone can lead us into the mystery. Everything else matters only if it is part of this atmosphere and functions within it" (24). By now the general points should be clear. According to Magrassi, spiritual reading, which is related to Christian worship but takes place beyond it, in more personalized modes, is not opposed to the various methodologies practiced within biblical scholarship with one crucial proviso: that all of these latter are practiced with, in, and under faith.[41] If faith is present, any and all interpretive methods can be a real benefit, "of greatest service to *lectio divina*" (72). But if faith and the various readerly dispositions described above are absent . . . well, then, as Magrassi puts it: "knowledge that does not lead to love is vain" (72). Without the "chief values," all our scientific categories and studies do not strengthen but only weaken the "living sense of the Word's transcendence" (24). All of our great learning becomes "more-or-less scientific dryness" (13).[42] Rightly practiced, though, all can be and all will be well. In this fuller perspective, this larger and synthetic vision, "Exegesis is not technique; it is mysticism" (52). The late Eugene Peterson agrees: "Exegesis is not pedantry; it is an act of love. Exegesis is about loving God enough to slow down and get the

40. Paul Delatte, *Commentaire sur la Règle de Saint Benoît* (Paris: Librairie Plon, 1948), 348–49; cited in Magrassi, *Praying the Bible*, 18–19 with n. 20.

41. Cf. Peterson, "Spiritual Reading," 768, on *lectio* as "a way of reading that places us under the text as obedient listeners instead of over the text." As Justin Walker has reminded me (personal communication) there are resonances here between Magrassi's understanding of *lectio* and Karl Barth's famous essay, "The Strange New World within the Bible."

42. Cf. Magrassi, *Praying the Bible*, 73–74: "Study is concerned with scientific certitude; *lectio* wishes to nourish a spiritual experience. Study takes place on the objective and detached level of investigation; *lectio* takes place in the contemplative atmosphere of prayer. Professional exegetes strive to prescind from personal feelings. Spiritual persons approach the Bible like Bernard, with open mouth and heart. Fervent before they start to read, they read in order to become even more fervent. Their aim is not to construct a science, but wisdom, which is contemplative knowledge."

words right. Exegesis is a sustained act of humility."[43] And so, to return to Magrassi, "Reading, too, is prayer" (112). Or at least *it can be* and one hopes it might!

3. Exegetical Details Crucial for Mysticism

In light of Magrassi's insistence—widely shared by exegetes everywhere, but notable for its presence even in the less technical and non-"scientific" approach of *lectio divina*—that the exegetical details matter, and crucially so, it is worth returning to 2 Kgs 2:23–25. In what follows, I offer some observations about this text that seem rather important for any and all kinds of reading; in the case of spiritual reading, the exegetical details I explore may very well be on the way to Magrassian mysticism.

The account in 2 Kgs 2:23–25 is spare and laconic. It is a very short episode that serves to get Elisha from Jericho to, ultimately, Samaria. The geographically low location of Jericho explains why Elisha "goes up from there" (*wayya'al miššām*) but it doesn't explain why the verb √'lh should be repeated four times in this brief account. Elisha "goes up" from Jericho (v. 23a), and the incident takes place while "he is going up on the road" (*wəhû' 'ōleh badderek*; v. 23b). The youths' mockery employs the same verb, telling Elisha to "get on up," not once but twice (*'ălēh . . . 'ălēh*; v. 23c). The last time the root √'lh appeared was in 2 Kgs 2:11 when Elijah went up to heaven in the tempest (*wayya'al . . . bas'ārâ haššāmāyim*). Elisha is not going to heaven but he is going to or toward "God's house," Bethel (*bêt-'ēl*).[44] Perhaps his journey *upward* with a destination (in v. 23) at God's domicile evokes Elijah's own itinerary in more ways than one.

Elisha is accosted, however, by young lads (*nə'ārîm qəṭannîm*). The noun *na'ar* is notoriously unspecific insofar as it can refer to full-grown adults, not just the chronologically young,[45] so presumably the adjective *qāṭān* is present to make clear these are indeed boys—a point confirmed, or so it would seem, by the use of *yəlādîm* ("youths") in v. 24.[46] Regardless of their precise age(s), this is evidently

---

43. Peterson, "Spiritual Reading," 769.

44. To be sure, Bethel has something of a mixed reputation in the larger literary context. See Joel S. Burnett, "'Going Down' to Bethel: Elijah and Elisha in the Theological Geography of the Deuteronomistic History," *JBL* 129 (2010): 281–97, who argues that Bethel is "a special place of scorn" in the Deuteronomistic History (282).

45. See Strawn, "Jeremiah's In/Effective Plea: Another Look at נער in Jeremiah I 6," *VT* 55 (2005): 366–77. Brichto, *Toward a Grammar*, 198, thinks the term "may refer to a male from the age of eight to eighty."

46. So also, similarly, Marcus, *From Balaam to Jonah*, 49–50, though both *na'ar qāṭōn* and

a very large group of youths: no less than forty-two are listed as mauled by the bears, but the prepositional phrase used with that verb (*mēhem*) likely contains an instance of the partitive use of *min*, which would mean that forty-two of "(only) *some* of them" were attacked.[47] That would mean, in turn, that there were *more* than forty-two youths involved in the incident, though it is unclear how many more there might have been. If forty-two is (only) *some*, then the group could have been very large indeed. Whatever the imagined total, the size of the numbered group alone is considerable: more than forty-two vs. Elisha's one.

These youths come out from the city (*min-hā'îr*), but it isn't clear if they are blocking Elisha's entrance or chasing after him as he passes by (or through) it.[48] The text seems to tilt ever so slightly toward the latter option—the boys following him—since Elisha is said to have turned (√*pnh*) behind him (*'aḥărāyw*) to see them (*wayyir'ēm*).[49] Verse 25 has Elisha going "from there" (*miššām*) to Mt. Carmel "and from there" (*ûmiššām*) returning to Samaria, so that Bethel is, at best, a temporary stop, if he is imagined to stop there at all.

Whatever the details of Elisha's itinerary, the text states that the boys *insult* or *mock* (√*qls*) him—that is what they do first upon coming out of the city[50]—though

---

yeled can be used of older individuals (see 1 Kgs 3:7; 12:8). Burnett, "'Going Down' to Bethel," 297, deems these youths "not children but a group of young adult males connected with the royal sanctuary of Bethel." Cf. Brichto, *Toward a Grammar*, 198: "The mockers of Elisha were not young children, they were 'worthless oafs, hooligans, hoodlums.'" Brichto offers "some mean-spirited rascals" in his translation of the unit (Brichto, 198).

47. I owe this and several of the observations that follow to James K. Mead, "'Elisha Will Kill'? The Deuteronomistic Rhetoric of Life and Death in the Theology of the Elisha Narratives" (PhD diss., Princeton Theological Seminary, 1999), 112–14 (here 112n45), who offers a very fine rhetorical-critical reading of the passage. For the partitive *min* in 2 Kgs 2:24, see *DCHR* 2:247–48.

48. Cf. Fretheim, *First and Second Kings*, 139, who speculates as to motive: "apparently to keep him away from Bethel (because he might speak against the shrine there? See 1 Kings 12:28–33)." But see further note 54 below. Note that Marcus, *From Balaam to Jonah*, 52n39, 55–56, argues that the youths are actually from Jericho.

49. So also Mead, "'Elisha Will Kill'?" 113n49: "The narrator may, then, be hinting that Elisha was on his way out of the city and meant the group no harm."

50. But note the plus in LXX^L (and OL): the youths "came out of the city *and stoned him* [*kai elithazon*] and mocked him." This is a doublet according to Montgomery and Gehman, *Kings*, 357, but Mordechai Cogan and Hayim Tadmor, *II Kings: A New Translation with Introduction and Commentary*, AB 11 (New York: Doubleday, 1988), 38, are not sure if it is "a true doublet or rather an embellishment which sought to explain the prophet's outburst." Perhaps it is a simple mistake due to metathesis: √*sql* for √*qls* (so also Marcus, *From Balaam to Jonah*, 57n61). Another possible cause of confusion might be the root √*ql'*, "to sling," which is sometimes used with stones, as in Judg 20:16 and 1 Sam 17:49 (both times with *'eben*). Perhaps the "stoning" reading might be

the specific root that is used here appears rather infrequently.[51] The narrative goes on to state that the boys speak (√ʾmr) to the prophet. It isn't entirely clear that their reported speech is coterminous with the previously mentioned mockery, though that is a likely inference. But before we assume as much, we might note that the repetition of verb + indirect object marked with a preposition + third masculine singular suffix (wayyitqalləsû-bô ... wayyōʾmərû lô) might also (or instead) suggest that the boys' insults included *more* than just their reported speech. The narrator could have simply used lēʾmōr after all: wayyitqalləsû-bô lēʾmōr, "they mocked him, saying (or as follows): ..." Whatever the case, the boys say only two words to Elisha though each word is repeated twice: ʿălēh qērēʾ(a)ḥ ʿălēh qērēʾ(a)ḥ: "Go on up, Baldy! Go on up, Baldy."[52] As noted earlier, the text has already indicated that Elisha is *already* going up (twice no less), so the boys' use of ʿălēh hardly seems much of an insult, though, as Seow notes, we "cannot be certain if the imperative in Hebrew means 'Go away!' (NRSV), 'Go on up!' (NIV), or simply 'Go up!' (KJV)."[53] If Elisha is already past Bethel, which seems to be the case, then "go away" doesn't make much sense and, again, doesn't have much force as an insult.[54]

What, then, of the other word that the youths repeat: qērēʾ(a)ḥ, "Baldy"? As one who is himself "folliclely-challenged" I can sympathize with those interpretations that think this term mocks the prophet's hairdo—or lack thereof: the text is all too real at this point! But, as Lissa Wray Beal has observed, interpretations that focus on "male-pattern baldness" don't fully satisfy; they feel a bit thin, as it were (pun fully intended).[55] Are we really to imagine that the prophet is just a wee bit overly sensitive about a receding hairline? If so, interpretations like Hens-Piazza's are waiting in the wings. In my own judgment, however, the question to be explored is not *if* Elisha is bald, but *why* is he bald? There are at least three options:

---

seen as evocative of what might have happened to Elisha had the bears not come; in this case, the bears could be viewed as providing the prophet with something like a rear guard. I thank Douglas Earl and Alex Kirk for their comments on these points (personal communication).

51. But see the nominal forms in Jer 20:8; Pss 44:14; 79:4.

52. The second instance of "Baldy" is omitted in LXX, and at least one Heb MS omits the second verb + qērēʾ(a)ḥ (see Montgomery and Gehman, *Kings*, 357).

53. Seow, "First and Second Books of Kings," 178.

54. In Burnett's interpretation, the youths are calling "for the prophet to worship at Bethel" ("'Going Down' to Bethel," 297; cf. also Lissa M. Wray Beal, *1 & 2 Kings*, Apollos Old Testament Commentary 9 [Downers Grove, IL: InterVarsity, 2014], 306). For Marcus, "the effect of the taunt would be ... that Elisha should 'go up' to heaven just like his master, Elijah" (*From Balaam to Jonah*, 61). If ʿălēh is euphemistic for dying, then it *would* be a kind of insult. Then again, Elijah's "passing" is hardly despicable, and so Marcus's option could actually be interpreted as a compliment. That it is not a compliment is confirmed by √qls.

55. Wray Beal, *1 & 2 Kings*, 305–6.

The first is that Elisha could be bald because he *just was*, actually, bald.[56] (As the old joke goes: God created a few perfect heads; to the rest God gave hair.) Texts like Lev 13:40 demonstrate that baldness was not unheard of in ancient Israel; neither was baldness necessarily deemed some sort of (religious) deficiency: "If anyone loses the hair from his head, he is bald [*qērē(a)ḥ*] but he is clean" (NRSV).[57] Even so, Elisha's *lack* of hair might be contrasted with how hair is associated with Elijah. In 2 Kgs 1:8 Elijah is described as a *baʿal śēʿar*, "a master of hair," which is idiomatic to say the least. Perhaps the phrase means "owner of hair," which may not be much better in English (cf. NRSV: "a hairy man"), but, given the mention of a leather belt immediately after *baʿal śēʿar*, some translations have taken the phrase to refer to a hairy garment of some sort (so CEB: "He wore clothes made of hair"). In either scenario, Elijah is associated with hair, even *owning* it; his successor, however, is identified as *lacking* in that same department. Elisha's *qērē(a)ḥ* does not equate with a double portion of Elijah's *śēʿar*! Could the youths thus be mocking Elisha because he is no Elijah, at least in this particular way (if not yet still others)? Perhaps.[58] Does such mockery depend solely on account of hair (loss)? Maybe, but the connection to Elijah isn't explicit in the text and, despite the association of hairiness with strength (e.g., Samson) and/or religiosity (e.g., Nazirites), this interpretation dissatisfies. If nothing else, it figures Elisha as exceedingly sensitive about his outward appearance with his curse-response to the boys' jeering grossly disproportionate. Once again, there seems to have been nothing inherently wrong about being bald in ancient Israel, as Lev 13:40 attests. It is possible, of course, that the need to mention baldness in the context of Lev 13's discussion of scale disease somehow signals that baldness *was* somewhat unusual, but that, despite that fact, it shouldn't be confused with *ṣāraʿat*. For reasons such as this, one can find a number of scholars who have opined that baldness was, in fact, atypical after all. Montgomery and Gehman, for example, state that "Elisha was not an old man,

---

56. So Cogan and Tadmor, *II Kings*, 38: "Perhaps it was Elisha's extreme natural baldness that caught the attention of the rude youngsters of Beth-el." Fritz, *1 & 2 Kings*, 239, too, thinks of natural hair loss, not tonsure (on which, see further below). Marcus, *From Balaam to Jonah*, 57–58, is both confident and specific: "If he was bald, it must have been with premature baldness. But it is more likely that the children were making fun of the fact that Elisha was just a bit thin on top."

57. Cf. Brichto, *Toward a Grammar*, 197: "Baldness is a natural and common phenomenon, not reserved for the old or the middle-aged and unlikely to have been perceived as a mark of shame anymore then than today." But see further below.

58. This is the opinion, for example, of Marcus, *From Balaam to Jonah*, 60. But he goes on to note another possibility: antiphrastic use, in which a term is used in the opposite sense (e.g., calling an overweight person "Mr. Slim"). If this were the case, the boys would be calling Elisha "Baldy" when he is actually quite hairy and so there would be no contrast between Elisha and Elijah on this point.

and natural baldness is infrequent in the open life of the East."[59] If Montgomery and Gehman are correct, natural baldness would seem to be neither the only nor best option to explain why Elisha is $qērē(a)ḥ$; it is time to consider a second.

According to Gray, a stranger on a journey (as opposed to a servant or laborer) would most likely have worn a head covering. Elisha's baldness, therefore, is "a kind of tonsure as a mark of the separation of the prophet from the profane sphere of life to the service of God."[60] Gray goes on to say that "this was inferred by the boys, who knew Elisha as a prophet by his mantle, and were familiar with tonsure, since many of them were themselves the progeny of prophets of Bethel and all were familiar with the conventions of the large . . . community there."[61] How Gray knows all of this about the boys, their origin, their knowledge, and their powers of inference is not clear; it seems best *not* to infer similarly, though the idea of prophetic tonsure is an interesting one. Writing much earlier than Gray, Montgomery and Gehman find it "suggestive," and trace the notion back to an even earlier essay by Bernhard Stade published in 1894.[62] Writing more than a century after Stade, Sweeney calls the tonsure notion "intriguing" and notes that head-shaving is sometimes associated with mourning for the dead.[63]

This latter point leads to a third option (unmentioned by Sweeney) for interpreting Elisha's baldness—namely, that it is not a sign of androgenetic alopecia, caused in turn by sensitivity to dihydrotestosterone, nor a sign of prophetic status (tonsure), but, rather, *a sign of his mourning the passing of Elijah.*[64] While this is not

---

59. Montgomery and Gehman, *Kings*, 355 (I do not know what they mean by "open life" here).

60. Gray, *I & II Kings*, 480; also Brichto, *Toward a Grammar*, 197–98. Cogan and Tadmor, *II Kings*, 38, think the tonsure idea has "little to support the suggestion. . . . Lengthy hair, rather than close shaving of the head, was an accepted feature of asceticism as is reflected in the Nazirite law in Num 6:5." See Marcus, *From Balaam to Jonah*, 59 and n. 67 for the Talmudic stricture that bald men are prohibited from being priests.

61. Gray, *I & II Kings*, 480.

62. See Montgomery and Gehman, *Kings*, 355.

63. Sweeney, *I & II Kings*, 275. See, e.g., Lev 21:5; Deut 14:1; Isa 15:2; Jer 7:29; 16:6; 48:37; Ezek 5; 7:18; 27:31; Amos 8:10; Micah 1:16; Job 1:20; and, further, Susan Niditch, *"My Brother Esau Is a Hairy Man": Hair and Identity in Ancient Israel* (Oxford: Oxford University Press, 2008), 99–106. Sweeney also notes the personal name (PN) Korah ("bald") which is "applied to a class of Levitical psalms (Pss 42; 44–49; 84; 85; 87; 88), and . . . is the name of the patriarch of a Levitical clan. . . . The name also appears in Edomite genealogies. . . . Such associations suggest that baldness may be the mark of a holy man, who perhaps is associated with the Transjordanian region" (Sweeney, *I & II Kings*, 275). For parts north, one might note the presentation of a bald Katamuwa (no hair extends beyond his hat) in the stela known by this royal official's name. See Eudora Struble and Virginia Rimmer Herrmann, "An Eternal Feast at Sam'al: The New Iron Age Mortuary Stele from Zincirli in Context," *BASOR* 356 (2009): 15–49 (esp. 22).

64. For more on shaving as a mourning rite, see Niditch, *"My Brother Esau,"* esp. 100–101;

his preferred interpretation, Fritz allows for it: "One could argue that Elisha had cut off his hair lamenting Elijah's departure."[65] This third option sees in the youths' mockery not ridiculing of Elisha's hairline per se, but of his mourning over the loss of his master, none less than the great prophet Elijah.[66] If this is accurate, the youths are disparaging *Elisha's grief* and, as an adjunct, are scorning the departed Elijah as well.[67] Perhaps they, too, like Ahab thought of Elijah as nothing more than a "troubler of Israel" (1 Kgs 18:17). Now that sounds like something that would draw the ire of Elijah's successor, who is apparently just making his way, sorrowfully, minding his own business on his way to Carmel (!), the very spot where Elijah had his greatest success against 450 prophets of Baal and 400 prophets of Asherah.

These three options for understanding Elisha's baldness are all lively ones, though in my judgment the few details the text provides lean toward the second or third, even if only ever so slightly.

In what happens next we are not told that Elisha *heard* the youths, only that he turned behind him and saw them. Then he cursed them *bə-šēm Yhwh*. Then come the bears: two she-bears (*dubbîm*) emerge from the forest and maul forty-two of these youths. As already noted, this figure of forty-two youths appears to be only *some* of them (*mēhem*) and so others are imagined to have gotten away unscathed or at least unmauled. This makes perfect sense: who wouldn't run if they saw two bears coming at them? This commonsense scenario leads to an exegetical question, however: How could two bears maul forty-two people? Didn't these forty-two also flee for their lives when they saw the bears coming? The oddity of the imagined scenario leads one to suspect that the number forty-two is hyperbolic

and Saul M. Olyan, "The Biblical Prohibition of the Mourning Rites of Shaving and Laceration: Several Proposals," in *"A Wise and Discerning Mind": Essays in Honor of Burke O. Long*, ed. Saul M. Olyan and Robert C. Culley, BJS 325 (Providence, RI: Brown Judaic Studies, 2000), 181–89.

65. Fritz, *1 & 2 Kings*, 239. Cogan and Tadmor, however, note that "the ritual cutting of hair is prohibited in Lev 19:24, 21:5" (*II Kings*, 38).

66. Keith Bodner, *Elisha's Profile in the Book of Kings: The Double Agent* (Oxford: Oxford University Press, 2013), 57, speaks of the irony of the insult to Elisha's head after he had lost his own "head," his master Elijah (see 2 Kgs 1:8; 2:3).

67. If one reconsiders *qrḥ* in unvocalized form, it is possible to read it, not as an adjective, but as a masculine singular imperative: *qĕrō(a)ḥ*, "shave!" (cf. Mic 1:16 which attests the feminine singular imperative *qorḥî*). An imperative might make the boys' insult even sharper: "Go on! Shave! Go on! Shave!" encouraging Elisha not only to go on his way but also to shave his hair, perhaps because of Elijah's "passing." Such an option is speculative, of course—it is not reflected in the Versions, for example. Further support of the revocalization might be found if the MT's adjectival form could be seen as secondary: the result of vowel harmonization with *ʿălēh*. Then again, the euphony presently found in MT, *ʿălēh qērē(a)ḥ*, might be seen as a sign of its originality.

if not also symbolic in some way.[68] Or is it that the mauling here must be seen as somehow *non*lethal because if the bears had stopped for any period of time on

---

68. Gray, *I & II Kings*, 480, takes forty-two as proof that the passage is "part of a prophetic saga rather than strict history." He goes on to posit that two was added to forty, "the conventional indefinite number in Semitic folk-lore," in order to "give the impression of accuracy" (Gray, 480; cf. 556, where Gray speaks of forty-two as "apparently at home in legend . . . and myth"). Montgomery and Gehman, *Kings*, 356, think forty-two "adds realism to the story; but for the figure as one of ill omen *cf.* 10[14], and Rev. 11[2], 13[5]" (cf. Montgomery and Gehman, 409, where they state that the number is "possibly round," an opinion shared by Cogan and Tadmor, *II Kings*, 114, who also wonder if forty-two simply expresses "a large number . . . common to the story-telling of that period" [Cogan and Tadmore, 38]). Sweeney, *I & II Kings*, 275, also refers to 2 Kgs 10:12–14 saying that the story about the boys and the bears "recalls the account of Jehu's slaughter of forty-two kinsmen of Ahaziah at Beth Eked." It seems "foreshadows" would be a better verb than "recalls." Of forty-two, Fritz says only that it is "a figure associated with death elsewhere too" (*1 & 2 Kings*, 240; n. 4 there cites Johannes Herrmann, "Die Zahl zweiundvierzig im AT," *OLZ* 13 [1910]: 150–52). In Rev 11:2 and 13:5 the number is *temporal*: forty-two months, and so in these passages the figure is likely nothing more than a designation (albeit symbolic) for three and a half years, with the use in the Apocalypse therefore unrelated to 2 Kgs 2:23–25 (see, e.g., Craig R. Koester, *Revelation: A New Translation with Introduction and Commentary*, AYBC 38A [New Haven: Yale University Press, 2014], 486–87, 572–73).

Trips into numerology/gematria are the ultimate rabbit hole: a quick Google search revealed that "Google" itself in Hebrew characters totals forty-two, which (on this site) was then correlated with Douglas Adams's satirical use of forty-two as the answer to "the Ultimate Question of Life, the Universe, and Everything" in his well-known Hitchhiker's Guide to the Galaxy book series (the ultimate question itself is "what do you get if you multiply six by nine?"). My own sense is that, as evocative as numerological connections are (the Google one notwithstanding), they are unlikely to do heavy lifting in narratives that are non-apocalyptic or non-eschatological. Then again there is at least some reason to suspect the number forty-two is odd in 2 Kgs 2:24, and Fretheim devotes an excursus to "On Symbolic Narrative" in conjunction with this part of Kings (*First and Second Kings*, 139–41). In my judgment, the following possibilities are listed from most reasonable to most speculative with regard to the number forty-two:

- foreshadowing of 2 Kgs 10:14 (cf. Montgomery and Gehman; Sweeney);
- use of a number normally used for a complete totality (forty) with two more added for good measure ("completeness plus," as it were)—perhaps for a sense of realism (cf. Gray; Cogan and Tadmor) or because the total number is only some of the youths (partitive *min*);
- a link to the forty-two stages of wilderness wanderings recounted in Num 33—perhaps connecting the youths of 2 Kings with the disobedient generation who wandered (?); or
- a numerological play on 7 x 6, the former being the so-called "perfect" number and the latter archetypally deficient—the forty-two youths are therefore somehow completely disobedient.

I note, finally, Burnett's statement that forty-two "figures regularly in the Hebrew Bible and the ancient Near East as a symbolic number of potential blessing or curse, confirming that the disaster was the result neither of a natural coincidence nor the prophet's own caprice but of divine

any one victim "to rip them to pieces" (√*bq'*, *piel*),[69] even more youths would have had time to escape.[70] This suggests that √*bq'*, too, might be hyperbolic or symbolic in some way. If so, ought we to understand that perhaps even the victims of this frightening encounter with two she-bears also escaped with their lives?[71] Or does the text mean to communicate the exact opposite: should we imagine that if the curse is disproportionate, so also is the power—and speed!—of these she-bears? Once again: *only two* of them but *forty-two youths*!

There is more to consider here. The youths are said to have "come out from the city" and the bears are reported to have "come out from the forest." The constructions are highly similar as also are the sounds of each: *yāṣə'û min-hā'îr* (v. 23), *watēṣe'nâ... min-hayya'ar* (v. 24). Is this euphony a sign of word-play?[72] If so, what would be its significance? Beyond (obviously and naturally) referring to these entities' respective abodes, do these constructions aurally capture a sense of poetic justice?

At this point we have reached the true crux of the text, or at least modern consternation over it: the relationship of Elisha's cursing in the name of Yhwh

---

intent" (Burnett, "'Going Down' to Bethel," 296). See further Joel S. Burnett, "A Plea for David and Zion: The Elohistic Psalter as a Psalm Collection for the Temple's Restoration," in *Diachronic and Synchronic—Reading the Psalms in Real Time: Proceedings of the Baylor Symposium on the Book of Psalms*, ed. Joel S. Burnett et al., LHBOTS 488 (New York: T&T Clark, 2007), 95–113, esp. 105–12.

69. Cf. Mead, "'Elisha Will Kill'?," 113, who believes that √*bq' piel* is "almost surely a lethal wound" (citing 2 Kgs 8:12; 15:16; Hos 13:8; cf. also BDB 131–32; DCHR 2:247–48). But perhaps not (see the citation of Mead in note 71 below), in which case √*bq' piel*, which can mean "split" (see Gen 22:3; 1 Sam 6:14), could connote something like "scatter" or "break apart" forty-two from the larger group. I thank Walter Moberly for discussing this point with me.

70. So also Marcus, *From Balaam to Jonah*, 53–54 with n. 49. Cf. Brichto, *Toward a Grammar*, 197, who comments at some length on the "incongruous" nature of the scene: "Either dozens of children standing fixed in place, waiting as if paralyzed to be struck down, or—if they took to flight—the two bears methodically pursuing them for the sheer lust of killing. And what was Elisha doing all the while—directing them to head off the few who seemed about to escape?" This is just one aspect that Brichto finds odd in the account; such oddities are often what led ancient interpreters to assume that a different kind of reading—a deeper, spiritual one—was in order.

71. Mead rightly notes that the narrator does not make use of √*mwt* in the passage: "In Jericho, death was obliterated by Elisha's oracle when the characters had not stated it as a problem; in Bethel, where fatalities were likely, the narrator avoids the word" ("'Elisha Will Kill'?" 113). See note 69.

72. Cf. Long, *2 Kings*, 33, who notes how "the narrative achieves a sense of artful play in the telling and of gravity in the tale." For more on literary design, see Marcus, *From Balaam to Jonah*, 61–65. Wray Beal understands such purposeful shaping as proof that "the narratives are theologically informed writing" (*1 & 2 Kings*, 307). The presence of word-play may explain the presence of "forest" in the first place—a detail that many interpreters have struggled to identify: which forest exactly? A later rabbinic saying derives from this story: *lō' dubbîm wəlō' ya'ar*, "no she-bears and no forest"; it is used to describe something that is entirely fabricated (see Marcus, *From Balaam to Jonah*, 47–48).

to the bears coming out of the forest. Much hangs on the *waw*-conjunction on *watēṣeʾnâ* ("and came out . . ."). Seow's remark provides an entry: "Elisha curses them . . . *whereupon* two female bears appear. . . ."[73] Seow's use of "whereupon" may be simply temporal, but it may also suggest causation, which is, in fact, how most interpreters have read the relationship of the two clauses: Elisha's curse *results in*, *leads to*, or otherwise *somehow causes* the mauling. So, for example, Cogan and Tadmor state that Elisha "drives off" these youths "with a curse, potent enough to cut down forty-two of their number."[74] In their reading Elisha's curse scatters the pack of insolent young men by design and they are hardly alone in offering such a directly causal interpretation.[75] But is that interpretation secure?

It is difficult to say. There can be no doubt that v. 24 begins with a *waw*-consecutive (*wayyiqtōl*) with Elisha as the subject, which is followed by another *waw*-consecutive, also with Elisha as the subject, and then yet another *waw*-consecutive, also with Elisha as the subject:

> and he turned (*wayyipen*)
> and he saw them (*wayyirʾēm*)
> and he cursed them . . . (*wayqallēm*)

This string of verbs must be seen as temporally sequential: he turned, *at which point* (or: *then*) he saw, *at which point* (or: *then*) he cursed. Sequentiality, however, is not necessarily the same as consequentiality.

The very next verb is also a *waw*-consecutive (*watēṣeʾnâ*) but the subject has changed: now it is the two she-bears. Does their action come after "he turned, he saw, he cursed"? It must; hence the use of *wayyiqtōl*. But how is this latest *waw*-consecutive with new subject(s) related to the prior sequence, especially the last verb about cursing? The grammar does not answer that question exactly. Sequentiality, yes, but consequentiality—causation, that is—perhaps not.

Now to be sure, the timing of the bears is fortuitous—for Elisha, at least. He is being pursued by no less than forty-two insolent youths who are mocking him, if not more than just that, and if not also jeering more than just him.[76] Perhaps he not only turned and saw (*wayyirʾēm*) this mob coming after him (*ʾaḥărāyw*), perhaps he turned and was "afraid of them"—if, that is, one repoints the consonantal

---

73. Seow, "First and Second Books of Kings," 178 (emphasis added).

74. Cogan and Tadmor, *II Kings*, 39.

75. E.g., Fritz, *1 & 2 Kings*, 239: "Elisha's curse *brings death* upon the boys jeering at him" (emphasis added); B. Long, *2 Kings*, 33: "*As though propelled* by the words, bears fall upon the boys" (emphasis added); Peter J. Leithart, *1 & 2 Kings* (Grand Rapids: Brazos, 2006), 176: Elisha "can *call out bears* from the forest as readily as Elijah can call out fire from heaven" (emphasis added).

76. See above, at notes 50, 64–65, 67.

text as *wayyīrā'ēm.[77] The timing is quite un-fortuitous for the youths; it is, instead, quite deleterious. But what the text *does not* say is as important to observe as what it does say. What the text leaves unsaid is the specific content of Elisha's "curse" (√qll piel),[78] which stands in sharp contrast to what the boys say not once, but twice (if they do not also add much more besides that; see above). It would have been perfectly possible for Elisha to have said "I curse you in the LORD's name" and left it at that. Whatever the case, Elisha himself does not explicitly mention bears; the bears just come. This fact is absolutely crucial: the bears just come, on their own, or so it would seem, since they are the subject of the verb watēṣe'nâ.[79] *Elisha does not summon them, neither does the text say Yhwh brought them.*[80] The bears just emerge from the forest.[81] The timing of all this is, once again, quite fortuitous for Elisha, but precise causation and origin of what is transpiring is left unsaid. This is important to note because the text could have put it otherwise—far

77. Full (*plene*) orthography of this word would require writing the *yod* twice (*wyyr'm* > *wayîrā'ēm*), which would disambiguate it from *wyr'm* (from √r'h), but defective writing is not uncommon with the verb √yr' (see, e.g., 1 Sam 18:12; 21:13; 28:5, 20; 2 Sam 6:9; Jer 26:21; 2 Chr 20:3; plural forms: Deut 17:13; 19:20; 21:21; Mic 7:17; with suffix: 1 Kgs 8:40), even if the specific form posited in the repointing above is not attested elsewhere. Cf. Mead's general assessment of the scene's mood: "With more than forty lads, it is difficult to say that Elisha did not perceive some danger. In any case, the text does not make an issue of Elisha's safety. Maybe he is in mortal danger; maybe not" ("'Elisha Will Kill'?" 114n53).

78. In the *qal*, the verb means to be small, insignificant, light, or trivial. The *piel* can have declarative or factitive sense: Elisha somehow *judged* the youths trivial, lightweight, or contemptible, or somehow *made* them such "in Yhwh's name." In so doing, Elisha treats these "little youths" as even smaller. Both declarative and factitive possibilities are worth pondering, though they may be functionally identical (see *HALOT* 3:1104). Note the use of the D stem (*piel*) of √qll in various cognates like Akkadian (*qullulu*) "to make insignificant, have scant regard for"; and Mandaic "to belittle" (*HALOT* 3:1103). The verb √'rr, which may be a slightly stronger term for the act of cursing, is not found in 2 Kgs 2:23–25. Brichto, who wrote a standard monograph on curse in the Hebrew Bible (*The Problem of "Curse" in the Hebrew Bible*, SBLMS 13 [Philadelphia: Society of Biblical Literature and Exegesis, 1963]), thinks that √qll in 2 Kgs 2:24 "may mean only upbraid" (*Toward a Grammar*, 198).

79. The arrival of the bears in v. 24 is syntactically different from Elisha's initial encounter with the youths in v. 23, which is twice presented with marked syntax, with the subject fronted before the verbal element: first, in terms of Elisha's going up (*wəhû' 'ōlēh*), and then when the youths come out of the city (*ûnə'ārîm qəṭannîm yāṣə'û*). The lack of similar markedness with the bears may lend further support to their simple arrival; there is no particle of attention (*hinnēh*), for example, or other means by which the narrator might have signaled an unexpected development. (I am grateful to Walter Moberly for his comments on this point.)

80. One might contrast at this point 2 Kgs 17:25, which explicitly notes Yhwh sending lions against the resettled inhabitants of Samaria.

81. As Richard Briggs and Alex Kirk have pointed out to me (oral communication), the bears might be a further sign of the somewhat out of control world represented in Kings.

more explicitly and far more directly, as exemplified in one of Anne Marie Kitz's reconstructions: "May Yahweh let two bears slaughter you." [82]

Among commentators, Brueggemann has seen the text's reticence with regard to causation best: "Notice how elliptical is the statement. There is a curse, and then there are bears. The narrative does not explicitly connect the two, thus adding to the inscrutability of the prophetic claim."[83] Exactly right! Brueggemann continues: "The incident puts Israel on notice. This Elisha is dangerous and is not to be trifled with, not by small boys, not by kings, not by anybody, for he has the spirit of Elijah."[84] These latter remarks, too, are no doubt correct, but they do not follow immediately or necessarily from the earlier comments on the ellipticalness of the passage. In other words, it may not be Elisha that is dangerous, but *the God of Elisha*. Such a judgment is nothing new, of course; Elijah's ministry made the same point abundantly clear. But then again: "Notice how elliptical is the statement." Insofar as the narrative "does not explicitly connect" the curse and the bears, nor God and the bears, the only thing that is dangerous for sure are *the two she-bears themselves*.

The text continues on, as does Elisha, who appears to survive this encounter relatively unfazed, despite √qls and qērē(a)ḥ. He proceeds on to Mt. Carmel, perhaps in homage to Elijah (especially after the taunting of his grief?), and then to Samaria, "where Elijah had his last stand against Ahaziah."[85] The text is once again terse. Seow's comments are suggestive but undeveloped, perhaps because the unit itself is the same: "Carmel . . . best known for the manifestation of the Lord's power over Baal . . . and then . . . Samaria, where the kings of Israel reign. These destinations signal to the reader that the prophet has truly taken up the mantle of his predecessor."[86] Fretheim, too, considers Elisha's journey symbolic: "In journeying to Mount Carmel and Samaria, Elisha visits familiar Elijah sites, returning finally to the burning center of both of their ministries."[87]

---

82. Kitz, *Cursed Are You!* 191 (cited also and more fully in note 31 above). One shouldn't ignore texts like Lam 3:10 or Hos 13:8, the latter of which figures Yhwh as a bear bereaved of cubs (kədōb šakkûl), which may suggest a close connection between the bears in 2 Kgs 2 and God. However, the Divine Bear in Hos 13 and Lam 3 is *one*, and 2 Kgs 2 explicitly identifies *two* bears, which may actually obviate too close of a connection between them and the Lord.

83. Brueggemann, *1 & 2 Kings*, 299. Cf. Fretheim, *First and Second Kings*, 140 (though this comment is not about 2 Kgs 2:23–25 specifically): "The narrator chooses not to 'explain' what occurs, or spell out the details, or even connect God closely with the wondrous events (only in v. 1 [of 2 Kgs 2] does the *narrator* explicitly make God the subject of what occurs)."

84. Brueggemann, *1 & 2 Kings*, 299.

85. Cohn, *2 Kings*, 17.

86. Seow, "First and Second Books of Kings," 178.

87. Fretheim, *First and Second Kings*, 139. Contrast Fritz's far less symbolic reading: "The

4. More Models to Follow: Ancient and Modern, Positive and Otherwise

Without wanting to appear too simple-minded about the situation—let alone appear cavalier about it—I nevertheless want to suggest that close attention to the exegetical details discussed above greatly problematizes many, if not most, expressions of modern dissatisfaction with 2 Kgs 2:23–25. Seow's general assessment is representative of the latter: "The episode of Elisha's cursing of the youngsters is challenging for anyone who comes to the Bible as Scripture."[88] While common, such a sentiment is, upon closer inspection, hardly necessary. There are quite a few instances of characters in the Bible cursing other characters (or things), and this holds true for none less than Jesus himself in the New Testament (Matt 11:21–24 // Luke 10:13–15; Matt 21:19 // Mark 11:14; see also Matt 23:13–36; Luke 23:28–31). Are these instances equally "challenging" for those who come to the Bible as Scripture? Perhaps that is true for some readers but for most the answer is probably not. Why, then, should Elisha and the bears be any different? If there is a difference, it likely stems from a latent and more general Marcionism, though it might also (or as a result) depend on two literary factors: the violence of the bears and the youth of the perpetrators. While the latter seems secure, especially given the use of both *yəlādîm* and *nəʿārîm*,[89] the mauling of the bears may not be nearly as straightforward as it seems. Be that as it may, Seow, a gifted interpreter, tries to redeem a worst-case scenario reading of the passage by saying that it "provides no paradigm of righteous conduct. . . . Ethics is not at issue. The point, rather, is a theological one."[90] I, for one, worry a bit about theological points that aren't much bothered with ethics or morality, but let such concerns pass for now. In support of his theological interpretation, Seow draws attention to the preceding episode in 2 Kgs 2:19–22 so as to arrive at "a dialectical understanding of the character of

---

detour over Mount Carmel is probably explained by the fact that this forested and mainly uninhabited mountain area was considered an attractive habitat by the early prophets, whose way of living on their own or in a community of followers put them outside the social order of Israel" (*1 & 2 Kings*, 240). Earlier, he writes that the text's "only presumption [!] is that there were bears in the central Palestinian mountains during the monarchy" (239).

88. Seow, "First and Second Books of Kings," 179.

89. But even this isn't beyond interpretive debate (see note 46 above). Whatever the case, note the remarks by Nelson, *First and Second Kings*, 161: "The ancient reader, untroubled by our post-industrial revolution apotheosis of childhood, doubtlessly found this a satisfying story. Those juvenile delinquents got exactly what they deserved! To insult God's prophet is to insult God"; and Brichto, *Toward a Grammar*, 198: "Our story is more in the comic vein than the tragic."

90. Seow, "First and Second Books of Kings," 179. Cf. Fretheim, *First and Second Kings*, 139: "The concern is not to discuss the morality of the prophet's action, but the nature of the prophetic task."

God. The sovereign deity is free to save and to punish, to bless and to curse, to give life and to take it away. . . . It is entirely up to God to bless or to curse." Such an understanding may be helpful to a degree, but perhaps only so far; it seems, at any rate, to be *only part* of what could and should be said about the text when it is read in the ancient practice of *lectio*.

Interestingly enough, ancient exegetes, like modern ones, also prove to be only partially useful.[91] This is because some of the less helpful interpretive moves made more recently are also found in antiquity. Ephrem the Syrian (306–373 CE), for example, opined that "the impudence of the children resulted from the teaching of their parents, because they were iniquitous and hostile to Elijah and all his disciples."[92] (How does one spell *Bubenmärchen* in Syriac?) St. Ephrem believes that the children

> did not only mention [Elisha's] baldness but also found further insults, which they said before him to outrage his fame, so that nobody might believe his word. . . . In fact, they had meditated on this evil thought and said, "This is the reason for his coming." Now, Elisha, even though he was upset by the effrontery of the children, was much more enraged by the craftiness and the iniquities of their parents, and he corrected both by a harsh and terrible sentence: he punished the former, so that they might not add to their iniquity by growing up to adulthood; the latter, so that they might be corrected and cease from wickedness.[93]

Much of this anticipates Gray's commentary (among others) by a millennium and a half. A little over a century after Ephrem, Caesarius of Arles (470–542 CE) wrote that "blessed Elisha was aroused with God's zeal to correct the people, rather than moved by unwholesome anger, when he permitted the Jewish children to be torn to pieces. His purpose was not revenge but their amendment, and in this fact, too,

---

91. C. T. Begg, "Kings," *DBI* 2:25–28, identifies the works by Ephrem (d. 373 CE) and Theodoret (d. 457 CE) as the only substantial interpretations of Kings from the patristic period. Begg also notes that while Ephrem's work "gives primary interest to an allegorical reading of Kings wherein the book's persons and events become symbolic foreshadowings of happenings in the life of Christ and of the church," in Theodoret's work, "allegorizing is virtually absent" (Begg, 25).

92. Ephrem, *On the Second Book of Kings* 2.20, cited in Marco Conti with Gianluca Pilara, eds., *1–2 Kings, 1–2 Chronicles, Ezra, Nehemiah, Esther*, ACCS 5 (Downers Grove, IL: InterVarsity, 2008), 149. Similar arguments involving the parents can be found in rabbinic literature (see Marcus, *From Balaam to Jonah*, 52 and n. 36).

93. Ephrem, *On the Second Book of Kings* 2.20, cited in Conti with Gianluca, *1–2 Kings*, 149.

the passion of our Lord and Savior was plainly prefigured. . . . What does 'Go up, you baldhead' mean except: Ascend the cross on the site of Calvary?"[94]

Caesarius's reading—no less than Ephrem's—doesn't satisfy because both his and the Syrian father's interpretations fail the standard of close evidentiary reasoning on the basis of the textual details as given.[95] That said, Magrassi would be perfectly fine with Caesarius's Christological move because Christological reading is a regular and important part of *lectio divina*. Magrassi is at pains to point out, however, that relating the text to God or Christ or the Spirit is *but one step* in *lectio*, and not the only one. Relating the text to the people of God is another, and relating the text to one's own self is a third (and last) move. Indeed, despite the importance of Christology, Magrassi points out that, even if Christians wish to say—as they so often do—that Scripture is "a Word that is summed up" in Christ, such a summary is "a short Word, a concise Word," even an "abridged" and "abbreviated" Word.[96] Magrassi is aware, in other words, of the reductive nature of Christological reading on its own, even within *lectio*.

While Christological readings are *permitted* within *lectio*, it is fair to say that the exegetical details of 2 Kgs 2:23–25 *do not require* such a reading in this instance.[97] We may turn, therefore, to ecclesiological and existential possibilities. Here again, Brueggemann's commentary is illuminating. He begins by noting a figural connection between the risen/ascended nature of Elijah and Christ, and how both of these figures will come again since they still have work to do (see Mal 4:5–6; Acts 1:11).[98] Until that happens, Elisha "is the focus of the narrative, as Israel continues to be dazzled and disrupted by him." Elisha is something of a surrogate, therefore, or "in between" replacement for Elijah/Christ. Brueggemann then draws a fascinating ecclesiological connection: "In parallel fashion, the book of Acts portrays the church responding to the departure of Jesus. The church is, in the meantime, to do its testimony and its mighty works. The church is situated like Elisha: Elisha has the spirit to do wonders. It is not different in Acts, a people propelled by God's Holy Spirit that is the spirit of Jesus."[99]

---

94. Caesarius, *Sermon* 127.2, cited in Conti with Pilara, *1–2 Kings*, 149.

95. Caesarius's interpretation disappoints in several other ways as well, esp. as he proceeds to anti-Jewish sentiments (see Conti with Pilara, *1–2 Kings*, 149–50). This latter move is at direct odds, it seems to me, with his earlier point that Elisha's purpose was "not revenge but . . . amendment."

96. Magrassi, *Praying the Bible*, 45 and n. 115.

97. For Christological readings as *permitted or allowed* but not *required or necessary*, see chapter 7 in the present volume.

98. Brueggemann, *1 & 2 Kings*, 302–4.

99. Brueggemann, *1 & 2 Kings*, 304.

After citing Acts 2:1–4, Brueggemann concludes in a highly evocative, almost staccato-like fashion: "None of this is explained. All of it is narrated and enacted. Elisha had detractors but the bears came against them. The early church had its detractors. The lions came. But the church persisted."[100] Then, after citing the end of Acts (28:30–31), he adds this line: "The story ends 'without hindrance.'"[101]

In this treatment, Brueggemann—who is himself a "living library" or "walking concordance"—has all of Christian Scripture somehow and simultaneously activated and so has no problem reading the church or Paul in Elisha's place.[102] In so doing, Elisha's curse is reframed and severely attenuated. We hear only that Elisha had his "detractors," but the bears came against them. The church, now seen as a corporate Elisha, also had its detractors, we learn—but no bears come against them; instead, it is the lions of the coliseum, those instruments of martyrdom. This is a profound switch—one not without Christological resonance—and yet the ends are similar: Elisha goes on his way and "the church persisted." "In the meantime," awaiting Elijah and the return of Christ, the church is "situated like Elisha"—opposed! detracted! mocked!—and so, as a result, "it is not different in Acts." Brueggemann's interpretation is a far cry from the postures of superiority struck by so many modern readers of 2 Kgs 2:23–25. In Brueggemann's treatment, one finds something drastically different. It turns out that Israel isn't the only one that "continues to be dazzled and disrupted" by the bald prophet. "It is no different" with Brueggemann, who proves to be equally dazzled and disrupted; following in his tracks, we see that it may also be no different with us.

For close to a decade now I have asked seminary students to practice *lectio divina* on 2 Kgs 2:23–25 as one of their assignments. They do not always like it; they do not always find it easy (quite to the contrary sometimes!). I have practiced *lectio divina* on the passage myself in concert with some doctoral students. The various *lectio*s vary, of course, with some more profound and insightful than others. I cannot even begin to categorize all of the readings I have seen, especially in brief compass, but, following Magrassi, it is clear to me that the exegetical details must play a central role in any spiritual reading that is rooted in the biblical text (and nowhere else), even as the practice of *lectio* keeps exegesis from being a matter of dry technique only, encouraging it to something more, something *mystical*.

100. Brueggemann, *1 & 2 Kings*, 304.

101. Brueggemann, *1 & 2 Kings*, 304.

102. Peterson, "Spiritual Reading," 769, would likely compare Brueggemann's practice here to *meditatio*, wherein one finds that "this world of biblical revelation is large; it is also coherent—everything is connected as in a living organism." There is profound resonance at this point with Jewish notions of the "literary simultaneity" of Scripture, for which see Levenson, *Hebrew Bible, the Old Testament, and Historical Criticism*, 62–81.

Here, then, is a personal attempt to do just that. I offer it with considerable trep-idation since in my experience the practice of *lectio*, unlike scholarly commentary, which strives for definitiveness, is highly episodic and subject to change the next time the text is read and the reader reads. Both entities, text and reader, have a way of changing, somehow, with the passage of time within the context of prayer.

I come to this text wanting to read it not in some detached fashion but eagerly, with full engagement. I know already that Elisha is a prophet, hand-picked by God and anointed by the great Elijah, so I watch his every move. He is a saint, after all, and one of the truly great ones; by definition, he is worth learning from, emulating.

He is heading upward, up to the very house of God and even further on, but something goes wrong. Youths, perhaps better yet, the brazen sins of youth—a vast horde of them it seems—arrest him on his way. They jeer him, seeking to distract him or perhaps yet worse still. But Elisha cannot be stopped! Look: he is already past them, he has to turn back to even see them. But they are intimidating and threatening. They mock him, everything about him that matters right now: his intended path, which retraces the steps of his master; and also his appearance, perhaps specific to him but perhaps much, much more—a physical sign of his grief for his great teacher Elijah, maybe, or an outward manifestation of his pro-phetic responsibility. The insults that come at him are many and also many-sided, therefore; they are also in the prime of their life, full of vigor. These are the kind of words that are impossible to ignore because they are so powerful and pointed. And so Elisha must turn and address them. But all he can do in the face of their quantity and force is respond with appeal to his only hope. "Where is the God of Elijah?" Elisha had asked earlier (2 Kgs 2:14). Now he has only to say the weighty name of Elijah's God, the Lord of Israel, Yhwh, and that alone, in and of itself, treats the mocking horde lightly, as altogether inconsequential (√qll). They and their comments are suddenly of no account, despite their power and quantity. Elisha has work to do. Divine work. He cannot be dissuaded from his path—and he is not dissuaded from it, despite this momentary but momentous interruption. He may not even know what happens next with the bears—that is all behind him, at his back; he leaves it all to God as he leaves it all behind. All that is certain is that Elisha is now back on his way, the way of obedience (cf. derek in 1 Kgs 2:2–4; 3:14; 8:25, 36, 58; 11:38), heading to Carmel, a place of respite, perhaps, but also of divine proving to Elijah and all Israel; then to Samaria, center of politics and religion, to do the work God has placed before him.

I am no prophet, nor the son of a prophet, but I can still situate myself with Elisha in my reading. Am I as single-minded as he in the work God has called me to do? Certainly not. Am I intimidated, stymied, and stopped up short by the sins of my youth or of others? Constantly. Do I fear or care overmuch about what those strong, jeering voices say about me and my vocation, often loud enough that others might overhear? All the time. Do I have the same sort of trust in the strong name of the Lord that Elisha had? Rarely. And what about this additional and difficult question: Do I dare curse in God's name? In truth, the answer to that question is probably yes, and likely too often, and not in the manner of Elisha, but only in my own *manner: cursing about and against those people or things that are in my own way, to my own displeasure,* not *which prohibit or frustrate the work and way of the God who calls. That situation raises even more profound questions: Do I even know my calling anymore? Am I pursuing it to the places it leads me, even if fraught with danger? I worry about the honest answers to both of those questions.*

These latter considerations suggest that I ought not, first and foremost, read myself in the place of the great prophet Elisha. Instead, it seems far better, far safer, and far more accurate to identify as one of the youths, quick to critique the called of God. Maybe I, like those youths, too frequently pose hindrance to, even withhold assistance from (are those the same?), the people who grieve on their way to God's house or travel to places of God's divine work, past and future. Maybe those bears will come for me. Maybe they are coming for me. Maybe they should *come for me. Will I survive the encounter? Perhaps I, too, will be split in pieces with only two legs or a piece of an ear left over from an all-too-close meeting with the Divine Bear (cf. Amos 5:19; Hos 13:8; Lam 3:10), the God who cannot be mocked (Gal 6:7). But maybe, just maybe, the worst, taunting, unhelpful, and unfaithful parts of me will be ripped away forever in the process. If only!*

My *lectio* could go on, but in short and in the end—and in sharpest contrast with Hens-Piazza's reading—it isn't Elisha who has a long and arduous journey ahead of him. *It's me.* And it isn't Elisha who is just beginning to figure out God's mysterious will as some sort of novice. *It's me.*[103] In the words of Gregory the Great

---

103. To further the contrast with Hens-Piazza, one might compare 2 Kgs 2:23–25 with Acts 5:1–11 (Ananias and Sapphira), which is structurally similar if not, in fact, more brutal in results. Peter, surely, is not portrayed as making a "rookie mistake" in this passage.

(d. 604 CE): "I will speak, I will speak! May the sword of God's word pass through me to pierce the heart of my neighbor! I will speak, I will speak! May I understand the word of God, even if it is against me!"[104] Or, in later but not so different words, from a poem by Hafiz (1315–1390 CE):

> Love wants to reach out and manhandle us,
> Break all our teacup talk of God. . . .
> Love sometimes gets tired of speaking sweetly
> And wants to rip to shreds
> All your erroneous notions of truth. . . .
> God wants to manhandle us,
> Lock us inside a tiny room with Himself
> And practice His dropkick.
> The Beloved sometimes wants
> To do us a great favor:
> Hold us upside down
> And shake all the nonsense out.
> But when we hear
> He is in such a "playful drunken mood"
> Most everyone I know
> Quickly packs their bags and hightails it
> Out of town.[105]

5. Conclusions

To return to the title of this chapter, can modern Christians read the most difficult—the so-called worst—biblical texts? Of course they can, provided they can stomach them for the duration of the experience. While modern readers often claim to find certain biblical texts distasteful, I suspect that this is not infrequently a case of protesting too much. If popular media is any indication, moderns have a very high tolerance for a vast number of (gross) *un*pleasantries.[106] Second Kings 2:23–25 is rather tame by comparison. But the titular question of

---

104. Gregory, *Homilies on Ezekiel* 11.1.5, cited in Magrassi, *Praying the Bible*, 101.

105. Hafiz, "Tired of Speaking Sweetly," widely available on the internet and, in print, in *The Gift: Poems by Hafiz the Great Sufi Master*, trans. Daniel Ladinsky (New York: Penguin Compass, 1999), 187–88. I am indebted to Mona Pineda for bringing this poem to my attention.

106. For some reflections, see Brent A. Strawn, "Projecting on Joshua: You Can't Worship Both God and Glock," in *God and Guns: The Bible against American Gun Culture*, ed. Christopher B. Hays and C. L. Crouch (Louisville: Westminster John Knox, 2021), 13–37.

this chapter is in truth a significant one, going beyond surface reading and initial impressions, whether disingenuous or otherwise. The deeper issue is if modern *Christians* can read, in a truly profound way, the most difficult of biblical passages. This is to ask, per Magrassi, not only about reading, but about *praying*: a kind of spiritual reading for formation and transformation, not just information. So: Can modern Christians read—that is, *pray*—the most troubling of biblical texts by means of *lectio divina* or some other habit of devotional attention? Here, too, the answer seems simple and straightforward: of course they can, if only because Christians *have done just that* for many thousands of years. Elisha and the bears may not be most contemporary readers' favorite Bible story but it hardly poses insurmountable difficulties, as I hope to have demonstrated above. And if that is true for this passage, which many modern readers—including well trained, world-class biblical scholars—deem so intractably off-putting, then other texts will be, as they say, "child's play."

At the end of the day, the problems with a text like 2 Kgs 2:23–25 (among others) would seem to have far less to do with this particular text than with its readers,[107] at least some of whom turn out to be, not theologians of the highest order, but "just" or "merely" exegetes *of a certain sort*: the most modern(ist) and mundane variety. Let me be clear that I do not intend this latter judgment as an *ad hominem* attack if only because in many corners of biblical interpretation it would be received not as an insult at all, but as the highest of compliments, especially after the triumph of objectivist, (quasi-)"scientific" (*wissenschaftlich*), historical-critical exegesis. This latter type of approach has become, in turn, the high point of the modern university's and (mainline) seminary's study of the Bible.[108] Alas, all of that appears in the end to be little more than *technique* that, by itself, can accomplish little to nothing for the soul of the Christian or for the larger world wherein Christians live and serve. Once again, exegesis of the highest theological order is precisely *not* technique, according to Magrassi—or, rather, not

---

107. Cf. the trenchant critique of R. W. L. Moberly, *The Bible in a Disenchanted Age: The Enduring Possibility of Christian Faith* (Grand Rapids: Baker Academic, 2018), 174: "How ... does one read a classic well? One regular assumption is that a work that has stood the test of time ... deserves a certain respect, a certain benefit of the doubt.... If countless others have found a book worthwhile, then if we don't—at least on first reading—it may be that the problem lies in us more than in the book. The person who reads Virgil's *Aeneid* or Shakespeare's *King Lear* and pronounces them to be 'rubbish' or 'mistaken' or even just 'boring' is likely to evoke reevaluation not of the *Aeneid* or *King Lear* but rather of their own quality of education and powers of judgment."

108. See further, among others, Michael C. Legaspi, *The Death of Scripture and the Rise of Biblical Studies* (Oxford: Oxford University Press, 2010).

only that—but is instead much, much more. It is nothing less than *mysticism. That* kind of approach, no less than historical-critical methodologies, can equally also be taught and learned, practiced well or not. That kind of approach, too, may have a great deal to teach more arid approaches, not least because it is obsessed with textual minutiae and how all of that contributes to larger webs of meaning and living. This larger, mystical approach begins, therefore, with Scripture itself and its morass of specific, sometimes off-putting and confusing details, but it ultimately depends on and ends with the listening heart.

> *Listen to this: obeying is better than sacrificing,*
> *paying attention is better than fat from rams.* (1 Sam 15:22 CEB)

PART 2

Biblical Theology

7

And These Three Are One: A Trinitarian Critique of Christological Approaches to the Old Testament

> Since the modern study of Old Testament theology developed, a great deal of discussion has been devoted to the question of what is the appropriate method for such a discipline. . . . The position I take is that . . . in so far as there are ultimate theological questions to be answered, about the Old Testament as about other matters, the resources for the answering of them within Christian theology must depend on the totality of theological insight and cannot be confined to an operation upon [only] the Old Testament.[1]

I am indebted to several individuals who read and discussed this chapter with me: Bill T. Arnold, Lewis Ayres, James K. Mead, Patrick D. Miller, and Christine Roy Yoder. Errors of fact or opinion that remain are my own and should not be attributed to these. I also acknowledge a grant from the Candler School of Theology, Emory University for the establishment of a one-year study group focused on "Toward Christian Reading(s) of the Old Testament" and my fellow participants in that study: Lewis Ayres (Emory), Carol A. Miles (Austin), and J. Ross Wagner (Princeton). Some of my thinking was worked out in this setting.

1. James Barr, *Old and New in Interpretation: A Study of the Two Testaments* (New York: Harper & Row, 1966), 167. Cf. Barr, *Old and New*, 168: "This kind of task, when properly examined, puts itself out of the reach of a branch of Old Testament scholarship and becomes an aspect of general Christian theology, working with the entirety of the Bible in its use of a biblical base. Such questions as, 'Where is revelation to be found?' cannot be answered from within any Old Testament study itself. But I do not think that they can be answered any more by taking a Christian theological point of view and then examining the Old Testament to see how it will turn out if this point of view is taken for granted or assumed." See further below.

These . . . considerations concerning the one and the many indicate that the way one thinks about God will decisively shape not only ecclesiology, but the entirety of Christian thought.[2]

In my opinion it is not Christian to want to take our thoughts and feelings too quickly and too directly from the New Testament.[3]

Christological approaches to the Old Testament are *ancient*, as early as the New Testament itself. The work of Donald Juel, among others, could be cited as proof of this point. In his book *Messianic Exegesis*, Juel argued that "the beginnings of Christian reflection can be traced to interpretations of Israel's Scriptures, and the major focus of that scriptural interpretation was Jesus, the crucified and risen Messiah."[4] Similar points have been argued both before and since, such that Juel's thesis, especially insofar as it bears on a christological approach to the Old Testament, could be repeated many times. But christological approaches are not only ancient, they are *formidable*. This is not due only to their antiquity and ubiquity. It is, instead, because in many of their "incarnations" (!), one gets the distinct impression that "the" christological approach is the only or at least the central, if not the ultimate, way to think about the Old Testament in a Christian manner. The descriptor *Christian*, after all, is based on the name Jesus Christ.

In reality, however, this formidable way of putting things—which I would like to term the "folk"[5] understanding of the christological approach—while rhetorically powerful, is not entirely accurate, primarily because "the" approach is not, in fact, singular, monolithic, or uniform. In the first place, the New Testament writers

2. Miroslav Volf, *After Our Likeness: The Church as the Image of the Trinity*, Sacra Doctrina (Grand Rapids: Eerdmans, 1998), 193.

3. Dietrich Bonhoeffer, *Letters and Papers from Prison*, enl. ed., ed. Eberhard Bethge (New York: Collier, 1972), 157.

4. Donald Juel, *Messianic Exegesis: Christological Interpretation of the Old Testament in Early Christianity* (Philadelphia: Fortress, 1992), 1. Cf. Wolfhart Pannenberg, "Problems in a Theology of (Only) the Old Testament," in *Problems in Biblical Theology: Essays in Honor of Rolf Knierim*, ed. Henry T. C. Sun and Keith L. Eades (Grand Rapids: Eerdmans, 1997), 276–77.

5. I mean by this term (and by setting it off with quotation marks) only that it is often used in popular, less precise, ways. I do not wish to imply that all christological readings are folksy or unsophisticated. Nor do I wish to give the impression that popular interpretations of issues are invariably wrong. Mostly, I wish to designate by this appellative a particular way of insisting on particular christological readings in lieu of all others. Note also the essay of Bill T. Arnold and David B. Weisberg, "A Centennial Review of Friedrich Delitzsch's 'Babel und Bibel' Lectures," *JBL* 121 (2002): 441–57, which has shown that problems in the "folk" approach are not limited to unsophisticated analyses. Even high-end academicians can fall prey to its worst possibilities.

themselves used the Old Testament materials in myriad ways—christological or messianic exegesis, while perhaps the most obvious and most important of these, is certainly not the only one. New Testament scholars like Juel and others have long noted this.[6] More to the point of the present chapter, however, it must be said that there is simply more to Christian theology than christology, as important as that is. Christian theology, regardless of its nominal (in the linguistic sense) origin in Jesus *Christ*, affirms faith in *the Triune God*. Despite that fact, at certain times in the history of the church the Trinity has received little emphasis. It is only in recent decades that Trinitarian theology has enjoyed a renaissance of theological interest and attention.[7]

In this chapter, I will argue that a thoroughly Trinitarian perspective of God necessarily involves a revisioning of christological interpretations of the Old Testament—at least as they are often construed and recounted in the "folk" understanding.[8] It should be said at the outset that my purpose here is not to establish the viability or cogency of Trinitarian theology *per se*. Nor do I wish to demonstrate the compatibility or generativity of a Trinitarian approach to the Old Testament or all of Scripture. Instead, I want to consider what difference it makes if one reads the Old Testament (and all of Scripture for that matter) with a theology that is Trinitarian in orientation and how that perspective may allow or disallow distinctively christological approaches. The last clause is quite intentional for, in my judgment, a Trinitarian perspective both permits and prohibits certain types of christological interpretation.

6. See esp. the work of Richard B. Hays, *Echoes of Scripture in the Letters of Paul* (New Haven: Yale University Press, 1989). Cf. also J. Ross Wagner, *Heralds of the Good News: Isaiah and Paul "In Concert" in the Letter to the Romans*, NTSup 101 (Leiden: Brill, 2002) and see further below.

7. See Elizabeth A. Johnson, "Trinity: To Let the Symbol Sing Again," *ThTo* 54 (1997): 303, who attributes the resurgence to the influence of Karl Barth and Karl Rahner. See E. Johnson, "Trinity," n. 9, for some important bibliography, including Jürgen Moltmann, *The Trinity and the Kingdom* (San Francisco: Harper & Row, 1981) and Catherine Mowry LaCugna, *God for Us: The Trinity and Christian Life* (San Francisco: HarperSanFrancisco, 1991). Add now Volf, *After Our Likeness*; Stephen T. Davis, Daniel Kendall, and Gerald O'Collins, eds., *The Trinity: An Interdisciplinary Symposium on the Trinity* (Oxford: Oxford University Press, 1999); Robert W. Jenson, *Systematic Theology*, 2 vols. (New York: Oxford University Press, 1997–2001); Samuel M. Powell, *Participating in God: Creation and Trinity*, Theology and the Sciences (Minneapolis: Fortress, 2003); and the other essays in *ThTo* 54 (October 1997): 293–380. A helpful collection of source material bearing on the Trinity can be found in William G. Rusch, *The Trinitarian Controversy*, Sources of Early Christian Thought (Philadelphia: Fortress, 1980).

8. An important issue that cannot be developed here but that must be noted is the relationship of modern christological approaches to christological readings from the early and medieval periods. One might well ask if these two types are coterminous or if, in fact, modern approaches are different in some fundamental and unhelpful ways.

One final comment: with a title that evokes 1 John 5:7–8 (the Johannine comma) and a subtitle that employs the terms "christological" and "Trinitarian," it is obvious that this chapter is an intra-Christian discussion. That being said, I still believe that the issues under discussion here have bearing on persons outside the Christian community—I think especially here of Jews and Jewish interpretation of the Tanak—if only regarding how Christians themselves view and perhaps ought to view others and their interpretations of the Old Testament/Hebrew Bible.

1. A Brief Primer of Christological Approaches

Before proceeding to Trinitarian theology proper, it is instructive to look briefly at some examples of christological approaches to Scripture and, particularly, the Old Testament. Again, while the christological approach is ancient—at least as old as the New Testament—in the last century the main theological proponents have been those who trace their heritage to Neo-Orthodoxy. Not surprisingly, then, Karl Barth looms large as one of the main examples, if not the architect, of modern christological approaches.

Barth placed consistent emphasis everywhere on Jesus Christ. George Hunsinger explains the centrality of Christ to Barth's project, citing from Barth's *Church Dogmatics*: "Jesus Christ is understood as the central content of its [the Gospel's] witness, for Jesus Christ is the name of the God who deals graciously with sinful humanity. 'To hear this is to hear the Bible—both as a whole and in each one of its separate parts. Not to hear this means *eo ipso* not to hear the Bible, neither as a whole, nor therefore in its parts.' The one thing said in the midst of everything, the center which organizes the whole, is 'just this: the name of Jesus Christ.'"[9] Barth again, this time *sans* Hunsinger: "All the concepts and ideas used in this report (God, humanity, world, eternity, time, even salvation, grace, transgression, atonement and any others) can derive their significance only from the bearer of this name and not the reverse. . . . They cannot say what has to be said with some meaning of their own or in some context of their own abstracted from this name. They can serve only to describe this name—the name of Jesus Christ."[10]

So pervasive and thoroughgoing is Barth's emphasis on Jesus Christ that he is sometimes accused of christomonism. I do not wish to support such an accusation

---

9. George Hunsinger, *How to Read Karl Barth: The Shape of His Theology* (New York: Oxford University Press, 1991), 59. The citations are from Karl Barth, *Church Dogmatics* I/2 (Edinburgh: T&T Clark, 1956), 720; cf. further Barth, *Church Dogmatics* I/2, 443; and note Hunsinger's conclusion on "Christ the Center" (*How to Read*, 225–33).

10. Karl Barth, *Church Dogmatics* IV/1 (Edinburgh: T&T Clark, 1956), 16–17; cited from Hunsinger's slightly revised translation (*How to Read*, 231).

here. Even so, as further evidence of his heavily christocentric approach one might note the wording of the Barmen Declaration (of which Barth was the main crafter) regarding the Confessing Church's opposition to Hitler and the Nazi movement: "Jesus Christ, as he is attested to us in Holy Scripture, is the one Word of God whom we have to hear, and whom we have to trust and obey in life and in death. We reject the false doctrine that the church could and should recognize as a source of its proclamation, beyond and besides this one Word of God, yet other events, powers, historic figures, and truths as God's revelation."[11] Here, exactly where one might have reasonably expected a statement about the unity of Scripture in its two Testaments and/or the continuity of Israel and Synagogue with the Church (or vice versa), the Declaration passes over such options in favor of a christological appeal.[12]

Barth's influence has been felt by many in the field of biblical studies, but it has been Brevard S. Childs who has most forcefully and eloquently continued Barth's legacy in the field of Old Testament.[13] Since Childs's writings are vast and deep, only a few representative citations can be given here. In his *Biblical Theology of the Old and New Testaments*, Childs writes: "Its [i.e., the church's] basic stance toward its canon was shaped by its christology. The authority assigned to the apostolic witnesses [the New Testament] derived from their unique testimony to the life, death, and resurrection of Jesus Christ. Similarly, *the Old Testament functioned as Christian scripture because it bore witness to Jesus Christ*. The scriptures of the Old and New Testament were authoritative in so far as they pointed to God's redemptive intervention for the world *in Jesus Christ*."[14] Later in the same book he states: "*Both testaments make a discrete witness to Jesus Christ* which must be heard, both separately and in concert. . . . As a result, a major task of Biblical Theology is to reflect on the whole Christian Bible with its two very different voices, *both of which the church confesses bear witness to Jesus Christ*. . . . Yet the challenge of Biblical Theology is to engage in the continual activity of theological reflection which . . . seeks to do justice to the witness of both testaments *in the light of its subject matter who is Jesus Christ*."[15] Other citations from this book, which is the culmination of

---

11. Clifford Green, ed., *Karl Barth: Theologian of Freedom*, The Making of Modern Theology (Minneapolis: Fortress, 1991), 149.

12. Daniel Jonah Goldhagen, *Hitler's Willing Executioners: Ordinary Germans and the Holocaust* (New York: Vintage Books, 1997), 113, 518n128, goes so far as to accuse Barth of anti-Semitism.

13. Childs cites Barth extensively in his writings, usually to positive effect, but note the passing criticism of Barth in Childs's *Old Testament Theology in a Canonical Context* (Philadelphia: Fortress, 1985), 4.

14. Brevard S. Childs, *Biblical Theology of the Old and New Testaments: Theological Reflection on the Christian Bible* (Minneapolis: Fortress, 1992), 64 (my emphases); see also 67–68, 74.

15. Childs, *Biblical Theology*, 78–79 (my emphases); cf. 67–68, 85–86, 452.

Childs's theological project, or from his earlier works could be added,[16] but these are sufficient both in content and complexity to guide the discussion.

Note, first, Childs's emphasis on christology in canon formation—not only for the New Testament where it is rather obvious but also for the Old Testament. Second, Childs claims repeatedly that what mattered most (and still does, one presumes) is how the Old Testament "bore witness to Jesus Christ." The Old Testament's authority or authoritative nature is contingent on its pointing to God's activity, not in the world in general or in Israel specifically, but "in Jesus Christ." Finally, there is the discussion of Scripture's "subject matter" (read: *Sache*!),[17] and the identification of that subject matter with Jesus Christ. More must be said about these positions below; for now, it is enough to note that Childs's debt to Barth at these points is both large and obvious.[18] To be fair, however, Childs's debt is not only to Barth but also to the Reformers, especially Luther and Calvin.[19]

It must be underscored that Barth and Childs, not to mention several others who could be adduced as proponents of a christological approach,[20] are subtle, sophisticated thinkers. Their work resists easy and hasty categorization. For instance, after Childs makes the bold claim that "it is a basic Christian confession

16. Cf. Childs's conclusion in his earlier *Introduction to the Old Testament as Scripture* (Philadelphia: Fortress, 1979), 671: "The Christian church confesses to find a witness to Jesus Christ in both the Old Testament and the New. . . . [T]he form of the Christian Bible as an Old and New Testament lays claim upon the whole scripture as the authoritative witness to God's purpose in Jesus Christ for the church and the world." See also Childs, *Old Testament Theology*, 8: Christianity's "relation to the Bible remains christologically conceived." Note also Childs's earlier discussion in his *Biblical Theology in Crisis* (Philadelphia: Westminster, 1970), 201–19.

17. Childs discusses Scripture's subject matter at several points, sometimes employing the term *Sache* or *Sachkritik* explicitly (*Biblical Theology*, 80–90, esp. 85; 721).

18. See James Barr, *The Concept of Biblical Theology: An Old Testament Perspective* (Minneapolis: Fortress, 1999), 401–12, for a treatment of Childs and Barth.

19. See Childs's discussion in *Biblical Theology*, 43–51; cf. Barr, *Concept*, 401.

20. One thinks of earlier works like Wilhelm Vischer's *The Witness of the Old Testament to Christ*, trans. A. B. Crabtree (London: Lutterworth, 1949). More recently, important thinkers who have weighed in on christology and the Old Testament include John Goldingay, *Approaches to Old Testament Interpretation*, rev. ed. (Downers Grove, IL: InterVarsity, 1990), 97–123; R. W. L. Moberly, *The Bible, Theology, and Faith: A Study of Abraham and Jesus*, Cambridge Studies in Christian Doctrine (Cambridge: Cambridge University Press, 2000), esp. 45–70, 225–42; and Francis Watson, *Text and Truth: Redefining Biblical Theology* (Grand Rapids: Eerdmans, 1997), esp. 216–18. Some of these prove to be even more christological than Childs. On F. Watson, e.g., see the important review essay by Christopher Seitz, "Christological Interpretations of Texts and Trinitarian Claims to Truth," *SJT* 52 (1999): 209–26, as well as Watson's response: "The Old Testament as Christian Scripture: A Response to Professor Seitz," *SJT* 52 (1999): 227–32. For a recent approach to the Old Testament with reference to Barth's theology, see Matthias Büttner, *Das Alte Testament als erster Teil der christlichen Bibel: zur Frage nach theologischer Auslegung und "Mitte" im Kontext der Theologie Karl Barths*, BEvT 120 (Gütersloh: Chr. Kaiser/Gütersloher, 2002).

that all scripture bears testimony to Jesus Christ," he immediately nuances his statement by writing that "the one scope of scripture, which is Jesus Christ, does not function to restrict the full range of the biblical voices."[21] Or, elsewhere, after stating that "the Old Testament functions within Christian scripture as a witness to Jesus Christ precisely in its pre-Christian form," he writes: "Although Christians confess that God who revealed himself to Israel is the God and Father of Jesus Christ, it is still necessary to hear Israel's witness in order to understand who the Father of Jesus Christ is. The coming of Jesus does not remove the function of the divine disclosure in the old covenant. Needless to say, for an Old Testament theology to avoid dogmatism on the right and historicism on the left requires both skill and wisdom."[22]

Skill and wisdom indeed. And Childs has a good deal of both. Qualifications such as these, then, may well emerge from his realization that the christological claims he has made are overstated, or, at least, that they are in need of careful (re)definition given some rather obvious problems. If so, such nuances are critical and evidence that the issues are complex and cannot be reified into the "folk" christological approach. Alternatively, such qualifications could be read by a less optimistic reader as special pleading or wishful thinking—a way to have one's "Old Testament christological cake" and eat it too. But insofar as nuances such as these are substantive, they reflect a level of sophistication in thinkers like Childs, Barth, and others, which means that they may well escape the Trinitarian critique that I will offer momentarily.[23] Moreover, it cannot be doubted that Childs and Barth (were either of them still alive) could offer substantial defenses of their positions. It may well be the case, then, that my criticism and concern lie not solely, perhaps not even primarily, with the likes of Childs and Barth—writers to whom I am indebted[24]— but with others who are not as subtle or sophisticated as they, and with how these others take up their perspectives in far less subtle and sophisticated ways.

I fear that all too often these latter types are found in pulpits and pews every Sunday morning. To be fair, the fault is not theirs alone. They *really can* trace a

---

21. Childs, *Biblical Theology*, 725.

22. Childs, *Old Testament Theology*, 9–10; see also 14. Cf. Childs, *Biblical Theology*, 85.

23. Note, e.g., that elsewhere Childs is much more nuanced and less christocentric. In *Biblical Theology*, 377, he states that the Bible's "subject matter . . . is God." See also the qualifications in Childs, *Biblical Theology*, 379; Childs, *Crisis*, 217.

24. Childs's comment about his disagreements with his own teachers—among them Eichrodt, von Rad, and Zimmerli—is apropos: "In those places where I have been forced to register my disagreement, it is done in the spirit of honest theological inquiry which is a concern first learned from them. In the end, my sense of continuity with these great scholars of the church exceeds that of rupture" (Childs, *Old Testament Theology*, xiii).

legacy, rightly or wrongly, to people like Childs, Barth, and even Luther.[25] The preachers among them can also find support in some of the homiletical literature, whatever its theological heritage and regardless (again) of its authors' theological subtlety. I am thinking here of recent work by Sidney Greidanus, Graeme Goldsworthy, or Elizabeth Achtemeier, some of which is a good bit more disturbing than others.[26] But there is still more to this story that is troubling because christological approaches to the Old Testament, especially in their "folk" manifestations, are often connected to (or degenerate into) easy notions of supersessionism wherein the Old Testament is always and invariably trumped by the New, or wherein the Old Testament God is seen as largely incompatible with the New Testament God—that is, Jesus.[27] (And who said Marcion was dead?) Even writers who mean quite well and often do quite well, at least here and there, fall prey to the temptation and, so, the criticism. Note Philip Yancey's comments in his immensely popular, best-selling treatment of the Old Testament, *The Bible Jesus Read*: "In the writings from this [Old Testament] period lay the seed, *but only the seed*, of God's grace. . . . In the Old Testament especially, God 'lisped.'"[28]

With all due respect to Calvin, from whom Yancey draws inspiration at this point, and the venerable notion of condescension, such sentiment clearly smacks of the kind of simplistic supersessionism that is no longer viable, and probably never was.[29]

25. Luther's christocentric analysis of Scripture, and the Old Testament in particular, is widely known. For a representative sample, see Sidney Greidanus, *Preaching Christ from the Old Testament: A Contemporary Hermeneutical Method* (Grand Rapids: Eerdmans, 1999), 120 and n. 35.

26. Greidanus, *Preaching Christ from the Old Testament*; Graeme Goldsworthy, *Preaching the Whole Bible as Christian Scripture: The Application of Biblical Theology to Expository Preaching* (Grand Rapids: Eerdmans, 2000); Elizabeth Achtemeier, *The Old Testament and the Proclamation of the Gospel* (Philadelphia: Westminster, 1973); and Achtemeier, *Preaching from the Old Testament* (Louisville: Westminster John Knox, 1989).

27. To be sure, not all of these issues are the same, but they seem to be closely related to, even contingent upon, one another. I agree, therefore, with Carol A. Miles who has shown that the fundamental question that must be asked and answered prior to the discussion of how the Old Testament ought to be preached in Christian contexts is the prior question of the relationship of the two Testaments. See Miles's "Proclaiming the Gospel of God: The Promise of a Literary-Theological Hermeneutical Approach to Christian Preaching of the Old Testament" (PhD diss., Princeton Theological Seminary, 2000).

28. Philip Yancey, *The Bible Jesus Read* (Grand Rapids: Zondervan, 1999), 12–13 (my emphasis). It should come as no surprise that in the intervening sentence (where the ellipsis is above), Yancey has a reference to Jesus. Note also that Yancey says the most important reason for reading the Old Testament is "perhaps" because it is the Bible Jesus read (24). At other points in the book, however, Yancey has statements that are more helpful and balanced.

29. See R. Kendall Soulen, *The God of Israel and Christian Theology* (Minneapolis: Fortress, 1998); Fredrick C. Holmgren, *The Old Testament and the Significance of Jesus: Embracing*

Indeed, it is the problems associated with easy and simplistic supersessionisms, especially since their track records often end in horrific fashion, that prompt us to re-think christological approaches (especially of the "folk" variety) in the first place.

I must be quick to emphasize that such rethinking need not be motivated purely or exclusively from historical-critical concerns or only from a changed climate in inter-religious, interfaith, and pluralistic dialogue. The former is a major worry of Childs; the latter is of central concern (positively and negatively) to many people today. Both aspects can and have motivated christological rethinking in the past. But at this point my interest in christological rethinking is not exclusively or even primarily because of them, but because of *theology*—theology proper, in this case the theology of the Triune God.

2. The Trinity, Perichoresis, and Inseparable Operations

To summarize to this point: the problem with the "folk" version of the christo-logical approach—and it should again be stressed that christological approaches are actually manifold, diverse, and not all "folk" versions—is not simply Marcion-ism as though one could simply assert in response that the Old Testament, too, is canon and part of Christian Scripture. This is, of course, a compelling point and should (!) be enough for most unwitting Marcionites.[30] But the main point to be wrestled with here is *theological* not simply canonical.[31] To put it bluntly: there is more to the Triune God than just the second member, incarnate in Jesus of Nazareth. Of course, in the present discussion the canonical and theological points are closely related: the Old Testament has largely been conceived of as testimony to God, the Father of Jesus Christ. Even in this Trinitarian formulation the emphasis lies on the first member of the Trinity.[32] As for Jesus Christ proper, he is simply not much present in the Old Testament[33]—at least not in any overt

---

Change—Maintaining Christian Identity: The Emerging Center in Biblical Scholarship (Grand Rapids: Eerdmans, 1999); Walter Brueggemann, *Theology of the Old Testament: Testimony, Dispute, Advocacy* (Minneapolis: Fortress, 1997), 729–30; and Rolf Rendtorff, *Canon and Theology: Overtures to an Old Testament Theology*, OBT (Minneapolis: Fortress, 1993).

30. One must be careful not to overuse the "Marcionite bogey," as Barr has pointed out (*Concept*, 670n16).

31. I realize that "canon," depending on its connotations, is *both* a theological and a historical concept.

32. Cf. Patrick D. Miller, "A Strange Kind of Monotheism," *ThTo* 54 (1997): 296.

33. Barr, *Old and New*, 150: "The Old Testament comes from the time when Jesus Christ was not yet come." See Barr, *Old and New*, 152–53; cf. Brueggemann, *Theology*, 731: "Any serious Old Testament interpretation, however, must be uneasy with such a procedure [a collapse of the Old Testament into the New Testament via christology], precisely because it is so clear that the

way.[34] Even when a christological approach is narrowed, historically or literarily, by means of messianism proper—that is, what the Old Testament says about the office of the Messiah/Christ, not Jesus Christ *per se*—the results are rather meager.[35] To cite Barr's formulation: "The Old Testament is the time in which our Lord is not yet come. It is as the time in which he is not yet come that we ought to understand it."[36]

But, again, this is not simply a matter of history, nor is it the stereotypical historical-critical problem with approaches that are more theological in nature. Among other things, one could say it is equally a *literary* problem: a christological approach—even if generously construed—is massively reductionistic. The Old Testament is about much more than just Christ—historically *and* literarily. And this judgment is equally *theological*. Perhaps Goldingay is right that "in the mind of God . . . [Old Testament] history looked forward to Christ,"[37] but at best that statement is predicated on knowledge after the fact which must then be retroverted backward. Such a move is not all bad nor is it all wrong.[38] But recent theological considerations, not just historical or literary ones, problematize Goldingay's statement.[39] Be that as it may, we might well ask of sentiments like Goldingay's (and

---

Old Testament does not obviously, cleanly, or directly point to Jesus or to the New Testament." On the collapse into christology, see also Brueggemann, *Theology*, 92, 730–31 and n. 12; also Soulen, *God of Israel*, 21.

34. This is not to deny that Christ may be "figured" there, especially in the church's (re)reading of Scripture. For some helpful thoughts on such figuring, (re)reading, and imaginative construal, see, respectively, Christopher R. Seitz, *Figured Out: Typology and Providence in Christian Scripture* (Louisville: Westminster John Knox, 2001); Moberly, *Bible, Theology, and Faith*; and Brueggemann, *Theology*, 731–32. See also Childs, *Biblical Theology*, 87–88; Watson, "Old Testament as Christian Scripture," 227–32; and further below.

35. See J. J. M. Roberts, "The Old Testament's Contribution to Messianic Expectations," in *The Messiah: Developments in Earliest Judaism and Christianity*, ed. James H. Charlesworth (Minneapolis: Fortress, 1992), 39–51, who notes that where messianic expectation occurs, the term "Messiah" (*māšyḥ*) almost never appears. See also Goldingay, *Approaches*, 117, who observes that "the NT is actually rather restrained in quoting 'messianic' prophecies. It does not refer to many of the texts which were later appealed to by Christians, but whose messianic reference historical criticism questions . . . nor even to many of the texts that scholarship does regard as originally messianic. . . . It is at least as interested in non-messianic eschatological texts."

36. Barr, *Old and New*, 152; cf. 150. It should be noted that, despite what one might expect from the earlier discussion, this fact is also acknowledged by Childs, *Biblical Theology*, 83, 85; and Goldsworthy, *Preaching the Whole Bible*, xii. In the case of Childs, the issue is probably one of further nuance; with Goldsworthy, it may be simple inconsistency.

37. Goldingay, *Approaches*, 97.

38. See Seitz, *Figured Out*, and the other works in note 34 above.

39. Without wishing to weigh in on the matter, I am alluding here to open and relational movements in systematic theology and the earlier, process theology, to which both are related.

they are legion) why we must start at *the end*, so to speak—that is, with the Christ event—and not with *the beginning*.[40] Indeed, it is hard to see how beginning at the beginning would pose much of a problem or even a question for discussion among Christians who find some sort of unity to the canon of Scripture and who identify the Lord God of Israel as the God and Father of the Lord Jesus Christ. Certainly Christians see Jesus as God's Son, the second member of the Trinity incarnate, but that just furthers the issue. While the Son is basic and foundational to the structure of Christian belief, the Son is not simply a mode of the Father, only to be replaced by the mode of the Spirit. The doctrine of the Trinity—"the central dogma of Christian theology"[41]—must be taken into account, and, when it is, it both refines and resists certain christological approaches.[42]

The question, then, is how does one speak appropriately of a christological reading of the Old Testament? Many answers have, of course, been proffered throughout history, including typology, allegory, the fuller sense, promise-fulfillment, law-gospel, messianic prooftexting, and the like. Another option, one that I suggest is more Trinitarian (and helpfully so), does not begin with Christ because such a move almost automatically requires these other reading strategies, some of which succeed far less well than others, and all of which can easily run into the kinds of problems mentioned above. Goldingay puts it succinctly: "They [allegory, typology, and the fuller sense] imply that the whole of Christianity is to be focused on Christ, so that the OT must be full of him if it is a Christian book. But if the OT is itself Scripture, the whole of it contributes to an understanding of the faith. . . . The NT is concerned with how Christ is to be preached, and a Christian concern with OT interpretation is broader than this."[43] While Goldingay's understanding of figurative readings might be challenged, he is right that Christian concerns with the Old Testament *should* be broader than "how Christ is preached." But, in truth, they frequently are not. If, however, we do not begin with the end, with Christ, perhaps we could begin at the beginning, with the Triune God, the

---

For a treatment with respect to the Old Testament, see Robert K. Gnuse, *The Old Testament and Process Theology* (St. Louis: Chalice, 2000).

40. Cf. Bonhoeffer, *Letters and Papers*, 157: "One cannot and must not speak the last word before the last but one."

41. F. L. Cross and E. A. Livingstone, *The Oxford Dictionary of the Christian Church*, 3rd ed. (Oxford: Oxford University Press, 1997), 1641.

42. Cf. the excellent formulation of Rolf P. Knierim, *The Task of Old Testament Theology: Method and Cases* (Grand Rapids: Eerdmans, 1995), 130: "Biblical *theo*logy codetermines New Testament *Christo*logy."

43. Goldingay, *Approaches*, 112–13. He goes so far as to accuse allegory, typology, and the fuller sense of being Marcion "in another form." This is surely overstating the case; see Barr's comment above (note 30). F. Watson, too, is fond of Marcionite accusations (*Text and Truth*, 127–76).

God who is the Father and who generates the Son and spirates the Spirit. Does the doctrine of the Trinity permit christological approaches to the Old Testament and actually help them avoid some of their potential problems?

In my judgment, the answer is affirmative. But before proceeding, a few cautions are in order. Simplistic Trinitarian approaches that are as unsophisticated as any "folk" christological approach are well known. These tend to find the Trinity explicitly mentioned or at least heavily hinted at here or there in the texts of the Old Testament. The parade examples, of course, are the "we"-language of Gen 1–11,[44] the three-visitors to Abraham in Gen 18 (cf. the famous icon by Andrei Rublev), or even the *trisagion* of Isa 6:3 (thrice-holy, after all: one for each member of the Trinity!), but many from church history could be adduced.[45] In this article, I am hoping for something a bit more subtle and logically prior to such figural readings, regardless of their merits or demerits.

I must also offer a retraction in addition to these cautions. Try as one might, in Christian theology, it is not completely possible (or desirable) to go back to the beginning and discuss the Triune God apart from reference to the Christ event. For Christian theology it is, after all, the Christ event that reveals God's Triune nature. While christology is not the same as Trinitarian theology, they are interdependent and must be considered together.[46] Part of the Trinity is its second member, incarnate in Jesus Christ. The experience of God at work in Jesus Christ (the economy of the Trinity) has revealed what was only hinted at here and there before Christ, namely that God is Triune in God's own being (the immanent Trinity). To a large extent, then, the Son is the revealer of God as Trinity.[47]

These remarks are already a good way down the road to indicating how a Trinitarian conception permits christological approaches. The discussion

---

44. Esp. Gen 1:26; cf. also 3:22; 11:7. For a helpful analysis of what the we-language is doing theologically in these three texts in Genesis, see Patrick D. Miller, *Genesis 1–11: Studies in Structure and Theme*, JSOTSup 8 (Sheffield: University of Sheffield, 1978), 9–26.

45. Cf., e.g., John Wesley's sermon "Upon Our Lord's Sermon on the Mount: Discourse the Sixth," §7, where he finds "discovery" of the Unity and Trinity of God "in the very first line of his Written Word, אלהים ברא—literally 'the Gods created', a plural noun joined with a verb of the singular number" (*The Works of John Wesley, Volume 1: Sermons 1: 1–33*, ed. Albert C. Outler [Nashville: Abingdon, 1984], 581).

46. I thus can agree only to a partial extent with Gerald O'Collins, "The Holy Trinity: The State of the Questions," in Davis, Kendall, and O'Collins, *Trinity*, 3, who argues that there is a false dichotomy between "trinitarian" and "christological." See also Michel René Barnes, "Rereading Augustine's Theology of the Trinity," in Davis, Kendall, and O'Collins, *Trinity*, 168n38; and Lewis Ayres, "'Remember That You Are Catholic' (*serm.* 52.2): Augustine on the Unity of the Triune God," *JECS* 8 (2000): 53n29.

47. See further below.

may gain precision, however, by recourse to the notions of perichoresis and inseparable operation.

Perichoresis, often called by its Latin equivalent circumincession (or circuminsession), is "the technical term for the interpenetration of the Three Persons of the Holy Trinity."[48] The notion was developed in a seventh-century work by John of Damascus (ca. 655–750 CE), but is already implicit in the Trinitarian theology of the Cappadocians and Dionysius the Pseudo-Areopagite (ca. 500 CE).[49] The Greek term was rendered into Latin by Burgundio of Pisa (d. 1193) as *circumincessio*.[50]

Even after perichoresis is neatly defined as the "mutually internal abiding and interpenetration of the trinitarian persons,"[51] significant questions remain. Indeed, while "the idea of perichoresis starts with the story of revelation (Father, Son, and Spirit as acting and speaking persons) . . . [it] admittedly leads into what comes close to being a conceptual labyrinth."[52] Miroslav Volf makes an attempt to escape the labyrinth:

> Perichoresis refers to the reciprocal *interiority* of the trinitarian persons. In every divine person as a subject, the other persons also indwell; all mutually permeate one another, though in so doing they do not cease to be distinct persons. In fact, the distinctions between them are precisely the presupposition of that interiority, since persons who have dissolved into one another cannot exist in one another. Perichoresis is "co-inherence in one another without any coalescence or commixture." . . . Being in one another does not abolish trinitarian plurality; yet despite the abiding distinction between the persons, their subjectivities do overlap. Each divine person acts as subject, and at the same time the other persons act as subjects in it.[53]

48. Cross and Livingstone, *Oxford Dictionary of the Christian Church*, 354.

49. Cross and Livingstone, *Oxford Dictionary of the Christian Church*, 1641. See G. W. H. Lampe, *A Patristic Greek Lexicon* (Oxford: Clarendon, 1961), 1078 s.v. περιχωρέω [*perichōreō*].

50. Cross and Livingstone, *Oxford Dictionary of the Christian Church*, 354; Lampe, *Patristic Greek Lexicon*, 1077–78, esp. 1078, for trinitarian use in John of Damascus.

51. Volf, *After Our Likeness*, 208. Cf. also Van A. Harvey, *A Handbook of Theological Terms* (New York: Collier, 1964), 181; Johnson, "Trinity," 308–9; and see the older articles by A. Deneffe, "Perichoresis, circumincessio, circuminsessio: eine terminologische Untersuchung," *ZKT* 47 (1923): 497–523; and [G.] L. Prestige, "ΠΕΡΙΧΩΡΕΩ [*perichōreō*] and ΠΕΡΙΧΩΡΗΣΙΣ [*perichōrēsis*] in the Fathers," *JTS* 29 (1928): 242–52.

52. Volf, *After Our Likeness*, 209n84.

53. Volf, *After Our Likeness*, 209; the citation is from G. L. Prestige, *God in Patristic Thought* (London: SPCK, 1956), 298. Note further Volf's use of John 7:16, where he argues that we must not resolve the tension between "mine" and "not mine." "Within personal interiority, 'mine' is simultaneously 'not mine' without ceasing to be 'mine,' just as 'not mine' is simultaneously

The accent in Volf's work, and in the work of others such as Catherine Mowry LaCugna, is the bearing of perichoresis on the divine (inter)relationships. Such a use of the notion of perichoresis may or may not be correct.[54] Divine relationality might better be discussed using the different, but related, notion of inseparable operations, which I will treat next. Still, it should be noted here that if perichoresis can be used in relational senses—and to some degree, even if not—the concept speaks to a conception of the Trinity in which testimony regarding one member can also be taken to refer to the others. So Volf wishes to speak of the divine persons' "catholicity": "In a certain sense, each divine person *is* the other persons, though is such in its own way, which is why rather than ceasing to be a unique person, in its very uniqueness it is a completely *catholic* divine person."[55] Here too, one begins to get a sense of why and how a Trinitarian perspective might permit christological approaches to the Old Testament.

The doctrine of inseparable operations is another, perhaps better, way to get at this same issue. Michel René Barnes and Lewis Ayres have recently explored the concept with reference to Augustine's Trinitarian theology.[56] Both have focused on Augustine's work *outside* his massive *De Trinitate*, demonstrating that most of Augustine's Trinitarian thought is already found in some of the early epistles (e.g., *Epistle* 11; ca. 389 CE) and treatises (e.g., *Eighty-Three Different Questions* 69; ca. 394–396 CE), as well as some of the later sermons (e.g., *Sermon* 52; ca. 410 CE; *Sermon* 117; ca. 418 CE). They have also argued against the widespread but erroneous notion that West and East were divided largely over whether theologians started with notions of God's unity and moved to the Trinity or the opposite (respectively).[57] Instead, Augustine's thought, far from being at odds with earlier, especially Eastern, exemplars, has notable antecedents there[58] and can be seen as a further example of pro-Nicene theology.

'mine' without ceasing to be 'not mine'" (Volf, *After Our Likeness*, 209). Note also Volf, *After Our Likeness*, 209n84, for a discussion of prophecy as a kind of perichoretic activity in which *both* the Spirit and prophet are active.

54. One is hard-pressed, e.g., to find relational uses of the term in Lampe, *Patristic Greek Lexicon*.

55. Volf, *After Our Likeness*, 209–10 (his emphasis).

56. Barnes, "Rereading," 145–76; Ayres, "Remember," 39–82.

57. This is especially apparent in Ayres who finds it in many authors, including Théodore de Régnon, John Zizioulas, and Catherine Mowry LaCugna. The problem has also been noted by Volf, *After Our Likeness*, 200; and James P. Mackey, "The Preacher, the Theologian, and the Trinity," *ThTo* 54 (1997): 350.

58. Barnes and Ayres lift up Hilary of Poitiers, especially his *De Trinitate* 7, where Hilary writes that "'the whole mystery of our faith' is contained in the teaching that the Son does the same work as the Father and that 'the same things the Father does are all done likewise by the Son'" (Barnes, "Rereading," 156, citing Hilary, *De Trinitate* 7.17–18; see also Ayres, "Remember," 77);

The finer points of Barnes and Ayres's treatments of Augustine need not detain us. For our purposes, the following passage from Augustine's *Epistle* 11.2 is a good entry point into the notion of inseparable operations and its meaning: "For, according to the Catholic faith, the Trinity is proposed to our belief and believed ... as so inseparable that whatever action is performed by it must be thought to be performed at the same time by the Father and by the Son and by the Holy Spirit. ... [T]he Son does not do anything which the Father and the Holy Spirit do not also do."[59] On the basis of this passage and others like it, Barnes and Ayres have mounted a compelling case that includes the following three points:

- the notion of inseparable activity is "the fundamental expression of divine unity";
- the incarnation is the decisive revelation of divine unity—i.e., the Trinity—and of the Trinity's inseparable activity; and
- faith or a certain type of life obedience leads to greater understanding of the Trinity and doctrinal insight into it.[60]

These points hold for understanding inseparable operations, in Augustine at least. The issue at stake here, however, is not simply how Augustine understands the unity and activity of the Trinity. It is, rather, to lift Augustine up as a major example in the tradition of the notion whereby the unity of the three members is found in "the understanding that *any action of any member of the Trinity is an action of the three inseparably*."[61] And, again, it should be pointed out that, not only does Augustine develop this doctrine elsewhere (especially in *De Trinitate*), but it is also found in his predecessors in both East and West. This is to say that the common, indeed inseparable, operation of the Trinity is a rather central point in Trinitarian doctrine.[62] Insofar as this conception has to do with actions *and* unity,[63] not only intra-trinitarian relationality (whether spatial or interpersonal), inseparable operation is even more helpful to the main point under discussion here. Through this

---

as well as Ambrose's *De fid.* 4.6.68 (Barnes, "Rereading," 171–72n49) and his commentary on Luke (Ayres, "Remember," 47); and Gregory of Nyssa's *On the Holy Trinity* (Ayres, "Remember," 48).

59. Cited in Ayres, "Remember," 46; cf. Barnes, "Rereading," 156–57; and see further Augustine's *De Trinitate* 1.8.

60. Barnes, "Rereading," 154 (the citation is from here), 158; Ayres, "Remember," 40, 41, 54–55, 80.

61. Barnes, "Rereading," 156 (his emphasis); cf. Rusch, *Trinitarian Controversy*, 25–27; Ayres, "Remember," 40, 48. See Ayres, "Remember," 57–58, for how Augustine is able to hold to this position and simultaneously avoid the charge of patripassianism (by distinction of persons despite inseparableness of operation).

62. This is one of Ayres's main points ("Remember," 39–82). One should also compare the related theological notions of appropriations and communion of properties (*communicatio idiomatum*). For a brief introduction, see Harvey, *Handbook*, 27 and 54–55, respectively.

63. See esp. Barnes, "Rereading," 158.

lens, testimony about the action of any one member of the Trinity is testimony about the actions of the others. This judgment holds true especially for and of Scripture and its comments about the Trinity's constituent members.

Augustine's own remarks from his later masterpiece may serve as an apt conclusion to this section:

> They are indeed one, as he tells us, *I and the Father are one* (Jn 10:30). In a word, because of this inseparability, it makes no difference whether sometimes the Father alone or sometimes the Son alone is mentioned as the one who is to fill us with delight at his countenance. Nor is the Spirit of each separable from this unity. . . . The actual truth is that *I and the Father are one* (Jn 10:30), and therefore when the Father is shown, the Son who is in him is shown also, and when the Son is shown, the Father who is in him is shown too.[64]

3. Revisiting Christological (Over)Statements in Light of Trinitarian Relations

Two major conclusions should be apparent from the discussion thus far:

1. Informed with the notions of perichoresis and inseparable operations, a Christian reader who is a Trinitarian (a connection that should be axiomatic) has every reason to adopt a christological approach to the Old Testament. What is witnessed there with regard to the Lord God of Israel, whom the New Testament speaks of as the God and Father of the Lord Jesus Christ and who is traditionally identified with the first member of the Godhead, *is also and simultaneously* a witness to the second member, the Son, incarnate in Jesus Christ (and, it should be added, also to the Spirit, the third member who is often given short shrift). Furthermore, the witness of the Old Testament that can be identified with other members of the Trinity need not be solely about the first member. I am thinking here of the oft-noted fact that the Old Testament also knows and speaks of God's Spirit. Certainly a Christian (re)reading can see the pregnancy of such references to the Spirit and find the same in references to the "Word of the Lord" so common in prophetic speech or implied in the first creation account. Perichoresis and, especially, the notion of inseparable operations thus permit christological readings of texts in the Old Testament that are nevertheless from the time "when Jesus

---

64. Augustine, *De Trinitate* 1.17–18; translation in Edmund Hill, *The Trinity*, The Works of Saint Augustine, ed. John Rotelle (Brooklyn: New City, 1991), 1.5:77, 79. Barnes calls *De Trinitate* 1.15–18 "a virtual checklist of references back to issues articulated in the earlier texts" ("Rereading," 170).

Christ was not yet come."[65] In light of the incarnation and the light it has shed on the Triune nature of the Godhead, testimony to God the Father (or the Spirit) is still testimony to the second member, belatedly incarnate in Jesus of Nazareth since these three are one.

2. And yet, while this Trinitarian understanding *permits* a christological approach, this is actually its minor contribution. Or, to put it another way, while christological approaches are permissible via perichoresis and inseparable operations, it is *only a certain type* of christological approach—namely, a heavily Trinitarian one—that employs these selfsame notions. The emphasis is here on the *Triune* God, not on the second member solely, not even on the second member primarily. Christological approaches that are not of this type (e.g., the "folk" variety) are discouraged, even resisted, and come in for significant critique.[66] This is *the major contribution* of Trinitarian doctrine to this discussion. If the Godhead is Triune, why do so many christological approaches focus only on the second member? Why do they neglect the first member? Why the almost total disregard of the third member?[67] Why, that is, the collapse into christology? Still further,

65. See Barr, *Old and New*, 150.

66. Such as that offered here. Note also Seitz's criticisms of F. Watson's christological approach in "Christological Interpretations," 221, and esp. 226: "A christological interpretation of the Old Testament—or of the New Testament—warrants our attention only to the degree to which it conforms with Trinitarian truth about God, and conveys exegetical and interpretive guidelines commensurate with that truth." See also Seitz, *Figured Out*, 10, 193. It is somewhat telling that Childs's section on the Trinity is not particularly long or helpful (*Biblical Theology*, 375–83), though his comments that the church's struggle with the Trinity was "a battle *for* the Old Testament, for the one eternal covenant of God in both unity and diversity" are significant (376; his emphasis).

67. The neglect of the third member (the Spirit) is, in fact, rather widespread in various theological circles. See, e.g., Ephraim Radner, "The Absence of the Comforter: Scripture and the Divided Church," in *Theological Exegesis: Essays in Honor of Brevard S. Childs*, ed. Christopher Seitz and Kathryn Greene-McCreight (Grand Rapids: Eerdmans, 1999), 355–94. This has begun to change due to the work of theologians like Badcock, Lodahl, Moltmann, and Welker, among others. See Gary D. Badcock, *Light of Truth and Fire of Love: A Theology of the Holy Spirit* (Grand Rapids: Eerdmans, 1997); Michael E. Lodahl, *Shekhinah/Spirit: Divine Presence in Jewish and Christian Religion*, Studies in Judaism and Christianity (New York: Paulist, 1992); Jürgen Moltmann, *The Spirit of Life: A Universal Affirmation* (Minneapolis: Fortress, 1992); Moltmann, *The Source of Life: The Holy Spirit and the Theology of Life* (Minneapolis: Fortress, 1997); Michael Welker, *God the Spirit* (Minneapolis: Fortress, 1994). Note also the telling title of Frederick Dale Bruner and William E. Hordern's book, *The Holy Spirit, Shy Member of the Trinity* (Minneapolis: Augsburg, 1984). An early exception to neglect of the Holy Spirit in Trinitarian perspective among Old Testament theologians may be found in Walther Eichrodt, *Theology of the Old Testament*, 2 vols., OTL (Philadelphia: Westminster, 1967), 2:79–80, though here too the emphasis is on the New Testament and its superiority to the "Old Covenant." It should be pointed out that

if testimony to one of the members is testimony to the others, because the three are one and act inseparably, such reductionism is not only made painfully obvious, it is also revealed to be completely unnecessary. Christ *can* be found in the Old Testament because of its witness to God, whom Christians know to be Triune—thanks to the Christ event but not it only (see below). But that is not the same thing as saying that Christ *is* or *must be* found in the Old Testament or that "the Old Testament is a witness to Jesus Christ" or that "the" subject matter of the Old Testament (!) or even of Scripture as a whole is Jesus Christ. In light of the doctrine of the Trinity, this is simply unnecessary. The subject matter of the Old Testament can simply be God.[68] The same might also be said of the New Testament, according to many New Testament scholars.[69] But even if one wants to retain the New Testament as a witness (only) to Jesus Christ, the entirety of Scripture can nevertheless be read as a witness to the Triune God. This is to say that theological reductionism of any sort, whether of the first member, second, or third, must be rejected. In orthodox Christian theology, one must avoid monarchianism, subordinationism, and patripassianism, to be sure, but there are other dangers as well: modalism is one, christomonism another. If God is Triune, even if we know that largely from our knowledge of Jesus Christ after his incarnation, the Triune God's being or presence or significance need not be reduced to just one of the members.[70] To do so runs the risk of serious theological error. The three

---

a number of those who advocate christological approaches do mention the Spirit, sometimes with regularity. This is true, for instance, of Childs who often refers to the Spirit (e.g., *Biblical Theology*, 86–87; *Old Testament Theology*, 12, 15; similarly Seitz, *Figured Out*, 6). Such references are, however, usually restricted to discussions of the interpretation of Scripture so that the Spirit is not so much active in the biblical texts themselves as in the (subsequent) *interpretation* of the texts. This is quite different from the kind of perspective on the Spirit provided by inseparable operations.

68. Rightly noted by Childs at a few points (*Biblical Theology*, 377, 379; *Crisis*, 217) but in marked contradiction with himself elsewhere. His clear emphasis is Jesus Christ.

69. I am thinking here of J. Christiaan Beker, who calls Paul a theocentric (*not* christocentric) theologian of hope, and Beverly Roberts Gaventa's work on Acts, which she argues is primarily about the work of God. See J. Christiaan Beker, *Paul the Apostle: The Triumph of God in Life and Thought* (Philadelphia: Fortress, 1984); Beker, *Paul's Apocalyptic Gospel: The Coming Triumph of God* (Philadelphia: Fortress, 1982); Beker, *The Triumph of God: The Essence of Paul's Thought* (Minneapolis: Fortress, 1990); and Beverly Roberts Gaventa, *The Acts of the Apostles*, ANTC (Nashville: Abingdon, 2003).

70. This is not to say that certain actions of the Trinity cannot be attributed to specific members and not the other(s). It is, in fact, a long-standing practice to do so and this is in part what permitted the early church to distinguish the suffering of the Son from the suffering of the Father. Cf. Ayres, "Remember," 53–54, and note 61 above.

are one and the one is three. As Augustine puts it: "They are each in each and all in each, and each in all and all in all, and all are one."[71]

In truth, there have been a number of important critiques of christological approaches to the Old Testament. Some have come from the domain of historical criticism, others from arenas that are generally non-religious; still others from Jewish authors.[72] These three loci are not the same and each has raised significant points, many of which I believe to be accurate, valid, and insightful. If the debate is intramural, however—within Christianity proper—many of these perspectives will fail to convince some Christians because they might be seen as stemming from communities or realms of discourse that are outside Christianity proper. Indeed, some Christians would probably go further, saying that such criticisms—*despite* their merits—should convince Christian theologians only so far for that very reason. I do not agree with such positions,[73] but, regardless, what I have offered here is a critique of christological approaches *from within the tradition*, from within the realm of Christian discourse. It is a theological criticism—one that advocates a thoroughly Trinitarian approach, obviating the need to find Christ everywhere in the Old Testament or even as the "culmination" of the Old Testament. A thoroughgoing Trinitarian approach *permits* christological readings but *does not require* such. Similarly, the means by which christological readings are often obtained—figurative reading strategies (allegory, typology, etc.), the fuller sense, and the like—are also permitted as possible interpretive approaches, but they, too, are not required or granted solitary or preeminent status. They are not the only Christian interpretive approaches nor are they inherently superior or more Christian than those that eschew their methodology. Methods that focus on God (the Father) alone, or the Spirit for that matter, are equally Christian—even equally christological—if one understands the Trinity as one, intermingled and inseparable in operation and being.

At this point one might well reverse the equation, however, and ask if a Trinitarian approach does not in fact *require* the christological move at some point down the line.[74] After all, so the logic goes, is not the Christ event *the* event that reveals God's self-differentiated nature? To respond to the first question from a

---

71. *De Trinitate* 6.10.12; translation in Hill, *The Trinity*, 214.

72. In particular note the incisive work of Jon D. Levenson, esp. the collected essays in *The Hebrew Bible, the Old Testament, and Historical Criticism: Jews and Christians in Biblical Studies* (Louisville: Westminster John Knox, 1993). In my judgment, Levenson is among the most important thinkers on the problem of biblical theology, and Christian biblical theology simply cannot be done without serious engagement with his work.

73. I agree rather with those who argue that valid theological criticisms ought to be heard *regardless* of their point of origin.

74. Cf. Childs, *Crisis*, 218; Barr, *Old and New*, 153–54.

Christian perspective, I think the answer is "perhaps so," but exactly how far down the line is exactly the question. The issue, again, is *permission* vs. *requirement*. Christological readings or interpretations are permitted via Trinitarian doctrine, but are not required, especially early on. That is due in part because of the answer to the second question, which is "not necessarily." A number of scholars have noted that the Old Testament itself knows of a kind of complexity or plurality to God;[75] the same holds true for early Judaism and later Jewish reflection.[76] So, to use the example of the Spirit, references to such in the Old Testament—or to the Word or Wisdom for that matter—need not be related solely to Christian, christological, pneumatological, or Trinitarian perspectives. So, even at this point, there might be room for dialogue between Christians and those who believe otherwise, especially Jews. Patrick D. Miller has put the point nicely:

> If one's exclusive and working sense about the Trinity is that it ... insists upon and guards the incarnation ... then the Trinity may serve to pull Christian faith away from its strong continuity with Israel. But if the Trinity also means that the God who is revealed in Jesus Christ is still one Lord, then it becomes a major piece of the church's understanding of its continuity with the Old Testament. The Trinity is as much a part of the church's insistence on the Shema and the oneness of God as it is a claim about the divinity of Christ. The latter could be claimed without the doctrine of the Trinity, but not the former.[77]

Even so, from their Trinitarian perspective, it seems likely that Christians will "at some point down the line" take up references to God's Spirit, Word, and Wisdom and relate them to what they believe to be the case regarding the Triune nature of the one God.[78]

4. Conclusion

By way of conclusion, I wish to revisit the epigraphs from Barr and Volf that began this chapter, as each highlights issues that this article has attempted to articulate.

---

75. See Miller, "Strange Kind of Monotheism," 293–95; and note Brueggemann who often speaks of God's rich interior life (e.g., *Theology of the Old Testament*, 267–313).

76. See Donald H. Juel, "The Trinity and the New Testament," *ThTo* 54 (1997): 312–24, esp. 314–15; O'Collins, "Holy Trinity," 7; Alan F. Segal, "'Two Powers in Heaven' and Early Christian Trinitarian Thinking," in Davis, Kendall, and O'Collins, *Trinity*, 73–95; Richard Bauckham, *God Crucified: Monotheism and Christology in the New Testament* (Grand Rapids: Eerdmans, 1998); and Childs, *Biblical Theology*, 83.

77. Miller, "Strange Kind of Monotheism," 293–94; cf. Pannenberg, "Problems," 280.

78. So also Miller, "Strange Kind of Monotheism," 294.

First, the question of the proper approach to Old Testament theology, *in Christian perspective*, depends on a good bit more than simply the Old Testament (Barr). In Christian perspective, it also involves the New Testament, *but still yet more*: the theology of the early and contemporary church, the creeds, and so forth impinge to greater or lesser degree on Christian readings. "Ultimate theological questions," as Barr indicates, "depend on the totality of Christian insight."[79] While they cannot depend only on the Old Testament, neither can they depend only on the New Testament (cf. the Bonhoeffer epigraph). This means that they cannot depend solely on christology.

Second, belief about the Trinity—a doctrine that only comes to full development in the first few centuries of the church—is one of these other aspects that impinge on Christian readings. Trinitarian belief, once it is fully articulated, has wide-ranging consequences (Volf).[80] Among other things, those consequences include how one can and cannot, should and should not, approach the Old Testament as a Christian who subscribes to classic Trinitarian theology.[81]

The latter point underscores yet again that the simplistic christological approach that is all (and far) too common—regardless of its antiquity and formidability—is only one Christian option for approaching the Old Testament. In Trinitarian perspective, it is no longer obviously the best, nor the most Christian, approach. The holy Trinity has three members—none of these may be slighted without repercussions. There is more to God than Christ despite the well-known christological overstatements to the effect that "all we know or need to know about God we learn or see or find in Christ."[82] The complete and total disregard

79. Barr, *Old and New*, 167; cf. Ayres, "Remember," 56: "Our task in understanding the Trinity . . . may be described as a task of understanding the traditional Catholic faith in inseparable operations *as* a reading of Scripture"; and Miller, "Strange Kind of Monotheism," 295: "The Trinity thus needs to be perceived as a feature of Old Testament theology if it is going to be a feature of Christian theology."

80. Cf. Colin Gunton, "The God of Jesus Christ," *ThTo* 54 (1997): 327: "Everything looks different when it is theologized with and through the doctrine of the Trinity."

81. For more on the Trinity and its impact on specific Christian practices, see Volf, *After Our Likeness*; LaCugna, *God for Us*; David S. Cunningham, *These Three Are One: The Practice of Trinitarian Theology*, Challenges in Contemporary Theology (London: Blackwell, 1998); Johnson, "Trinity," 306–9; Ellen T. Charry, "Spiritual Formation by the Doctrine of the Trinity," *ThTo* 54 (1997): 367–80. Some of this work is based on human reflexes or analogies of the Trinity, which are oftentimes based on Augustine's notion of "trinitarian vestiges" (*vestigia Trinitatis*). But Augustine was also quite aware of the limitations of such analogies and, indeed, of the presence of dis-analogy. See Barnes, "Rereading," 161; Ayres, "Remember," 58–59 and n. 44; Volf, *After Our Likeness*, 198–200; and Seitz, *Figured Out*, 69–79.

82. Cf., e.g., Ian A. McFarland, "The Ecstatic God: The Holy Spirit and the Constitution of the Trinity," *ThTo* 54 (1997): 344: "We know *most profoundly* who God is when we know that in the person of Jesus" (my emphasis); similarly Juel, "Trinity," 322–23; and, to a disturbing degree,

such statements have for God's work in Israel, in Torah, in prophet, in proverb and psalm—things that the New Testament itself says witness to God and to God in Christ (cf. Luke 24:27)!—not to mention God's work in the Spirit is staggering.

But a Trinitarian approach is two-edged. There is more to the Trinity than Christ, to be sure, but the second member, incarnate in Christ, *is* part of the Trinity. Consider, in closing, a formulation by Walter Brueggemann. He writes that, because the Old Testament "is polyphonic and elusive and insists on imaginative construal, it is then credible and appropriate to say that the early church, *mesmerized by the person of Jesus*, found it inescapable that it would draw this elusive, polyphonic text to its own circumstance, close to its experience, and its continuing sense of the transformative presence of Jesus. Thus as a confessing Christian, I believe that *the imaginative construal* of the Old Testament toward Jesus is a credible act and one that I fully affirm."[83] I share Brueggemann's confessional stance and much of his sentiment here. Yet the argument advanced in this chapter is that if, because of the Trinity and its inseparable operation, the Old Testament is not all just christology, then we must also say on the basis of that same Trinitarian belief that neither is it all just mesmerism or imagination that sees the God revealed there to be connected to the God known in Jesus Christ. Instead, we have to do, in both instances, with the Triune God. A God who is actually three, and yet these three are one. Scripture has much to teach us about both.

Goldsworthy, *Preaching the Whole Bible*, 115–16 and passim. Statements such as these superabound. They are often used to draw problematic practical conclusions; e.g., a sermon is not Christian if it does not mention Christ or utilize a New Testament text (see, e.g., Achtemeier, *Preaching from the Old Testament*, 56–57; Achtemeier, *Old Testament and Proclamation*, 142–44; similarly the works of Goldsworthy and Greidanus, cited above). These statements are also often couched in terms of *primacy*—whether that is temporal or qualitative is not always clear (e.g., we know God "first and foremost" because of Christ). Again, one must not neglect the second member, but the shape of the canon as well as the shape of the Nicene and Apostles' Creeds do not begin first with the second member but with "God the Father Almighty, Maker of Heaven and Earth," one with the Son (and the Spirit), and yet distinguishable from the other members as the Father who generates (and who spirates).

83. Brueggemann, *Theology*, 731–32 (my emphases).

8

"Israel, My Child":
The Ethics of a Biblical Metaphor

Even before they've been lived through, a child can sense the great human subjects: time which breeds loss, desire, the world's beauty.[1]

The quality of childhood is largely determined by the care and protection children receive—or fail to receive—from adults.[2]

When the father dies he will not seem to be dead,
for he has left behind him one like himself,
whom in his life he looked upon with joy
and at death, without grief. (Sir 30:4–5 NRSV)

T he notion (really, metaphor) of God as a divine parent—typically a "father"—with human offspring is deeply embedded in numerous religions. In the Jewish and Christian traditions, this rootage stems from the metaphor's presence in Scripture, where it is found in both the Old Testament/Hebrew Bible and the New Testament (note also Wis 14:3; Sir 23:1, 4). Admittedly, it occurs with much greater

My thanks to the members of the consultation for their helpful feedback, esp. William P. Brown, Marcia J. Bunge, and Terence E. Fretheim. I also thank Bill T. Arnold, Steve Kraftchick, Mark Roncace, Brad D. Strawn, and Christine Roy Yoder for reading drafts of the chapter and/or for discussing it with me. I dedicate this chapter to my children, Caleb Verner, Annie Jean, and Micah Reese, who, in this subject as in so many other subjects in life, have been my best teachers.

1. Louise Glück, *Proofs and Theories: Essays on Poetry* (Hopewell, NJ: Ecco, 1994), 7.
2. Carol Bellamy, ed., *The State of the World's Children 2005: Childhood Under Threat* (New York: The United Nations Children's Fund [UNICEF], 2004), 11.

frequency in the New Testament than in the Old,[3] and this fact is not without certain literary effects—one of which is that the New Testament presentation of God is, overall, far more "father-ish" than that of the Old.[4] Regardless, the metaphor's presence in both testaments serves as a uniting factor between them and helps to explain the "fatherhood" of God as a common conception in Judaism and Christianity.

The metaphor is not only Scriptural; it is powerful, and this in several ways. To mention but one example, many find it of great significance that in the New Testament Jesus often calls God "Father."[5] Whatever one might think about how this practice speaks to contemporary concerns over proper God-language—and whatever this practice's precedents in the Old Testament and elsewhere[6]—it is especially noteworthy that by means of this language Jesus is figured as (and figures himself as) God's *child*. Moreover, in the Lord's Prayer, according to both the Matthean and Lukan versions, Jesus encourages his followers to do the same by addressing God as "(our) father" (Matt 6:9; Luke 11:2). In this way, every Christian who prays this prayer becomes (is "metaphorized" as) the child of God. Not surprisingly, the children of God metaphor is found elsewhere in the New Testament (e.g., John 1:12; 1 John 3:1–2, 10; 5:2; Rom 8:16; Phil 2:15) and, of course, also in the Old.[7]

These examples—a few among many—demonstrate the significance of the "Divine Parent–Human Child" metaphor: it is deeply rooted, widely attested in Scripture, and legitimated by important figures and worship practices. Indeed,

3. By Marjo Christina Annette Korpel's count there are twenty-one instances of God being figured as a father in the Old Testament vs. 255 instances in the New Testament (*A Rift in the Clouds: Ugaritic and Hebrew Descriptions of the Divine*, UBL 8 [Münster: Ugarit-Verlag, 1990], 237). Both numbers would increase if one includes passages where parental imagery is alluded to or evoked in subtle ways.

4. Said differently, the Old Testament permits other metaphors more play; this functions to restrict and critique the father (alone) metaphor. See further §§2–3 below.

5. Some examples: Matt 7:21; 10:32–33; 11:27; 12:50; 15:13; Mark 14:36; Luke 10:22; 22:29, 42; 23:46; 24:49; John 5:17; 6:32, 40; 8:19, 49, 54; 10:18, 29, 37; 15:8, 15, 23–24; 20:17. One should perhaps distinguish passages where Jesus calls God "my father" from those where Jesus speaks of God as a father more generally. See further the essays on the Gospels in *The Child in the Bible*, ed. Marcia J. Bunge, Terence E. Fretheim, and Beverly Roberts Gaventa (Grand Rapids: Eerdmans, 2008), 143–214.

6. On these points, see Marianne Meye Thompson, *The Promise of the Father: Jesus and God in the New Testament* (Louisville: Westminster John Knox, 2000).

7. For the Johannine texts, see Marianne Meye Thompson, "Children in the Gospel of John," in Bunge, Fretheim, and Gaventa, *The Child in the Bible*, 195–214. For the Old Testament, see §§3–4 below. Note esp. Isa 63:16 where Israel prays to Yhwh, twice addressing God as "our father." A third instance, belonging to the same prayer, is found in Isa 64:8. See Paul Niskanen, "Yhwh as Father, Redeemer, and Potter in Isaiah 63:7–64:11," *CBQ* 68 (2006): 397–407.

the metaphor is so compelling that the ultimate proof of its power may be that many devout persons do not realize that the statement "God is (my/our) (Heavenly) Father" is a metaphor in the first place. But it is. And it is a metaphor with profound effects, in part because of the power of major, macro-metaphors such as this one (see §2). The present study (re)considers some of the most important of these effects. Its thesis can be stated as follows:

Construing the relationship between Yhwh and Israel as that between a parent (whether father or mother) and a child (whether daughter or son) has impact on at least two different areas:

1. explicitly, the metaphor shaped how Israel represented and understood God's actions toward itself and its actions toward God (see §3)—making what might otherwise be misunderstood on both sides of the metaphor (parent and child) available, evocative, and insightful;

2. implicitly, the metaphor affected how Israelite parents may have (and ought to have) treated their own children, providing them a divine example to emulate at its best moments (see §4).

The first area concerns the theology (including the theological anthropology) of the parent-child metaphor; the latter, the metaphor's ethics. The present chapter will argue that the latter can be understood in positive ways with beneficial results. This leads to a final piece of the thesis—one closely related to the second:

3. in its best aspects the God:Israel::parent:child analogy bears within itself ethical significance for present communities (and their families) that claim allegiance to these texts and the God they portray—offering them, like Israel, modes and models of action and relationship that can benefit all concerned (see §4).

This last item might be restated as a question: Does the portrayal of God as our parent make any difference when we consider our own relationship with our children? Once we have children of our own, do we parent differently and better if we believe God is a parent both to us and to others?[8] Before proceeding any further in answering these questions or addressing the various parts of this thesis, it is imperative to acknowledge some important and far less positive assessments

---

8. God's parenthood of "other children" means that the ethics at work need not concern only one's own biological children. See further §4 below, and Walter Brueggemann, "Vulnerable Children, Divine Passion, and Human Obligation," in Bunge, Fretheim, and Gaventa, *The Child in the Bible*, 399–422.

of the metaphor (§1). Thereafter, Wayne C. Booth's work on the ethics of metaphor will be discussed (§2) before I turn to the theology and ethics of the divine parent–human child metaphor proper (§§3–4, respectively).

1. Two Opposing Readings

In recent years vigorous criticism has been leveled at the God-as-parent metaphor, especially in its masculine-gendered version. Two writers can be lifted up as exemplary and paradigmatic. First, from a psychoanalytical perspective, is Sigmund Freud.[9] In several of his writings on religion, Freud argued that humanity (as species and civilization) evolved on analogy with the life of the individual. Consequently, the "traumata" associated with individual psyches were also present in larger, societal ways in extreme (prehistoric) antiquity. That ancient history was marked by the brutal rule of a tyrannical male father only belatedly conquered by a horde of victimized sons who wished to both be and to replace him. Reflexes of that drama (specifically, neurotic symptoms) are found by Freud in a number of religious systems and their beliefs. What is important for the present study is Freud's assertion that the problems manifested in both that tragic ancient history and in more recent religious phenomena stem from and pertain to the family, especially the father. Most striking in this regard is Freud's belief that the ancient despotic male ruler is ultimately what lies behind the (return of the) notion of "the one and only father deity whose power is unlimited"—namely, God the Father.[10]

Some fifty years later, writing from a feminist perspective, Mary Daly leveled a withering critique at "father religion." Like Freud before her, but in a different mode, Daly exposed the history of violence against women that has often accompanied the God-as-Father metaphor: "If God in 'his' heaven is a father ruling 'his' people, then it is in the 'nature' of things and according to divine plan and the order of the universe that society be male-dominated. Within this context a mystification of roles takes place: the husband dominating his wife represents God 'himself.' . . . If God is male, then the male is God."[11] There can be no doubt

---

9. For what follows, see Sigmund Freud, *Moses and Monotheism*, trans. Katherine Jones (New York: Vintage, 1939), esp. 101–17, 164–76. Many of the ideas in that book are already found in his earlier *Totem and Taboo: Some Points of Agreement between the Mental Lives of Savages and Neurotics*, trans. and ed. James Strachey (New York: Norton, 1950), esp. 182.

10. Freud, *Moses and Monotheism*, 106.

11. Mary Daly, *Beyond God the Father: Toward a Philosophy of Women's Liberation* (Boston: Beacon, 1985), 13, 19. Among others, Karl Barth would debate the equation; we only know fatherhood, he argues, because of God—not vice versa. See his *Credo* (New York: Scribner's, 1962), 19–27. Cf. Eph 3:14–15.

that the critiques of Freud and Daly are on target on a number of points. Insofar as the God-as-father/parent metaphor has been associated with and served to legitimate inappropriate and unjust "rule" by male figures, especially fathers, the problems these writers are critiquing are longstanding and in gross need of rectification. It is especially noteworthy that the difficulties they have identified are not confined solely to issues of *gender* but also and obviously concern *age* and *family relationships*: it is *the children*—whether boys or girls—who have typically suffered the ill effects of the father (or mother). Not surprisingly, then, both Freud and Daly have worried about the metaphor's capacity to permanently restrict humans to infantile status.[12]

However, simply because the metaphor has been problematic at points in the past does not constitute proof that it need necessarily be so always and everywhere. Freud's psychohistorical reconstruction, in particular, has been critiqued and challenged given its highly speculative nature.[13] Daly's gender-based argument is far more substantial, but its conclusions, too, are neither exhaustive nor foregone. Some women and children *can* relate (and evidently have done so) to the God-as-father metaphor with apparently no ill effects; conversely, some women and children (and men) *cannot* relate to the God-as-mother metaphor or have done so to ill effect.[14] Moreover, not all fathers are despotic—some have been known to be quite loving and nurturing; conversely, and unfortunately, even motherhood is not beyond the reach of tyrants. What is crucial, regardless, is that we remember, despite the power of the God-as-father/mother/parent metaphor, that we are dealing with a *metaphor*: God, even in biblical construction, is beyond gender.[15] Metaphors, furthermore, function as tropes of both resemblance and

---

12. See Freud, *Moses and Monotheism*, 172; Daly, *Beyond God the Father*, 25.

13. The post-Freudian critiques are too numerous to list. For a beginning, see Stephen A. Mitchell and Margaret J. Black, *Freud and Beyond: A History of Modern Psychoanalytic Thought* (New York: Basic Books, 1995).

14. See Jane R. Dickie et al., "Parent-Child Relationships and Children's Images of God," *Journal for the Scientific Study of Religion* 36 (1997): 25–43. This study of two diverse samples indicated that *both* fathers and mothers impact children's God-concepts. Interestingly, if the mother was perceived as powerful and the father as nurturing—a reversal, the authors note, of stereotypical gender roles—then God was perceived as both nurturing and powerful. Important for the conclusions of Daly is the fact that the children sampled tended to use God as an ideal substitute attachment figure, "the more perfect parent," *even and especially* if the actual parent was imperfect and/or absent (regardless of gender, though it was the fathers who were most often absent).

15. See Num 23:19; Hos 11:9; Job 32:13; Tikva Frymer-Kensky, *In the Wake of the Goddesses: Women, Culture, and the Biblical Transformation of Pagan Myth* (New York: Free Press, 1992), esp. 188–89; and Mayer I. Gruber, *The Motherhood of God and Other Studies*, SFSHJ 57 (Atlanta: Scholars Press,

dissemblance.[16] To say that God is a father is thus to say that God is both like and unlike fathers—especially, of course, fathers of the human variety.[17] The same holds true for the predication "God is a mother."

This is not to argue that the God-as-father metaphor (or God-as-parent metaphor, for that matter) is problem-free; on the contrary, it clearly has been problematic at many times and in various ways. That negative history lives on with us and in us such that the metaphor must always be viewed as potentially volatile.[18] It is only to say that this negative reception of the metaphor need not be so, at least not always, and this judgment is due, in part, to the ethics of metaphor in general and the ethics of this particular metaphor—points that must now be addressed.

2. On the Ethics of Metaphors

It is imperative to assess the parent-child metaphor precisely because of its potential for abuse and real (mis)use *against* children. And yet, when the metaphor

---

1992), 8; contra Daly, *Beyond God the Father*, xxiii–xxiv. For the argument that the biblical authors knew they were speaking metaphorically when they spoke of God's fatherhood, see Korpel, *Rift in the Clouds*, 237, 263, and note the earlier, similar sentiments of Roland de Vaux, *Ancient Israel: Its Life and Institutions* (New York: McGraw-Hill, 1961), 51–52; and W. Robertson Smith, *The Religion of the Semites: The Fundamental Institutions* (New York: Schocken, 1972), 41–42.

16. See Paul Ricoeur, *The Rule of Metaphor: Multi-Disciplinary Studies of the Creation of Meaning in Language*, trans. Robert Czerny, Kathleen McLaughlin, and John Costello (Toronto: University of Toronto Press, 1977), 6–7, 216–56, and passim; cf. Korpel, *Rift in the Clouds*, 48. The dissimilarity or difference inherent in metaphor is what makes Daly's equation of "God = male, therefore male = God" logically unnecessary.

17. By itself, the term for "father" in Hebrew may not refer only to humans. The term used for animal mothers is the same as that used of human mothers: *ʾēm* (see Exod 22:30 [29]; 23:19; 34:26; Lev 22:27; Deut 14:21; 22:6–7; cf. Job 17:14). While there is no clear reference in biblical Hebrew to a male animal by the term "father" (*ʾāb*), it is likely—given the use of *ʾēm*—that an animal father would also have been called *ʾāb*. So, while it is common for readers, when hearing of God as father, to think of human fathers, it is possible that this was not always the case in ancient Israel. Note that some parental metaphors used of God are mammalian and are marked for gender (Nah 2:13: male lion; Hos 13:8: female bear).

18. The same is true for many metaphors; see §2. For the history of violence against children remaining with us note the chilling remark of Alice Miller, *Thou Shalt Not Be Aware: Society's Betrayal of the Child*, trans. Hildegarde Hannum and Hunter Hannum (New York: Farrar, Straus and Giroux, 1998), 315: "The truth about our childhood is stored up in our body, and although we can repress it, we can never alter it. Our intellect can be deceived, our feelings manipulated, our perceptions confused, and our body tricked with medication. But someday the body will present its bill, for it is as incorruptible as a child who, still whole in spirit, will accept no compromises or excuses, and it will not stop tormenting us until we stop evading the truth." See further Alice Miller, *The Body Never Lies: The Lingering Effects of Cruel Parenting*, trans. Andrew Jenkins (New York: Norton, 2005).

is seen through their eyes, a way forward might be found. It may be the case that, when viewed with children "foregrounded," this metaphor is revealed to be one with great potential for and real use *on behalf of* children. If so, a reexamination of this metaphor is imperative as it can benefit children everywhere.

Assessment of the parent-child metaphor is also required because every metaphor contains within itself ethical potential. Figurative language, of whatever stripe, is powerful: it can "figure" the mind in tenacious ways. Wayne C. Booth, in his noted work on the ethics of fiction, writes: "Every art of the imagination, benign or vicious, profound or trivial, can colonize the mind."[19] In this colonization process, the one who experiences the art becomes, as it were, a part of the work of art itself. The effort that is involved in engaging or resisting art (or, here, figurative language) means that it "will always figure the mind more incisively than plain language."[20] This leads to an equation of sorts: the more engaging the figure, the more ethical power is needed and exerted. Most engaging and most powerful of all figures—and therefore most representative of the power of figurative language—is metaphor: "the figure that we . . . conduct our lives *with* and *in*."[21]

Not all metaphors are created equal, however; some are more powerful than others. The most powerful "do not simply *allow*" one to engage them or to wonder about possible ethical outcomes, "they *require* every reader to do so."[22] Booth calls these especially large and generative metaphors "cosmic myths" or "macro-metaphors."[23] These metaphors are world-creators—or, perhaps better, world-devourers: they demand "a choice between . . . imaginative worlds. . . . Each invites us to come and live within a given culture, sharing the assumptions of all who live there. Our entire way of life is thus at stake."[24] Metaphors derived from the sphere of the family and household are of this macro-type. Indeed, it is hard to imagine a more fundamental societal metaphor—whether we are speaking of antiquity or of today's world. The ethical assessment of metaphors drawn from the family sphere is thus particularly urgent. Such assessment has already taken place, especially around the problems of the gendered divine parent and *his* (!) human child. But Booth's work demonstrates that macro-metaphors are never taken in "as isolated propositions, nor even as developed fragments."[25] Instead, as

19. Wayne C. Booth, *The Company We Keep: An Ethics of Fiction* (Berkeley: University of California Press, 1988), 298.

20. Booth, *Company We Keep*, 298.

21. Booth, *Company We Keep*, 300; his italics; cf. 304 and, further, George Lakoff and Mark Johnson, *Metaphors We Live By* (Chicago: University of Chicago Press, 2003 [1980]).

22. Booth, *Company We Keep*, 331 (his italics).

23. Booth, *Company We Keep*, 325–73.

24. Booth, *Company We Keep*, 335.

25. Booth, *Company We Keep*, 336.

we encounter them, we re-constitute them within "a vast articulated network of interrelated images, emotions, propositions, anecdotes, and possibilities. . . . We find ourselves dwelling in a newly created, animated *uni*-verse of possibilities, in which each particular obtains its full life by virtue of being *in* the whole."[26] Among other things, this means that, even if the God-as-parent metaphor is represented in gendered fashion, it cannot be simplistically interpreted as "God = Father/Male Superpower" and/or/therefore "Father/Male Superpower = God" in purely negative fashion. Instead, the larger context(s) of the metaphor mean(s) that more is happening in the construction and reception of the metaphor. That "more" in the case of this particular metaphor is that the world created by the metaphor is, in context and at root, *familial*. This means that not only fatherhood, but also motherhood, and even childhood, are all on the table—the artist's table, as it were, taking their place in a larger, sculptured world.

That point being granted, macro-metaphors like those derived from the realm of family discourse remain powerful (and dangerous) precisely because of their capacity to co-opt the imagination and all other narratives completely. Once a macro-metaphor has been established and readers become aware of it (or entrapped by it), everything can and will be seen through its lens, even as that lens is modified, reinforced, or strengthened.[27] As Northrop Frye remarked: "In examining the relation of one subject to another, the initial choice of metaphors and conceptual diagrams is a fateful choice."[28] It is fateful because subsequent events, later metaphors, and succeeding images are all able to be read with—all *will* be read with—the initial choice. A macro-metaphor draws all narratives unto itself.

3. The Theology of the Divine Parent–Human Child Metaphor

Biblical family metaphors are macro-metaphors largely due to the importance of the family and household in the ancient world. In antiquity it was, quite simply, family "all the way down."[29] While the larger familial context means that family metaphors are never solely a matter of fathers, it is nevertheless apparent that ancient Israel,

---

26. Booth, *Company We Keep*, 336 (his italics).

27. See Booth, *Company We Keep*, 325.

28. Northrop Frye, "Expanding Eyes," *Critical Inquiry* 2 (1975): 204.

29. See the massive study by J. David Schloen, *The House of the Father as Fact and Symbol: Patrimonialism in Ugarit and the Ancient Near East*, Studies in the Archaeology and History of the Levant 2 (Winona Lake, IN: Eisenbrauns, 2001); as well as Mark S. Smith, *The Origins of Biblical Monotheism: Israel's Polytheistic Background and the Ugaritic Texts* (New York: Oxford University Press, 2001), 54–66, 90–91, 102–3; Leo G. Perdue, Joseph Blenkinsopp, John J. Collins, and Carol Meyers, *Families in Ancient Israel*, The Family, Religion, and Culture (Louisville: Westminster

as other ancient Near Eastern (and Mediterranean) societies, was "patri-central"—organized around a central male father figure. While traditional family structures have slowly changed in recent generations, especially in the industrialized world, it is no less true today that the family remains a (if not the) dominant nexus wherein humans live, move, and have their being. And every human being had parents, even if they played only biological functions. The sheer ubiquity of family, parents, and children—which is to say the human life-cycle and societal structures—means that family metaphors are set and function within a context that is quite literally everywhere. They are, as a result, eminently sensible. Construing God as a parent in this family-rich context is thus also thoroughly understandable. Indeed, the metaphor corresponds to such a degree with human society that—as noted above—many people do not realize that the construction is metaphorical in the first place.[30]

Turning directly to the Old Testament, Leo G. Perdue has argued that the family sphere had profound impact on the presentation of virtually all aspects of Israelite thought:

> Much of what the Old Testament says about the character and especially the activity of God is shaped by discourse concerning the family. . . . Major metaphors for Israel's self-presentation were drawn from household roles, especially those of the wife (the bride/wife of YHWH), the son and the daughter, the impoverished kin (redeemed by YHWH), and marginal members (debt servant, slave, resident alien, and sojourner). . . . Indeed, the household not only grounded Old Testament theology in Israel's social reality but also became the primary lens through which to view the character and activity of God, the identity and self-understanding of Israel in its relationship to God, the value and meaning of the land as the *naḥălâ* [inheritance] God gives to Israel, and Israel's relationship to the nations.[31]

Perdue's comment underscores for the Old Testament what we have already seen elsewhere: (1) the *power* of the family sphere as a locus for major theological metaphors; and (2) the ability of the family metaphor to become all-powerful: a macro-metaphorical lens through which all else is viewed—God, Israel, the land, the nations.

John Knox, 1997); and Karel van der Toorn, *Family Religion in Babylonia, Syria and Israel: Continuity and Change in the Forms of Religious Life*, SHCANE 7 (Leiden: Brill, 1996), passim, esp. 205.

30. Schloen, *House of the Father*, 349, points out that the parent-child metaphor endures because it is not a "free invention of discourse but is 'bound' to actual preverbal experience of the world."

31. Leo G. Perdue, "The Household, Old Testament Theology, and Contemporary Hermeneutics," in Perdue et al., *Families in Ancient Israel*, 225–26; cf. 251, 254.

And yet, interestingly enough, when we turn to Genesis, we do not encounter the family metaphor under discussion here, that of parent-child, in the beginning, where we might expect it. Instead, apart from creation, which in the ancient Near East was often associated with various gods' "fatherly" status,[32] we have no indication of God's "fathering" in the first book of the Bible.[33] The metaphor is withheld until Exod 4. When it finally appears there, it is shocking in force:

> Yhwh said to Moses: "When you return to Egypt, make sure that you do all the wonders that I have placed in your power before Pharaoh. But I will harden his heart so that he will not release the people. Then say to Pharaoh, 'Thus says Yhwh: Israel is my firstborn son [bny bkry yśr'l]. I said to you: Release my son [bny] that he might worship me, but you have refused to release him. So, now I will kill your firstborn son [bnk bkrk].'" (Exod 4:21–23)[34]

The placement of this metaphor is significant in at least two ways. The first is that it comes on the scene relatively early in the book of Exodus. The narrative of Moses's call and commission has only just finished in Exod 4:17, and, though v. 20 indicates that Moses and his family went back to Egypt, the subsequent materials indicate that vv. 21–23 occur (in narrative time) prior to the first encounter with Pharaoh (see vv. 21, 24, 27). These temporal and geographical confusions may reflect redactional seams and compositional layers; but even so, that judgment

---

32. That is, as begetter or engenderer. Some scholars (e.g., David R. Tasker, *Ancient Near Eastern Literature and the Hebrew Scriptures about the Fatherhood of God*, StBibLit 69 [New York: Peter Lang, 2004]) have argued that the avoidance of "father" language with reference to the creation of the world is a polemical move on Israel's part vis-à-vis its neighbors. This claim appears dubious in light of Deut 32:6, which employs *'āb* ("father") along with the verbs *qnh* ("to create"), *'śh* ("to do/make"), and *kwn* ("to establish"). Moreover, even if father-language is absent from Genesis, the power of the parent-child metaphor is such that the creation stories can easily be read through its lens. Cf. Mal 2:10; 1 Cor 8:6.

33. A possible exception, depending on certain interpretations, would be the "God of the fathers" motif that recurs throughout Genesis. *Prima facie*, however, the metaphorical construction here appears different. Regardless, the power of the metaphorical lens means that these references can also be read as reflecting the parent-child metaphor. For example, covenant terminology in the ancient Near East and Old Testament often uses family terms, sometimes with adoption overtones. The covenant and calling of Abraham (e.g., Gen 12:1–9; 15:1–21; 17:1–27), therefore, can be read (esp. via the parent-child metaphor) as a kind of divine adoption. For more on the child in Genesis, see Terence E. Fretheim, "'God Was with the Boy' (Genesis 21:20): Children in the Book of Genesis," in Bunge, Fretheim, and Gaventa, *The Child in the Bible*, 3–23; for adoption, see David Bartlett, "Adoption in the Bible," in Bunge, Fretheim, and Gaventa, *The Child in the Bible*, 375–98.

34. Translations are my own unless otherwise indicated.

only serves to underscore the importance of the current canonical placement of vv. 21–23. As it now stands in the book of Exodus, this unit is a summary of the showdown with Pharaoh *before the fact*, and the climax of that summary is the explanation offered in vv. 22–23, predicated on the identification of Israel as Yhwh's firstborn son.[35] This predication suggests that Yhwh is Israel's parent, but no specific term for parent is used of Yhwh until much later (Deut 32:6; *'āb*, "father").[36] Whatever the case, the placement of the metaphor so early in the Exodus narrative (and the Pentateuch as a whole)[37] indicates that the metaphor should not be understood solely as a reflex of the covenant, nor simply as covenantal language.[38] For Exodus (and the Pentateuch), God's parenting of Israel is earlier and prior to covenant-making. From whence the metaphor comes is not explicitly stated, though the use of the "God of the fathers" motif in Exod 3:6, 15–16; 4:5, and throughout Genesis, is probably sufficient indication that it has to do with the ancestors (cf. Deut 4:37; 7:8).[39] Regardless, in the narrative form of Exodus, the

---

35. The initial positioning of *bny bkry* and the double construction in v. 22 suggest emphasis: "*My son, my firstborn (son)* is Israel." The *inclusio* with v. 23 (which ends with *bnk bkrk*, "your son, your firstborn [son]") should not be missed. At the center of this structure is the command in v. 23a to "release my son (*bny*) that he might worship me." Pharaoh's refusal (*m'n*) to release leads directly to Yhwh's statement that he will kill Pharaoh's firstborn. Everything hinges, then, on *bny*, "my son." What is done, or not done, to *bny*, "*my* son," directly affects *bnk*, "*your* [i.e., Pharaoh's] son." Cf. Jon D. Levenson, *The Death and Resurrection of the Beloved Son: The Transformation of Child Sacrifice in Judaism and Christianity* (New Haven: Yale University Press, 1993), 38: "In no small measure, the story of the Exodus turns on the contrast between the first-born son whom God enables to survive enslavement and attempted genocide and the first-born son whom he slays."

36. Cf., earlier, the metaphors in Deut 1:31; 8:5 (both of God, with *k'šr*, "just as"); and 14:1 (of Israel).

37. This placement also means that the metaphor occurs early in the presentation of Israel as a nation-group (regardless of what that group is called) since that is often thought to lie in the book of Exodus itself (cf. *bny yśr'l* in Exod 1:1 with 1:9 [*'m* "people"]) or in the Exodus event (see Exod 15; esp. the use of *qnh*, "to create," in v. 16).

38. Contra F. Charles Fensham, "Father and Son as Terminology for Treaty and Covenant," in *Near Eastern Studies in Honor of William Foxwell Albright*, ed. Hans Goedicke (Baltimore: Johns Hopkins Press, 1971), 121–35; Dennis J. McCarthy, "Notes on the Love of God in Deuteronomy and the Father-Son Relationship Between Yahweh and Israel," *CBQ* 27 (1965): 144–47; Niskanen, "Yhwh as Father," 397–407; and others. But, again, the covenant can be read with the parent-child metaphor and vice versa (see notes 32–33 above). In this light, one wonders if "becoming like a child" in the New Testament involves entering into relationship (or into covenant) with God (see Matt 18:1–5; Mark 9:33–37; 10:15; Luke 9:46–48; 18:17; John 1:12; 12:36). For relationship *preceding* covenant, see Terence E. Fretheim, *God and World in the Old Testament: A Relational Theology of Creation* (Nashville: Abingdon, 2005), 14–16.

39. Cf. Schloen, *House of the Father*, esp. 345–60; and van der Toorn, *Family Religion*, 155–60, on the West Semitic god *Ilib* (literally: "the god of the father"—that is, the divine ancestor), who

metaphor is not only covenantal, though it can easily include that. It is, at times at least, "literal"—that is, real, whether biological or adoptive.[40]

The second critical observation about the placement of Exod 4:21–23 is that it occurs *in* the context of the exodus event with all that that means, both socio-politically and theologically. A large part of what that means is that God's parental claim of "child Israel" involves *protection and deliverance* of God's child. That these values are at work in the very first instance of the metaphor is of no small import. In Tasker's words, "when God liberates his people from bondage and allots them their inheritance, he is 'acting like a father.'"[41] But note that Exod 4:21–23 does *not* mention inheritance; instead, it is apparent that Tasker has succumbed to the power of the parent-child macro-metaphor. Given its early placement in the Pentateuch and its conceptual, explanatory power, Tasker has read the entirety of the narrative of Exodus–Joshua through the metaphorical lens. Such is the power of a macro-metaphor! Even so, the presence of protection and deliverance in the first clear instance of the parent-child metaphor in Scripture lends support to Tasker's further comment: "It appears that this metaphor was chosen by the Bible writers to best describe their experience of God's protection and care from the perspective of human fatherhood, as they knew it."[42] This statement is full of ethical potential for human parents (see §4 below), but it also has ethical ramifications for this particular text. Quite apart from the vexed issue of the hardening of Pharaoh's heart (v. 21), the difficulty of v. 23 should not be skirted. To be sure, there are protection, care, and liberation for child Israel. But it comes at the expense of Pharaoh's (Egypt's) firstborn. Some children live, some die: both at the hands of the Parent who is Yhwh. These two outcomes concerning the firstborn son are

---

was a primeval deity—father of the gods—at Ugarit and elsewhere. For the general antiquity of the parent-child metaphor in Israel and elsewhere, see McCarthy, "Notes on the Love of God," 144–47; Tasker, *Ancient Near Eastern Literature*; Smith, *Religion of the Semites*, 41–48; Korpel, *Rift in the Clouds*, 236; and Thorkild Jacobsen, *The Treasures of Darkness: A History of Mesopotamian Religion* (New Haven: Yale University Press, 1976), 145–64, esp. 158–60. Note also Num 21:29 which applies the metaphor to the Moabite people and their god Chemosh.

40. For the latter option, see Janet L. R. Melnyk, "When Israel Was a Child: Ancient Near Eastern Adoption Formulas and the Relationship between God and Israel," in *History and Interpretation: Essays in Honour of John H. Hayes*, ed. M. Patrick Graham, William P. Brown, and Jeffrey K. Kuan, JSOTSup 173 (Sheffield: Sheffield Academic, 1993), 245–59. For the "literal" option, see Tasker, *Ancient Near Eastern Literature*, 191. Note also Fensham, "Father and Son," 132, who points out that Deut 32:19 cannot be a covenantal instance of the metaphor because it mentions daughters and "nowhere in the Old Testament or the ancient Near East is 'daughters' used as a covenant term." Of course, this verse could be the exception.

41. Tasker, *Ancient Near Eastern Literature*, 5. See also Niskanen, "Yhwh as Father," 406.

42. Tasker, *Ancient Near Eastern Literature*, 5–6.

inextricably conjoined in this text. How, then, does this text speak for and about children (can it?), who in our day are so often the victims in armed conflicts not unlike (and certainly as deadly) as the battle between Yhwh and Pharaoh?[43]

Exodus 4:21–23, like so many other difficult texts, cannot be "fixed," especially not easily, but it is worth paying attention to the fact that this first indication of Yhwh's onslaught against Pharaoh and Egypt via the plague of the firstborn is crafted as a metaphor and, further, *as a metaphor* that highlights *the childlike status of Israel*. Perhaps we will never understand the hardening of Pharaoh's heart, the plague narratives, or, especially, the final plague, all of which testify to an odd, violent, and certainly biased deity. But we can understand or at least *feel* this metaphor with its evocation of childlike helplessness and parental passion. Children are the most vulnerable of human beings, easily preyed upon, most in need of protection. And what parent would not go to the end of the world to protect their child? Especially a child that has been imprisoned, beaten, enslaved, or worse? Who would not, if they could, wreak havoc (or at least wish to) on the perpetrator of their child's death?[44] This does not fix a very difficult text, but seeing the violence of Yhwh against Egypt through the metaphorical lens of the parent-child may make it more understandable and affective, even if it remains unpalatable.[45] (But is it unpalatable, when *our* children are at stake?)

Co-opting (All) Other Metaphors

Certainly more could be said about this text from Exod 4. For now, however, it is important to reconsider the parent-child metaphor in Exodus in light of Booth's work on macro-metaphors. When this is done, the early placement of the metaphor in the book of Exodus and in the context of Egyptian slavery becomes even

43. See Bellamy, *State of the World's Children 2005*, 39–66; and Danna Nolan Fewell, *The Children of Israel: Reading the Bible for the Sake of Our Children* (Nashville: Abingdon, 2003), 19, for the grisly statistics. For the difficulties the book of Exodus poses for children, see Claire Mathews McGinnis, "Exodus as a 'Text of Terror' for Children," in Bunge, Fretheim, and Gaventa, *The Child in the Bible*, 24–44.

44. Israel is, of course, a collective "child." For these children's deaths, see Pharaoh's attempts at genocide in Exod 1:15–22. Note also Deut 32:43: "Praise, O heavens, his people, worship him, all you gods! For he will avenge the blood of his children" (NRSV).

45. Perhaps the lack of an explicit term for a parent (whether father or mother) in Exod 4:21–23 is a hint that in this particular instance of the metaphor the parental passion is restricted to the Deity, not to be replicated (or replicable) by humans. In this interpretation, the metaphor allows us to sympathize with Yhwh's parental passion but not act/requite in the same way. For more on parental passion, mobilized in the defense of the child, see Brueggemann, "Vulnerable Children."

more significant as does the fact that the first occurrence establishes the relationship between God and Israel as one of concerned/impassioned parent with needy/victimized child. These factors are important because Booth argues that once a macro-metaphor such as the parent-child one is established—especially if it is done powerfully and if it is repeated—subsequent events will be seen to reinforce the metaphor.[46]

It is not surprising, then, to find God figured as a parent elsewhere in the Bible—often times quite explicitly (e.g., Deut 1:31; 8:5; 32:6; Jer 3:4; Ps 68:5[6]),[47] at other times by means of the identification of Israel (or a representative thereof) as the child(ren) of the Lord (e.g., Deut 14:1; 2 Sam 7:14; Isa 1:2, 4; 30:1, 9; 63:8; Jer 3:14, 22; 4:22; 31:20; Hos 1:10 [2:1]; 1 Chr 17:13; 22:9–10; 28:6), or, occasionally, both (see Deut 32:5–6, 18; Isa 43:6–7; 45:10–11; 63:16; 64:8[7]; Jer 3:19; 31:9; Ezek 16; Hos 11; Mal 2:10–11; 3:17; Pss 2:7; 89:26–27[27–28]; Sir 23:1, 4). Each of these texts can and should be read for how they reinforce the parent-child metaphor begun in Exod 4—a task that lies outside the scope of the present essay.[48] Even so, it can be stated that *nurture and care* are aspects of some of these metaphors (see, e.g., Deut 1:31; Jer 31:9; Hos 11:1, 3–4, 8–9; Mal 3:17; Pss 68:5–6[6–7]; 103:13; Wis 14:3; cf. Deut 32:10–11); *covenant and discipline* belong to others (see, e.g., Deut 8:5; 14:1; Prov 3:11–12; Mal 1:6); *adoption* seems implied in still others (see, e.g., Ps 27:10; cf. 2 Sam 7:14; 1 Chr 17:13; 22:9–10; 28:6; Ps 2:7); and so on and so forth. Most of these passages figure God as a father and Israel as God's son (usually), God's daughter (cf. Lam 2:13; Deut 32:19; Isa 43:6; 2 Cor 6:18), or a (female) foundling saved by the Lord (Ezek 16). All of them reinforce the parent-child metaphor even as they simultaneously modify it, adding various nuances to its first occurrence in Exod 4. One way to put this is to say that these additional metaphors reveal Yhwh to be not just any parent, but a certain kind of parent—a father who carries and protects, for instance (Deut 1:31), and a mother who will not forget her child (Isa 49:15; see further below).[49]

The second observation regarding the parent-child metaphor established in Exod 4:22 (if not earlier) is that, as a macro-metaphor, it creates a powerful world

46. See the next paragraph and cf. the use of *bkwr* in Exod 11:5; 12:12, 29; 13:15; cf. 13:2, 13; 22:28; 34:20. The only other instance of *bkwr* in God's mouth with reference to Israel is Jer 31:9. Cf. Ps 89:27(28) for Yhwh making the king "(as) the firstborn" (*bkwr*).

47. Mythological passages such as Ps 82:6–7 and the like (cf. Gen 6:2, 4; Job 1:6; 2:1; 38:7; Ps 29:1), while not completely unrelated, lie at some remove from the concerns of the present chapter.

48. Tasker, *Ancient Near Eastern Literature*, offers brief analyses of most of the father-passages. For other passages, see further below.

49. See Terence E. Fretheim, *The Suffering of God: An Old Testament Perspective*, OBT (Philadelphia: Fortress, 1984), 12.

that captures all other narratives. It co-opts (lesser) metaphors in subsequent con-texts, creating a lens through which they can and will be seen as part and parcel of the macro-metaphor. In this way, the events following Exod 4—*all* the events, not just those that explicitly utilize the metaphor—can be "read with" the parent-child image. Assuming and granting that this is true, we can focus on two specific ways the metaphor functions when the rest of Scripture is seen through its lens: Israel's perceptions and representations of (1) God as its parent and (2) itself as God's child. Co-inhering with both of these, but perhaps forming a third distinct category, is another function: viewing other people as God's children (see further below).[50]

God-Perceptions

There is a tendency, perhaps even pressure, to read the parent-child metaphor's impact on God-perceptions positively. So, for example, Tasker argues that the ba-sic tenor of the portrait of God as a father in Scripture is God's passion for God's children,[51] such that God's parenting is best described in terms of *rḥm* ("mercy, pity") and *'hb* ("love").[52] He concludes his study with a list of attributes of God's fatherhood: creative, personal and loving, universal, covenantal, powerful, salv-ific, nurturing, vindicating, just and merciful, educational, proactive, relational, humanitarian.[53]

All of these divine qualities are laudable. But, as Exod 4 demonstrates, the texts themselves reveal other qualities as well, showing that disturbing aspects can be inextricably joined to the most beautiful of things. These other, more negative,

50. As Terence E. Fretheim reminds me (oral communication), this latter category may indi-cate that family is fundamentally a *creational* category. One thinks of how the book of Genesis is structured as a genealogy: "These are the generations [*tôlĕdôt*] . . ." (see Gen 2:4; 5:1; 6:9; 10:1, 32; 11:10, 27; 25:12, 13, 19; 36:1, 9; 37:2). If so, it would indicate that Israel's self-understanding is based on the more basic creational understanding of God's relation to the entire world. See Fretheim's extensive treatment of this motif in his *God and World in the Old Testament*.

51. Tasker, *Ancient Near Eastern Literature*, 197, 207, who argues that this is in contrast to other ancient Near Eastern deities. So, similarly, John W. Miller, "God as Father in the Bible and the Father Image in Several Contemporary Ancient Near Eastern Myths: A Comparison," *SR* 14 (1985): 347–54.

52. Tasker, *Ancient Near Eastern Literature*, 198. Note that Phyllis Trible has argued that *rḥm* has female connotations (*God and the Rhetoric of Sexuality*, OBT [Philadelphia: Fortress, 1978], esp. 31–59).

53. Tasker, *Ancient Near Eastern Literature*, 204–6. See also Miller, "God as Father," esp. 353; John W. Miller, *Calling God "Father": Essays on the Bible, Fatherhood and Culture*, 2nd ed. (New York: Paulist, 1999), 44; Melnyk, "When Israel Was a Child," 245–59; Willem A. VanGemeren, "*'Abbā'* in the Old Testament?" *JETS* 31 (1988): 393.

qualities must not be neglected. They, too, are real and have potentially real impact on real children. And, as Exod 4 also demonstrates, it is often the distinctly familial aspect of the metaphor that allows one to understand and empathize with, if not appropriate, the negative instances of the metaphor.[54]

1. Whether "positive" or "negative,"[55] it is clear that the parent-child metaphor impacts Israel's depictions of God. Given the urgency of the negative instances of the metaphor, these merit special attention. As a first example, one might lift up the issue of *parental impatience with children*. Simplistically (too simplistically), one might contrast a human parent's impatience with their child with God's supposedly infinite patience so as to produce a particular ethic (a work-ethic, no doubt!): namely, parents who *try* to be more patient with their children. The problem with this scenario is that parent Yhwh is sometimes portrayed as impatient with child Israel. Does this obviate the ideal of a truly patient parent (whether divine, ancient, or modern)? Does it, rather, recommend impatience with children? Perhaps someone would want to argue that; it makes far more sense, however, to reverse the metaphor, so to speak, and examine God's impatience through the parent-child lens. Seen in this way, God's impatience becomes quite understandable, maybe even forgivable. Who, after all, has not been similarly exasperated with their children at one point or another? Moreover, there are times when impatience with one's children is not only natural but expected, even justified. A look at the murmuring accounts in the Pentateuch casts light on this.

In the murmuring stories, Israel complains about various matters, including a lack of basic necessities during their sojourn in the wilderness: water, bread, meat. Jay A. Wilcoxen has noted a marked difference between these kinds of stories prior to Sinai (e.g., Exod 15:22–27; 16:1–36; 17:1–7) and those after Sinai (e.g., Num 11:1–35).[56] Prior to Sinai, there are no serious punishments associated with the Israelites' complaints regarding food and water. After Sinai, there are major punishments, including death. Sinai, in short, makes a difference: it formalizes the God-Israel

54. Some readers will take issue with the suggestion that we could "appropriate" negative aspects of the parent-child metaphor. Space precludes a refutation of that objection; I can only defer and refer to Booth's work which masterfully shows that *all* metaphors must be evaluated and that we do, in fact, perform such evaluation all the time—indeed, every time we encounter a metaphor—and that we do so on the basis of pre-existing metaphors that we already know and have already evaluated. "Appropriation," that is, is not an option and need not and must not be understood simplistically in positive or utilitarian fashion. The term Booth coins for the kind of engagement he describes is "coduction." See *Company We Keep*, esp. 70–77, 371–81.

55. These terms are heuristic; I do not wish to imply a simple dichotomy. Several of the metaphorical constructions are exceedingly complicated and do not permit easy reification.

56. Jay A. Wilcoxen, "Some Anthropocentric Aspects of Israel's Sacred History," *JR* 48 (1968): 333–50.

relationship and, therefore, Israel's responsibilities (see, e.g., Exod 19:1–8). When viewed through the lens of the parent-child metaphor, this narrative development can be seen on analogy with human development: "The divine promise to the patriarchs is the 'conception' of 'Israel,' the exodus is the 'birth' (the 'delivery') of 'Israel,' Sinai is the 'bar mitzvah' of 'Israel' (the point at which moral responsibility formally begins), the two parts of the wilderness period are preadolescent childhood and the period from adolescence to adulthood. . . . Prior to Sinai their responsibility in these respects had not been formalized. 'Israel' was still a child to be scolded not yet a 'son of the commandment.'"[57] Israel "grows up" at Sinai, or is supposed to at any rate. By means of the parent-child metaphor God's parental impatience is made understandable, and, in some cases—such as in the murmuring stories or the golden calf debacle (see Exod 32:1–34:28)—it is portrayed as justifiable.

Related to the issue of impatience is that of *parental fatigue*. Perhaps the universal experience of being a tired parent affords insight into some of the habits and attitudes of "God the father." The parent-child lens suggests that parental fatigue might explain "lapses" in God's (stereo)typical qualities such as patience, tolerance, love, and the like. "If God is a parent," the metaphorical logic runs, "and parents sometimes get tired and impatient with their children, then maybe that is why God is impatient with me/us now." This logic is obviously well down the road to theodicy—making sense of or at least considering God's mysterious and problematic ways. The logic is also putting the metaphor's power to good use on the child-referent of the metaphor—that is, Israel's self-perception—a topic that will be engaged momentarily.

Third, the parent-child metaphor proves helpful in understanding *divine regret*. Parents sometimes (in truth, oftentimes) have regret regarding their parenting. Parents sometimes (oftentimes) regret things they did or did not do, or wish they had done things differently, because they realize too late that their children were incapable of certain attitudes or behaviors or were unable to understand certain concepts. Hosea 11 is a good example of this process at work in the parent-child metaphor (see also Jer 42:10). Here Yhwh is figured as a parent, loving Israel as a "young boy" (*n'r*) and calling "my son" (*bny*) from Egypt (Hos 11:1). But Israel rebelled, sacrificing to the Baals and offering incense to idols (v. 2). Yhwh then recounts a history of parental goodness: teaching Israel to walk, carrying Israel, feeding them (vv. 3–4). This mismatch between parental beneficence and childish rebellion is more than the divine parent can stomach: Israel will return to Egypt, be ruled by Assyria; the sword rages and devours (vv. 5–6). But it is precisely at this juncture, at the very moment when the people call out to the Most High to no avail, that avail occurs.

57. Wilcoxen, "Some Anthropocentric Aspects," 347–48, 349.

> How could I hand you over, O Ephraim?
> > How could I give you up, O Israel?
> How could I make you like Admah?
> > How could I make you like Zeboiim?
> My heart is changed within me;
> > all my compassion grows tender.
> I will not act upon my fierce anger;
> > I will not turn to destroy Ephraim;
> for I am God, not a human,
> > the Holy One in your midst,
> and I will not come in rage. (Hos 11:8–9).

Yhwh, like other parents, realizes—partially in retrospect, but also (and largely) in a self-conflicted sort of way—that he was too hard on child Israel. Divine compassion wins out: Yhwh's children will return from Egypt and Assyria, Yhwh returns them to their homes (vv. 10–11).

Does the parent-child metaphor "sanctify" passages like this one, which can recount divine judgment in violent detail? Or does the metaphor simply suggest the image of an abusive (divine) parent? Many have worried about the latter option, and with good cause.[58] But the ethical criticism of macro-metaphors cuts both ways: the divine parent can be seen in some passages as a violent one, but the violent passages can also be reframed, chastened, modified in light of other instances and aspects of the parent-child metaphor, including (and especially) those of love and nurturance. That modification may not solve all of the problems at work in passages that involve divine violence, but it does create a heuristic matrix through which they can be seen and understood in more sympathetic fashion. Perhaps God is, at times at least, an impatient and exhausted parent. Perhaps, at times at least, God is even provoked by a child's rebellion, such that divine judgment is warranted. And, perhaps, at times at least, if and when God *over*-punishes, even God regrets.[59] But the Hos 11 passage also indicates that dissemblance is part of the parent-child metaphor. God is God, after all, not a human (v. 9b), and that predication both justifies and motivates God's decision not to punish (v. 9a, c). Perhaps it is significant to note that the term for human here is specifically *'îš*, which generically means "man," but which can be a term used for

---

58. See, e.g., Terence E. Fretheim, "'I Was Only a Little Angry': Divine Violence in the Prophets," *Int* 58 (2004): 365–75.

59. See further Fretheim, "'I Was Only a Little Angry,'" on the regret having to do, at least in part, with the fact that the human agents chosen and used by the Lord overdo it and go too far.

fathers (e.g., Deut 1:31; Eccl 6:3). Yhwh is like a father, yes, but also *unlike* a father: in this case, Yhwh's patience and decision to forgo punishment distinguish him from human counterparts even as they set a model example for human parents to emulate (see §4 below).

2. Other positive aspects of the portrayal of God as a parent in the Old Testament can also be seen by means of the metaphor's power to co-opt other narratives. Positive aspects of *parental passion* have already been noted above for Exod 4 and Hos 11. Another example: the constant reminders of God's gift of land or other gracious acts to Israel in Deuteronomy (cf. also Jer 3:19) could be seen as *assurances of parental goodness.*[60] The protection and care begun in Exod 4 are reinforced here through seemingly endless repetition with the result that God appears—again: at times at least—as the ideal parent, one who is not above *parental indulgence*, providing the child with all the best gifts.[61] *Parental forbearance* is another positive aspect and serves to balance instances of *parental impatience*. Indeed, both were at work in the play of the poetry in Hos 11. Still further on this point, when some of the pentateuchal legislation pertaining to children is seen through the metaphorical lens, God is depicted as *ultra*-patient.

According to Deut 21:18–21, the incorrigible son (*bn*)—one who is stubborn (*srr*) and rebellious (*mrh*), who will not listen (*'yn* + *šm'*) to the voice of his father and mother and who will not heed (*l'* + *šm'*) their discipline—deserves death after a public trial with the elders at the city gate (cf. also Exod 21:17; Lev 20:9; Prov 20:20). The verbs used to describe this rebellious child are often used of Israel. In fact, "most of the vocabulary that describes the rebellious son in the Hebrew Bible is used to portray Israel's rebellion against YHWH."[62] Through the metaphorical lens—especially with a little help from the prophets—one can see child Israel often and repeatedly cursing its parent, Yhwh (see, e.g., Isa 1:2–3). But, while Yhwh repeatedly engages in legal proceedings with the rebellious child (especially with a little help from the prophets), the prescribed punishments are

60. See, e.g., Deut 1:8, 11, 20–21, 25, 35–36; 2:7, 12, 29, 36; 3:18; 4:1, 21, 38, 40; 5:16, 31; 6:10, 18, 23; 7:8, 12–13; 8:1, 10; 9:6, 23; 10:11; 11:9, 17, 21, 31; 12:1, 7, 9, 15; 14:24, 29; 15:4, 6–7, 10, 14, 18; 16:10, 15, 20; 17:14; 18:9; 19:1–2, 10, 14, 28; 21:1, 23; 23:20(21); 24:4; 25:15, 19; 26:1–3, 9, 15; 27:2–3; 28:8, 11–12, 52; 30:16, 20; 31:7, 20–21, 23; 32:49, 52; 34:4.

61. Positive aspects such as these argue against McCarthy, "Notes on the Love of God," 145–46, who finds no trace of tenderness or love in the parent-child metaphor, evidently because the love that is discussed is one that can be commanded. For a thorough refutation of such a position, see Jacqueline E. Lapsley, "Feeling Our Way: Love for God in Deuteronomy," *CBQ* 65 (2003): 350–69. Note also Leo G. Perdue, "The Israelite and Early Jewish Family: Summary and Conclusions," in Perdue et al., *Families in Ancient Israel*, 171.

62. Melnyk, "When Israel Was a Child," 256. Cf., e.g., Neh 9:29; Ps 78:8; Isa 1:23; 30:1; 65:2; Num 27:14; Deut 1:26.

repeatedly deferred. God's threatened punishments look increasingly like empty parental threats: they are not lies per se, but the loving parent never wishes to act on them. And, even when the death penalty is finally executed in 596/586 BCE—if the destruction of Jerusalem and the Judean deportations into Babylonian exile can be described in such a way[63]—even this is not the final word. There is, for both parent and child, *life after death*. Moreover, the life that happens then is, according to Jeremiah and Ezekiel, completely at God's gracious initiative. The child is resurrected, as it were, purely because of the parent's surpassing love and grace; the child does nothing to provoke or promote this restoration.[64] But, long before the climactic drama of exile and return, parent Yhwh is repeatedly shown to be "slow to anger" (see, e.g., Exod 34:6; Num 14:18; Jonah 4:2; Nah 1:3; Sir 5:4), forgiving, and non-punitive.

3. Two items bear emphasizing in the impact of the parent-child metaphor on Israel's depiction of Yhwh: First, the themes identified above and those like them need not and should not be seen as originating solely from within the parent-child metaphor. Each may well have its own distinct lineage. Still, the fact that each can be profitably understood by means of the parent-child metaphor underscores the metaphor's power. Simply put, it has the two characteristics (or tests) that Booth deems necessary for macro-metaphors: comprehensiveness and correspondence.[65]

Second, the fact that Israel knows the ups and downs of its parent's "moods" or "tempers"—that it can read the Deity's various affect states and is able to recognize, characterize, and record them—is worth worrying about in light of Alice Miller's notion of the "gifted child." Is Israel such a gifted child, which in Miller's estimation is not a positive characteristic in the least since it is the product of inappropriate parenting?[66] Or, on the contrary, at its best moments, does the parent-

---

63. See Donald E. Gowan, *Theology of the Prophetic Books: The Death and Resurrection of Israel* (Louisville: Westminster John Knox, 1998).

64. See Thomas M. Raitt, *A Theology of Exile: Judgment/Deliverance in Jeremiah and Ezekiel* (Philadelphia: Fortress, 1977). One might contrast Luke 15:11–32 where the prodigal must first return.

65. *Comprehensiveness*: "It 'covers' the essential territory with astonishing breadth: it provides a ground for our responsibilities; it accounts for our human origins and nature; it provides particular standards for choosing between plausible moral requirements; and it provides a motive for obeying the moral law that it reveals." *Correspondence*: It corresponds "to our common-sense experience of our own ambiguous natures and that of our fellows. . . . It does not deny but rather explains our capacity for nobility—and yet both acknowledges and provides remedies for our inherent love of vice. . . . It is open to new historical experience; in the domain of history, it is pluralistic . . . [it] is implicitly *shareable* by all humankind" (Booth, *Company We Keep*, 359–61).

66. See Alice Miller, *Prisoners of Childhood*, trans. Ruth Ward (New York: Basic Books, 1981).

child metaphor show God to be the paradigmatic "good enough" parent if not, in fact, more than that?[67] Perhaps child Israel—better, Israel as fully-grown adult child—is affectively gifted because it had a parent that appropriately attended to it via mirroring, parental matching, empathetic attunement, and the like.[68] When the parent-child metaphor is drawn widely, given its fullest, most comprehensive scope, it certainly looks that way. The Psalms, for example, especially the laments, become a means by which God mirrors Israel's pain, granting its legitimacy and reality.[69] The canon of Scripture itself becomes a family scrapbook or picture album of sorts, preserving not only moments of the family's history for posterity's sake, but also occasions for *parental pride*.

4. One final text must be mentioned: it is the notoriously difficult Ezek 16, which depicts Jerusalem as an abandoned baby girl, a foundling, evidently left to die of exposure (vv. 1–5). Yhwh saves Jerusalem (vv. 6–7), then marries her (vv. 8–14), but after she "plays the whore" (vv. 15–34), Yhwh promises punishment that is rife with themes of sexual violence (vv. 35–43).[70] Like Hos 11, when Ezek 16 is viewed through the parent-child lens it seems to be at great pains to describe

67. For the notion of the "good enough" parent, see D. W. Winnicott, *The Maturational Processes and the Facilitating Environment: Studies in the Theory of Emotional Development* (Madison, CT: International Universities, 1965), 140–52.

68. See Miller, *Prisoners of Childhood*, 10; Miller, *For Your Own Good: Hidden Cruelty in Child-Rearing and the Roots of Violence*, trans. Hildegarde and Hunter Hannum (New York: Farrar, Straux, Giroux, 1990), 284: people whose integrity has not been damaged in childhood, who were protected, respected, and treated with honesty by their parents, will be—both in their youth and in adulthood—intelligent, responsive, empathetic, and highly sensitive. They will take pleasure in life and will not feel any need to kill or even hurt others or themselves. They will use their power to defend themselves, not to attack others. They will not be able to do otherwise than respect and protect those weaker than themselves, including their children, because this is what they have learned from their own experience, and because it is this knowledge (and not the experience of cruelty) that has been stored up inside them from the beginning. One might compare, in passing, the repeated emphases in the Torah on taking care of the stranger, orphan, widow, and similar personages. In these ways, child Israel seems to have learned from its Exodus parent. See further §4 below.

69. See Brad D. Strawn and Brent A. Strawn, "From Petition to Praise: An Intrapsychic Phenomenon?" (paper presented at the annual meeting of the Society of Biblical Literature, Denver, Colorado, 2001); Walter Brueggemann, "The Costly Loss of Lament," *JSOT* 36 (1986): 57–71; Erich Fromm, *You Shall Be as Gods: A Radical Interpretation of the Old Testament and Its Tradition* (New York: Henry Holt, 1991), 201–23. Cf. also Tasker, *Ancient Near Eastern Literature*, 119, for the Psalms' depiction of God's fatherhood as the care of orphans, widows, the estranged, and released prisoners (and see previous note).

70. For a discussion of the problematics at work in the latter section and related passages, see Renita J. Weems, *Battered Love: Marriage, Sex, and Violence in the Hebrew Prophets*, OBT (Minneapolis: Fortress, 1995), and the literature cited there.

the heights and depths, the passion and compassion of God's parental relationship with Israel. In family contexts, of course, passion and compassion always run perilously close to "out-of-control." Unlike Hos 11, however, where God's compassion wins out, Ezek 16 is (in)famously more complicated than that. The discussion of this terrifying text in the secondary literature is massive and cannot be rehearsed here. It is enough to suggest that the use of the parent-child metaphor in this passage might offer another way into and through (but not around) its many difficulties.

Without wanting to oversimplify the situation, it seems that a major shift occurs at verse 15. Verses 1–14 set a more "positive" beginning to the chapter, recounting Yhwh's saving of the exposed baby girl (Jerusalem), raising her, and then marrying her,[71] though it must be admitted that even this first unit is not without problems and that this "positive" beginning is quickly overturned. After the turn in verse 15, which begins to recount Jerusalem's rebellion, it is noteworthy that God's wrath in the latter part of the chapter is connected in no small degree to children and childhood: Jerusalem is criticized for having forgotten the days of "your youth" (*ymy n'wryk*; vv. 22, 43), a reference to Yhwh's earlier act of saving her. Even more significantly, Jerusalem is condemned for what it has done to *her own* sons and daughters, including sacrificing them (v. 20), slaughtering and offering them up (v. 21), even loathing them (v. 45). God cares about these little ones: they are the children borne by Jerusalem following her marriage to Yhwh (v. 20). God even calls them "*my* children" (*bny*; v. 21). The end of the chapter, which speaks of restored fortunes and consolation (vv. 53–54), also does so in terms of children— specifically *daughters* (vv. 53, 55; cf. 57)—and, again, the days of Jerusalem's youth (*bymy n'wryk*; v. 60, cf. vv. 22, 43).

Ezekiel 16 is difficult and disturbing, but, among other things, the lens of the parent-child metaphor reveals within this chapter what might be called *God's preferential option for the child*, especially *the weakest, most vulnerable child*. God's care for the exposed baby girl Jerusalem is not unlike God's care for firstborn son Israel in Exod 4; only the child's sex has changed. In both texts, it is the weakest, abused, left-for-dead child that is cared about and attended to. And yet, not unlike the murmuring episodes, when the child grows up, different expectations are in place. After Sinai, son Israel ought to murmur less. When grown, daughter Jerusalem ought not forget the days of her youth, when Yhwh rescued and cared for her. And if (when) she does forget her parent's example of protection and care, goes after other "parents" (see Jer 2:27), and the result is the victimization of her own

---

71. It is twice emphasized that Yhwh is *not* Jerusalem's biological parent: "Your father was an Amorite and your mother a Hittite" (v. 3; cf. v. 45).

(and God's own!) children, the divine parent will see to them.[72] God's parental passion is mobilized especially on behalf of the youngest, the weakest, the most helpless, the most victimized child. God's older children, if (when) they are grown and forget the days of their youth—how they were rescued and nurtured—and if (when) they abuse their own (and God's own) children, will find themselves on the other side of God's mercy.[73]

It is at this juncture that one might consider the divine curses that threaten children (e.g., Deut 28:54–57). Via the metaphoric lens these might be thought of as *hyper*-curses: a way to shock the Israelites into an awareness of the severity of their wrongdoing and the profundity of their imminent punishment insofar as God's preferred concern—the littlest children—are here targeted. It is worth recalling that these types of curses are typically set in covenant contexts, where the parent-child metaphor is often at work.

Israel-Perceptions

The fact that it is the child, Israel, who presents and preserves these God-depictions says much about Israel itself. This is, after all, how Israel perceived and represented its Lord. That being granted, the parent-child metaphor also has direct bearing on Israel's self-understanding and self-representation. The world-creating lens of the parent-child means that all of Israel's life with God can be seen through it from both sides of the relationship. Here, too, a full presentation lies outside the scope of this chapter; space permits mention of only two significant dyads.

1. *Special (firstborn) child* and *one of many children*. Israel is Yhwh's *firstborn*— it is special, favored, the recipient of unusual care and attention.[74] But the very

---

72. The leitmotif of "blood" (*dm*) in Ezek 16 is a critical point here; compare v. 22 with vv. 36, 38: Jerusalem forgets how she was bloody, left for dead (v. 22), and then perpetrates violence on her children, who are bloody as a result (v. 36). So Yhwh will now visit bloody fury against Jerusalem (v. 38). It is almost as if the sight of blood should automatically remind Jerusalem of her plight when the Lord rescued her. How awful, then, that the sight of blood on Jerusalem's own children—at her own hand—does nothing of the sort. Note also the tragic cycle of abuse recounted in v. 45.

73. Perhaps the spy debacle and the shift from old to new generation belongs in this discussion (see Num 13:1–14:45). Though no mistreatment of the children is mentioned, the faithless generation does use them in their argument: the children, they lament, will become booty (Num 14:3). Yhwh's response is to see that the children do nothing of the sort: "But your toddlers, whom you said would become war-booty, I will bring them in, and they will know the land that you have despised" (v. 31).

74. In ancient Israel primogeniture included preferential status that was manifested in a double portion of property, a special blessing from the father, and fatherly succession as the next

language of "firstborn child" suggests that there are *other children* who also belong to the Lord. God has "other stories," other children who are "not of this fold."[75] Child Israel lives in this tension: special and privileged as eldest child, but always in the presence of other children, younger ones, who threaten and compete for parental favor in various ways.[76]

2. *In need (immature)* and *growing up (maturing)*. Israel's self-presentation as a child and the self-understanding that comes by means of this metaphor constitute a profound confession of immaturity, need for further growth, and dependent status. To return to the examples already mentioned: (a) the murmuring narratives witness an Israel that realizes (after the fact) that things were different prior to Sinai. It could get away with more back then. Following Sinai, its murmurings are not acceptable. A new stage has been reached. It is time to grow up, take more responsibility, especially given the repeated parental provision of food and drink, deliverance and care. Similarly, (b) in prophetic passages of judgment, Israel presents itself as the rebellious child, in need of parental correction, even discipline.[77] In still other places—(c) the psalms come to mind—child Israel clings to its parent, refusing to be separated, refusing to be silenced, insisting on saying the parent's name, over and over again if necessary, until it is heard, until its questions are answered.[78] Surely, if God is a parent who carries children through the

---

head of household (Philip J. King and Lawrence E. Stager, *Life in Biblical Israel*, LAI [Louisville: Westminster John Knox, 2001], 47–48; de Vaux, *Ancient Israel*, 41–42).

75. See Carol Meyers, *Exodus*, NCBC (New York: Cambridge University Press, 2005), 62. For some intriguing texts, see Deut 2:1–25; 4:19; 32:8; Amos 9:7; Isa 19:19–25; and the discussion in Patrick D. Miller, "God's Other Stories: On the Margins of Deuteronomic Theology," in *Israelite Religion and Biblical Theology: Collected Essays*, JSOTSup 267 (Sheffield: Sheffield Academic, 2000), 593–602.

76. See the problems between the firstborn and the youngest throughout Genesis (e.g., 4:1–16 [Cain and Abel]; 16:1–15 and 21:1–21 [Ishmael and Isaac]; 25:19–34 and 27:1–40 [Jacob and Esau]) and beyond. For discussion, see further Frederick E. Greenspahn, *When Brothers Dwell Together: The Preeminence of Younger Siblings in the Hebrew Bible* (New York: Oxford University Press, 1994); Fewell, *Children of Israel*, 43–53; Levenson, *Death and Resurrection*.

77. On discipline, see William P. Brown, "To Discipline without Destruction: The Multifaceted Profile of the Child in Proverbs," in Bunge, Fretheim, and Gaventa, *The Child in the Bible*, 63–81. Note also Tasker, *Ancient Near Eastern Literature*, 135, who points out that the parallelism at work in Prov 3:12 connects correction with favor: "The importance of the association is that it qualifies the concept of correction-discipline and removes it from the realm of abusive father-child relationships by linking it to an everlasting covenant based on concepts of . . . mercy and truth . . . love and delight." Whether it is the poetics of Prov 3:12 alone that does this or the power of the macro-metaphorical lens is open for discussion.

78. See Ludwig Köhler, *Hebrew Man*, trans. P. R. Ackroyd (Nashville: Abingdon, 1956), 68–69,

wilderness (Deut 1:31), who lifts them to the cheek (Hos 11:4)—surely that kind of parent will listen to this child's voice!

Even as it acknowledges immaturity by means of the parent-child metaphor, Israel also portrays itself as in process and maturing. Human development does not happen overnight, not even over many years. So, the metaphor confesses, on the one hand, and indicts on the other. It indicts because it chastens the over-bearing parent.[79] Children cannot understand everything—Israel admits that. Shouldn't God admit it too? Children are not capable of everything—Israel admits that. Shouldn't God admit it too? God gets tired, impatient, frustrated—Israel understands that (see above). But doesn't that mean that God should pause before punishing? After all, God is dealing with a *child*, one that is maturing, to be sure, but one that is still in need, still dependent—in a word, still a child—and God cares for children, especially small, weak, and vulnerable children. At this point, God's quality of being "slow to anger" (Exod 34:6; Num 14:18; Jonah 4:2; Nah 1:3; Sir 5:4) takes on increased significance.

In these examples (and others like them), the parent-child metaphor is shown to work its power on both the human community and the divine partner. One further example of this, developed more extensively below, can be briefly mentioned here: maturing Israel is given increased responsibilities, as is the case with any developing child. A process of independence might be traced; at the very least, God's use of human agency in Israel (and beyond) indicates that God and Israel are *inter*dependent—like any and every other family unit.

(M)other Metaphors

The parent-child macro-metaphor is obviously quite productive. It has had an espe-cially lively reception in its gendered form as that of father-son. Most of the passages recounted above are crafted in this way. But several are not. In fact, the metaphor is not always explicitly marked for gender. This indicates that the male/father version of the metaphor is, in truth, *yet another macro-metaphor* that has been layered onto the macro-metaphor of parent-child. The divine parent in Exod 4 is not explicitly gendered by means of a "father" term. The same is true for Hos 11. Indeed, there are other metaphors—*mother* metaphors—that should be considered when we take

on children's insistent and insatiable question-asking. See also Miller, "That the Children May Know," in Bunge, Fretheim, and Gaventa, *The Child in the Bible*.

79. One might compare the U.N. Convention on the Rights of the Child article 31:1, which provides for the right of the child "to rest and leisure, to engage in play and recreational activities appropriate to the age of the child"—that is, to truly be a child and not a "miniature adult." Note Tasker, *Ancient Near Eastern Literature*, 203, who speaks of the child's right to veto.

up the parent-child metaphor. When this is done, it becomes apparent that the parent-child metaphor can just as easily be read through the lens of mother-child as that of father-child. This is, of course, most especially true for those passages that explicitly or implicitly invoke God as a mother. Famous here are the passages from Second Isaiah (Isa 42:14; 45:10–11; 49:15; 66:13), but there are a number of other instances as well (Pss 22:9–10 [10–11]; 131:1–3; note also Luke 13:34 // Matt 23:37; cf. 2 Esdr 1:30).[80] In fact, a closer look at the "father" texts demonstrates that several of them employ language that is an amalgam of mother and father imagery (e.g., Deut 32:18; Jer 31:20; Ps 103:13; cf. also 1QH 17.35–36)[81]—underscoring by means of the mixed-metaphorical construction that God is neither mother or father, male or female, or at least neither of these exclusively. These are, and remain, *metaphors*.

Be that as it may, if the lens employed for the parent-child macro-metaphor is that of mother and child, many God-depictions are equally understandable if not more so. God's provision of food to Israel in the wilderness, for example, makes perfect sense within the world of mothers and their young.[82] In the wilderness, then, perhaps the parent who carries the child is a mother (cf. Isa 46:3–4; 63:8–9).[83] Viewing some of these God-depictions through the lens of motherhood rather than fatherhood may "fix" them in some ways and "break" them in others: Positive aspects are shown to be equally applicable to mothers; they are not the sole possession of fathers. But the same holds true for negative aspects: mothers are as capable of these as are fathers. But not to worry; even if mothers forget their children, Yhwh will not forget Israel (Isa 49:15).[84] That is, as was the case with fathers, Yhwh is both like and unlike human mothers.

---

80. Korpel, *Rift in the Clouds*, 241–42, believes that Moses's statement in Num 11:12 figures Yhwh as a mother. For the possibility that Ps 131 was written by a mother, see Patrick D. Miller, *They Cried to the Lord: The Form and Theology of Biblical Prayer* (Minneapolis: Fortress, 1995), 239–43; see also Melody D. Knowles, "A Woman at Prayer: A Critical Note on Psalm 131:2b," *JBL* 125 (2006): 385–89.

81. In some of these texts, the maternal aspects are evoked by use of *rḥm*. See note 52 above.

82. See L. Juliana Claassens, *The God Who Provides: Biblical Images of Divine Nourishment* (Nashville: Abingdon, 2004).

83. See Jacqueline E. Lapsley, "'Look! The Children and I Are as Signs and Portents in Israel': Children in Isaiah," in Bunge, Fretheim, and Gaventa, *The Child in the Bible*, 82–102. See also Frederick J. Gaiser, "'I Will Carry and Will Save': The Carrying God of Isaiah 40–66," in *"And God Saw That It Was Good": Essays on Creation and God in Honor of Terence E. Fretheim*, ed. Frederick J. Gaiser and Mark A. Throntveit, Word and World Supplement 5 (Saint Paul: Luther Seminary, 2006), 94–102. Gaiser's article demonstrates that the carrying motif is broader than just that of parent.

84. As with the father lens, the net can be widely drawn with the mother macro-metaphor. For example, it seems to have been the mother's prerogative to name the children (see Joseph

The existence of mother metaphors to express the parent-child metaphor demonstrates that the metaphor is capable of more than one reception. The divine parent is not exclusively or irreducibly male; nor is the child invariably a son. The father-son version is just that: *one* version that must come in—like any metaphor—for modification and critique given the existence of female-gendered versions. Mother metaphors offer irrefutable proof that father metaphors are metaphorical—no matter how powerful—and that no metaphor is beyond reproach. Still further on this point, it should be recalled that both human and divine partners—not to mention their relationship—are metaphorized in Scripture in ways that go beyond and that are other than the familial.[85] Yhwh can be an animal—a bird or bear, a lion or a maggot (see Exod 19:4; Deut 32:11; Hos 5:12, 14; 13:8). And Israel can be a cow, a sick body, an abandoned booth, or a vineyard as easily as it can be a child (see Amos 4:1; Isa 1:6, 8; 5:7).

What all that means is that no one cosmic myth, no one macro-metaphor will do—not even one as pervasive as that of parent-child, whether mother or father, son or daughter. While cosmic myth metaphors are all-consuming and world-constituting, it is for this very reason that they must be critiqued by means of other metaphors. "Metaphoric criticism of metaphors for ultimate commitments is one of the most important kinds of talk we can ever attempt," Booth writes, because "no single myth can give any culture all that is needed both to ensure its survival and to enable its individual inhabitants to build rewarding life stories for themselves"[86]—not even, it should be underscored, a myth that is deeply ingrained and profoundly loved.[87]

Yet even when we grant the veracity of these claims—that other metaphors are important, and that the parent-child metaphor is not above critique—it is nevertheless clear that this particular metaphor remains a macro-metaphor *in* Scripture and *in* human society, *because* of Scripture and *because* of human society. And, because of that, this particular metaphor remains both powerful and

---

Blenkinsopp, "The Family in First Temple Israel," in Perdue et al., *Families in Ancient Israel*, 68; de Vaux, *Ancient Israel*, 43). What does that mean for those instances where Yhwh (re)names key individuals like Abraham and Sarah (Gen 17:5, 15), Jacob (to Israel; Gen 32:28), the people of Israel (from "not-my-people" to "children-of-the-living-God"; Hos 1:10 [2:1]), the city of Jerusalem (to "Yhwh is there"; Ezek 48:35)?

85. Perdue, "Household," for instance, believes the sphere of kingship is the main alternative to that of the household. But according to Schloen (*House of the Father*) and others, kingship and family structures are profoundly related in the ancient Near East.

86. Booth, *Company We Keep*, 335, 350. See also 345.

87. It is especially the metaphors we like, repeat, and dwell on that are most tenacious and most potentially destructive (Booth, *Company We Keep*, 295).

dangerous.[88] We would be remiss, then, especially if we care about our children, not to inquire after the ethics of this particular metaphor.

4. The Ethics of the Divine Parent-Human Child Metaphor

If energy expended in engagement equals ethical power (see§2), then much of ethical significance has already been said in the preceding discussion. There are nevertheless two areas deserving special attention in the ethics of the parent-child metaphor: (1) how it may have functioned in ancient Israelite families and (2) how it might function in contemporary families. In both cases the question is: Did/does the metaphor help people parent better?[89] And if so, how?

The Metaphorical Ethics Back Then

The evidence pertaining to the impact of the metaphor on Israelite parents is mostly circumstantial, barring the existence of a text that clearly depicts a reflex of God's benevolent parenting activities in a human familial context.[90] That being said, the

88. But also especially useful (see further below). In passing, it might be noted that the usefulness and ubiquity of the parent-child metaphor may commend its necessity at some level. It *can* be used negatively, but also positively; that it *must* be used at all is suggested by the fact that metaphors must not be too idiosyncratic or they will not communicate effectively. See Mary Kinzie, *A Poet's Guide to Poetry*, 2nd ed. (Chicago: University of Chicago Press, 2013).

89. One should be careful not to romanticize the lives of ancient children or the parent-child relationship in antiquity. Images of family closeness—by our standards—are rare (for an exception, see depictions of the royal family in Egyptian art of the Amarna Age). It is widely acknowledged that children occupied the bottom rung of ancient societies and were largely powerless vis-à-vis the near absolute authority of their parents and other adults (see Joseph A. Grassi, "Child, Children," *ABD* 1:905; Blenkinsopp, "Family in First Temple Israel," 66–68; Köhler, *Hebrew Man*, 59–62). Artistic depictions often portray children as "miniature adults," and we know of cruel and physical means of punishment and education in antiquity (see Prov 13:24; 22:15; 23:13; Sir 30:1, 12; and Brown, "To Discipline without Destruction"). With these caveats duly entered, it should nevertheless be stressed that other images of children are known in Scripture (see esp. Isa 11:8–9; Zech 8:5). Children were valued, pregnancy was a time for rejoicing, and birth was an occasion to celebrate. See Perdue, "Summary and Conclusions," 171; de Vaux, *Ancient Israel*, 470; King and Stager, *Life in Biblical Israel*, 41; Grassi, "Child, Children," 904; and Fretheim, "God Was with the Boy."

90. The closest non-biblical analogue of which I am aware is the presentation of *Tkmn-w-šnm*'s treatment of his father El (see *KTU* 1.114:18–22) in light of the description of the "ideal" son in the Aqhat text from Ugarit (*KTU* 1.17 i 23–33, 42–48; ii 1–9, 14–23). The parallel is inexact insofar as the parent and child here are both divine, though the list of filial duties in Aqhat applies to human children. The list may be translated as follows: "Bless him, Bull, El my father, / Prosper him, Creator of Creatures. / Let him have a son in his house, / Offspring within his palace, / To set up his Ancestor's stela, / The sign of his Sib in the sanctuary; / To rescue his smoke from

metaphor can be read "backward," as it were, investigated with reference to socio-political (i.e., familial) realities.[91] What social order permitted, authorized, and made sense of the parent-child metaphor? How does the metaphor reflect sociological realities "on the ground"? One can then investigate the instances of the metaphor for potential reflexes in "real life." One possible correlation: when Yhwh is depicted as a man (אִישׁ) carrying his son (Deut 1:31; cf. Hos 11:4), it may be an indication that Israelite fathers (and mothers)—some of them at any rate—did the same. The parent-child metaphor thus casts light on theology and theological anthropology (perceptions of God and Israel) but also on real family dynamics.[92] There is a synergy of sorts in the metaphor between theology and anthropology, psychology and sociology.

If so, the parent-child metaphor can be seen as descriptive of and (potentially) prescriptive for actual parent-child relationships in ancient Israel. The latter item makes it imperative that we investigate "negative" aspects of the metaphor be-cause the stakes are so high. Given negative instances, their prescriptive potential, and possible outcome scenarios, we need to work hard to uncover and critique the metaphor even as we work equally hard to reclaim its best possible outcomes. Again, some steps toward critique and reclamation are evident in the preceding discussion. But, given the extent and power of the parent-child metaphor, there is more work to be done and much grist for the ethical mill. As but one example, we might consider the role of instruction.[93] Could the role of Israelite parents in

---

the Underworld, / To product his steps from the Dust; / To stop his abusers' spite, / To drive his troublers away; / To grasp his arm when he's drunk, / To support him when sated with wine; / To eat his portion in Baal's house, / His share in the house of El; / To daub his roof when there's [mu]d, / To wash his stuff when there's dirt" (Simon B. Parker, "Aqhat," in *Ugaritic Narrative Poetry*, ed. Simon B. Parker, SBLWAW 9 [Atlanta: Scholars Press, 1997], 52–53). For discussion, see Schloen, *House of the Father*, 343–45, 352; A. van Selms, *Marriage and Family Life in Ugaritic Literature* (London: Luzac, 1954), 100–103; and David P. Wright, *Ritual in Narrative: The Dynamics of Feasting, Mourning, and Retaliation Rites in the Ugaritic Tale of Aqhat* (Winona Lake, IN: Eisenbrauns, 2001), 48–69, who thinks the list is synecdochic.

91. Cf. Booth, *Company We Keep*, 335: "Whenever we look closely at any powerful cluster of metaphors, we can infer from it the maker's world"; and Schloen, *House of the Father*, 350: "The programs of action evident in Ugaritic literary texts are best explained in terms of a patrimonial conception of the social order. . . . These programs of action are thus subplots within a larger plot formed by the typical lifecourse of the ideal (male) protagonist."

92. This kind of analysis is facilitated by metaphorical constructions in which the source domain is real, knowable, and derived from common, lived experience (as, e.g., in Deut 1:31). In other constructions, with different source domains, analysis is more difficult. But note Schloen, *House of the Father*, 356, who finds the relationship of the Ugaritic gods El and Baal to neverthe-less capture "fundamental experiences of fatherhood and sonship and their dynamic interrela-tion that constituted the social world of those who sacrificed to these gods, heard and recited the myth, and wrote it down."

93. On education/instruction, see King and Stager, *Life in Biblical Israel*, 45–47; de Vaux,

the (religious) instruction of their children, especially as that is emphasized in Deuteronomy, be a reflection on and the result of the divine instruction found throughout Scripture itself (even and especially in Deuteronomy)? If so, then as parent Yhwh teaches child Israel, so Israelite parents instruct their children.[94] Moreover, the fact that the divine instruction in Deuteronomy so often concerns life and well-being, not to mention care for others, including persons who lie outside of the immediate kinship structure (e.g., debt slaves, widows, fatherless children, etc.), is no small ethical point.[95]

As another example, consider Prov 19:18 (NRSV):

> Discipline your children [*bnk*] while there is hope;
>   do not set your heart on their destruction.

In the human family, this instruction sounds like encouragement for parents to imitate Yhwh as the long-suffering parent painted in several passages by means of the parent-child metaphor (see above). Or, via the mother-child version of the metaphoric lens, one might note that in Isa 66:11–13 the consolation mother Jerusalem offers corresponds in no small way to the consolation mother Yhwh extends:

> [Mother Jerusalem]
> that you may nurse and be satisfied
>   from her [Jerusalem's] consoling [√*nḥm*] breast;
> that you may drink deeply with delight
>   from her glorious bosom.
> For thus says the LORD:
> . . .
>
> [Mother Yhwh]
> As a mother comforts [√*nḥm*] her child,
>   so I will comfort [√*nḥm*] you;
>   you shall be comforted [√*nḥm*] in Jerusalem. (Isa 66:11–13 NRSV)

Ancient Israel, 48–50; Perdue, "Summary and Conclusions," 190; Köhler, *Hebrew Man*, 68–69; and Miller, "That the Children May Know." It is apparent that both mothers and fathers were active in education (Prov 1:8; 6:20; de Vaux, *Ancient Israel*, 49).

94. See Brown, "To Discipline without Destruction," and his comparison of the father's teaching in Prov 6:21–22 with the Shema in Deut 6:6–9.

95. Perdue, "Summary and Conclusions," 171–72. See also Lapsley, "Children in Isaiah"; Brueggemann, "Vulnerable Children."

The Metaphorical Ethics Now

At many points the preceding discussion has drifted into, or revealed potential for, today's parents and children. Ultimately, for our children's sake, it is the contemporary significance of the parent-child metaphor that is most important. Can it, does it, help us parent better? Many parents would have to admit that they have said things to their children like "I should only have to tell you *once.*" But in the play of the parent-child metaphor, that dictum is simply not true. If God tells God's children the same thing more than once—at times over and over again, even if to no avail—why do we imagine that our parenting will be "better" than that?

Many writers have argued that the image of God as a parent does (and should) impact human parenting.[96] The point is especially pressing in the light of studies that have demonstrated the effect—both direct and indirect—that parents have on children's images of God.[97] These two—the divine and human parent, as well as the metaphorical and real human child—are conjoined, for better or for worse.

But which is it, better or worse? There are people who have had poor parents and, as a result, have profound difficulty with God(-images). Given the awesome power and virtually unlimited extension of the parent-child macro-metaphor, what then? Here again the importance of ethical engagement, "metaphoric criticism," is underscored and leads to several responses. First, the perduring power of the parent-child metaphor demonstrates that it works because it has been lived.[98] Second, it has been lived in positive, not just negative ways—that is, it has been lived *well*—and this is true quite apart from the human source domain of the metaphor. Despite poor parenting, that is, some have found in God the "perfect substitute attachment figure" for an imperfect caregiver.[99] Booth points out that "surviving metaphors survive because . . . they continue to uncover truth about us."[100] There is something true about the parent-child metaphor, in part because it reflects the social reality of the family—a reality that remains crucial for the well-being, health, and future of children—even though that social reality

---

96. E.g., Miller, "God as Father," 353; Miller, *Calling God "Father,"* esp. 55–70; Tasker, *Ancient Near Eastern Literature,* 5, 158, 195–97; Perdue, "Household," 252; Fretheim, *Suffering of God,* 10. See also Brueggemann, "Vulnerable Children." For the gods as paradigms for human parenting in Greco-Roman sources, see Margaret Y. MacDonald, "A Place of Belonging: Perspectives on Children from Colossians and Ephesians," in Bunge, Fretheim, and Gaventa, *The Child in the Bible,* 278–304.

97. Dickie et al., "Parent-Child Relationships and Children's Images of God," esp. 25, 31, 42.

98. Booth, *Company We Keep,* 350–52, 368.

99. Dickie et al., "Parent-Child Relationships and Children's Images of God," esp. 25–26, 31, 42.

100. Booth, *Company We Keep,* 368.

has often fallen short.[101] So, while the parent-child metaphor is fraught with peril and checkered with actual disasters—as *all* metaphors are—it is not uniformly or unequivocally so. We must resist "the temptation to make global claims when what we need are discriminations. . . . Come, let us abandon these general moves and start talking, first about *this* one, and then about *that* one."[102] And let us do so armed with the full range of metaphors from the entirety of Scripture and how these both strengthen and reinforce but also modify and critique the parent-child metaphor. The result may be an interpretation of the text as the best text possible and an understanding of God as the best possible parent[103]—one that inspires us to behave similarly toward our children.

I conclude this section on ethics—ancient and modern—by considering an interesting facet of the parent-child metaphor that has not garnered much discussion, but which, in the end, may contain its greatest ethical power. That facet is related to this simple fact: parents age, and children grow up and, in time, become parents to their own children. And on it goes. What this means is that when the parent-child metaphor is utilized, unless it is completely frozen,[104] it carries with it implications of family dynamics that are both synchronic and diachronic. The former means that different members of the family play different roles and interact in various ways; the latter means that these family roles change and develop, again in various ways and through time, as the members mature and age (cf. 1 Sam 2:26; Luke 2:52; Hos 11:1; 1 Cor 13:11).[105] In ancient Israel, as children grew up, they helped with the family's work, apprenticed themselves to their parents'

101. Bellamy, *State of the World's Children 2005*, 15: "Families form the first line of defence for children: the further away children are from their families, the more vulnerable they are to risks." Cf. the Convention on the Rights of the Child, preamble and article 7: the right to know and be raised by one's parents. For a recent statement on the importance of good fathering in particular, see Linda J. Waite and William J. Doherty, "Marriage and Responsible Fatherhood: The Social Science Case and Thoughts about a Theological Case," in *Family Transformed: Religion, Values, and Society in American Life*, ed. Steven M. Tipton and John Witte Jr. (Washington, DC: Georgetown University Press, 2005), 143–67.

102. Booth, *Company We Keep*, 312–14; his italics.

103. For an argument for interpreting the biblical text as "the best text it can be," see Dale Patrick, *The Rhetoric of Revelation in the Hebrew Bible*, OBT (Minneapolis: Fortress, 1999), 193, and the literature cited there. For the "good enough" parent, see note 67 above.

104. Cf. Schloen, *House of the Father*, 356, on the frozen nature of the Ugaritic pantheon "around which the narrative must flow." In my judgment, the pluralistic nature of the metaphorical world of Scripture works against any similar freezing.

105. The maturational dynamic implicit in the parent-child metaphor speaks against both Freud and Daly's concern about the metaphor confining humans to infantile states (see note 12 above).

tasks, and continued those after the parents' death.[106] On the human level, that is, children replace their parents in no small way—as in the epigraph used for this study from Sir 30:4–5 (cf. also Ps 127:3–5). That text, manifestly about *human* fathers and sons, takes on a different hue when viewed through the lens of the divine parent–human child metaphor. The child, "one like" the parent, is apprenticed to the parent's work, who has learned from the parent's instruction—all of that begins to place Israel's son- and daughter-ship in a distinctly different light. It begins to look like it has as much to do with mission and God's purposes as it does with Israel's election or status. There are, of course, connections to both status and election in the parent-child metaphor.[107] In Egypt, it was the Pharaohs who called themselves the gods' sons; at Ugarit, use of the epithet "son of El (god)" for humans was apparently reserved for kings.[108] In this light, child Israel begins to look not just like an heir, but like an heir *to the throne*. But even in the royal house there are profound connections to mission. It was, after all, the duty of kings in the ancient Near East to care for orphans and to judge the case of widows.[109] Is it surprising, then, to find such a concern often on the lips of Yhwh's intermediaries, the prophets? The divine parent, who is also the just ruler, requires correlate behavior from the royal offspring. It is thus not surprising to find another child of God, later, saying that he "must be about his Father's business" (Luke 2:49; cf. Matt 5:44–45).

God's (grown) child must model parental care for other children not only because it is *God's* child, about God's business, but also because it knows that *all* children are God's children.[110] Recall, after all, that the child prays *"our* Father," not *"my* Father"; and remember that this child is the firstborn, not the only child. Among other things, these observations suggest that care for children must extend beyond one's own biological children. And so, in this regard, even those without

---

106. For data on work in ancient Israel, see Carol Meyers, "The Family in Early Israel," in Perdue et al., *Families in Ancient Israel*, 27–30; King and Stager, *Life in Biblical Israel*, 46; Perdue, "Summary and Conclusions," 189–90; Pamela J. Scalise, "'I Have Produced a Man with the LORD': God as Provider of Offspring in Old Testament Theology," *RevExp* 91 (1994): 579–81.

107. See Tasker, *Ancient Near Eastern Literature*, 175; Melnyk, "When Israel Was a Child," 259.

108. Tasker, *Ancient Near Eastern Literature*, 49; Korpel, *Rift in the Clouds*, 253.

109. See Korpel, *Rift in the Clouds*, 238; further, Moshe Weinfeld, *Social Justice in Ancient Israel and in the Ancient Near East* (Minneapolis: Fortress, 1995). These social-justice aspects of the parent-child metaphor obviate Daly's critique of the metaphor as devoid of such (*Beyond God the Father*, 24).

110. See note 75 above and the discussion there; also Tasker, *Ancient Near Eastern Literature*, 198, 207; Melnyk, "When Israel Was a Child," 246. For the capacity of beautiful things—like an adorable child—to exert pressure on observers to care for them and to extend such care to other items of the same category and beyond, see Elaine Scarry, *On Beauty and Being Just* (Princeton: Princeton University Press, 1999).

biological children can (and must) still be loving "parents" toward children.[111] The concern for the orphan in Scripture, commanded by the divine (adoptive) parent and modeled by the children, makes the same point.[112] For the grown child of the Lord, parental care must be imitated whether through parenting proper, adoption, surrogate parenthood, or just plain old mentorship. Whatever the case, it clearly takes a metaphor to raise a child.

The family dynamic in diachronic mode means that child Israel develops, but so does Israel's divine parent, as does the relationship between these two. Possible connections at this point between the parent-child metaphor and other realities are several. Steven A. Rogers has attempted to map development onto the portrayal of God's relationship with the main figures in Genesis.[113] His schema appears too rigid and imposed, but his ability to trace stages of maturation in the parent-child relationship—including separation, individuation, and reintegration—between God and the ancestors is evocative. With each maturational stage, God seems to recede, giving more control to the human "children." The parent-child metaphor, that is, with its associated dynamism, may help to explain the slow disappearance and silence of God that has been noted in Scripture.[114] In Rogers's words, with reference to the ancestors: "Like the parent of an adult, God's silence may be taken as respect for Joseph's psychic integration and spiritual health. This does not mean that God is inactive, but rather that God's activity is subtle and designed to operate behind human events to support and sustain Joseph's psychic integration, instead of directing and guiding it, as occurs with Abraham and even Jacob. . . . What this requires for God and any parent relating with an adult child is a comfort with paradox and metaphors."[115] This includes, it would seem, metaphors of the fam-

111. Cf. P. A. H. de Boer, *Fatherhood and Motherhood in Israelite and Judean Piety* (Leiden: Brill, 1974), on various authority figures as "mothers" and "fathers" in ancient Israel. Note also the presentation of apostolic figures as parents, with their churches as their children. See Beverly R. Gaventa, "Our Mother St. Paul: Toward the Recovery of a Neglected Theme," *PSB* 17 (1996): 29–44; Gaventa, "Finding a Place for Children in the Letters of Paul," in Bunge, Fretheim, and Gaventa, *The Child in the Bible*, 233–48. Note also de Vaux, *Ancient Israel*, 49 on calling priests "father"—a practice as early as Judg 17:10; 18:19.

112. See Exod 22:21–25; Deut 14:28–29; 16:9–11, 13–14; 24:17, 19–21; 26:12; 27:19; Prov 23:10; etc. Perdue, "Summary and Conclusions," 193, believes orphans were "children . . . from broken families that no longer provided nurture and protection" for them.

113. Steven A. Rogers, "The Parent-Child Relationship as an Archetype for the Relationship Between God and Humanity in Genesis," *Pastoral Psychology* 50 (202): 377–85; this is not completely unrelated to Freud's work in *Moses and Monotheism*. See also Wilcoxen, "Some Anthropocentric Aspects," esp. 350.

114. See esp. Jack Miles, *God: A Biography* (New York: Alfred A. Knopf, 1995); Richard Elliott Friedman, *The Disappearance of God: A Divine Mystery* (Boston: Little, Brown, 1995).

115. Rogers, "The Parent-Child Relationship," 383.

ily and of the maturing relationship between a parent and child with its various paradoxes (and sub-metaphors). These paradoxes encompass, on the one hand, the child who grows into an adult and continues the parent's legacy, all the while remaining its parent's child; and, on the other hand, the "good enough" parent who remains benevolent and of use to the child, largely by not-retaliating, despite the child's attempt to control the parent (cf. Prov 19:18).[116]

Among other things, then, *growth, mission,* and *purpose* are at work in the dynamics of the parent-child metaphor. Carrying on the parental legacy is part of what is expected of children, including the children of Israel. A well-known rabbinic story gets at these issues in a delightful way:

> Again (Rabbi Eliezer) said to them: "If the *halachah* agrees with me, let it be proved from Heaven!" Whereupon a Heavenly Voice cried out: "Why do you dispute with R. Eliezer, seeing that in all matters the *halachah* agrees with him!" But R. Joshua arose and exclaimed: "*It is not in heaven* (Deut 30:12)." What did he mean by this?—Said R. Jeremiah: "That the Torah had already been given at Mount Sinai; we pay no attention to a Heavenly Voice, because Thou has long since written in the Torah at Mount Sinai, *After the majority must one incline* (Exod 23:2)." R. Nathan met Elijah and asked him: "What did the Holy One, Blessed be He, do in that hour?—He laughed [with joy], he replied, saying, 'My sons have defeated Me, My sons have defeated Me.'" (*b. B. Metzi'a* 59b)

In addition to maturation and growth, there is conflict of a kind in this account, though in this case the halakic contest is in service to the purposes of Torah, and God is said to be delighted that the children have become even more adept (!) in Torah than God. Whatever the case, at all times we should remember that children come to grips with their parents in different (and sometimes difficult) ways as they mature and age. The lament process, especially as encapsulated in the Psalms, both facilitates and attests to such maturation on the part of the pray-er. On the other side of lament, everything looks different (see, e.g., Ps 30)—including God, the self, and the enemy. That different perspective may be quite sobering, even if it is, despite that fact, liberating in its own way. Sobriety and a lack of easy or happy endings is the way things are, sometimes, with lament. And that is the way they are, sometimes, with the complexities of family life. We should not be surprised, then, to see reflexes of that same dynamic worked out in the God-Israel metaphor, whether that is in the lament psalms or, more broadly, elsewhere in Scripture (e.g., Job or Ecclesiastes) where disappointment with the divine "father" reaches its apex (better: nadir).

---

116. These latter notions are taken from D. W. Winnicott, "The Use of an Object and Relating through Identifications," in *Playing and Reality* (London: Routledge, 2005), 115–27.

But even here, the metaphor continues to operate. It is, after all, a *comprehensive* macro-metaphor. Even in the midst of parental disappointment, that is, comes the old commandment—heard afresh, perhaps, in a new metaphoric register: "Honor your father and mother, *as the* LORD *your God commanded you*, so that your days may be long *and that it may go well with y*ou in the land that the LORD your God is giving you" (Deut 5:16 NRSV; cf. Exod 20:12; Mal 1:6).[117] One of the things children were to do in ancient Israel was honor their parents. One of the things children still do now, sometimes, is forgive them. There is more than just *growth and conflict* in the parent-child dynamic, then. There is also the possibility for *resolution and reconciliation*. Perhaps it is no coincidence that, in the end, Yhwh commends Job four times as "my servant" (Job 42:7–8) and that Ecclesiastes concludes with an epilogue urging proper worship of God and obedience to the commandments (Eccl 12:13).

5. Conclusion

The present study has suggested that there is (and *should* be) something similar and familiar, perhaps even more than that, between the God-human relationship and that of the human parent and child. The metaphor of God-as-our-parent/us-as-God's-children casts light on depictions of God in Scripture, depictions of Israel in Scripture, and depictions of children in Scripture. Even more profoundly, it suggests that human parents must strain to the highest and best levels of that metaphorical construction so that their parenting, care, and nurture of their children are indeed worthy of the divine image. If so, this would be no small contribution of Scripture's child-image to and for *all* children *everywhere*, including the children in our own midst, who are so often neglected, victimized, and abused.

---

117. Words in italics are found only in the Deuteronomic version. Scholars have long noted the connection between honoring (√kbd) one's parents and the honor due the Lord (note kəbôd yhwh, "the glory of the LORD"). Both of the Deuteronomic plusses tie the command closely to other passages where obedience is mandated by God and directed toward God. King and Stager (*Life in Biblical Israel*, 42) believe that the law concerning rebellious children (Deut 21:18–21) "underscores the importance of showing gratitude for the care that they have shown their children." The same could also hold true for the fifth commandment. Of course, if a parent did not show care to their children, keeping the commandment becomes far more complicated. See Walter J. Harrelson, *The Ten Commandments and Human Rights* (Macon, GA: Mercer University Press, 1997), 92–105.

9

What Would (or Should) Old Testament Theology Look Like If Recent Reconstructions of Israelite Religion Were True?

> But whatever else it is, the Old Testament is a set of religious texts—a witness to faith. Ultimately, to treat it as anything different is to deny the witness, and what caused the texts to be written.[1]

> Out of experience comes literature, and out of religious experience comes religious literature.[2]

> Historical criticism has long posed a major challenge to people with biblical commitments, and for good reason. . . . The reverse is also the case: the Bible poses a major challenge to people with historical-critical commitments.[3]

The initial title for this chapter was slightly different: "What Would (or Should) Old Testament Theology Look Like *If Everything They Said about Israelite Religion Were True*?" This title raises an immediate question: who are these "they"

Thanks to several individuals for their feedback: James K. Mead, Patrick D. Miller, R. W. L. Moberly, and J. J. M. Roberts.

1. John W. Rogerson, *A Theology of the Old Testament: Cultural Memory, Communication, and Being Human* (Minneapolis: Fortress, 2010), 195.

2. Mark S. Smith, "Recent Study of Israelite Religion in Light of the Ugaritic Texts," in *Ugarit at Seventy-Five*, ed. K. Lawson Younger (Winona Lake, IN: Eisenbrauns, 2007), 5.

3. Jon Levenson, *The Hebrew Bible, the Old Testament, and Historical Criticism: Jews and Christians in Biblical Studies* (Louisville: Westminster John Knox, 1993), 126.

who are saying things about Israelite religion? In addition to being *anonymous*, "they" can be rather *ominous* (as in "they are out to get me"), and it is, regardless of any threatening overtones, *plural*, which means that whatever "they" are saying is not going to be one thing at all but *several different things*, and that would no doubt also hold true for "their" reconstructions of Israelite religion. Paulist Press has a long-standing and successful series entitled *What Are They Saying About . . . ?* which faces the same problem of the "they," but at least those treatments are book length. Given the limitations of space afforded me here, far greater selectivity is in order. "They" is too high a mark to achieve and so I altered the earlier title.

Selectivity means that difficult decisions must be made in any overview of reconstructions of Israelite religion and their bearing on Old Testament theology.[4] And, despite the crucial caveat that whoever "they" are would no doubt *disagree*, it is also the case that there is occasionally something called "scholarly consensus," though that is always a moving target and subject to constant revision and (re)construction. There is also such a thing, or rather *things*, as "leading lights"— *persons*, in fact, who are crucial in shaping such consensus. In what follows, then, I take a fascinating essay written by Karel van der Toorn as generally illustrative if not also representative of recent scholarly reconstructions of Israelite religion.[5] While my focus on this one essay is somewhat arbitrary, van der Toorn is without doubt a leading scholar in the field, having written a series of brilliant studies on the religion of ancient Israel and the Near East, as well as on the composition of the Hebrew Bible.[6] Furthermore, this particular essay, in addition to being a highly imaginative and engaging piece, is also, by van der Toorn's own account, "informed by a tiresome amount of reading."[7] Even so, while I take van der Toorn's work as

4. For now I leave the distinctions between "Israelite religion" and "Old Testament theology" conveniently *un*defined.

5. Karel van der Toorn, "Nine Months among the Peasants in the Palestinian Highlands: An Anthropological Perspective on Local Religion in the Early Iron Age," in *Symbiosis, Symbolism, and the Power of the Past: Canaan, Ancient Israel, and Their Neighbors from the Late Bronze Age through Roman Palaestina: Proceedings of the Centennial Symposium W. F. Albright Institute of Archaeological Research and American Schools of Oriental Research, Jerusalem, May 29–31, 2000*, ed. William G. Dever and Seymour Gitin (Winona Lake, IN: Eisenbrauns, 2003), 393–410.

6. I mention here only his significant trilogy: Karel van der Toorn, *From Her Cradle to Her Grave: The Role of Religion in the Life of the Israelite and Babylonian Woman*, trans. Sara J. Denning-Bolle, Biblical Seminar 23 (Sheffield: JSOT Press, 1994); van der Toorn, *Family Religion in Babylonia, Syria and Israel: Continuity and Change in the Forms of Religious Life*, SHCANE 7 (Leiden: Brill, 1996); and van der Toorn, *Scribal Culture and the Making of the Hebrew Bible* (Cambridge: Harvard University Press, 2007).

7. Van der Toorn, "Nine Months among the Peasants in the Palestinian Highlands," 409. Note his selected bibliography on 409–10.

representative and illustrative, one must not forget that he is just one of the "they" who say many different things about Israelite religion and who reconstruct it in various ways.

In what follows, then, I will first summarize van der Toorn's essay (§1) before asking what (an) Old Testament theology would (or should) look like if a reconstruction like his were accurate (§2). In order to round out that answer—or more properly, the lingering questions—I next contemplate how Job (or even a reconstructed *Job) fits into a reconstructed *Israelite religion (§3).[8] A conclusion completes the study (§4).

To anticipate my argument, I hope to show that reconstructions of Israelite religion are often rather *un(der)*religious if not *non-* or *a*-religious—and certainly *un(der)*theological—which leaves so much of the Old Testament's religious/theological literature[9] hard to account for, or, if one is to account for it, that must be done by seeing it as the product of a much later, perhaps hostile but certainly elitist takeover, with all that means for a theology written about that literature. Said theology, that is, would presumably also be elitist if not oppressive to boot.[10] And yet, the stubborn existence of the religious literature that is the Old Testament, on the one hand, and the at-least-partially-speculative nature of reconstructions of Israelite religion, on the other, suggest that, in some details (to say the very least), scholarly takes on Israelite religion are not yet definitive—or exhaustive—and therefore Old Testament theology remains not only viable but crucial, even for the study and reconstruction of ancient Israelite religion. In the end, then, Old Testament theology contributes to the study and reconstruction of ancient Israelite religion, even as it retains something of a (semi-)independent status insofar as it is not necessarily beholden to the latter.

---

8. In this chapter an asterisk (*) will precede any hypothetical and/or reconstructed text, tradition, or entity, even if I myself remain agnostic about the nature or contents of such reconstructions, their cogency as such, or even their putative existence. This particular use of the asterisk, regardless, is standard in the field especially in redaction-critical studies.

9. Here too I prefer to leave the niceties of distinguishing between religion and theology to others. I admit to using them somewhat interchangeably in what follows, though I am also comfortable with conceding the point that, in biblical studies at least (this is not always the case in ancient Near Eastern studies, especially Egyptology), "theology" is reserved for higher, second-order reflection that can (but need not) be marked by more comprehensive scope and coverage (including, at times, a systematizing tendency). I am also quite happy with a more narrow and etymological definition of "theology"—namely, discourse about God and/or the gods.

10. William G. Dever's *Does God Have a Wife? Archaeology and Folk Religion in Ancient Israel* (Grand Rapids: Eerdmans, 2005) comes to mind at this point, and for more than one reason. See the insightful critique of this kind of position in Luke Timothy Johnson, *Religious Experience in Earliest Christianity* (Minneapolis: Fortress, 1998), 25–26 (and passim).

1. What Are "They" Saying about Israelite Religion?
Van der Toorn's Imaginative Ethnography

As already noted, it is impossible to summarize what "they" are saying about Is-raelite religion(s), how "they" are reconstructing it (or, better, *them*),[11] for two primary reasons: first, there is no clear delimitation of who "they" are; and, second, what "they" say, how they reconstruct, is too diverse to homogenize. So not only does space prohibit a full treatment here, so does the very (complex) nature of the researchers and their work. Even so, Karel van der Toorn's 2003 essay, "Nine Months among the Peasants in the Palestinian Highlands: An Anthropological Perspective on Local Religion in the Early Iron Age," is a useful example of recent scholarly reconstructions of Israelite religion for at least three reasons: (1) it is authored by an expert, (2) depends on extensive research, and (3) is intentionally synthetic. Still further, the essay is particularly engaging since it is written as a fictional first-person account.[12]

In the essay, van der Toorn recounts something of "a dream report" in which he speculates on "what it would have been like to spend nine months in an early Isra-elite village in the highlands."[13] While van der Toorn is clear that this is a fictional account (and so also should his readers be), he also indicates that "it attempts to get as close to the historical reality as the data and imagination allow."[14] It is pre-sented as an account of a "scholar-of-religion-turned-anthropologist" who spends nine months "in a hamlet in the central Hill Country, enough to get at least an idea of the inhabitants' customs and beliefs."[15]

As one might expect on the basis of van der Toorn's other publications, the essay places great emphasis on family and ancestor cult. In his dream report, van der Toorn finds himself in the village of Ramat-Yachin, "Hill of Yachin," which is named after an ancient ancestor, Elyachin. Van der Toorn resides with the family of the village chief, who is named Elḥanan, and immediately stresses the impor-tance of Elḥanan's family unit to the (small) society, to agriculture, and to subsis-

---

11. The plural form is becoming increasingly commonplace. Note, e.g., the titles to two re-cent Israelite religions: Ziony Zevit, *The Religions of Ancient Israel: A Synthesis of Parallactic Approaches* (London: Continuuum, 2001); and Richard S. Hess, *Israelite Religions: An Archaeo-logical and Biblical Survey* (Grand Rapids: Baker Academic, 2007).

12. The only thing comparable is the (quite different) account in James A. Michener, *The Source: A Novel* (New York: Random House, 1965). (Thanks to R. W. L. Moberly for reminding me of Michener's book.)

13. Van der Toorn, "Nine Months among the Peasants," 393; see also 409.

14. Van der Toorn, "Nine Months among the Peasants," 393.

15. Van der Toorn, "Nine Months among the Peasants," 393.

tence living. Also in light of van der Toorn's previous work, it is not surprising to find him paying special attention to women's lived experience, and also to how it differed drastically from that of men.[16]

Despite van der Toorn's intention "to get at least an idea of the inhabitants' customs *and beliefs*" and despite the title of the essay, which speaks of "local *religion*," it is actually quite striking to see how much religion is downplayed in his account: "I was especially eager to follow up on conversation topics that had to do with their beliefs. *Religion was hardly on the minds of these men, however.* They did not even have a word for it. They did hold certain beliefs about the supernatural, but these were rarely discussed."[17] Van der Toorn repeats this sentiment on more than one occasion. Religion just wasn't very important at Ramat-Yachin, and it certainly wasn't a topic of frequent discussion. Even so, van der Toorn continues:

There was a common, mostly tacit, understanding that the land they lived on was made and governed by El, a word that simply means "god" but was used as a proper name. *This belief elicited little enthusiasm from my hosts, much less devotion.* The deity they most frequently referred to was Baal, held to be responsible for the growth of the crops and the fertility of the cattle. Baal means "lord," and at first I took it as an epithet of El. The villagers located both of them in the sky, or said they lived on a mountain in the north; when asked about the shape of these gods, they came up with contradictory information: some said they looked like giants, others said they were heavenly bulls. The two seemed

16. See, e.g., van der Toorn, "Nine Months among the Peasants," 394–95, and passim; further van der Toorn, *From Her Cradle to Her Grave*.

17. Van der Toorn, "Nine Months among the Peasants," 395 (my emphasis). The "they don't have a word for *x*" is a common but ultimately fallacious argument, and is a problem for translation more than it is conceptualization. Ancient Israelites didn't have a word for "poetry" either, but they clearly had the art form. Indeed, it is more accurate to say that they had *words* for poetry (e.g., *šîr* in Ps 129:1; or *maʿăśê* in Ps 45:2 [1]); they just weren't the same as the word "poetry." So also with "religion." Why wouldn't *ʿăbōdâ* suffice, or, to take a clue from later rabbinics, *hălākâ*? Other possibilities include various derivatives of √*šmr*, √*šmʿ*, √*ʿbd*, and √*yrʾ*. (On the latter root, see, e.g., R. W. L. Moberly, *Old Testament Theology: Reading the Hebrew Bible as Christian Scripture* [Grand Rapids: Baker Academic, 2013], 245; and Brent A. Strawn, "The Iconography of Fear: *Yirʾat Yhwh* [יראת יהוה] in Artistic Perspective," in *Image, Text, Exegesis: Iconographic Interpretation and the Hebrew Bible*, ed. Izaak J. de Hulster and Joel M. LeMon, LHBOTS [Edinburgh: T&T Clark, 2014], 91–134). Note also Jonathan Z. Smith, "Religion, Religions, Religious," in *Critical Terms for Religious Studies*, ed. Mark C. Taylor (Chicago: University of Chicago Press, 1998), 269, who writes, "'Religion' is not a native category. It is not a first-person term of self-characterization. It is a category imposed from the outside on some aspect of native culture" (see also 281–82). In this perspective, no native language (or culture) has a "word" for "religion."

indistinguishable, but it turned out that El and Baal were really two separate gods. Baal was the lord, and more particularly, the lord of the village; El was a dim deity by comparison.[18]

This is a fascinating paragraph—a synthesis of a gaggle of controversial points—but, for purposes of the present article, the real bombshell is when van der Toorn writes, almost in passing, "A god named 'Yahweh' was unknown to the villagers, although a visiting divine once mentioned him as the deity worshiped in some settlements to the south."[19] And that's all we hear of Yhwh in the balance of the article and the rest of the nine months spent in Ramat-Yachin: just one mention of Yhwh worship, limited to southern climes, and even there only found in a few ("some") villages!

There are other religious factoids that van der Toorn details: for example, the villagers had images—both of Baal and of their ancestors—and one could pray to such images but one didn't have to do so since "Baal could also hear you from the sky."[20] "In general," however, "the men were not forthcoming with details on their religion." While they admitted that the sun and moon were gods ("everybody knew that"), the villagers weren't clear as to "their particular field of activity, apart from the obvious fact that they were the 'lamps of heaven.'"[21] "In the end," van der Toorn writes, though still early in his article, "I had to resign myself to the idea that the villagers had a religion, but that it was more a religion of action than of speculation."[22] So, in the absence of a "resident religious specialist," van der Toorn restricts the balance of his essay "to a description of the rituals that I witnessed. Their deeper meaning is a matter for others to discover."[23]

Already there is much to chew on here with an eye on Old Testament theology, but van der Toorn's essay continues on for ten more pages, much of which goes a good bit beyond mere description of ritual.[24] So, for example, he describes gestures of greeting the sun and the moon, though he is quick to qualify this action

18. Van der Toorn, "Nine Months among the Peasants," 395 (my emphasis).

19. Van der Toorn, "Nine Months among the Peasants," 395.

20. Van der Toorn, "Nine Months among the Peasants," 396.

21. Van der Toorn, "Nine Months among the Peasants," 396.

22. Van der Toorn, "Nine Months among the Peasants," 396. The categorization of religions into action vs. speculation—and what each one may or may not entail—is an important issue that is not discussed by van der Toorn. See further below and esp. note 52.

23. Van der Toorn, "Nine Months among the Peasants," 396.

24. For description of ritual as an alternative to (and occasionally an end run around) theological analysis, see Brent A. Strawn, "The History of Israelite Religion," in *The Cambridge Companion to the Old Testament/Hebrew Bible*, ed. Stephen B. Chapman and Marvin A. Sweeney (Cambridge: Cambridge University Press, 2016), 86–107.

with an interpretive assessment: "No particular fervor was implied by this practice: it was a matter of recognizing the universe in which the villagers lived." No basis is provided for this assessment, nor any definition of what it would mean—especially in the Iron Age—to "recognize the universe."

The impression one gets, then, is not one of mere description of various religious elements, nor heavy-handed interpretation of them, but, instead, a *disallowing* of certain interpretations, especially of the "speculative" (= theological?) sort. For example: "Although they used religious phrases ('El be with you'—'And with you, too'), the significance is comparable to our 'Good to see you'—'Good to see to [*sic*] you, too'; an affirmation of membership in the community."[25]

Despite the tabooistic origins of, say, the English word "Goodbye," our modern "Good to see you" is far indeed from a greeting (even if is only that!) that invokes a divine name. It is quite intriguing, then, if somewhat odd that, while van der Toorn downplays religion among the (big) gods—and erases it altogether with reference to Yhwh—he trumps it up elsewhere, especially in family religion (ancestor cult),[26] in what might be called "folk" religion, and in demonic powers. So, for example,

> Religious songs were rare, although the lyrics did recognize unusual events as acts of God. . . . It was presumed to be dangerous to work in the early afternoon; the sun might strike you or a demon might catch you. . . . Religious topics were rare, as I have noted—with one exception. The men loved to tell each other dreams. Their dreams were perhaps not religious in the strict sense of the term, but many of them involved actors from another world, be they gods, demons, or ghosts. It was as though the excitement of the night had to make up for the dullness of the day. These men enjoyed an intimacy with the other world that one would not expect in a people of so practical a bent of mind. As I came to discover, however, the discussion of dreams was their way of expressing their inner life. You must realize that these people were hardly ever alone, nor would they speak about their feelings—to such an extent that you might believe they simply did not have them. . . . Only asleep were they alone, and dreams were the outlet for their feelings. Feelings of desire, guilt, ambition, jealousy, love, and hatred assumed the shape of visitors from beyond, commanding them to do things and involving them in strange adventures.[27]

---

25. Van der Toorn, "Nine Months among the Peasants," 396.

26. Note van der Toorn, "Nine Months among the Peasants," 398, where an informant's reference to "the gods" is equivalent to "speaking about the ancestors."

27. Van der Toorn, "Nine Months among the Peasants," 397. On the lack of individuality,

The latter sentiments, in particular, are not just interpretive; they are psychoanalytic, striking one as particularly Freudian, perhaps even excessively so, but without sufficient theoretical support.[28] It is hard, then, to not see this part of van der Toorn's analysis—fictive though it may be—as rather reductionistic vis-à-vis religion proper.[29]

Unfortunately this trend continues. The women are reported to have put "a small part of the food in a separate basket . . . not to be eaten, but to be given to the ancestors, present in the *teraphim*"; but, van der Toorn quickly notes, "this small rite" did not "trigger particular demonstrations of devotion."[30] His later remark that "there is little religious activity"—although said about a particular period in the lunar month—holds true, it would seem, for all of Ramat-Yachin's (non)religious life.

Despite the rather understated or minimalistic presentation of religion in van der Toorn's essay, there is nevertheless—to go back to Freud for a moment—the

---

see also 408: "In Ramat-Yachin no one is ever alone; it is a condition the villagers do not know. Introspection, which requires at least mental withdrawal, is foreign to them." Cf. similarly van der Toorn, *Family Religion in Babylonia, Syria and Israel*, 3–4, 374. These sentiments sound like Alfred North Whitehead's definition of religion in his *Religion in the Making* (New York: World, 1969), 60: "Religion is solitariness; and if you are never solitary, you are never religious" (cited in J. Gerald Janzen, "Solidarity and Solitariness in Ancient Israel: The Case of Jeremiah," in *When Prayer Takes Place: Forays into a Biblical World*, ed. Brent A. Strawn and Patrick D. Miller [Eugene, OR: Cascade, 2012], 211–17 [214n8]). As J. J. M. Roberts reminds me, however, it is not hard to be alone, even in a hard-working familial, agricultural environment. Cf. Isaac meditating in the field in Gen 24:63. Communal religious experiences refute the overly simplistic equation of religion and solitariness in Whitehead (and van der Toorn). In point of fact, a vast amount of van der Toorn's conclusions depend on his understanding of individuality (or its lack) in the ancient world (see, e.g., *Family Religion in Babylonia, Syria and Israel*, 115–18). I have no doubt that ancient conceptions of the self differed from modern ones, and that cultural differences, too, are to be reckoned with most seriously. I am unconvinced, however, that there was a total lack of subjectivity, interiority, or introspection in antiquity—"no inner life to speak of" (van der Toorn, *Family Religion in Babylonia, Syria and Israel*, 117)—and only group/social role and character with all that this means for religious experience. A far more compelling perspective on the fundamentally individual nature of religious experience is found in Johnson, *Religious Experience in Earliest Christianity*, esp. 46–52.

28. Of course the nature of the essay as a fictive dream report does not allow for extensive theoretical discussion. That granted, note also the interpretation in van der Toorn, "Nine Months among the Peasants," 398, where he speculates that a dream reported by a family who lost a young child reflected their need "to come to terms with their grief before she [the wife] could conceive again." For Sigmund Freud's classic statement on dreams, see his *The Interpretation of Dreams*, trans. James Strachey (New York: Basic, 2010).

29. Cf. the trenchant critique of "the enlightenment project" offered in Levenson, *Hebrew Bible, the Old Testament, and Historical Criticism*, 106–26. Though Levenson's interlocutors do not include van der Toorn, many of the issues and moves are comparable.

30. Van der Toorn, "Nine Months among the Peasants," 399.

return of the repressed. So, inexplicably, we learn—beyond the demons that some-how motivate ethics that the gods do not[31]—that "the burning of incense has a reli-gious dimension. . . . It is thought to please the gods."[32] How this is so or which gods are pleased we are not told, presumably because the villagers didn't know either. The "repressed" religion that returns is thus far from what one might designate as "orthodox"—however the latter is defined, whether in (later) biblical or Yahwistic perspectives[33]—and it is certainly not very developed. It is telling, regardless, that it is the less "orthodox" religious aspects (judging from later periods and texts) that are alive and well at Ramat-Yachin. So, for example, "the women think most of the goddesses of fertility and lactation. . . . [T]o the peasant women these goddesses, represented by roughly carved wooden statuettes, are of paramount importance." While "El and Baal are the all-important gods . . . they are the gods with whom the men are concerned; their territory lies beyond the house. In the domestic realm, the goddesses prevail." The confidence of this statement—recall that no one even knows Yhwh's name at Ramat-Yachin—is remarkable, as is the fact that these god-desses are said to be "[k]nown as Asherah and Astarte"! Van der Toorn goes so far as to write that the women's "lives depend on" these goddesses.[34]

Where there is mention of the male gods, it is invariably Baal. A ceremony unites the men of the village, their ancestors, and Baal; there is a greeting or blessing (apparently the same thing; see above) of Baal at the same time.[35] What happened to El along the way is unclear. As "a dim deity," perhaps he is already otiose,[36] though the personal name (PN) of the village chief, "Elḥanan" ("El has shown mercy" or the like) shouldn't be forgotten.[37] Why is he not named

---

31. Prophylactic actions, if nothing else (see van der Toorn, "Nine Months among the Peas-ants," 399); for more on demons and warding them off, see van der Toorn, "Nine Months among the Peasants," 402–3. On ethics in Old Babylonian religion, see van der Toorn, *Family Religion in Babylonia, Syria and Israel*, 94–118 (cf. further below).

32. For other examples see van der Toorn, "Nine Months among the Peasants," 398, who mentions the gods "call[ing]," blessing formulae that are used ("my grandfather, blessed be his memory"), or certain aspects of quotidian life ("the women put an almost religious zeal into" preparing food).

33. I realize the term is anachronistic, especially in the earliest periods. I use it only heuristically.

34. Van der Toorn, "Nine Months among the Peasants," 399.

35. Van der Toorn, "Nine Months among the Peasants," 401–2; cf. 405.

36. Van der Toorn, "Nine Months among the Peasants," 395.

37. For this name in the Bible and epigraphic record, see Jeaneane D. Fowler, *Theophoric Per-sonal Names in Ancient Hebrew: A Comparative Study*, JSOTSup 49 (Sheffield: JSOT Press, 1988), 82, 111, 147, 345; and Ran Zadok, *The Pre-Hellenistic Israelite Anthroponymy and Prosopography*, OLA 28 (Leuven: Peeters, 1988), 25, 179, 228, 313–14.

"Baalḥanan"?[38] Maybe "Elḥanan" is just an old trace of a naming tradition that goes as far back as the eponymous founder of the village, "Elyachin" ("El established"). Whatever the case, Baal is clearly the most important deity for Ramat-Yachin—any religious "thought" (if it could even be called such) that rises to some level of expression concerns him. Or demons.[39] But the victory for the cloud-rider is a muted one. Even in a ritual held at a *bāmâ* that appears to recognize Baal's fructification of the earth,

> no fervent prayers were spoken, and there was no show of devotion. . . . The ceremony might strike onlookers as a tepid performance, [but] the participants derived comfort from its regularity. . . . It . . . strengthened their belief that they lived in a world of order and of mutual goodwill between Baal, the dead, and the living. Such thoughts were never spoken out loud, nor did they need to be. The ritual, performed as a pious duty, spoke for itself to the participants; they did not ask for its meaning, nor did they care to talk about it.[40]

How van der Toorn draws these conclusions when so much goes unspoken and no one cares to discuss these matters is unclear.[41] But a similar question obtains at a later point in the story when we find Elḥanan giving "something amounting to a speech at a ritual"[42] held at the *bāmâ*. In a voice "higher [pitched] than usual," Elḥanan describes Baal's rejuvenated rule of the land after his sojourn in the world below (with the ancestors), which left "the land a playground for Death, his adversary."[43] "But now," the elder goes on to say,

> Baal had returned and had brought the ancestors with him. He showed his presence in the new wine, reinvigorating all those who drink it. Death had been defeated; Baal reigned supreme. In a few weeks' time he would shower his rains upon them, preparing the fields for a new sowing. The coming year would be even better than the last one: the flocks would multiply, women would hold new children on their laps, and the efforts of the men would bear fruit. As

---

38. For this name, see Fowler, *Theophoric Personal Names in Ancient Hebrew*, 62, 82, 338, 345; and Zadok, *Pre-Hellenistic Israelite Anthroponymy and Prosopography*, 25, 180, 232.

39. Van der Toorn, "Nine Months among the Peasants," 402–3.

40. Van der Toorn, "Nine Months among the Peasants," 403.

41. One suspects that van der Toorn's dream report is being interfered with at this point by (his) other knowledge bases. It was only fiction after all!

42. Van der Toorn, "Nine Months among the Peasants," 405; 406 calls it a "peroration"!

43. Van der Toorn, "Nine Months among the Peasants," 405.

Elḥanan spoke about the future, his words had the quality of an incantation. The audience responded now with shouts, now with whispers.[44]

So, at that rare point when something approaching an extended articulation of religious belief is expressed, it is for Baal. Even more striking than that fact is the observation that the belief that is finally expressed corresponds largely to a Baal mythology known (so far, at least) from the textual record of Late Bronze Age Ugarit, which is removed from isolated Ramat-Yachin by many miles and a goodly number of years. How that religious mythology—preserved, we might recall, by a scribal elite[45]—came to be the religion of these highland village peasants is not clear in the article; perhaps it is not available to anthropological ways of knowing.

For a moment it seems like Yhwh *may* make a comeback at the end of van der Toorn's essay, in the description of a case of illness which is treated by a visiting divine known as "the man of God," who defines the problem not as a physical malady at all but as the result of communal sin—a religious vow left unfulfilled, to be precise.[46] This may be the same divine who knew of Yhwh worship in parts south, but it needn't be, and by the end of the account it is more than clear that he is no card-carrying member of the Yhwh-alone party (see §2 below) because he accepts a statement that the village had "kept the covenant [N.B.!] with Baal [N.B.!] and the ancestors," even as he notes that "the dead are dissatisfied" with their actions, and later deduces that "El would speak" on behalf of the village elders via the drawing of lots.[47] Evidently this "man of God(s)" is an equal opportunity soothsayer with the notable exception, or so it would seem, of Yhwh.

Not only is there a return of the repressed (religion) at various points in van der Toorn's description of Ramat-Yachin, there are also moments where this essay seems to be in some conflict with his earlier work on family religion in Babylonia, Syria, and Israel. We learn there, for instance, that despite diachronic change in Israelite family religion, the latter entity is actually "the prolongation of a Bronze Age phenomenon into the Iron Age."[48] In this way, especially because family reli-

---

44. Van der Toorn, "Nine Months among the Peasants," 406.

45. Cf. §2 below, and note, for example, the role of the scribe Ilimilku in the mythological texts from Ugarit, and Yanḥamu for the lexical texts from there. See Richard S. Hess, "The Onomastics of Ugarit," in *Handbook of Ugaritic Studies*, ed. Wilfred G. E. Watson and Nicolas Wyatt, HdO 1/39 (Leiden: Brill, 1999), 499–528, esp. 512; and, further, Juan-Pablo Vita, "The Society of Ugarit," in *Handbook of Ugaritic Studies*, 455–98, esp. 465, 472–73.

46. The language of "sin" and religious "vows" that must be fulfilled are additional examples of the return of the repressed (religion).

47. Van der Toorn, "Nine Months among the Peasants," 407.

48. Van der Toorn, *Family Religion in Babylonia, Syria and Israel*, 375; cf. 4.

gion in the biblical text "has survived mainly as a substratum," knowledge of Old Babylonian family religion is absolutely essential. Without it, "it would be very difficult to interpret the few and mostly oblique references to family religion in the Bible."[49] And yet, in some contrast to the downplayed role of religious devotion in the Ramat-Yachin essay, van der Toorn is at pains in his larger book to *insist* on the importance of religious belief and practice: "The vitality of religious beliefs and customs in the context of the family belies Oppenheim's assessment that 'the influence of religion on the individual, as well as on the community as a whole, was unimportant in Mesopotamia.' . . . The absence of these [religious themes, specifically the cult of the ancestors and the worship of local patron deities] . . . promotes a myopic vision of the Old Babylonian reality."[50]

Now, to be sure, van der Toorn's nine months in the village of Ramat-Yachin revealed a good bit of ancestor cult—though it was quite nondescript in the end, and also rather unceremonial and not highly meaningful, at least in any descriptive sort of way—but "vitality," "religious beliefs," and "worship," to borrow just three of van der Toorn's terms used above, seem curiously absent in the religion of Ramat-Yachin. One wonders if we too are left with "a myopic vision," only this time of the early Israelite, not Old Babylonian, reality.

Still further on this point, in his earlier book van der Toorn states that "it is impossible to attain a real understanding of the Babylonians without taking into account what their religion did to them,"[51] but in the essay on Ramat-Yachin one gets the sense that if there even is a "religion" of which to speak (perhaps there isn't),[52] it doesn't seem to have "done" much at all to the villagers—at least not in the same way that it did for the Old Babylonians.[53] Or, one might consider how, in the earlier book, van der Toorn seems more comfortable with the symbolic nature of ritual acts and their cognitive content than he is in the later essay on early Israelite religion: "To say that solidarity with the ancestors and the neighbourhood

---

49. Van der Toorn, *Family Religion in Babylonia, Syria and Israel*, 5.

50. Van der Toorn, *Family Religion in Babylonia, Syria and Israel*, 373, citing A. Leo Oppenheim, *Ancient Mesopotamia: Portrait of a Dead Civilization*, rev. ed. (Chicago: University of Chicago Press, 1977), 176.

51. Van der Toorn, *Family Religion in Babylonia, Syria and Israel*, 373.

52. Cf. van der Toorn's definition of "religion" in van der Toorn, *Family Religion in Babylonia, Syria and Israel*, 7: "Religion refers to the various notions, values and practices involving nonempirical powers." This is certainly not the only, nor an exhaustive, description of religion. See, inter alia, Daniel L. Pals, *Eight Theories of Religion*, 2nd ed. (New York: Oxford University Press, 2015); and Smith, "Religion, Religions, Religious," 269–84.

53. "Historical identity" and "a sense of belonging to a specific place"—two central leitmotifs in van der Toorn's *Family Religion in Babylonia, Syria and Israel*—are very vague indeed when it comes to Ramat-Yachin.

preceded its ritual celebration is not quite true. The sentiment of such solidarity does not fully exist until it takes place in certain symbols. Family religion can be seen as the complex of symbols (*a term that covers beliefs and values* as well as certain practices) which give substance to the identity and mutual affinity of its followers."[54] But beliefs and values evidently do not pertain to Iron Age Israelite Ramat-Yachin—or at least everyone is tight-lipped about them—despite the facts that (1) such beliefs and values obtained for Old Babylonian religion long beforehand; and (2) Iron Age Israel is in some sort of profound continuity with the latter (once again: "a prolongation of a Bronze Age phenomenon into the Iron Age").

One final important point of disjuncture between van der Toorn's earlier work and the later essay deserves mention. It concerns the "personal" nature of "personal devotion." In his earlier monograph on family religion van der Toorn emphasizes the "collective" nature of Babylonian religion: "There was, in a sense, no identity outside the group, just as there was no religion outside the community. Left to himself man would be a non-entity, and his religion a private delusion."[55] Such sentiment mandates that we be very careful with the use of adjectives like "personal" and "individual," though van der Toorn also asserts that they "should not be simply dismissed."[56] There was, he writes, "hardly any privacy to family religion. The Near Eastern civilizations were unfamiliar with contemplation or silent prayer; acts of devotion always had a public aspect."[57] But while the non-private nature of lived experience at Ramat-Yachin *is* strongly emphasized in the essay, the public nature of the religion there is *not*, but seems, again, rather downplayed. Even more to the point I wish to explore here, the diachronic focus of the monograph's attention on Israelite religion leads van der Toorn to speak of a move *"from* family religion *to* personal devotion."[58] This movement suggests that something happened to change the old (Babylonian or Babylonian-*ish*) family religion into something more familiar to moderns, something that was marked by personal (eventually individual?) devotion and that was presumably characterized by "beliefs and values."[59]

I will say more about the "something" that happened below (§2); the problem to

---

54. Van der Toorn, *Family Religion in Babylonia, Syria and Israel*, 374 (my emphasis).

55. Van der Toorn, *Family Religion in Babylonia, Syria and Israel*, 374; cf. 3–4.

56. Van der Toorn, *Family Religion in Babylonia, Syria and Israel*, 3.

57. Van der Toorn, *Family Religion in Babylonia, Syria and Israel*, 4.

58. Van der Toorn, *Family Religion in Babylonia, Syria and Israel*, 6, 375; see further all of part III, on Israel, which is actually subtitled in this way (179–372).

59. Van der Toorn, *Family Religion in Babylonia, Syria and Israel*, 6: "The third and most extensive part of the book has been called 'From Family Religion to Personal Devotion', since it describes the waning of the traditional forms of family religion and the emergence of a religion

be noted here is that—from the front (early) side of the development—"beliefs and values" *already characterized early religion* according to van der Toorn. And, from the back (later) side of the development, we end up learning from van der Toorn that this personal devotion is ultimately nothing less than "what might be called a national religion."[60] It is hard indeed to know what a national religion would look like except something that is thoroughly public and presumably also a good bit more systematized or, to borrow from van der Toorn's language, dogmatized.[61]

Let me be clear that I do not intend an overly pedantic critique by this extended summary and analysis of van der Toorn's essay in light of his earlier work. I find van der Toorn's publications consistently insightful and incisive; there are good reasons that he is a leading light and that his work has helped shape scholarly consensus! And if there are points of disjuncture between the book on family religion and the essay on Ramat-Yachin, there are also obvious points of profound similarity. The latter essay could simply not have been written without the earlier monograph on family religion, and the seminal ideas of the book are on repeated display throughout the essay.[62]

Even so, there does seem to be a bit of a pulling back on some things—ideas, terms, and subjects—in the Ramat-Yachin essay vis-à-vis the comparative data amassed in the monograph on family religion.[63] It is hard to judge why that should be the case. Perhaps it is because the essay is explicitly "anthropological" whereas the monograph is not.[64] Maybe there are other reasons as well.

Whatever the case, the upshot of van der Toorn's imaginative essay on what it would be like to spend nine months in an early Israelite village is that the religion therein is of a certain and rather understated sort. "Primitive" is the first descriptor that comes to mind, but "superstitious" and "magical" aren't far behind. That is to be expected, one supposes, in an ancient, primitive (there's that word again) culture-*cum*-religion. But what is not expected—even and perhaps especially among ancient cultures and their religions—is how thoroughly *non-affective* this religion

---

of personal commitment to beliefs and values that transcend the immediate interests of the family and the local community."

60. Van der Toorn, *Family Religion in Babylonia, Syria and Israel*, 375.

61. See van der Toorn, *Family Religion in Babylonia, Syria and Israel*, 2.

62. See above. Note also that in *Family Religion in Babylonia, Syria and Israel*, van der Toorn is well aware of potential reductionism: "One should beware not to overrate the explanatory potential of the notion of identity"—and one might add, history or social scientific categories; "Religion fulfils a variety of functions" (8).

63. This is not to say that I find the monograph fully satisfying on matters of religion, religious experience, or theology. I do not.

64. See van der Toorn, *Family Religion in Babylonia, Syria and Israel*, 4–6, for its method as historical and comparative.

is and how deeply *non-cognitive* to boot.[65] Where there is any developed, though hardly fully-formed, articulation of religious experience and/or belief, it relates to Baal worship, especially as that is known (at least to us now) via the finds at Ugarit and not, pointedly, from any textual remains from ancient Israel/Palestine.[66]

Van der Toorn is no maverick in offering such a reconstruction of ancient Israelite religion even if he is rather unique in offering such a creative presentation of such (a creativity for which he is to be commended, in my opinion). As I indicated earlier, I take his essay as generally representative of something approaching scholarly consensus in reconstructions of Israelite religion, at least of the earliest variety, and at least of late.[67] My criticisms, then, should not be taken as singling him out unfairly. To broaden the net a bit further, for example, I note that Tammi J. Schneider's recent volume on Mesopotamian religion is similarly marked by extreme reticence to say anything about the meaning of various rituals and an aversion to speculate at all about the cognitive content of religious belief.[68]

65. Cf. van der Toorn, *Family Religion in Babylonia, Syria and Israel*, 2 (cited more extensively below in §2). For the indispensable neurological connections between emotions and cognition see, inter alia, Antonio R. Damasio, *Descartes' Error: Emotion, Reason, and the Human Brain* (New York: Quill, 1994); and Damasio, *The Feeling of What Happens: Body and Emotion in the Making of Consciousness* (San Diego: Harcourt, 1999). For the fundamental role of conceptual analogy or metaphor in the religious symbol system of "Syro-Canaan," see David P. Wright, "Syro-Canaanite Religions," in *The Cambridge History of Religions in the Ancient World*, vol. 1: *From the Bronze Age to the Hellenistic Age*, ed. Michele Renee Salzman and Marvin A. Sweeney (Cambridge: Cambridge University Press, 2013), 129–50.

66. This is not to say that the name "Baal" does not appear in the epigraphic record, which it certainly does (see esp. the Samaria ostraca), but there is no extended mythology of Baal available from the soil of ancient Israel/Palestine, and there are good reasons to question too-simple an identification of the material from Ugarit with that from "Canaan" let alone "ancient Israel." See Lester L. Grabbe, "'Canaanite': Some Methodological Observations in Relation to Biblical Study," in *Ugarit and the Bible: Proceedings of the International Symposium on Ugarit and the Bible, Manchester, September 1992*, ed. George J. Brooke, Adrian H. W. Curtis, and John F. Healey, UBL 11 (Münster: Ugarit-Verlag, 1994), 113–22. Still further, if the epigraphic record was to be relied on, Yhwh would certainly have to figure more prominently than he does at Ramat-Yachin. On the PN evidence, see most recently Stig Norin, *Personennamen und Religion im alten Israel untersucht mit besonderer Berücksichtigung der Namen auf El und Ba'al*, ConBOT 60 (Winona Lake, IN: Eisenbrauns, 2013). Note also Jeffrey H. Tigay, *You Shall Have No Other Gods: Israelite Religion in the Light of Hebrew Inscriptions*, HSS 31 (Atlanta: Scholars Press, 1986); Miller, *Religion of Ancient Israel*; Fowler, *Theophoric Personal Names*; and Zadok, *Pre-Hellenistic Israelite Anthroponymy and Prosopography*. Or, if the Bible is summoned to fill in gaps about Baal, then it would certainly have to be allowed to fill in gaps on Yhwh as well.

67. There are, as R. W. L. Moberly has kindly reminded me, some very marked differences between these more recent reconstructions and those of, say, the mid-twentieth century. See further below.

68. Tammi J. Schneider, *An Introduction to Ancient Mesopotamian Religion* (Grand Rapids:

In the end, though, one wonders if some important elements have been left out in these reconstructions. Perhaps the title of van der Toorn's essay says it all: it is about time spent with "peasants in the Palestinian Highlands," and that description seems fair enough. But the essay also speaks of an "Israelite" village, not an "Israbaalite" one,[69] and the village in question is located in Iron Age Israel/Palestine, *not* in Late Bronze Age Ugarit. Or then again the title announces an "anthropological perspective on local religion," but this approach seems unable to get a good grasp on the local inhabitants' religious "beliefs."[70] Does something as simple as a personal name signify anything of the latter? The PN Elḥanan, after all, means "El/God had mercy," and raises a host of questions: What does "mercy" mean in this construction and how is it an action of El/God? To whom was the mercy shown and when? How so? Is that a "real" and "true" assertion in the user's perspective or simply a piece of traditional tripe? Or then there is the PN of the eponymous ancestor, Elyachin, which means "God established." Here too questions abound: What did El/God establish? And for whom? When and how? Really and truly? It is hard to imagine even people "of so practical a bent of mind" not having an idea or two about these questions, precisely because, if the PNs aren't simply "traditional" (in the modern conceit), they would seem to be the result of intentional choice.[71] Furthermore, devoid of any religious conceptions, a PN like "Spear" (*qayin*) or "Lion" (*'aryê*) would seem to have done just fine. Why include a deity name, especially if the deity in question is non-functional, uninspiring, and (apparently) downright unimportant? If good old-fashioned and all-pervasive "primitive superstition" is invoked as the likely reason, the dream report from Ramat-Yachin would indicate that names like *Nāṣûr* ("Protected") or *Māgēn* ("Shield") would have made just as much sense, given the reality of the demons (see above), than anything invoking the gods proper. It seems preferable, then, to treat the theophoric names at Ramat-Yachin as van der Toorn himself does in his

---

Eerdmans, 2011). Cf. van der Toorn, *Family Religion in Babylonia, Syria and Israel*, 112: "Devotion must not be confused with fervor. A true [Babylonian] gentleman avoids extremes."

69. The relationship between "Palestinian" and "Israelite" is never clarified in the essay.

70. See Levenson, *Hebrew Bible, the Old Testament, and Historical Criticism*, 114–15, for an incisive critique of anthropological ways of knowing that fall short of "native belief." He cites Lesek Kolakowski's work, *Religion* (New York: Oxford University Press, 1992), 15–16: "We need more than [the empirical material of the anthropologist] to assert that when people speak of God or the gods, of invisible forces purposely operating behind empirical facts, of the sacred quality of things, they are in fact, and without knowing it, speaking of something entirely different" (Levenson, *Hebrew Bible, the Old Testament, and Historical Criticism*, 115).

71. Not to mention the intimacy they enjoyed with the other world (van der Toorn, "Nine Months among the Peasants," 397).

earlier monograph: "Such names [in the Old Babylonian period] are miniature confessions illuminating the conceptual universe of family religion."[72]

2. What Would (Should) Old Testament Theology Look Like? A First Probe

With the preceding overview of one, particularly fascinating, reconstruction of Israelite religion in place, we may now turn to a first probe of what (an) Old Testament theology would (or should) look like in light of it.

1. The first thing one might say is that it is hard to say what (an) Old Testament theology should look like in light of the reconstruction offered in the Ramat-Yachin essay. The focus there is resolutely on (very) early Israel such that one might easily say that, since there is no Old Testament at that point in time, there can be no such thing as an "Old Testament theology."[73] Somewhat analogously, in his family religion book van der Toorn writes that certain differentiations (such as the opposition between "popular" and "official" religion) are "of little use when we are dealing with religions that have no dogmatics." And, he continues, "both the Old Babylonian and Early Israelite religion belong to this class—as do most ancient religions."[74]

---

72. Van der Toorn, *Family Religion in Babylonia, Syria and Israel*, 95.

73. The question that immediately follows is: when is there an Old Testament such that there can be something called "Old Testament theology"? Cf. Levenson, *Hebrew Bible, the Old Testament, and Historical Criticism*, 37: "The juxtaposition of . . . various sorts of literature in the same book is a matter of literary context; it becomes a fact of history per se only very late in the period of the Second Temple—long after the original historical contexts of the pentateuchal literature and perhaps also the proverb collections had vanished. The construction of a religion out of all the materials in the Hebrew Bible violates the historian's commitment to seeing the materials in their historical contexts. The result will correspond to the religion of no historical community, except perhaps some parties very late in the period of the Second Temple. The argument that Old Testament theology can maintain both an uncompromisingly historical character and its distinction from the history of Israelite religion is therefore not valid." See further §4 below.

74. Van der Toorn, *Family Religion in Babylonia, Syria and Israel*, 2. But contrast Ziony Zevit, "False Dichotomies in Descriptions of Israelite Religion: A Problem, Its Origin, and a Proposed Solution," in Dever and Gitin, *Symbiosis, Symbolism, and the Power of the Past*, 223–35, esp. 232:

Insofar as there is no reason to assume that cultic observances at the level of the father's house were less formal, regulated, or tradition-bound than at the poly-tribal level, and because there is no reason to assume any significant difference in formality between the observances of consanguine groups and those of affiliations of unrelated individuals, the digitized dichotomies simply do not apply. Their words lack a social or ideological referent in the culture of ancient Israel. They mislead.

There was no state or elite or official or popular religion in ancient Israel. There was a political body that we may label "state"; there were social and economic elites; there were sacerdotal and royal officials; there was a populace; and there was the so-called "man in the street." But data do

Quite apart from the questions of whether (an) Old Testament theology must be "dogmatic" (a particularly fraught term in the history of doctrine)—or, perhaps better, "systematizing"[75]—or whether ancient religions are capable of such thought,[76] the Israelite religion reconstructed by van der Toorn is one that, despite its obvious dependence on parts of the Bible, seems to bear very little resemblance to much of the religion captured therein. To begin with just the most obvious point of distinction: there is no Yhwh at Ramat-Yachin! And what is a religion (at least in the ancient Near East) if it is not something to do with its gods?[77] Ramat-Yachin has no Yhwh; for the Old Testament, Yhwh is indispensable.[78] So, in the old adage, "Never the twain shall meet" . . . or so it seems. To put things slightly differently, borrowing words from van der Toorn, the data "that any reconstruction of local religion . . . must take into account" are "few" and offer "the dissembled bones of a skeleton, at best. Let these bones live!"[79] But vis-à-vis the Old Testament, one may be pardoned in thinking that these particular bones simply *can't* live—not, at least, in terms of (an) Old Testament theology. These bones are too far desiccated even for the *rûaḥ yhwh* (Ezek 37:1–14; notwithstanding Jer 32:17, 27; Matt 19:26;

---

not support the proposition that a particular type of pattern of credo or praxis may be associated with them.

75. I tend to agree with Rolf P. Knierim that systematizing of some sort is inevitable when it comes to Old Testament theology (*The Task of Old Testament Theology: Method and Cases* [Grand Rapids: Eerdmans, 1995], 475–86, 548). Even someone as emically oriented as Walter Brueggemann (*Theology of the Old Testament: Testimony, Dispute, Advocacy* [Minneapolis: Fortress, 1997]) evidences thematizing or systematizing trends. See Brent A. Strawn, "On Walter Brueggemann: (A Personal) Testimony, (Three) Dispute(s), (and On) Advocacy," in *Imagination, Ideology, and Inspiration: Walter Brueggemann and Biblical Studies*, ed. Jonathan Kaplan and Robert Williamson Jr., Hebrew Bible Monographs (Sheffield: Sheffield Academic, 2015), 9–47. R. W. L. Moberly has suggested (personal communication) that "synthesizing" might be a better term.

76. It is interesting that scholars of ancient Egyptian religion do not evidence problems with the word "theology." Cf. Strawn, "History of Israelite Religion."

77. See, inter alia, Miller, *Religion of Israel*, 1–45. For van der Toorn's definition of religion, see note 52 above.

78. Note, e.g., Henning Graf Reventlow's notion that Yhwh should be the center (*Mitte*) of Old Testament theology (see, e.g., *Problems of Old Testament Theology in the Twentieth Century* [Philadelphia: Fortress, 1985], 125–33; cf. also Hasel, *Old Testament Theology: Basic Issues in the Current Debate*, 4th ed. [Grand Rapids: Eerdmans, 1991], 139–71). Gerhard von Rad's famous retort ("What kind of a Jahwe is he?") (*The Theology of Israel's Prophetic Traditions*, vol. 2 of *Old Testament Theology*, trans. D. M. G. Stalker [San Francisco: Harper & Row, 1965], 415) effectively counters Reventlow's (and others') quest for a center but does not challenge the centrality of Yhwh for "Old Testament religion."

79. Van der Toorn, "Nine Months among the Peasants," 409.

Mark 10:27; Luke 1:37; 18:27), precisely because that spirit is the spirit *of Yhwh*, a persona otherwise unknown! Maybe Baal's spirit would have a better go of things.

2. Now, to be sure, van der Toorn's essay appears to concern only (very) early Israel. It could be seen, that is, as the first chapter in a much longer history of Israelite religion that would develop and unfold through time. While that may well be true, it leads to a second thing that can be said about the interface of the Old Testament and Israelite religion: the disjuncture between early Israelite religion as reconstructed in the Ramat-Yachin essay and the religion and/or theology[80] found in the Old Testament means that to make a reconstruction of Israelite religion such as van der Toorn's fit with, work toward, or otherwise have an impact on (an) Old Testament theology, one must somehow explain what the Old Testament is and/or how it came to be. That means, in the case at hand, that one must explain why the Old Testament at full stretch looks so drastically different than the dream report about Ramat-Yachin. What one must do, therefore, is create some sort of diachronic model to explain or justify the rise of the Old Testament and its religion and/or theology since it does not appear to relate—at least not directly—to early Israelite religion.

Van der Toorn offers just such an explanation in his book on family religion and in his more recent book on scribal culture.[81] The gist of the former can be briefly recounted: Since family religion is so profoundly social, social changes of any sort lead directly to religious change. In Israel, the rise of the state brought "the possibility of an identification with the supra-local collectivity of the nation," no longer just that of the family.[82] There is now "a kind of competition between state religion and family religion, the former validating a national identity, the latter a local identity."[83] State religion can only win this battle by "the creation of a charter myth that might mobilize a sense of national identity among the population"—the priests and prophets are responsible for that step[84]—and by "an attempt at integrating family religion in the religion of state," which is a task

---

80. See note 9 above on "religion" and "theology." In what follows I use both, often with "and/or" to show their possible interrelations as well as their potential distinctions.

81. See also van der Toorn's essay "Scribes and Scribalism," in *The Oxford Encyclopedia of the Bible and Law*, ed. Brent A. Strawn (Oxford: Oxford University Press, 2015), 2:278–85.

82. Van der Toorn, *Family Religion in Babylonia, Syria and Israel*, 375.

83. Van der Toorn, *Family Religion in Babylonia, Syria and Israel*, 375.

84. Van der Toorn, *Family Religion in Babylonia, Syria and Israel*, 375–76. This is, of course, the exodus myth, even if, as van der Toorn allows, it may depend on some small shred of historical fact. Note that in "Nine Months among the Peasants," 402–3, van der Toorn details a practice of anointing a door with blood in Ramat-Yachin, but it has nothing to do with the exodus proper, but rather with averting demons that might prowl around the houses of the village.

for kings.[85] But the coexistence of family and state religion in Israel "was never harmonious. The two were in constant competition"[86] and the integration of Baal worship, in particular, proved too much for the theological conservatives (where they come from—apart from the south—is curious since, if the Ramat-Yachin reconstruction holds any water, most people—at least early on—were Baalists), who eventually congealed into "the incipient [and famous or infamous, depending on one's perspective] Yahweh-alone movement . . . the zealots of a strict monolatry of Yahweh."[87] The architects (or culprits) of the demise of old family religion and rise of late state religion were, big surprise, those stodgy Deuteronomists! But not all is lost: "One may regret the oblivion to which much Ephraimite family religion abroad has been reduced, but one should rejoice over the understanding of the Deuteronomists which a study of the competition between family religion and state religion produces."[88]

It is the Deuteronomists, then, who are ultimately responsible for bringing about "a new religion," though "it must be recognized that they were the exponents of a much wider trend."[89] But whence comes this Deuteronomism, or how it reflects a "wider trend," and who those additional "exponents" might be, is not fully described, simply postulated. And yet, despite its dissatisfyingly hypothetical nature, this sort of postulation seems absolutely necessary in the grand scheme of things, owing its existence mostly, if not exclusively, to the fact that one must explain how one gets to the material presently found in the Old Testament from a reconstruction of Israelite religion that is so drastically different.

It is a short next step from this sort of historical reconstruction of Israelite-religion-into-Old-Testament-literature to a compositional model that posits that the Hebrew Bible, in the aggregate, is the result of scribal elite circles.[90] How else to explain material that seems so much more "Yahwized"—even if not dogmatized or systematized (though perhaps more "dogmatizable/systematizable")? Average Joe- and Judy-Elḥanan from Ramat-Yachin are not well represented in the pages

---

85. Van der Toorn, *Family Religion in Babylonia, Syria and Israel*, 376.

86. Van der Toorn, *Family Religion in Babylonia, Syria and Israel*, 376.

87. Van der Toorn, *Family Religion in Babylonia, Syria and Israel*, 377. Cf. earlier Morton Smith, *Palestinian Parties and Politics That Shaped the Old Testament*, 2nd ed. (London: SCM, 1987).

88. Van der Toorn, *Family Religion in Babylonia, Syria and Israel*, 378.

89. Van der Toorn, *Family Religion in Babylonia, Syria and Israel*, 379.

90. See van der Toorn, *Scribal Culture in the Making of the Hebrew Bible*. Once again, van der Toorn is not alone in this regard and there is a recent spate of books on the composition history of the Hebrew Bible, or its constituent parts, many of which are highly speculative (how could they be otherwise?). For a recent reaction—also not without problems—see John Van Seters, *The Edited Bible: The Curious History of the "Editor" in Biblical Criticism* (Winona Lake, IN: Eisenbrauns, 2006).

of the Old Testament, after all. They would not find themselves or their religious experiences therein—of course they wouldn't be able to read the Bible anyway, being illiterate, and there wasn't any Bible to speak of until long after their deaths. Even so, the very little trace that they leave in the pages of Holy Writ seems an ominous indicator that they were victims of more than just the vagaries of history. Elite scribal erasure may be to blame.

Unlike some other, more simple-minded theorists, van der Toorn states clearly (and admirably) that he does not wish to posit a simplistic or "uniform development,"[91] but it is hard to avoid the impression that exactly such a development is common among so many reconstructions of Israelite religion, along with their correlate (non-)bearing on the Old Testament and its religion and/or theology. To put this development rather too simply, one might delineate at least four stages in the argument:

> **STAGE 1:** Radical disjuncture between early Israelite religion and anything later
> *(leads to)* ↳ **STAGE 2:** various political-historical developments, especially of the hierarchical, royal, and elite kind
>   *(leads to)* ↳ **STAGE 3:** production of religious literature ultimately culminating in the Old Testament but only much, much later
>   *(leads to)* ↳ **STAGE 4:** theological readings of the Old Testament literature that are even more belated than stage 3 (up to the present).

Once again, if Israelite religion is the kind "on the ground," especially of the average person ("folk religion," to use a problematic term for the moment), especially in earlier periods prior to state "corruption" or "imposition," then the obvious conclusion seems to be, again, that when it comes to Israelite religion of this sort (stage 1) and Old Testament theology (stage 4), never the twain shall meet—despite the intervening stages.[92]

Let me be clear that I do not mean to suggest that all of the above is completely wrong or erroneous somehow. There is no doubt that much of the scholarly consensus depends on good modeling, decent data, and reasonable argumentation. I would not want to challenge, for instance, that few ancient individuals were

---

91. Van der Toorn, *Family Religion in Babylonia, Syria and Israel*, 377.

92. It is worth noting (as R. W. L. Moberly has kindly reminded me), how different this gross distinction between Old Testament theology and Israelite religion is when compared to works in the early twentieth century where Old Testament theology (at least of a sort) was virtually identified with Israelite religion. See, e.g., the debate between Otto Eissfeldt and Walter Eichrodt reprinted in Ben C. Ollenburger, ed., *Old Testament Theology: Flowering and Future*, SBTS 1 (Winona Lake, IN: Eisenbrauns, 2004), 12–29.

literate, which means that the vast majority were illiterate (at least by modern standards), leaving *literary production*, at least, in scribal hands and the circles that supported them.[93] All of that seems quite reasonable and decently supported, thanks to the work of people like van der Toorn and others.

I do wish to suggest, however, that much of this kind of model is dissatisfying, not necessarily due to a general lack of explanatory power (though that power may depend on a certain circularity) but because of its *lack* of explanatory power *at certain key junctures*. One such juncture is that *the Old Testament itself* provides some of the key data to build the model—say, Baalistic tendencies that are mentioned in Judges or Kings or the like (cf. also Baalistic PNs in the Samaria ostraca). This is a case of having the proverbial cake and wanting to eat it too. But if the Baalistic tendencies of the Hebrew Bible are legitimate, why shouldn't the Yahwistic ones be as well? Or, at a second, but not unrelated juncture, if the end result that is the Old Testament is (solely) the work of a scribal elite, why is there so much in the Old Testament that simply doesn't seem to fit such "elitism"—that resists it or challenges it?[94]

The biggest problem, then, is and remains the existence of the Old Testament itself—especially the burrs it sticks in the saddle of any developmental model that moves seamlessly from something early and almost entirely non-Yahwistic (if not also non- or a-religious) to something that is heavily, if not thoroughly, Yahwistic with its full complement of (admittedly non-uniform) "theological" or "dogmatic" material, all of which would have been unimaginable in the imaginary village of Ramat-Yachin. It should be recalled that, for his part, van der Toorn resists any uniform development, but it seems more common than not for many scholars to assume something very much like it. The development that is postulated is neither wholly unreasonable nor completely unimaginable, but does it have any more claim to reality than the imaginative reconstruction of early Israelite religion at Ramat-Yachin? Is one any less (or more?) speculative than the other? The developmental model needs significant thickening and revision—it must not only resist simplistic uniformity but

93. Even so, see Carolyn Routledge, "Parallelism in Popular and Official Religion in Ancient Egypt," in *Text, Artifact, and Image: Revealing Ancient Israelite Religion*, ed. Gary Beckman and Theodore J. Lewis, BJS 346 (Providence, RI: Brown Judaic Studies, 2006), 223–38, for other types of religious literacy that do not depend on reading or writing.

94. Similar literature is found in the Near East as well, of course. One thinks of anti-royal oracles in, say, the Mari letters, but while these were no doubt recorded by literate scribes, many do not seem to reflect inner-circle dynamics that support—and certainly not invariably—the royal hierarchy. Whatever the case, note that van der Toorn also attributes Old Babylonian religion, including its theology and ethics (N.B.!), to the upperclass ("gentility," *awīlutum*), but also states that "most Babylonians, it seems, cherished religious notions and ideas very similar to those held by the class of the *awīlū*" (*Family Religion in Babylonia, Syria and Israel*, 95), which renders the class distinction somewhat moot. See also note 74 above.

must also resist simplistic linearity, and those are only two of the more important qualifications that should be made. Others could be mentioned.[95]

So far, however, all I have offered is an analysis of just a small portion of van der Toorn's work—work that I continue to find insightful, even indispensable, despite the fissures I have identified here and there along the way. I admit that it is easy to conduct this kind of "armchair scholarly analysis"; it is far harder to do the extensive data collection, sifting, and interpretation that van der Toorn and others have done. One may justifiably ask, then, if there are any data to support what are, so far, my rather theoretical observations. Do these latter finally comprise nothing more than a small-minded critique—a gnat bothering a lion? Is there any evidence for an alternative? Obviously I do not have the room here that van der Toorn had to develop his ideas across three book-length studies. I have only a few pages left, but as a further gesture toward the question(s), if not also the solution(s), of what Old Testament theology should look like in light of reconstructions of Israelite religion, I wish to turn now to the book of Job.

3. Fitting Job into *Israelite Religion

Job has problems fitting into reconstructions of Israelite religion like the one(s) recounted above for several reasons, but an excellent entrée into the larger issues is provided by J. J. M. Roberts's classic study, "Job and the Israelite Religious Tradition."[96]

Roberts's essay is rather strongly anti-historical-critical, at least when it comes to Job's intersection with Old Testament theology. Roberts speaks of "history's

---

95. For example, what kind of social mechanism, especially of the elite-political variety, could explain the religiosity one finds in later literature? This is never adequately addressed in my view (see further below). An essay like that of Ryan Byrne, "Lie Back and Think of Judah: The Reproductive Politics of Pillar Figurines," *NEA* 67 (2004): 137–51, attempts such an explanation—though with reference to pillar figures not biblical literature—but in the end I find it unconvincing and reductionistic in terms of lived religious experience. For a similar critique, with reference to Hobbesian and Foucauldian views of power see Levenson, *Hebrew Bible, the Old Testament, and Historical Criticism*, 113–14. It is better, in Levenson's opinion, to pay attention to those ""microrelations" of power' that suffused the society and acquired an enduring literary testament in the Hebrew Bible.... Scholars ... [should] concentrate less on the elites and ... show the masses more respect" (114). Cf. also Johnson, *Religious Experience in Earliest Christianity*.

96. J. J. M. Roberts, "Job and the Israelite Religious Tradition," *ZAW* 89 (1977): 107–14, reprinted in Roberts, *The Bible and the Ancient Near East: Collected Essays* (Winona Lake, IN: Eisenbrauns, 2002), 110–16. Citations are taken from the latter. See also J. Gerald Janzen, "The Place of the Book of Job in the History of Israel's Religion," in *Ancient Israelite Religion: Essays in Honor of Frank Moore Cross*, ed. Patrick D. Miller, Paul D. Hanson, and S. Dean McBride (Minneapolis: Fortress, 1987), 523–37.

stranglehold on biblical theology and Old Testament scholarship" that "in general remains unbroken"; of the "persisting theological *tyranny* of history"; the "theological *bias* for history"; and "the *temptation* to historicize."[97] That such "history remains the touchstone of a genuine, normative, biblical theology" is not, in his view, at least vis-à-vis Job, a good thing. This is largely because such an approach must assume a "historical background extraneous to the text of the book" to properly understand or interpret it. More often than not, according to Roberts, this kind of historicizing approach "reduces Job to a mere cipher for Israel, and his theological problem becomes the problem of understanding Israel's national experience" (Job stands for Israel in exile, for example); the book itself, however, presents the theological issue in question as thoroughly "individualistic" in nature.[98]

A further problem identified by Roberts is that historicizing attempts have been unsuccessful in terms of chronology and typology—consider, for example, the individual doctrine of retribution which is sometimes tied to Ezekiel's time with Job consequently following Ezekiel at some later point in history. But it might be contested that such a "doctrine" first appeared with Ezekiel (or in his time) and/or that Ezekiel is the fount for Job's "situated" theology. This chronological-typological reconstruction is just that: a reconstruction—one that seems like a house of cards that Roberts brushes aside with a single, poignant question: "What legitimacy can an interpretive background of history claim in the absence of any clear textual references to that history?" As if "the subjective nature of all . . . attempts to interpret Job by reference to a particular historical background" weren't enough, Roberts goes on to note "the total lack of consensus in the dating of the book."[99] While the range of possibilities may be more limited now than when he originally penned his essay,[100] Roberts is certainly right that, barring certainty in such matters, "one cannot use the date of the book . . . to provide a ready-made background for its interpretation, and lacking this, an historical framework is hard to establish."[101]

In brief, overly historicized approaches to Job have come up empty.[102] What

---

97. Roberts, "Job and the Israelite Religious Tradition," 110–11 (my emphasis).

98. Roberts, "Job and the Israelite Religious Tradition," 110–11.

99. Roberts, "Job and the Israelite Religious Tradition," 111–12.

100. Roberts delineates a range "as early as the eleventh or tenth centuries and as late as the fourth century," after which he concludes wryly: "In view of this seven-hundred-year discrepancy, it should be obvious that most of the criteria advanced for dating carry little conviction" (Roberts, "Job and the Israelite Religious Tradition," 112). For recent discussions of the date of Job, see, e.g., David J. A. Clines, *Job 1–20*, WBC 17 (Dallas: Word, 1989), lvii; C. L. Seow, *Job 1–21: Interpretation and Commentary*, Illuminations (Grand Rapids: Eerdmans, 2013), 39–45.

101. Roberts, "Job and the Israelite Religious Tradition," 113.

102. Not on all fronts, of course. One thinks of older views on the authorship of Job by Moses or its location in the ancestral period as now permanently debunked, in no small part due to historical considerations (e.g., historical philology).

then? Roberts advocates for "simply stick[ing] to the text," and when one does so, "the poetic dialogue presents the problem as that of a religious individual who was experiencing what appeared to him as undeserved suffering. There is no hint that the suffering extended beyond his immediate family; indeed 19:13–17 implies that even within his own household Job's agony was his alone."[103] But of course Job's agony is not, ultimately, just his own: "A similar theme appears numerous times in Israelite and Mesopotamian individual laments. . . . The same motifs also appear in the narrative portions of the individual thanksgiving song . . . and several of the Mesopotamian 'wisdom' texts often compared to Job actually belong to this genre. Their resemblance to Job stems not from wisdom per se, but from their roots in *the existential experience of rejection, lament, and restoration*."[104] In the end, then, Roberts concludes that "the actual date of the composition of Job is largely irrelevant for its exegesis." He explains:

> If its author stood in a long literary tradition in which basically the same problem had been dealt with before, and if the human experience necessary for this problem to arise in Israel was independent of any necessary connection to the national history, it is illegitimate to read that history into the book simply because the book could have come into its present form during an acute national crisis. Not every work written in a period of great upheaval deals with or is strongly influenced by that upheaval, not even when the work could plausibly be interpreted in that fashion.[105]

And so, Roberts concludes, "the historical method has its own peculiar temptation toward eisegesis."[106]

In sum, Roberts argues that Job is something of a "timeless text," in at least two ways: the first is due to the scholarly inability to fix the text firmly in a time and space that could be definitive for its interpretation (especially for all interpreters); the second is that insofar as Job deals with "the same problem" that "had been dealt with before," one that was not uncommon to "the human experience," especially when considered—via the textual clues—as an individual problem, not a theodicy

---

103. Roberts, "Job and the Israelite Religious Tradition," 114.

104. Roberts, "Job and the Israelite Religious Tradition," 114–15 (my emphasis).

105. Roberts, "Job and the Israelite Religious Tradition," 116. Roberts helpfully refers at this point to J. R. R. Tolkien's Lord of the Rings trilogy. Note that this observation gives the lie to any assumption that any and every social change must directly and invariably impact religious change. For sentiments on Job similar to those expressed in Roberts's article, though formulated more briefly, see Moberly, *Old Testament Theology*, 244.

106. Roberts, "Job and the Israelite Religious Tradition," 116.

for some national catastrophe, then it can be read, interpreted, and understood independently of 587 BCE—or 722 BCE or 332 BCE or 167 BCE, for that matter.

In one sense, then, Roberts cannot "fit" Job into Israelite religion, whatever the historical reconstruction "they" offer (once again, because "they" can't agree), but this does not bother him. Job, in his estimation, doesn't need to be fit into (the history of) Israelite religion due to the book's nature, content, and problem—all of which are somehow "timeless."

To be sure, even "timeless" literature comes into being at a particular point in time at a particular place amidst certain circumstances,[107] all or at least some of which would seem to be important to, if not somehow determinative for, its interpretation. I do not wish to challenge Roberts's main conclusions here, however, so much as put them to slightly different use. If Roberts is right—and I think he is—that Job and other texts like *Ludlul* or *The Babylonian Theodicy* are rooted in "the existential experience of rejection, lament, and restoration,"[108] then that is an important datum for considering the interface between Old Testament theology and Israelite religion. To be specific: what was missing in the preceding discussion of reconstructions of Israelite religion, at least in the early Iron Age highlands, was, for lack of a better word, any *soul*—that is, real, lived religion that impacted persons in profound and affectual ways.[109] For its part, the book of Job has a good

---

107. Or in the case of composite timeless literature, which has grown through various compositional processes, plural forms are probably in order: particular *points* in time at particular *places*. Job may be one such work, given ongoing questions regarding its compositional unity. See, e.g., Leo G. Perdue, *The Sword and the Stylus: An Introduction to Wisdom in the Age of Empires* (Grand Rapids: Eerdmans, 2008), 118. But contrast Clines, *Job 1–20*, lviii; and Seow, *Job 1–20*, 26–38.

108. Roberts, "Job and the Israelite Religious Tradition," 115. For *Ludlul* see the sensitive treatment in William L. Moran, "The Babylonian Job," in *The Most Magic Word: Essays on Babylonian and Biblical Literature*, ed. Ronald S. Hendel, CBQMS 35 (Washington, DC: Catholic Biblical Association, 2002), 182–200; also Thorkild Jacobsen, *The Treasures of Darkness: A History of Mesopotamian Religion* (New Haven: Yale University Press, 1976), 162; Jacobsen, "Mesopotamia," in *The Intellectual Adventure of Ancient Man: An Essay on Speculative Thought in the Ancient Near East*, ed. Henri Frankfort and H. A. Frankfort (Chicago: University of Chicago Press, 1977), esp. 212–16. For more on texts such as these, see Kenton L. Sparks, *Ancient Texts for the Study of the Hebrew Bible: A Guide to the Background Literature* (Peabody, MA: Hendrickson, 2005), 56–83, and, for translations, see *ANET* 589–91, *COS* 1.179:573–75 (*A Man and His God, the "Sumerian Job"*); *ANET* 596–600, *COS* 1.153:486–92 (*Ludlul*); *ANET* 601–604, *COS* 1.154:492–95 (*The Babylonian Theodicy*); *ANET* 600–601, *COS* 1:155:495–96 (*The Dialogue of Pessimism*).

109. In Johnson's terminology: "religious experience" (see *Religious Experience in Earliest Christianity*, passim). While benefiting immensely from a reading of Johnson's work at the end of my work on this chapter, I note that he has a different and more negative view of theology than what I express here (Johnson, *Religious Experience in Earliest Christianity*, 2–4). My use sees profitable overlap between "theology" and "religion" and "religious experience" (see notes 9 and 80 above). While that is somewhat fuzzy, and Johnson's more consistent terminology might be

bit of "soul": "the existential experience of rejection, lament, and restoration," as Roberts calls it. This "existential experience" is in Job (so also in *Ludlul* and *The Babylonian Theodicy* et al.) at root religious and theological in so far as it concerns the pious person and his God. And, if Roberts can't fit Job into Israelite religion due to problems pertaining to the insufficiency of diachronic analysis, many recent reconstructions of Israelite religion suffer the same problem—not because of diachrony, but because there seems to be very little room for any religious experience whatsoever in them, and certainly no room for the most profound variety like that attested in Job. Early Israelite religion seems to be little more than subsistence survival, with a dash of primitive "magic" or "superstition." There's certainly no thought, and no high thought at that, that would reflect profound wrestling with substantive theological problems—"existential experiences," that is, "of rejection, lament, and restoration," which involve humanity coming face-to-face with what it deems *not* human or *supra*human: namely, the divine. Many reconstructions of early Israelite religion cannot account, then, for a book like Job, or the predicament(s) and issue(s) it raises. At this point, Job is a microcosm of the problem the Old Testament as a whole poses for reconstructions of Israelite religion like those discussed in the previous section. What explains Job in these reconstructions? Where does it come from, especially when it is antedated, in most scholarly reckonings, by ancient Near Eastern materials that address the same issues hundreds of years earlier?

The problem with the non-fit of Job (or *Job)[110] in reconstructions of Israelite religion is thus two-fold. (1) First, the inability of reconstructions of Israelite religion to account for Job neglects in a rather odd way the fact that these existential-theological-religious issues are attested *outside* Israel, *long before* Israel. Van der Toorn knows this better than most scholars, having written a brilliant treatment of the problem of sin and theodicy in the Hebrew Bible and the ancient Near East already as his dissertation.[111] The problem of the non-fit of Job, then, is not because

---

preferable, it may be that the issues he faces in the study of Christian origins differ from those under examination here. In any event, I do not deem "theology" to be a problem as he does, but see it as a subset of religious experience: faith seeking understanding, as it were, or, in William P. Brown's memorable reformulation, "fear seeking understanding" (*Wisdom's Wonder: Character, Creation, and Crisis in the Bible's Wisdom Literature* [Grand Rapids: Eerdmans, 2014]).

110. The problem persists even in composition-critical approaches that would break the book into its constituent parts or otherwise fillet it into earlier or later pieces. Cf. note 107 above.

111. See Karel van der Toorn, *Sin and Sanction in Israel and Mesopotamia: A Comparative Study*, SSN 22 (Assen/Maastricht: Van Gorcum, 1985). Note also van der Toorn, "The Ancient Near Eastern Literary Dialogue as a Vehicle of Critical Reflection," in *Dispute Poems and Dialogues in the Ancient and Mediaeval Near East*, ed. G. J. Reinink and H. L. J. Vanstiphout, OLA 42 (Leuven: Peeters, 1991), 59–75; and Karel van der Toorn, "Sources in Heaven: Revelation as a Scholarly Construct in Second Temple Judaism," in *Kein Land für sich allein: Studien zum Kulturkontakt in*

van der Toorn doesn't know of these other ancient Near Eastern texts, their content, or even their "existential" aspects. The problem is that those texts and their concomitant religious experience and theological content are not permitted to function, analogously, in so many reconstructions of ancient Israelite religion.[112] This religious experience is, to crib from Luke Timothy Johnson's work, "what's missing from Israelite religion."[113]

Let me be clear that my point in noting the attestation of these religious/ theological aspects in extra-biblical literatures that antedate Israelite instances of the same should not be understood as an argument about influence or dating, the latter of which, at least, would be subject to the same problems Roberts's essay identifies (debate over chronology, mechanisms of influence, and so forth).[114] It is, instead, to simply observe that, if someone in the Kassite period can struggle with these sorts of existential-religious-theological issues,[115] or an Egyptian can do it in *The Dispute of a Man with His Ba*,[116] then certainly Job can. And if Job can—that is, if the author or authors of Job can—then reconstructions of Israelite religion need to become *more biblical* and *more textual* than they have been of late (cf. Roberts's "stick[ing] to the text"), and *far more theological* to boot. The dirt is only going to tell us so much and it won't tell us as much as we need to know if we

---

Kanaan, Israel/Palästina und Ebirnâri für Manfred Weippert zum 65. Geburtstag, ed. U. Hübner and E. A. Knauf, OBO 186 (Freiburg: Universitätsverlag, 2002), 265–77.

112. Van der Toorn is certainly not alone at this point. Note, famously, Frank Moore Cross's opinion that "there is a sense in which Job brought the ancient religion of Israel to an end," because the argument of Job "repudiated the God of history" (*Canaanite Myth and Hebrew Epic: Essays in the History of the Religion of Israel* [Cambridge: Harvard University Press, 1973], 344); cf. Roberts, "Job and the Israelite Religious Tradition," 114: "What F. M. Cross fails to stress is that such a God did not reveal himself to Job's friends either. His friends do not appeal to the sacred history, and they seem as much at home with the god of myth as Job is." Note that Job does not show up in the subject indices of either Zevit, *Religions of Ancient Israel*, or Hess, *Israelite Religions*, its use being confined in those works to small citations of particular verses. Similarly King and Stager, *Life in Biblical Israel*, 76. Rainer Albertz's work is notable for devoting an extended section to Job (*A History of Israelite Religion in the Old Testament Period*, trans. John Bowden, OTL [Louisville: Westminster John Knox, 1994], 2:511–17), but Albertz presents Job as a crisis of personal theology of the upper class. While accounting for Job in one sense, Albertz's treatment falls prey to many of Roberts's criticisms. Cf., similarly, van der Toorn, "Sources in Heaven," 265–77, for an account of Job that is strikingly similar to Albertz's and that is also subject to Roberts's critique.

113. See Johnson, *Religious Experience in Earliest Christianity*, chap. 1, "What's Missing from Christian Origins" (1–38).

114. Roberts, "Job and the Israelite Religious Tradition," 115, cites both *Ludlul* and *The Babylonian Theodicy*, indicating that the latter "must have exercised at least an indirect influence on the biblical work."

115. For the date, see Moran, "The Babylonian Job," 183; *BWL* 21–29.

116. See *AEL* 1:163–69; *ANET* 405–7; *LAE* 178–87 for translations.

care about religious experience, affect, and the like. For the latter, we need access to the larger symbolic systems that reflect and shape these aspects of religion, and the textual data, while not comprising a complete picture by any means, are nevertheless crucial for that.[117]

(2) The non-fit of Job faces a second problem because, in the historical and literary reconstruction evidenced in van der Toorn's work, what one encounters in Job can only be the product of a much, much later development. Once again clarity at this point is crucial: I do not wish to challenge developmentalism writ large. Things change, including ideas, and such change often includes thickening, increased precision, and complexity. That is not the only way things develop, however;[118] regardless, we still have to deal with Job-like parallels in the ancient Near Eastern materials that precede Job (whenever Job is to be placed). Again, I am not interested in dating Job early, I only wish to observe the existence of its existential-religious-theological issues in *antecedent* cognate data. So, in the positing and articulation of certain developmental schemata—especially of the overly uniform or linear kind—it would seem that many reconstructions of Israelite religion fare no better than classic "Wellhausenianism" when it comes to the finally rather simple-minded idea that complex presentations must be (much) late(r), if not also somehow devolved (an odd development, to be sure!) despite their complexity (so, e.g., for Wellhausen: P long after J/E).[119] A correlate result (equally problematic it seems) is that the Hebrew Bible becomes the ultimate in late constructivism with its use for understanding Israelite religion deeply problematic at best and perhaps completely irrelevant at worst.

More on this last point—what the Old Testament and its theology are good for in the wake of reconstructions of Israelite religion—in the next section (§4). Before (re)turning to that, however, let me just point out again (cf. §2 above) that Job is not alone in highlighting these sorts of problems that face the interface (or not) of reconstructions of Israelite religion and Old Testament theology. The Psalms pose the same problem. At least some of them, at least according to some scholars, originate from

---

117. To be sure, archaeology can get at symbol systems in various ways, perhaps most especially via iconography. See the insightful comments of Othmar Keel and Christoph Uehlinger, *Gods, Goddesses, and Images of God in Ancient Israel*, trans. Thomas H. Trapp (Minneapolis: Fortress, 1998), 7–13, 393–96. For a recent iconographical attempt to get at emotion-language, see Strawn, "Iconography of Fear." See L. Johnson, *Religious Experience in Earliest Christianity*, 39–68, for an approach that is phenomenological.

118. E.g., languages can simplify, over time, not just become more complicated, even if such simplification is often caused by outside interference of some sort (e.g., linguistic contact, insufficient language acquisition, etc.).

119. Cf. Johnson, *Religious Experience in Earliest Christianity*, 182, on how developmental schemata are often ways to avoid dealing with the phenomenon of religious experience.

Iron Age Israel, if not Late Bronze Age "Canaan"—even if we can't be certain about all the details.[120] Or, moving backward, it seems safe to say that not all of the Psalms are Hasmonean! It isn't the date that is the primary point, however; it is *the religious experience* that they represent. Consider but one simple line from Ps 127:2 (NRSV):

He [Yhwh] gives sleep to his beloved.

This line seems utterly unexplainable in any depictions of Israelite religion that are insufficiently . . . well, religious and/or theological.[121] Why would a deity "give" ($\sqrt{ntn}$) sleep to an individual if not out of some sort of care for such a person—a point underscored by calling said person the deity's "beloved" (*yādîd*)? An intimate term to be sure! And why "sleep" (*šēnā'*)?[122] Sleep is fundamental to human health and life; it is also an activity that suggests safety and security. The God depicted in just this one line of Ps 127 apparently feels strongly, even passionately, about human beings and seems to care for them enough to provide them with something essential for human existence along with the circumstances needed to experience it (cf. Ps 3:5: "I lie down and sleep; / I wake again for the LORD sustains me" [NRSV]).[123]

And it doesn't stop with an example like this one from the Psalms—which could be repeated *ad infinitum*—what of the heart language in 1 Sam 2:1; 4:13; and 10:26?[124] Or the love language in Deuteronomy, not all of which need be seen as politicized speech?[125] If one is looking for a rather acerbic religious experience vis-

120. So (perhaps!), Pss 29, 68, 104. Others could be added to this list, but all could be seriously debated. Once again, the dating of texts seems an insufficient foundation on which to build.

121. See Moran, "Babylonian Job," 188, for an Old Babylonian text which also captures a great deal of religious affect: "A young man weeps to his god as to a friend."

122. On the form of $\sqrt{šn'}$ (rather than $\sqrt{šnh}$), see John Goldingay, *Psalms 90–150*, vol. 3 of *Psalms* (Grand Rapids: Baker Academic, 2008), 497n3; Hans-Joachim Kraus, *Psalms 60–150: A Continental Commentary*, trans. Hilton C. Oswald (Minneapolis: Fortress, 1993), 454.

123. Cf. Moran, "Babylonian Job," 188, for an Old Babylonian exemplar of comparable deity-care: "I am your god, your creator, your refuge. My guards are awake for you, are strong for you. I will open for you a hiding place. Long life will I give you." The god who says this is a personal god, but note the description of Marduk in *Ludlul* I:19–20 as a cow who constantly looks behind for its calf (the worshiper). See Amar Annus and Alan Lenzi, *Ludlul bēl nēmeqi: The Standard Babylonian Poem of the Righteous Sufferer*, SAACT 7 (Helsinki: The Neo-Assyrian Text Corpus Project, 2010), 15, 31; also Moran, "Babylonian Job," 194.

124. First Samuel 2:1: "Hannah prayed and said, 'My heart exults in the LORD'"; 4:13: "Eli was sitting upon his seat by the road watching, for his heart trembled for the ark of God"; 10:26: "with him [Saul] went warriors whose hearts God had touched" (NRSV).

125. *Pace* William L. Moran, "The Ancient Near Eastern Background of the Love of God in Deuteronomy," *CBQ* 25 (1963): 77–87 (reprinted in *Most Magic Word*, 170–81, and in Frederick E. Greenspahn, *Essential Papers on Israel and the Ancient Near East* [New York: New York University

à-vis the Deity, one may perhaps locate that in Qoheleth (though I myself would understand that book somewhat differently), but—and here is further proof of the point—that book is almost universally dated to the Hellenistic period, not the early Iron Age.[126]

4. Conclusion: What Is the (*)Old Testament Good For?

It should be clear by now that the preceding section on Job was no detour but actually quite important as it showcased some of the problems involved in relating reconstructions of Israelite religion to Old Testament theology. This was, of course, also discussed in §§1–2, but considering Job allowed us to see the problems from the other side—a more textual(ized) side rather than a historical or anthropological one. The problems are several, but can be glossed with the question "What is the Old Testament?" or "What is the Old Testament good for?" especially vis-à-vis recent reconstructions of Israelite religion. There is clearly no going back from key insights that have been hard won over decades of painstaking historical research on ancient Israel and its cultural congeners. To the extent that those insights are accurate, they are not only true but are profoundly helpful; no one would *want* to retreat from them. One of the most important of these insights is that the Old Testament does not provide a direct or unmediated picture of ancient Israelite religion.[127] Things on the ground were far more complicated than what one might otherwise think upon a facile reading of the Old Testament.[128] One aspect of this complexity is precisely religious: religious experience was no doubt more complex and diversified in ancient Israel than what scholars of previous generations envisioned largely because they relied (overmuch) on the Old Testament.[129] In

---

Press, 1991], 103–15). See Jacqueline E. Lapsley, "Feeling Our Way: Love for God in Deuteronomy," *CBQ* 65 (2003): 350–69.

126. A notable exception is Choon-Leong Seow, who places Qoheleth in the Persian Period. See his *Ecclesiastes: A New Translation with Introduction and Commentary*, AB 18C (New York: Doubleday, 1997), 11–21.

127. Cf. Levenson, *Hebrew Bible, the Old Testament, and Historical Criticism*, 107: "The basis of religion in biblical times was not a Bible: the religion *in* the Book is not the religion *of* the Book."

128. See, e.g., Francesca Stavrakopoulou and John Barton, eds., *Religious Diversity in Ancient Israel and Judah* (London: T&T Clark, 2010). Note, however, Johnson, *Religious Experience in Earliest Christianity*, 21, for the problem in assuming that "each dissected strand of literature adequately represents the ideology of a separate 'community.'"

129. See, e.g., Helmer Ringgren, *Israelite Religion*, trans. David E. Green (Philadelphia: Fortress, 1966), 4–14; Georg Fohrer, *History of Israelite Religion*, trans. David E. Green (Nashville: Abingdon, 1972), 24–25; and Elmer Leslie, *Old Testament Religion* (Nashville: Abingdon, 1936). Of course this, too, must be qualified. Close attention to the entire Old Testament reveals a large range in terms of religious experience or affect—the difference, for example, between starchy

one sense, then, it is no surprise at all that reconstructions of Israelite religion à la van der Toorn's dream report about Ramat-Yachin are drastically different than what one finds in the Old Testament. That is to be expected, part of the deal.

Then again, part of the problem in relating studies of Israelite religion and Old Testament theology is the notorious specter of "the facile reading of the Old Testament." Any such reading—from whichever perspective (and it can come from several sides)—simply will not do, especially when there is a good bit of complexity and diversity present in the pages of the Bible itself, and because at least some of that biblical material is drawn upon and used, even if only selectively, in reconstructions of Israelite religion, especially in those that highlight diversity and difference from the Hebrew Bible and the religion and/or theology it contains or somehow reflects or represents.

This is to say that the Old Testament *itself* is a datum that should—indeed *must*—be considered in reconstructions of Israelite religion. And that means that the religion and/or theology that it contains is also a datum for Israelite religion. Further, the book of Job is a datum, as is the issue(s) that it represents. So also are *Ludlul* and other such texts, along with their comparable issues, data.[130] These too, that is, are, as it were, pieces of historical evidence that are every bit as important and valid as, say, the texts from Ugarit or Baalistic PNs among the Samaria ostraca.[131] But, if one only attends to items such as the latter, what the Old Testament is and what it (re)presents becomes impossible—virtually unexplainable in terms of its origins and its content, or is explainable only in terms of a certain kind of greatly reduced historicism or ideology. The Old Testament in the aggregate, in this per-

---

Qoheleth and the rapturous hymns of praise in the Psalter. It is not, then, only historical or archaeological data that produce this kind of differentiated insight, but also attentive reading of the literature. In this way, relying "overmuch" on the Old Testament could actually lead to the very same results as another kind of developmental or diachronic approach. Furthermore, the giants of the previous generation—e.g., Hermann Gunkel, Walther Eichrodt, and Gerhard von Rad—were anything but facile readers.

130. See Moran, "Babylonian Job," 187, for his opinion that in *Ludlul*, the sufferer ("Mesopotamian Everyman") is, "in his hour of deepest desperation . . . made aware of another and, to him, new reality, the reality of Marduk, and there is revealed to him a new personal religion, the religion of Marduk, a religion that transforms and transcends the religions and problems of the past." Cf. 198: "*Ludlul* seems to be almost the logical extension of Marduk's lordship over creation and history into the domain of individual lives. If he rules the world and all that happens in it, he should rule the individual as well. A sovereignty less pervasive would not be absolute." Cf. Annus and Lenzi, *Ludlul bēl nēmeqi*, xxxvi: "Whatever else *Ludlul* is, it is certainly a text that we would intuitively call 'religious' because it praises a deity, Marduk, and commends his veneration."

131. That is to say that a focus on religious experience and/or theology need not be *a*-historical. See L. Johnson, *Religious Experience in Earliest Christianity*. Cf. analogously the thoughtful revisioning of historical criticism in F. W. Dobbs-Allsopp, "Rethinking Historical Criticism," *BibInt* 7 (1999): 235–71.

spective, is good for almost nothing when it comes to reconstructing Israelite religions.[132] If the most un(der)religious presentations of Israelite religion, especially vis-à-vis Yahwism as known from the Hebrew Bible (a diverse phenomenon, let it be again underscored), were true, Old Testament theology would become ethereal, abstract, even "mythic" (in the fictive sense)—something far removed, if not completely severed, from so much reality in ancient Israel, especially of earlier periods. In such a scenario Old Testament theology must be(come) something that treats the Old Testament as a product (only) of later elite culture, an ideological product of scribes or priests or kings, that can and perhaps should be mistrusted, not only because it is elite and ideological, but because it is so grossly inaccurate when it comes to the "facts on the ground."[133] Old Testament theology would need to traffic in the realm of fable, make-believe, fiction, as something concocted by later religious ideologues—first priests, then scribes, then rulers, until then, even more belatedly, believers (no doubt conservative ideologues themselves) of whatever stripe, whether Jewish or Christian. Old Testament theology, in this view, could simply be dispensed with—for more than one good reason—as secondary and inferior to the more real and substantive work emerging from historical reconstruction and archaeology, whether the stratification in question is of a tell or of a text. This is the rather sad and dismal picture of what Old Testament theology would, and perhaps should, look like if recent reconstructions of Israelite religion were accurate.[134]

But, as I have tried to show in this chapter, not everything "they" say about Israelite religion is true. Consider, for example, Yhwh's servant Job.

132. Or, to provide a slightly different angle in light of van der Toorn's reconstruction vis-à-vis Deuteronomism, one could say that Deuteronomy and its exponents changed Israelite religion so drastically that the Old Testament, which is post-Deuteronomy, is of little if no help whatsoever for what was pre-Deuteronomy, simply because the latter has been so drastically and irrevocably altered.

133. Cf. Dever, *Did God Have a Wife*, passim. It is worth noting that in his most recent book, van der Toorn discusses Job only in passing in a few instances, one of which states "there can be little doubt that the Book of Job goes back to a scribe as well" (*Scribal Culture and the Making of the Hebrew Bible*, 116). Cf. note 112 above on Albertz's and van der Toorn's readings of Job in Israelite religion.

134. The only alternative of which I am aware would be to take the Old Testament as intentionally polemical *against* much (most?) of Israelite religion and self-consciously so. See, e.g., John W. Wright, "Toward a Holiness Hermeneutic: The Old Testament against Israelite Religion," *Wesleyan Theological Journal* 30 (1995): 68–90. I deem this approach unsuccessful and unsatisfying as well, in part because—at least in Wright's case—it depends entirely too much on reconstructions of Israelite religion that are not yet certain.

10

The Old Testament and Participation with God (and/in Christ?): (Re)reading the Life of Moses with Some Help from Gregory of Nyssa

To participate means to have acquired, to have received from without, though, of course, not necessarily in a passive and unconscious manner. The participant stands in a continuous causal dependence on the transcendent Source.[1]

In one brief utterance, the grand intention of God has become a specific human responsibility, human obligation, and human vocation.[2]

In God [*bēʾlōhîm*] we will act valiantly, and/but [*wəhûʾ*] it is he who will trample our enemies. (Pss 60:12[14]; 108:13[14])

I am thankful to the conveners of the North Park symposium for their kind invitation to participate in the 2017 colloquium. I also thank my interlocutor, J. Nathan Clayton, for his gracious and helpful response. I also wish to thank Mark McInroy for helpful discussions on participation and for many bibliographical suggestions prior to my writing as well as for commenting on an initial draft. I am also thankful to Collin Cornell and Anthony Briggman for giving me feedback on the piece. Early in my thinking Klyne Snodgrass was gracious enough to share a copy of his own paper on participation, which is now published as "The Gospel of Participation," in *Earliest Christianity within the Boundaries of Judaism: Essays in Honor of Bruce Chilton*, ed. Alan J. Avery-Peck, Craig A. Evans, and Jacob Neusner, BLRJ 49 (Leiden: Brill, 2016), 413–30.

1. David L. Balás, Μετουσία Θεοῦ: *Man's Participation in God's Perfections according to Saint Gregory of Nyssa*, Studia Anselmiana 55 (Rome: I.B.C. Libreria Herder, 1966), 124.

2. Walter Brueggemann, "The Book of Exodus: Introduction, Commentary, and Reflections," in *NIB* 1:713.

"Participation with Christ" is not the most obvious topic for an Old Testament professor to address—not, at least, for the past few centuries of biblical scholarship. Some, maybe even most, scholars presently active in the guild would deem the topic completely out of bounds since Christ as such does not appear in the Old Testament, the Greek translation of "Messiah" as *Christos* in the Septuagint[3] and/or other so-called "messianic prophecies" notwithstanding.[4] To be sure, if the Old Testament professor at hand is a Christian, especially one open to the kind of figural interpretation that marked Jewish and Christian exegesis before the modern era (and still does, to no small degree, at least homiletically), the theme of participation with Christ in the Old Testament may not be impossible to imagine. The rock that accompanied the people of Israel, after all, was Christ according to Paul (1 Cor 10:4)—let the reader understand (Matt 24:15 // Mark 13:14)! Or, in a different vein, the biblical texts were written also for us and for our sake (1 Cor 9:10), if only one has ears to hear (Mark 4:9 // Luke 8:8; Mark 4:23; Luke 14:35).[5]

The shadow of historical criticism—or at least its thin veneer of historicism—still looms large in the guild of biblical scholarship, however, and is usually accompanied by a strong distaste of so-called "pre-modern" interpretations of the Bible, even among Christian exegetes, and so a figural approach, while viable and in many ways resurgent in certain circles,[6] will probably make a number of people uncomfortable, whether they are religious adherents or not: such is the power

---

3. See, e.g., Lev 4:5, 16; 6:15; 1 Sam 12:5; 16:6; 24:6[7], 10[11]; Isa 45:1; Hab 3:13; Amos 4:13; Lam 4:20; Dan 9:26; etc.

4. Some such prophecies are applied to Christ already within the New Testament itself. See, e.g., Donald Juel, *Messianic Exegesis: Christological Interpretation of the Old Testament in Early Christianity* (Philadelphia: Fortress, 1992). Of course, messianic prophecies from the Old Testament need not apply directly or only to Jesus of Nazareth, as evidenced, inter alia, by non-Christian Jewish messianic expectation at Qumran and elsewhere. See, generally, James H. Charlesworth et al., eds., *The Messiah: Developments in Earliest Judaism and Christianity* (Minneapolis: Fortress, 1992), esp. the essay therein by J. J. M. Roberts, "The Old Testament's Contribution to Messianic Expectations," 39–51.

5. Immediacy in terms of applicability is a widely shared assumption by those interested in and practicing the reading of the Bible for the life of faith. In my judgment, this assumption depends on a prior disposition—namely, to hear Scripture as a word of address. For some general reflections on this matter, especially in the light of Christian preaching of the Old Testament, see Ellen F. Davis, *Wondrous Depth: Preaching the Old Testament* (Louisville: Westminster John Knox, 2005).

6. See, e.g., David C. Steinmetz, "The Superiority of Pre-Critical Exegesis," in *The Theological Interpretation of Scripture: Classic and Contemporary Readings*, ed. Stephen E. Fowl (Malden, MA: Blackwell, 1997), 26–38; and John David Dawson, *Christian Figural Reading and the Fashioning of Identity* (Berkeley: University of California Press, 2002); more recently, consult Ephraim Radner, *Time and the Word: Figural Reading of the Christian Scriptures* (Grand Rapids: Eerdmans,

and the rootedness of historical criticism in the study of Holy Scripture. Stepping back somewhat, then, but in some ways depending on a deeper foundation (or assumption), one might appeal to orthodox Trinitarianism such that any instance of "participation with God" (however that phase is defined—and it isn't yet here)[7] would be equally an instance of participation with the Son, though of course also with the Spirit who ought not be neglected. I myself have advocated such an approach for reading the Old Testament in a way that *permits* but *does not require* christological connections.[8] But, insofar as a Trinitarian approach is decidedly *post*-textual (insofar as the full-blown doctrine of the Trinity is the distinguished achievement of later Christian centuries) or, probably better, *pre*-textual (insofar as it operates with some form of preunderstanding that informs and guides the interpretation of the text), and insofar as this a priori situation may be quite totalizing but at the same time rather non-specific (i.e., every place where one member is operative/present all members are operative/present . . . but what does that mean, specifically, for text *x*, *y*, or *z*?), it, too, may not be particularly helpful in specific cases beyond reiterating the general principle that, wherever one might participate in God in the Old Testament, one must also understand such participation as being "in Christ" (and the Spirit!). So what, then, can we say about the subject at hand—"participation with Christ"—from the perspective of the Old Testament?

I shall return to a Trinitarian (pre)understanding at the end of this chapter, but, thus far in the secondary literature—or so it seems to me—the place of the Old Testament's contribution to the notion of divine participation has been

---

2016); and see also John L. Thompson, *Reading the Bible with the Dead: What You Can Learn from the History of Exegesis That You Can't Learn from Exegesis Alone* (Grand Rapids: Eerdmans, 2007).

7. This is at least partly by design and for at least two reasons: the first is that Gregory's own work depends on various philosophical positions that are not operative, at least to the same degree, in the biblical texts, and I do not want to force Gregory's categories on the Old Testament's unduly. The second is that, precisely given the difference delineated in the first reason, I think it would be most helpful to treat the general idea of participation inductively, touching on various themes and texts which seem to be of most pertinence to the notion. I fully concur with Gary A. Anderson, when he writes (of purgatory) that "a proper grasp of what the doctrine intends to teach is crucial for determining whether it has a biblical basis" (*Christian Doctrine and the Old Testament: Theology in the Service of Biblical Exegesis* [Grand Rapids: Baker Academic, 2017], 185). Even so, the present essay proceeds intentionally with a somewhat underdefined or undertheorized notion of participation so as to not constrain the biblical text unduly and to let Scripture say things back to the idea that might otherwise be ignored (cf. at note 46 below).

8. See chapter 7 in the present volume. The only thing that might be forbidden in a Trinitarian approach is an overly wrought Christocentrism; all varieties of Christomonism would definitely be out of order.

somewhat staid or lackluster, limited largely to the question of "background." Any decent and thorough investigation of the idea of participation will include at least some summary treatment of its antecedents. There are actually a large number of antecedents for the idea of participation, and one of them, to be sure (and also to say the very least), is the Old Testament. So it is that scholars appeal to various notions in the Old Testament as precursors or anticipations of the idea.[9] Studies disagree, of course, on just *how* important the Old Testament is to this "background" especially vis-à-vis other possible datasets. In some instances, that is, the Old Testament is deemed to be only one of several helpful resources; in others, it might be considerably less than that.[10] So, even if it is a source or fount,

---

9. See, e.g., Norman Russell, *The Doctrine of Deification in the Greek Patristic Tradition* (Oxford: Oxford University Press, 2004), 53–55 (on ancient Israel, just one of five parts of what he calls "the Jewish paradigm," and which focuses almost exclusively on Enoch and Elijah, both of which are deemed to be "comparatively late accounts of extraordinary events which did not in any way affect the expectations of the ordinary Israelite" [55]); Gregory Glazov, "Theōsis, Judaism, and Old Testament Anthropology," in *Theōsis: Deification in Christian Theology*, ed. Stephen Finlan and Vladimir Kharlamov, PTMS 52 (Eugene, OR: Pickwick, 2006), 16–31 (who, of "Israelite royal-sonship ideology," says only that it "could have contributed to the later emergence of Christology and theōsis" [25] and that "biblical anthropological models taken from covenant salvation history and wisdom narratives provide many bases for a biblical theōsis theology" [29]); and Jules Gross, *The Divinization of the Christian according to the Greek Fathers*, trans. Paul A. Onica (Anaheim, CA: A&C, 2002), 61–69 (who speaks of "the seeds of a doctrine of deification contained in the oldest books of the Old Testament" which were fertilized by the author of Wisdom to "prepare the way for the Christian revelation" [69]). There is wide agreement that Ps 82:6 was an important text for the doctrine, esp. as read through John 10:34–38. See esp. Carl Mosser, "The Earliest Patristic Interpretations of Psalm 82, Jewish Antecedents, and the Origin of Christian Deification," *JTS* 56 (2005): 30–74. Prior still to the Old Testament, see the comment by Thorkild Jacobsen about ancient Mesopotamian religion: "As it was thought possible for a man to achieve partial identity with various gods, so could one god enjoy partial identity with other gods and thus share in their natures and abilities" ("Mesopotamia," in *The Intellectual Adventure of Ancient Man: An Essay on Speculative Thought in the Ancient Near East*, ed. Henri Frankfort and H. A. Frankfort [Chicago: University of Chicago Press, 1977], 133). Erik Hornung, *Conceptions of God in Ancient Egypt: The One and the Many*, trans. John Baines (Ithaca, NY: Cornell University Press, 1982), does not think Egyptians had a similar notion. An intriguing ritual that highlights the complexity of divine and human interworkings is the Mesopotamian *mīs pî* ceremony; a similar ritual is attested in Egypt. See Michael B. Dick, ed., *Born in Heaven, Made on Earth: The Making of the Cult Image in the Ancient Near East* (Winona Lake, IN: Eisenbrauns, 1999).

10. See the previous note. Note also that many studies omit explicit and extended treatment of the Old Testament: e.g., Michael J. Christensen and Jeffery A. Wittung, *Partakers of the Divine Nature: The History and Development of Deification in the Christian Traditions* (Grand Rapids: Baker Academic, 2007); and Pedro Urbano López de Meneses, *Theosis: La Doctrina de la Divinización en las Tradiciones Cristianas: Fundamentos para una Teología Ecuménica de la Gracia* (Pamplona: Ediciones Universidad de Navarra, 2001), though studies like these often

the Old Testament is just one such and maybe not the most important; that takes the wind out of the sails a bit, to say the least.

Whatever the case, the present study will not rehearse this kind of approach once more, though it is tempting to do so to see if it makes any difference if the writer in question is first and foremost an Old Testament professor rather than, as is so often the case, a New Testament or patristic one. Instead, I propose to look at one specific but extended instance of divine-human participation in the Old Testament—namely, the life of Moses, especially as found in the book of Exodus. Justification of this choice, as opposed to some other, will be mostly implicit in what follows insofar as the material proves useful to the subject.[11] Even so, an appeal to Moses as a test-case (and a text-case) may need no more (explicit) justification than the well-known fact that Gregory of Nyssa's classic treatise on the spiritual life, too, takes as its paradigm Moses's life. It is equally well known that Gregory depends heavily on Philo of Alexandria's prior treatment (*De Vita Mosis* I–II), which is to say that understanding Moses as exemplar in the life of faith and in the life with (and in) God has both Jewish and Christian precedent.[12]

In what follows, I begin with a brief overview of Moses's life via Gregory's filtering of that story (or sequence) and its contemplation as instruction for the

---

do have Scripture indexes demonstrating at least some engagement with Old Testament texts here and there.

11. For other possibilities, one may perhaps compare the notion of seeing God. Cf., e.g., Mark S. Smith, "'Seeing God' in the Psalms: The Background to the Beatific Vision in the Hebrew Bible," *CBQ* 50 (1988): 171–83; and Brent A. Strawn, "To See/Not See God: A Biblical-Theological Cutting on the Knowability of God," *Koinonia* 7 (1995): 157–80. Another kind of approach to participation—one via literature and literary effect focused on the *piyyutim*—can be found in Laura S. Lieber, "The Rhetoric of Participation: Experiential Elements of Early Hebrew Liturgical Poetry," *JR* 90 (2010): 119–47. Note also, most recently, Tim Meadowcroft, "'One Like a Son of Man' in the Court of the Foreign King: Daniel 7 as Pointer to Wise Participation in the Divine Life," *JTI* 10 (2016): 245–63; Meadowcroft, "Daniel's Visionary Participation in the Divine Life: Dynamics of Participation in Daniel 8–12," *JTI* 11 (2017): 217–37. On this latter option, see further below (§3).

12. Perhaps one should consider 2 Cor 3:7–4:6 at this point, though what I (and Gregory!) say about certain details of Moses's life below offers at least a slightly different take than some of this text's more dismissive and supercessionist aspects. In any event, due to time and space constraints, as well as the focus of the North Park symposium on Christian notions of participation, I leave aside discussion of Philo. The notes in Abraham J. Malherbe and Everett Ferguson, ed., *Gregory of Nyssa: The Life of Moses*, CWS (New York: Paulist, 1978; hereinafter the text is cited as *LM* followed by book and section number according to this edition) are good on connecting the *LM* and Philo (and many other antecedent and contemporary works). For Philo's treatment, see conveniently *The Works of Philo: Complete and Unabridged, New Updated Edition*, trans. C. D. Yonge, repr. ed. (Peabody, MA: Hendrickson, 1993), 459–517.

progress of the soul (§1).[13] Next, I revisit several key moments in Exodus that seem particularly important for an understanding of participation with God and assess them once more in that light (§2). In these instances, I do not intend to try and go one better than the great Cappadocian father, but seek, instead, to (re)assess these texts once more from the perspective of contemporary (i.e., *non*-premodern) study of the Old Testament, on the one hand, and with an eye on some of the more recent developments and controversies in the study of participation, on the other. I conclude the study by returning to the question of how a Trinitarian pre-understanding proves useful, and in the most foundational of ways, for a biblical approach to the issue of participation (§3).

1. Gregory on the Life of Moses in Nuce

Gregory of Nyssa (ca. 335–395 CE) probably wrote the *The Life of Moses* some-time in the early 390s.[14] It has two unequal parts (books), the first, shorter book taking up the challenge of presenting its reader with "some counsel concerning the perfect life" (*LM* I, 2),[15] especially the question of perfection in virtue,[16] which is discussed more generally before mention is finally made of Moses as "our example for life in our treatise" (*LM* I, 15).[17] Once Moses has been selected, Gregory proposes to "go through in outline his life as we have learned it from the divine Scriptures" (*LM* I, 15). This "history" (*historia*) comprises the balance of Book I (*LM* I, 16–77). After this "outline," Gregory indicates that "we shall seek out the spiritual understanding which corresponds to the history in order to obtain suggestions of virtue" (*LM* I, 15). This understanding (*dianoia*) or contemplation (*theōria*) is what is found in Book II (*LM* II, 1–318). "Through such understanding," Gregory concludes, "we may come to know the perfect life" for humankind (*LM* I, 15).

---

13. For Gregory's use of "sequence," see, e.g., *LM* II, 39, 49–50, 136, 148, 150, 188; also Malherbe and Ferguson, *Gregory of Nyssa*, 13 (cf. also 164n59), who think it "should not be pressed in an absolute sense. Moses's life is not made to fit a schematized progression of spiritual experience." For the use of *historia* and *theoria* in Gregory, see Malherbe and Ferguson, 7.

14. See Malherbe and Ferguson, *Gregory of Nyssa*, 1–2.

15. The reader is identified by name as a certain "Caesarius": see *LM* II, 319; Malherbe and Ferguson, *Gregory of Nyssa*, 2–3 and 143n13; and Herbert Musurillo, ed., *Gregorii Nysseni: De Vita Moysis*, Gregorii Nysseni Opera 7.1, ed. Werner Jaeger and Hermann Langerbeck (Leiden: Brill, 1964), 1, 143, for other possibilities represented in the manuscript tradition.

16. "Concerning Perfection in Virtue" is, in fact, the treatise's alternative (or complete) title. See Malherbe and Ferguson, *Gregory of Nyssa*, 3; Musurillo, *De Vita Moysis*, 1.

17. In his *On Perfection* (*De perfectione*), Gregory instead proposes Paul as the example. See Malherbe and Ferguson, *Gregory of Nyssa*, 149n4. For other passages that refer to Moses in Gregory's corpus, see Malherbe and Ferguson, 20–22 and 148nn82–85.

Gregory's treatment is rich and detailed, as is the history of scholarship surrounding it; this is not yet to mention its status as a classic of spirituality. For present purposes, then, the following three key points should be underscored.

1. First, the pursuit of true virtue is defined early on in the *LM* in terms of *participation*—and one that is ongoing, indeed never-ending: "Certainly whoever pursues true virtue participates in nothing other than God, because he is himself absolute virtue. Since, then, those who know what is good by nature desire participation in it, and since this good has no limit, the participant's desire itself necessarily has no stopping place but stretches out with the limitless" (*LM* I, 7). Perfection, therefore, is a matter of participation and is one that is ultimately processual or progressive: constantly able to be perfected further or susceptible to further growth in grace.[18] "For," Gregory writes, "the perfection of human nature consists perhaps in its very growth in goodness" (*LM* I, 10).[19]

2. In response to the problems that face humans seeking perfection in virtue, Gregory suggests turning to "Scripture as a counselor in this matter" (*LM* I, 11), particularly the memories of those distinguished individuals who might serve as beacon lights: "It may be for this very reason that the daily life of those sublime individuals is recorded in detail, that by imitating those earlier examples of right action those who follow them may conduct their lives to the good" (*LM* I, 13). *Imitation*, generally, and *imitation of Scriptural examples*, specifically, is the way forward, therefore, though Gregory immediately admits of a problem someone might raise—a problem that is largely due to a flat-footed (and overly literal?)[20]

18. Philippians 3:13 is in many ways the key text for the treatise. See *LM* I, 5; II, 239; also Malherbe and Ferguson, *Gregory of Nyssa*, 12–13, 146n61, 149n11, 186n322. Note also *LM* II, 224–27, on how it is the nature of the soul to move "upward, soaring from below up to the heights" (*LM* II, 224); and *LM* II, 191 on how the blue color of the priestly vestments may signify the sky and air, so that "we should be close to what rises upwards and is light and airy, in order that when we hear the last trumpet we may be found weightless and light in responding to the voice of the One who calls." See also Malherbe and Ferguson, *Gregory of Nyssa*, 16: "Bodies, once having received an initial thrust downward, continue in that direction, whereas the soul, incorporeal and airy, unless hindered rises upward toward God."

19. This makes perfection profoundly paradoxical: "undoubtedly impossible to attain . . . since . . . perfection is not marked off by limits" and yet commanded by the Lord (Gregory cites Matt 5:48) so that "we should show great diligence not to fall away from the perfection which is attainable, but to acquire as much as is possible" (*LM* I, 8–10).

20. In the contemporary setting discussed in passing above, it seems better to deem this a kind of "historicizing" position. Insofar as such an approach reads the text wrongly (misinterpreting, say, a poetic figure for a historical report) it is "literal(izing)" in the worst sense of the term, for which see Brent A. Strawn, "Focus on Jonah: Jonah and Genre," *Oxford Biblical Studies Online* (https://global.oup.com/obso/focus/focus_on_jonah/) and the various uses in the *Oxford English Dictionary* cited there, especially the adjective "literal-minded": "having a literal mind;

understanding of such imitation: "Some one will say, 'How shall I imitate them, since I am not a Chaldaean as I remember Abraham was, nor was I nourished by the daughter of the Egyptian as Scripture teaches about Moses, and in general I do not have in these matters anything in my life corresponding to anyone of the ancients? How shall I place myself in the same rank with one of them, when I do not know how to imitate anyone so far removed from me by the circumstances of his life?'" (*LM* I, 14). Gregory responds by pointing out that not everything in Scripture is to be imitated, especially in so wooden a fashion: "To him we reply that we do not consider being a Chaldean a virtue or a vice, nor is anyone exiled from the life of virtue by living in Egypt or spending his life in Babylon, nor again has God been known to the esteemed individuals in Judaea only, nor is Zion, as people commonly think, the divine habitation. We need some subtlety of understanding and keenness of vision to discern from the history how, by removing ourselves from such Chaldaeans and Egyptians and by escaping from such a Babylonian captivity, we shall embark on the blessed life" (*LM* I, 14). This strategy of "subtlety of understanding" and "keenness of vision" is then immediately put to work by lifting up Moses as "our example for life" (*LM* I, 15).

3. To participate in God and make progress in perfection, therefore, one must imitate Scriptural examples and, in this treatise, the example par excellence is Moses. The final point that should be made before moving on is that Gregory's reading of Moses's life with reference to virtue, participation in God, progress in perfection, and so forth takes place on at least two levels:

· The first level is represented by *the numerous comments found throughout the work that relate specific details from Moses's life to the life of faith.* There are too many of these to list here, but, regardless per the second point above, the whole idea of using Moses as an exemplar is precisely to identify imitable elements for those who would also choose to progress in virtue as he did. This first level is thus quite obvious and explicit.

· The second level is more implicit but equally as obvious given the nature, purpose, and execution of the work—it is simply this: that Gregory's recommen-

characteristic of one who takes a matter-of-fact or unimaginative view of things. Hence *literal-mindedness*." For Gregory the kind of "literal(izing)" reading that is best avoided would seem to pertain not only to specific textual details (e.g., being a Chaldean) but to the entirety of Scripture and its macrogenre. How does one read it rightly? The answer is in no small measure to read it as a collection of models to imitate in the spiritual life toward perfection in virtue—a far cry indeed from excessively historicizing/literalizing approaches. Note also Anthony Briggman, "Literary and Rhetorical Theory in Irenaeus, Part 2," *VC* 70 (2016): 31–50, esp. 33–39, for the interest among early church writers for type and antitype to correspond to each other in reasonable fashion.

dation to imitate Moses's life depends on *the prior participation of his reader(s) with the story of that life*. It is, indeed, this foundational participation with the Scriptural text that facilitates an imitation of Moses, which, in turn, permits participation with God. The participation with Scripture is also what super-charges the biblical text with meaning such that its many details—virtually its every detail—has meaning *beyond* what Gregory calls "the bare history of the man." In point of fact, the bare history of Moses is not worth dwelling on extensively (*LM* I, 21).[21]

Gregory's words from the conclusion of his work (*LM* II, 319–321) nicely capture the three points highlighted above:

> These things concerning the perfection of the virtuous life . . . we have briefly written . . . tracing in outline like a pattern of beauty the life of the great Moses so that each one of us might copy the image of the beauty which has been shown to us by imitating his way of life. . . . Since the goal of the virtuous way of life was the very thing we have been seeking, and this goal has been found in what we have said, it is time for you, noble friend, to look to that example and, by transferring to your own life what is contemplated through spiritual interpretation of the things spoken literally, to be known by God and to become his friend. This is true perfection. . . . This, as I have said, is the perfection of life. (*LM* II, 319–320)

2. The Life of Moses: Revisiting Moments in (Non-)Participation

With this brief overview of Gregory's *Life of Moses* in place, and with the Cappado-cian father as inspiration at least, if not guide (at points), we may now re-examine a few of the most salient moments in the life of Moses for an understanding of participation with God therein. Following Gregory's focus on the primary human protagonist in the Pentateuch,[22] we may begin with Moses's formal introduction to God in the call narrative of Exod 3, but, before doing so, two points should be made.

21. Dwelling on it at least in part, however, is the work of Book I. Here is not the place to comment on exactly how closely Book I and Book II are correlated. It is obvious that Book II goes into far greater detail than Book I, though Book I, too, is not entirely without comments that could fit the contemplation found in Book II (see, e.g., *LM* I, 46–47). Gregory admits, at the conclusion of Book I, that he has "of necessity . . . amplified the account as to bring out its intention" (*LM* I, 77).

22. For an excellent overview of the importance of Moses in the Torah, but especially in Deuteronomy, see Patrick D. Miller, "'Moses My Servant': The Deuteronomic Portrait of Moses,"

First, Moses is introduced in the Torah, and in significant ways, *before* Exod 3. It is possible in hindsight to "find" or somehow retroject Moses's post-call life into his pre-call life such that the latter is seen as providentially guided and protected, even vocationally anticipated, and in various ways—though such anticipations are probably best seen as by definition incomplete and premature.[23] Second, and moving beyond Moses himself, the narrative of Exodus prior to chapter 3 suggests a good bit of *non*-participation with God. God may very well be lurking behind the prosperity of Israel in the opening verses of Exod 1, especially given the obvious connections of these verses with the opening of Genesis,[24] but God is mostly absent during the struggles of Exod 1–2 (with the notable exception of 1:21), and, indeed, according to the internal biblical chronology, God is largely out of touch for 430 years (12:40). God's first major appearance is found in 2:23–25, where God, as it were, "wakes up" to the people's plight (cf. Pss 35:23; 44:23; 59:4; 80:2). The newly awakened divine attention is motivated by two things: (1) Israel's suffering and (2) God's remembrance of the covenant with Israel's ancestors.[25] The attention God pays in this passage is extensive and intimate, with the verbs for God corresponding (four-to-four) to the words used to describe Israel's pain (*šmʿ, zkr, rʾh, ydʿ*; and *ʾnḥ, zʿq, šwʿh, nʾqh*, respectively). Significantly, what transpires in 2:23–25 leads directly into the next chapter and what takes place there in what appears to be a close, even causal relationship (note especially the repetitions between 2:23–25 and 3:7–9). Before 2:23, however, one may worry about a noticeable *lack* of participation and that at least some of that absence is on the part of the divine (again excepting 1:21). Perhaps this second point suggests that participation can be frustrated or complicated by the divine side of the equation as much as by the human side: failure to participate in God, in other words, isn't solely a problem with human will or desire; it would seem that such failure can originate from the divine (non-)participant as well.[26] That is a sobering

---

in *A Song of Power and the Power of Song: Essays on the Book of Deuteronomy*, ed. Duane L. Christensen, SBTS 3 (Winona Lake, IN: Eisenbrauns, 1993), 301–12.

23. Cf., e.g., Dennis T. Olson, "Violence for the Sake of Social Justice? Narrative, Ethics and Indeterminacy in Moses' Slaying of the Egyptian (Exodus 2:11–15)," in *The Meanings We Choose: Hermeneutical Ethics, Indeterminacy and the Conflict of Interpretations*, ed. Charles H. Cosgrove, JSOTSup 511 (London: T&T Clark, 2004), 138–48.

24. Particularly the use of the verbs "to be fruitful" (*prh*), "to be prolific" (*šrṣ*) and "to multiply" (*ṣm*) with the result being that "the land was filled" (*mlʾ* + *ʾereṣ*) with the Israelites in Exod 1:7. Note the presence of these key terms also in Gen 1:22, 28; 9:1, 7.

25. Note the debate on this point between John J. Collins, "The Exodus and Biblical Theology," *BTB* 25 (1995): 152–60; and Jon D. Levenson, "The Exodus and Biblical Theology: A Rejoinder to John J. Collins," *BTB* 26 (1996): 4–10.

26. Note, mostly by way of contrast, Gregory's treatment of the hardening of Pharaoh's heart in *LM* II, 73–88, where he goes to great lengths to see that situation as the result of free will, which

observation, chastening any overly confident or triumphalistic understanding of divine participation—namely, that it is always available to the human participant or always desired by God.[27] But, be that as it may, it must also be quickly asserted that all that follows 2:23–25 is predicated on God's extensive and intense participation with Israel's pain (*šmʿ, rʾh, ydʿ*) and with Israel's ancestors (captured via the weighty syntagm *wayyizkōr... bərîtô*, "he remembered his covenant"), precisely in the experience of Israel's grief and suffering.

The Call of Moses

The call of Moses in Exod 3:1–4:17 is remarkable for many reasons, but of necessity our discussion should focus on what is most pertinent to the notion of participation (for this unit, see *LM* II, 19–41). The repetition of key verbs of 2:23–25 in 3:7–9 has already been noted above (viz., *rʾh, šmʿ*, and *ydʿ*). Indeed, there is so much repetition that readers may be forgiven if they occasionally miss three significant differences that are present in 3:1–12 vis-à-vis 2:23–25. The first is that 2:23–25 was third-person narration *about God*, but in 3:7–9, *God speaks directly* in first-person discourse. The narrator is validated, therefore, regarding what was said in 2:23–25, and so the narrator may be trusted: God does indeed do the things the narrator had previously claimed about God.[28] The second difference is that beyond *the verbs of attention* found in 2:23–25, which are repeated in 3:7–9, God now adds *a decisive (compound) verb of action*:

> I have seen . . . heard . . . know (3:7; cf. 2:23–25) → I have come down to deliver. (3:8a)

This verbal act of deliverance is instantly glossed by another: "to bring them up," which is immediately described as an action that leads "out of Egypt" and "into a

---

"through its inclination to evil does not receive the word which softens resistance" (*LM* II, 76). For more on "the place of the freedom of human choice in Gregory's thought," which "is fundamental to the *Life of Moses*," see Malherbe and Ferguson, *Gregory of Nyssa*, 16–17. It should be observed in this general connection that, according to Gregory, there are also *poor* examples to be found in Scripture that one might imitate to their detriment, the Egyptians being one such instance (*LM* II, 83).

27. Cf. Gregory's sober reflections in *LM* II, 279, where he notes that sometimes "individuals punish the passion of desire by living a disciplined life," but then "thrust themselves into the priesthood, and with human zeal and selfish ambition . . . arrogate to themselves God's ministry."

28. Of course, it goes without saying that the narrator is also responsible for the discourse in chapter 3. For reliable narrators, see, inter alia, Wayne C. Booth, *The Rhetoric of Fiction*, 2nd ed. (Chicago: University of Chicago Press, 1983), esp. 211–40. Note also Paul J. Kissling, *Reliable Characters in the Primary History: Profiles of Moses, Joshua, Elijah, and Elisha*, JSOTSup 224 (Sheffield: Sheffield Academic, 1996).

good and spacious land" (3:8b). *To come down* in order *to deliver* and *to bring up from* and/in order (*to bring*) *into* appears to comprise yet another set of four key terms like the twinned set found earlier in 2:23–25:

> To groan—to cry out—cry for help—moan (*'nḥ, z'q, šw'h, n'qh*)
> To listen—to remember—to see—to know (*šm', zkr, r'h, yd'*)
> To come down—to deliver—to bring up from—(to bring) into
> (*yrd, nṣl, 'lh mn, ['lh] 'l*)

though the most recent quartet advances the action considerably, providing us with information that the narrator either didn't know in chapter 2 or just did not report.[29]

The third and most important difference is that *God's* verbal actions that were noted in 2:23–25 and then repeated and advanced in 3:7–9 are now intimately and immediately conjoined with another subject, *Moses*: "So, therefore, go: I will send *you* . . ." (v. 10).

The sequencing of chapter 2, especially 2:23–25, with chapter 3 (at a larger level) and the sequencing of 3:7–8 and 3:10[30] (at the more immediate level) suggest that God has heard Israel's "prayer" (reinforced by the repetition in 3:9 of "seen" and "heard") and is now answering that prayer *by, through, and with Moses*.[31] This is remarkable and mustn't be passed over too quickly without considerable reflection: God answers Israel's prayer by sending, not a divine messenger (at least not a nonhuman one) but a human being to Pharaoh. A divine-human synergy is initiated here in a way unlike anything that has come before in the Old Testament. To be sure, Moses's call sets a pattern for other call narratives,[32] but the synergistic relationship manifested in the call of Moses is stunning, not only because it is first, but because it is so massive in scale: it flies in the face of the greatest entities in the narrative world (Pharaoh, Israel, Egypt) and the most profound of human issues (suffering, oppression, slavery). Perhaps only the call of Mary in Luke 1 can be compared in terms of sheer scale and import.[33]

---

29. See previous note.

30. See note 13 above on Gregory's use of the (literary) sequence.

31. Israel's articulation in 2:23–24 is not explicitly directed at God but it needn't do so to qualify nevertheless as prayer, especially since God eventually attends to it (cf. Gen 4:10). Furthermore, at least one of the key terms used there, *z'q* (and its by-form *ṣ'q*), is frequently used in prayer. See Patrick D. Miller, *They Cried to the Lord: The Form and Theology of Biblical Prayer* (Minneapolis: Fortress, 1995), 44–46.

32. The classic study remains that of N. Habel, "The Form and Significance of the Call Narratives," *ZAW* 77 (1965): 297–323.

33. See Brent A. Strawn, "Luke 1:26–38," in *The Lectionary Commentary: Theological Exege-*

Nothing short of divine participation is found in Moses's call, therefore—participation in God: participation in God's own verbs of attention and action, and thus participation in the very mission of God in the world, which is, via those selfsame verbs, traced to God's own being.[34] This participation is not beatific but instead profoundly perilous, a fact that is clearly not lost on Moses, who immediately protests that he is not up to the job (v. 11).

Moses's concerns vis-à-vis his calling drive the rest of the account, but it is v. 10's call to participate in God's missional activity that should most arrest our attention and summon our deepest reflection. I know of no better formulation of what is at stake here than that of Walter Brueggemann: "Verse 10 makes a radical and decisive break, which must have stunned Moses when he heard it, and must have stunned Israel each time it was reiterated. What had been all pious promise now becomes rigorous demand: 'Come.' *In one brief utterance, the grand intention of God has become a specific human responsibility, human obligation, and human vocation.*"[35] Not only is this so, but *no other missional strategy is considered or deemed plausible*—not, at least, from what is given to us in the text of Exodus. *This* way, and *only* this way—through divine-human participation or synergy—is how God's most foundational salvific act in the Old Testament, if not the entire Christian Bible, will, and indeed *must*, take place.[36]

---

sis for Sunday's Texts, The Third Readings: The Gospels, ed. Roger E. Van Harn (Grand Rapids: Eerdmans, 2001), 286–90. To be sure, Jeremiah's call to be a prophet to the nations is also quite expansive in scope (Jer 1:4–10). Beyond the texts that are formally related to Moses's call narrative, the figures of Abraham and Paul would also loom large in considering divine-human synergy in the Bible.

34. Perhaps Gross would deem this kind of connection "external" (*Divinization of the Christian*, 66), and, in Glazov's terms, it seems to relate to what he calls the divine "energies" and thus not divine essence or being ("Theōsis, Judaism, and Old Testament Anthropology," 16–31), but I'm not sure the biblical texts, at least the Old Testament ones, will always permit a hard and fast division on divine ontology and economy. For the place of participation in creating missional individuals, see Jacobus (Kobus) Kok and John Anthony Dunne, "Participation in Christ and Missional Dynamics in Galatians," in *Participation, Justification, and Conversion: Eastern Orthodox Interpretation of Paul and the Debate between "Old and New Perspectives on Paul,"* ed. Athanasios Despotis, WUNT 2.442 (Tübingen: Mohr Siebeck, 2017), 59–85.

35. Brueggemann, "Book of Exodus," in *NIB* 1:713 (emphasis added), used also in the second epigraph above. Brueggemann's use of "come" reflects the NRSV. The translation offered earlier, "So, therefore, go: I will send you" is my own. The key verb is *ləkâ* (an imperative of *hlk*), and either translation, "come" or "go," works in English translation, though "go" may underscore the missional aspect more: Moses is not to come to or toward God but rather to go to Pharaoh. Cf. CEB: "So get going. I'm sending you to Pharaoh . . ."

36. For the Exodus as the fundamental salvific act in Scripture, see, inter alia, Brent A. Strawn, "Exodus," in *The New Interpreter's Bible One Volume Commentary*, ed. Beverly Roberts Gaventa and David L. Petersen et al. (Nashville: Abingdon, 2010), 33–34.

Now perhaps the human participant needn't have been Moses. Despite his pre-call "credentials," and even if we speculate that Moses might have somehow escaped his task, the textual logic implies that someone else would have had to be found to replace him. Indeed, the closest we get to proving this hypothesis true is when, as a last-ditch effort, Moses begs God, "O my Lord, please send someone else" (4:13 NRSV). Note: *someone else*; not: "Do it *yourself*, Lord!"[37] Furthermore, God's (angry) response to this final request from Moses is to provide Moses with a companion, Aaron. Aaron is added to the leadership team—Moses is no longer alone (3:12a notwithstanding!)—but the addition is precisely of "an Aaron": another person, that is, not a divine or semi-divine partner (contrast, for example, the angel's role in the story of Balaam in Num 22). Now to be sure, the Exodus narrative will go on to speak of additional entities that play key roles in what happens. Several are already mentioned in Exod 3:1–4:17: an angelic messenger (3:2) and various divine signs (3:12b; 4:5, 8, 9), especially those done with "the staff of God" (4:2–6, 20). Others that will come into the narrative include another (?) angel or angels (14:19; 23:20, 23; 32:34; 33:2; cf. 3:2; Ps 78:49) and the pillar(s) of fire and cloud (Exod 13:21–22; 14:19, 24; 33:9–10).[38] But it does not seem to be going too far to say that these other things are, at best, bit players serving specific and limited roles. So much of what happens next, therefore, is specifically Moses's (and Aaron's) "work."[39] This leads directly into the next section on agency in Exodus writ large, but before moving to that material four important points from Exod 3:1–4:17 should be underscored.

1. The first, and most obvious, is that the divine-human participation that is at work in the life of Moses, which begins at the burning bush, comes *at the initiative of God.* This may be the narrative counterpart to the non-participation of God in Exod 1–2 noted earlier. That is, just as God can *prohibit, frustrate, or be absent from* participation, God is also the one who *inaugurates, permits, and facilitates* participation.

---

37. The Hebrew construction is admittedly somewhat vague here and perhaps not as clear with regard to the "someone else" as the NRSV would make it seem. See William H. C. Propp, *Exodus 1–18: A New Translation with Introduction and Commentary,* AB 2 (New York: Doubleday, 1999), 212–13, for discussion. Indeed, it is perhaps possible that *šəlaḥ-nāʾ bəyad-tišlāḥ* ("send by the hand you will send") might be construed as something close to "doing it yourself," though one could imagine clearer constructions. Whatever the case, the next verse makes it unmistakable that, whatever the precise sense of Moses's statement, it was a cause of anger to God who does not, in fact, "do it himself" but simply adds another human to the mix.

38. These have their own complexities regarding symbiosis and/or synergy, as reflected in 14:19 (angel) and 14:24; 33:9 (Yhwh). Cf. more generally on the issue Benjamin D. Sommer, *The Bodies of God and the World of Ancient Israel* (Cambridge: Cambridge University Press, 2009).

39. Cf. Brueggemann, "Book of Exodus," 713: "It is Moses (not God) who will 'bring out' (יָצָא *yāṣāʾ*) 'my people.' It is Moses who acts in God's place to save God's people." But see further below on the thoroughly intermixed nature of divine-human synergy in Exodus. Brueggemann's formulation may favor Moses overmuch.

2. The second point concerns the divine name that is given to Moses in 3:14: "I AM WHO I AM" (NRSV). Much has been written about the origin and significance of this name that needn't be rehearsed here. For present purposes, the most important observation is that God's "I am" in 3:14 echoes God's "I am" in 3:12. There, in 3:12, in response to Moses's first objection that he was not up to the job for which God had commissioned him (but who is?)—"Who am I that I should go to Pharaoh . . . ?" (3:11)—Yhwh speaks not to *who Moses is*, but addresses *Who is with Moses*. "*I* will be with you" (*'ehyeh 'immāk*; 3:12a) is the divine reply. Now, in response to a second objection from Moses (potential Israelite disbelief over who sent him), God's name is given in this enigmatic, elusive, and rather unclear "I AM WHO I AM" (*'ehyeh 'ăšer 'ehyeh*; 3:14). God's name, it seems, is given and yet not given, offered and yet held back by means of this odd verbal construction—the precise meaning and nuance of which is ambiguous, perhaps by design. And yet, whatever confusions may remain, one thing is quite clear about this God "who is": precisely because of the earlier text in 3:12, this God is a God who is "with Moses." This is to say that God may be *'ehyeh 'ăšer 'ehyeh*, "I am who I am" or "I will be who I will be" (inter alia), but one of those things God is or will be is precisely *'ehyeh 'immāk*, "I am with you." God will not (cannot?) answer Israel's prayer without Moses, but neither must Moses answer that prayer alone. Instead, divine-human synergy is the order of the day and in equal part(icipation)s, or so it would seem.

3. Third, it must be observed that God's call for participation in the divine mission can be resisted, though perhaps not ultimately: Moses's string of objections proves unsuccessful and the same can be said for other call narratives in Scripture. That would be the fourth point developed further below: that God can, and frequently does, overcome human resistance to the invitation to participation.[40] But this third point is simply to underscore what seems implicit in the English word "participation"—namely, that participation is not a given but volitional.[41] One cannot be forced to participate but, rather, is invited to do so, and that invitation

40. God can also overcome *divine* resistance to participation, as is evidenced in 2:23–25 and its relationship to 3:1–12. The sequencing of these two units, as well as the specific content, however, suggests that such overcoming is in no small way the result or work of human beings: their grief, suffering, and cries for help, as well as their history of faithful forebears. This is just another instance of divine-human synergy (or perhaps symbiosis in this case), and it anticipates not only the point made here but also the key moments of Mosaic intercession in the Pentateuch (especially surrounding the golden calf debacle).

41. Despite the formulation above which stresses the *will*, I think the point actually negotiates the dichotomy found in more recent debates on divine-human participation in Martin Luther, which has set ontology against volition. It may be that volitional obedience need not be entirely contrasted with ontological participation. See Carl E. Braaten and Robert W. Jenson's remarks in the preface to *Union with Christ: The New Finnish Interpretation of Luther*, ed. Carl E.

can be rejected, or at least delayed. This is to say that the invitation to participate is *limitable*.[42] Further invitations may be necessary; additional motivations and reasons might need to be provided. Participation, according to Exod 3:1–4:17, is thus quite interactive if not downright dialogical. If, per Gregory, participation is a matter of following God's leading (which is what he thinks it means "to see God's back"; *LM* II, 252), it is also, contra Gregory, the case that God apparently turns around, at least on occasion, to participate in dialogue and discussion—even face to face (see Exod 33:11; contrast *LM* II, 253). Still further, taking the life of Moses as a paradigmatic pattern for the human soul and its progress (or lack thereof), perhaps it is not going too far to say that the default position—our first response as humans—is to *resist* God's call to participate in the divine mission which is rooted in the very life of God.

4. The fourth point, already indicated above, is that Moses's resistance is overcome in Exod 3:1–4:17. In the end, if he does not happily assent, he at least succumbs to God's call to be a participatory agent in the *missio Dei*. Other individuals who are called in the pattern of Moses do the same, though some texts in Jeremiah and Ezekiel, especially, suggest that this kind of assenting or succumbing is not always smooth, nor does it signal an end of the dialogue or an absence of problems for the divine-human synergy moving forward.[43] Perhaps those texts should make us reread Moses's participation similarly: that it was not all smooth sailing, after all;[44] if so, it would be true, not only that participation can be *resisted*, but that it can be *varied* in its experience and "success" (efficacy) as well. Even so, the life of Moses writ large, now in the canon and read in Gregory's way, suggests that even resistance is brought into the life of faith and obedience via the dialogics of call and response.[45] It is worth noting, however, that for his part Gregory does not mention Moses's resistance or objections to God's call. Does he deem such

---

Braaten and Robert W. Jenson (Grand Rapids: Eerdmans, 1998), viii–ix. See note 26 above for the importance of free will in Gregory's *Life of Moses*.

42. Cf. Everett Ferguson, "God's Infinity and Man's Mutability: Perpetual Progress according to Gregory of Nyssa," *Greek Orthodox Theological Review* 18 (1973): 59–78 (68): one "receives a knowledge of God and participates in his goodness 'according to his capacity.' [Humans'] knowledge of God is limited by [their] capacity, not by the transcendent object."

43. I am thinking especially of Jeremiah's "confessions," which reveal a tumultuous relationship between the prophet and God (see, e.g., Jer 15:15–18). Similarly, Ezek 3:14b may suggest that the prophet was bitter and angry about having to perform the prophetic task that lay ahead of him.

44. See Propp, *Exodus 1–18*, 213, for the possibility that Moses's response in 4:13 "arguably betrays sullenness."

45. Perhaps the same should be said of Moses's "radical and dangerous" prayers/protests (see Walter Brueggemann, *Old Testament Theology: Essays in Structure, Theme, and Text*, ed.

negativity outside the pale of participation altogether, only a hindrance to the soul's perfection in virtue—a regression as it were?[46]

Agency in Exodus: Thoroughly (Inter-)Mixed

The fact that God's deliverance of Israel from Egypt necessarily involves Moses (and Aaron) in what is a profound instance of divine-human synergy leads one to consider agency in Exodus more generally. This is a large topic and so it suffices to depend on a recent essay on the matter by Terence Fretheim.[47]

"A close study of the book of Exodus," begins Fretheim, "generates complex theological reflections regarding issues of agency." His own analysis leads him to claim that "God works in both history and creation in and through agents. God does work directly, but *always* through means/agents, ranging from human words and deeds (both within and without Israel) to nonhuman activities such as natural events."[48] Indeed, at one point in his essay, Fretheim goes so far as to state: "One might ask whether God *ever* acts . . . unilaterally."[49] In his opinion, divine action via human agents—what I have referred to as divine-human synergy above—is the order of the day. Questions remain, however. So, while "one must not diminish the distinction between God and God's agents, discount the real power of the agent (a divine gift), or claim that God acted alone," it is equally the case that "just how God is involved in this activity cannot be fully factored out."[50]

The first part of that statement leads Fretheim to distinguish his reading from others that differ from his own—to greater or lesser degrees.[51] He ultimately commends the "major emphases in Brueggemann's interpretation," and proceeds to "move through key texts that both support and expand upon such an understand-

---

Patrick D. Miller [Minneapolis: Fortress, 1992], 30): these, too, are part of his life and his example for other souls on the journey.

46. See *LM* I, 21, which is where Moses's objections would fit in the *historia* account, but which is exactly where Gregory encourages the reader to "not dwell extensively on the bare history of the man" (cited more fully above). Similarly, the contemplation section in Book II also passes over the objections without comment (*LM* II, 19–41). Gregory only treats the book of Numbers briefly and so does not discuss the crucial (but highly ambiguous) moment of Mosaic disobedience in Num 20.

47. Terence E. Fretheim, "Issues of Agency in Exodus," in *The Book of Exodus: Composition, Reception, and Interpretation*, ed. Thomas B. Dozeman, Craig A. Evans, and Joel N. Lohr, VTSup 164 (Leiden: Brill, 2014), 591–609.

48. Fretheim, "Issues of Agency in Exodus," 591.

49. Fretheim, "Issues of Agency in Exodus," 599n33.

50. Fretheim, "Issues of Agency in Exodus," 592.

51. See Fretheim, "Issues of Agency in Exodus," 592–95.

ing of [divine-human synergistic] agency in Exodus."[52] He specifically discusses Exod 1–2; 3:1–7:7; 7:8–12:51; 13:1–15:21; 15:22–18:27; and 32:1–34:35,[53] before concluding his study by stating that "God *always* uses agents in God's working in Israel and the larger world." He adds that "God does not perfect human beings (or other creatures), with all their foibles and flaws, before deciding to work in and through them.... Hence, such work by the agents will always have mixed results, and will be less positive than what would have happened had God chosen to act alone."[54]

Fretheim is obviously concerned with matters other than the ones relating to participation that are the focus of the present chapter, but his analysis is useful nevertheless. It affirms, first, that the kind of synergy identified earlier is not an idiosyncratic interpretation but one also noticed by other interpreters and, more importantly, an extensive and repeated motif in Exodus. And not only there. Inspired by Gregory who does not stop at the book of Exodus but continues on into Numbers to discuss a few key points in the narrative there (particularly the spy story and the account of Balaam; see Num 13–14; 22–24; cf. LM II, 264–68, 291–304), I would note that the "confusion of properties" that is at work in Yhwh and Yhwh's messenger seems to also be at work at certain moments with Moses. One particularly curious instance of this in Exodus is considered in the next section. But, beyond Exodus, one might note other examples like the ambiguity in the Hebrew text of Deut 1:4, which states "this was after he had defeated [*hakkōtô*] King Sihon ... and King Og." Syntactically, the subject of this verb could be either Yhwh or Moses. The nearest antecedent is Moses but the last-mentioned verbal subject is God: so who, exactly, did the smiting? Perhaps Deut 2:24, 31; 3:2–3; and especially 31:4 would clinch the matter for God, not Moses (cf. also Pss 135:11; 136:19–20), and if *only one* agent can take the credit, it is likely that the Deity is the one in view. But Fretheim's work would query any hard and fast division in this regard: "God *always* uses agents ... ," he would assert. And, in this vein, it is worth noting that Moses claims the victory for the Israelites (see 3:3–4; 29:7) or with them (4:46) in a few passages in Deuteronomy. All of this is to say that Deut 1:4, also, may showcase the divine-human synergy between Moses and God, and perhaps still more: that their work can be "interconfused." The very last chapter of the last book in the Torah contains a passage that is very much apropos on this point:

---

52. Fretheim, "Issues of Agency in Exodus," 595 (my addition). These emphases in Brueggemann's work are very much like the ones cited above; indeed, Fretheim quotes the same passage from Brueggemann on Exod 3:10 that I provided earlier (see at note 35 above; Fretheim, "Issues of Agency in Exodus," 597–98n28).

53. One has to look to Fretheim's earlier commentary for treatment of Exod 19–31, 35–40. See Terence E. Fretheim, *Exodus*, Interpretation (Louisville: John Knox, 1991).

54. Fretheim, "Issues of Agency in Exodus," 606.

> No prophet like Moses has yet emerged
> —the LORD knew him face to face!—
> with regard to all the signs and wonders that the LORD sent Moses to
>   do in the land of Egypt
> —to Pharaoh, to all his servants, and to his entire land—
> and with regard to all the great power and all the awesome deeds
>   that Moses did before the eyes of all Israel. (Deut 34:10–12;
>   my translation)

Here too the syntax is somewhat complicated, with the lineated version offered here clarifying that with only partial success. The most important point, regardless, is that language that is usually used elsewhere of God (e.g., "great power," "awesome deeds," and actions performed "before the eyes" of others) is here attributed, not to Yhwh first and foremost, but to the agency of Moses. One might counter that Moses's actions here are dependent on God's primary verb of sending (*šlḥ*), but that does not counter the fact that the passage ascribes to Moses language that is typically reserved for God. If both the beginning and ending of Deuteronomy "ambiguate" the work of God and Moses—what belongs to whom?[55]—this is just further proof of Fretheim's point about agency in Exodus. But it is also, for our purposes, additional evidence that speaks to the question of participation in the divine—one that extends so far that the two subjects are intertwined, intermixed, at times even confused.[56]

Moses's Face and Two Bodies

A text like Deut 34 can be confusing, syntactically no less than theologically, but the kind of synergism, replete with a good bit of unresolved if not unresolvable ambiguity, that is especially pronounced at the beginning and end of Deuteronomy is also traceable in Exodus. An example might be the event at the Red (or

---

55. Cf. Fretheim, "Issues of Agency in Exodus," 607–8: "Both God and agents have crucial roles to play, and their spheres of activity are interrelated in terms of function and effect. God is not only independent and the agents involved only dependent." Instead, Fretheim argues for a profound God-world relationality, one that inevitably involves a divine vulnerability. For these themes elsewhere in Fretheim's work, see his *The Suffering of God: An Old Testament Perspective*, OBT (Philadelphia: Fortress, 1984), and *God and World in the Old Testament: A Relational Theology of Creation* (Nashville: Abingdon, 2005).

56. Many other passages could be noted in this regard. So, e.g., in Num 12, the complaint against Moses eventuates in a divine curse, implying the closest of connections between God and "my servant Moses" (Num 12:8).

Reed) Sea in Exod 14–15, where we encounter different perspectives on what, exactly, took place there. It has been the special burden of historical critics to worry about the "exactly" part, with much of the results unfortunately and finally atomizing—succeeding by attributing this perspective to one tradition/source, and that perspective to another tradition/source, mostly due to a priori assumptions that traditions/sources within themselves must somehow be logical or consistent, or, even better (!), logically consistent. In my judgment, such filleting never satisfactorily answers the problem of the current, overfull text as it now stands. Exodus as it now stands, furthermore—however multilayered it may be, and no doubt is—does not require or even invite such textual dissection. Instead, Exod 14–15, no less than Deut 1 or 34, stubbornly presents a full-orbed if confusing synergistic picture in which God and Moses, Moses with God, God through Moses, and perhaps still other iterations are responsible for the miracle at the sea.

In my judgment, another profound example of the commingling of the divine and human agents, and thus their participation, one with the other, may be found in the short account about the shining of Moses's face in Exod 34:

> Moses came down from Mount Sinai. As he came down from the mountain with the two covenant tablets in his hand, Moses didn't realize that the skin of his face shone brightly because he had been talking with God. When Aaron and all the Israelites saw the skin of Moses' face shining brightly, they were afraid to come near him. But Moses called them closer. So Aaron and all the leaders of the community came back to him, and Moses spoke with them. After that, all the Israelites came near as well, and Moses commanded them everything that the LORD had spoken with him on Mount Sinai. When Moses finished speaking with them, he put a veil over his face. Whenever Moses went into the LORD's presence to speak with him, Moses would take the veil off until he came out again. When Moses came out and told the Israelites what he had been commanded, the Israelites would see that the skin of Moses' face was shining brightly. So Moses would put the veil on his face again until the next time he went in to speak with the LORD. (Exod 34:29–35 CEB)

The key interpretive question concerns the verb translated in the CEB as "to shine brightly."[57] In Hebrew, this verb (*qrn*) is apparently a denominative from the noun

---

57. See the studies by William H. C. Propp, "The Skin of Moses' Face—Transfigured or Disfigured?" *CBQ* 49 (1987): 375–86 (popularized in Propp, "Did Moses Have Horns?" *BR* 4/1 [1988]: 30–37, 44); and Propp, *Exodus 19–40: A New Translation with Introduction and Commentary*, AB 2A (New York: Doubleday, 2006), 620–23. Propp's own suggestion is that Moses's face became dry or hard in some fashion such that it was disfigured, an "example of a symbolic wound in-

qeren, which means "horn." Several of the ancient versions (especially the LXX, which uses *doxazō*, "to glorify"; cf. Peshitta and Targum) also understand the sense of the verb to be the shining that is reflected in CEB and so many other modern translations (e.g., NRSV, NJPSV). The Vulgate, however, has *cornuta esset facies sua*, "his face was horned"—an image made most famous, perhaps, in Michaelangelo's sculpture *Moses* in the church of San Pietro in Vincoli in Rome, but common in many depictions of Moses in religious art.

While Moses's horns in artistic renderings may strike contemporary viewers as a bit devilish, the Latin translation of the Hebrew text deserves consideration, the venerable "shining" approach notwithstanding. This is not only due to the relationship between the verb *qrn* and the noun *qeren* already noted, but also due to the widely known fact that in ancient Near Eastern art divinities were often portrayed with horns.[58] Indeed, various anthropomorphic figures, especially in series or larger tableaus, are often *only* identifiable as deities by means of horns, with the equation usually running as follows: the more horns present, the higher up the god in question is in terms of power or pantheon structure. Gary Rendsburg has noted a similar artistic detail in depictions of the pharaoh in Dynasties 18–19 (ca. 1550–1186 BCE).[59] Pharaohs during this period sometimes wore a ram's horn on their face, apparently to signal their deification.

Both the Mesopotamian portrayal of gods with horns and the Egyptian depiction of the pharaoh with a horn (apparently also under divine influence) lend contextual support to the notion that Moses's face was, in fact, horned and not just shining. To be sure, the two possible understandings of *qrn* aren't entirely unrelated, since the gods who wore horns on their heads were also often depicted with radiant light.[60] In any event, in both cases (or a combined one), the possibility that

curred during a rite of passage" (623). While novel, I do not find this option compelling, mostly given the overall sense and content of the unit (despite Propp's correct attention to the text's emphasis on "skin").

58. Pictures may be found in *ANEP*.

59. Gary A. Rendsburg, "Moses as Equal to Pharaoh," in *Text, Artifact, and Image: Revealing Ancient Israelite Religion*, ed. Gary Beckman and Theodore J. Lewis, BJS 346 (Providence, RI: Brown Judaic Studies, 2006), 201–19, esp. 216–18.

60. See, e.g., Menahem Haran, "The Shining of Moses' Face: A Case Study in Biblical and Ancient Near Eastern Iconography," in *In the Shelter of Elyon: Essays on Ancient Palestinian Life and Literature in Honor of G. W. Ahlström*, ed. W. Boyd Barrick and John R. Spencer, JSOTSup 31 (Sheffield: Sheffield Academic, 1984), 159–73, who relates Moses's shining face to the Mesopotamian concept of *melammu*: a brilliant light that radiated from the gods, particularly from their heads (cf. *Enuma Elish* IV 58). The weapons of the gods, too, and other things belonging to the gods, could also radiate *melammu*. The gods were able to grant *melammu* to others, particularly kings, but could also take it away (see Haran, "Shining of Moses' Face," 168). Finally, *melammu*

Moses's face is *qrn*-ed suggests a truly close encounter with the Divine—an interaction that is so close, in fact, that qualities of the Deity are, as it were, rubbing off on Moses and being physically manifested by him. His face looks this way, after all, "because he had been talking with God" (*bədabbərô 'ittô*; 34:29). Moses has been exposed to divinity in close quarters, for extended periods, and so is now taking on divine characteristics himself.[61] It is no wonder, then, that the people are in awe of Moses, or fear him (34:30). Such language is mostly proper with reference to the Lord, but Moses's intermediary function in this unit makes him God's stand-in, and so it comes as no surprise that the people are afraid; nor is it surprising that, as they earlier asked Moses to serve as covenant mediator (20:18–21; cf. Deut 5:5), so now some other or new thing must come between Moses-with-Godlike-features and the people—namely, the veil.[62] This, too, underscores how Moses's communion, or perhaps better, participation, with God is of the most intimate sort, since the human participant in the divine reality is manifesting divine characteristics and must be managed accordingly.[63]

---

was often combined with *pulḫu*, which was the awe created or inspired by the god or monarch (see Haran, "Shining of Moses' Face," 172n19; and A. L. Oppenheim, "Akkadian *pul(u)ḫ(t)u* and *melammu*," *JAOS* 63 [1943]: 31–34). Propp notes: "In Mesopotamian iconography, a stack of horns bears some relationship to the gods' radiant aura called *melammu*" (*Exodus 19–40*, 620) and cites the horn = light equation of Ps 132:17. While the details of Propp's unspecific "some relationship" remain elusive, the relationship seems (once more) to resist an overly precise distinction between energy and essence (see note 34 above and note 61 below).

61. This, too, might be seen as a kind of "externality," *à la* Gross (*Divinization of the Christian*, 66), or something to do with energies, *à la* Glazov ("Theōsis, Judaism, and Old Testament Anthropology," 19), but it is one that is related to the divine being and so related to essence if not also inwardness, individuality, and transcendence. Indeed, the question raised by Gross of the book of Wisdom: "Is this not a genuine deification of the soul—even though it is not so described—to the entire extent in which its position as creature, which, of course, never disappears, allows?" (*Divinization of the Christian*, 68) seems equally applicable to Moses in Exod 34. It might not be going too far, therefore, to say that what one finds in this chapter may be the Old Testament equivalent of receiving the stigmata, perhaps especially if Propp's interpretation of the *qrn*-ed nature as disfigurement/wounding is deemed accurate. See further below.

62. Cf. Propp, *Exodus 19–40*, 621: "If this is the true meaning of *qāran* ["to shine, be luminous"], the veiled, shining Moses may be regarded as a walking Tabernacle, manifesting and yet concealing Yahweh's splendor."

63. Rendsburg goes so far as to say, even in the case of the encounters between Moses and Pharaoh earlier in Exodus, that "for the purposes of this story, Moses is elevated to divine status. This is the plain meaning of the two passages cited at the outset [Exod 4:16; 7:1]" ("Moses as Equal to Pharaoh," 203). Rendsburg asserts (though without explicit support) that "in Israel the elevation of a human being from human status to divine status certainly was heretical," but that this "standard theology of the Bible . . . is set aside in the case of Moses's appearance before Pharaoh" ("Moses as Equal to Pharaoh," 202–3). Note also Fretheim, *Exodus*, 311: "Moses now

Another, not unrelated way to understand this unit is via the idea of the ruler's two bodies. *The King's Two Bodies* is the title of a famous book by Ernst Kantorowicz, in which he argued that the king was understood to have two distinct bodies in the medieval period: the body politic and the natural body.[64] The notion of a monarch having two bodies was known for centuries, indeed millennia, before many of the sources Kantorowicz cites, however, and this is particularly true for Egypt, which also knew of two bodies for the king.[65]

Pharaoh's two bodies correspond to the ones also identified by Kantorowicz in his much-later corpus—namely, the physical, natural body of the specific monarch in question (Egyptian *niswt*), and the "body" or office of Pharaoh that the specific individual inhabited (Egyptian *ḥm*). There has been a good bit of debate in Egyptological circles with regard to the Egyptian king's status: whether he was, in fact, a god or not, or somehow instead semi-divine, and it seems that attitudes on this matter may have varied through the course of Egyptian history or segments of Egyptian society.[66] Whatever the case, it seems at least safe to say that "the king *reveals* the deity by being a visible incarnation of it."[67] Furthermore, even if the physical person of the king (*niswt*) was not (always) considered divine, at least while he was still alive, he nevertheless inhabited a divine office (*ḥm*) since kingship belonged first to the gods before it was handed down to humans.[68]

Seen in the light of this background, Moses, too, might be seen as two-bodied: "this man, Moses" (Exod 32:1), on the one hand, and, on the other, the Moses who is close confidant of the Lord, who begins to take on divine qualities (ones also depicted among *pharaohs* of the Eighteenth and Nineteenth Dynasties!). Moses, too, that is, may be seen as human and (semi-)divine, just like the pharaoh was.[69] One

---

functions as a divine messenger. . . . We are told in 33:11 that God speaks to Moses face-to-face. Yet it is twice stated that God's face cannot be seen in all its fullness, even by Moses (33:20, 23). One might then say that *Moses' shining face is the fullness of the face of God which is available to the community*" (his emphasis). Cf. Propp, *Exodus 19–40*, 623: Moses's face, "branded by Yahweh—whether horned, beaming or hardened—becomes the Mask of God."

64. Ernst H. Kantorowicz, *The King's Two Bodies: A Study in Medieval Political Theology* (Princeton: Princeton University Press, 1997).

65. See Siegfried Morenz, *Egyptian Religion*, trans. Ann E. Keep (Ithaca, NY: Cornell University Press, 1996), 37–40; and, briefly, Brent A. Strawn, "Pharaoh," in *Dictionary of the Old Testament: Pentateuch*, ed. T. Desmond Alexander and David W. Baker (Downers Grove, IL: InterVarsity, 2003), 631–36, esp. 633.

66. See the previous note and the essays in David B. O'Connor and David P. Silverman, eds., *Ancient Egyptian Kingship*, PdÄ 9 (Leiden: Brill, 1995).

67. Morenz, *Egyptian Religion*, 41 (his emphasis); cf. also O'Connor and Silverman's introduction to *Ancient Egyptian Kingship*, xxv.

68. Strawn, "Pharaoh," 632 (with literature).

69. For Moses and royal imagery, see Danny Mathews, *Royal Motifs in the Pentateuchal Por-*

way to parse this would be to say that Moses is becoming a new kind of pharaoh—not a tyrannical, despotic one, but a new and ideal type: an "Israelite pharaoh," the ultimate intermediary and priest between Yhwh and Yhwh's people,[70] one who even inaugurates a new kind of office, that of the prophet, even if the Torah is clear that none who come after, whatever office they hold, can quite compare to the first to hold the post (see Deut 18:15–22 and 34:10).[71]

Yet another way to parse this situation would be in terms of divine participation: that Moses is becoming more and more like God. It is worth observing in this regard that the passage about Moses's horns comes quite late in the book of Exodus. Moses is progressing, that is, in his participation and his upward journey toward perfection in virtue—that is how Gregory would put it at any rate. At the start, Moses's participation with God, while synergistic to be sure, had mostly to do with God's mission and was regularly accompanied by other "helps": God's staff, Aaron, the pillar and cloud, and so on. Later in Exodus, however, the participation seems far more direct and intimate, more physical, and perhaps, therefore, more ontological or essential. If so, we might posit a kind of participation equation—namely, that participation in mission precedes incorruptibility, not unlike incarnation precedes resurrection. If the latter parallel with the ministry of Christ seems too far-fetched for some readers, it seems nevertheless quite clear that the narrative of Exodus begins with a sharing in *divine work or activity* and only later progresses to a sharing in *divine attributes or quality*. Whatever the case, paying attention to the narratival and dramatic contours of participation in Exodus suggests something that is more dynamic than generalized and too-static notions of "deification."[72]

In the final analysis, deciding whether Moses's participatory development in Exodus makes him look more like Pharaoh or more like God may be a distinction without significant difference, since, in the case of the Egyptian monarch at least,

---

trayal of Moses, LHBOTS 571 (New York: T&T Clark, 2012), whose thesis is that the "Pentateuchal authors adapted tropes and traditions, well-attested elsewhere in biblical and other ancient Near Eastern sources, to identify Moses as an exalted, even divinized figure." This formulation (and his book as a whole) reveals that Mathews is not primarily or exclusively concerned with *Egyptian* kingship, though his work is helpful to the point at hand.

70. For the pharaoh as high priest, if not, in principle, the *only* priest of Egypt, see Morenz, *Egyptian Religion*, 40.

71. See Miller, "Moses My Servant," esp. 302: Moses is "the mediator of the divine word, the spokesman for God to the people. He has that function and distinction in a way that no other figure has. . . . Thus Moses' words are coterminous with God's words."

72. My thanks to Anthony Briggman and Mark McInroy for discussion on this point, which may also connect, in their own way, to the study by Bruce L. McCormack, "Participation with God, Yes; Deification, No: Two Modern Protestant Responses to an Ancient Question," in *Orthodox and Modern: Studies in the Theology of Karl Barth* (Grand Rapids: Baker Academic, 2008), 235–60.

the divine and human categories bled together a good bit, especially at certain points in the history of ancient Egypt.

Before moving on, I wish to note a possible (major) point of contact between the life of Moses here and the so-called new Finnish interpretation of Luther, which, according to Braaten and Jenson, sees faith as "a real participation in Christ" such that "in faith a believer receives the righteousness of God in Christ, not only in a nominal and external way, but really and inwardly."[73] They continue: "If through faith we really participate in Christ, [then] we participate in the whole Christ, who in his divine person communicates the righteousness of God. Here lies the bridge to the Orthodox idea of salvation as deification or *theosis*."[74] The story of Moses's shining face at the end of Exodus seems to be a type of biblical instanti-ation of such theosis, replete with the communication of the divine person to the human person who, as a result, participates in the divine. To be sure, the story in Exodus, given its specific content, context, and nature is not about participation "in Christ" or receiving "the righteousness of God in Christ" (but see the beginning of this chapter above, and, further, §3 below), but it is important to observe that the Exodus story chastens what appears in Braaten and Jenson to be a denigration of external manifestations of participation ("not only in a nominal and external way, but really and inwardly"). In the case of Moses's face, proof of participation is in fact "external"—visible to all (*sans* veil, at any rate)—and not solely internal, even as this externality is not simply "nominal" but "really" manifest.[75]

Participation Democratized

One final text from Exodus deserves discussion: it is Israel's successful completion of the tabernacle in Exod 35–40. These chapters repeat, in close but not entirely verbatim fashion, the instructions first given in Exod 25–30. What comes between these two units is, of course, the golden calf debacle where nearly all is lost and things are saved only by Moses's bold intercession. The repetition of details in Exod 35–40 is quite necessary, then, even if mind-numbing to modern readers,[76]

---

73. Braaten and Jenson, *Union with Christ*, viii.

74. Braaten and Jenson, *Union with Christ*, viii.

75. See note 62 above.

76. It needn't be so: see chapter 3 in this volume for how repetition can sharpen the mem-ory and play out ethically. See also the insightful study of Amy H. C. Robertson, "'He Kept the Measurements in His Memory as a Treasure': The Role of the Tabernacle Text in Religious Ex-perience" (PhD diss., Emory University, 2010), which raises the possibility that the repetition found in the tabernacle texts may have served a meditative function, especially for those readers living away from or long after the destruction of the tabernacle (and temple).

because it demonstrates precisely obedient execution of the commands issued in Exod 25–30. What one finds at the end of Exodus, that is, is Israel "at full stretch."[77] Israel has been disobedient to the extreme: opening a deep fissure at the very moment of covenant-making—a fissure that threatens to destroy everything—but after the delicate negotiation of Mosaic intercession and divine forgiveness (33:12–34:9),[78] Israel shows itself faithful . . . repeatedly, obsessively, *minutely.*

One way to gloss such faithfulness is to see it as a kind of participation: Israel here participates in the divine life and mission in the world by faithfully executing God's commands and constructing a place for God's presence, to which, according to later texts, God's people and even the nations will come and pray (see 1 Kgs 8; Isa 2:1–5; 56:3–8; Mic 4:1–4; Matt 21:13 and parallels). To be sure, the divine commands are mediated through Moses, but that is nothing new; furthermore, it is all Israel that performs the work (see Exod 39:32, 42–43). And even if Israel participates somehow only through, with, or in Moses, we know that Moses's participation, in Exodus, is with God, from front to back.[79]

It should be underscored that the specific commandments in question concern the tabernacle, the very meeting place—a tent of meeting!—for God and Israel. It is no small thing that Exodus culminates not only with Israel's faithful completion of God's commands concerning this site of divine-human interactivity, but also with the successful filling of that tabernacle with God's own presence (40:34). If the beginning of Exodus raised questions about God's *absence* and *non-*participation, there is no question, as the book concludes, that God desires close, intimate relationship with all Israel, not just with Moses. And if participation in Exodus is largely begun with Moses's call and mediated throughout the book through Moses, there can be no doubt that at the end, divine-human participation is fully democratized or communalized: made available to all.[80]

---

77. I use this language for Exod 35–40 in Strawn, "Exodus," 53–55.

78. For an analysis of the poetry in this unit, see chapter 2 in this volume.

79. Cf. the arresting comment by Anderson, *Christian Doctrine and the Old Testament*, 37: "Through the prophets, God has invited Israel into his own person."

80. This is also true in Leviticus and not only in the holiness code of Lev 17–26, which extends holiness to the entire community, but to no small degree also in the first part, which, while having the flavor of a technical priestly manual, nevertheless lets readers see "behind the curtain" or "backstage," as it were. Propp, *Exodus 19–40*, 621–22, cites A. H. McNeile, *The Book of Exodus*, Westminster Commentaries (London: Methuen, 1908), cxxiii, on how the shining of Moses's face might also pertain to all of Israel: "Moses alone stood in a relation to God close and intimate enough for such a transfiguration to be possible or bearable; the people durst not gaze even upon the reflexion. But Moses was the representative of his nation, and the glory upon his face was a pledge and symbol of the abiding of the divine glory upon the whole people."

3. Conclusion: On Participatory Reading with Christ and/in God

There are no doubt other details that could be lifted up from the life of Moses in the book of Exodus (and beyond), (re)read, and (re)assessed with an eye toward participation. Gregory's own treatment is lengthy and I have left aside most of the many details he discusses while only barely mentioning many items that would repay far greater scrutiny.[81] While this admission is obvious to the reader of the present chapter, I hope that at least some of what has been discussed here is useful in thinking about or rethinking the contribution of the Old Testament to the idea of participation. Furthermore, while I have not drawn extensive connections between the biblical texts I have focused on and more recent theological discussions of participation, I trust that the relationships are clear enough, along with the various implications that may be drawn and that might be developed further, especially for those with great interest in the subject. At the very least, the present analysis has attempted to account for some aspects that Gregory, for one, doesn't reckon with as much as he might have—among these, I would mention above all *the problem of divine (!) and human non-participation, human resistance to participation*, and *the democratization or communalization of participation*.[82] But, again,

81. I am thinking particularly of the intercessions of Moses, as well as his profile as suffering servant. For both things, see Miller, "Moses My Servant," 307–10, esp. 308, on the great intercessors of the Old Testament and how they are most passionate when the sin is greatest ("It is as if they know that the mercy of God is equal to and indeed more intense than the judgment of God"); and 310, on Moses's failure to enter the promised land, in Deuteronomy, on account of Israel (1:37; 3:23–28; 4:21–22) ("Moses does not share the fearful perspective of the people, but he shares existence with them and so must suffer with them. . . . We do not have here a full-blown notion of the salvation and forgiveness of the many brought by the punishment of the one, but we are on the way to that . . . reminding all hearers that the special way in which judgment becomes grace in the work of this God is when the Lord's own servant receives the judgment 'on your account'"). One might also see more generally the studies by John Barton, "Imitation of God in the Old Testament," in *The God of Israel*, ed. Robert P. Gordon, UCOP 64 (Cambridge: Cambridge University Press, 2007), 35–46; and by Cyril S. Rodd, *Glimpses of a Strange Land: Studies in Old Testament Ethics* (Edinburgh: T&T Clark, 2001), 65–76.

82. The latter, at least, is probably implicit in Gregory, however, since he believes readers of *LM* can in fact make progress in virtue by following Moses's example. In any event, perhaps some of the problematic texts I have lifted up do not rise to serious problems for notions of participation. Perhaps they are simply bits of the "bare history of the man" that Gregory would say need not detain us overmuch (*LM* I, 21; see further above). But these, too, are part of the life of Moses in Scripture and I have not sought to challenge Gregory with these details so much as *follow* him: attending closely to *all* aspects of Moses's life as recounted in Scripture and subjecting them to contemplation. Again, several of these texts may well be of a sort that would urge Gregory to move on quickly in the "sequence," but, even if he leaves some of these matters aside in *LM*, it seems reasonable to believe that Gregory would be agreeable to a deeper contemplation of them if that were possible—and that is the task I have at least tried to begin in my remarks here.

more could be said—both generally on the subject matter and on the specific details mentioned here.

I wish to conclude with one final connection between the life of Moses, Gregory's account, my own study, and the idea of participation. On the one hand, this connection is almost too obvious to mention; on the other hand, its obviousness may be its genius (and hope) insofar as it provides what may be the main and most achievable way to participate with God. It is simply this: *we participate with God in no small way by reading Scripture.* In *The Life of Moses*, Gregory selects the story of Moses and then reads it as a model for progress in the life of virtue. But, as noted earlier, in another of his major studies on the same topic, *On Perfection*, Gregory chooses Paul as the exemplar to study. Paul, Moses, it makes no difference.[83] The point, or, rather, the method, is to read with the saints so as to participate, via such reading, with them and their exemplary lives in God so as to grow in grace, perfection, even divinity.[84]

Although much has been written of late on how stories—narrative proper, that is—are somehow ideal to facilitate such existential engagement, my own sense is that generic specificity and the valorization of narrative at this point are greatly overstated. One *may* and perhaps often *does* read stories in existentially engaged, participatory ways, but one may just as well *not* and, more to the point, *need not* do so. Other genres—but above all others, poetry—seem just as likely to facilitate participatory reading.[85] Still further, it is not just the genre, nor the process of reading alone; in communities of faith, there are other things that accompany and facilitate the best reading practices—things like prayer, for instance.[86] Of course, it has long been

83. Still, given the often-beleaguered state of the Old Testament in many Christian circles, it should be underscored that Moses, not just Paul, is worthy of such attention and contemplation. On the dire state of the Old Testament today, see Brent A. Strawn, *The Old Testament Is Dying: A Diagnosis and Recommended Treatment*, Explorations of the Church Catholic (Grand Rapids: Baker Academic, 2017).

84. For recent studies, see Meadowcroft, "One Like a Son of Man"; and Meadowcroft, "Daniel's Visionary Participation." Note also the comments of Angus Paddison, "Scripture, Participation and Universities," in *Scripture: A Very Theological Proposal* (London: T&T Clark, 2009), 122–44.

85. Cf. Lieber, "Rhetoric of Participation," 145: "In his *piyyutim*, Yannai, one of the first and foremost liturgical poets of Judaism, brings both the Torah portion and the liturgy vividly alive for his community. His listeners did not merely hear the stories of the Torah. In a diversity of ways, they *experienced* their own sacred history, and they did so *in the context of prayer*—a ritual that, in and of itself, *offers access to another realm*. Through techniques of form, such as refrains and patterned repetition, the community had the opportunity to *physically participate* in these poems. And by means of rhetorical devices, Yannai was able to *involve the community emotionally and intellectually as he collapsed the distance* along both horizontal and vertical axes: between past and present and between heaven and earth" (emphases added).

86. See previous note.

thought that the most profound type of reading, spiritual reading (*lectio divina*) is, in fact, a kind of prayer.[87]

I end with two remarks on this score. The first is that, according to Luke 4:16–21, Jesus also read Scripture—specifically, of course, the Old Testament—in this participatory sort of way. According to Luke, Jesus read the words of Isa 61 as applying immediately to him and to his ministry. Isaiah was a guide, therefore, not unlike Moses or Paul for Gregory, whose words were to be trusted and enacted in the life with and toward God. It is no small matter, furthermore, that the text Jesus selected to read speaks of God's spirit being upon him (see Luke 4:18; Isa 61:1).

The second remark builds from this first one, especially with the tantalizingly Trinitarian evocations of Luke 4 still in mind (even if those are, as yet, seriously underdeveloped and only inchoately present). It is to return to where I began with the possibilities of "participating in Christ" in reading the Old Testament via Trinitarian preunderstandings or predispositions. The passage from Luke suggests that even Jesus participated with God's spirit through reading Isaiah. Jesus's reading in Luke 4 also indicates that the model found in Gregory—reading for participatory engagement with the life and mission of God—is already at work *in* the pages of Scripture, not simply a task to be performed *on* the pages of Scripture. But of course the latter performance on Scripture (or from it) is very much possible, assuming that the participation is willed and enabled (see above). So, per Gregory and per Luke 4, one may participate in God *through reading* and, in Trinitarian mode, *such reading also participates in Christ* (and the Spirit!). And so, in this fuller perspective, Moses, too, can be said to be participating in Christ when he participates in God. Perhaps that is why Moses is present at the transfiguration (Matt 17:3 and parallels), and why he can be an exemplar for the *Christian* soul (per Gregory) as well as the Jewish soul (per Philo). But insofar as (or at those times when) a Christian reads in these sorts of participatory ways, they also participate in Christ, who also read in the same way, and so they also participate in God, since these three are one—one also, perhaps, in the grandest vision, with the human reader-prayer-participant (cf. John 17:21).

Let the final words be Gregory's, with a gloss that the finding of which he speaks is dependent in no small way and perhaps entirely on *reading*: "As your understanding is lifted up to what is magnificent and divine, whatever you may find (and I know full well that you will find many things) will most certainly be for the common benefit in Christ Jesus. Amen" (*LM* II, 321).

---

87. See esp. Mariano Magrassi, *Praying the Bible: An Introduction to Lectio Divina* (Collegeville, MN: Liturgical Press, 1998).

11

Tolkien's Orcs Meet the Bible's Canaanites:
The Dynamics of Reading Well . . . or Not
(Or, How to Critique Scripture and Still Call It Scripture)

> The language of criticism now often reflects an emotional alien-
> ation from the imaginative life of the text under discussion, often
> seems in its bristling conceptuality empty of an experiential ground
> in reading.[1]

> For children are innocent and love justice; while most of us are
> wicked and naturally prefer mercy.[2]

> I hope in your word. (Ps 119:74, 81, 114, 147)

A version of this chapter was presented at the Durham University Research Seminar in Old
Testament in February 2021. I am thankful to Walter Moberly for his invitation to present on that
occasion and I am grateful for the helpful feedback I received at that time from the participants,
especially Brandon Hurlbert, Nicholas J. Moore, Richard Briggs, Douglas Earl, and Madhavi Ne-
vader. I am further indebted to Will Kynes, Stephen Chapman, Michael Rhodes, Walter Moberly,
and the editors of the present volume for their careful and helpful reviews of the chapter (for
which they should not be blamed). Some of what follows depends on an earlier publication:
Brent A. Strawn, "Canaan and Canaanites," in *The Oxford Encyclopedia of the Bible and Theology*,
ed. Samuel E. Balentine et al. (Oxford: Oxford University Press, 2015), 1:104–11.

1. Robert Alter, *The Pleasures of Reading in an Ideological Age* (New York: Norton, 1996), 15.
2. G. K. Chesterton, "On Household Gods and Goblins [1922]," in *The Coloured Lands* (London: Sheed and Ward, 1938), 195–200 (195).

1. The Problem of the Canaanites

The Canaanites are a real problem in the Old Testament, and for more than one reason. First and foremost, of course, they pose a problem *for the Israelites*, and here, too, in more than one way, insofar as they represent both a military (e.g., Num 13:28–29) and religious threat (e.g., Lev 18:24–28; Deut 7:3–4). Second—and in no small way, consequently—the Canaanites pose a problem *for contemporary readers* who are often upset, even scandalized, by the poor treatment the Canaanites receive in the Old Testament. This second, contemporary problem is shared by readers both inside and outside communities of faith. So, for example, in the latter camp one can find atheist Christopher Hitchens speaking "sympathetic words for the forgotten and obliterated Hivites, Canaanites, and Hittites, also presumably part of the Lord's original creation, who are to be pitilessly driven out of their homes to make room for the ungrateful and mutinous children of Israel."[3] Another atheist, Richard Dawkins, piles on by mentioning the "poor slandered, slaughtered Midianites, to be remembered only as poetic symbols of universal evil in a Victorian hymn."[4] (I'm not sure which fate Dawkins deems more ignominious.) Remarkably similar sentiments can also be found among those "inside" the fold. The Christian theologian C. S. Cowles, for instance, challenges any attempt to justify the "indiscriminate and promiscuous slaughter" of the Canaanites, even when such *apologia* is found in giants like John Calvin: "What could possibly be 'just' about the wanton and indiscriminate slaughter of 'women and children, the aged and decrepit'?" he asks.[5] Cowles—an Arminian and so no Calvinist himself—thinks the great reformer's admission that "the decree is dreadful indeed"[6] is "a gross understatement," preferring by far John Wesley's opinion that "to attribute such atrocities to God is an outrage against his character and makes him 'more false, more cruel, and more unjust than the devil. . . . God

3. Christopher Hitchens, *God Is Not Great: How Religion Poisons Everything* (New York: Twelve, 2007), 101.

4. Richard Dawkins, *The God Delusion* (Boston: Houghton Mifflin, 2006), 278.

5. C. S. Cowles, "The Case for Radical Discontinuity," in *Show Them No Mercy: 4 Views on God and Canaanite Genocide*, ed. Stanley N. Gundry (Grand Rapids: Zondervan, 2003), 11–44 (17), citing John Calvin, *Commentaries on the Book of Joshua*, trans. Henry Beveridge (Edinburgh: Calvin Translation Society, 1855), 97.

6. John Calvin, *Institutes of the Christian Religion*, trans. Ford Lewis Battles, ed. John T. McNeill (Philadelphia: Westminster, 1960), 2:955 (§3.23.7). It should be noted, however, that Calvin makes this admission with reference to God's predestination of the fall to sin, *not* the conquest proper.

hath taken [Satan's] work out of [his] hands. . . . God is the destroyer of souls."[7] To come full circle and unite the two camps—religious and not—Walter Wink's comment seems apt: "Against such an image of God the revolt of atheism is an act of pure religion."[8]

The present chapter engages the problem(s) of the Canaanites once again with a more recent comparative tool: the presentation of the Orcs in J. R. R. Tolkien's many writings about Middle-earth, especially *The Lord of the Rings* and *The Silmarillion*.[9] After briefly overviewing the mythology of the Orcs in Tolkien's oeuvre (§2), I will argue, first, that the Old Testament's Canaanites are—at least in some passages—presented in ways that are *quite like* Tolkien's Orcs (§3). That means, on the one hand, that they merit little or no pity (see, e.g., Deut 7:2), and a failure to recognize this fact is a failure to attend to the warp and woof of the literary presentation—that is, it is to be a poor reader of the literature *qua* literature. This would mean that "the problem of the Canaanites" is, nowadays at least, mostly of the *second* and distinctively *modern* type: modern readers (and, to be sure, I am inescapably one of them) are bothered by any and all specters of racism, genocide, and ethnic cleansing—as well we should be! Unfortunately, a number of modern readers evidence little to no knowledge of the *first* problem posed by the Canaanites (military and religious), nor of its relationship to, whether in problematizing or exacerbating, the second problem, though much can be (and often is) assumed about topics like these.[10]

---

7. Cowles, "Case for Radical Discontinuity," 18, citing John Wesley, "Free Grace," in *The Works of John Wesley* (London: Wesleyan Conference Office, 1872), 7:373–86.

8. Walter Wink, *Engaging the Powers* (Minneapolis: Fortress, 1992), 149.

9. J. R. R. Tolkien, *The Lord of the Rings* (Boston: Houghton Mifflin, 2004); Tolkien, *The Silmarillion*, 2nd ed., ed. Christopher Tolkien (Boston: Houghton Mifflin, 2001). For other pertinent works, see further below.

10. So, for example: is it appropriate to speak of the conquest of the land of Canaan as "holy war," "genocide," or "ethnic cleansing" in the first place? For various opinions on these matters, see, e.g., Lawson G. Stone, "Ethical and Apologetic Tendencies in the Redaction of the Book of Joshua," *CBQ* 52 (1991): 25–36; Stephen B. Chapman, "Martial Memory, Peaceable Vision: Divine War in the Old Testament," in *Holy War in the Bible: Christian Morality and an Old Testament Problem*, ed. Heath A. Thomas, Jeremy A. Evans, and Paul Copan (Downers Grove, IL: IVP Academic, 2013), 47–67; John H. Walton and J. Harvey Walton, *The Lost World of the Israelite Conquest: Covenant, Retribution, and the Fate of the Canaanites* (Downers Grove, IL: IVP Academic, 2017); John J. Collins, *Does the Bible Justify Violence?* (Minneapolis: Fortress, 2004); and Christian Hofreiter, *Making Sense of Old Testament Genocide: Christian Interpretations of* Herem *Passages* (Oxford: Oxford University Press, 2018).

But more needs to be said—and said very quickly—lest I miscommunicate or be misunderstood. And so, after noting the similarities between the Canaanites and Tolkien's Orcs, I will proceed to the proverbial "on the other hand," by first considering some of the real concerns such (literary) descriptions raise, especially for us now (§4). After that, I will proceed to argue that in several crucial ways the Canaanites are presented in ways that are *quite unlike* Tolkien's Orcs after all (§5). This judgment in its best forms—at least in *my* judgment—depends on the habits and skills of careful reading, not on a priori decisions about any number of issues drawn from elsewhere. In sum, I propose to use the problem of the Canaanites and its (im)proper assessment(s) as a vignette on how to read Scripture well, or not—or, to put the matter slightly differently, how to critique Scripture and still view it as Scripture (§6). The stakes, in both cases, are high.

2. *Tolkien's Orcs*

In J. R. R. Tolkien's *The Lord of the Rings*, the Orcs are presented as a wicked race of beings that comprise the primary military force of the chief antagonist, the evil lord Sauron. At his stronghold, Isengard, the traitorous wizard Saruman breeds a specialized subgroup of Orcs, the Uruk-hai, to serve as an even more elite fighting force; Sauron evidently does the same from his stronghold in Mordor.[11] In Tolkien's initial outing, *The Hobbit* (1937), a prequel to *The Lord of the Rings*, the preferred term is *goblin* rather than *orc*. In a note to the 1966 edition of *The Hobbit*, Tolkien clarified that *goblin* was an English translation of those beings that Hobbits called Orcs,[12] and is used particularly of mountain-dwelling Orcs in the North.[13] In light of Tolkien's larger oeuvre, and his extensive attention to the languages (and linguistics) of Middle-earth, it is thus possible to define *uruk* (*orch* in the Elvish language Sindarin) as a "goblin, particularly a large fighting Orc."[14] In the

---

11. The word for *orc* in what Tolkien called "the Black Speech" is *uruk*. See Ruth S. Noel, *The Languages of Tolkien's Middle-earth* (Boston: Houghton Mifflin, 1980), 203. In *The Lord of the Rings*, 1131, Tolkien commented that *uruk* "was applied as a rule only to the great soldier-orcs that at this time issued from Mordor and Isengard. The lesser kinds were called, especially by the Uruk-hai, *snaga* 'slave.'"

12. J. R. R. Tolkien, *The Hobbit or There and Back Again* (Boston: Houghton Mifflin, 1966), 8.

13. See David Day, *Tolkien: A Dictionary* (San Diego: Thunder Bay, 2013), 105.

14. Noel, *Languages of Tolkien's Middle-earth*, 203. See David Salo, *A Gateway to Sindarin: A Grammar of an Elvish Language from J. R. R. Tolkien's Lord of the Rings* (Salt Lake City: University of Utah Press, 2004), 278 (with bibliography), for the plural form of *orch* and its

end, then, the two terms are interchangeable, with *Orc* the governing, albeit not exclusive, term for what is the largest and most dastardly group of enemies in *The Lord of the Rings*.

Tolkien did not comment extensively on the history of the Orcs in *The Lord of the Rings*. But, given the remarkable thoroughness of his world-building, it is not surprising to find that he had formulated ideas about the Orcs which are hinted at and/or discussed to greater or lesser degrees elsewhere in his many other writings.[15] So, for example, according to *The Silmarillion*, the evil entity Melkor (*Morgoth* in Elvish) initially bred the Orcs "in envy and mockery" of the good and wise Elves. For this purpose, Melkor used Elves he had captured and corrupted

---

relationship to Old (!) Sindarin. Anderson Rearick III, "Why Is the Only Good Orc a Dead Orc? The Dark Face of Racism Examined in Tolkien's World," *Modern Fiction Studies* 50 (2004): 861–74, esp. 870–71, traces the use of *orc* in Old English (also Latin *orcus*) in order to argue that, in "one way or another, the term links Orcs to the infernal world of demons." In correspondence dated to December 29, 1968, Tolkien wrote to Sigrid Fowler that "in my work *Orc* is not an 'invention' but a borrowing from Old English *orc* 'demon'" (see Wayne G. Hammond and Christina Scull, *The Lord of the Rings: A Reader's Companion* [Boston: Houghton Mifflin, 2005], 25); elsewhere, Tolkien explained to his publisher that he "originally took the word from Old English *orc* (*Beowulf* 112), *orcneas* and the gloss *orc* = *þyrs* 'ogre', *heldoefel* 'hell-devil' (*Beowulf*, 24, 762)" (Humphrey Carpenter, ed., *The Letters of J. R. R. Tolkien* [Boston: Houghton Mifflin Harcourt, 2000], 177–78). An infernal connection also holds true, in Rearick's opinion, for *goblin* in Middle English and its use in Wycliffe's translation of Ps 90:6 (Rearick, "Why Is the Only Good Orc a Dead Orc?" 873n8). For Rearick, these linguistic connections indicate Tolkien's Orcs are not to be considered "mortal beings" but *super-* or at least *non-*natural agents of evil (870–71). In yet another place, a short note on the origin of the Orcs, Tolkien attributes the name to Elvish: "The Elves from their earliest times invented and used a word or words with a base (*o*)*rok* to denote anything that caused fear and/or horror. . . . Its application (in all Elvish tongues) specifically to the creatures called *Orks*—so I shall spell it in *The Silmarillion*—was later" (J. R. R. Tolkien, *Morgoth's Ring: The Later Silmarillion*, Part One: *The Legends of Aman*, The History of Middle-earth 10, ed. Christopher Tolkien [Boston: Houghton Mifflin Harcourt, 1993], 413–14; see further there, 422).

15. See, e.g., the compendia provided in Day, *Tolkien: A Dictionary*, 181–86; and, especially the scholarly discussion in Christina Scull and Wayne G. Hammond, *The J. R. R. Tolkien Companion and Guide: Reader's Guide*, rev. and exp. ed. (London: HarperCollins, 2017), 2:908–10.

"by slow arts of cruelty."[16] And so it was that "the hideous race of the Orcs" were "the bitterest foes" to the Elves.[17]

Another discussion is found in an appendix in *The Lord of the Rings* on the languages of Middle-earth:

> The Orcs were first bred by the Dark Power of the North in the Elder Days. It is said that they had no language of their own, but took what they could of other tongues and perverted it to their own liking; yet they made only brutal jargons, scarcely sufficient even for their own needs, unless it were for curses and abuse. And these creatures, being filled with malice, hating even their own kind, quickly developed as many barbarous dialects as there were groups or settlements of their race, so that their Orkish speech was of little use to them in intercourse between different tribes.[18]

16. Tolkien, *Silmarillion*, 50; see also *Morgoth's Ring*, 74, 109; and Robert Foster, *The Complete Guide to Middle-earth: From the Hobbit through the Lord of the Rings and Beyond*, rev. ed. (New York: Random House, 2001), 387–89; Ralph C. Wood, *The Gospel according to Tolkien: Visions of the Kingdom in Middle-earth* (Louisville: Westminster John Knox, 2003), 51–52; and Patrick Curry, *Defending Middle-earth: Tolkien, Myth and Modernity* (New York: Houghton Mifflin Harcourt, 2004), 30. A similar situation obtains for the trolls who were bred in mockery of the Ents (see Tolkien, *Lord of the Rings*, 486) or of "primitive human types" (Tolkien, *Morgoth's Ring*, 414). Sometime in the late 1950s, after the publication of *The Lord of the Rings*, Tolkien seems to have changed his mind on the Elf-Orc relationship, writing himself a note: "Alter this. Orcs are not Elvish" (*Morgoth's Ring*, 80, 127–28; see further *Morgoth's Ring*, 408–13; and Scull and Hammond, *Tolkien Companion and Guide*, 2:909). At this later stage, Tolkien seems inclined to think that the Orcs had been bred from both Elves *and* humans (both considered *Eruhíni*, the children of *Ilúvatar*, the Elvish name for the supreme deity Eru), but especially from the latter, in a perversion/conversion process (*Morgoth's Ring*, 413–14; but note Christopher Tolkien's editorial caution about avoiding any too simple explanation of Orc origins [*Morgoth's Ring*, 421]). One of the main theological drivers in Tolkien's mythology of Orc origins has to do with creative power: he is at pains to make clear that only Eru had such power; Melkor (or any other) "could not 'create' living 'creatures' of independent wills" (*Morgoth's Ring*, 413, see also 74, 413n6, 416–17; cf. Carpenter, *Letters*, 195). A problem Tolkien encountered, however, was his own complicated chronology, which forced him to posit that at least some Orcs were corrupted from spirits (the Maiar), not, that is, solely from Elves or humans; corrupted Maiar types "would exhibit terrifying and demonic characteristics" (*Morgoth's Ring*, 414). And so, while "the idea of breeding Orcs came from Morgoth . . . the accomplishment was left to Sauron" (Scull and Hammond, *Tolkien Companion and Guide*, 2:910; *Morgoth's Ring*, 420–21).

17. Tolkien, *Silmarillion*, 50. Also, "deep in their dark hearts the Orcs loathed the Master whom they served in fear, the maker only of their misery. This it may be was the vilest deed of Melkor" (Tolkien, *Silmarillion*).

18. Tolkien, *Lord of the Rings*, 1131 (see also 1132); cf. J. R. R. Tolkien, *The Peoples of Middle-earth*, The History of Middle-Earth 12, ed. Christopher Tolkien (Boston: Houghton Mifflin, 1996),

Elsewhere, Tolkien writes briefly and similarly that the Orcs were "fluent only in the expression of abuse, of hatred and fear."[19]

Tolkien continued to think and rethink the Orcs, their origins, will power, and so forth in other writings after the publication of *The Hobbit* and *The Lord of the Rings*: it remains uncertain if he ever settled his own mind on these matters, and so discrepancies are apparent across his corpus on several important details.[20] Indeed, in one place he jotted a note to himself that the "nature and origin [of the Orcs] require more thought. They are not easy to work into the theory and system."[21] Be that as it may, the longer citation immediately above demonstrates that language is not the only way Tolkien indexes the wickedness and brutality of the Orcs. A host of other literary techniques conspire to paint them as evil—and naturally so.[22] Among other things, especially in the aggregate, these strategies seem designed to produce a narrative world and reading experience that are not bothered in the least when one—or, hopefully, *many*—Orcs are killed. The Orcs are, after all, little more than, or, perhaps more accurately, *nothing more* than, the "bad guys" in Tolkien's fictional world.[23] They deserve, therefore, exactly what they

---

35, where Tolkien indicates that Orkish (i.e., the language) was originally "devised for them by the Dark Lord of old, but it was so full of harsh and hideous sounds and vile words that other mouths found it difficult to compass, and few indeed were willing to make the attempt." See also Tolkien, *Morgoth's Ring*, 413n8.

19. Tolkien, *Peoples of Middle-earth*, 21.

20. See, e.g., note 16 above and, further, the letter to Peter Hastings of September 1954, drafted but never sent (Carpenter, *Letters*, 188–96, esp. 190–91); Scull and Hammond, *Tolkien Companion and Guide*, 2:908–10; and Tolkien, *Morgoth's Ring*, 123–24, 127–28. In the last-mentioned work, Tolkien writes that the Orcs "had little or no *will* when not actually 'attended to' by the mind of Sauron. Does their cheating and rebellion pass that possible to such animals as dogs, etc.?" (413n6 [emphasis his]; elsewhere he speaks of ant-like obedience). See further *Morgoth's Ring*, 408–13, and esp. 415–22—the latter an essay on the Orcs that seems to have been written by Tolkien in 1959–1960. Tolkien writes there of the Orcs' comprehensive corruption that left them "pitiless, and there was no cruelty or wickedness that they would not commit; but this was the corruption of independent wills, and they took pleasure in their deeds" (417–18).

21. Tolkien, *Morgoth's Ring*, 409; cf. J. R. R. Tolkien, *The Nature of Middle-earth: Late Writings on the Lands, Inhabitants, and Metaphysics of Middle-earth*, ed. Carl F. Hostetter (Boston: Houghton Mifflin Harcourt, 2021), 360: "The history of the Orks is naturally obscure . . ."

22. See, e.g., Tolkien, *Peoples of Middle-Earth*, 35: "These creatures, being filled with all malice and hatred . . . did not love even their own kind." In a letter, Tolkien admits that the "horribly corrupted" nature of the Orcs may not be any "more so than many Men to be met today" (Carpenter, *Letters*, 190) and goes on to actively resist calling them "irredeemably bad" because "that would be going too far" (195). See further §6 below.

23. Tom Shippey writes that "there can be little doubt that orcs entered Middle-earth originally just because the story needed a continual supply of enemies over whom one need feel no compunction" (*The Road to Middle-earth*, 2nd ed. [London: Grafton, 1992], 207). Even so, as

get, whenever they get it. Still further, the Orcs aren't just "bad"—they are truly *dangerous*: they represent a real, constant, and imminent threat to the life, health, and safety of the "good" peoples who stand for what is right in Middle-earth. Further and final testimony to the enduring ill effects of Orcs (and similar groups or individuals aligned with evil in Tolkien's world) is found in the fact that, even after the destruction of the One Ring, the Hobbits are faced with a dire situation in the Shire upon their return home.[24]

3. The Canaanites Are (Basically) Orcs

Just this far and one can easily imagine a number of points at which Tolkien's Orcs and the Canaanites might be compared. While I will nuance such a judgment momentarily, it nevertheless seems to be the case that in many texts and traditions in the Old Testament the Canaanites are presented in literary ways that seem entirely akin to Tolkien's representation of the Orcs. The Canaanites, too, are wicked, dangerous, aggressive, monstrous, and so on and so forth. Already in Gen 15:16, for instance, "the iniquity of the Amorites" who inhabit Canaan is mentioned in what looks like anticipatory justification for the Israelites' later taking of that territory.[25] In Deuteronomy, the prior inhabitants of the land are called by strange names like Emim, Zamzummim, Horim, and Avvim (Deut 2:10–23)—terms S. Dean McBride has glossed as "frighteners," "mumblers," "troglodytes," and "ruiners."[26] These groups are discussed in mythic categories, presented as unnaturally tall and/or unusually wicked, with origins that go back, ultimately, to the Nephilim (see Gen 6:1–4; Deut 1:28; 2:10–11, 21; 9:2, 4; 20:18).[27] King Og of Bashan is explicitly

---

Rearick notes, there is "a very troubling quality in Tolkien's depiction . . . specifically the expendable nature of the Orcs" ("Why Is the Only Good Orc a Dead Orc?" 864).

24. See the chapter entitled "The Scouring of the Shire" (Tolkien, *Lord of the Rings*, 998–1020), which makes mention of a number of antagonists, including "Goblin-men" (or half-orcs) also bred by Saruman. Tolkien speculated that "orc-cults" continued on in Middle-earth after the time in which *The Lord of the Rings* is set (see Carpenter, *Letters*, 419; Hammond and Scull, *Lord of the Rings*, 591).

25. See Gary A. Anderson, "What about the Canaanites?" in *Divine Evil? The Moral Character of the God of Abraham*, ed. Michael Bergmann, Michael J. Murray, and Michael C. Rea (Oxford: Oxford University Press, 2011), 269–82, esp. 279–80, 282; and Anderson, "Reply to Wolterstorff," in Bergmann, Murray, and Rea, *Divine Evil?* 289–90, esp. 290.

26. S. Dean McBride, "Deuteronomy," in *The HarperCollins Study Bible*, ed. Harold W. Attridge et al., rev. ed. (San Francisco: HarperSanFrancisco, 2006), 255–309 (here 259–60). It is important to note that Emim is a Moabite, not Israelite, designation (Deut 2:11), and Zamzummim is an Ammonite, not Israelite, term (Deut 2:20).

27. See Brent A. Strawn, "Deuteronomy," in *Theological Bible Commentary*, ed. Gail R.

said to be the last of the related and equally mythic Rephaim (Deut 3:11), with the Canaanites direct descendants of the dreaded Anakim (Deut 1:28; cf. Num 13:33; also Josh 11:21–22; 14:12, 15).

The Canaanites are, in this kind of light, downright *Orcish*; indeed, names like "Og" and "Anak" sound as if they might belong to characters living in Tolkien's Middle-earth—say, in the Tower of Cirith Ungol or the fortress of Barad-dûr. More to the point at hand, the literary presentation of the Canaanites described thus far may well function, perhaps even be *designed* to function, analogously to that of Tolkien's depiction of the Orcs. If so, readers of such descriptions ought not to worry overmuch about the dispatching of the Canaanites because they, like the Orcs, are the quintessential "bad guys." As A. R. Millard once put it, the prior inhabitants of the land of Canaan "command little attention beyond the generality of their wickedness by which their extermination was justified."[28] And so, again, in terms of literary presentation and readerly effect, the Canaanites can be seen as (basically) Orcs. Perhaps this explains (even if it does not yet justify) what appears to be Jesus's rather harsh treatment of the "Canaanite" woman in Matt 15. Maybe Jesus had been reading *The Lord of the Rings*—or, rather, the book of Deuteronomy—the night before!

Before moving on to question certain aspects of this "Orcish presentation" and wonder about its (inevitable?) effect on readers, we should pause and acknowledge that similar depictions that paint individuals or groups of individuals in strongly negative terms are ubiquitous in literature.[29] In these contexts—even in works where enemy-depictions are not especially harsh—literary works often manifest a decided *lack* of interest in secondary, supporting characters who turn out to be little more than props for the plot.

An example from the book of Job is instructive. In his well-known book *Answer to Job*, Carl Jung worried about what he deemed the insensitivity of the narrator with regard to the loss of Job's family, servants, and possessions. According to

---

O'Day and David L. Petersen (Louisville: Westminster John Knox, 2009), 63–76 (here 67); cf. Jerome F. D. Creach, *Violence in Scripture*, Interpretation (Louisville: Westminster John Knox, 2013), 130–32 (on Judges).

28. A. R. Millard, "The Canaanites," in *Peoples of Old Testament Times*, ed. D. J. Wiseman (Oxford: Clarendon, 1973), 29–52 (here 29).

29. Umberto Eco suggests that enemy-depictions are somehow *necessary*: "Having an enemy is important not only to define our identity but also to provide us with an obstacle against which to measure our system of values and, in seeking to overcome it, to demonstrate our own worth. So when there is no enemy, we have to invent one" (*Inventing the Enemy: And Other Occasional Writings*, trans. Richard Dixon [Boston: Houghton Mifflin Harcourt, 2012], 2). Note also Andrew Delbanco, *The Death of Satan: How Americans Have Lost the Sense of Evil* (New York: Farrar, Straus and Giroux, 1995), esp. chap. 5 ("The Age of Blame").

R. W. L. Moberly, however, Jung's concern is a classic case of missing the literary point. This is because

> the fate of Job's animals, servants, and family is, *in the story's own frame of reference*, a diminution *of Job*. They are considered not in their own right but *only for their bearing* upon Job as paterfamilias. Thus there is a genuine difference of assumption between the ancient world of the narrative and that of today, where most people rightly would not make that particular "patriarchal" assumption. Historical distance and difference can be real and problematic. However, the way Jung formulates his objection is surely tone-deaf to *the dramatic tenor of the text*, in which the narrative is *speedy and stylized, not to be lingered on.*[30]

Jung was troubled by the book's all-too-brief treatment of these minor characters and their untimely demises; Moberly's response is to redirect attention to the "dramatic tenor of the text" and its narrative, which is "speedy and stylized." Moberly illustrates his counterpoint further with a scene from the movie *Where Eagles Dare* (1968), in which a number of German soldiers are gunned down:

> These German soldiers are not dramatically significant: they play a minor role, to create dramatic tension and action in the struggle around escape from the fortress. To concentrate on the carelessness with which they are gunned down, or to lament the abuse of their human dignity, is *to fail to appreciate or follow the nature of the drama.* One is not obliged to like a certain kind of action movie, but that is a different issue from not understanding how its conventions work. Comparably, Jung comes across as a superficial reader of the ancient text, so eager to make it serve his own agenda that he does not bother to *attend properly to its (hardly obscure) conventions.*[31]

In a footnote, Moberly makes the same point with reference to expressions of sympathy for Job's wife, who goes unnamed in the book and who seems to be treated harshly by Job in his reply to her (Job 2:10):[32] "In ordinary life these would

---

30. R. W. L. Moberly, *Old Testament Theology: Reading the Hebrew Bible as Christian Scripture* (Grand Rapids: Baker Academic, 2013), 260 (emphases added).

31. Moberly, *Old Testament Theology*, 260–61 (emphases added); note also 261n31: the dramatic presentation "is hardly different in kind from a child at play who knocks down and 'kills' a whole group of models/figurines with a sweep of the hand."

32. For discussion of Job's wife, see, e.g., C. L. Seow, *Job 1–21: Interpretation and Commentary*, Illuminations (Grand Rapids: Eerdmans, 2013), 292, 294–97. Will Kynes has drawn attention to the comparative construction, "you speak *as* . . ." (*kǝ-*), to argue that Job does *not* think of his

be appropriate sentiments. But in a narrative where Job's wife has no existence other than the narrative function of expressing an inappropriate thought (i.e., she is not really a character at all), *one's imaginative energies are better directed elsewhere.*"[33] Moberly's point could be applied to and traced in—*ad infinitum, ad nauseam,* and *ad maximum*—a host of entertainment media from late last week if not yesterday night. It isn't just literature or World War II movies, that is, but also television shows or major motion pictures that feature heroes killing countless "bad guys" on their way to accomplishing whatever they need to accomplish: usually rescuing someone important (and attractive) and/or saving countless lives of some sort—ideally both. The sheer number of these henchmen, both pre- and postmortem, is usually nothing short of stunning (where do they all come from?). Equally remarkable is how they are constantly on guard around every single corner and extraordinarily well armed to boot (who is bankrolling all that?). And yet, despite their vast numbers and good equipment, these henchmen barely slow our heroes down; neither, evidently, does our heroes' killing of these antagonists register even a blip on their consciences, nor, apparently, on the consciences of those who are watching—namely, us, the audience.[34] Or, to switch genres, consider the murder victims on so many police dramas, where the deceased serves as a more or less grisly backdrop for the romantic relationship between the sexy detectives assigned to the case. If cop shows aren't one's favorite, no worries: there are endless hospital dramas, where the traumatized dead—murdered or otherwise—provide similarly slim background for the primary action: the young aspiring doctors who are forever engaging in behavior that would surely get them fired from any *real* hospital. This is not yet to mention violent song lyrics across a host of musical genres or, perhaps most troubling of all, violent video games that not only depict violence but require simulated participation therein, and where headshots are usually awarded extra points.

One could worry about all this—indeed, one *should* worry about it—but the point is simply that artistic presentations across multiple media exist, and in truth are fantastically widespread, that depict some characters as far more important than others, with still other characters of absolutely no importance whatsoever,

---

wife as foolish, at least not generally or normally. I first encountered Kynes's interpretation on the podcast *The Two Testaments* (episode 3, October 13, 2021); it can also be found in Bill Kynes and Will Kynes, *Wrestling with Job: Defiant Faith in the Face of Suffering* (Downers Grove, IL: IVP Academic, 2022), see chaps. 3 and 5.

33. Moberly, *Old Testament Theology*, 260n30 (emphasis added).

34. Nothing could be further from the truth of the matter when it comes to actual killing. See Dave Grossman, *On Killing: The Psychological Cost of Learning to Kill in War and Society*, rev. ed. (New York: Back Bay, 2009), esp. 74, 97–98, 131–33, 225–26, 238–39.

and this valuation extends to these characters' mortality. That is to say, characters of little or no importance frequently find themselves dead before the end of the art form: the final page, the final scene, the curtain's close. That is simply the *nature* of these presentations, the way they work—the way they are *designed to work*—within their respective media.

4. Cause(s) for Concern

The preceding, rather quick comparison of the Bible's Canaanites and Tolkien's Orcs suggests, not only that Moberly's comments contra Jung on Job are accurate, but also that they are widely applicable. It is possible to see, that is—as Moberly has done with the "minor characters" in the prologue to Job—that the biblical presentation of the Canaanites functions not unlike Tolkien's depiction of the Orcs, the Uruk-hai, the trolls, and all the rest, and that such a presentation is wrought, *by design*, so that readers do *not* feel sympathy for these characters who are, at the end of the day, simply not of much narrative importance.[35] Instead, these characters are, to borrow Moberly's terms, "not really characters at all." They are props for the plot but little else, rarely, if ever, rising to what E. M. Forster called "round characters."[36] Sympathetic sentiments for the Canaanites, especially postmortem, would be, as Moberly writes about Job, appropriate "in ordinary life"—though our rapacious consumption of violent entertainment media likely suggests otherwise—but not in a narrative world where they are hardly characters at all. If such a judgment seems too harsh and too unkind, comparison should be made, again, to Tolkien's world (inter alia), where such a judgment is indubitably true of the Orcs: one is hard pressed indeed to find any narrative reason to feel any sympathy for them,[37] and, again, the Bible's literary depictions of the Canaanites seem similar—at least at some points and in some ways.

---

35. In an important letter that lays out some of his thinking on the metaphysics and theology of Middle-earth, Tolkien expresses some regret that he named the troll in *The Hobbit* "William," perhaps because it was too endearing, though Tolkien clarifies that this troll showed no evidence of true pity (Carpenter, *Letters*, 191).

36. See E. M. Forster, *Aspects of the Novel* (San Diego: Harcourt, 1955), 67–78.

37. Note, again, the ways the Orcs refer to themselves, or their "hideous names to suit their persons" (Fleming Rutledge, *The Battle for Middle-earth: Tolkien's Divine Design in the Lord of the Rings* [Grand Rapids: Eerdmans, 2004], 150n6), or the way they fight with all other peoples in part to keep from slaying each other (Tolkien, *Morgoth's Ring*, 420n*), though they frequently fight themselves, too, as in the scene that takes place in the tower of Cirith Ungol (Tolkien, *Lord of the Rings*, 905–7; see also Tolkien, *Nature of Middle-earth*, 370). In *The Hobbit*, Tolkien writes: "It is not unlikely that they [the Goblins, i.e., the Orcs] invented some of the machines that have since troubled the world, especially the ingenious devices for killing large numbers

Now if this comparison be granted, even if only momentarily for the sake of argument, questions immediately arise that demand careful consideration. One of these would be to wonder if the two presentations—the Bible's and Tolkien's—are exactly or exhaustively the same. The answer here, obviously, is *of course not*. (More on this crucial distinction later.) Another rather large question that is equally important and closely related is to wonder if and how literary presentations like these are (or might be construed as) racist, whether intentionally or otherwise. Put most directly, the question is simply this: was Tolkien racist?

Was Tolkien Racist?

Not a few readers have thought Tolkien so and for more than one reason, with others weighing in strongly to the contrary. In a 2004 essay, Anderson Rearick argued that it was high time for Tolkien's work to be subjected to academic scrutiny along lines such as these,[38] though at the time of his essay, discussions accusing Tolkien of racism were mostly popular in nature: an exchange in the novel *The Rotters' Club*, for example, along with a few websites, blog posts, and newspaper articles.[39] Enough material was available, however, to convince Rearick that questions about "Tolkien's possible racism" went back at least as far as the 1970s; writing more than three decades later, Rearick stated that "the silence of the academy must end" on this matter, and he sets out to do exactly that in his essay.[40]

First, however, Rearick must engage in a bit of deck-clearing before he can directly address the charge of racism in Tolkien—a charge he wishes to refute. So, for example, Rearick points out that any racist connotations that are evoked by film adaptations of *The Lord of the Rings*, particularly with regard to costume, make-up, and acting, cannot be properly (or at least fully) laid at Tolkien's door.[41] That point duly noted, there is a comment Tolkien once made in a letter to Naomi Mitchison

---

of people at once" (73). In *The Lord of the Rings*, the Ent named Treebeard describes the Orcs as "evileyed-blackhanded-bowlegged-flinthearted-clawfingered-foulbellied-bloodthirsty" (979).

38. See Rearick, "Why Is the Only Good Orc a Dead Orc?" 862.

39. Jonathan Coe, *The Rotters' Club* (New York: Vintage, 2001), 143.

40. Rearick, "Why Is the Only Good Orc a Dead Orc?" 864.

41. In his programmatic essay, "On Fairy-Stories" (in *The Monsters and the Critics and Other Essays*, ed. Christopher Tolkien [London: HarperCollinsPublishers, 2006], 108–61), Tolkien is adamant that "Fantasy is a thing best left to words, to true literature" (140). In other art forms, like painting, "the visible presentation of the fantastic image is technically too easy; the hand tends to outrun the mind, even to overthrow it" ("On Fairy-Stories"; see also 141 where he speaks of Drama as attempting "a kind of bogus, or shall I say at least substitute, magic: *the visible and audible presentation of imaginary men in a story*" [his emphasis]). In an associated note, Tolkien states that the "radical distinction between all art (including drama) that offers a *visible* presen-

(December 8, 1955) that compares the Dwarves to Jewish people: "I do think of the 'Dwarves' like Jews: at once native and alien in their habitations, speaking the languages of the country, but with an accent due to their own private tongue."[42] If this starts making some readers nervous, Rearick's interpretation may settle them down: "Tolkien's connection [here] is more historically linguistic and cultural than racial," he writes. "So even this documented connection between a known human race and Tolkien's imaginary ones is a dead end" when it comes to the charge of racism.[43] If one is not yet convinced, other letters from Tolkien provide further support, though the record is admittedly not uniform. So, for example, in one letter Tolkien objects to a reader's equation of Sauron with Stalin: "To ask if the Orcs are Communists is to me as sensible as asking if Communists are Orcs."[44] In another, he derides unnecessary gloating over Germany's demise in the war as akin to the hooting of an "orc-crowd."[45] "We were supposed to have reached a stage of civilization" beyond such mean-spirited activity, Tolkien writes.[46] But on the other side of things is Tolkien's 1958 letter to Forrest J. Ackerman about a proposed film adaptation of *The Lord of the Rings* in which he states that the Orcs were "corruptions of the 'human' form seen in Elves and Men. They are (or were) squat, broad, flat nosed, sallow-skinned, with wide mouths and slant eyes, in fact degraded and repulsive versions of the (to Europeans) least lovely Mongol-types."[47] The fact that Tolkien qualifies his comment with "least lovely" and "to Europeans," or that his remark here or his writings elsewhere can (and have) been read as racist with regard to different groups—and thus not focused on any one in particular[48]—or that he was quite against visual representation of fantasy stories more generally, doesn't seem enough to prevent one from worrying about racism. But, according to Rearick, the most important evidence—in this case of "evidence of Tolkien's anti-racism"—"appears in his correspondence in which his disgust toward the racism especially prevalent in his time—anti-Semitism—is clear."[49] Rearick summarizes the data:

---

tation and true literature is that it imposes one visible form. Literature works from mind to mind and is thus more progenitive. It is at once more universal and more poignantly particular" (159).

42. Carpenter, *Letters*, 228–29 (here 229).

43. Rearick, "Why Is the Only Good Orc a Dead Orc?" 864. For an extensive study that supports Rearick's interpretation, see Renée Vink, "'Jewish' Dwarves: Tolkien and Anti-Semitic Stereotyping," *Tolkien Studies* 10 (2013): 123–45.

44. Carpenter, *Letters*, 262; see also Rutledge, *Battle for Middle-earth*, 8–9n21.

45. Carpenter, *Letters*, 111; see also Rutledge, *Battle for Middle-earth*, 14–15.

46. Carpenter, *Letters*, 111.

47. Carpenter, *Letters*, 274.

48. So, e.g., Christopher J. Ferguson, "No, Orcs Aren't Racist," *Psychology Today* (April 29, 2020), online at: https://www.psychologytoday.com/us/blog/checkpoints/202004/no-orcs-arent-racist.

49. This is an especially important point in light of the "racist tradition of anti-Semitism"

In a letter to Graham Tayler who had noted a similarity between Sam Gamgee and Samson Gamgee, a name included in an old list of Birmingham Jewry, Tolkien reflects on the suggestion that his own [sur]name might have a Jewish source: "It [Tolkien] is not Jewish in origin, though I should consider it an honour if it were" (*Letters* 410). More overt is Tolkien's response to Nazi publishers who wanted a *Bestätigung* or confirmation of his Aryan, racial "purity." To his own publisher, Allen and Unwin, Tolkien expressed his misgivings of allowing such a statement to appear on his text even if it cost the company money, or as he put it, "let the German translation go hang" if such a statement created the appearance that he agreed with the Nazi concept of racial purity: "I should regret giving any colour to the notion that I subscribed to the wholly pernicious and unscientific race-doctrine" (*Letters* 37). Later, in a letter dripping with sarcasm in which he pretends to not understand the Nazi publisher's definition of Aryan, Tolkien points out that true Aryans are, in fact, an "Indo-iranian" [*sic*] group and none of his ancestors spoke "Hindustani, Persian, Gypsy, or any related dialects." Tolkien finally writes if "you are enquiring whether I am of *Jewish* origin, I can only reply that I regret that I appear to have *no* ancestors of that gifted people" (*Letters* 37).[50]

On the basis of these remarks, Rearick concludes that "Tolkien's own words seem to lay to rest the charge that he was racist in his thinking."[51]

I am finishing this chapter in early 2022, in North Carolina, a southern state in the United States and many things are different, now, than they were when Rearick wrote. Well, in truth, many things are *not* different when it comes to racial equality—or rather *in*equity—and that is precisely the problem. Even so, discussions of ethnicity and racism are now more widespread and common, with critical thinking about the same considerably more developed than when Rearick wrote, or, at least, than is reflected in his essay. To cite an example: many people now (and earlier!) would be altogether dissatisfied with Rearick's assertion that "living in a racist society does not predestine one to be racist. Other factors can play a role in forming a personality."[52] Such a statement underestimates the power and perniciousness of racist systems that need not and frequently do not depend

---

that Rearick says "tinged" Tolkien's "young man's world of academia" ("Why Is the Only Good Orc a Dead Orc?" 866).

50. Rearick, "Why Is the Only Good Orc a Dead Orc?" 866–67. The parenthetical citations are from pages in Carpenter, *Letters*.

51. Rearick, "Why Is the Only Good Orc a Dead Orc?" 867. He goes on to cite Julia Houston that Tolkien "often wrote of the evils of apartheid and racism."

52. Rearick, "Why Is the Only Good Orc a Dead Orc?" 866, and further there.

on acts of individual will. Similarly, Rearick's carefully executed argument that Tolkien's "treatment of dark forces in general and Orcs in particular is based more on an archetypal and Judeo-Christian parameter than a racial one" will likely not satisfy all contemporary readers. Indeed, such an argument could be seen as not settling the matter in the least but just punting it further up the line, offering additional proof, that is, of a larger racist system, one that is (still worse!) *religiously* authorized. A study that reflects more recent thinking and that, as a result, is significantly more critical—and successfully so—of Tolkien and other fantasy writers is Helen Young's book, *Race and Popular Fantasy Literature: Habits of Whiteness*.[53]

Space precludes a full analysis of the many issues at work here, and so a few points must suffice for now. First, one might ask if the question "Is Tolkien racist?" is well put, or if a better formulation would be to ask "Is Tolkien's *narrator* racist?" or "Is Tolkien's *Middle-earth* a racist system?" Much depends here on definitions of racism: contemporary, on the one hand, and "fantasy," on the other, not to mention their connections (or lack thereof). But much also depends on the relationship of authors to their texts. With regard to the latter, if Middle-earth or its narrator is racist, does that mean Tolkien himself was? That is a hard line to argue on this side of the (now not so new) New Criticism—not without committing the intentional fallacy.[54] As already noted, Rearick, among others, mounted a case that Tolkien was actually *anti*-racist in several important ways.[55] Then again, there can be no doubt that Tolkien was born into one racist system (in South Africa) and spent the rest of his life in another system (the United Kingdom) which had yet another set of societal and class issues.[56] That makes Tolkien—no less than any human being—part of a much larger system(s) of race and class regardless of his own

---

53. Helen Young, *Race and Popular Fantasy Literature: Habits of Whiteness* (New York and London: Routledge, 2016), esp. 15–39, 88–113. It should be noted that Young's work is as much interested in (and concerned about) gaming products inspired by Tolkien, and by Peter Jackson's film renditions of *The Lord of the Rings*, as she is Tolkien's own works, especially in their full compass as described in *The History of Middle-Earth*, which is not much cited. It remains unclear, however, how (or if) that larger corpus would affect Young's argument. Note, again, Vink, "'Jewish' Dwarves," for a thoughtful study that offers a very different perspective to that of Young.

54. In the case of Middle-earth, it is obvious that Tolkien's mind was constantly changing and evolving as he worked on the vast stretch of worlds he had created. In the draft letter to Peter Hastings cited earlier, Tolkien wrote (rather tellingly) that his fictive creation "seems to have grown out of hand, so that parts seem (to me) rather *revealed through* me than by me" (Carpenter, *Letters*, 189 [emphasis added]). Tolkien never sent the letter, adding, at the top of the draft: "Not sent. It seemed to be taking myself too importantly" (196).

55. See also Ferguson, "No, Orcs Aren't Racist"; Vink, "'Jewish' Dwarves."

56. Noted by Rearick, "Why Is the Only Good Orc a Dead Orc?" 865–66.

proclivities; furthermore, few people in Tolkien's era would qualify as "anti-racist" by current definitions.[57]

To repeat: definitions of *racism* that depend on individual dispositions, while not uncommon, are now widely recognized as insufficient. Rearick appears to espouse such a definition himself, but, regardless of that, describes "the central racist presumption" as the belief "that individuals can be categorized and judged by their physical, racial appearances."[58] That presumption typically comes with a correlate—namely, the inherent superiority of some people over others, precisely because of their physical features.[59] By this definition, Tolkien's Middle-earth and/ or its narrator seem almost certainly racist: Elves are not humans are not Orcs are not hobbits are not trolls and so forth, with some peoples of Middle-earth clearly superior to others, with the Elves the very best of all.[60] This, in turn, raises the specter of *systemic racism*, defined as "prejudice, antagonism, or discrimination" at an institutional or societal level.[61] Middle-earth seems precisely such a system since the various people groups are carefully distinguished and mostly rigidly ordered.[62] Even so, systemic racism as known in today's world, say within the United States, is not easily applied to Tolkien's Middle-earth.[63] A British critic, John Yatt, has

57. See, e.g., Ibram X. Kendi, *How to Be an Antiracist* (New York: One World, 2019), 18, who prefers to speak specifically of "racist policy."

58. Rearick, "Why Is the Only Good Orc a Dead Orc?" 864.

59. Cf. *OED*: "Prejudice, antagonism, or discrimination by an individual, institution, or society, against a person or people on the basis of their nationality or (now usually) their membership of a particular racial or ethnic group, typically one that is a minority or marginalized. Also: beliefs that members of a particular racial or ethnic group possess innate characteristics or qualities, or that some racial or ethnic groups are superior to others; an ideology based on such beliefs" (online 3rd edition revised June 2008). See further Stephen Jay Gould, *The Mismeasure of Man*, rev. ed. (New York: Norton, 1996).

60. Rearick, "Why Is the Only Good Orc a Dead Orc?" 869: "Far more troubling might be the fact that all the races portrayed by Tolkien in *The Lord of the Rings* seem to share his sensibilities and to be internally attracted to the fair qualities of the elven people."

61. *OED* (online 3rd edition revised June 2008).

62. Exceptions exist (e.g., "half-elves") and so qualifications are in order. See, e.g., Rearick, "Why Is the Only Good Orc a Dead Orc?" 867–68, for "a much larger and mixed description of good and evil," including Sam's empathy for a fallen Southron soldier, which caused him to wonder if many of Sauron's troops were unwilling agents and thus not themselves evil. See further below on the Hobbits.

63. Rearick, "Why Is the Only Good Orc a Dead Orc?" 867, cites Julia Houston, who thinks one particular critic's "conclusions about Tolkien's racism are based more on his being an American who does not understand the European ideas of class that Tolkien seems to have held than to any actual elements of racism in Middle-earth." "Other countries don't write literature," Houston continues, "on uniquely American sins." Unfortunately, Houston's essay entitled "Tolkien, Racism, and Paranoia," proved unavailable via the webpage Rearick cited.

derided Tolkien's work because it is filled with "basic assumptions that are frankly unacceptable in 21st-century Britain."[64] Yatt's judgment is straightforward enough, commonsensical even, but fails as a substantive critique because of course Britain is not Middle-earth, nor Middle-earth Britain. Tolkien's is, and remains, a *fictive* world.[65] There simply are no Orcs in the *real* world—Tolkien was quite clear about that in his rebuff of their possible connection to Communism!

There is another issue to consider, beyond the definition(s) of racism and the relationship(s) of a text to its author, and that is whether and how literary works generate subsequent and consequent ethical activity. Does *The Lord of the Rings* produce—necessarily and inevitably—racism now? On the one hand, such a scenario is not hard to imagine if, say, some hypothetical reader chose to self-identify with the Elves and saw all other people, especially people they didn't like very much, as equivalent to some other type of person from Tolkien's world. The Orcs *could* be that "other type of person," but in truth the Orcs are only one possibility: Hobbits and humans, too, are far less than Elves in the world of Middle-earth. On the other hand, such a scenario seems extremely unlikely. Most modern people would deem such a scenario—someone self-identifying as an Elf of Middle-earth—to be very odd to say the very least, and this despite the fact that a decent number of people attend comic book conventions dressed up as their favorite characters. I don't know of any empirical evidence demonstrating a causal relationship between Tolkien's literary depiction of the Orcs and contemporary racist policies or behaviors.[66] That is not to say that such evidence doesn't exist or couldn't, at least in theory. Perhaps it is only to say, as Young does in her book, that *The Lord of the Rings* and a number of other popular fantasy works are simply further instantiations of widespread racism throughout contemporary society, extending to and manifested in its various art forms. Fair enough, but if the charge of racism in Tolkien envisions (or entails) a negative ethics, it would be helpful to have some way of establishing a causal connection between the (racist) literature

64. John Yatt, "Wraiths and Race," *Guardian* (December 2, 2002), https://www.theguardian.com/books/2002/dec/02/jrrtolkien.lordoftherings; cited in Rearick, "Why Is the Only Good Orc a Dead Orc?" 864.

65. Ferguson, "No, Orcs Aren't Racist," asks "Can you be racist toward a race that doesn't exist? . . . Sometimes an orc is just an orc." Despite the fictive nature of Middle-earth, it is intriguing to note how the work of Tolkien and his fellow Inklings demonstrates an interest in tying their stories into the larger history and mythology of England. See Philip Zaleski and Carol Zaleski, *The Fellowship: The Literary Lives of the Inklings* (New York: Farrar, Straus and Giroux, 2015).

66. According to Ferguson, "No, Orcs Aren't Racist": "there's little empirical reason to suspect that playing Dungeons and Dragons [a major point of concern for Young, *Race and Popular Fantasy*, given Middle-earth's influence on that role-playing game] or watching Lord of the Rings is associated with real-life racism."

and the (racist) ethics. Barring that connection, the case is simply much harder to make: *perhaps* it is true, but *perhaps not.*

More generally—and at this point I likely reveal too much of my own robust doctrine of sin—I suspect that bad human behavior rarely needs *literary* justification. Furthermore, if and when people who behave badly appeal to literary precedent, I admit that I'm not convinced that the rest of us are compelled to believe them or their warranting. Such justification is coming, after all, from people who are *behaving badly*. Why should we trust them as accurate interpreters of the texts they cite, especially if the texts in question aren't so clear?[67] *Maybe* these persons are right in their appeal to their textual authority, but *maybe not*—they could be quite wrong. In point of fact, a great number of readers of *The Lord of the Rings*—indeed, the vast majority of them, if not in fact, every single one of them—have *not* declared war on other people, calling them "Orcs" or "Trolls" or "Goblins" or whatever else. The point to be made, at any event, is that complex human behaviors are rarely, if ever, monocausal. Still further, according to some scholars, texts don't have ideologies, *readers do*.[68] If that is accurate, *The Lord of the Rings* isn't racist *in se*—indeed, it *cannot* be racist in such a view, even though its readers very well might be. But then again, its readers might be otherwise and the exact opposite: *anti*-racist.

This last point leads to a final consideration: if Tolkien's presentation of the Orcs is deemed racist and is somehow determined to be directly connected to reprehensible behavior in the present moment, must the opposite case also hold true? Would, that is, traces of other, more inclusive visions in Tolkien's world lead also, automatically and necessarily, to virtuous behavior, to a positive ethics? If one direction of influence is operative (the negative), so also must the other be (the positive)—at least in theory, all things being equal. This is an intriguing point to consider because much in Tolkien's fictive world would seem to resist racist ideology. The ultimate heroes of *The Lord of the Rings* are, after all, the Hobbits, a group of people that *everyone*—even the most noble characters (Wizards, Elves, Ents, monarchs)—consistently underestimate, ignore, and (quite literally) look down upon.[69] If literature and ethics are conjoined, then shouldn't readers of *The Lord of*

---

67. See the similar and highly pertinent argument of R. W. L. Moberly, *The Theology of the Book of Genesis*, OTT (Cambridge: Cambridge University Press, 2009), 179–99, esp. 182–84, 195–99.

68. Stephen Fowl, "Texts Don't Have Ideologies," *BibInt* 3 (1995): 15–34; also Bo H. Lim and Daniel Castelo, *Hosea*, Two Horizons Commentary (Grand Rapids: Eerdmans, 2015), 232. But see Brennan W. Breed, *Nomadic Text: A Theory of Biblical Reception History* (Bloomington: Indiana University Press, 2014), on textual "potential."

69. See, inter alia, Rearick, "Why Is the Only Good Orc a Dead Orc?" 867, and, further, 872.

the Rings emerge on the other side of their reading thinking very differently about the "least of these"?[70] Rearick makes this point by paraphrasing 1 Sam 16:7, "Man [Elf, Dwarf, and Ent] looketh on the outward appearance, but the LORD looketh on the heart," before offering his final conclusion: "Nothing could be more contrary to the assumptions of racism than a Hobbit as a hero."[71] Or consider a more specific, non-Hobbit case—the reconciliation experienced between the Dwarf Gimli and the Elven queen Galadriel, each representing groups that were often at profound enmity in Middle-earth. Gimli, the narrator reports, "looked suddenly into the heart of an enemy and saw there love and understanding."[72] Shouldn't readers of *The Lord of the Rings* come away from this kind of scene with a new appreciation of the Other, even one who has traditionally been a sworn enemy? Then too is the compassion Frodo shows Sméagol/Gollum, who not only differs from Frodo and Sam in a number of ways,[73] but who is profoundly ill, troubled, and prone to treachery due to his twisted love of the One Ring—Middle-earth's equivalent, as it were, of a serious drug addict. Shouldn't readers of *The Lord of the Rings* come away from their reading with greater sympathy for the profound complexity of good and evil in someone—anyone, everyone!—who finds themselves chained to an addiction beyond their control? Indeed, even the Orcs (!), as despicable and contemptible as they are, are not to be treated poorly in cases of surrender. In one of his explanatory writings, Tolkien explicitly stated that while Orcs "must be fought with the utmost severity" as "fingers of the hand of Morgoth," they must also "not be dealt with in their own terms of cruelty and treachery. Captives must not be tormented, not even to discover information for the defence of the homes of Elves and Men. If any Orcs surrendered and asked for mercy, they must be granted it, even at a cost."[74] Or one might consider Frodo's instruction to kill no Hobbits even if they've gone over to "the other side," or Frodo's insistence on mercy for Saruman.[75] Shouldn't readers of passages like these think very differently about their enemies and the use of "cruel and unusual punishment"?

70. Cf. Rearick, "Why Is the Only Good Orc a Dead Orc?" 872: "A lesson that many of the individuals in *The Lord of the Rings* must learn is not to judge individuals by their outward appearances."

71. Rearick, "Why Is the Only Good Orc a Dead Orc?" 872.

72. Tolkien, *Lord of the Rings*, 356. Rearick sees in this exchange "the hope for a coexistence of races more than the dominance of one over the other" ("Why Is the Only Good Orc a Dead Orc?" 870).

73. In point of fact, Sméagol/Gollum was a Hobbit of the southern, Stoor variety, but the power of the One Ring "warped him beyond recognition" (Day, *Tolkien: A Dictionary*, 106). See Tolkien, *Lord of the Rings*, 1130 with n. 1, 1135.

74. Tolkien, *Morgoth's Ring*, 419; see further there with n. *.

75. See Tolkien, *Lord of the Rings*, 1006 and 1018–19, respectively; see also Rutledge, *The*

If negative outcomes are allowed for in the reading process—as well they should, since readers *definitely do* have ideologies—then the same should hold true for positive outcomes. At the very least, possible (though certainly not invariable) positive outcome scenarios show that negative outcome scenarios, while certainly possible, are (also) not unavoidable or invariable. One suspects, moreover, that the larger and more complex the literature is, the more difficult and complicated the hermeneutical processes become, with the range of potential outcomes (of whatever sort) correlatively increased.

* * *

EXCURSUS ON RACISM IN THE ANCIENT NEAR EAST

Since the ultimate comparand of this chapter is the Bible, not modern fantasy literature, the question might more properly be put as: Is the Bible racist? One entry into that question is another: the presence of racism in the broader ancient Near East. In a treatment of "The Subhuman Barbarian" in his edition of *The Curse of Agade*, Jerrold S. Cooper writes that "Mesopotamian sources of all periods are surprisingly free of racist ideology."[76] Given the date of Cooper's study, one may wonder if his definition is up to present standards in our own time of careful attention to "racist ideologies" (plural). To his credit, Cooper immediately explains his understanding:

> That is to say, different ethno-linguistic groups are rarely characterized as inherently inferior, subhuman, or deserving extermination or servitude, and this is true of groups within Mesopotamia proper as well as groups from neighboring lands. Enemies, to be sure, are reviled in the strongest terms, both as groups and as individuals, but the ruler of a neighboring Babylonian city can be showered with as much (or more) abuse as the ruler of a distant land. In Sumerian literary tradition, there *was* a feeling that sovereignty over Babylonia should rest in native hands, but the only expression of ethno-linguistic superiority in Sumerian literature is placed in the mouth of the ruler of Aratta, who is not a Sumerian.[77]

Battle for Middle-earth, 363–64 and 363n50 there. Cf. Sam's assessment of the Southron soldier (note 62 above).

76. See Jerrold S. Cooper, *The Curse of Agade*, JHNES (Baltimore: Johns Hopkins University Press, 1983), 30–33 (here 30).

77. Cooper, *Curse of Agade*, 30 (his emphasis).

As was the case with Rearick, Cooper's definition falls short of twenty-first century understandings of systemic racism; even so, in his considered judgment, there simply was no comparable thing in the ancient Near East. Cooper must admit, however, of two exceptions to the "non-racist" nature of the Mesopotamian world, the Gutians and the Amorites, both of whom were often subjected to serious literary abuse. Of these two, the former group gets the worst of it: "The Gutians are characterized as savage, beastlike imbeciles, whereas the Amorites are usually curious primitives, less horrible, if every bit as threatening militarily, than the Guti."[78] Some sampling of what the texts say about these groups follows:

- *The Gutians* are "not classed among people, not reckoned as part of the land"; they are "people who know no inhibitions, with human instinct but canine intelligence and monkey's features"; "apelike" in appearance, "monkeys who came down from their mountains," or "serpents of the mountains," or "dogs." They are "stupid people" (*nišē saklāti*), "with sheldrake bodies" and "raven faces," who were suckled by Tiamat. Despite this rather inhuman presentation, "they do turn out to be sorts of human beings after all, because they bleed when pricked."[79]
- *The Amorites* are described as largely ignorant of the basics of human civilization: shelter, agriculture, food, and proper burial customs. The Amorite knows "neither house nor city" and is a "fool who lives in the mountains," "with instincts like dogs or like wolves."[80] Cooper describes the presence of such traits in what he thinks could be "the earliest recorded ethnic joke":
    Pease flour is made up like a confection,
    The Amorite eats it, but doesn't recognize its ingredients![81]

Cooper believes that "these ethnic slurs on the Amorites and Guti are almost unique" in the ancient Near East—*almost*, because he proceeds to note the presence of similar sentiments made with reference to the Elamites, Subarians, and Su-people.[82] For example, the Elamites are as "overwhelming as lo[cust swarms]" and "not among the living," while the Su are as "numerous as grass, whose seed is wide-spread," but who are nomadic, irreverent, and base:

---

78. Cooper, *Curse of Agade*, 30.
79. See Cooper, *Curse of Agade*, 30–31, for all of these citations.
80. See Cooper, *Curse of Agade*, 31–32.
81. Cooper, *Curse of Agade*, 32 and 36n69.
82. Cooper, *Curse of Agade*, 32.

Who lives in a tent, and knows not the places of the gods,
Who mates just like an animal, and knows not how to make offerings
of (*eše*)-flour.[83]

Cooper's brief treatment could easily be rounded out by more recent work.[84] His treatment remains instructive, however, because it seems that what is said of the Canaanites in the Old Testament could constitute another exception to Cooper's general rule: perhaps they, too, ought to be considered alongside the Gutians and Amorites—at least in biblical perspective. And yet, insofar as the Canaanites are often seen as related to, or a subsection of the Amorites (cf., e.g., Gen 15:16, 21; Ezek 16:3, 45; Amos 2:9–10), perhaps their literary presentation in the Old Testament is not an exception at all but a further exemplification, outside the cuneiform corpus, of what Cooper has discerned therein. If so, the "Israelite presentation" (if it may be called that for the moment) would be an additional instance of a wider, decently attested bias against the Amorites.[85] That is cold comfort, on the one hand—the bias is *still there*, after all—but it does add further support to the suggestion that the presentation in the Old Testament may well be *ad litteram*, according to the letter, which is to say conventional, in the literary sense of that term.

83. Cooper, *Curse of Agade*, 33 and 36n72.

84. See, e.g., Mario Liverani, *Assyria: The Imperial Mission*, trans. Andrea Trameri and Jonathan Valk, MC 21 (Winona Lake, IN: Eisenbrauns, 2017), 55–65; T. M. Lemos, "Neither Mice nor Men: Dehumanization and Extermination in Mesopotamian Sources, Ḥērem Texts, and the War Scroll," in *With the Loyal You Show Yourself Loyal: Essays on Relationships in the Hebrew Bible in Honor of Saul M. Olyan*, ed. T. M. Lemos et al., Ancient Israel and Its Literature 42 (Atlanta: Society of Biblical Literature, 2021), 249–66; Lemos, "Dispossessing Nations: Population Growth, Scarcity, and Genocide in Ancient Israel and Twentieth-century Rwanda," in *Ritual Violence in the Hebrew Bible: New Perspectives*, ed. Saul M. Olyan (New York: Oxford University Press, 2015), 27–66; and, more generally, Kenton L. Sparks, *Ethnicity and Identity in Ancient Israel: Prolegomena to the Study of Ethnic Sentiments and Their Expression in the Hebrew Bible* (Winona Lake, IN: Eisenbrauns, 1998), esp. 23–93.

85. The Gutians do not appear in the Old Testament for reasons related to chronology (they were expelled from southern Babylonia ca. 2100 BCE) and geography (they lived far to the East, apparently originally coming from the central Zagros mountain range). See, briefly, Piotr Bienkowski, "Guti," in *Dictionary of the Ancient Near East*, ed. Piotr Bienkowski and Alan Millard (Philadelphia: University of Pennsylvania Press, 2000), 135; and Marc Van De Mieroop, *A History of the Ancient Near East, ca. 3000–323 BC*, 3rd ed. (Malden, MA: Wiley Blackwell, 2016), 76, 79. For problems in defining the Amorites, see Van De Mieroop, *A History of the Ancient Near East*, 111–12; and Daniel E. Fleming, "The Amorites," in *The World around the Old Testament: The People and Places of the Ancient Near East*, ed. Bill T. Arnold and Brent A. Strawn (Grand Rapids: Baker Academic, 2016), 1–30.

Further on this point: the textual data collected by Cooper show that the literary presentation of the Canaanites in the Old Testament fits rather hand-in-glove with the kinds of disapproved characteristics found elsewhere in the ancient Near East for the Gutians and the Amorites. So it is that the Canaanites, too, are presented as overwhelming, numerous and widespread, and irreverent (at least to Yahwistic tastes), if not also quite base in certain practices. Even so, the biblical presentation of the Canaanites, in comparative perspective, seems to stop well short of the slurs—"fighting words," as Melissa Mohr calls them[86]—found in the cuneiform texts. The Canaanites are never described as animals in the Bible, whether serpents or dogs or apes.[87] It is, rather, the Israelites who are compared to animals—insects, to be precise—when compared with the inhabitants of the land (Num 13:33). Neither are the Canaanites ever described as stupid; quite to the contrary, in fact, some inhabitants of the land prove to be quite shrewd (e.g., the Gibeonites), and, as a result, escape the fate of other groups discussed in Joshua. Neither are the people of Canaan invariably irreverent: Rahab is the most obvious counterexample at this point. In her case, her reverence of Yhwh leads to the survival of her and her family (Josh 2:8–14; 6:25). Finally, the Canaanites do not seem to be the brunt of any joke that has survived in the Bible. A text like Gen 19:30–38, which recounts incest between Lot and his daughters, is obviously unflattering, but it is unclear if it was meant to be humorous in any way. That specific account, regardless, refers to the origins of the Transjordanian groups of Ammon and Moab, not the Cisjordanian Canaanite peoples proper (though of course the groups and issues are closely intertwined).[88] Even if Gen 19:30–38 is meant to be disparaging, other texts speak differently, and more appreciatively, of Transjordanian groups: for example, Deuteronomy prohibits military engagement with the Edomites and Moabites because they are kin (Deut 2:2–13). The former group traces back to none other than Isaac and Rebekah, of course, through their son Esau (Gen 25:25, 30; 36:1–43), while the latter group (Gen 19 aside) will even-

---

86. Mohr, *Holy Sh*t: A Brief History of Swearing* (Oxford: Oxford University Press, 2013), 233–39.

87. See further Lemos, "Neither Mice nor Men." Interestingly enough, the Psalms frequently do animalize their enemies—though these latter are often *other Israelites*. See the insightful treatment in William P. Brown, *Seeing the Psalms: A Theology of Metaphor* (Louisville: Westminster John Knox, 2002), 135–66, who points out that not only are the enemies animalized, but such animalization may, in the end, be redeemed by the Psalter's theme of non-human praise (164–65).

88. Note, e.g., how Sihon, king of Heshbon, is repeatedly described as an Amorite (Num 21:21, 26, 29, 34; 32:33; Deut 1:4; 2:24; 3:2; 4:46; Josh 12:2; 13:10, 21). Deuteronomy 31:4 calls both Og and Sihon kings of the Amorites.

tually boast of Ruth, who becomes great grandmother to Israel's most famous king. Other groups—Cisjordanian or otherwise—are presented in varied ways, including the positive: Abram's allies include the Amorites Mamre, Eschol, and Aner (Gen 14:13), for instance, and only slightly later, Abraham purchases property from Ephron the Hittite (Gen 23:1–20). Other texts could easily be cited in this same vein[89] with the point being that none of these people groups is presented as univocally, consistently, or invariably *bad*.[90]

In the final analysis, then, the Old Testament's presentation(s) of the Canaanites at its worst may be less *sub*human, when compared to the ancient Near Eastern material, than it is *super*human. If the Canaanites are somehow *in*human, that is, it is not because they are inferior but because they are superior in some, if not several, ways: they are children of Anak, related to the Nephilim, the great heroes of old, giants such that the Israelites seem, at best, like grasshoppers in comparison. To be sure, the presentation is not meant as flattery—not all of it, at any rate. It seems, instead, designed to terrify if not also justify: to *terrify* Israel, which stands no chance against such odds and such peoples, and to *justify* the coming conflicts by offering an *apologia*—one that stretches all the way back to Gen 15:16—on why the removal of such frightening, superhuman peoples was both necessary and legitimate.

The additional detail that this military action is divinely authorized is far from *nonpareil* throughout the ancient Near East as K. Lawson Younger has shown.[91] The Mesha Stele famously speaks of the Moabite god Chemosh authorizing military action against Israel (line 14), and also employs the (in)famous verbal root √ḥrm (line 17), though that text does not present the Israelites in any hyperbolic way like one finds in the case of the Canaanites in the Old Testament. For many

---

89. See, inter alia, the more thorough treatments found in John R. Bartlett, *Edom and the Edomites*, JSOTSup 77 (Sheffield: Sheffield Academic, 1989); Diana V. Edelman, ed., *You Shall Not Abhor an Edomite for He Is Your Brother: Edom and Seir in History and Tradition*, ABS 3 (Atlanta: Scholars Press, 1995); and Erika J. Fitz, "A Significant Other: Moab as Symbol in Biblical Literature" (PhD diss., Emory University, 2012).

90. Cf. Van De Mieroop, *History of the Ancient Near East*, 112, who concludes that the sense of "several so-called 'ethnic' terms" found throughout ancient Near Eastern texts "depended on the context in which they were used. . . . We cannot see them as simple and clear-cut categorizations of people within Near Eastern societies. Their use was flexible and depended on circumstances we today can rarely recognize." The contrast to more recent instances of racism (e.g., anti-Semitism) could not be stronger. For a collection of truly horrifying racist and sexist remarks, see Eco, *Inventing the Enemy*, 1–21; note also Gould, *Mismeasure of Man*; and Delbanco, *Death of Satan*, esp. 155–83.

91. K. Lawson Younger Jr., *Ancient Conquest Accounts: A Study in Ancient Near Eastern and Biblical History Writing*, JSOTSup 98 (Sheffield: JSOT Press, 1990), esp. 258–60.

modern readers, the divinely authorized nature of the biblical action against the Canaanites makes it exponentially more problematic than what one finds in the Mesha Stela or other comparables, if only due to the otiose nature of the respective deities mentioned in the latter. In the ancient context, however, divine legitimation may have made the whole notion of conquest and settlement more palatable and more justifiable, in part by making it less immediately personal or vindictive. That is to say that what happened in Canaan is not Israel's *own vendetta*; rather, this is *God's doing* because of affronts made to God, on the one hand (e.g., Gen 15:16; Lev 18:25, 27), and because of promises made by God, on the other (e.g., Gen 12:7; 13:15, 17; 15:7, 18; 17:8; 26:3; 28:4, 13, 15; 35:12).[92] Both "hands" matter because God claims sole proprietary rights over this land and can thus distribute and redistribute it at will (Lev 25:23)—including to *non*-Israelites (see Deut 2:21–22; cf. Amos 9:7)![93] If the Canaanites learn the consequences of Yhwh's root of title in Joshua, the Israelites themselves learn the very same lesson only a bit later, in 2 Kings, twice (for north and south), and *definitively*.[94]

* * *

---

92. The nature of all this as God's prerogative constitutes what Ellen F. Davis has called (in a different context) "a severely limiting condition" (*Getting Involved with God: Rediscovering the Old Testament* [Cambridge, MA: Cowley, 2001], 27). Indeed, Millard Lind, *Yahweh Is a Warrior: The Theology of Warfare in Ancient Israel* (Scottsdale, PA: Herald, 1980), has argued that divine agency is the ultimate warrant for human pacifism. For further, more general reflections, see Brent A. Strawn, *Honest to God Preaching: Talking Sin, Suffering, and Violence*, Working Preacher Books 7 (Minneapolis: Fortress, 2021), 99–138; and Strawn, "Who's Afraid of the Old Testament? Tough Texts for Rough Times," in *The Oxford Handbook of the Bible in Orthodox Christianity*, ed. Eugen J. Pentiuc (Oxford: Oxford University Press, 2022), 539–55. Psalm 44:3[4] is particularly important in this regard: "For not by their [the ancestors'] own sword did they win the land, / nor did their own arm give them victory; / but your [God's] right hand, and your arm, / and the light of your countenance, / for you delighted in them."

93. See Miller, "God's Other Stories: On the Margins of Deuteronomic Theology"; and Brent A. Strawn, "What Is Cush Doing in Amos 9:7? The Poetics of Exodus in the Plural," *VT* 63 (2013): 99–123.

94. For an instructive analysis of the conquest in light of property law, see Geoffrey Parsons Miller, "Property," in *The Oxford Encyclopedia of the Bible and Law*, ed. Brent A. Strawn et al. (New York: Oxford University Press, 2015), 2:175–82, esp. 176–77. Note also William Ford, "The Challenge of the Canaanites," *TynBul* 68 (2017): 161–84, esp. 181–82 on how this kind of interchange ("Israelites can become Canaanites and Canaanites can become Israelites") demonstrates that "what matters in the end is not ethnicity, but one's attitude to YHWH."

Cowboys, Indians, and . . . Canaanites?

The similarities in literary presentation between the two people groups, Tolkien's Orcs and the Bible's Canaanites, suggests that the same concerns facing Middle-earth may also obtain for the Old Testament. If anything, these questions will likely be even yet more complex since, in the case of the Bible, we have not just one author (narrator) as in *The Lord of the Rings* but only God knows how many. Which of these mostly unknown and unquantifiable authors would be the one properly termed "racist"? All of the biblical authors, furthermore, belong to a people group that has been harshly mistreated, exactly and precisely for their ancestry, and for centuries, most horrifically of all in the Holocaust. In this light, and in light of what was said above, querying these authors' racism may be ill-put. Regardless of that, there is the other, closely related question—perhaps more easily answered, perhaps not—that concerns the possibly *racist effect* of the literature the biblical authors bequeathed to posterity.

A now famous essay by Robert Allen Warrior, first penned in 1989, addresses these issues more or less directly, with attention focused on the problem of the Canaanites.[95] Warrior—a Native American himself (Osage Nation)—takes issue with what he deems to be liberation theology's overdependence on the Exodus narrative. This dependence is "an enormous stumbling block," according to Warrior; in his judgment, "the story of the Exodus is an inappropriate way for Native Americans to think about liberation" (22). The reasons for Warrior's discomfort is that the Exodus narrative flows directly into the conquest narrative: one moves from the departure from Egypt into the taking of the land in Joshua. In this process, Warrior writes, "Yahweh the deliverer became Yahweh the conqueror" (22).[96] "The obvious characters in the story for Native Americans to identify with are the Canaanites," he avers (22). And so, he writes, "I read the Exodus stories with Canaanite eyes" (22).

95. Robert Allen Warrior, "Canaanites, Cowboys, and Indians: Deliverance, Conquest, and Liberation Theology Today," originally published in *Christianity and Crisis* 49/12 (Sept 11, 1989): 261–65, and reprinted many times since—e.g., in *The Postmodern Bible Reader*, ed. David Jobling, Tina Pippin, and Ronald Scheifer (Oxford: Blackwell, 2001), 189–94. Citations here follow the reader-friendly PDF that is easily available on the web at https://www.rmselca.org/sites/rmselca.org/files/media/canaanites_cowboys_and_indians.pdf. In the discussion that follows, page references will be given parenthetically in the text. For a brief summary and analysis of Warrior's essay, see Jobling, Pippin, and Scheifer, *The Postmodern Bible Reader*, 188–89; and George Aichele et al., *The Postmodern Bible* (New Haven: Yale University Press, 1995), 284–86.

96. The force of the verb "became" is unclear, but see note 97 below. Warrior later asserts that, "as long as people believe in the Yahweh of deliverance, the world will not be safe from Yahweh the conqueror" (Warrior, "Canaanites, Cowboys, and Indians," 26).

It is important to note that Warrior allows for the possibility, if not the likely fact, that "the actual events of Israel's history are much different than what was commanded in the narrative. The Canaanites were not systematically annihilated, nor were they completely driven from the land. In fact, they made up, to a large extent, the people of the new nation of Israel" (22). This would seem to soften the blow of the critique. But it doesn't, as Warrior goes on to argue:

> Scholarly agreement [on such matters, insofar as it exists] should not allow us to breathe a sigh of relief. For, historical knowledge does not change the status of the indigenous in the narrative and the theology that grows out of it. The research of Old Testament scholars, however much it provides an answer to the historical question—the contribution of the indigenous people of Canaan to the formation and emergence of Israel as a nation—does not resolve the narrative problem. People who read the narratives read them as they are, not as scholars and experts would like them to be read and interpreted. History is no longer with us. The narrative remains. (23)

There is much that could and should be unpacked in this citation, but, as Warrior continues on, it becomes more and more clear that he sees the main problem to be a *literary* not historical one: "The narrative remains," in his phrasing. And "the danger," he asserts, is that Christian communities "will read the narratives, not the history behind them" (25). The narrative is dangerous, problematic, racist. The history *behind* the narrative is safer in some fashion in Warrior's view, evidently because the history didn't *actually* happen or because the Israelites *were*, to some degree, Canaanites. And so, again, the problem is primarily a textual one: *within* the narrative itself. Warrior next states that "the text itself will never be altered by interpretations of it, though its reception may be" (25). The only way forward, therefore, for Warrior, is to place the Canaanites "at the center of Christian theological reflection and political action. They are the last remaining ignored voice in the text, except perhaps for the land itself" (25).

Herein lies the crux of the matter since, in Warrior's reading, "the narrative tells us that the Canaanites have status only as the people Yahweh removes from the land in order to bring the chosen people in" (24). Considering the Canaanites will thus help to prevent inattention toward the conquest stories "with all their violence and injustice," as well as the blindness "evident in theologies that use the Exodus motif as their basis for political action. The leading into the land becomes just one more redemptive moment rather than a violation of innocent peoples' rights to land and self-determination" (25). Once again, there is a great deal to unpack here; the last sentence in particular reveals that Warrior's analogy between the Canaanites and Native Americans is a profoundly generative one in terms of his overall argument and its various moves.[97] Furthermore, there can be no doubt that appeal to the conquest narratives of Joshua (less the exodus proper, contra Warrior) did indeed play a role in the rhetoric about the "New World" and subsequent conflicts between European settlers and the indigenous First Nations.[98] Such data would seem to speak directly to the question raised earlier about ethics caused by texts. In Warrior's words: "Those who act on the basis of these texts . . . must take responsibility for the terror and violence they can and have engendered" (25; see further 25–26). We may see, therefore—with Holy Scripture no less—far more clearly, even empirically, than with *The Lord of the Rings* that the Bible's literary presentation of the Canaanites really *can* and *has* engendered terror and violence, and precisely so for Native Americans.[99] But taking responsibility is not enough for Warrior, or rather, he ultimately charts a different way. He speaks repeatedly of the "god [the lower-case *g* is no doubt intentional] of the Old Testament" or "the god represented" in the text (25), and concludes his essay with the following: "We will perhaps do better to look elsewhere for our vision of justice, peace, and political sanity—a vision through which we escape not only our oppressors, but our oppression as well. Maybe, for once, we will just have to listen to ourselves, leaving the gods of this continent's real strangers to do battle among themselves" (26).[100]

In light of this ending, and Warrior's essay as a whole, it seems that not only is the literary presentation of the Canaanites capable of causing real trauma, it can

97. The connections are analogical and thus not always precise. For example, a number of laws regarding land and also regarding treaties (esp. treaties *about* land) would support—and *should* have supported—the claims of Native Americans against European settlers. The presentation of Canaan in the Bible is of a different sort, however, as shown by G. Miller, who details the several different ways the Bible undercuts the Canaanite claim to the land ("Property," 2:176–77). Once more: in biblical perspective, the land/earth (either being an appropriate translation of Hebrew *'ereṣ*) is claimed *by Yhwh*, which means that the root of title belongs to God, not to any Canaanite, not to any Israelite, and not to any other. In this way, Warrior's comment "Yahweh the deliverer *became* Yahweh the conqueror" ("Canaanites, Cowboys, and Indians," 22; emphasis added) is inaccurate on more than one level: prior to both, that is, is Yhwh the "maker of heaven and earth" (see, e.g., Pss 115:15; 121:2; 124:8; 134:3; 146:6; Isa 37:16; Rev 14:7), and thus owner of *kol hā'āreṣ*, "all the earth" (see, e.g., Exod 19:5; Lev 25:23).

98. See Hofreiter, *Making Sense of Old Testament Genocide*; see also, within the commentary genre, Carolyn J. Sharp, *Joshua*, SHBC (Macon, GA: Smyth & Helwys, 2019).

99. One wonders if this oppressive situation might also (or instead) have led, as it sometimes did in the case of enslaved African peoples, to Native Americans' identification with the Israelites (not the Canaanites), maltreated and oppressed by a tyrannical Pharaoh (read here: European settlers). If so, Warrior's unequivocal decision of which characters are most or only to be identified with in the reading process becomes somewhat less obvious.

100. Note also (on the same page): "With what voice will we, the Canaanites of the world, say, 'Let my people go, and leave my people alone?'"

apparently also lead directly to a rejection of Christian faith altogether. At this point, thanks to the "Orcish" presentation of the Canaanites in the Old Testament, all seems lost . . .

5. The Canaanites Aren't (Basically) Orcs After All

. . . until . . . well, until *it isn't*. As powerful as Warrior's essay is, it can be challenged, and challenged precisely on the grounds on which he himself depends and from which he argues—namely, that of the text itself, the narrative that "remains." Reconstructed history *may* save the Old Testament's morality for some people or to some degree, but not for long, since even if the Iron Age Israelites (whoever they were) *didn't* destroy all the Canaanites, several of the texts seem to wistfully hope that they *had* insofar as several of the texts seem to mandate as much. The various qualifications in the preceding sentence are crucial, and shouldn't be missed: *several* texts (certainly not all) *seem to* mandate (but may not). In what follows, I leave aside the latter qualifier—in the best-case scenario, "seem(s) to" may be a trace of academic humility; in the worst, it is often a scholarly hedge or anticipatory parrying of one's critics. Whatever the case, "seem(s) to" raises the real problems and potentials of interpretative practice, and it is not my intention to delve deep into the weeds of the *ḥērem* texts, or the socio-historical origins of the Israelites, and so on, especially when that work has been done capably by others in venues with more space and greater expertise than I have at hand. It must suffice to say that I concur with those who have argued that *even* the dreaded *ḥērem* texts may not be what they seem. So, in what follows, I focus on the first qualification—namely, the bit that "several" of the texts seem to mandate such-and-such.

The first point to make here, quite simply but oh-so-crucially, is that "the text" itself is not of a piece; "the narrative" that causes Warrior consternation is highly variegated. I do not mean that remark exclusively in a composition-critical sort of way (*viz.*, that the texts are composites of originally discrete traditions, texts, etc., however that is imagined), though that, too, is entirely likely and not unimportant. Instead, I simply mean to say that the judgment that the Bible's literary presentation of the Canaanites is comparable to Tolkien's Orcs holds true only for *some of the texts* and only for *some of the time*. Alongside these there are *other texts*, at *other times*, that tell a *very different* story (or, rather, stories—plural), and that include accounts of Canaanites who end up setting exemplary models for the faithful of Israel.[101] This latter type of presentation—*equally* textual, *equally* a part of the narrative that remains—is quite *unlike* Tolkien's Orcs, who could

---

101. Cf. Creach, *Violence in Scripture*, 122–23, on how positive stories about the Canaanites

never boast of the same. In this way and at precisely these points, the Canaanites (some of them, at any rate) are downright *non-Orcish*, perhaps even *anti-Orcish*. At these points and in this way, "the narrative" parts company with Warrior's interpretation thereof.[102]

Let's begin slowly and build out from there. First, while it is true that the predominant literary presentation of the Canaanites appears far from positive, we should be wary of overestimating texts that discuss Canaanite "wickedness" especially in excessive ways. There are not nearly as many of these texts as one might suspect,[103] and even those that exist often appear to serve other purposes. So, for example, Deut 9:4–5 states that it is "because of the wickedness of these nations that the LORD is dispossessing them before you," but this remark is little more than an aside within a larger rhetorical context wherein the major emphasis is on the wickedness, not of the Canaanites, but of the *Israelites* (see Deut 9:6–24).[104]

Second, on the matter of the conquest and settlement of the land, the Bible's "narrative" once again offers more than one perspective. Judges 1, which speaks of unconquered areas in Canaan, comes as something of a surprise to many readers after the impression left by the book of Joshua (see also Judg 3:1–6). But that impression from Joshua is a somewhat careless one. In point of fact, Joshua himself, at the end of his life, is informed—by God no less—that a great deal of land remains to be taken (see Josh 13:1–7; cf. 23:5, 7, 12–13). Or then there is the curious caveat found in Deut 7:22, which indicates that God "will clear away these nations before you little by little; you will not be able to make a quick end of them, otherwise the wild animals would become too numerous for you," which sounds like nothing so much as a hedging of one's bets, especially after what appears to be an unremitting (and unmerciful) injunction in Deut 7:1–5. What should one do with these "minority opinions" on the conquest? Ought the texts that strike us now as more "down-to-earth" or closer to "how things actually happened" be favored in some way,[105] with the other, more dominant (and idealized?) texts

---

"mitigate ideas about Israel's exclusive virtue." Ford, "Challenge of the Canaanites," 182, adds Uriah the Hittite as a later, similar example.

102. Jobling, Pippin, and Schleifer, *Postmodern Bible Reader*, 189, rightly identify Warrior's essay as a "revisionist biblical reading."

103. Cf. Nicholas Wolterstorff, "Comments on 'What about the Canaanites?'" in Bergmann, Murray, and Rea, *Divine Evil?* 283–88, esp. 286.

104. See Norbert Lohfink, "Reading Deuteronomy 5 as Narrative," in *A God So Near: Essays on Old Testament Theology in Honor of Patrick D. Miller*, ed. Brent A. Strawn and Nancy R. Bowen (Winona Lake, IN: Eisenbrauns, 2003), 261–82; also Brent A. Strawn, "Slaves and Rebels: Inscription, Identity, and Time in the Rhetoric of Deuteronomy" (chapter 4 of the present work).

105. Nicholas Wolterstorff, "Reading Joshua," in Bergmann, Murray, and Rea, *Divine Evil?*, 236–56 (here 253–54).

discounted altogether?[106] Or are the former some kind of clue that the latter are somehow symbolic, allegorical, or hagiographic,[107] with all that that might mean for subsequent interpretation?[108]

Third, but continuing in this same vein, some scholars have looked at Joshua and have noted that, upon closer inspection, all of its campaigns after Ai are presented as *defensive reactions*, not aggressive engagements.[109] The narrative thus presents the Canaanites as well-organized and well-supplied *aggressors* who *initiate* military action *against* Israel.[110] Still further, the narrative presents the source of their aggression as an unwillingness to hear and heed what God has done (both failed actions adequately conveyed by the weighty Deuteronom[ist]ic verb √*šmʿ*). This scenario does not portray the inhabitants of the land as "morally decadent," as some might put it,[111] so much as "increasingly resistant to the action of Yahweh."[112] Indeed, what Lawson Stone has called "the ethical and apologetic tendencies" in the final redaction of the book of Joshua shift "the level of the material perceptibly and significantly," such that the stories of the Canaanites "become object lessons in responsiveness to Yahweh's action and warnings against

106. Jobling, Pippin, and Schleifer, *Postmodern Bible Reader*, 189, believe Warrior's essay shows "how privileged readings of texts obscure the totality of multiple experiences," but fail to observe how Warrior's own essay appears guilty of the same charge.

107. For these options see, inter alia, Wolterstorff, "Reading Joshua," 252–53; Wolterstorff, "Reply to Antony," in Bergmann, Murray, and Rea, *Divine Evil?*, 263–64 (here 264); Wolterstorff, "Comments," 287; and Creach, *Violence in Scripture*, 99, 105. Once again, see Stone, "Ethical and Apologetic Tendencies," to which add Douglas S. Earl, *Reading Joshua as Christian Scripture*, JTISup 2 (Winona Lake, IN: Eisenbrauns, 2010).

108. Cf. the intriguing comment by Eco, *Inventing the Enemy*, 17–18: "It seems we cannot manage without an enemy. The figure of the enemy cannot be abolished from the process of civilization. The need is second nature even to a mild man of peace. In his case the image of the enemy is shifted from a human object to a natural or social force that in some way threatens us and has to be defeated, whether it be capitalistic exploitation, environmental pollution, or third-world hunger. But though these are 'virtuous' cases, even hatred of injustice, as Brecht reminds us, 'makes the brow grow stern.'" See also the stunning essay by Corrine Carvalho, "The Beauty of the Bloody God: The Divine Warrior in Prophetic Literature," in *The Aesthetics of Violence in the Prophets*, ed. Julia M. O'Brien and Chris Franke, LHBOTS 517 (New York: T&T Clark, 2010), 131–52.

109. See Chapman, "Martial Memory, Peaceable Vision," 49; Stone, "Ethical and Apologetic Tendencies," 33; Creach, *Violence in Scripture*, 99, 117.

110. Stone, "Ethical and Apologetic Tendencies," 33. This is quite different from Warrior's presentation that what Israel does constitutes "a violation of innocent peoples' rights to land and self-determination." Warrior's remark is exactly right with reference to the sordid history of the United States of America but is inaccurate with reference to the Old Testament.

111. For an example from older scholarship, see Ulf Oldenburg, *The Conflict between El and Ba'al in Canaanite Religion* (Leiden: Brill, 1969).

112. Stone, "Ethical and Apologetic Tendencies," 34.

resistance."[113] If so, the final form of Joshua shifts the "semantic level" of the conquest account in a profound way. These stories are no longer merely, solely, or primarily *military* accounts (whether real or imagined); they are now "primarily a theological paradigm."[114] The "conquest" of the land of Canaan becomes, in this way, an extended metaphor for the life of faith.[115] More recently, Jean-Louis Ska has made the same point:

> According to the text, Joshua is more like a rabbi or a doctor of the law than a great conqueror, a *conquistador*. The true ideal of Israel is a scholar and a scrupulous observer of the law. In fact, Joshua's conquests and great achievements are due not to his military genius and administrative talents but rather his fidelity to the law of Moses. In more modern terms, Joshua will be decorated not with a military medal but rather with a medal of the Order of the Torah.... It is quite clear ... that the story of the conquest has been reread in the shadow of the Torah.[116]

Fourth, there are notable exceptions to the conquest and its "ban"—most famously Rahab in Josh 2 and the Gibeonites in Josh 9. These stories demonstrate that, in point of fact, mercy actually *can* be shown even on those to whom no mercy was to be shown, and covenantal agreements can be made with those with whom there were to be no covenants.[117] Ford goes so far as to say that, since "these are the only two examples of Canaanites who seek to side with Israel in the book of Joshua ... we can say that in the conquest, *any* Canaanite who seeks to side with Israel and YHWH is accepted."[118] These accounts further highlight the fact

---

113. Stone, "Ethical and Apologetic Tendencies," who lifts up Josh 2:9–11; 5:1; 8:30–35; 9:1–4; 10:1–5; 11:1–5.

114. Stone, "Ethical and Apologetic Tendencies," 35.

115. Cf. Creach, *Violence in Scripture*, 105, 108; also Anderson, "What about the Canaanites," 272: "a means of focusing the mind on the horrors of turning aside from the worship of the one true God."

116. Jean-Louis Ska, *A Basic Guide to the Old Testament* (New York: Paulist, 2019), 49–50; cf., similarly, Stone, "Ethical and Apologetic Tendencies," 36.

117. I am fully aware that it is possible to look quite skeptically at these texts, especially the so-called "conversion" of Rahab as an instance of imperial fantasy or colonial collaboration. While I admit I do not find such readings ultimately satisfying, the main point is that skeptical readings are unlikely to be of much help to Warrior, who speaks repeatedly of the straightforward meaning of the narrative.

118. Ford, "Challenge of the Canaanites," 181, see further there and 182. Cf. Stone, "Ethical and Apologetic Tendencies," 33: "The text comes close to suggesting that war would not have been necessary had the Canaanite response been more cooperative."

that even the archetypal "non-Israelite" Canaanites can, at least on occasion, serve as models of faithful and shrewd behavior, even to Israel.[119]

Perhaps even to Jesus Christ according to some New Testament scholars. In Matt 15, Jesus retreats to the district of Tyre and Sidon (15:21), where "a Canaanite woman" (*gynē chananaia*) meets him, shouting for mercy (*eleēson me*) because of her demon-tormented daughter. She addresses Jesus as both "Lord" and "Son of David" (15:22). Jesus meets her shouting with silence until the disciples implore him to send her away, "for she keeps shouting after us" (15:23). Jesus then answers (the woman or the disciples? the text isn't clear) with the statement that he was "sent only to the lost sheep of the house of Israel" (15:24).[120] At this point the woman kneels (*prosekynei*)[121] before Jesus and begs once more with a simple, "Lord, help me" (15:25). Jesus, however, appears unmoved, and proceeds to compare helping this woman to the unfair (or bad: *ouk . . . kalon*) situation of taking food meant for children (i.e., Israel) and throwing it to dogs (i.e., Canaanites) instead (15:26). "Yes, Lord," she replies, "yet even the dogs eat the crumbs that fall from their masters' table" (15:27). At that point, Jesus commends the woman's great faith (*megalē . . . hē pistis*). "Let it be done for you as you wish," he says, and instantly her daughter is healed (15:28).

The description of this woman as "Canaanite" is quite significant, especially given the parallel in Mark 7:26, which calls her *hellēnis, syrophoinikissa tō genei*, "a Gentile, of the Syrophoenician race" (NASB). Equally noteworthy is her thrice-repeated address of Jesus as *kyrie*, "Lord." This is not yet to mention her tenacious perseverance in the face of not one but two rebuffs, which according to some scholars reflect a racist mentality of superiority, whether on the part of Jesus or his disciples or both (and/or the Evangelists). It is, of course, hard to know the precise tone of Jesus's remarks—tone is rarely self-evident in literature but must be deduced and argued for; interpreted, that is[122]—but what is clear, in the end, is that the resolve of a Canaanite who begs for relief for *her tortured child* is ultimately

---

119. Creach, *Violence in Scripture*, 118–24; on shrewdness, see the parable in Luke 16:1–9. By way of comparison, it would be impossible to imagine the same sort of scenario in Middle-earth: a morally upright Orc who joined the Fellowship of the Ring, for example. Cf. Rutledge, *Battle for Middle-earth*, 150.

120. Joel Willitts, *Matthew's Messianic Shepherd-King: In Search of 'the Lost Sheep of the House of Israel'*, BZNW 147 (Berlin: de Gruyter, 2007), has argued that this phrase refers to remnants of the Northern Tribes and is somewhat archaizing; it may not, therefore, be a sign of some sort of ethnic prejudice. (I owe this reference to Nicholas J. Moore.)

121. It is perhaps intriguing to note that "Canaan" derives from the root √*knʿ* which has to do with "being low" or "humbled" (BDB 488–89; *HALOT* 2:484–86).

122. See, e.g., David Marno, "Tone," in *The Princeton Encyclopedia of Poetry and Poetics*, ed. Roland Greene et al., 4th ed. (Princeton: Princeton University Press, 2012), 1441–42.

met with acquiescence, and, even more, with an enthusiastic commendation of her faith by the one she calls "Lord." Here too, then, is another Canaanite exemplar of faith—perhaps the ultimate one—and here, if nowhere else in the Bible, is definitive proof that the Lord sanctions exemptions to "anti-Canaanite-ism."

In the end, I judge Warrior to be exactly right when he states that "the research of Old Testament scholars," as that is glossed in historical modes regarding the facticity of the conquest accounts, "does not resolve the narrative problem." It is, instead, the *narrative* that resolves the narrative problem. Warrior himself does not recognize this for whatever reason, and his conclusion "the narrative remains," which is apparently a dread assessment in his view, can be taken, not as some sort of disappointing death-knell for the unconscionable parochialism (or worse) of Scripture, but cause for celebration because the *variegated, non-monolithic* narrative not only remains, it also *continues.* Warrior is also quite correct that "historical knowledge does not change the status of the indigenous in the narrative and the theology that grows out of it."[123] It is, instead, *the variegated, non-monolithic, and ongoing narrative itself* that does that, even if that change is as slow as it is inexorable.[124] That same narrative change problematizes any monolithic summary of "the" status of the indigenous Canaanites (according to which account and where?), and soundly refutes Warrior's reduction of that status to only one: "the people Yahweh removes from the land."[125]

I want to underscore that these counterpoints are not a matter of special pleading or grasping after straws—not, at least vis-à-vis Warrior's essay—because Warrior himself makes ultimate appeal to the *narrative*, not to its historical background, source-critical complexity, or interpretive reception, any of which could also problematize his conclusions. That being said, I am under no false pretense that what I've said here would convince Warrior or others who think similarly. Finally, it is important to observe that it is possible—indeed, necessary—to recognize and decry the unjust treatment of Native Americans in the United States quite apart from how the hermeneutical matters surrounding Joshua are decided. Part of the point is that those two things can (and likely should) be teased apart.

123. Warrior, "Canaanites, Cowboys, and Indians," 23.

124. The status change is also in some ways self-wrought in the case of Rahab, the Gibeonites, and the Canaanite woman in Matt 15. I am, again, aware of interpretations that would see "the narrative" otherwise, but the success of such interpretations (if and when they are deemed successful) often depends on reading "against the grain" of the text itself (see note 102 above). Such readings are always possible, but remain contrarian, and, regardless of that, are hardly necessary, not the only sort of reading available. Part of the point of the present chapter is, of course, to recommend an alternative to that type of reading.

125. Warrior, "Canaanites, Cowboys, and Indians," 24.

To repeat: the Canaanites are basically Orcs until they aren't, which is to say when the narrative says otherwise. And so it is that the Canaanites aren't basically Orcs *after all*—with "after all" meaning we have to read the *entire* "narrative."[126] We also have to read it closely and read it well. That means, in part (per Moberly), reading in terms of its literary presentation, the "dramatic tenor of the text," "attend[ing] properly to its (hardly obscure) conventions" and appreciating and following "the nature of [its] drama." What I have attempted to show is that the Old Testament's predominant literary presentation of the Canaanites (or at least its most memorable one, if only because it is so off-putting)—or, perhaps better, the Bible's "hardly obscure conventions" about the prior inhabitants of the land—is something quite akin to Tolkien's presentation of the Orcs. The effect, in both instances, suggests that these groups are frighteningly larger than life, maybe even (and precisely because of that) more symbolic than real. In this way, these literary presentations could easily be seen as instances of "demonization." If so, there is more than one way to respond. One way is to see in such presentations *much more* than merely banal, post hoc ways to legitimize the subsequent defeat and displacement of antagonistic individuals or groups that pose problems in the plot; instead, the presentations confront us with *super-* and/or *supra-*human antagonists.[127] It is essential, regardless, to recognize that these types of literary presentations only work as long as the reader "plays along"—that is, as long as the reader is able and/or willing to submit and succumb to the rhetoric, even if only for the duration of the reading.[128] If and when "we are so enchanted" (to use

126. The scare quotation marks are necessary because at this point the discourse concerns Scripture as a whole, which is not, in my opinion, best (or only) described as a narrative. See, provisionally, Brent A. Strawn, "Lyric Poetry," in *Dictionary of the Old Testament: Wisdom, Poetry and Writings*, ed. Tremper Longman III and Peter Enns (Downers Grove, IL: IVP Academic, 2008), 437–46; and Strawn, *The Old Testament: A Concise Introduction* (London: Routledge, 2019), esp. 168–71.

127. One might counter that the Old Testament is intended as realistic narrative, but this is only partly true, especially in contemporary reception. There simply are no Girgashites (etc.), which suggests their figural interpretation, at least now, at which point we may be poised to enter what Karl Barth called "the strange new world within the Bible." Cf. John Cassian's (360–432 CE) (re)interpretation of the "seven nations mightier and more numerous than you" (Deut 7:1) as the innumerable vices that outnumber the virtues (*Conference* 5.16.1–2; Joseph T. Lienhard, ed., *Exodus, Leviticus, Numbers, Deuteronomy*, ACCS 3 [Downers Grove, IL: InterVarsity, 2001], 286).

128. For more on such dynamics, see Brent A. Strawn, "Keep/Observe/Do—Carefully—Today! The Rhetoric of Repetition in Deuteronomy" (chapter 3 of the present volume). Note Erich Auerbach, *Mimesis: The Representation of Reality in Western Literature*, trans. Willard R. Trask (Princeton: Princeton University Press, 2013), 15: "The Scripture stories do not, like Homer's, court our favor, they do not flatter us that they may please us . . . —they seek to subject us, and if we refuse to be subjected we are rebels."

Tolkien's terms),[129] we may well find ourselves agreeing with Rearick in asserting that the only good Orc is a dead Orc in the same way that the only good demon is an exorcised demon.[130] Of course, the variegated, non-monolithic narrative that continues knows and shows that the Canaanites are *not*, in fact, demons but people, some of whom are good, some of whom are bad—just like God's elect people, Israel—and so are people who suffer or enjoy the same benefits or punishments that also face Israel. Small wonder, then, that they still live in Israel, even in Jerusalem, "to this day" (see Josh 13:13; 15:63; 16:10; 17:12; Judg 1:21).[131]

Even if the above understanding of this kind of literary presentation is accurate—and it may be challenged, not least given the existence of contrariwise literary presentations—I candidly admit that it does not solve every problem. Real dangers remain which must not be trivialized (see above, esp. §4). Moreover, and this is directly to the point at hand, there seem to be plenty of *un*sympathetic readers, who *refuse* to succumb to the "demonized" portrait of the Canaanites (less so in the case of Tolkien's Orcs). Whenever that happens, it may constitute proof that the literary devices in the Old Testament, if not also in Tolkien's Middle-earth,[132] have failed to prove successful, though such a situation might just as well indicate that these readers have not been sufficiently attuned to the literary effects or sufficiently sympathetic in their reading—once again in marked contrast to how some of these same readers likely consume violent entertainment media nowadays. But another possibility exists—namely, that the very best of these "unsympathetic" readings are not against the grain of the text due to some sort of a priori modern sensibility about violence (whether duplicitous or genuine), or due to a failure to attend to literary convention, but *exactly because of their careful attentiveness to the full range of the text in all its subtleties*: the exceptions, for instance, represented by Rahab and the Gibeonites, or the texture offered by Josh 13:1–7; Judg 1:1; 3:1–6, and so on and so forth. In this best case scenario, readers are aware that the Canaanites are, yes, sometimes presented *exactly like* Orcs, *but also* know that

---

129. Tolkien, "On Fairy-Stories," 113; see also and esp. 132 and 139 ("Many people dislike being 'arrested' by their reading"). The entire essay repays close attention and careful consideration.

130. Rearick, "Why Is the Only Good Orc a Dead Orc?" 871. Rutledge, *Battle for Middle-earth*, 24, compares the Orcs to Legion in Mark 5:9. Despite the material cited in note 14 above, Tolkien is clear that the Orcs "were not of demon kind, but children of earth corrupted by Morgoth" (*Morgoth's Ring*, 109).

131. It is far from clear that these Canaanites who continued in the land (even into the New Testament!) are seen as converts, in contrast to Warrior's confident assertion that such people "were worthy of annihilation" if they refused to "be converted" ("Canaanites, Cowboys, and Indians," 25).

132. See the critical review of Edmund Wilson, "Oo, Those Awful Orcs!" *The Nation* 182 (April 14, 1956): 15. Wilson is unimpressed with Tolkien's narrative, its heroes and its foes.

sometimes they are *precisely unlike* Orcs because these readers are aware of the dramatic tenor of the text, the entire warp and woof of Scripture.[133] The grandest sweep of Scripture knows that anti-Canaanite violence is constrained to a particular period of Israel's history, that it may be viewed as a divine concession in the face of the vagaries of (violent) human history, that it is about religious matters as much as it is about anything else, and—ultimately—that it is not the final goal or endgame of Scripture or its Lord.[134]

This means, to cite Umberto Eco, that the issue of morality "intervenes" in this matter, as in analogous ones, "not when we pretend we have no enemies but when we try to understand them, to put ourselves in their situation. . . . Trying to understand other people means destroying the stereotype without denying or ignoring their otherness."[135] This is easier said than done, of course, as Eco goes on to note: "Let us be realistic. These [kinder] ways of understanding the enemy are the prerogative of poets, saints, or traitors. Our innermost impulses are of quite another kind."[136] I think Eco is exactly right: our deepest and ungenerous impulses are, indeed, "of quite another kind." And yet, in its both like-and-unlike-Orcish unfolding, Scripture charts a middle way—not pretending "we have no enemies," but slowly and certainly "destroying the stereotype." Perhaps this is why the presentation in Deuteronomy is one way, seemingly more consistently strident, with the presentation in Joshua and Judges reflecting another, ever more differentiated way.[137] Perhaps it is also why, much later, texts in the Pauline corpus traffic in a then–now dynamic which points out (to use the terms at hand here) the formerly "Orcish" nature of St. Paul's audience which has, now, been transformed (see, e.g., Rom 6:16, 19; 1 Cor 6:11; Eph 2:1–3; 4:22–25, 31; Col 3:5, 8).[138]

---

133. This suggests, I think, that the readers and their readings need not—indeed should not and cannot—overly identify with one interest to the complete exclusion of other readers and their readings, ending up in what begins to look like a zero-sum game of power (cf. Aichele et al., *Postmodern Bible*, 286).

134. See Strawn, "Canaan and Canaanites," esp. 1:110; and, further, Chapman, "Martial Memory, Peaceable Vision," which to my mind is the most compelling treatment of the issues.

135. Eco, *Inventing the Enemy*, 18.

136. Eco, *Inventing the Enemy*, 18.

137. Cf. further Ford, "Challenge of the Canaanites," 161–84, esp. 177, who notes distinctions between the literary presentation of the Canaanites as a whole vs. as individuals. Ford demonstrates (in contrast to, e.g., Sharp, *Joshua*, 19) that the presentation of individual Canaanites in both the Pentateuch and Joshua can be positive.

138. As Nicholas J. Moore has noted (personal communication), heresiologists sometimes admitted (or let slip) that the other group in question—the "them"—was part of "us." I thank Moore for this insight and for pointing me to Daniel Boyarin, *Border Lines: The Partition of Judaeo-Christianity* (Philadelphia: University of Pennsylvania Press, 2004); and Alain Le Boul-

6. On Getting to the Right Conclusions, or: What Remains of the Old Testament after Critique?

Hermann Gunkel's famous book *What Remains of the Old Testament and Other Essays* appeared in 1928.[139] Its intriguing title is based on the first essay in the volume, which put the statement as a question,[140] but the answer Gunkel offered was disappointing: not much. After critical scholarship carved this or that bit of traditional belief out, earmarking it for the trash heap, there just wasn't much left—except for traces of what appear to be romantic and idealistic influences on Gunkel: powerful poetry, prophecy, and so forth. But, despite the no-doubt-well-meaning surgical procedure, Doctor Gunkel's prognosis of what survived of his patient seems unduly dire. The Old Testament has somehow retained its chunkier, non-cut-away-by-criticism form, and so Gunkel's skeletal "not much" now seems passé. We live, after all, on this side of theologians like Karl Barth and the great generation of confessing biblical scholars who endured the Second World War. We also live on this side of the rise of literary criticism, on the one hand, and Brevard Childs with his attention to canonical form and function, on the other, not to mention, most recently of all, the "theological interpretation of Scripture" movement. All of the above makes Gunkel and his survival-by-critical-attrition approach—as genius as both he and that was, back then—look thin; it is a relic of an earlier, and, when considered now, backward time.

But one may still wonder if the question Gunkel pressed needs to be mounted once more, albeit updated and upgraded for present circumstances. In these latter days, the Old Testament has again been subject to surgical removals of various sorts, particularly in light of various ethical and ideological interventions. These, no less than the critical approaches at work in Gunkel's time, are not without considerable merit and many mean well—*very well*. They are certainly not all wrong

---

luec, *La notion d'hérésie dans la littérature grecque, IIe-IIIe siècles*, 2 vols. (Paris: Etudes augustiniennes, 1985). An instructive New Testament example may be "insider" Pharisees like Nicodemus (John 3:1) or Gamaliel (Acts 5:34–39; cf. 22:3). Worth pondering, too, is John 8:31–59, a particularly sharp exchange between Jesus and "the Jews *who had believed in him*" (v. 31; emphasis added).

139. Hermann Gunkel, *What Remains of the Old Testament and Other Essays*, trans. A. K. Dallas (New York: Macmillan, 1928).

140. "What Is Left of the Old Testament?" The German original appeared as Hermann Gunkel, "Was haben wir am Alten Testament?" *Deutsche Rundschau* 161 (1914): 215–41, then as *Was bleibt vom Alten Testament?* (Göttingen: Vandenhoeck und Ruprecht, 1916). Note the modified translation by K. C. Hanson in Hermann Gunkel, *Water for a Thirsty Land: Israelite Literature and Religion*, ed. K. C. Hanson, Fortress Classics in Biblical Studies (Minneapolis: Fortress, 2001), 1–30, where the essay appears as "Why Engage the Old Testament?" Citations that follow are from Hanson's edition.

and many make a great deal of sense, especially to us here and now, in our present hermeneutical context, which is itself highly differentiated, though it shares at least some commonalities as part of the twenty-first-century technologized world. Our critical engagement, no less than Gunkel's, that is, has significant value and disciplinary coherence. It is usually carefully reasoned and articulate; it is, again, most certainly not all wrong.

But what remains of the Old Testament after we are done? After Gunkel and all his generation were done, precious little was left—at least for them. What, then, for us, and our present moment now? In my judgment, Gunkel's approach fails most profoundly because so much is conceded, given or cut away, on the basis of the so-called assured results of critical scholarship. After all that, the Old Testament doesn't remain—not in a full robust form, at any rate, but only in part, in pieces: only bits remain, "not much." Might the same hold true for us and so many of our own approaches? Time will tell.

To repeat: a great deal of what Gunkel and others did heretofore and what we do now makes good sense and may even be quite right. But if that "doing" (in whatever form it takes) leaves the Old Testament decimated—a shadow of its full self—it simply won't do. That kind of doing will only accelerate the demise of the Old Testament and of the various faiths (plural) that depend on it. Obsolescence may be the goal of a particular type of interpreter, but it obviously cannot be the long game for those who have real investment in the Old Testament as Holy Scripture and in its descendent faith communities. The Old Testament must somehow survive even our most withering critiques. I believe, in point of fact, it will—or rather that it *does* (Ps 119:96)—but my opinion needn't be viewed as wishful, fideistic thinking. I am fully aware of, and profoundly concerned about, the mortality of the Old Testament.[141] I don't mean to suggest, therefore, that critiques of whatever sort don't touch the Old Testament, don't leave a mark, don't do some sort of damage (sometimes considerable). Our critiques do *all* of these things if not still more, but for those invested in Scripture as Scripture, such criticism can only be a preliminary step. Something *further*, something *else*, something *more* must be said. The truly hard work must begin *after critique*. It may be, as it now stands with Gunkel, that one hundred years hence new developments will have taken place that will make our own critical approaches look thin, passé. But it may also be the case that we have work to do to ensure the survival of the Old Testament *despite* any and all legitimate concerns and worries. There *are* ways

---

141. See Brent A. Strawn, *The Old Testament Is Dying: A Diagnosis and Recommended Treatment*, Explorations of the Church Catholic (Grand Rapids: Baker Academic, 2017).

to balance or contain difficult texts, redress and reinterpret troublesome matters. Some of those come *ab extra*, from outside the text, at least to some degree, at least with reference to the specific troublesome passage at hand. But they needn't be entirely extra-textual, a kind of *deus ex machina*. Instead, as I have tried to argue here, it may be that the best strategies begin, if not also sometimes end, with the text itself and with how we read it, whether well or not. There is a way to critique Scripture and still call it Scripture.

So . . . are the Canaanites of the Old Testament equivalent to Tolkien's Orcs? Yes and no. To borrow from a few other texts that are not about Canaanites—at least not on the face of it (!)—perhaps we might say that, yes, for a moment (*rega'*) the Canaanites were like Orcs (cf. Isa 54:7–8). God hid the divine visage from them because they were wrongdoers unable to inherit the kingdom of God. But with everlasting love, God will yet have compassion; the old ways were what used to be, prior to washing, prior to sanctifying, prior to justification (cf. 1 Cor 6:11). Things are different now. That, at least, seems to be the testimony of Rahab according to Josh 2, Matt 1, Heb 11, and Jas 2; and the testimony of an unnamed Canaanite woman still roaming the countryside in Jesus's day according to Matt 15.

I end with a final fascinating bit of information from Tolkien: there is a hint that even the despicable Orcs of Middle-earth might ultimately be redeemed within the largest vision of the supreme deity Eru (*Ilúvatar*).[142] If so, that would be an-

---

142. See Tolkien, *Morgoth's Ring*, 409, where he wonders if the Orcs "were ultimately re-mediable, or could be amended and 'saved'?"; 411, where it is pondered if Melkor could ever fully or "wholly corrupt any work of Eru"; and esp. 419: "They [the Orcs] might have become irredeemable (*at least by Elves and Men*), but they *remained within the Law*" (emphases added). What this "Law" is isn't specified, but it is presumably the divine law of Eru Ilúvatar (see Jennifer G. Hargroves, "Law," in *J. R. R. Tolkien Encyclopedia: Scholarship and Critical Assessment*, ed. Michael D. C. Drout [New York: Routledge, 2007], 347–48). Whatever the case, as Shippey notes, "If evil could not create, [and] was only good perverted, then presumably the orcs had been by nature good and might in some way be saved" (*Road to Middle-earth*, 207; cf. Rearick, "Why Is the Only Good Orc a Dead Orc?" 871). In a letter to W. H. Auden, Tolkien wrote that he intended his story "to be consonant with Christian thought and belief, which is asserted somewhere, Book Five, page 190, where Frodo asserts that orcs are not evil in origin. We believe that, I suppose, of all human kinds and sorts and breeds, though some appear, both as individuals and groups to be, by us at any rate, unredeemable" (Carpenter, *Letters*, 355; see also Hammond and Scull, *Lord of the Rings*, 605). In the letter draft to Peter Hastings quoted earlier, Tolkien states that "by [God's] accepting or tolerating their making—necessary to their actual existence—even Orcs would become part of the World, which is God's and ultimately good" (Carpenter, *Letters*, 195; see also note 22 above).

other way that Tolkien's Orcs and the Old Testament's Canaanites might be compared—this time in the best, most beatific of ways. It is, perhaps, a small step from that vision, to even grander views: Christian theological discussions of demonic conversion (*apocatastasis*), for instance, even the very salvation of Satan.[143]

143. See, e.g., C. A. Patrides, "The Salvation of Satan," *Journal of the History of Ideas* 28 (1967): 467–78; Sergius Bulgakov, *Apocatastasis and Transfiguration*, trans. and ed. Boris Jakim (New Haven: The Variable Press, 1995); and Ambrose Andreano, "The True Fate of 'the so-called Devil' in Origen," https://www.academia.edu/44789518/The_True_Fate_of_The_So_Called_Devil_in_Origen. Frodo's mercy toward Saruman (Sharkey) at the very end of the novel is instructive: "I do not wish him slain in this evil mood. He was great once, of a noble kind that we should not dare to raise our hands against. He is fallen, and his cure is beyond us; but I would still spare him, in the hope that he may find it" (Tolkien, *Lord of the Rings*, 1019).

12

Docetism, Käsemann, and Christology: Can Historical Criticism Help Christological Orthodoxy (and Other Theology) After All?

IN MEMORIAM ERNST KÄSEMANN

[Primitive Christianity] agreed only in one judgment: namely that the life history of Jesus was constitutive for faith, because the earthly and the exalted Lord are identical.[1]

The function of recalling the historical Jesus is thus, within the framework of the Gospel, a permanent necessity.[2]

My thanks go to several colleagues who read and commented on earlier drafts of this chapter, none of whom should be held responsible for its contents: B. T. Arnold, L. Ayres, B. R. Gaventa, J. B. Green, S. J. Kraftchick, J. K. Mead, R. A. Reese, and J. L. Walls. I would also like to thank A. K. M. Adam for graciously offering constructive and critical remarks on an earlier version and for encouraging me. I hope Adam's comments elsewhere apply to my own essay—namely, that it "suggest[s] both an increase in the degree to which our positions converge and an increase in the nuance of our disagreements. . . . [Such a situation] signals noteworthy progress toward a discourse in which arguments actually contribute to clarity" (A. K. M. Adam, "Toward a Resolution Yet to Be Revealed," in *Reading Scripture with the Church: Toward a Hermeneutic of Theological Interpretation*, ed. A. K. M. Adam, Stephen E. Fowl, Kevin J. Vanhoozer, and Francis Watson [Grand Rapids: Baker Academic, 2006], 143–48 [143]).

1. Ernst Käsemann, "The Problem of the Historical Jesus," in *Essays on New Testament Themes*, trans. W. J. Montague (Philadelphia: Fortress, 1964), 33–34. This essay was originally presented in 1953 and first published in *ZTK* 51 (1954): 125–53.

2. Ernst Käsemann, "Blind Alleys in the 'Jesus of History' Controversy," in Käsemann, *New Testament Questions of Today*, trans. W. J. Montague (Philadelphia: Fortress, 1969), 64.

1. On Thinking Theology and History

The role of history—along with its correlate: the study of history, most particularly historical criticism—in theology (and vice versa, the role of theology in history) has been a vexed question for some time now.[3] Do history and theology go together? The prior question, of course, is: *can* they go together at all? Even more pointedly, can they go *together*? Or is it the case that one must always go first with the other following? And which would (or should) do which?

In a recent attempt to "think theology and history together," Murray A. Rae has again demonstrated that this problem is rather longstanding.[4] The nondescript "for some time now" in the first sentence above is, in Rae's view, a time span of at least four hundred years. He traces the refusal to think theology and history together back to Descartes (1596–1650), who "revived the ancient belief of the philosophers that the realms of history and of eternal truth were mutually exclusive."[5] As that statement reveals, and as Rae proceeds to expound, the rift between theology (or, in alternative vernacular: "ideas, wisdom, timeless truths," and so forth) and history has a pedigree at least two-and-a-half millennia long.[6]

In latter days, the genetics of this theology-history divide has produced scholarly offspring who have largely inherited only one of the two chromosomal possibilities. Scholars have thus tended to fall (mostly) into one of two camps: on one side are those who emphasize theology; on the other, are the historian types.[7] Practically speaking, each camp has been mistrustful of the other, not fully understanding the "genetic makeup" of its sibling. And, as with any good sibling rivalry, self-definition has often come at the expense of the other. Rae states: "The divorce between historical and theological study has taken two forms. The first

---

3. E.g., N. T. Wright has claimed that the compartmentalization of history and theology belongs to the worldview that has dominated the West for two hundred years but that is now under attack and suffering collapse (*The New Testament and the People of God*, Christian Origins and the Question of God 1 [Minneapolis: Fortress, 1992], 24).

4. Murray A. Rae, *History and Hermeneutics* (London: T&T Clark, 2005).

5. Rae, *History and Hermeneutics*, 1. Rae subsequently recounts the development from Descartes through Spinoza, Reimarus, Lessing, Kant, Hegel, Marx, Strauss, von Ranke, and Troeltsch (Rae, *History and Hermeneutics*, 6–17).

6. See Rae, *History and Hermeneutics*, 5–6, on the rootedness of the problem in "the metaphysics of classical Greek philosophy," especially Plato.

7. Among the scholars discussed by Rae, it would seem that he categorizes the camps as follows: theology types include Kähler, Bultmann, Barth, and Frei (see Rae, *History and Hermeneutics*, 22–30, 39–44); the historians include Käsemann, Cullmann, Pannenberg, and N. T. Wright (Rae, *History and Hermeneutics*, 30–39). Of course, this typology should not be too rigidly understood.

seeks to protect theology from the alleged vagaries of history, while the second seeks to protect history from the allegedly ephemeral and speculative claims of theology."[8]

Among other things, such "protection" has sometimes taken a more aggressive, offense-minded approach, with scholars from one camp openly disparaging those from the other, or at least disparaging the other's approach. As but one example of historians "protecting" themselves and their approach from theologians, one could note how easily the Jesus Seminar dismisses theology, in part by speaking approvingly of Thomas Jefferson, who wanted "to separate the real teachings of Jesus, the figure of history, from the encrustations of Christian doctrine."[9] Encrustations, of whatever sort, are rarely considered commendable!

The pendulum has swung back and forth on which sibling—history or theology—has been dominant in the history of biblical interpretation. For the last several centuries, of course, biblical criticism has mostly sided with the history camp. But in recent days, the theological interpretation of Scripture has experienced something of a Renaissance, even in academic publication. One might note at least three commentary series devoted especially to theological interpretation,[10] an encyclopedic dictionary on the topic,[11] and even the journal in which this chapter originally appeared as proof of the point.[12]

Something of an example of both the resurgence of theological interpretation and the propensity of one side to dismiss the other (perhaps too hastily)—in this case, theology protecting itself against history—may be found in the work of A. K. M. Adam. Adam has rightfully taken his place as a leading voice advocating for the theological interpretation of Scripture.[13] Among other things, he has

---

8. Rae, *History and Hermeneutics*, 4.

9. Robert W. Funk, Roy W. Hoover, and the Jesus Seminar, *The Five Gospels: The Search for the Authentic Words of Jesus* (San Francisco: HarperSanFrancisco, 1993), 2–3. In fact, this book is dedicated (along with Galileo Galilei and David Friedrich Strauss) to Thomas Jefferson, "*who took scissors and paste to the gospels*" (v; emphasis original).

10. The Two Horizons Old Testament Commentary, ed. J. Gordon McConville and Craig Bartholomew (Grand Rapids: Eerdmans, 2008–); The Two Horizons New Testament Commentary, ed. Joel B. Green and Max Turner (Grand Rapids: Eerdmans, 2005–); and Brazos Theological Commentary on the Bible, ed. R. R. Reno et al. (Grand Rapids: Brazos, 2005–).

11. Kevin J. Vanhoozer et al., ed., *Dictionary for Theological Interpretation of the Bible* (Grand Rapids: Baker Academic, 2005).

12. *Journal of Theological Interpretation* (*JTI*). Note that *JTI*'s editor includes the role of history and historical criticism in theological interpretation among the important and difficult questions that the journal is intended to address (see Joel B. Green, "The (Re-)Turn to Theology," *JTI* 1 [2007]: 3).

13. See, e.g., the collected essays in A. K. M. Adam, *Faithful Interpretation: Reading the Bible*

leveled a number of significant critiques against the hegemony of the historical-critical method. While Adam is quite prolific and his agenda multi-faceted, his critique of historical criticism and his advocacy of theological interpretation come together nicely in an article on Ernst Käsemann that was recently republished in a volume of his collected essays.[14]

In the present chapter, I propose to use Adam's essay on Käsemann as a case study to think further about the role of history in the theological interpretation of Scripture. In so doing, I will not only examine Adam's argument, but also Käsemann's own work—especially on the genre of the Gospels and on the theological importance of the historical Jesus—to analyze the history-theology rift (as Adam's article might seem to have it) or the theology-history nexus (as Rae's work would seem to have it). In particular, I will argue here that, while Adam has made a number of excellent points about historical criticism generally, his critique falls wide of Käsemann himself. Said differently, Adam's critique may be on target, but the target isn't quite Käsemann. In fact, a closer look at Käsemann, especially Käsemann-in-historical-context (!), reveals that the Old Marburger is still useful as a model to think theology and history together, not least because he continues to hold these two together (albeit in a somewhat messy way). If these points are correct, then it may well follow that Adam, despite the cogency of much of his argument, (inadvertently?) falls overmuch into Rae's first camp (all theology or "ideas") without sufficient clarity (albeit a somewhat messy one) regarding the role of history in theological interpretation. And yet, at this very juncture, it may be that Adam is not far removed from Käsemann himself, since the latter is, in the final analysis, *thoroughly* theological—not just due to his engagement with the likes of Rudolf Bultmann and Karl Barth but also, and more fundamentally, with Martin Luther.[15]

The first task is to lay out Adam's critique of Käsemann's historicism.

---

in a Postmodern World (Minneapolis: Fortress, 2006), as well as his original foray: *Making Sense of New Testament Theology: "Modern" Problems and Prospects*, StABH 11 (Macon, GA: Mercer University Press, 1995).

14. A. K. M. Adam, "Docetism, Käsemann, and Christology: Why Historical Criticism Can't Protect Christological Orthodoxy," *SJT* 49 (1996): 391–410; reprinted in slightly altered fashion in *Faithful Interpretation*, 37–56 (all citations are to the *SJT* version). Cf. also *Making Sense*, esp. 164–65.

15. On Luther: "No old Marburger will forget how passionately Luther was studied in the early days" (Ernst Käsemann, "Vom theologischen Recht historisch-kritischer Exegese," *ZTK* 64 [1967]: 259–81 [273]; cited in Roy A. Harrisville and Walter Sundberg, *The Bible in Modern Culture: Baruch Spinoza to Brevard Childs*, 2nd ed. [Grand Rapids: Eerdmans, 2002], 270). For Barth's influence, see R. P. Martin, "Käsemann, Ernst (1906–1998)," in *Dictionary of Major Biblical Interpreters*, ed. Donald K. McKim (Downers Grove, IL: IVP Academic, 2007), 602; and Rae, *History and Hermeneutics*, 30.

2. Historical Criticism, Docetism, and Käsemann—
Or Was That Bultmann?

Adam's primary purpose, to put it rather over simply, is to argue against Käsemann's claim that history in general, and the historical-critical method in particular, can be a "prophylaxis" against docetism. The main statement with which Adam takes issue is the following: "The legitimacy of historical criticism lies theologically in its breaking through the docetism which dominates the community."[16] To counter this claim, Adam first shows that the term "docetism" as employed by patristic heresiologists is rather slippery. The appellation does not seem to denote a specific group or faction, but is applied rather to a wide range of peoples who are *not* united by a particular heretical Christology. Moreover, even when the heresy described seems to correspond to contemporary understandings of docetism, one often looks in vain for the actual term *dokeō*.[17] How, then, Adam asks, can historical criticism protect against something that historical criticism itself cannot define or identify precisely?[18] Still further, historical criticism must (presumably) be "objective," and objective to such an extent that it cannot suppress or ignore, say, the persuasiveness of heresies like "docetism," nor their sometimes positive effects.[19] Since historical critics are not permitted to play favorites, "historical criticism is constitutively ill-suited for a role as *defensor fidei*."[20] Thus, "in the end . . . historical interpretation lacks the distinctive capacity to detect and root out docetism which alone could warrant enshrining historical exegesis as the primary criterion of the church's interpretation of Scripture. Classical docetism does indeed pose a threat to theologically sound readings, but we avoid these dangers

---

16. "Das Recht der historischen Kritik liegt theologisch darin, daß sie durch den die Gemeinde beherrschenden Doketismus hindurchbricht" (Käsemann, "Vom theologischen Recht," 281). Käsemann continues: "That is not its concrete task or intention, which consists in uncovering historical reality. But that is its effect . . . it frees for a sight of the cross" (cited in Harrisville and Sundberg, *The Bible in Modern Culture*, 258).

17. See Adam, "Docetism," 392–95. Adam refers to the *Oxford Dictionary of the Christian Church*, ed. F. L. Cross and E. A. Livingstone, 2nd ed. (Oxford: Oxford University Press, 1983), 413 (= 3rd ed.; 1997, 493), which states that docetism was "a tendency, rather than a formulated and unified doctrine." Cf. also B. Studer, "Docetism," in *Encyclopedia of the Early Church*, ed. A. Di Berardino (New York: Oxford University Press, 1992), 1:244: "We are not dealing with a definite sect."

18. This is not as compelling as it might at first appear. One can imagine protections against things like the common cold, cancer, or terrorism, even though these are not always precisely understood or defined, at least by those who experience (or fear) them.

19. Adam, "Docetism," 397.

20. Adam, "Docetism," 397.

by Chalcedonian interpretation, not by a historical rigor that is constrained in principle to examine only Christ's humanity."[21]

Adam proceeds next to demonstrate that Käsemann's own use of the terms "docetism" and "docetic" is just as slippery as that of the ancients. Furthermore, most of the problems for which Käsemann employed the term do not seem to correspond exactly to Christological error *per se*. Rather, they are more (or less!) generally or loosely related issues: for example, a vague notion of anti-historicism or anti-intellectualism—an avoidance, that is, of critical thinking. Analogically or metaphorically, these may approximate docetic tendencies insofar as they may lead to "a doctrine of Scripture which apparently denies full humanity to the production of the Bible."[22] But, even so, most of Käsemann's usages do *not* correspond to a *dogmengeschichtliche* definition of docetism, which, as Adam has already demonstrated, is rather confused anyway. Adam concludes that what Käsemann was arguing for, then, is not historical criticism proper, but *Käsemann's own particular type* of interpretive process and result.[23] Armed with these data, Adam goes on to argue that there is no *essential* or *necessary* reason that historical criticism protects against docetism. Indeed, "exclusive attention to the *actual* Jesus, accessible to historical investigation, runs a grave risk of nurturing Ebionism."[24] At this point, then, historical criticism can actually be a hindrance, not a help to theological investigation, and just as susceptible to theological heresy as a protection against it.

There can be little doubt that there is much to commend in Adam's article.[25] Indeed, perhaps the first thing that might be said is that his critique of Käsemann does not go far enough. Käsemann's work suffers from a number of weaknesses, especially from our present vantage point, and several of these are closely related to Adam's main concern. A primary example of such a "weak spot" would be Käsemann's argument on the uniqueness of the Gospel genre. However, in examining this issue below (§3), it will be seen that the main point in Käsemann's argument was not generic *per se*, but *theological*. To be more precise, Käsemann's main point

---

21. Adam, "Docetism," 399.

22. Adam, "Docetism," 400.

23. Adam, "Docetism," 404.

24. Adam, *Making Sense*, 165. Note, however, that (ironically) Ebionism, too, is rather ill-defined historically.

25. I hope it will be clear that, in the main, I agree with Adam's trenchant critique of historical criticism *when elevated as sole interpretive option*, esp. in ecclesial contexts. I am in full agreement, for instance, with Adam, "Docetism," 410: "Historical criticism cannot justify claims that it is the *only sound theological* approach to biblical interpretation, or the *necessary first step* for Christological reflection" (emphasis added). Despite this agreement, there remain crucial points of Adam's argument with which I disagree, as will become clear below.

has to do with the relationship of history to theology, or, at least, the importance of "history" (vaguely defined at this juncture) to theology. Moreover, Käsemann's argument was not primarily or simply about literature, but constituted part of his disagreement with his teacher, Rudolf Bultmann. This same situation obtains for Käsemann's discussion of docetism where his argument with Bultmann over the historical Jesus was also at work, at least in the background (see §4). This, along with other considerations, demonstrates that Adam's argument, as serious and compelling as it may be, is not yet definitive and is, in fact, somewhat off the mark, at least when it comes to Käsemann understood in (dare one say it?) *historical* context, which is to say *Bultmannian* context. That context reveals a New Testament scholar who is a historian-theologian—or, better: a theologian-historian—who is not, contrary to Adam's presentation, primarily after the exaltation or "enshrining" of historical criticism proper, least of all as "the primary criterion of the church's interpretation of Scripture," but who is instead *using the category of history in a thoroughgoingly theological way*. To return to Rae's terms, Käsemann is doing nothing less than thinking theology and history together. But these individual points must be set forth more fully before this larger conclusion can be reached.

3. Käsemann on the Genre of the Gospels, Or: Contra Bultmann, Part I

At several key junctures in his argument with Bultmann on the importance of the historical Jesus, Käsemann cites the genre of the Gospels as evidence for his position. He characteristically calls this genre "unique."[26] Scholarship of the past few decades, however, has cast considerable doubt on such a statement.[27] Certainly

---

26. E.g., Käsemann, "Blind Alleys," 62: "This tradition was embodied in the form of Gospels—here we have something which remains unique." Cf. also his comments in Käsemann, "Blind Alleys," 40, 41, 49, 56–57, etc. The uniqueness of Christian literature was a common position in earlier biblical scholarship. See, e.g., Franz Overbeck, *Über dei Anfänge der patristischen Literatur* (Darmstadt: Wissenschaftliche Buchgesellschaft, 1954), 36.

27. The literature on this question is immense. See, among others, David E. Aune, *The New Testament in its Literary Environment* (Philadelphia: Westminster, 1987), esp. 17–76; J. Arthur Baird, *A Comparative Analysis of the Gospel Genre: The Synoptic Mode and Its Uniqueness* (Lewiston, NY: Mellen, 1991); Richard Burridge, *What Are the Gospels? A Comparison with Greco-Roman Biography*, 2nd ed. (Grand Rapids: Eerdmans, 2004); L. W. Hurtado, "Gospel (Genre)," in *Dictionary of Jesus and the Gospels*, ed. J. B. Green, S. McKnight, and I. H. Marshall (Downers Grove, IL: InterVarsity, 1992), 276–82; P. L. Shuler, *A Genre for the Gospels* (Philadelphia: Fortress, 1982); Charles Talbert, *What Is a Gospel? The Genre of the Canonical Gospels* (Philadelphia: Fortress, 1977); Michael E. Vines, *The Problem of Markan Genre: The Gospel of Mark and the Jewish Novel* (Atlanta: Society of Biblical Literature, 2002); C. W. Votaw, *The Gospels and Contemporary Biog-*

the particular constellation that is a canonical Gospel *is* unique, but then again, so is *every* literary work, including each of the four Gospels respectively.[28] In that respect the claim for uniqueness doesn't go very far. Furthermore, despite some generic *dis*similarities, there is much in common between the canonical Gospels and the non-canonical Gospel material, whether that be apocryphal, Gnostic, or otherwise. Still further, the narrative quality of the Gospels makes it possible to speak of them as a sub-genre of narrative in general, a macro-genre that is hardly unique or parochial.[29]

In this light, scholars have attempted to explain the origin and development of the (canonical) Gospel genre in antiquity. In an overview article, Willem S. Vorster has highlighted two main approaches: the evolutionary model and ana-logical explanations.[30] The former discusses the Gospel as the result of a process of collection of various forms or legends, virtually all of which typically have some sort of antique parallel. It is not surprising to find that, on this basis, form critics (of which Käsemann was one) could claim uniqueness for the composite that is a Gospel, despite widespread attestation of the individual forms that make up said Gospel. The second explanation, on the other hand, views genre as the total orga-nization of a work and has thus posited various analogues for the Gospels (again, primarily narrative) in the history of literature. Among possible candidates are classical Greek biographies and memoir literature (e.g., Xenophon's *Memorabilia*, Arrian's *Epictetus*, and so forth); Hellenistic aretalogies, tragedies, or discourses; Semitic apocalypses; and Rabbinic *midrashim*—to name a few. Many scholars today maintain that the most likely choice is Greco-Roman/Hellenistic biogra-phy, specifically the *encomium* or "laudatory biography," the purpose of which is "to praise a person by accentuating his life, works, and teachings."[31] In sum then,

---

raphies in the Greco-Roman World (Philadelphia: Fortress, 1970); Lawrence M. Wills, *The Quest of the Historical Gospel: Mark, John, and the Origins of the Gospel Genre* (New York: Routledge, 1997); Adela Yarbro Collins, *Is Mark's Gospel a Life of Jesus? The Question of Genre* (Milwaukee: Marquette University Press, 1990).

28. See, e.g., Willem S. Vorster, "Gospel Genre," *ABD* 2:1077, on the "uniqueness" of Mark. So also Bart D. Ehrman, *The New Testament: A Historical Introduction to the Early Christian Writings*, 2nd ed. (New York: Oxford University Press, 2000), 58.

29. Vorster, "Gospel Genre," 1078.

30. See Vorster, "Gospel Genre," 1077–79.

31. Vorster, "Gospel Genre," 1079. Examples of the genre can be found in Polybius, Cicero, Lucian, and others. Scholars who subscribe to the Hellenistic biography comparison include Burridge, *What Are the Gospels?*; Talbert, *What Is a Gospel?*; Aune, *New Testament in Its Literary Environment*, esp. 63–67; Luke Timothy Johnson, *The Writings of the New Testament: An Interpre-tation*, rev. ed. (Minneapolis: Fortress, 1999), 157; and Ehrman, *New Testament*, 55–59. Raymond E. Brown, after noting both similarities and differences between the Gospels and Greco-Roman

contemporary scholarship has shown, in the main, that the Gospels are *not*, in fact, unique in light of the commonalities shared between them and extra-biblical parallels, especially—and above all—given the Gospels' narrative superstructure. In this light, Käsemann's argument for the "uniqueness" of the Gospel genre seems to crumble and lose its force.

To a large extent this is true. Of course, one must admit that at least some members of the jury are still out on the Gospel-biography comparison, and that indecisive situation may last for some time, if not indefinitely.[32] And it must also be granted that Käsemann himself would likely have disagreed most vehemently with the biography comparison, especially with such a bold (if not cavalier) statement as "they [the Gospels] are nothing less than biographies."[33] But Käsemann's argument must be put in context. His ultimate purpose is not so much to assert the uniqueness of the Gospels in the history of literature or genre for some sort of literary, generic, or "supernatural" purpose, so much as to make a point *against Bultmann*. That point, quite simply, is that the canonical Gospels, in their combination of kerygma with narrative, refuse to separate the earthly Jesus from the risen Lord.[34] Stated in this way, Käsemann's point stands quite unrelated to the

---

biographies, cut the genre-knot as follows: "It is likely that many 1st-century hearers/readers familiar with Greco-Roman biographies would not have been so precise [on dissimilarities with the Gospels] and would have thought of the Gospels almost as lives of Christ, particularly Matthew and Luke which begin with an infancy narrative" (*An Introduction to the New Testament*, ABRL [New York: Doubleday, 1997], 103).

32. I.e., while Mark, for example, may be similar to Hellenistic "biography"; Luke-Acts may be more akin to Hellenistic "historiography." In any event, consider the comments by Helmut Koester, *Introduction to the New Testament* (Philadelphia: Fortress, 1982), 2:169, who states that the "genre of Hellenistic biography provides [only] a partial precedent." Similarly, Hurtado, "Gospel (Genre)," 282.

33. Vorster, "Gospel Genre," 1079. On the other hand, if the argument is to be weighted toward one side or the other, Käsemann would appreciate a lean toward the biography idea. After all, in his view, "the form of the Gospels . . . [is] essentially *not* preaching but reporting" ("Blind Alleys," 49; emphasis his).

34. Of course, there is more to it than just this, but this is the crux of Käsemann's argument. If Bultmann is right, on the other hand, the Gospels remain "in the last resort an incomprehensible and superfluous sport in the natural history of the kerygma, which is, however, itself threatened with diminished status if no theological justification can be found for the wide range of mutations which occur within it" (Käsemann, "Blind Alleys," 57). Käsemann is not alone in his assessment of the Gospel as combining kerygma and narrative, "earthly/historical Jesus" and "risen Lord/Christ of faith," or even that such a combination is "unique." See, among others, Brevard S. Childs, *The New Testament as Canon: An Introduction* (Valley Forge, PA: Trinity Press International, 1994), 65–67, 85–86; Johnson, *Writings of the New Testament*, 158; Koester, *Introduction to the New Testament*, 2:169; Udo Schnelle, *The History and Theology of the New Testament Writings* (Minneapolis: Fortress, 1998), 153–61; Edward Schillebeeckx, *Jesus: An Experiment in Christology* (New York: Seabury, 1979), 76; Eduard Schweizer, *A Theological Introduction to the*

uniqueness of the Gospel *qua* literary genre in the history of literature. Hence, a criticism of Käsemann on the uniqueness of the Gospel-genre issue, while accurate from literary and historical perspectives, falls wide of the mark when *his theological commitment* is considered. Indeed, Käsemann himself indicated that he was well aware of the tenuous nature of claims to uniqueness.[35] Instead, what matters is the theological point: that the resurrected Christ is, through the medium of the Gospels, inextricably connected with the historical Jesus of Nazareth.[36] The latter, then, is essential and irreplaceable when speaking of the former.

4. Käsemann on Christology and Docetism, Or: Contra Bultmann, Part II

I would argue that the same situation—the primacy of the theological datum over all others, including the historical—obtains for Käsemann's discussion of docetism and historical criticism, and this significantly undercuts the force of Adam's contra-Käsemann argument if it doesn't in fact obviate it altogether. In Adam's attempt to counter historical-critical hegemony, that is, he has perhaps missed or underestimated Käsemann's (more) profound theological convictions. Even so, Adam's argument still has much to commend it. Indeed, despite the fact that there seems to be more to "historical docetism" than Adam would allow—that is, the jury is still out here, too[37]—and despite some admissions on his

---

New Testament (Nashville: Abingdon, 1991), 128; and Georg Strecker, *History of New Testament Literature* (Harrisburg: Trinity Press International, 1997), 97–100, who actually cites Bultmann on the point (97n27)!

35. See esp. Käsemann, "Blind Alleys," where he acknowledges that uniqueness is difficult to establish since it is always possible that someone might find something that would disprove uniqueness. For other "uncertainties" of which Käsemann was well aware, see further below.

36. Note Käsemann's unpublished manuscript entitled *Theologie des Neuen Testaments*, 102: "The exalted Lord creates continuity with the historical Jesus"; and 107: "We have known Jesus in the exalted Lord" (both cited in Harrisville and Sundberg, *The Bible in Modern Culture*, 253n18).

37. Note, e.g., that Ignatius uses *dokein* to speak of persons with docetic-like Christological errors (e.g., Ignatius, *To the Trallians* 10.1 [2×]; see also *Trallians* 9.1, where Ignatius states that Jesus Christ was "truly" [*alēthōs*] born; both ate and drank; was "truly" persecuted; and was "truly" crucified and died). In this light, the observation that Ignatius does not use the label "docetic" does not strike one as particularly significant (cf. Adam, "Docetism," 396). The evidence from Irenaeus is also quite impressive. As Studer points out ("Docetism," 244), the Valentinians, at least, can be considered docetists (for a nice example, see Bentley Layton, *The Gnostic Scriptures*, ABRL [New York: Doubleday, 1995], 238–39), and, if so, their doctrine can be compared to that found elsewhere, for example, that combated by Tertullian (esp. "On the Resurrection of the Flesh," in A. Cleaveland Coxe, *Latin Christianity: Its Founder, Tertullian*, ANF 3 [Grand Rapids: Eerdmans, 1993], 545–95). Thus, while the labels and terms may be somewhat fluid or imprecise, the cumulative evidence would seem to be indicative, in the main, of what have become

part that would seem to grant Käsemann's side of the debate,[38] Adam's argument against an unrivaled hegemony of historical criticism is exceedingly well made and well taken. However, with respect to Käsemann proper, it seems that, while Adam has the right package, he has sent it to the wrong address. The argument is misplaced—at least partially.

There can be no doubt, of course, that Käsemann's work *is* thoroughly historical-critical.[39] Writing when he did, how could it be otherwise? It must also be admitted that Käsemann *did* argue quite strongly regarding the importance of the historical enterprise in theological reflection. To this extent his work bears directly on the question of the relationship of history and theology;[40] hence, to a degree in some areas, he is subject to Adam's critique. However, Käsemann's position can be understood only in the light of the specific situation in which it arose and to which it was a response. The brunt of Käsemann's anti-docetic argument is leveled at (again) Bultmann.[41] To be sure, it is also aimed in the other

---

"stereo-typical" definitions of docetism in the scholarly literature. One should also note here the discussion of docetism in Johannine scholarship and the literature cited there. See esp. Georg Strecker, *The Johannine Letters: A Commentary on 1, 2, and 3 John*, Hermeneia (Minneapolis: Fortress, 1996), 69–76, cf. 222–26; and Rudolf Schnackenburg, *The Gospel according to St. John* (New York: Crossroad, 1982), 1:21–23. Note on this point that Polycarp's discussion of the antichrist denying Christ's flesh (*To the Philippians* 7.1) cites 1 John 4:2–3 and 2 John 7. The number of New Testament scholars who agree that docetism is a problem, already in the New Testament period, is large. In addition to the literature already cited, see, e.g., Oscar Cullmann, *The Christology of the New Testament*, rev. ed. (Philadelphia: Westminster, 1963), 324; Udo Schnelle, *Antidocetic Christology in the Gospel of John: An Investigation of the Place of the Fourth Gospel in the Johannine School* (Minneapolis: Fortress, 1992); and Strecker, *History of New Testament Literature*, 167–68.

38. See below, esp. note 60.

39. Cf., e.g., Käsemann's passing comments about historical criticism in *Jesus Means Freedom* (Philadelphia: Fortress, 1974), 55, 81 (but note also his *theological* [N.B.!] positivism on 154). Adam, *Making Sense*, 165n47, cites another example from Käsemann's "The Problem of a New Testament Theology," *NTS* 19 (1973): 242: "A New Testament theology is therefore of necessity a historical discipline." It is hard to tell how much history actually plays into Käsemann's nonmethodological work, esp. with Paul. Even so, Käsemann's *The Testament of Jesus: A Study of the Gospel of John in the Light of Chapter 17* (Philadelphia: Fortress, 1978), passim, is a rather thorough example of his use of and reliance upon history.

40. A full assessment obviously lies outside the scope of this chapter. See, however, the important book-length treatments in the following: Bernhard Ehler, *Die Herrschaft des Gekreuzigten: Ernst Käsemanns Frage nach der Mitte der Schrift* (Berlin: de Gruyter, 1986), esp. 161–273; and Pierre Gisel, *Vérité et histoire: La théologie dans la modernité: Ernst Käsemann*, Théologie Historique 41 (Paris: Éditions beauchesne, 1977). Cf., on the latter work, Ghislain Lafont, "La pertinence théologique de l'histoire," *RSPT* 63 (1979): 161–202.

41. James F. Kay, *Christus Praesens: A Reconsideration of Rudolf Bultmann's Christology* (Grand Rapids: Eerdmans, 1994), 110, has pointed out that Käsemann is not alone in making such a

direction—at "enthusiasts" (*die Schwärmerei*), both ancient and modern—but the basic point is a simple one, altogether in line with that of his argument regarding the uniqueness of the Gospel genre. Again, it is simply this: the early church refused to sacrifice the historical, earthly Jesus in either its oral kerygma or in its written records (the Gospels). To be sure, much of the force of Käsemann's argument depends on a particular historical reconstruction that seemed certain in his day and is far less so now. To that extent his ideas regarding the early rise of enthusiasm-docetism prior to the writing of the Gospels and to which the Gospels were a response seem, in today's context, at best arguable and problematic.[42] Adam rightly challenges the consensus (both specifically and theoretically) that Käsemann presupposes. There can be little doubt, however, that, were he alive today, Käsemann would sufficiently nuance his argument in light of these newer (and more precise? for how long?) data regarding the history of docetism, enthusiasm, early Christianity, and so on. After all, Käsemann repeatedly showed himself aware of the finitude of his own method—including, particularly, the *historical-critical* method[43]—not to mention the limitations of his own results; he also knew that problems must ever be investigated anew.[44] Regardless, with these

---

charge. Barth, too, accused Bultmann of docetism and since then it has become something of a fad, though the charge is probably untrue insofar as Bultmann does not go to the far left-wing position of, for example, Fritz Buri. Cf. also Martin, "Käsemann," 604; and, further, Jacques Schlosser, "Le débat de Käsemann et de Bultmann à propos du Jésus de l'histoire," *RSR* 87 (1999): 373–95.

42. But see note 37 above.

43. See, e.g., Käsemann's comment in "The Saving Significance of the Death of Jesus in Paul," in Käsemann, *Perspectives on Paul* (Philadelphia: Fortress, 1971), 50: "The person who wants to build on historical facts as such is bound to fall into uncertainty of salvation, and historical criticism confirms that this is the case." See also Käsemann, "Saving Significance," 51–52, and "Blind Alleys," 28, on the inability of the historical process to be an object of faith. Cf. E. F. Osborn, "Käsemann, Ernst," *DBI* 2:15: "Historical criticism without theological reflection [for Käsemann] . . . is merely playing with mirrors." Similarly, Harrisville and Sundberg, *Bible in Modern Culture*, 257: "History, Käsemann contends, cannot define and interpret the gospel, for the simple reason that history is ambiguous. The eschatological contingency of the revelation makes clear that the true God as well as true human existence is totally hidden in the fallen world."

44. See esp. Käsemann, *Commentary on Romans* (Grand Rapids: Eerdmans, 1980), viii: "In true theology there is no place for global judgments, and concreteness is always required. Awareness of the provisional nature of the solutions offered at any time and expected from theology does not release it from, but obligates it to, unceasing labor. Each of its statements is to be thought through by the reader either in assent or rejection, and it thus remains a question instead of lulling to sleep or granting secure possession. . . . Having arrived at the limits set for me, I accept the provisional nature of my own thought and deeds, and willingly leave the way clear for others." See also Käsemann, *The Wandering People of God: An Investigation of the Letter to the Hebrews* (Minneapolis: Augsburg, 1984), 15; Käsemann, *Essays on New Testament Themes*, 9; Käsemann, *New Testament Questions of Today*, ix; Käsemann, *Jesus Means Freedom*, 9, 156; Käsemann, "What I Have Unlearned in 50 Years as a German Theologian," *CurTM* 15 (1988): 335; and even Käsemann, *Testa-*

caveats entered, Käsemann's theological and analogical argument is still pressing and worth consideration. Whether the Gospels are unique or not, exactly when "docetism" becomes a historically accurate term for early Christian Christological error, matters, in the end, quite little. What matters for Käsemann is that the early Christian communities preserved a connection between the earthly Jesus and the risen Lord. More than that, *they identified the two*. Bultmann's program, which was content to let the earthly Jesus fade to "presupposition" or mere background (is this the "mere history" of which Käsemann so often spoke?),[45] is thus wrong on several fronts. In the context of this debate with Bultmann, one can easily see that for Käsemann the issue is fundamentally or at least primarily *theological* and not purely or only *historical*.[46] Here again, then, Käsemann shows both sides of his scholarly soul—historical-theological, or, better: theological-historical— and, in so doing, shows that both are, for him at least, deeply and profoundly connected, though the theological takes precedence. It is quite telling on this score that Adam must admit that, "to the extent that his argument is theologically motivated, it is not distinctively modern and therefore escapes some of the force of my counterargument."[47]

---

ment of Jesus (see 1–2, 74–77), which is over(t)ly historical. Several of these passages demonstrate that Käsemann is also well aware of his own subjective involvement in his scholarship (see, e.g., *Jesus Means Freedom*, 9) and of differences in opinion—even in the earliest periods of Christian history. Indeed, the latter point was one of the hallmarks of his scholarship, particularly in his work on the canon (see Harrisville and Sundberg, *Bible in Modern Culture*, 260–67). See further Käsemann, *Jesus Means Freedom*, 14; G. C. Chapman Jr., "Ernst Käsemann, Hermann Diem, and the New Testament Canon," *JAAR* 36 (1968): 3–12; Heikki Räisänen, *Beyond New Testament Theology: A Story and a Programme* (Philadelphia: Trinity Press International, 1990), 82; and Osborn, "Käsemann," 15: "The historical objections may be taken seriously; they belong to the enterprise that K[äsemann] regarded as least secure." At all of these points, then, Adam's assessment of Käsemann as the great defender of historicism misses the mark. Moreover, as Adam admits elsewhere (see *Making Sense*, 165, 187), according to his own scheme, these aspects of Käsemann's thought are actually more similar to the non- or postmodern situation than the "modern" one.

45. Käsemann, "Problem of the Historical Jesus," 24: "Mere history is petrified history, whose historical significance cannot be brought to light simply by verifying the facts and handing them on." Note that in "What I Have Unlearned," 329, Käsemann actually stated that Bultmann "may be called the last significant representative of that radical historical criticism founded 150 years earlier by . . . Ferdinand Christian Baur." The famous line from Bultmann to which I am alluding is found in his *Theology of the New Testament*, trans. Kendrick Grobel, 2 vols. in 1 (New York: Scribner's Sons, 1951–55), 1:1: "*The message of Jesus* is a presupposition for the theology of the New Testament rather than a part of that theology itself" (emphasis original). Many would argue, however, that Käsemann has misrepresented Bultmann's program to some degree.

46. See Käsemann's comments in *Essays on New Testament Themes*, 8; *New Testament Questions of Today*, x; consider also Robert Morgan's assessment of the theological subtext(s) at work here: *The Nature of New Testament Theology*, SBT 25 (London: SCM, 1973), 52–53, 54, 56, 60, 177n128.

47. Adam, *Making Sense*, 165; cf. 187. This admission obviates or seriously nuances much of

Still further—and this is of no small importance—one must recall that Käsemann explicitly disagrees, not simply with Bultmann, but equally also with Jeremias.[48] The latter's overly historical work constituted the first "blind alley" in the
"Jesus of history controversy." Ernst Käsemann is no William Wrede *Redivivus*. The
influence of Barth and Adolf Schlatter, not to mention Luther, was too strong on
him; and his pastoral background would not let him drift completely into the *re-
ligionsgeschichtliche Schule*, despite his deep affinities for it.[49] *Mere* history means
nothing to Käsemann; for history to be significant it must be mediated via interpretation.[50] Hence, Käsemann deemed Jeremias profoundly mistaken insofar as
Jeremias was ultimately arguing for faith in an object of critical research.[51] But
the historical-critical data make such a conclusion untenable. The theological
problem at play in Jeremias's work (and others like it) is thus the otiose kenosis
of the liberal historicizers.[52] While the earthly Jesus *is* the eschatological event,
he is *not* the object of faith. Rather, Jesus is the *eph' hapax*—the historical "once"
(Jeremias's emphasis) who also became the eschatological "once for all" (Käsemann's emphasis).[53] Both elements must be preserved, but "revelation ceases

---

Adam's critique in "Docetism," 406–7 (see further notes 43–45 above and note 60 below). It is
also not entirely clear why, for Adam, theology does not (or cannot) approximate, at least at
times, "modernity," or be related, at points, to "history" (cf. "Docetism," 405). What of "historical
theology," "history of dogma," or even "modern" theology? Furthermore, to what extent, if at all,
does "theological reflection"—which Adam seems at times to divorce rather cleanly from historical reasoning—actually depend on history? At the very least, knowledge of texts written in
languages not our own is dependent in part on historical research (historical linguistics, among
other things). How would we know of Chalcedon or "Chalcedonian interpretation" if not, in
part, for history? Again, the issues are too complex to resolve here, but the point is simply that
theology and history are not as completely noncontiguous or as neatly discrete—at least not
necessarily—as Adam would sometimes make it seem (e.g., Adam, "Docetism," 407–8). Here,
then, might be a case where Adam is guilty of the very same charge he levels at Käsemann:
namely, that his "case is a good deal weaker than is his prose."

48. It is noteworthy that in the "Docetism" article, Adam mentions Bultmann only once and
never refers to Jeremias by name (though he does cite the larger issue Jeremias represents).
Adam includes this mention within a passage "to be fair" to Käsemann, and admits that Käsemann "may have been right on both counts" (405–6).

49. Cf. Käsemann, "Problem of the Historical Jesus," 19.

50. Käsemann, "Problem of the Historical Jesus," 18.

51. Käsemann, "Blind Alleys," 28.

52. See Käsemann, "Problem of the Historical Jesus," 25.

53. Käsemann, "Problem of the Historical Jesus," 30–31. See also Käsemann, *Theologie des
Neuen Testaments*, 75–76 and esp. 85: "Das Hapax im Eph' Hapax ist nicht nur die Basis für das
Ein-für-allemal, sondern zugleich der Schutz vor dem Enthusiasmus des Synergismus und jeg-
lichen Schwärmertums. Das Kerygma ersetzt niemals den hist. Jesus!" (thanks to Rolf Jacobson
for sharing this manuscript with me).

to be God's revelation once it has been brought within a causal nexus."[54] This is to say that an exclusively historical, "Enlightenment-rationality" project must be avoided, because it is only the constant re-entering of the *Christus praesens* that prevents the particular history of Jesus from becoming "mere history." Thus the kerygma is central and essential. Christian faith is not built on *bruta facta* but (also) on eschatological interests. The resolution of the problem of both history and eschatology, earthly Jesus and risen Christ, is thus not easy, and many (partly contradictory) answers were given by the early Church (e.g., the Gospels).[55] Nevertheless, these agreed on one thing and one thing only: "namely that the life history of Jesus was constitutive for faith."[56] Even so, "neither our sources nor the insights we have gained from what has gone before permit us to substitute the historical Jesus for the exalted Lord."[57]

As can be seen from the above, at a number of points Käsemann's arguments are quite close to Adam's—so close, in fact, that one wonders if Adam's primary opponent is not Käsemann but rather Jeremias! In a word, Käsemann is no "mere" historicist, no theologically naïve historical critic. And yet, for Käsemann, *both* Bultmann and Jeremias are mistaken. Just as the genre of the Gospels dispels the myth that the historical Jesus is the complete content of the faith or is to be simply equated with the Christ of Faith (contra Jeremias, but with Bultmann), so also the Gospels dispel (demythologize?) the "myth"—in this case, Bultmann's—that the Christ of Faith has no relation whatsoever to the historical Jesus. Using the words of 2 Cor 5:16, Bultmann would no doubt emphasize that, though we once knew Christ "according to the flesh" (*kata sarka*), *we no longer know him that way.*[58] Käsemann would agree to a large extent, but would equally emphasize the other part

54. Käsemann, "Problem of the Historical Jesus," 31. Similarities to Barth at this point are rather obvious. Cf. Rae, *History and Hermeneutics*, 30.

55. Note Käsemann's observation that the various answers posed by the Gospels show that the historical Jesus is a "genuine theological problem" (Käsemann, "Problem of the Historical Jesus," 34). It also shows that there could be more than one good answer to solving it. Whatever the case, Adam's appeal to the existence of a plethora of historical-critical options for Jesus as evidence of historical criticism's inability to impact theological debate ("Docetism," 406) loses much of its force.

56. Käsemann, "Problem of the Historical Jesus," 33. The use of "constitutive" here is of crucial importance.

57. Käsemann, "Problem of the Historical Jesus," 34.

58. See Bultmann's treatment of this verse in his *The Second Letter to the Corinthians*, trans. Roy A. Harrisville (Minneapolis: Augsburg, 1985), 155–56. Note also J. Louis Martyn's discussion in "Epistemology at the Turn of the Ages: 2 Corinthians 5:16," in *Christian History and Interpretation: Studies Presented to John Knox*, ed. W. R. Farmer, C. F. D. Moule, and R. R. Niebuhr (Cambridge: Cambridge University Press, 1967), 269–87.

of the equation: *we once did know* Christ *kata sarka*, and that "once" still impacts our "non-fleshly" understanding of Christ.

To sum up, what one finds in Käsemann is a fascinating fusion. His is a middle or third way between Rae's two options of the overly theological (in this case, Bultmann) or overly historical (in this case, Jeremias).[59] As a hybrid of sorts, Käsemann's position will not allow itself to be easily classified or categorized. In short, Adam's criticism of Käsemann about historical criticism and docetism, which at first seemed so devastating—and which is not without merit for, and may well still be pertinent to, historical criticism in general (or at least certain practitioners thereof)—turns out to be more applicable to a contemporary "(stereo)type of Käsemann" than Käsemann himself. As Adam admits, there does seem to be quite a bit to "the historical Käsemann's" argument.[60] So, while historical-criticism *doesn't necessarily* protect against Christological error (Adam's well-taken point), it still seems that—in Käsemann's case at least—it is equally true that there is *no necessary reason why it cannot* protect against such,[61] *if* it be granted that historical data derived from historical criticism can be used in a theological way (especially against docetic tendencies).[62] Or, said differently, if a theological use of history like that evident in Käsemann is permitted, one can see how that particular use could be employed in theological debates, be they Christological or otherwise.[63]

---

59. A point acknowledged by Adam, "Docetism," 405. For a historical Jesus discussion that at points sounds remarkably similar to Käsemann and that tries to follow his middle road see John P. Meier, *A Marginal Jew: Rethinking the Historical Jesus*, ABRL (New York: Doubleday, 1991–2001), 1:196–201.

60. Adam, "Docetism," 397, 398, 399, 400, 405–6, 407. These admissions would seem to prove or at least grant Käsemann's points to no small degree. They make one wonder, moreover, if Adam's Käsemann is actually a "docetic" one!

61. Indeed, if Adam wants to say that historical criticism *necessarily cannot* do something, he may be succumbing to epistemological tendencies in the very "modern" project with which he is taking issue. This tension between the "modern" and non- or postmodern recurs throughout the "Docetism" article, though I suspect Adam is well aware of this and has good (rhetorical) reasons for it. Perhaps, then, in the case of Christological error, one might say that historical criticism is a *necessary but not sufficient* criterion, though one must hasten to add, as Adam astutely points out, that even if so, historical criticism can only protect against *certain* Christological errors, namely those that underemphasize Jesus's humanity. It would be unable to guard against the opposite problem: an under-emphasis on Christ's divinity.

62. Such a theological use of history seems to be granted in Adam, *Making Sense*, 187, which speaks of "Käsemann's theological adherence to the importance of historical interpretation." More pointedly (and ironically), Adam seems to be doing something quite similar: using historical criticism against itself in order to defend orthodoxy against historical criticism!

63. Once more the issues are thorny and cannot be fully discussed, let alone resolved here. Suffice it to say that the "that-ness" of Jesus's existence is probably not enough, at least not in

5. Conclusion, Part I: Käsemann on History (and Theology)— Or Was That Theology (and History)?

Other facets of Käsemann's work could be raised in connection with the issues at hand. One thinks, for instance, of his analysis of Pauline theology and the concept of the "justification of the godless," which may well showcase him as more a Lutheran theologian than historian of the early church.[64] The present chapter—something of an *apologia* for Käsemann—has centered instead on the historical Jesus debate which demonstrates that Käsemann was trying to wage a war on two theological fronts, not unlike Luther himself.[65] To be sure, not all will deem Käsemann to have been successful. And yet, it may be his broader commitments, not his specific

---

our own, post-Enlightenment context. The "that-ness" must take on some sort of content, at least if the Apostles' Creed is to be believed, which locates the "that-ness" under the rule of a particular Roman prefect. This content is, in part, precisely the relation to the historical Jesus that Käsemann talks about in terms of the importance of the historical Jesus in the kerygma, the genre of the Gospels, and so forth. For further reflection on the differences among and relationships between historical knowledge, "historic" knowledge, and faith knowledge, see the still useful discussion in Norman Perrin, *Rediscovering the Teaching of Jesus* (New York: Harper, 1976), 207–48. More recently, see Rae, *History and Hermeneutics*, passim; and, somewhat relatedly, Rae, "Texts in Context: Scripture and the Divine Economy," *JTI* 1 (2007): 1–21.

64. For an example of Käsemann's Lutheran tendencies, see "Worship and Everyday Life: A Note on Romans 12," in Käsemann, *New Testament Questions of Today*, 188–95. See also the following important works on Paul by Käsemann: "'The Righteousness of God' in Paul" (in Käsemann, *New Testament Questions of Today*, 168–82); "Some Thoughts on the Theme 'The Doctrine of Reconciliation in the New Testament,'" in *The Future of Our Religious Past: Essays in Honour of Rudolf Bultmann*, ed. J. M. Robinson (New York: Harper, 1971), 49–64; "On Paul's Anthropology," in Käsemann, *Perspectives on Paul*, 1–31; "The Saving Significance," 32–59; "Justification and Salvation History in the Epistle to the Romans," in Käsemann, *Perspectives on Paul*, 60–78; *Commentary on Romans*, passim; and *Theologie des Neuen Testaments*, 5–6. Cf. also Ehler, *Die Herrschaft des Gekreuzigten*, 277–342; and the translator's preface to *Wandering People of God*, 11. Note also the title of Käsemann's Festschrift: *Rechtfertigung: Festschrift für Ernst Käsemann zum 70. Geburtstag*, ed. Johannes Friedrich, Wolfgang Pöhlmann, and Peter Stuhlmacher (Tübingen: Mohr Siebeck, 1976). Clearly, other less Lutheran interpretations of Paul are possible. See, e.g., Krister Stendahl, *Paul among Jews and Gentiles* (Philadelphia: Fortress, 1976), esp. 78–96; also J. Paul Sampley, "Reasoning from the Horizons of Paul's Thought World: A Comparison of Galatians and Philippians," and Paul J. Achtemeier, "The Continuing Quest for Coherence in St. Paul: An Experiment in Thought," both in *Theology and Ethics in Paul and His Interpreters: Essays in Honor of Victor Paul Furnish*, ed. E. H. Lovering Jr. and J. L. Sumney (Nashville: Abingdon, 1996), 114–31 and 132–45, respectively.

65. See David V. Way, *The Lordship of Christ: Ernst Käsemann's Interpretation of Paul's Theology* (New York: Oxford University Press, 1991), 25–29, esp. 28–29, who points out that Käsemann's two fronts were virtually the same as, if not identical to, Luther's (nomism and enthusiasm). See similarly, Martin, "Käsemann," 604.

results (already dated), which will be of lasting significance.[66] Part of that significance is found, and is perhaps encapsulated, in the fact that Käsemann simply refuses to let the historical go.[67] In his opinion, all theological work—*including the historical-critical task when it is employed for theological purposes*—can and must have a constructive purpose.[68] As an example, one might note that, for Käsemann, even a problem like that of the historical Jesus is, ultimately and finally, not in the historian's hands to solve. In his own words, the problem of the historical Jesus

> is only solved by those who since the Cross and the Resurrection confess him as that which, in the days of his flesh, he never claimed to be and yet was— their Lord, and the bringer of the liberty of the children of God, which is the correlate of the kingdom of God. For to his particularity there corresponds the particularity of faith, for which the real history of Jesus is always happening afresh; it is now the history of the exalted Lord, but it does not cease to be the earthly history it once was, in which the call and the claim of the Gospel are encountered.[69]

This, surely, represents both the unique perspective that Käsemann brings to the material as well as his weakness, at least when viewed from the perspective of a Bultmann or a Jeremias or, perhaps, an Adam.

But the preceding discussion also shows that while Käsemann's work is susceptible to Adam's critique at several points, there is another, deeper sense in which Käsemann's project is thoroughly theological,[70] not to mention tending

---

66. Cf. Robin Scroggs, "Ernst Käsemann: The Divine Agent *Provocateur*," *RelSRev* 11/3 (1985): 260; Osborn, "Käsemann," 2:15.

67. This is purposefully vague and echoes Käsemann himself, who often seems to be concerned only with a general notion of history or "the historical" even though he often speaks specifically of "historical criticism"—a tendency, I would argue, that has as much to do with his historical location as it does with methodological (im)precision.

68. Adam's recent emphasis on biblical theology as a signifying practice (e.g., *Faithful Interpretation*, 155–63; "Poaching on Zion: Biblical Theology as Signifying Practice," in Adam, Fowl, Vanhoozer, and Watson, *Reading Scripture with the Church*, 17–34) also resonates with much of Käsemann's life and work. When was he ever willing to let Christianity be solely a matter of academic theology? See, inter alia, Harrisville and Sundberg, *The Bible in Modern Culture*, 249–70, esp. 265.

69. Käsemann, "Problem of the Historical Jesus," 47.

70. Many would argue that it is the theology that wins out in Käsemann's work. Note John K. Riches, *A Century of New Testament Study* (Valley Forge, PA: Trinity Press International, 1993), 201: "Käsemann wrote consciously as a church theologian, and for all the controversy he provoked within church circles his historical work was intended as church theology." Later, Riches writes

toward the non- or postmodern, and thus escapes Adam's well-formulated argument. Of course, Käsemann was certainly *not* non- or postmodern, if that term is taken to mean (among any number of other things) little or no emphasis on the old standard of historical-critical inquiry. Instead, Käsemann struggled to hold together—albeit and admittedly in a messy tension—the two sides of his "Old Marburger" soul: the historical and the theological. If he does so in a way that is not altogether satisfying, does that mean that his attempt is in vain or meaningless? Is anyone who recites the Apostles' Creed excused from a similar task? *Passus sub Pontio Pilato*, after all! And, while there can be no doubt that Käsemann was a child of his time, unaware of the epistemological developments that would change the landscape of the field of biblical studies (how could he be otherwise?), aren't we all such children (how could we be otherwise?)? As for Käsemann, his work—despite its demerits—remains a significant if not seminal contribution to the question of the always-vexed question of the relationship of theology and history, the historical use of theology, and, most importantly perhaps, the *theological* use of history. Though he is no longer with us, he still has some important things to teach us on these points.

6. Conclusion, Part II: Back to Thinking Theology and History

In conclusion, Käsemann represents an approach that, with appropriate modifications or updates for the present scene, remains viable insofar as it refuses to be pigeon-holed in either of the two camps delineated by Rae. To be sure, Käsemann's way is certainly not *exclusively* theological, which is Adam's point against him, but neither is he *exclusively* historicist, which is the point of the present chapter *for* him. Instead, Käsemann reflects a serious and studious attempt to think theology and history together. In this way, Käsemann can be seen as a partner, with Adam, *against* the sole hegemony of historical criticism at the expense of theological interpretation. But he also chastens approaches to theological interpretation that are, sometimes, too light-handed when it comes to the problems, vicissitudes, and study of history; or too quick to dismiss historical approaches; or too hasty to deem "modern" theorists passé in our postmodern context. Theological interpretation of Scripture, that is, needs to be careful to resist the rift between history and theology that Rae has documented.[71] Historical criticism may not be the problem so

---

of Käsemann as a transitional figure straddling "the era of Barth and Bultmann and the political reaction of the late 1960s."

71. Rae, *History and Hermeneutics*, 18, effectively accuses Spinoza, Lessing, Hegel, Strauss and the rest of "the roll call of Modern . . . interpreters [that] could continue at length," of docetism.

much as particular practitioners thereof.[72] Käsemann and others like him—and here one thinks, in Old Testament studies, of Hans Walter Wolff, Claus Westermann, Walther Zimmerli, and Gerhard von Rad (why are so many form critics? why were so many active around World War II?)—show skillful use of history in service to broader theological goals.[73] They are far from Wrede or Jeremias and their offspring (on both left and right wings of the ideological spectrum). Instead, Käsemann and (theological) company refuse what Rae thinks is "typical of Modernity"—namely, "the prising apart of history and theology."[74] Moreover, if Rae is right, that "orthodox Christian theology, confessing as it does that the Word has become flesh, requires that the Jesus 'behind the text'—the one who went his way among us in the flesh—is one and the same person as the risen and ascended Lord whom the New Testament proclaims"[75] then Käsemann and his *modus operandi* do, in fact, demonstrate a helpful approach to Christological orthodoxy and, perhaps, other theological issues or questions as well.[76]

If, on the other hand, theological interpretation of Scripture does not resist the bifurcation of theology and history, then it will simply perpetuate the problem that has been with us for some time now—centuries, really—just on the polar opposite side of the playing field. Käsemann, in his stubborn way, seems to stand in the middle, between the two opposing teams, offering us another way to think theology *and* history—yes, *together*.

---

72. Elsewhere, Adam seems to admit as much. It is not so much *the fact* that historical criticism has dominated, but *the way* it has done so ("Toward a Resolution," 144).

73. Compare Adam, who speaks of "the most sophisticated exegetes and theologians (who until recent years frequently turned out to be the same people)" (*Faithful Interpretation*, 155). In my judgment, Käsemann and the others listed above (and more could be added) are precisely such people. Or, consider Adam, *Faithful Interpretation*, 13: "The strongest ventures in biblical theology demonstrate insight and critical judgment that draw on historical-critical scholarship but cannot be limited to the horizons that circumscribe modern technical conventions of reading." Again: Käsemann!

74. Rae, *History and Hermeneutics*, 3.

75. Rae, *History and Hermeneutics*, 24.

76. See note 16 above: historical criticism's effect is to *free us to see the cross!*

PART 3

Practice

13

Is God Always Anything?

Text: The book of Job; also Isa 43:14–21 and 1 John 1:1–5

Then the LORD answered Job out of the whirlwind: . . .
"Where were you when I laid the foundation of the earth?
Tell me, if you have understanding." (Job 38:1, 4)

I sometimes tell my students who are beginning their preaching careers to start with something easy when preaching. Some easy text. And short, too. Short and easy. That would be a good idea. But professors often seem completely incapable of following their own advice! And so it is that I have chosen a very difficult text: Job. And not just one little part, but *the whole book* of Job.

Now don't worry: I'm not going to read the whole book to you. But if I'm going to preach on Job, you might wonder what gives with those Old and New Testament readings. Here's what gives—when we read those well-beloved portions of scripture together, they seem to pose a question: Is God always anything? That is, is God always one thing consistently whether it is light, as 1 John says, or something else? Or does God—at least on occasion—change God's mind, forgetting the old ways and doing new things, as Isaiah asserts? Which is it? Consistency or changeability? One, both, neither? And how might we decide?

Enter the book of Job.

This sermon was preached at the Kinfolk Campmeeting, Brownsville, TN, July 18, 2012. Prior to that, it was first preached at Asbury Theological Seminary, Wilmore, KY, in Spring 1999.

Job's Predicament (1:1–2:13)

This question—"Is God Always Anything?"—is just one of many that arise from the book of Job. And I think Job gives us an answer or two.

Now I'm sure you are already quite familiar with Job. In fact, I have no doubt that many of you feel intimately acquainted with him for whatever reason—for a whole host of reasons! "Know him?" some of you might be saying right now, "I AM him! I *am* Job. Or at least it feels like it."

It really does feel like it sometimes doesn't it? And that's what makes this material so crucial—crucial for our theologies and crucial for our souls.

The story begins with a nice guy in a nice place with all the nice trappings: nice wife, nice kids—though they party a bit much—and lots of nice stuff. But then something strange happens: we are suddenly ushered into the divine throne room and catch a glimpse of what goes on there. In come the heavenly beings and with them comes one called "the Satan," which means "the accuser" since that is his job. Unfortunately for Job, God is quite proud of him and brags to the Satan about Job: "Have you considered my servant Job?" God asks. "There is no one like him on the earth, a blameless and upright man who fears God and turns away from evil" (1:8 NRSV). Then the Satan answers God: "Does Job fear God for nothing? Have you not put a fence around him and his house and all that he has, on every side? . . . But stretch out your hand now, and touch all that he has, and he will curse you to your face" (1:9–11 NRSV).

God takes this challenge; the wager is set. It's a bet of cosmic proportions. Heaven and earth will strain to see if Job really serves God "for nothing." He has been blessed and supported and loved and nurtured. Take it away, though, and will he still be faithful? Or will he curse God and call it quits? That's the gist of the opening chapters.

And so the story begins. In one day, Job loses all his material possessions—oxen, donkeys, sheep, and camels—and he loses his loved ones—all but four messengers and all of his ten children, dead. And, amazingly, we come to find out that without all this—without all of the trappings, the hedge of protection, even without his children and servants—Job is still able to say: "The LORD gave and the LORD has taken away; blessed be the name of the LORD" (1:21 NRSV).

Such words! Almost unfathomable in the face of such tragedy. Unfortunately for Job, the tragedy has only just begun.

Back in God's throne room, the heavenly beings file in and wouldn't you know it, the Satan is back too. God won the first round but the accuser wants double-or-nothing: "All that people have they will give to save their lives," he says. "But stretch out your hand now and touch his bone and his flesh, and he will curse you to your face" (2:4–5 NRSV).

Then, of course, Job is afflicted with loathsome sores from the sole of his foot to the crown of his head. All he can do is sit on the ash heap and scrape his blisters with a piece of broken pottery. But still he persists, despite the discouraging words of his wife that he should curse God and die. "Should we accept only good from God and not accept evil?" he asks her (2:10).

Well, that's Job's story—up to this point at least. That's his predicament. And it is certainly a tragic one: once rich, he is now impoverished; once a father of many children, he is now bereaved; once a husband, he is now estranged from his wife; once healthy, he is now a portrait of sickness and suffering. But it's actually *worse* than all that.

You see, Job didn't have the benefit of seeing God's throne room like we have. He knows of no "Satan"-figure and doesn't know that his situation is the result of an elaborate cosmic wager on whether or not he will prove faithful in the end. On the one hand, maybe it's better that Job didn't know that! But on the other hand, this also makes his predicament much worse because Job only knows of God. All there is, then, is Job's painful encounter with the one ultimately responsible for his very great suffering: God.

Oh, there is something else: Job's friends. Eliphaz the Temanite, Bildad the Shuhite, and Zophar the Naamathite "met together to go and console and comfort" Job (2:11 NRSV). When they find him they don't recognize him so twisted is he from his pain. "They sat with him on the ground seven days and seven nights," the Scripture says, "and no one spoke a word to him, for they saw that his suffering was very great" (2:13 NRSV).

Job, Job's Friends, and Their Answers (3:1–37:24)

Finally someone speaks out of the silence. It is Job. And his voice is both less and more confident than it had been in the preceding chapters. It is less confident in that Job wishes he were dead. Wishes he had never been born. Is uncertain about the character and quality of the God whom he has served with such uprightness and blamelessness. But Job's voice is more confident in that he is certain that his suffering is undeserved. He *has*, truly and in fact, served this God with uprightness and blamelessness. How then could this have happened?

Then Job's friends break their silence. They have an answer for Job. He won't like it, but they have it all figured out. They tell him that he is absolutely right—this shouldn't have happened to an innocent, upright, and blameless chap like Job. That's the whole point—it did happen and that is proof that Job is not so innocent, upright, blameless, perfect, sanctified, you name it. On the contrary, he is guilty, sinful, perverse, ignorant, arrogant, you name it. That's the answer. That is why Job suffers.

353

In theological terms we call this type of thinking retribution theology. It means that you always get what you've got coming. If you do good, good things will happen to you. If you do bad, bad things will happen to you. It's as simple and un-complex as that. This is the way God works, the friends say: "Since you got the bad end of the deal, it means, logically, necessarily, inescapably, that you were the bad start of the deal. God is just, God is fair, God rewards according to one's deeds. *Always*. There is no use complaining about that. Give up, give in, repent, and everything will be alright again—of course, the sheep and the children and the servants are all still dead, but no matter. You suffer, Job, because you *deserve* to suffer."

Several fascinating things happen in this dialogue between Job and his friends. The first is that Job actually agrees. His friends are right. This *is* the way God works. But they are wrong too, Job avows. He is, despite what they say, innocent. Completely and totally. That's what makes their theology, which sounds so right and good, in actuality so utterly wrong and horrible. You see, it is not applicable here. Here, we have a good man, a good Job, at the start—but instead of a good end to the story, there is a tragic one. This system, this retribution theology, that the friends espouse just doesn't work. God may work this way sometimes, but certainly *not always*. "I am innocent!" Job maintains. The friends disagree. They become more and more hostile in their condemnation of Job and Job becomes more and more adamant about his innocence and the injustice of his situation. And it goes on like this for thirty-three chapters.

In the middle of this maelstrom, another fascinating thing happens. Since his friends refuse to listen, Job decides to take his case to the One who is responsible in the first place. He complains to God. And with such pathos! And with such honesty! And with such boldness, if not arrogance! Listen to what he says:

> "If I summoned [God] and he answered me,
>   I do not believe that he would listen to my voice.
> For he crushes me with a tempest,
>   and multiplies my wounds without cause;
> he will not let me get my breath,
>   but fills me with bitterness. . . .
>   He destroys both the blameless and the wicked.
> When disaster brings sudden death,
>   he mocks at the calamity of the innocent. . . .
> He has torn me in his wrath, and hated me;
>   he has gnashed his teeth at me. . . .
> I was at ease, and he broke me in two;
>   he seized me by the neck and dashed me
> to pieces;

> he set me up as his target. . . .
>
> He slashes open my kidneys, and shows no mercy;
>
> > he pours out my gall on the ground." (9:16–18, 22b–23; 16:9a, 12–13 NRSV)

Who among us would dare say such things—of God no less?! But that is what Job says. In such pain, all he can end with is simply, plaintively: "Where then is my hope? Who will see my hope?" (17:15 NRSV).

All the while the friends are getting more and more nervous. They smell heresy here! It won't do to have such talk in church! And friendship and compassion get thrown to the wind in their attempt to justify God and God's ways. Their systematic theology—if we might call it that—is inflexible, absolutely rigid, completely settled. There is no room for a Job in it. And there is definitely no room for this Job.

Then comes the most fascinating part of all. At the end of the book, as you know, God finally comes on the scene to survey the situation and to have a word with those involved. God speaks primarily to Job; there is only one comment to the friends, and it is directed to Eliphaz. Listen to what God says to him: "My wrath is kindled against you and against your two friends; for you have not spoken of me what is right, as my servant Job has" (42:7 NRSV; cf. 42:9).

Now wait a minute. Let me get this straight. Those things Job said about God, about the universe, about everything—all that anger, that pain, that suffering speech—that was *right*? And all those things that the friends said about God always rewarding the just and always punishing the unjust—that was not right? That was wrong?

The book of Job seems to be telling us that just when you feel like you have God all figured out and just when you are ready to box God up into a nice little package of theology, religion, spirituality, whatever—watch out! God may just end up bursting out. God may end up freer than our systems allow! God may end up saying and showing that our little finite minds and our little finite theologies are not equipped to deal ultimately and exhaustively with the Infinite. Indeed, it may be that some of our talk of God will end up being wrong: "You have not spoken right of me as my servant Job has."

You see, Job's God, *our God*, is not subject to our whims, our pleasures, our every desire, not even our every prayer. Job's God, *our God*, is God. No less! Our theologies—even our best constructed, best informed, and most well-meaning ones—are not God. That is what Job's friends learn, and they learn it from God's own mouth.

Job's God and God's Answer (Job 38:1–42:17)

But they end up getting off easy. Job learns what they learn too, but he learns more because God has more to say to him. Job finally gets what he has wanted, begged for, demanded: audience with Almighty God. But it ain't all it's cracked up to be!

> Then the LORD answered Job out of the whirlwind:

> "Who is this that darkens counsel by words without knowledge?
> Gird up your loins ...
>> I will question you, and you shall declare to me.

> "Where were you when I laid the foundation of the earth?
>> Tell me, if you have understanding.
> Who determined its measurements—surely you know!"
>> (38:1–5a NRSV)

Now hold on. The Scripture says that God *answered* Job. *This* is supposed to be an answer? It's no answer at all. Instead, all Job gets for all his eloquence, for all his suffering, for all his pain-full theology is the question: "Where were you, boy, when I laid the foundation of the earth?"

Job can say nothing. How could he? How could he respond to this odd, this uncontrollable, this radically free God? This God who is God—no less!? All Job can say is

> "I have uttered what I did not understand,
>> things too wonderful for me, which I did not know. . . .
> I had heard of you by the hearing of the ear,
>> but now my eye sees you;
> therefore I recant,
>> and repent of dust and ashes." (42:3b, 5–6 NRSV with v. 6 altered)

Maybe when everything is said and done, then, Job's innocence and uprightness and all that don't really matter. At least not in the face of the question "Where were you?" That question views Job's suffering on a cosmic scale and from that perspective, as tragic and significant as Job's suffering is, it just isn't that tragic or significant. Job says it himself: "I am of small account; what could I possibly say to you?" (see 40:4). And yet this overwhelming, almighty God is the same God who says "Job, my servant, spoke right of me." And this is the same God who comes to Job, in his suffering, exactly where he needed God most and where he has longed to see God most, and where he has begged for God to meet him most. This God of the universe, this God of the whirlwind and of the cosmic perspective, this God who asks, "Where were you?"—this is the God who nevertheless, despite all that, still shows up at the ash heap where Job scrapes his latest blister with a piece of broken pottery.

Conclusion

When you stop and think about that, it is absolutely stunning. But before we get caught up in it, I think we should ponder God's question to Job further. For as harsh as that question seems, we mustn't shirk it because it is of critical importance for people like us—people who faithfully attend church, who go to camp meetings even!—committed Christian folks who know their way around a hymnal and a Bible and thus presumably know something about God and can speak about God knowingly and wisely. We—our type—we have God down, don't we? We know what God would say on subject *x*, *y*, or *z*! That's our job!

But where were *we* when God laid the foundation of the earth? Oh, I know, I know, I know: when the pressure is on, we can always defer to our forebears who certainly knew more than we do! We have traditions, don't we, and doctrine and theologians and denominations! But the question won't die: Where were *you*, Martin Luther? Where were *you*, John Calvin? And, perish the thought, you good Methodists among the Kinfolk: Where were *you*, Mr. Wesley?

But most humbling of all, the question hits close to home: Where were *you*, Brent? "Uhh, me? Umm, nowhere." Could any answer be more obvious? I wasn't there! You weren't there! Luther, Calvin, Wesley, and all the others, weren't there! But could any question be harder to hear? It bespeaks our limitations, our finitude, our lack of knowledge about all that God might be and all that God might be up to in this world. It warns us that we ought to be careful with our theology—let it not be too precise, too rigid, too settled. For there is seldom room for a Job in a theology like that. And God might just break out of a theology like that. God may just end up appearing in a whirlwind, asking "Where were you?"

And that is no small question. For you see, in the final analysis, this is not just a *theological* question—it is also a *pastoral* question, even for those of us who are not ordained. Don't forget that these well-meaning but ill-informed friends (every one of them un-ordained) who came and sat down next to Job came to comfort him and console him in his time of need. But they did nothing of the sort. They placed their system of belief above their compassion for their friend, and in their concern to be true to the system, they betrayed him. His words were more than they could bear. Too irreverent they thought. He must be crushed somehow. Or at least corrected. But it is *their* words that are finally and ultimately condemned, not by Job or by the harsh facts of life, but by God's own lips. And, in the end, it is

Job who becomes their pastor, interceding on their behalf for their forgiveness as he offers sacrifices for them and prays for them.

So too for us, I think, when we encounter the many Jobs that will cross our paths. Some will only think they are Job, some will really be Job. But it doesn't matter—the effect is the same: Job is always with us and Job always wants an answer.[1] Ultimately, only God can provide that answer. So the question is whether or not we will rush in after Job's friends giving *their* answers, saying things like:

"God wanted this—wanted your brother to die this way . . ."
"That atrocity overseas happened to get those people's attention . . ."
"You probably lost your job because you aren't right with God . . ."
"Look, I'm really sorry about your cancer, but it happened so that God would bring good of it . . ."
"Those people deserve everything they get . . ."

Those are words worthy of Eliphaz the Temanite, Bildad the Shuhite, and Zophar the Naamathite. They are not worthy, however, of Job. Not the book and not the man. And they are not worthy of Job's God. And so, they are not worthy to be spoken to the Job you will be staring at in the eyes sooner or later, scraping his or her latest sore with a piece of broken pottery.

So: Is God always anything? It would seem that the book of Job says no. At least on some points. God has the freedom and ability to break out and do new things (like Isaiah says), to act in new ways, to not be confined by systems or ideologies, well-meaning or not. And that means we can't be too quick in presuming that we know *what* God is doing in someone's life and *why* God is doing it or even *if* God is doing it—*especially* if we are talking about someone's suffering. So, no, God isn't always anything—if that anything in any way limits the freedom of God to be God.

But that just shows that God is always something in the book of Job and that is that God is always God. No less!

And there is something else to be said about this God who is always God: this God is with us when we suffer. When we sit on the ash heap. And that's why we know that God is light, in God there is no darkness—not even one bit. We know this, not from our own experience—for if we are honest, truly honest, we must admit that we don't always experience God that way. But we know of God's goodness nevertheless, not only from the First Epistle of St. John or because the God of the whirlwind shows up at the ash heap in the book of Job. We also know of God's goodness because of the pathos of the one who suffered not only with us,

1. Cf. Archibald MacLeish, *J.B.: A Play in Verse* (Boston: Houghton Mifflin, 1986), 12–13.

but for us, our Lord Jesus Christ. And if he has suffered then we can too—whether it be as bad as, worse than, or less than his servant Job. And when we suffer, maybe God will meet us there, too. For God met Christ in his suffering, at the ash heap of Golgotha. And God also met us in Christ's suffering, just as God met Job in his.

Amen.

14

On Pharaohs: Egyptian and Otherwise

Text: Isa 19:19–25; Ps 87; Ezek 32:31–32

I confess that I've been thinking a lot about Pharaoh lately—something one does in my line of work I suppose. Not the famous racehorse, "American Pharoah"— whose name actually misspells "Pharaoh," which is a terrible tragedy to someone in my line of work. No, I've been thinking a lot about the *Egyptian* Pharaoh. We all know that *that* Pharaoh is the ultimate bad guy in the Bible. But as Netflix, Hulu, and all the rest have taught us, even bad guys can be . . . well, complex. Maybe there is more to Pharaoh, then, than pure unadulterated evil. So I'd like to revisit three portraits of Pharaoh found in Scripture. The most familiar, "bad guy" one is the second of the three, but surrounding that meaty and malicious middle are two quite different perspectives. All three portraits are important, however, because these days, even if you aren't in my line of work, it's not hard to find yourself thinking a lot about Pharaoh—even if you don't use that name for him.

Pharaoh: Sort of Okay at the Start

So, if we begin at the beginning, with Genesis, Pharaoh and Egypt are there, right from the start. One of Noah's sons, Ham, is the father of the Cushitic peoples, including Egypt according to the genealogy in Gen 10. More familiar than that

This sermon was preached on January 15, 2019, in Cannon Chapel, at the Candler School of Theology, Emory University, at the Spring Convocation during which I was installed as William Ragsdale Cannon Distinguished Professor of Old Testament. Versions have also been preached at Church Street United Methodist Church in Knoxville, TN; Kingsway Christian Church in Germantown, TN; the Kinfolk Camp Meeting at Brownsville, TN; and Point Loma Nazarene University in San Diego, CA.

genealogy is the story of how, immediately after God calls Abraham to Canaan, there's a famine in that land. So Abraham and Sarah head off to Egypt. Egypt is a land of plenty, evidently because Pharaoh is an acquisitive kind of guy. No surprise, then, that he quickly acquires Sarah for his harem. But it isn't really his fault. It's Abraham's fault for pawning Sarah off as his sister. Once Pharaoh learns that Sarah is married, he wants nothing to do with the situation. He returns her to Abraham and expels both of them from the country.

So far (in Genesis) and not so bad. Not so great, if you're Abraham—worse if you're Sarah!—but not so bad if you're Pharaoh because Egypt at this early point in Genesis is a haven in need, and Pharaoh is someone who rights wrongdoings when they come to his attention.

Later in Genesis, Pharaoh—same title, different guy this time—continues to do the right thing by listening to Joseph. He realizes Joseph is wise and so promotes him to second in command (41:38–45; cf. Acts 7:10). Just a bit later, Pharaoh is delighted to hear that Joseph's family is immigrating to Egypt, and he assists (not resists) their relocation (45:16–17, 21; 46:5; cf. Acts 7:13). Upon meeting Pharaoh, the elderly patriarch Jacob blesses him and that's no small thing: that Pharaoh, the head of the world's greatest superpower, would consent to be blessed, not once but twice, by an ancient, dry, and dusty nomad who worshipped a very different God (47:7, 10).

To sum up this first portrait of Pharaoh: he's a decent guy—pretty okay at the start and even better than that by the end of Genesis. But this is just the first portrait of the Egyptian king and it's an exceedingly thin one compared to the second one.

Pharaoh: Horrific in the Meaty Middle

Everything changes drastically when we go from Genesis to Exodus. We are only eight verses in when we read that a new Pharaoh is in power (same title, but *very* different guy this time). This Pharaoh has no memory of someone named Joseph (Exod 1:8)—a very revealing detail! Regime change can change a lot . . . not always for the better. I suspect you knew that already, but Exodus drills it home. Unlike Genesis, the Pharaoh of Exodus isn't okay at all. Quite to the contrary. He's a despot. He's also a hardcore ultranationalist, an Egypt-Supremacist, you might say. And you wouldn't be wrong. Pharaoh is worried about *all those other people*—the kind with a different language, different customs, different clothes, different skin: the Hebrews. He wants them gone—wiped out. So, in a direct reversal of the opening of Exodus, which tells of God's fruitful blessing of Israel, Pharaoh decides, instead, to kill them all off. When that doesn't pan out—thanks to the civil disobedience of some very brave midwives who refused to take their assigned seats on Pharaoh's murder bus (so to speak)—he enslaves the Israelites and makes "their lives miserable with hard labor" by forcing them to work in the fields doing all sorts of cruel tasks, according to Exodus (1:14 CEB). We wouldn't be surprised in the least, I suspect, if some Egyptologist told us that Pharaoh grew cotton along the Nile on the back side of the pyramids. But back then, Pharaoh had his own brand of toilsome despair: mud brick without straw (5:5–13). And he was already expert in human trafficking.

No wonder, then, that the Israelites groaned and cried out, begging to be rescued from their slavery (see 2:23–24a). And, Scripture says, God heard them. And God remembered God's promises. God saw the Israelites and God knew (2:24–25).

That is the Good News of the Gospel, already in Exodus chapter 2, verse 25, but there's a long way to go because Pharaoh is nowhere near the decent guy he was in Genesis. Now he is a murderous megalomaniac. An egotistical tyrant who would never consent to be blessed by Jacob or his children, let alone their God. "Who is this LORD?" he asks Moses derisively. "I don't know this LORD and I certainly won't let Israel go" (5:2 CEB).

But Pharaoh learns, doesn't he (cf. Rom 9:17)? Slowly, excruciatingly, through the ten plagues and at the Red Sea, Pharaoh learns who this Lord is. This is:

- the Lord, who is not to be trifled with
- the Lord, who will brook no rivals, no competing masters or monarchs, no politicians who claim, falsely, power over God's people
- the Lord, who will go to ultimate lengths to save God's oppressed people from the house of bondage.

Pharaoh and all Egypt, including the animals—yes, even the firstborn children—learn how seriously the Lord takes tyrannical dictators who care only for nation and money and power and more and more and more. Small wonder that the Sabbath commandment in Deuteronomy says everyone gets a day off work because Pharaoh never ever gave them a break. He's an acquisitive guy, after all—greedy—and a power-monger. And a racist.

To sum up this second portrait of Pharaoh, his semi-decent rating is long gone—a thing of ancient history. And the negative portrait established here in Exodus persists for a very long time to come. In fact, you might say it persists *for the rest of time*. Pharaoh and the Egypt he represents, along with God's deliverance of Israel in the exodus, are standard and oft-repeated tropes throughout the rest of the Bible, and throughout Christian thought as well—both early and late. Pharaoh is and becomes the archetypal enemy of God and God's people, and thus also of the evil and sin that enslaves us. Leaving Egypt and crossing the Red Sea is equivalent to salvation, therefore: redemption, like being baptized, with the promised land the place of God's favor and blessing, the inheritance of the saints.

Pharaoh in this second, extended and extensive portrait is thus a cipher for all that stands opposed to God's ways. Have you ever noticed, in this regard, how he is never given a name, just called by the title, "pharaoh," which simply means "king" in the Egyptian language? Pharaoh *had* a name for heaven's sake—a very long, flowery, royal one in fact. But Pharaoh's name isn't significant in Scripture. What is significant in Scripture is who Pharaoh is *generally*, what he stands for *generically*. That's one reason why it's not hard nowadays to think about Pharaoh, because we all know him, don't we, even if he goes unnamed in the Bible. We see him *all* the time. He's lurking in the pages of our American history books, particularly where I live, in the South. But he's also all over television, on the news crawl, on Twitter and Facebook and all the rest. And if we are honest, we also sometimes spot him—more often than we care to admit—looking back at us in the mirror.

That hits a bit close to home, doesn't it? Or it *should* because we know how God feels about Pharaohs—all of them, *plural*. We know how God deals with them, the extreme lengths God will go to set things straight, to do justice and show mercy, to bring good news to those under the poverty line, to announce a release date for inmates, to grant pardons for overfull prisons (cf. Mic 6:8; Isa 61:1–2). And if we are on the wrong side of all that—as we so often are, as our country has so often been, as even the Christian church so often is—well, then, we should be on notice. We, too, may soon learn who this Lord really is. We may already be learning it!

Pharaoh: Repentant, Even Saved at the End?

But there is one last portrait of Pharaoh to consider. It is in a minor key, but no less important for that. This final portrait shows that, despite the horrific image of Pharaoh that dominates Scripture, there is still something more to say, and that something more is quite remarkable. It's found here and there in nooks and crannies of the Bible that are often overlooked or under-known. Among other texts, we might consider Isa 19, which says that one day even Egypt, that ultimate symbol of evil and sin (both societal and systemic)—one day *even* Egypt will have an altar devoted to the Lord; and that when the Egyptians—the paradigmatic oppressors—when the Egyptians are themselves oppressed, God will send them a savior and rescue them. On that day the Egyptians will worship the Lord, make promises to God, and make good on their promises. And, Isaiah tells us, God will heal the Egyptians and listen to them on that day.

That is simply unbelievable. It's amazing what you can find in that Bible of ours if you read it! It might just blow us away! But Isa 19 isn't done: it goes on to say that Israel will just be one in a trio of God's favorite people. The other two are, wait for it: Egypt—horrific Egypt!—and Assyria, another brutal archenemy. And then, listen to this: God *blesses* this trio, going so far as to call Egypt "my people"—the

Egypt that God systematically took down to the studs in Exodus. And then God proceeds to call Assyria "my handiwork." Those are pet names normally reserved for Israel alone. But now God uses them of Israel's worst enemies.[1] Just think about that for a moment. Let that sink in for a minute. Today it might sound something like calling brutal drug lords, "precious brothers in the Lord," or ISIS, "my church," or Al-Qaeda, "the bride of Christ." Like I said: simply unbelievable.

And get this: Pharaoh himself, that horrific head of state, also gets into the act. In an obscure corner of the somewhat obscure book of Ezekiel, he, too, is said to participate in this "come-to-Jesus" moment. He will be sorry, Ezekiel tells us, about all the people "slain by the sword of Pharaoh and all his army" (Ezek 32:31; my translation). That is *repentance* language: Ezekiel is saying that Pharaoh will *repent* of his violence and killing.[2]

This last portrait of Pharaoh, drawn from Isaiah and Ezekiel, among other texts, suggests that Egypt and its despotic king will come around, in the end. For Pharaoh himself, that end might really be *the end*: it seems he makes his confession in the afterlife, down in Sheol somewhere.[3] But Ezekiel, that priest who was exiled to Babylon, knows firsthand that there is no place that God cannot reach. Paul knew that too when he wrote that not even death could separate us from the

1. See Walter Brueggemann, *Theology of the Old Testament: Testimony, Dispute, Advocacy* (Minneapolis: Fortress, 1997), 522: "Thus Israel has lost two of its pet names. . . . In this daring utterance we witness the process by which other peoples are redesignated to be Yahweh's chosen peoples so that, taken paradigmatically, all peoples become Yahweh's chosen peoples. . . . The [inexplicable] promise [of God] is an invitation to Israel to move beyond itself and its self-serving ideology, to reposition itself in the family of beloved nations, and to reimagine Yahweh, beyond any self-serving, privileged claim, into the largest possible horizon, as the one who intends well-being for all the nations, including the ones formerly defiant and condemned."

2. Brueggemann, *Theology of the Old Testament*, 506: "Pharaoh will at long last, at the eleventh hour, repent and become a willing vassal of Yahweh. . . . The brutal, sad tale of Egypt unexpectedly portrays even Egypt coming, at the last moment, out of the fissure of devastating punishment to new life with Yahweh." Brueggemann depends on a study by Ellen F. Davis, "'And Pharaoh Will Change His Mind . . .' (Ezekiel 32:31): Dismantling Mythical Discourse," in *Theological Exegesis: Essays in Honor of Brevard S. Childs*, ed. Christopher Seitz and Kathryn Greene-McCreight (Grand Rapids: Eerdmans, 1999), 224–39, esp. 234–35. Davis thinks "the prophet conceives the ideological conversion of Israel's oldest enemy as the final movement of the exodus. This marks an end to Pharaoh's vacillating changes of heart that began when he first encountered the power of Israel's God. . . . Pharaoh's change of mind is the ultimate confirmation of the reality of Israel's God. The conversion of Egypt is a witness even more powerful to compel belief—even Israel's own belief—than would be Egypt's extinction" (235). There may be points of connection here with the centurion's remark in Mark 15:39.

3. See Walther Eichrodt, *Ezekiel: A Commentary*, OTL (Philadelphia: Westminster, 1970), 441.

love of God (Rom 8:35–39). And we know it, too, when we confess in the Apostles' Creed that Christ's descent went all the way to hell.

Good-and-Not-Easy News

Just imagine that—oppressive Egypt, despotic Pharaoh—coming around to God: to God's ways, God's views, God's *side*; and being blessed, not by old Jacob but by old Jacob's God who calls Egypt "my people" with its king "my son." That is simply unbelievable. But if you can believe it, it is the Good News of the Gospel, especially if you are or have been on the Egyptian side of things—if you know what I mean—or if you've glimpsed a bit of Pharaoh around your house lately if not also in your heart. It means there is hope, too, for you, for me, for us—in the end—even if we have been backing the wrong guy for far too long.

But you know as well as I do that good news is rarely easy news. The good news that even Pharaoh can be saved is hard news to stomach if you've ever been on *the other side* of Egypt—if you know what I mean—under Pharaoh's thumb, on the wrong side of his sword for far too long. And all of us have, in one way or another, but some of us have *far, far* more than others. From this perspective, it just doesn't seem right, does it, that Pharaohs and oppressors and all the rest who've benefited for hundreds of years suddenly get to be numbered with God's chosen, even get called special names that God normally reserves only for the most beloved. No, it doesn't seem right at all, nor fair. But those of us who are Christians confess something about this, too, in our Creed: "I believe," we say, "in the forgiveness of sin." Not just *my* sin, you see, but just sin—*all* sins, presumably—even, one worries, the sins of others against us. Christians confess that those, too, can be forgiven, which is why we pray about "those who sin against us" every time we recite the prayer our Lord taught us. And if that's not bad enough, there's that parable our Lord taught us—the one about the landowner who paid the people who worked only one hour, at the very end of the day, the exact same amount as those who worked the whole hot day long (Matt 20:1–16). "Don't I have the right to do what I want with what belongs to me?" that landowner asks the disgruntled early bird workers. "Or are you resentful because I'm generous?" And if we aren't clear on his point, Jesus—as he so often does—drills it home: "Those who are last will be first," he says. "And those who are first will be last" (Matt 20:15–16 CEB).

That's not easy either. *None* of that is easy. But if you're asking me, the scenario that is most applicable is the first one I described, since many of us have often spent far too much time enjoying the fleshpots of Egypt-land worshiping its god-king Pharaoh, benefiting from his system. And so, as you'll no doubt have deduced by now, in point of fact I *really have* been thinking about American Pharaoh lately.

Not the equine kind, but American Pharaoh in every one of his innumerable incarnations—American Pharaohs *plural*: living and walking among us now, today, *in* us, even *as* us. And so the possibility of his repentance and his ultimate redemption is quite poignant, isn't it? Because it isn't just about him. It's also about us. It's about our country. It's about our church. It's about *us*. Lord, have mercy; Christ, have mercy; Spirit, have mercy.

> So, now, finally, brothers and sisters, be strong in the Lord and in the power of his might. Put on the full armor of God, so that you can take your stand against the devil's schemes. For our struggle is not against flesh and blood, but against the rulers, against the authorities, against the powers of this dark world and against the spiritual forces of evil in high places. Therefore put on the full armor of God, so that when the day of evil comes, you may be able to stand firm, and after you have done all that is required of you, you can remain standing. So stand firm, with the belt of *truth* around your waist, with *justice* as your breastplate, and as shoes for your feet put on whatever will make you ready to proclaim the gospel of *peace*. In addition to all this, take up the shield of *faith*, which can extinguish all the flaming arrows of the evil one. Take the helmet of *salvation* and also the sword of the *Spirit*, which is *the word of God*. And pray in the Spirit on all occasions with all kinds of prayers and requests. Keep this in mind, stay alert, and always keep on praying for *all* the Lord's people. (Eph 6:10–18)[4]

Amen.[5]

---

4. The translation is an adaptation of NIV, CEB, and NRSV.

5. Only after finishing this sermon did I have opportunity to read closely Walter Brueggemann's "American Pharaoh's Last Race," in *Tenacious Solidarity: Biblical Provocations on Race, Religion, Climate, and the Economy*, ed. Davis Hankins (Minneapolis: Fortress, 2018), 149–73. There are some obvious points of resonance, though Brueggemann's essay is far more extensive and wide-ranging than my sermon. Since I had looked at his volume at some point before writing my sermon, and must have glanced at this essay (or at least its title), I suspect that I was somehow influenced by it, even if only subconsciously, since Brueggemann's influence always lies heavily on me—even, evidently, when I'm not fully conscious of it!

15

Designated Readers: Deuteronomy's Portrait of the Ideal King—or Is It Preacher?

> When he [the king] sits on his royal throne, he himself must write a copy of this Instruction on a scroll . . . and he must read in it every day of his life. (Deut 17:18–19 CEB)

If you know anything about preaching, you'll know that a number of famous preachers and teachers of preaching have encouraged us to preach *like* Scripture itself.[1] Put slightly differently, this means that our practices of teaching and preaching should be *formed and informed* by Scripture itself. I agree wholeheartedly, and, in a related vein, have often encouraged students to develop their theologies of Scripture on the basis of specific texts from Scripture. Wanting to set a good example, I've tried to do this myself—I have five texts on my "for sure" list. They include:

Versions of this sermon have been preached in both seminary chapels (e.g., Candler School of Theology, Atlanta, GA; September 2006) and local churches (e.g., Oconee Presbyterian Church, Oconee, GA; September 2006). Its origins lie in a reflection for a gathering of theological educators at the Wabash Center for Teaching and Learning in Theology and Religion (Summer 2005). The present iteration is most similar to a reflection offered to a group of biblical scholars concerned with teaching exegesis in theological schools (Columbia Theological Seminary; August 2007) and a sermon at a continuing education event for United Methodist pastors (Orlando, FL; March 2008). I have retained many of the elements that mark it as an originally oral address.

1. See especially the works of Thomas G. Long, *Preaching and the Literary Forms of the Bible* (Philadelphia: Fortress, 1989); T. Long, *The Witness of Preaching*, 2nd ed. (Louisville: Westminster John Knox, 2005), esp. 117–71; and Fred B. Craddock, *Preaching* (Nashville: Abingdon, 1985), esp. 170–93. See also Mike Graves, *The Sermon as Symphony: Preaching the Literary Forms of the New Testament* (Valley Forge, PA: Judson Press, 1997).

- John 6:68: "Simon Peter answered him, 'Lord, to whom can we go? You have the words of eternal life.'" (NRSV)
- Eccl 5:2: "Never be rash with your mouth, nor let your heart be quick to utter a word before God, for God is in heaven, and you upon earth; therefore let your words be few." (NRSV)
- Job 2:10: "[Job] replied... 'Shall we accept good from God, and not trouble?'" (NIV)
- Gen 32:31: "The sun rose upon him as he passed Penuel ['the face of God'], limping because of his hip." (NRSV)

The fifth, very important one is Deut 17:14–20, Deuteronomy's law of the king:

> When you have come into the land that the LORD your God is giving you, and have taken possession of it and settled in it, and you say, "I will set a king over me, like all the nations that are around me," you may indeed set over you a king whom the LORD your God will choose. One of your own community you may set as king over you; you are not permitted to put a foreigner over you, who is not of your own community. Even so, he must not acquire many horses for himself, or return the people to Egypt in order to acquire more horses, since the LORD has said to you, "You must never return that way again." And he must not acquire many wives for himself, or else his heart will turn away; also silver and gold he must not acquire in great quantity for himself. When he has taken the throne of his kingdom, he shall have a copy of this law [Hebrew: *torah*] written for him in the presence of the levitical priests. It shall remain with him and he shall read in it all the days of his life, so that he may learn to fear the LORD his God, diligently observing all the words of this law [Hebrew: *torah*] and these statutes, neither exalting himself above other members of the community nor turning aside from the commandment, either to the right or to the left, so that he and his descendants may reign long over his kingdom in Israel. (NRSV)

Deuteronomy 17 and Old Testament Kingship

It is a striking and rather under-known fact that in all of the Pentateuch, with its dizzying and seemingly countless laws, there is only one that concerns the king. Several monarchs are mentioned in the Torah, of course, but there are no laws about the native Israelite king apart from this one single passage in Deut 17.

Now, despite the venerable status of Deut 17 as Holy Writ, or the long tradition of the threefold office of Christ and his ministers as prophets, priests, and kings, I know that royal imagery is often in bad company these days. It's too autocratic, too hierarchical, too dictatorial, hegemonic, you name it. I mean, it's just plain anti-democratic. Nevertheless, despite the many and real problems we may have with royal imagery, I have become convinced that this text holds great promise for us as preachers and servants of the Gospel (or is it servants of Torah?). Let me make a few comments.

As you may already know—but if not, now you do—most biblical scholars are agreed that the foibles of the Israelite monarchy and, especially, the mistakes of Solomon, are on the brain of the author of Deut 17. In the canonical flow, of course, Deut 17 long precedes Israel's demand for a king in 1 Sam 8, let alone Solomon's rule as described in 1 Kgs 1–11. But the links, both lexical and thematic, are strong—so strong that when readers get to those later passages they already know something about them and how they are at odds with Deuteronomy's law of the king. They hear the echoes and catch the allusions. Of course, that is probably exactly what Scripture wants us to catch and to hear—or at least those authors responsible for Samuel and Kings, called the Deuteronomists, who apparently crafted their work with Deuteronomy on *their* brains. So it is not impossible—and, in fact, according to many, quite likely—that Deut 17 was written after firsthand exposure to the exploits and exploitations of the monarchy. The deuteronomic law of the king, that is, is to no small degree *against* kingship. Rejoice all who dislike tyrants!

The "Designated Reader" Back Then

Now the "against-ness" of kingship in Deut 17 is rather obvious and stark when set against Solomonic excess in 1 Kings, but it is apparent already in the words of the text itself. Note the severe restrictions placed on the executive branch:

- First, *required membership in the community* (17:15; cf. 17:20a). The king must be an Israelite. A foreigner may not be king "over you"; at least, a foreign-born king may not be selected by Israel itself. The language used here is quite familial: literally, "one of your brothers" you may set over you as king, but not a stranger—not someone Israel doesn't know. This keeps leadership all in the family, so to speak, and already hints at some of the restrictions that will follow.
- Second, *limitations on economic excess* (17:16; cf. 17:17b). The acquisition of horses is connected in real ways to exploitation: returning the people to Egypt *in order to* multiply horses. The king can't do that.
- Third, *limitations on personal excess* (17:17; cf. 17:20a). This includes both sexual and economic excess. Even what might be called "interpersonal excess" is forbidden: the king shall not exalt himself (literally, "his heart") over the other members of the community (literally, again, "his brothers"). In the old days, this was called "pride"; the king can't have any.

These significant restrictions are answered by a series of positive injunctions, which can be boiled down to two (and ultimately, probably, just one):

- First, *he must write a copy of this Torah in a book.* Against the NRSV, the verb for writing used here is singular and active and implies, I think, the king's *own* copying of the document. This king is, in short, *a Torah scribe.* In contrast to general ancient Near Eastern practice, the deuteronomic king is not a promulgator of the law so much as its servant and faithful transmitter.
- Second, *this Torah must be with him and he must read in it all the days of his life.* This personally written copy of the Torah "shall remain with him" (NRSV) and it will get a lot of use: he must read in it constantly. Note the length and specificity of the injunction: "all the days"—that means *every day*—"of his life"—that means *all of it.* This king is, in short, *a Torah reader.* A devoted and expert one at that.

There's more to the passage, but the heat and light are at the collision of the negative prohibitions and the positive injunctions. By any standards, let alone ancient Near Eastern ones, what Deuteronomy is describing here is *by no stretch of the imagination* a king. I mean, sure, no problem with the king being indigenous or monogamous—we're probably okay with that (even if our politicians often aren't!). But what kind of king, of any substance at least, doesn't have lots of stuff? What king is not proud, exalted over his people? Those are hallmarks of monarchy—"monarchy," by definition, means "rule" (Greek: *archē*) of "one" (Greek: *monos*) over all others. *By definition*—even if those are, in fact, the *negative* hallmarks of monarchy. But the Israelite monarch imagined by Deuteronomy has none of those negative hallmarks. In their place, Deuteronomy envisions not a king but *a designated reader*: someone—you can't even call him a king; if you do, make sure you put it in quotation marks—someone who copies the Torah, who has it at his elbow at all times, and who reads in it incessantly with the result being that this person serves the Lord, keeps the Torah and the statutes, remains humble, is faithful, and thus ensures a long rule for himself and his descendants. And who wouldn't want a king or a dynasty like that?

The "Designated Reader" Now

This notion of the designated reader has stuck with me ever since I first happened upon it. No external and certainly no exploitive accoutrements of power here. Instead, *service by means of reading.* I often tell students—especially those preparing for ministry, but also other folks: pastors, even liturgists in training—that

Deut 17 is not a bad model for them. They are, or will be soon enough, designated readers, designated to read things that those whom they serve have neither time, desire, or, let's face it, interest in reading. Things like Scripture!

The designated reader is a good model for all kinds of people, but I think it is an especially pregnant image for those of us who preach and teach the Bible, the good news of the Gospel of God. Imagine having—imagine being!—a preacher or teacher who wears no external and exploitive accoutrements of power whether those are manifested in heavy-handedness in a board meeting; intellectual posturing by means of the well-placed but perhaps mispronounced Greek, Hebrew, or Latin term in the midst of the sermon; or the ever-expanding and thoroughly careerist resume, but who is, instead, a member of the community, kin with students and parishioners, and, among other things—no scratch that, not among other things, but as *the only thing*—is their designated reader. Talk about a subject-centered classroom! Talk about a Scripture-centered community! Talk about a Bible-oriented church!

This is a counterintuitive, counter-cultural model of leadership, but an empowering one for those whom we serve, the community of God's people. It is an image of a queen robbed of queenship as humanly constructed, void of all the marks of success as commonly understood: money, sex, power—that unholy trinity that rules our churches as much as it does our economy. Instead, in their place, we have a ruler envisioned as God desires: a designated reader. And a designated reader *of Torah*. For we must not forget that it is not just any book or every book that this ruler reads and writes. It is Deuteronomy itself. It is Torah. It is Scripture.

Now I know that last bit is easy for me to say, being a biblical scholar, Old Testament at that, who's worked a bit in Deuteronomy with more of that ahead of me. Not everyone is so lucky, I'm afraid! But whatever our interests and expertise, mine included, we know we have to read a lot of books, not just Deuteronomy, not just Torah, and not just Scripture. (Alas!) But even then we can still be designated readers for our people. Indeed, Deuteronomy's model of a humble ruler (better: reader) might be even more important vis-à-vis these other "books" (or subjects or areas) since they are often arcane, esoteric, in other tongues like seminary-speak, and so completely inaccessible to our people. How easy to lord it over them! To impress them with our learning and insight! But the designated reader does not exalt her heart over her brothers and sisters.

Whatever books we must read in as part of our disciplines and as part of our callings, if we wish to learn from Deut 17, then we must not neglect its emphasis on Torah. I think that means that our pursuit, our designated reading—whatever the subject—must come back to and be rooted in our life with God and our pursuit of God; that it must be rooted in God's instruction, in God's designs and purposes. All these things and more are evoked by the Hebrew word *torah*, which means "law" or "instruction," on the one hand, and, on the other, can be used to designate the five books of Moses, or even all of Scripture itself. Deuteronomy's emphasis on reading the Torah, not something else, at all times means that ours is a properly *theological* task. There is more to that task than Scripture, though Scripture plays a preeminent role (in my humble Old Testament opinion!). But, regardless, our task involves everywhere and always *God*. *That* discipline must be with us always and we must read in it all the days of our life. And we must write it, write *in* it, ourselves, not remaining content merely with *someone else's* copy.[2]

What Good Is Designated Reading?

Now I think all this business about reading makes a lot of sense. But let's face it: I'm an academic. I get paid to read. I get paid to read my Bible! And while the same is true for you, even folk like me are keenly aware that the time pressures facing ministers—facing *anyone* these days—are, in a word, overwhelming. So, if we stop and think for a minute—outside this nice occasion and these nice words about Deuteronomy—we may have real doubts about the relevance of all this reading business. When viewed from a larger perspective reading may seem like a highly *un*important luxury in the face of the real difficulties plaguing our world. What use is reading, in the face of war, I.E.D.s, famine, suffering, political races, murdered student body presidents, and all the rest?

I don't think that Deuteronomy is naïve—nor that we ourselves should be naïve—at this point, *about* these points. Huge social ills and large matters of public policy will not be fixed easily by simply reading a scroll.[3] But then again, this scroll, this Torah we are talking about is not just any book; it isn't *like* any other book. The book that we've been called to read—chosen by the Lord to serve as designated reader of—what goes on in this book, as you know (and if you don't, then I suggest you start reading!), is an alternative vision of how the world can be, a transforming vision of God, of society, of humanity, and all points in between and even beyond. It is a book, a vision, a place where the lowly are exalted, the powerful and wicked brought low (Luke 1:51–53); where widows and orphans count as much as the married and the parented; where money is left out on office desks for the nighttime cleaning crew to pocket; where a no-name Moabitess might just end up great-grandmother to Israel's greatest king (Ruth 4); where the

2. Note Jeffrey H. Tigay, *Deuteronomy*, 168, who points out that "writing makes a more lasting impression than does merely reading."

3. See Brueggemann, *Deuteronomy*, 186–87, which is influential on me here.

weapons of war are melted down and made into John Deere tractors just in time for harvest; where nations not only sign non-proliferation treaties, they decide to disband their armies altogether and do away with intelligence agencies (Isa 2:4); and where the very incarnation of tyranny—the monarch (*tyrannus*)—turns out to be the ideal worshipper of God, first in her seminary class, attuned to the Lord's ways and the Lord's word because she reads about it and in it every single day. Oh, and every night too. Don't forget that. "All the days of her life."

And if this reading is going to matter, we mustn't miss the fact that it is done *on behalf of others*—on behalf of future generations—so that not only the rulers themselves can live long in the land of God's promise, but also their children after them, ensuring that this benevolent, Torah-obsessed, God-preoccupied designated reading on behalf of others never ends.[4] The fact that our world leaders—*all* of them it seems—evidently do not care much for such rule or such reading only underscores the urgency of it. Far from being irrelevant or unimportant, then, the image of the designated reader is desperately needed, even if, for the moment, reading seems like the last thing one should be doing.

The Results of Designated Reading

And what's the result of all this reading? Perhaps it is too optimistic, but for Deuteronomy the result is as automatic as it is axiomatic: right worship of the Lord, obedience, humility, fidelity, and a long rule—if in fact "rule" is the best word, a long "reading and preaching" might be more appropriate. Now let me ask you: who would not want to have a pastor or a preacher like that? And who wouldn't want to *be* a preacher or pastor like that?[5]

---

4. Compare Brueggemann, *Deuteronomy*, 188: "The Torah keeps the managers of power fixed on the social fabric and the neighbor who has no horses, no silver, no gold, and perhaps only one wife or one husband who is underfunded."

5. Thanks to Walter Brueggemann for his help and encouragement. I'd like to dedicate this sermon to him as a very small token of my appreciation to him as a model scholar, powerful preacher, and delightful friend.

16

On Priesting

OT Lesson: Selections from Lev 13–14 (esp. 13:1–8, 45–52; 14:33–42, 54–57); NT Lesson: 1 Pet 2:1–10

But you are a chosen race, a royal priesthood, a holy nation, God's own people. (1 Pet 2:9 NRSV)

The priest will examine the infection on the skin. (Lev 13:3 CEB)

The Priesthood of Believers

Let me begin by answering the question that's on everyone's mind: "Is he really going to preach on that stuff about skin disease from Leviticus?" The answer to that question is: Oh yes. Oh yes, I am!

But it'll take me a minute to get there.

We need to begin with some background, which in the case of this sermon means the New Testament lesson and the statements in 1 Pet 2 that "you are a chosen race, a royal priesthood, a holy nation, God's own people" (v. 9 NRSV) and that you should "let yourselves . . . be a holy priesthood" (v. 5 NRSV). The "you" in those statements is plural: "y'all" if you will, or "all y'all" if you're originally from the South (I'm not, so had to learn that fine point of grammar).

This plural "you" in 1 Peter who are becoming a holy priesthood provides us with biblical precedent for what has come to be called "the priesthood of all believers"—a notion made famous by Martin Luther. But that idea is much earlier

---

This sermon was first preached at the Candler School of Theology in November 2010.

than Luther, as 1 Peter clearly demonstrates. But it's also much earlier than 1 Peter since the sentiment expressed there surely goes back to Exod 19. In that chapter, on the cusp of the covenant at Sinai, Israel is informed that if they will only obey God's voice and keep God's covenant, then they will be God's treasured possession, a holy nation, and a priestly kingdom (Exod 19:5–6). That's where 1 Peter gets that language from: 1 Pet 2 read Exod 19!

So that's our starting point, *the* starting point, you might say: according to both New and Old Testaments, God's people—originally Israel, but now also, belatedly, the Church—are priests. "The priesthood of all believers" is a biblical doctrine from start to finish. All well and good. But what, you may be asking, is a priest? I mean, I know we know about priests—Roman Catholic ones, for instance, but also Episcopalian ones (one kind can marry, the other can't, if you didn't know). But what is a priest according to the Bible such that all of Israel, and all of the church, and all of us can be called "priests"? So, again: what, exactly, is a priest?

On the Verb "to Priest"

On the one hand, that is a very good question; on the other hand, it may be poorly put. Let me explain. Let's stick with the Exodus text, since it is the foundational one, and talk about Hebrew for a minute. In Hebrew, the word for priest is *kōhēn*. Now in English, "priest" is a noun,[1] but Hebrew *kōhēn* isn't a noun so much as a verb—well, truth be told, it appears to be a *participle*, which means it's *both*: it is "a verbal noun" to be precise.[2] But the *verbal* aspect of the word, and the verbal quality of the root from which it derives,[3] means that one shouldn't ask what a priest *is* but what a priest *does*.

"To *be* a priest" isn't quite right, then; it is better to think of "*acting* the priest" or "acting *as* (a) priest." That means the noun "priest" isn't quite right either; instead, it would be better to think of "one who priests" or, even, with the gerund ending

---

1. The *Oxford English Dictionary* (*OED*) also lists a verb "to priest," with two definitions. *OED* deems the first, "to exercise the ministry or functions of a priest," obsolete with the most recent reference dating to 1642. The second, "to make [a person] a priest; to ordain to the priesthood" (normally used in the passive) includes a citation as recent as 1994, but it, too, seems largely archaic if not extinct.

2. Most Hebrew lexicons list *kōhēn* as a noun, in part because the verb itself is only attested in the *piel*, and *kōhēn* is an active participle of the *qal* stem. The dictionaries thus tend to treat the *piel* verb as deriving from an original noun form (hence, technically, a "denominative" verb), rather than vice versa, which is more often the case with verbal roots. Comparative Semitic evidence suggests, however, that a *qal* verbal form may well have existed.

3. Unless the verb is a denominative (see the previous note).

common to English participles, "one priesting." Well, enough grammar! The point is simply that the notion of being a priest is more about *acting* the priest, *doing* what a priest *does*, than it is about *being* or *existing* as one. In fact, that's really the only way to make sense of texts like Exod 19 or 1 Pet 2, or the idea of the priesthood of all believers for that matter, because we all know, as did the biblical writers, that despite this crucial point about "acting the priest" there *really* are people who really *are* priests—preeminently, of course, "Aaron & Sons," but also other priestly authorities of various sorts, including, belatedly, our own priests, pastors, ministers, and so forth. Those kinds of folks *are* priests in the *being* sort of way—well, that's what their ordination papers say at any rate. But insofar as being a priest is about *acting* the priest—*priesting*, as it were—then *anyone*, even those not formally ordained, can be part of the royal priesthood, the holy priesthood, the priestly kingdom. And that's exactly what 1 Pet 2 and Exod 19 teach us: Anyone can be—or rather anyone *is*—a priest *if* they act the part, *precisely because* they act the part. They *priest* even if they aren't "priests" (in the formally ordained sort of way).[4]

Well, again, all well and good. But we haven't really answered the question have we? "Priests" are those who "priest," who act the part, who "do" priesting—and that includes (or *could* include) all of us. But what exactly is the content of the verb "to priest"? How, exactly, does one *priest*?

Leviticus on Priesting—Or, Priesting Back Then

Here we come at last to the Old Testament lesson from Leviticus. As you know, probably because Leviticus is your favorite book of the Bible (here I jest), Leviticus is *the* book for priests and for priesting (here I do *not* jest). The English title, "Leviticus," says as much, tying it directly to the Levites. The rabbis called the book *tōrat kōhănîm*, "priestly law," which makes the same point but in Hebrew instead of Latin.

It is precisely because of the book's relationship to the priests that so much of Leviticus seems pertinent only for the kind of priests who *are* priests—by birth and training and service—you know, Aaron and all the rest. After all, not everyone was qualified to officiate at those bloody sacrifices. Not everyone would *want* to officiate at those bloody sacrifices! But Leviticus, *the* book for priests, also knows that priesting is about *doing*, not just being. Especially at the end of the book, starting in chapter 17, Leviticus indicates that the qualities of priesting—especially holiness and purity—should mark *all* of Israel, not just the ordained few. You'll probably remember how Lev 19:1–2 famously puts it: "The LORD spoke to Moses, saying: Speak to all the congregation of the people of Israel and say to them: You shall be

---

4. The reverse is also true: even those ordained as priests aren't priests if they don't act the part!

holy for I, the LORD your God, am holy."[5] Yes, here too the "you" is a plural all y'all: it refers to the entire congregation of the people of Israel, not just the priests.

So in light of that fact, not to mention Exodus, 1 Peter, Martin Luther, and all the rest, it pays to take a second, closer look at the priestly manual of Leviticus to see what we can learn from it about priesting.

When we do that we see that we can actually learn quite a lot—the book is twenty-seven chapters, after all. So while I'm tempted to break into lecture mode and cover the whole book in twenty to thirty PowerPoint slides with handouts and a pop quiz, we need to focus a bit, and the Old Testament lesson from chapters 13–14 will do the trick.

Now, I imagine that you might have felt a bit confused, perhaps even bored, as you read this Old Testament lesson. These chapters of Leviticus are unlikely to comprise the basis for the next blockbuster sermon series from Rick Warren, Joel Osteen, T. D. Jakes, or Beth Moore (though I wouldn't put it past Beth!).[6] I mean, come on, these chapters are about some sort of skin disease for heaven's sake! (By the way, this disease has traditionally been called "leprosy," but it is almost certainly not the same thing we call leprosy today.[7])

On a second look, though, these chapters on skin disease might be more exciting than initially thought. Priesting, in this section of Leviticus, is quite similar to the things they do at the Centers for Disease Control (CDC) or in a medical school or back in the lab on a C.S.I. (Crime Scene Investigators) episode. Priesting here involves examining infections to see how far they've penetrated the epidermis, looking for telltale signs of disease, quarantining sick parties to see if they get better, watching for the spread of the pathology, and finally making a determination as to the state of the afflicted individual: healthy and whole or not.

Now I suppose how exciting that is could be debated, but there can be no question whatsoever that it is *disgusting*. Priesting, in this section of Leviticus, involves a number of gross *un*-pleasantries: infection, rash, swelling, boils, scabies, burns, raw flesh, and fungus to name a few. And the priest is the one who has to examine such nastiness, not only on people, but also on their clothes and similar

---

5. Lev 19:1–2; notably, v. 2b is cited in 1 Pet 1:16.

6. In point of fact, it is well known that former pastor Rob Bell preached an extended expositional series on Leviticus when he began his Mars Hill church.

7. Modern day "leprosy" is Hansen's disease. For an exhaustive discussion, see Jacob Milgrom, *Leviticus*, AB 3–3B, 3 vols. (New York: Doubleday, 1991–2001), 1:768–826, esp. 816–20. Also of interest are the various causes of skin disease in Leviticus (see Milgrom, *Leviticus*, 1:820–24). The difference between the biblical disease (which in Hebrew is called ṣāra'at) and modern "leprosy" are particularly obvious if (a) ṣāra'at is actually a combination of diseases, not just one; and/or if (b) ṣāra'at isn't a disease at all but rather a ritual impurity of some sort.

items. And as if that weren't nauseating enough, the priest has to do the same for houses and for *everything*—animate and inanimate—that is found in them. Exciting? Maybe. Disgusting? Most definitely.

Since "priest" is as much a verb as it is a noun, the verbs that describe the priestly duties in these chapters are significant: the priest *examines*, which means the priest *looks at closely and sees*; the priest *quarantines*; the priest *declares* clean or unclean; the priest *orders* washing, the priest *burns* infected items. There are other verbs, but those are the main ones.

Well, once again, all well and good. But who cares? What does all that obscure priestly lore—what Leviticus calls "the Instruction concerning every infection of . . . skin disease" (14:54, 57 CEB)—what does all that have to do with being a priest now or being a priestly nation today? If 1 Pet 2 and Exod 19 are right about everyone being a priest, what does that have to do with us?

Well, quite a lot actually. Among other things, these chapters in Leviticus show that the priestly function is a *hermeneutical* one—that means it is an *interpretive* one, and that means if you're going to be a priest, if you're going to act the priest, you better know what you're talking about and you better know what you're looking for. Let me repeat that: *if you're going to be a priest, if you're going to act the priest, you better know what you're talking about and you better know what you're looking for*. And, since all of us are priests according to 1 Pet 2 and Exod 19 that means *we* better know what we're talking about and know what we're looking for. The priest on duty who receives the 911 call in the middle of the night regarding a possible outbreak of skin disease doesn't saunter over to the infected house armed with a few platitudes, a soft-but-warm handshake, and some nondescript but well-intentioned good wishes, perhaps a tepid prayer. Not in Leviticus. In Leviticus, the priest who gets the late night 911 call gears up—probably in a Level 4 Biosafety suit! Then the priest packs the microscope, the surgical glasses with the built-in magnifying loupes, plenty of plastic gloves, and makes sure his brain is clear, his hand is steady, and the knowledge he needs is at the ready.

I'm stretching things a bit, of course. Ancient Israelite priests lacked the medical apparatus, but you can be certain of this: they didn't lack the *knowledge* necessary to make the crucial and critical determination of "clean" or "unclean." Nor did they lack the *powers of observation* that were just as crucial to making that call. Nor were they afraid to make that call. Well, let me take that last part back. I suspect that sometimes the priests *were* afraid to make that call. Quarantining people (especially important people), destroying infected items (especially expensive items), even whole houses if need be, is time consuming, costly, and difficult work. And it's risky work. What if you're wrong? At least occasionally, the priests must have gulped before pronouncing the diagnosis—perhaps they even took some extra time to have one more look at that rash to make sure the hair really was white, the skin really raw. Maybe they took time to utter one more quick prayer for divine guidance in the diagnosis. But make no mistake: they couldn't shirk that task. That task was part of their priesting.

Now why should *that* be the case? Why not just declare everything clean?[8] That seems much nicer, much more happy, far more *Christian*. Well, in part, because not everything was clean. Not everything *is* clean. But we need to be absolutely clear about something: the priestly determination of clean and unclean wasn't willy-nilly. It wasn't a mean-spirited way to keep some people down, other people out, and the priests on top. In Leviticus, the determination of holy, clean, and unclean states was what permitted access to God (or not). And those states even seem to have affected God's presence with Israel. If someone was unclean, that is, they weren't allowed access to worship and were even barred from basic aspects of communal life; and if too many people were unclean, the community itself—and its worship—might become so polluted that God would punish Israel or leave altogether.[9] So, far from being some odd archaic ritual or mean-spirited device, this time-consuming, costly, and difficult task of declaring someone or something unclean and then rectifying whatever problems might obtain—that was the difference between life with God and life apart from God, which is to say that it was the difference between life and death. *Everything* hung on this priestly task—not just for an individual, but also for their family, their houses, even their wardrobe. Even more: this priestly task affected the people of God as a whole, their relationship with the Lord, and their nature and function as God's people, which was, don't forget, to be a priestly nation in the first place.

So, that's the priestly task according to Lev 13–14. Exciting? Maybe. Disgusting? Most definitely. Whatever the case, make no mistake about this: it was one of life-and-death importance. And if it wasn't for those with weak stomachs, then neither was it for the faint of heart.

Priesting Now

Well, once again, and for one last time, all well and good, but what does that have to do with us? Quite a lot actually—if, that is, we care about Exod 19 and 1 Pet 2

---

8. Though one might be tempted to think of Acts 10, that story is particularly about clean and unclean *food*, and the lesson Peter needs to learn about gentiles, whom, it might be said, Peter once considered unclean, but who now, through the gospel, have been given access—which is to say that they have been given a means by which to become clean.

9. Cf. Lev 10 and Ezek 8–10, respectively.

or all those places where Jesus commissions his followers—the disciples and the church that followed them—to act like priests.[10] If we care about any of that, we must care about the life-and-death importance of the priestly duties in Leviticus and, belatedly, also now.

Now I know there are other models out there—in the Bible and in our culture—that we might entertain instead of this priestly one. Who wouldn't like to play the part of the monarch every now and then? I mean, sure, it's not exactly democratic, but there *are* a few good kings in the Bible—like one or two! And there's no question that some of our CEOs make as much money as some ancient kings and wield as much power as they did over as many people as they did. But then again there are a lot of bad kings in the Bible, and a lot of bad CEOs for that matter. Maybe the king/queen/CEO isn't such a great model after all.

What about the prophet, then? Who wouldn't want to be a firebrand like one of them? Speaking truth to those in power, representing God to humanity, completely fearless. But then again, prophets—both the biblical and contemporary variety—often end up dead before their time with no one to collect the life insurance. Seems too dangerous, if we're being honest.

So I guess there's nothing for it but the priestly role.

"And why not? Priests are nice, right? They're *ministers*, after all. They bind up the broken-hearted. In contrast to the fiery prophets, who represented God to humans, priests represent humans to God and that means they're compassionate, kind, you know, always-on-our-side-kind-of-folks. Maybe a bit wishy-washy at times, but hey, I mean, who am I to judge, right?"

No, not right. Quite wrong in fact. If you're a priest, if you are acting the priest, you are *precisely* the one tasked with the difficult determination—the difficult *judgment*—of clean and unclean, holy or profane, remediable or not. Don't get me wrong: I understand the sentiment—the desire to always be nice and accommodating, accepting and generous—I really do understand it; I have the same desire! And while I would like to say a lot more about that right now, some of which would be *against* that, I have to content myself with saying this: that any mundane, lackluster, easy-way-out vision of the priest and priestly service, whether ordained or not, is a far, far cry from the emergency room life-and-death circumstances and actions of priesting in Leviticus. If you want to be a priest, if you want to act the priest—and that's who we are and what we are to do according to Exodus, 1 Peter, and all the rest—then it's time for us to brush up on the priestly torah, practice our skills in diagnosis, and be ready to make some difficult calls. It's time to *examine, look closely, see*. It's time to *quarantine*. It's time to *declare* "clean" or

---

10. See, e.g., Matt 10:1, 8, 13; 16:19; 28:19–20; John 20:22–23.

"unclean." *Everything*—our very nature and purpose as God's people and the very nature and purpose of the people among whom we live—might be depending on *that* kind of priesting. But that other kind of priesting? The kind with nothing but easy platitudes, band-aids, and cheap grace? Not much of anything hangs on it. Certainly nothing important.

Everyone a Priest, like Jesus

In the past year or two I've taken to calling the students in my classes "priests." I used to call them "saints," a practice I borrowed from one of my old professors. "Well the saints are here," I'd say (as did my old prof), "now we can start class." But not every saint is an ordained priest, nor is every priest a saint—as much as we wish it were so—and so "priests" seems more appropriate to me. Not because my students aren't saints (of course they are!) but because they are in training to be priests. Put better, they are in training *to priest*, to *act* the priest. Calling them "priests" at the beginning of class reminds me of that—that I'm talking to priests and I shouldn't forget it. Perhaps it reminds them of the same—that they are studying for the priesthood, even if they're not Catholic or Episcopalian or Anglican.

If they remember this fact, and if I remember it too, then it seems that we'll be on the same page about the big priestly tasks:

- *the task of interpreting*—interpreting on the basis of priestly lore, that technical knowledge that not everyone knows nearly as well as they should, but on which everyone and so much depends;
- *the task of examining closely*, of really seeing things as they are;
- *the task of declaring* what is clean and what isn't; and
- *the task of offering* the remedies that restore the unclean back to their community and back to their God.

You might recall that in the first chapter of the Gospel of Mark, a leper—someone with skin disease like that described in Lev 13–14—comes to Jesus and says to him, "If you choose, you can make me clean." And Jesus, moved with pity,[11]

---

11. There is a famous variant in the Greek text at this point in Mark, which indicates that Jesus was not moved with pity but with "anger." Angry at what, we might ask: the leper's condition? how he had been ostracized? that he had to ask if Jesus "so willed"? The text does not say, but if the "angry" reading is more original, one sees again that the priestly task is not all about wish-washy, syrupy-sweet kind-heartedness. Sometimes it is conducted with indignation.

stretched out his hand and touched him, and said "I do choose. Be made clean!" (Mark 1:40–41 NRSV).

Listen: When Jesus did that, he was *acting the priest*. He wasn't pretending not to see the leper, he wasn't pretending not to notice the leprosy, and he certainly wasn't pretending he didn't know the difference between clean and unclean or what to do about that. Let anyone with ears to hear, listen. Let any who would be a part of God's priestly kingdom and holy nation, listen.

I want to end where I started: by reiterating that 1 Pet 2 and Exod 19, the book of Leviticus and Martin Luther, and many others all agree that all of this priestly business applies to all of us—whether we are ordained priests or not. *All of us* already *are* priests. It only remains to be seen if we'll act the part.

So, once again, hear the New Testament lesson:

Come to him, a living stone, though rejected by mortals yet chosen and precious in God's sight, and like living stones, let yourselves be built into a spiritual house, to be a holy priesthood, to offer spiritual sacrifices acceptable to God through Jesus Christ. (1 Pet 2:4–5 NRSV)

Amen.

17

Four Thoughts on Preaching and Teaching the Bible—Mostly the Old Testament

---

For whatever was written in former days was written for our instruction, so that by steadfastness and by the encouragement of the scriptures we might have hope. (Rom 15:4 NRSV)

[Rabbi] Ben Bag Bag said: Turn it [the Torah] and turn it (again) because everything is in it. And look in it and grow gray and old in it. And do not turn away from it because there is no better rule for you than it.[1]

True to its title, this chapter offers four thoughts on preaching and teaching the Bible—mostly the Old Testament. While I originally formulated these thoughts for teaching future pastors about the specific task of preaching from the Old Testament, I believe they also apply to teaching as well as preaching and to the New Testament as well as the Old.

Before getting to these four thoughts, both a disclaimer and a caveat are in order. First, the disclaimer: I am an Old Testament professor and teach Old Testament studies exclusively. One job hazard is that I must frequently justify this vocational focus. For example, I sometimes find it necessary to point out to my students that I am an Old Testament professor both by training and by choice. It is not because I failed the New Testament exam! A more significant and worrisome job hazard is that I often must justify the Old Testament itself. I will return to this last point momentarily.

---

1. *m. Avot* 5.22 (my translation).

Second is the caveat: I have intentionally left the title of this chapter—particularly the last part—open to more than one interpretation. On the one hand, I offer these four thoughts mostly *about* preaching the Old Testament, because that is how I originally formulated them. However, I believe they also apply to the New Testament and thus the whole of the Christian Bible. On the other hand, the second meaning of "Mostly the Old Testament" is that, if I had my druthers, Christian preaching and teaching from Scripture would be mostly preaching *from* the Old Testament! I do not have space or time to argue this point extensively or explicitly, but I do believe such a position is justifiable.[2] It must suffice here to observe that the sheer size and mass of the Old Testament alone indicate that one should preach from it far more often than from the New Testament. The Old Testament comprises approximately 77 percent of the Christian Bible, so one could easily imagine, statistically speaking alone, preaching from it three times as often as the New Testament. One might also appeal to the great German theologian-turned-martyr Dietrich Bonhoeffer, who wrote the following: "In my opinion it is not Christian to want to take our thoughts and feelings too quickly and too directly from the New Testament."[3] Bonhoeffer's statement is stunning—all the more so when we remember that one of his most famous books, *Psalms: The Prayer Book of the Bible*, is a thoroughly Christological reading of the book of Psalms.[4] I believe what enabled Bonhoeffer to make his statement is precisely the first point I wish to make on preaching and teaching the Old Testament. It concerns *address*.

Address

I agree completely with Ellen F. Davis who, in her excellent book *Wondrous Depth: Preaching the Old Testament*, states that the fundamental starting point for all good preaching of the Old Testament treats the Old Testament as *an urgent speaking presence that exercises salutary pressure on our lives*.[5]

---

2. On this and some of the other topics that follow, see further Brent A. Strawn, *The Old Testament Is Dying: A Diagnosis and Recommended Treatment*, Theological Explorations for the Church Catholic (Grand Rapids: Baker Academic, 2017).

3. Dietrich Bonhoeffer, *Letters and Papers from Prison*, enl. ed., ed. Eberhard Bethge (New York: Collier, 1972), 157.

4. See Dietrich Bonhoeffer, *Psalms: The Prayer Book of the Bible* (Minneapolis: Augsburg Fortress, 1970). For a brief analysis, see Brent A. Strawn, "Bonhoeffer on Enemies and Imprecation in the Psalms: A Biblical-Theological Commentary," *TJT* 37 (2021): 156–67.

5. See Ellen F. Davis, *Wondrous Depth: Preaching the Old Testament* (Louisville: Westminster John Knox, 2005), xiv: the Old Testament is "an urgent and speaking presence"; and p. 2: the Old Testament is "an immediate presence that exercises shaping force in Christian lives—indeed that serves as a source of salutary pressure on our lives."

Most Christians, I suspect, believe that about the New Testament or at least *think* they believe that about the New Testament. But many Christians are disturbingly open about the fact that they do *not* feel that way about the Old Testament. That is a very serious problem that good preaching and teaching can and must correct.[6] *Why* this is a very serious problem goes back to the heresy of Marcion, who already in the second century CE wanted to dismiss the Old Testament and "the Old Testament God" as fundamentally different from Jesus and the writings that would eventually become the New Testament. However, the Christian church decreed Marcion a heretic. By doing so, the church reasserted its belief in the inseparable and fundamental unity of the Old and New Testaments and their conjoined witness to the one God.[7]

How good preaching and teaching of the Bible will correct this very serious problem is precisely by treating the Old Testament and New, whether taught or preached, as an urgent speaking presence exercising salutary pressure on our lives. This is what I mean by "address," and I believe that the best preaching and teaching, from either Testament or from both, proceeds from this fundamental starting point: that Scripture demands our attention and obedience. And Scripture especially makes *these* demands because it is not just talking *at* us or *past* us, but is rather bearing in *on* us, bearing in *upon* us, and exercising pressure on us. But that pressure is ultimately of the best, most benevolent, and salvific kind.

Again, I believe most Christians, preachers, and teachers of Scripture believe this about the Bible (at least the New Testament) or *think* they believe this about the Bible (at least the New Testament). But I think they may be wrong, because in actual practice the use and function (or *non*-use and *non*-function) of the Old Testament in many churches bears little similarity to the demands of attention

---

6. I agree with Gerhard von Rad, who wrote not only that we *can* preach the Old Testament but that we *must* (see his *Biblical Interpretations in Preaching*, trans. John E. Steely [Nashville: Abingdon, 1977], 11: "The biblical texts *must* be preached—under all circumstances and at any cost. The people for whom we each have a responsibility need them for living [and for dying].... The biblical texts *can* be preached. This is a battleground, and there is much that must be clarified here"). *Can* and *must* went together in powerful and dangerous ways for von Rad who was a member of the Confessing Church movement amidst the terrible circumstances of Nazi Germany during World War II. They also go together in the situation we face today which attests to widespread devaluation and denigration of the Old Testament in much Christian experience and practice. Stated differently, I think very highly of the sacred task of preaching and its capacity to set theological and biblical matters "right" in the local church among contemporary believers.

7. The classic statement remains the five books against Marcion written by the early church writer Tertullian (ca. 160–220 CE).

and obedience. This is why "address" is so important, and this is why I mention it here as the first of my four thoughts.

Sola Scriptura

The import of Scripture's address leads directly to the second thought: *sola Scriptura* or "Scripture alone." This was, of course, one of the clarion calls of the Reformation.[8] By invoking it in this context, I mean that the Bible is sufficiently deep and significant that good preaching and teaching rarely, if ever, need to move beyond it.

Stated more pointedly with reference to preaching, *sola Scriptura* means the preacher need not worry about finding just the right illustration, movie clip, or image from the internet to "make" the sermon. The biblical text, *rightly preached*, is more than enough; the rest is often only a distraction. That is, the perfect illustration, image, or story *is* the biblical text itself or perhaps other related biblical texts. Again, I quote Davis, who makes this point nicely with particular reference to the biblical psalms: "What I am suggesting is that the psalms have nearly inexhaustible potential for making connections with the larger biblical story. This relieves the preacher of the anxiety that has become a modern trademark of the profession, namely, the perceived need to 'find an illustration,' on which the success of the sermon is often supposed to depend. That is a pernicious idea, for very often the illustration proves to be the tail that wags the dog of the sermon (and I use that last phrase advisedly)."[9] Elsewhere, Davis states, "The plain fact is that no preacher can ever be astonishing (in a positive sense!) unless she has first been astonished. And the only regular and fully reliable source of astonishment for the Christian preacher is Scripture itself."[10] To put this in language borrowed from Walter Brueggemann, we might say that the task of the preacher or teacher is to create and nurture a reality alternative to the dominant one around us. Thus, Scripture is the primary way we encounter that reality, live it, and live into it.[11] But

---

8. The others were *sola gratia* ("grace alone"), *sola fide* ("faith alone"), *solus Christus* ("Christ alone"), *soli Deo gloria* ("glory to God alone"). The existence of no less than five "solas," indicates that there are always more than one "sola" operative at any given point in time.

9. Davis, *Wondrous Depth*, 28.

10. Davis, *Wondrous Depth*, 2. M. Craig Barnes's wonderful book, *The Pastor as Minor Poet: Texts and Subtexts in the Ministerial Life* (Grand Rapids: Eerdmans, 2009), esp. 24–27, makes similar points.

11. Walter Brueggemann, *The Prophetic Imagination*, 2nd ed. (Minneapolis: Fortress, 2001), 3: "The task of prophetic ministry is to nurture, nourish, and evoke a consciousness and perception alternative to the consciousness and perception of the dominant culture around us."

all such lofty goals are forfeited if, instead of *sola Scriptura*, Scripture is just one item on the menu and maybe the least important and appetizing one at that (but the movie clip is amazing!).

Among other things, *sola Scriptura* underscores that the locus of authority for teachers and preachers of Scripture is *not* the teacher or preacher themselves, *nor* their charisma, *nor* their wisdom, *nor* even their really interesting stories from church camp. Instead, the locus of authority is *Scripture—its* authority, *its* wisdom, *its* stories and hymns, *its* prayers and poems, *its* prophecies and the like. Here, too, I think we believe this, at least in theory, but I fear we act otherwise. I fear we often preach and teach otherwise.

To be sure, the best preachers and teachers know they must "translate" and (re)present Scripture for and to the contemporary scene. That is never an easy task or a simplistic proposition. Nevertheless, a *sola Scriptura* kind of disposition as defined here remains completely essential. And it is felt (or not felt), I think, even in *how* Scripture is read and *how much* of it is read in church on any given Sunday morning.

Honesty

The third thought, *honesty*, notes that Scripture, especially the Old Testament, is characterized by a remarkable and at times even unbearable honesty about a number of different topics. Although the Old Testament is brutally candid about many things, at the very least two subjects must be mentioned as especially obvious: its honesty about *sin*, and its honesty about *suffering*.[12]

The New Testament, too, is honest, but I think we tend to read it in flat ways so its honesty is often lost on us.[13] But it is very hard indeed to miss the brutal honesty of the Old Testament and the stories of God's people contained there.

It seems to me that the Old Testament sets us an example at precisely this point. Instead of beating up on the Old Testament on account of these moments of extreme candor, we ought to emulate its brutal honesty. Stated differently, the old preaching strategy that repeatedly belittles Israel for "yet again" failing or "yet again" sinning needs to die a quick and painful death. In its place, sensitive preach-

---

12. Violence is yet another honest topic. For these three and for more on what follows, see Brent A. Strawn, *Honest to God Preaching: Talking Sin, Suffering, and Violence*, Working Preacher Books 7 (Minneapolis: Fortress, 2021).

13. Cf., e.g., Paul's not infrequent mentions of his own suffering, esp. in 2 Cor (e.g., 1:4–6, 8–10; 2:1–5; 11:23–29; 12:7–10; cf. Gal 4:19). In my experience, however, one hears less of these matters from the pulpit and far more about "Rejoice always, pray without ceasing, give thanks in all circumstances" (1 Thess 5:16–18a; cf. Phil 4:4).

ers and teachers will recognize we only know of Israel's sins and failings because Israel was honest enough to tell us about all that. We ought to take a clue from this and model similarly honest—even brutally honest—dispositions toward and in our life with God.[14] That would mean, at very least, that we become more honest about our own sin and suffering.[15]

Philip Yancey, in his book on the Old Testament, *The Bible Jesus Read*, captures something of this third point about honesty:

> From initial resistance, I moved to a reluctant sense that I *ought* to read the neglected three-quarters of the Bible. As I worked past some of the barriers (much like learning to read Shakespeare), I came to feel a *need* to read, because of what it was teaching me. Eventually I found myself *wanting* to read those thirty-nine books, which were satisfying in me some hunger that nothing else had—not even, I must say, the New Testament. They taught me about Life with God: not how it is supposed to work, but how it actually does work.[16]

Another example that underscores the power and function of the trenchant honesty found in the Old Testament is the well-known passage from a letter that Franz Kafka wrote to his friend Oskar Pollak, dated January 27, 1904, when Kafka was only twenty years old:

> If the book we are reading does not wake us, as with a fist hammering on our skull, why then do we read it? So that it shall make us happy? Good God, we would also be happy if we had no books, and such books as make us happy we could, if need be, write ourselves. But what we must have are those books which come upon us like ill-fortune, and distress us deeply, like the death of one we love better than ourselves, like suicide. A book must be an ice-axe to break the sea frozen inside us.[17]

14. For the benefits of such disclosure, see, among others, James W. Pennebaker, *Opening Up: The Healing Power of Expressing Emotions*, rev. ed. (New York: Guilford, 1997). See also, and further, Strawn, *Honest to God Preaching*, esp. 91–98.

15. The dynamics of, e.g., Isa 6:5–7 and the Psalms, respectively, show the stunning results of such honesty.

16. Philip Yancey, *The Bible Jesus Read* (Grand Rapids: Zondervan, 1999), 20–21 (his emphasis).

17. George Steiner, *Language and Silence: Essays on Language, Literature, and the Inhuman* (New Haven: Yale University Press, 1998), 67. Apparently this is Steiner's own translation of the letter and other, slightly different versions can be found (see, e.g., http://www.languagehat .com/archives/001062.php). The German original reads "My God" (*Mein Gott*), which Steiner translates as "Good God." Although this phrase may be nothing more than an interjection, the presence of the divine name in this passage is nevertheless important, suggesting that Kafka

Kafka is speaking of reading *any* kind of literature, *any* sort of book. Yet surely his insight holds true for Scripture as well. Surely we also need it to break the sea frozen inside us. That kind of work is not accomplished by cover up and denial but only by the honest, hard, and often gruesome work of the ice-axe, which turns out, in the end, to be a scalpel.

Poetry

In my judgment, honesty is one of the signal contributions the Old Testament makes to Christian Scripture. Another is poetry, since fully one-third of the Old Testament is poetic, whereas the New Testament itself has very little poetry. In several ways, the first three thoughts on preaching and teaching the Bible come together in this fourth and final one:

Samuel Taylor Coleridge (1772–1834) famously described poetry as "the best words in their best order." Among other things, the superiority of poetry allows it to be re-uttered, and therefore re-appropriated. In this way, for example, the psalms become *our* prayers, not just David's or Asaph's, and therefore poetry involves *address* (the first thought). The best poetry is also heavily imagistic and metaphorical. Thus, those images and metaphors can potentially stay with us forever, changing our ways of thinking and living. Someone might think, for example, of a life-decision in terms of Robert Frost's two roads that diverge in a yellow wood and then decide to take the road less traveled. Or, more biblically, someone might think of the righteous as a tree planted by streams of water, bringing forth its fruit in season, with no withering leaves of which to speak, succeeding in all endeavors, and so decide to crack open the Lord's law and start meditating on it day and night (Ps 1). All this is a way of saying that poetry can be all-encompassing literature, and so Scripture in poetic mode is *sola Scriptura* (the second thought). Poetry is also *honest* literature, often heart-wrenchingly so (the third thought). That point is as old as the prophets and the psalms, of course, and supported philosophically from Aristotle forward. Much more recently, Garrison Keillor has stated that good poems matter because "they offer a truer account than what we're used to getting."[18]

---

thought God somehow figures into the need to read difficult literature. Steiner's version goes further, suggesting that God's very *goodness* plays a role—that God's goodness might even be what difficult literature (and reading it) is about. In any event, after citing this passage at the end of an essay on how literature impacts humanity and civility, Steiner comments: "Students of English literature, of any literature, must ask those who teach them, as they must ask themselves, whether they know, and not in their minds alone, what Kafka meant."

18. Garrison Keillor, *Good Poems* (New York: Penguin, 2002), xxv.

These considerations, especially the last one, provide motivation to read the poetry of Scripture—to get a truer account than we're used to getting. They also motivate one to preach and teach in similar ways—to *give* a truer account than what we or our people are used to getting.

Now thinking about teaching and preaching Scripture as a poetic act is one thing; thinking about Scripture *itself* as poetry is another but equally important thing. In my judgment, the categories of story or narrative, while important, are not fully adequate descriptions of Scripture, in part because so much of the Bible is not a unified narrative and so much of it is poetic.[19]

Not all of Scripture is poetry, of course, but thinking of Scripture in poetic ways and as poetry creates interesting opportunities and has significant benefits. For one thing, it suggests that it is going to take time and energy, hard work and discipline to understand Scripture.[20] I fear that we often treat Scripture otherwise, implying that it is straightforwardly transparent or easily understood and applied. *But Scripture is more like a poem than a newspaper.* Like poetry, it requires slow and careful reading and reflection. And also like poetry, it will probably require rereading, and will benefit from that practice.

Expert testimony supports this point. The great poet and agrarian Wendell Berry has written that a "good poem ... cannot be written or read in distraction."[21] Gerhard von Rad said something quite similar about the Old Testament specifically: "To be sure, the Bible *never was easy reading*; and the finest interpretation cannot and should not make it so. Whatever one wrote in ancient Israel, it was *not for speed-reading.... Reading the Bible has always demanded that one be prepared for contemplation.*"[22] With reference to pastoral ministry proper, M. Craig Barnes has put forth the image of the poet as a particularly apt metaphor for the minister. According to Barnes, the minister is one of those "who have been blessed with a vision that allows them to explore, and express, the truth behind the reality. Poets see the despair and heartache as well as the beauty and miracle that lie just

19. I have explored these points and what follows more fully in Strawn, "Lyric Poetry," in *Dictionary of the Old Testament: Wisdom, Poetry and Writings*, ed. Tremper Longman III and Peter Enns (Downers Grove, IL: IVP Academic, 2008), 437–46.

20. One should note that the metaphors and parables in the Bible are rarely explained, so situations like Isa 5:1–7 or Matt 13:1–9, 18–23 are exceptions, not the rule. Indeed, according to Matt 13:10–17 the reason Jesus speaks in parables is precisely so people do *not* understand (cf. Isa 6:9–10)! A statement from David Shapiro, "Gold and Cardboard," *Poetry* 196/5 (Sept. 2010): 423, is evocative at this point: "Even the literal is a metaphor."

21. Wendell Berry, "The Responsibility of the Poet," in *What Are People For? Essays* (Berkeley: Counterpoint, 2010), 90.

22. Gerhard von Rad, "How to Read the Old Testament," in *God at Work in Israel*, trans. John H. Marks (Nashville: Abingdon, 1980), 10, 18 (emphasis added).

beneath the thin veneer of the ordinary, and they describe this in ways that are recognized not only in the mind, but more profoundly in the soul."[23]

The poetry of Scripture helps with these crucial ministerial roles, tasks, arts— especially those concerning contemplative reading and careful interpretation. Indeed, I believe that the Bible itself is the very best schoolhouse for the very best poetic preachers and teachers of Scripture, which is nothing less than the poetry of God.

23. Barnes, *Pastor as Minor Poet*, 17.

18

On Not Bifurcating: Faith and Scholarship
in the Life of a Bible Professor

Is it not much shorter and more direct to do everything for the love
of God? . . . There is no finesse about it; one has only to do it generously and simply.[1]

When I stop to crunch the numbers, it's hard to believe that I have been
teaching for over twenty years. It simply doesn't seem that long ago that I
was in graduate school or struggling through my first few years of teaching. Since I
was hired "ABD" (all but dissertation complete), the last two periods overlap: I was
very much still in graduate school during my first few years of teaching with my
dissertation hanging over my head amidst six new preps. In any event, twenty-
plus years of teaching means that I'm getting ever nearer to the gold standard of
"old and curmudgeonly"—or, at least, I'm too old to be a member of a group of
promising young theologians and can only be included in such august company
by being invited to give a "mentor" address. Since I'd like to think I'm still in the
middle of my career (perhaps this is denial), "mentor" strikes me as perhaps a wee
bit optimistic (that is not denial). Well, nevertheless!

In this chapter, I plan on sharing what I would want to say to a group of gifted
young theologians if I only had one shot. You are precisely such a group and this
is exactly my one shot! After giving you my big idea, which has to do with resisting

---

This chapter was initially delivered as a mentor talk to the very promising but very short-lived
North American Society of Early Career Theologians in Baltimore, MD, on November 21, 2013.

1. Brother Lawrence, *The Practice of the Presence of God* (Pittsburgh: Whitaker House, 1982),
81. Citations from Lawrence that follow also come from this edition, but many others are available. One such, and more recent, edition is Brother Lawrence, *The Practice of the Presence of
God: Contemporary English Version*, ed. Hal M. Helms (Brewster, MA: Paraclete Press, 2010).

the tendency to bifurcate the scholarly life and the life of faith, I want to round it out further by discussing some items that have helped me practice—or at least *try* to—what I am preaching.

One caveat before I begin: I am painfully aware that you are all very smart people and have no doubt thought a lot about the topics I will touch on. Said differently, please forgive any pedantry, paternalism, or patronizing in advance. I certainly don't intend any of those things!

The Big Idea: Resist Bifurcation

So here's the big idea, the one thing I want to commend. It's clear already from my title. I want to encourage you—better yet *urge* you—to resist the temptation to bifurcate the life of faith and the life of scholarship. On the one hand, such an admonition is the proverbial "preaching to the choir" with a group like this one, comprised of theologians and biblical scholars who are also committed persons of faith, but on the other hand we need to be candid that the temptation toward such bifurcation is both real and powerful. And it comes at us, even if we are disposed against it, from more than one angle. I will delineate the two most obvious angles in a moment, but let me say something even more obvious first, which is simply this: bifurcation of faith and scholarship suggests that scholarship is somehow *not* faith or faithful, even as it also indicates that faith is somehow *not* scholarly or intellectually rigorous.[2] This is the rift and division that I want you to resist and that I have tried hard to resist myself throughout my career, beginning already in my first semester of seminary and continuing on to this very day.

Two Angles on Bifurcation

Now as I said, the temptation to divide faith and scholarship comes from at least two angles. First, it comes from *the scholarly side of things*. This could be called

---

2. Patrick R. Keifert, "The Bible and Theological Education: A Report and Reflections on a Journey," in *The Ending of Mark and the Ends of God: Essays in Memory of Donald Harrisville Juel*, ed. Beverly Roberts Gaventa and Patrick D. Miller (Louisville: Westminster John Knox, 2005), 165–82, relying on language from my former Emory colleague Martin Buss, speaks of the opposing categories of "critical description" vs. "capricious faith." I conveniently leave un(der)defined the word "faith." Speaking personally, it would involve the practices of a life of faith which would include religious commitment and adherence, creedal belief, church attendance and/or membership, and so forth. I take as instructive, too, the point made by Luke Timothy Johnson, *The Creed: What Christians Believe and Why It Matters* (New York: Doubleday, 2003)—namely, that one cannot confess something like the creed and go on "believing in" everything else as well. Believing some things means disbelieving some other things. See on this matter Christopher Morse, *Not Every Spirit: A Dogmatics of Christian Disbelief*, 2nd ed. (New York: Continuum, 2009).

the "research-one university pressure," even for those who do not work at such institutions, if only because the vast majority of professors take their degrees at R1 institutions and so this pressure is in the air, and we pick it up there, quite like an airborne pathogen (I use the last image advisedly). And even if you took your terminal degree at a free-standing seminary, as I did (and mine was far from free of this pathogen), there's always the professional guild to worry about, filled with R1 university types, not to mention certain scholars in the guild—often among the very cream of the crop—who seem to have no problems with bifurcating, perhaps by resolving the faith/scholarship dialectic once and for all by dispensing with the faith side altogether or at least by burying it so deep that who would ever *know*? And then there's tenure and promotion to think about. What counts as "real scholarship"? And by whom? It isn't hard to imagine that whoever "they" are, they might not like matters of faith popping up in your portfolio.

All these pressures are real—I don't mean to make light of them. And to quote someone I read once, I suspect you have to be as innocent as doves and as shrewd as snakes about matters like these (Matt 10:16). Some institutions may actually *require* bifurcation in favor of 100 percent "pure" scholarship devoid of faith (whatever *that* is or whatever it would look like)—at least for the sake of a tenure run. If so, the way you will have to resist bifurcation—and I still urge you to resist it!—is by *doing yet more*: writing *additional* pieces or working on *additional* projects other than just those ones that will get you promoted. Or by doing *additional* speaking or teaching or other such things that will enable you to bring your scholarship into vibrant engagement and interaction with the life of faith, *to the enrichment of both*.[3]

There is another important item to mention at this point: don't be tempted to *temporarily* bifurcate, imagining that until tenure you'll be a real, hardcore, "pure" scholar (again, whatever *that* is or whatever it would look like) but that after tenure you'll be somehow (miraculously?) ready and able to do other more "faith-ish" things. Why shouldn't you think that? Well, because after tenure and promotion is the run up to full professor. And after that you'll be hoping for a chair. And at that point you may be dead. Or at least near retirement. I'm joking . . . but only a little! There's always, to cite one of my favorite singers (at least for purposes of classroom instruction), St. Alanis Morissette, "the everelusive kudo, the transparent dangling carrot," which bifurcating *may*, but *equally also may very well not* (!), get you. More immediately, before retirement, that is, what you do—and I think this is especially true for what you do early in your career—will establish patterns of

---

3. I am of the mind that some of my best scholarly ideas have emerged while teaching in non-academic contexts.

creativity, habits of working, and ways of thinking and being. Seven lean years of bifurcating will not lead inevitably to seven fat years of something more holistic or integrative or faith-full. As you well know, the pattern is quite the opposite in Pharaoh's dream (Gen 41).

The second way we are tempted to bifurcate comes from *the faith side of the equation*. We can feel this sort of pressure from our institutions if they are religiously affiliated in vibrant and lively, not just historic, ways. Such institutions can sometimes look askance at scholarship that is not somehow generative of or for religious people or religious contexts, especially in an immediate sort of way (will it preach? what would pastors do with it?). And even if we don't feel this pressure from our institutions, we might feel it from some of our more religiously inclined students, or, even if not from them, then from our own upbringings, our families of origin, or our own faith communities (whether past or present doesn't really matter, does it?). "So," the question goes after church one day, or in the hallway after class, or on faculty coffee break, "what *does* Ugaritic [or the Nag Hammadi codices or . . .] have to do with *Jesus*?" Well, much and in every way, of course: to be continued!

If you find yourself facing this latter sort of scenario it will likely also lead to *more work*: working above and beyond or after hours or on semester break on some piece of research that you deem important or that is crucial for your tenure portfolio even if it doesn't make an immediate contribution to the Seven Habits of Highly Effective Christians (God forbid). But one more point is important here: don't be tempted—perhaps when you find yourself quite tired of working more, maybe even ruing your institution's pragmatism—to think that those additional scholarly projects are *not* somehow related to the life of faith. For that would be just another instance of bifurcating, and if unchecked could easily lead to a kind of cynical disposition toward matters or persons, especially students and colleagues, of faith and the wearing of a scholarly chip on one's tweed-clad (above an elbow-patched) shoulder. I don't think that's good for your school, neither for your place in it, nor for your students, nor for your soul. Unfortunately, it's all too common among people who feel the pressure to bifurcate from this second angle.

Resources for Resistance and Integrations

So the big idea is simply: don't bifurcate! Instead, work hard at holding the life of faith and scholarship together. Don't bifurcate! Integrate! That's easier said than done for all the reasons I mentioned and many, many more. And so the big question that must be put to my big idea concerns execution: how does one resist bifurcation and integrate instead? At this point I want to mention four things that have proven useful to me on this matter. Being someone trained in evidentiary reasoning (in other words, a textualist), you will not be surprised to hear that they are associated with or derived from specific texts.

1. The first text is a little book that I was required to read for some bureaucratic reason early in my teaching career entitled *Scholarship Assessed: Evaluation of the Professoriate* by Glassick, Huber, and Maeroff.[4] The main point of this slender little volume is that there is more than one way to evaluate what counts as "scholarship." The authors advocate that, in truth, *many aspects* of a professor's work are scholarly, not just the publication of a peer-reviewed article or critical monograph. Scholarly activity is defined, they say, by no less than six standards: clear goals, adequate preparation, appropriate methods, significant results, effective presentation, and reflective critique.[5] These six standards (not just one: the "scholarly" monograph or article) allow us to see that discovery, integration,[6] application, and teaching are all scholarly activities, at least potentially, and therefore count as "scholarship"—yes, even for the purposes of a tenure portfolio (or at least *they should* count for a tenure portfolio). There is, therefore, *a scholarship of teaching* and *a scholarship of praxis* just as much as there is *a scholarship of discovery* or *a scholarship of integration*—the latter two being the kind that are usually valued in terms of scholarly print production.[7]

Thinking analogically, the volume by Glassick, Huber, and Maeroff suggests to me that there could and should also be a kind of scholarly way to conduct work that is concerned with or influenced by matters of faith. Among other things, following these authors' lead, such work would be marked by clear goals, adequate preparation, appropriate methods, significant results, effective presentation, and reflective critique. According to the path offered in *Scholarship Assessed*, work that deals with matters of faith, if it satisfies these criteria, is justifiably entitled "scholarship."[8] Mission complete: bifurcation avoided!

4. Charles E. Glassick, Mary Taylor Huber, and Gene I. Maeroff, *Scholarship Assessed: Evaluation of the Professoriate* (San Francisco: Jossey-Bass, 1997).

5. Glassick, Huber, and Maeroff, *Scholarship Assessed*, 35 and passim.

6. Obviously, the authors do not mean "integration" as I am using it here, to unite faith and scholarship. Instead, they are referring to works of scholarly synthesis.

7. See previous note. A work of scholarly integration/synthesis might be the writing of an introductory textbook.

8. I am reminded here of two works: A. K. M. Adam, *Making Sense of New Testament Theology: "Modern" Problems and Prospects*, StABH 11 (Macon, GA: Mercer University Press, 1995), which offers "aesthetic" criteria (= Glassick, Huber, and Maeroff's "effective presentation"?) alongside others for the proper evaluation of works in New Testament Theology; and Ellen T. Charry, *By the Renewing of Your Minds: The Pastoral Function of Christian Doctrine* (New York: Oxford University Press, 1999), which is helpful in thinking about "significant results" and "reflective critique" in a highly thoughtful, yet profoundly theological-pastoral synthesis.

To be honest, *Scholarship Assessed* has not been a major resource for me on the problem of bifurcation—not nearly as existentially important as the other three texts I will mention—but I still deem it helpful in thinking about various dynamics, especially institutional ones, on this thorny problem. Of course I must admit that, even if my analogy works, not all institutions will agree that such a beast as *a scholarship of faith* really exists. But that doesn't mean their doubt is accurate. If anything, it just means we will be back at the necessity for those of us who are both believers and scholars, scholars and believers to do *more*. That's not easy, but who said it was going to be? Those of us who have slogged through graduate degrees know none of that is easy. More to the point, nothing that I've read in my favorite book says the life of faith is going to be *easy*. The luxury of a faculty office or a home study should not trick us into thinking otherwise.

Although *Scholarship Assessed* hasn't been a major influence on me, I find it intriguing that its arguments have stuck—I suspect that is because I read it early on in my teaching career, which is such a formative, and fraught, time.[9] In any event, the three texts that I turn to now have been perennial resources that I have continued to return to throughout the course of my career as I've contemplated the problem of bifurcation and tried to resist it. You may know one or all of these texts intimately, but if you don't, I encourage you to do so, as soon as possible—they will repay reading and rereading. Each one is a great gift. Each one suggests a way around bifurcation by transcending the (false) dichotomy so often drawn between the life of faith and the life of scholarship, the life of the mind and the life of the heart.

2. The second text is Simone Weil's little essay, "Reflections on the Right Use of School Studies with a View to the Love of God," from her book *Waiting for God*.[10] In this piece Weil suggests that any school exercise (she specifically mentions math and Latin) can be helpful to our spiritual life as long as "they are carried out with a view to this purpose and this purpose alone."[11] School exercises are spiritually helpful, according to Weil, in two ways: first, they develop in us *the power of atten-*

---

9. Another piece I read about the same time, indeed *before* I took my first teaching post, and that has proven similarly, or rather *much more enduring*, is Paul Rorem, "Empathy and Evaluation in Medieval Church History and Pastoral Ministry: A Lutheran Reading of Pseudo-Dionysius," *PSB* 19 (1998): 99–115. Rorem's essay, too, in its own way, navigates a way to hold together scholarship and faith.

10. Simone Weil, "Reflections on the Right Use of School Studies with a View to the Love of God," in *Waiting for God*, trans. Emma Craufurd (New York: Harper & Row, 1951), 105–16. I first learned of Weil's essay from Stephanie Paulsell, "Spiritual Formation and Intellectual Work in Theological Education," *ThTo* 55 (1998): 229–34. See also, in the same issue, David Tracy, "Traditions of Spiritual Practice and the Practice of Theology," *ThTo* 55 (1998): 235–41.

11. Weil, "Reflections on the Right Use of School Studies," 105.

tion without which we can neither pray nor be present with those who suffer. The practice of simply concentrating on something other than ourselves—a verbal form, a mathematical problem, an ancient text, a contemporary theorist—can help us develop habits that are crucial for prayer and compassionate ministry.[12] Without the capacity to pay attention, she points out, we can neither pray nor be present with those who suffer.[13]

The second way school exercises help us spiritually is *by cultivating humility*, especially in the face of bad grades. There is a great temptation, Weil notes, to justify ourselves when we receive a bad grade—it is the teacher's fault, not ours. And lest any of us think we are above such things, now, on the other side of the lectern, with this problem residing solely among the ungrateful student bodies we serve (!), let me ask you about the last time one of your journal articles was rejected or the last time you received a critical review of any sort—say in a class evaluation from some ungrateful student body. How'd that go over? Likely with painkillers. But the virtue of humility, Weil asserts, is "a far more precious treasure than all academic progress."[14] No knowledge is more desirable than the knowledge of our own mediocrity because we can't make progress without redressing our weaknesses, some of which, we have to admit, seem intractable.

So, Weil writes, "if these two conditions"—attention and humility—"are perfectly carried out there is no doubt that school studies are quite as good a road to sanctity as any other."[15] "Every school exercise," she continues, "thought of in this way, is like a sacrament."[16] Now, if all that works for students, for learners, it also holds true for professors who are, among many other things, life-long learners, lifetime students. The question then becomes quite pointed: how sacramental have you been with your "school exercises" of late? Weil offers us a way around, or perhaps better through or beyond, bifurcation. Every professorial exercise, thought of in this way, is like a sacrament. Could it be? Even grading? Perish the thought!

3. Weil's insights lead directly to my third text, *The Practice of the Presence of God*, a small classic in spirituality, by the seventeenth-century Carmelite monk Brother Lawrence. Brother Lawrence's take on the presence of God is to find it

---

12. Cf. Weil, "Reflections on the Right Use of School Studies," 114: "Whoever goes through years of study without developing this attention within himself has lost a great treasure."

13. Weil, "Reflections on the Right Use of School Studies," 105, 109, and 114, where she writes: "Those who are unhappy have no need for anything in this world but people capable of giving them their attention. The capacity to give one's attention to a sufferer is a very rare and difficult thing; it is almost a miracle; it *is* a miracle" (her emphasis).

14. Weil, "Reflections on the Right Use of School Studies," 109.

15. Weil, "Reflections on the Right Use of School Studies," 109.

16. Weil, "Reflections on the Right Use of School Studies," 112.

and practice it *everywhere*. It was a serious mistake, he thought, "to think of our prayer time as being different from any other"; our sanctification, he said, did not depend on "*changing* our activities" as it did on "doing them for God rather than for ourselves."[17] The following citation nicely captures Lawrence's fundamental teaching on matters of faith and practice:

> People seek for methods of learning to love God. They hope to arrive at it by I know not how many different practices; they take much trouble to remain in the presence of God in a quantity of ways. *Is it not much shorter and more direct to do everything for the love of God*, to make use of all the labors of one's state in life to show [God] that love, and to maintain [God's] presence within us by this communion of our hearts with [God's]? There is no finesse about it; one has only to do it generously and simply.[18]

So, Brother Lawrence might say, *just do* your scholarship for the love of God and it *will be* for the love of God. No need to do this bit now, and *then* do that. Or write this piece now, *then* that. Or think about things this way now, and *only then* think about them that way. There's no finesse about it, he says. Just do it generously and simply, which I suspect also means do it *holistically, integratively*—as one piece, not two.

Here is a final quotation from Brother Lawrence, as a bonus free of charge: "Do not forget [God]! Think of [God] often; adore [God] ceaselessly; live and die with [God]. That is the real business of a Christian; in a word, it is our profession. If we do not know it, we must learn it."[19] Not bad advice, even for theology professors— perhaps *especially* for theology professors and other theological professionals.

4. Several of the points from Simone Weil and Brother Lawrence, maybe all of them, are found in my fourth and final text which is, I'm happy to report, a biblical one. It's found in Deut 17:14–20: Deuteronomy's law of the king. Among other things that could be said about this text, it offers a striking, countercultural model of kingship.[20] The king can't have lots of money, lots of stuff, lots of wives, can't be

---

17. Lawrence, *Practice of the Presence of God*, 20 (emphasis original). Note also *Practice of the Presence of God*, 21: "Never tire of doing even the smallest things for [God], because [God] isn't impressed so much with the dimensions of our work as with the love in which it is done."

18. Lawrence, *Practice of the Presence of God*, 81 (emphasis added); cf. the epigraph above. Cf. 90: "The good brother found God everywhere, as much while he was repairing shoes as while he was praying with the community. He was in no hurry to go on retreats, because he found the same God to love and adore in his ordinary work as in the depth of the desert."

19. Lawrence, *Practice of the Presence of God*, 48.

20. What follows depends on Brent A. Strawn, "Designated Readers: Deuteronomy's Por-

proud, etc., etc., etc. (How do you spell "Solomon" again? *S-O-L*-Deut 17!) In brief, all the things that define monarchy as the rule of one over all others, especially in the ancient world—all of that is firmly and emphatically denied of the Israelite king in Deuteronomy. The Israelite king, instead, is to be *a Torah scribe*, writing a copy of the Torah in a scroll in the presence of the priests, and he is to be *a Torah reader*—an obsessed and obsessive one, having the Torah with him always, and reading in it all the days of his life. This is by no stretch of the imagination a king, but, instead, and at best, a kind of "designated reader"—someone who sits around and reads all day long on behalf of others.[21] Deuteronomy 17 does not envision royal rule so much as *leadership and service by means of reading*—by means of reading Deuteronomy, reading Torah, reading Scripture.

Ever since I hit upon this idea it has proven useful to me in thinking about my own vocation and the vocation of the (mostly) seminary students I teach. It's easy to think that the life of faith or my ministry or what not is *something else, somewhere else*—within a local church proper, for instance—but not in my academic institution, not in my office, and not in my classroom. But that's bifurcating. Deuteronomy 17 helps me to integrate these things, faith/ministry and my profession, especially as a Scripture scholar: the designated reader is supposed to read Torah for heaven's sake! So, even when I'm studying—*especially* when I'm studying—I am a designated reader *on behalf of others*, reading things they have neither time, nor desire, nor interest (!) in reading. Things like Torah. Things like Scripture. Things like theology. But here's an important observation: the designated reader does not emerge from her study lording it over the "babes in Christ." The monarch in Deut 17 is explicitly forbidden from exalting his heart over his kin. This, then, is Weil's virtue of humility once again, even if in a slightly different key. And who couldn't be humble in our profession—in the face of all there is to know, not to mention due to the specific content (and Subject) of what (and Whom) there is to know?

The answer to this last question, it would seem, is actually, in truth, "a lot of people," all of whom appear quite impressed with their own great learning. In the end, though, I think that is nothing else but the unfortunate outcome of the second type of bifurcation I mentioned earlier. Whatever the case, it's in egregious violation of the law of the designated reader (a.k.a. "monarch" in quotation marks!) according to Deut 17.

---

trait of the Ideal King—or Is It Preacher?" *Journal for Preachers* 32 (2008): 35–40, reprinted as chapter 15 in the present volume.

21. See further Strawn, "Designated Readers."

An Unbalanced Integration

So those are the four texts that have been useful to me in trying to unite what so many (including me) are prone to separate. My own effort in this regard, in brief, is to try not to think of *different* steps or *different* things—certainly not linearly or sequentially—but to think of *one thing* happening *at the same time, all the time* via the lenses afforded by *Scholarship Assessed*, Simone Weil, Brother Lawrence, and Deut 17 (inter alia, of course). Most recently, I've contemplated how this simultaneous work is not unrelated to the idea of transference and countertransference in therapy. In *transference*, clients transfer their feelings and issues with, say, their moms (always their moms!), on to their therapists. This may initially strike one as odd, but it turns out to be quite typical and a crucial process by which psychoanalysis becomes a place for redressing poor relationships or retraining problematic ways of relating. In *countertransference*, the therapist does the exact same thing only this time back on to the client. The therapist, too, that is, is working things out at the same time and in the very midst of the patient's working things out and in the midst of the therapist helping the patient work things out.[22] The "things" in question may not be the same issues, or not in equal measure, between the therapist and the client, but the therapeutic work is going both ways and is happening concurrently.

I've come to think that I'm doing something very similar, and you are too, whenever we teach or think or write about our fields of study. There is a clientele of some sort, even if only implied or imagined, and they are putting their "stuff" on us, whatever it is. (It's usually stuff about faith and/or scholarship.). And, in all candor, we are putting our "stuff" on them. (Also usually about faith and/or scholarship.) That's not all bad; it's probably just the way the world works, just like it is with how therapy works. And it's also *okay*. Once again, we see that we simply don't have to bifurcate: figuring it all out first, ahead of time, on our own, perhaps in our offices, and only then going out and performing it all in the real world in some unmatched performance. We can figure it out—can be figuring it out—*in the midst of doing it*. Put differently, we can resist bifurcating by resisting bifurcating. We can work on holding faith and scholarship together if we work on holding faith and scholarship together. Shades of Brother Lawrence! Once again: there's no finesse about it.

---

22. Heinrich Racker, *Transference and Counter-Transference* (New York: International Universities Press, 1968), 137: "These countertransference situations may be repressed or emotionally blocked but probably they cannot be avoided; certainly they should not be avoided if full understanding is to be achieved."

In the end I should confess that, despite all that I've said above, maybe I am a bifurcator after all. At the very least I have to admit that I acknowledge a difference, at least in practice, between the life of faith and scholarship, especially in the professional life of many biblical scholars, who often succumb to bifurcation. To which I say, "Alas!" If I'm right about that practical difference—how biblical scholars conduct themselves in bifurcating modes—then I want to weigh in heavily and clearly that, if push comes to shove, you need to cultivate spiritual depth more than your *curriculum vitae* (CV). Here, then, is where I might be a bifurcator myself, or, more to my preference, one who advocates for an unequal integration of faith and scholarship. Let us not forget, after all, the noted theologian and bishop who runs a theological society down in hell in C. S. Lewis's novel *The Great Divorce*.[23] Resumé building will happen as a matter of course—especially if you want to keep your job, make money, have a career, feed your family, etc.—but spiritual depth is not a simple matter of course; it is intentional work. It is not easy work and it's not the kind of work you can put on your CV. You don't get awards for it. Not here. Not *down here*, you realize. But where you lay up your treasures . . . well, that's where your heart will be also (Matt 6:19–21; Luke 12:32–34).

---

23. C. S. Lewis, *The Great Divorce: A Dream* (New York: Macmillan, 1946).

Acknowledgments

The author and publisher gratefully acknowledge permission to reprint the following materials that originally appeared elsewhere:

Chapter 1 originally appeared as "From *Imago* to *Imagines*: The Image(s) of God in Genesis," in *The Cambridge Companion to Genesis*, ed. Bill T. Arnold (Cambridge: Cambridge University Press, 2022), 211–35.

Chapter 2 originally appeared as "YHWH's Poesie: The *Gnadenformel* (Exodus 34:6b–7), the Book of Exodus, and Beyond," in *Biblical Poetry and the Art of Close Reading*, ed. J. Blake Couey and Elaine T. James (Cambridge: Cambridge University Press, 2018), 237–56. Reproduced with permission of the Licensor through PLSclear.

Chapter 3 originally appeared as "Keep/Observe/Do—Carefully—Today! The Rhetoric of Repetition in Deuteronomy," in *A God So Near: Essays on Old Testament Theology in Honor of Patrick D. Miller*, ed. Brent A. Strawn and Nancy R. Bowen (Winona Lake, IN: Eisenbrauns, 2003), 215–40.

Chapter 4 originally appeared as "Slaves and Rebels: Inscription, Identity, and Time in the Rhetoric of Deuteronomy," in *Sepher Torath Mosheh: Studies in the Composition and Interpretation of Deuteronomy*, ed. Daniel I. Block and Richard M. Schultz (Peabody, MA: Hendrickson, 2017), 161–91.

Chapter 7 originally appeared as "And These Three Are One: A Trinitarian Critique of Christological Approaches to the Old Testament," *Perspectives in Religious Studies* 31 (2004): 191–210.

Chapter 8 originally appeared as "'Israel, My Child': The Ethics of a Biblical Metaphor," in *The Child in the Bible*, ed. Marcia Bunge, Terence E. Fretheim, and Beverly R. Gaventa (Grand Rapids: Eerdmans, 2008), 103–40.

Chapter 9 originally appeared as "What Would (or Should) Old Testament Theology Look Like If Recent Reconstructions of Israelite Religion Were True?" in *Between Israelite Religion and Old Testament Theology: Essays on Archaeology, History, and Hermeneutics*, ed. Robert D. Miller II, CBET 80 (Leuven: Peeters, 2016), 129–66.

Chapter 10 originally appeared as "The Old Testament and Participation with God (and/in Christ?): (Re-)Reading the Life of Moses with Some Help from Gregory of Nyssa," *Ex Auditu* 33 (2017): 25–52 [appeared 2018]. Used by permission of Wipf and Stock Publishers, www.wipfandstock.com.

Chapter 12 originally appeared as "Docetism, Käsemann, and Christology: Can Historical Criticism Help Christological Orthodoxy (and Other Theology) After All?" *Journal of Theological Interpretation* 2 (2008): 161–80. This article is used by permission of The Pennsylvania State University Press.

Chapter 13 originally appeared as "Is God Always Anything?" *Journal for Preachers* 37 (2014): 56–61.

Chapter 15 originally appeared as "Designated Readers: Deuteronomy's Portrait of the Ideal King—or Is It Preacher?" *Journal for Preachers* 32 (2008): 35–40.

Chapter 17 originally appeared as "Four Thoughts on Preaching and Teaching the Bible—Mostly the Old Testament," in *The Bible Tells Me So: Reading the Bible as Scripture*, ed. Richard P. Thompson and Thomas Jay Oord (Nampa, ID: SacraSage, 2011), 33–42.

Bibliography

Achtemeier, Elizabeth. *The Old Testament and the Proclamation of the Gospel*. Philadelphia: Westminster, 1973.

———. *Preaching from the Old Testament*. Louisville: Westminster John Knox, 1989.

Achtemeier, Paul J. "The Continuing Quest for Coherence in St. Paul: An Experiment
in Thought." Pages 132–45 in Lovering and Sumney, *Theology and Ethics in Paul
and His Interpreters*.

Adam, A. K. M. "Docetism, Käsemann, and Christology: Why Historical Criticism Can't
Protect Christological Orthodoxy." *SJT* 49 (1996): 391–410.

———. *Faithful Interpretation: Reading the Bible in a Postmodern World*. Minneapolis:
Fortress, 2006.

———. *Making Sense of New Testament Theology: "Modern" Problems and Prospects*.
StABH 11. Macon, GA: Mercer University Press, 1995.

———. "Poaching on Zion: Biblical Theology as Signifying Practice." Pages 17–34 in
Adam, Fowl, Vanhoozer, and Watson, *Reading Scripture with the Church*.

———. "Toward a Resolution Yet to Be Revealed." Pages 143–48 in Adam, Fowl, Vanhoozer, and Watson, *Reading Scripture with the Church*.

Adam, A. K. M., Stephen E. Fowl, Kevin J. Vanhoozer, and Francis Watson, eds. *Reading
Scripture with the Church: Toward a Hermeneutic of Theological Interpretation*.
Grand Rapids: Baker Academic, 2006.

Aejmelaeus, Anneli. "Function and Interpretation of כִּי in Biblical Hebrew." *JBL* 105
(1986): 193–209.

Ahn, John. "Psalm 137: Complex Communal Laments." *JBL* 127 (2008): 267–89.

Aichele, George, et al. *The Postmodern Bible*. New Haven: Yale University Press, 1995.

Albertz, Rainer. *A History of Israelite Religion in the Old Testament Period*. Translated by
John Bowden. 2 vols. OTL. Louisville: Westminster/John Knox, 1994.

Allen, Leslie C. *Psalms 101–150*. Rev. ed. WBC 21. Nashville: Nelson, 2002.

Alter, Robert. *The Art of Biblical Narrative*. New York: Basic Books, 1981.

———. *The Art of Biblical Narrative*. Rev. ed. New York: Basic Books, 2011.

———. *The Hebrew Bible*. 3 vols. New York: Norton, 2019.

———. *The Pleasures of Reading in an Ideological Age*. New York: Norton, 1996.

Anderson, A. A. *The Book of Psalms*. 2 vols. NCB. Grand Rapids: Eerdmans, 1972.

Anderson, Gary A. *Christian Doctrine and the Old Testament: Theology in the Service of Biblical Exegesis*. Grand Rapids: Baker Academic, 2017.

———. "Joseph and the Passion of Our Lord." Pages 198–215 in *The Art of Reading Scripture*. Edited by Ellen F. Davis and Richard B. Hays. Grand Rapids: Eerdmans, 2003.

———. "King David and the Psalms of Imprecation." Pages 29–45 in *The Harp of Prophecy: Early Christian Interpretation of the Psalms*. Edited by Brian E. Daley and Paul R. Kolbet. Notre Dame: University of Notre Dame Press, 2015.

———. "Reply to Wolterstorff." Pages 289–90 in Bergmann, Murray, and Rea, *Divine Evil?*

———. *Sin: A History*. New Haven: Yale University Press, 2009.

———. "What About the Canaanites?" Pages 269–82 in Bergmann, Murray, and Rea, *Divine Evil?*

Andreano, Ambrose. "The True Fate of 'the So-called Devil' in Origen," https://www.academia.edu/44789518/The_True_Fate_of_The_So_Called_Devil_in_Origen

Annus, Amar, and Alan Lenzi. *Ludlul bēl nēmeqi: The Standard Babylonian Poem of the Righteous Sufferer*. SAACT 7. Helsinki: The Neo-Assyrian Text Corpus Project, 2010.

Aristotle. *On Rhetoric: A Theory of Civic Discourse*. Translated by George A. Kennedy. New York: Oxford University Press, 1991.

Arnold, Bill T. *Genesis*. NCBC. Cambridge: Cambridge University Press, 2008.

———. "Reexamining the 'Fathers' in Deuteronomy's Framework." Pages 10–41 in *Torah and Tradition: Papers Read at the Sixteenth Joint Meeting of the Society for Old Testament Study and the Oudtestamentisch Werkgezelschap, Edinburgh 2015*. Edited by Klaas Spronk and Hans Barstad. Oudtestamentische Studiën 70. Leiden: Brill, 2017.

Arnold, Bill T., and David B. Weisberg. "A Centennial Review of Friedrich Delitzsch's 'Babel und Bibel' Lectures." *JBL* 121 (2002): 441–57.

Arnold, Bill T., and John H. Choi. *A Guide to Biblical Hebrew Syntax*. Cambridge: Cambridge University Press, 2003.

Astour, Michael C. "*Rdmn*/Rhadamanthys and the Motif of Selective Immortality." Pages 55–89 in *"Und Mose schrieb dieses Lied auf": Studien zum Alten Testament und zum Alten Orient: Festschrift für Oswald Loretz zur Vollendung seines 70. Lebensjohres mit Beiträgen von Freuden, Schülern und Kollegen*. Edited by Manfried Dietrich and Ingo Kottseiper. AOAT 250. Münster: Ugarit-Verlag, 1998.

Auerbach, Erich. *Mimesis: The Representation of Reality in Western Literature*. Translated by Willard R. Trask. Princeton: Princeton University Press, 2013.

Augustine. *The Trinity*. Translated by Edmund Hill. Vol. 1, part 1 of *The Works of Saint Augustine*. Edited by John E. Rotelle. Brooklyn: New City Press, 1991.

Aune, David E. *The New Testament in Its Literary Environment*. Philadelphia: Westminster, 1987.

Awabdy, Mark A. *Immigrants and Innovative Law: Deuteronomy's Theological and Social Vision for the גר*. FAT 2.67. Tübingen: Mohr Siebeck, 2014.

———. "Teaching Children in the Instruction of Amenemope and Deuteronomy." *VT* 65 (2015): 1–8.

Ayres, Lewis. "'Remember That You Are Catholic' (*serm.* 52.2): Augustine on the Unity of the Triune God." *JECS* 8 (2000): 39–82.

Badcock, Gary D. *Light of Truth and Fire of Love: A Theology of the Holy Spirit*. Grand Rapids: Eerdmans, 1997.

Bahrani, Zainab. *The Graven Image: Representation in Babylonia and Assyria*. Philadelphia: University of Pennsylvania Press, 2003.

Bainton, George. *The Art of Authorship: Literary Reminiscences, Methods of Work, and Advice to Young Beginners*. New York: D. Appleton and Company, 1890.

Baird, J. Arthur. *A Comparative Analysis of the Gospel Genre: The Synoptic Mode and its Uniqueness*. Lewiston, NY: Mellen, 1991.

Bal, Mieke. *Narratology: Introduction to the Theory of Narrative*. 3rd ed. Toronto: University of Toronto Press, 2009.

Bar-Efrat, Shimon. "Love of Zion: A Literary Interpretation of Psalm 137." Pages 3–11 in Cogan, Eichler, and Tigay, *Tehillah le-Moshe*.

Barker, Kit. "Divine Illocutions in Psalm 137: A Critique of Nicholas Wolterstorff's 'Second Hermeneutic.'" *TynBul* 60 (2009): 1–14.

———. *Imprecation as Divine Discourse: Speech Act Theory, Dual Authorship, and Theological Interpretation*. JTISup 16. Winona Lake, IN: Eisenbrauns, 2016.

Barnes, M. Craig. *The Pastor as Minor Poet: Texts and Subtexts in the Ministerial Life*. Grand Rapids: Eerdmans, 2009.

Barnes, Michel René. "Rereading Augustine's Theology of the Trinity." Pages 145–78 in Davis, Kendall, and O'Collins, *The Trinity: An Interdisciplinary Symposium on the Trinity*.

Barr, James. *The Concept of Biblical Theology: An Old Testament Perspective*. Minneapolis: Fortress, 1999.

———. "The Image of God in the Book of Genesis—A Study of Terminology." *BJRL* 51 (1968): 11–26.

———. "Man and Nature: The Ecological Controversy and the Old Testament." *BJRL* 55 (1972): 9–32

―――. *Old and New in Interpretation: A Study of the Two Testaments.* New York: Harper & Row, 1966.

Barth, Karl. *Credo.* New York: Scribner's Sons, 1962.

Bartlett, David. "Adoption in the Bible." Pages 375–98 in Bunge, Fretheim, and Roberts, *The Child in the Bible.*

Bartlett, John. *Familiar Quotations.* 10th ed. New York: Blue Ribbon Books, 1919.

Bartlett, John R. *Edom and the Edomites.* JSOTSup 77. Sheffield: Sheffield Academic, 1989.

Barton, John. "Imitation of God in the Old Testament." Pages 35–46 in *The God of Israel.* Edited by Robert P. Gordon. UCOP 64. Cambridge: Cambridge University Press, 2007.

Bauckham, Richard. *God Crucified: Monotheism and Christology in the New Testament.* Grand Rapids: Eerdmans, 1998.

Bean, Martha S., and G. Genevieve Patthey-Chavez. "Repetition in Instructional Discourse: A Means for Joint Cognition." Pages 1:207–20 in Johnstone, *Repetition in Discourse.*

Beckman, Gary, and Theodore J. Lewis, eds. *Text, Artifact, and Image: Revealing Ancient Israelite Religion.* BJS 346. Providence, RI: Brown Judaic Studies, 2006.

Begg, Christopher T. "Contributions to the Elucidation of the Composition of Deuteronomy with Special Attention to the Significance of the Numeruswechsel." PhD diss., Louvain University, 1987.

―――. "Kings." *DBI* 2:25–28.

Beker, J. Christiaan. *Paul the Apostle: The Triumph of God in Life and Thought.* Philadelphia: Fortress, 1984.

―――. *Paul's Apocalyptic Gospel: The Coming Triumph of God.* Philadelphia: Fortress, 1982.

―――. *The Triumph of God: The Essence of Paul's Thought.* Minneapolis: Fortress, 1990.

Bellamy, Carol, ed. *The State of the World's Children 2005: Childhood Under Threat.* New York: The United Nations Children's Fund (UNICEF), 2004.

Bergmann, Michael, Michael J. Murray, and Michael C. Rea, eds. *Divine Evil? The Moral Character of the God of Abraham.* Oxford: Oxford University Press, 2011.

Berlin, Adele. "Psalms and the Literature of Exile." Pages 65–86 in *The Book of Psalms: Composition and Reception.* Edited by Peter W. Flint and Patrick D. Miller. VTSup 99. Leiden: Brill, 2005.

Berry, Wendell. "The Responsibility of the Poet." Page 88 in *What Are People For? Essays.* Berkeley: Counterpoint, 2010.

Biberger, Bernd. *Unsere Väter und Wir: Unterteilung von Geschichtsdarstellungen in Generationen und das Verhältnis der Generationen im Alten Testament.* BBB 145. Berlin: Philo, 2003.

Bienkowski, Piotr. "Guti." Page 135 in *Dictionary of the Ancient Near East*. Edited by Piotr Bienkowski and Alan Millard. Philadelphia: University of Pennsylvania Press, 2000.

Bird, Phyllis. "'Male and Female He Created Them': Gen 1:27b in the Context of the Priestly Account of Creation." *HTR* 74 (1981): 129–59.

Blair, Edward P. "An Appeal to Remembrance: The Memory Motif in Deuteronomy." *Int* 15 (1961): 41–47.

Blenkinsopp, Joseph. "The Family in First Temple Israel." Pages 48–103 in Perdue et al., *Families in Ancient Israel*.

Blumfeld, Laura. *Revenge: A Story of Hope*. New York: Simon & Schuster, 2002.

Boda, Mark J. *A Severe Mercy: Sin and Its Remedy in the Old Testament*. Siphrut 1. Winona Lake, IN: Eisenbrauns, 2009.

Bodner, Keith. *Elisha's Profile in the Book of Kings: The Double Agent*. Oxford: Oxford University Press, 2013.

Boer, P. A. H. de. *Fatherhood and Motherhood in Israelite and Judean Piety*. Leiden: Brill, 1974.

Bonhoeffer, Dietrich. *Creation and Fall: A Theological Exposition of Genesis 1–3*. Translated by Douglas Stephen Bax. Edited by John W. de Gruchy. DBW 3. Minneapolis: Fortress, 1997.

———. "Lecture on Christ in the Psalms." Pages 386–93 in *Theological Education at Finkenwalde: 1935–1937*. Translated by Douglas W. Stott, edited by H. Gaylon Barker and Mark S. Brocker. DBW 14. Minneapolis: Fortress, 2013.

———. *Letters and Papers from Prison*. Enlarged edition. Edited by Eberhard Bethge. New York: Collier, 1972.

———. *Psalms: The Prayer Book of the Bible*. Minneapolis: Augsburg Fortress, 1970.

Booth, Wayne C. *The Company We Keep: An Ethics of Fiction*. Berkeley: University of California Press, 1988.

———. *The Rhetoric of Fiction*. 2nd ed. Chicago: University of Chicago Press, 1983.

Boyarin, Daniel. *Border Lines: The Partition of Judaeo-Christianity*. Philadelphia: University of Pennsylvania Press, 2004.

Braaten, Carl E., and Robert W. Jenson. "Preface: The Finnish Breakthrough in Luther Research." Pages vii–ix in *Union with Christ: The New Finnish Interpretation of Luther*. Edited by Carl E. Braaten and Robert W. Jenson. Grand Rapids: Eerdmans, 1998.

Braude, William G. *The Midrash on Psalms*. 2 vols. New Haven: Yale University Press, 1959.

Braulik, Georg. "The Sequence of the Laws in Deuteronomy 12–26 and in the Decalogue." Pages 313–35 in D. Christensen, *A Song of Power and the Power of Song*.

———. "Wisdom, Divine Presence and Law." Pages 1–25 in *The Theology of Deuteron-

omy: Collected Essays of Georg Braulik. Translated by Ulrika Lindblad. North Richland Hills, TX: BIBAL Press, 1994.

———. "Zur Abfolge der Gesetze in Deuteronomium 16,18–21,23: Weitere Beobachtungen." *Bib* 69 (1988): 63–92.

Breed, Brennan W. *Nomadic Text: A Theory of Biblical Reception History.* Bloomington: Indiana University Press, 2014.

Brenner, Athalya. "'On the Rivers of Babylon' (Psalm 137), or between Victim and Perpetrator." Pages 76–91 in *Sanctified Aggression: Legacies of Biblical and Post Biblical Vocabularies of Violence.* Edited by Jonneke Bekkenkamp and Yvonne Sherwood. JSOTSup 400. London: T&T Clark, 2003.

Brichto, Herbert Chanan. *The Problem of "Curse" in the Hebrew Bible.* SBLMS 13. Philadelphia: Society of Biblical Literature and Exegesis, 1963.

———. *Toward a Grammar of Biblical Poetics: Tales of the Prophets.* New York: Oxford University Press, 1992.

Briggman, Anthony. "Literary and Rhetorical Theory in Irenaeus, Part 2." *VC* 70 (2016): 31–50.

Briggs, Charles Augustus, and Emilie Grace Briggs. *A Critical and Exegetical Commentary on the Book of Psalms.* ICC. Edinburgh: T&T Clark, 1906–1907.

Briggs, Richard S. "Humans in the Image of God and Other Things Genesis Does Not Make Clear." *JTI* 4 (2010): 111–26.

Brown, Raymond E. *An Introduction to the New Testament.* ABRL. New York: Doubleday, 1997.

Brown, William P. "Happiness and Its Discontents in the Psalms." Pages 95–115 in *The Bible and the Pursuit of Happiness: What the Old and New Testaments Teach Us about the Good Life.* Edited by Brent A. Strawn. New York: Oxford University Press, 2012.

———. *Seeing the Psalms: A Theology of Metaphor.* Louisville: Westminster John Knox, 2002.

———. "To Discipline without Destruction: The Multifaceted Profile of the Child in Proverbs." Pages 63–81 in Bunge, Fretheim, and Gaventa, *The Child in the Bible.*

———. *Wisdom's Wonder: Character, Creation, and Crisis in the Bible's Wisdom Literature.* Grand Rapids: Eerdmans, 2014.

Brueggemann, Walter. "The Book of Exodus: Introduction, Commentary, and Reflections." Pages 677–981 in vol. 1 of *NIB.*

———. "The Costly Loss of Lament." *JSOT* 36 (1986): 57–71.

———. *Deuteronomy.* AOTC. Nashville: Abingdon, 2001.

———. *1 & 2 Kings.* SHBC. Macon, GA: Smyth & Helwys, 2000.

———. *The Message of the Psalms: A Theological Commentary.* Minneapolis: Augsburg, 1984.

———. *Old Testament Theology: Essays in Structure, Theme, and Text*. Edited by Patrick D. Miller. Minneapolis: Fortress, 1992.

———. *The Prophetic Imagination*. 2nd ed. Minneapolis: Fortress, 2001.

———. *Tenacious Solidarity: Biblical Provocations on Race, Religion, Climate, and the Economy*. Edited by Davis Hankins. Minneapolis: Fortress, 2018.

———. *Theology of the Old Testament: Testimony, Dispute, Advocacy*. Minneapolis: Fortress, 1997.

———. "The Travail of Pardon: Reflections on *slḥ*." Pages 283–97 in Strawn and Bowen, *A God So Near*.

———. "Vulnerable Children, Divine Passion, and Human Obligation." Pages 399–422 in Bunge, Fretheim, and Gaventa, *The Child in the Bible*.

Brueggemann, Walter, and William H. Bellinger Jr., *Psalms*. NCBC. Cambridge: Cambridge University Press, 2014.

Bruner, Frederick Dale. *Matthew: A Commentary*. Vol. 1: *The Christbook: Matthew 1–12*. Rev. ed. Grand Rapids: Eerdmans, 2004.

Bruner, Frederick Dale, and William E. Hordern. *The Holy Spirit, Shy Member of the Trinity*. Minneapolis: Augsburg, 1984.

Bulgakov, Sergius. *Apocatastasis and Transfiguration*. Translated and edited by Boris Jakim. New Haven: The Variable Press, 1995.

Bultmann, Rudolf. *The Second Letter to the Corinthians*. Translated by Roy A. Harrisville. Minneapolis: Augsburg, 1985.

———. *Theology of the New Testament*. Translated by Kendrick Grobel. 2 vols. in 1. New York: Scribner's Sons, 1951–55.

Bunge, Marcia, Terence E. Fretheim, and Beverly Roberts Gaventa, eds. *The Child in the Bible*. Grand Rapids: Eerdmans, 2008.

Burke, Kenneth. *The Philosophy of Literary Form: Studies in Symbolic Action*. 3rd ed. Berkeley: University of California Press, 1973.

Burnett, Joel S. "'Going Down' to Bethel: Elijah and Elisha in the Theological Geography of the Deuteronomistic History." *JBL* 129 (2010): 281–97.

———. "A Plea for David and Zion: The Elohistic Psalter as a Psalm Collection for the Temple's Restoration." Pages 95–113 in *Diachronic and Synchronic—Reading the Psalms in Real Time: Proceedings of the Baylor Symposium on the Book of Psalms*. Edited by Joel S. Burnett et al. LHBOTS 488. New York: T&T Clark, 2007.

Burnside, Jonathan. *God, Justice, and Society: Aspects of Law and Legality in the Bible*. Oxford: Oxford University Press, 2011.

Burridge, Richard. *What Are the Gospels? A Comparison with Greco-Roman Biography*. 2nd ed. Grand Rapids: Eerdmans, 2018.

Büttner, Matthias. *Das Alte Testament als erster Teil der christlichen Bibel: zur Frage nach theologischer Auslegung und "Mitte" im Kontext der Theologie Karl Barths.* BEvT 120. Gütersloh: Chr. Kaiser/Gütersloher, 2002.

Byrne, Ryan. "Lie Back and Think of Judah: The Reproductive Politics of Pillar Figurines." *NEA* 67 (2004): 137–51.

Calvin, John. *Commentaries on the Book of Joshua.* Translated by Henry Beveridge. Edinburgh: Calvin Translation Society, 1855.

———. *Institutes of the Christian Religion.* Translated by Ford Lewis Battles, edited by John T. McNeill. 2 vols. Philadelphia: Westminster, 1960.

Carmichael, Calum. *The Spirit of Biblical Law.* Athens: University of Georgia Press, 1996.

Carpenter, Humphrey, ed. *The Letters of J. R. R. Tolkien.* Boston: Houghton Mifflin Harcourt, 2000.

Carvalho, Corrine. "The Beauty of the Bloody God: The Divine Warrior in Prophetic Literature." Pages 131–52 in *The Aesthetics of Violence in the Prophets.* Edited by Julia M. O'Brien and Chris Franke. LHBOTS 517. New York: T&T Clark, 2010.

Cassuto, Umberto. *A Commentary on the Book of Exodus.* Translated by I. Abrahams. Repr. ed. Skokie, IL: Varda, 2005.

Chapman, G. C., Jr. "Ernst Käsemann, Hermann Diem, and the New Testament Canon." *JAAR* 36 (1968): 3–12.

Chapman, Stephen B. "Martial Memory, Peaceable Vision: Divine War in the Old Testament." Pages 47–67 in *Holy War in the Bible: Christian Morality and an Old Testament Problem.* Edited by Heath A. Thomas, Jeremy A. Evans, and Paul Copan. Downers Grove: IVP Academic, 2013.

Charlesworth, James H., et al., eds. *The Messiah: Developments in Earliest Judaism and Christianity.* Minneapolis: Fortress, 1992.

Charry, Ellen T. *By the Renewing of Your Minds: The Pastoral Function of Christian Doctrine.* New York: Oxford University Press, 1999.

———. "Spiritual Formation by the Doctrine of the Trinity." *ThTo* 54 (1997): 367–80.

Chesterton, G. K. "On Household Gods and Goblins." Pages 195–200 in *The Coloured Lands.* London: Sheed and Ward, 1938.

Childs, Brevard S. *Biblical Theology in Crisis.* Philadelphia: Westminster, 1970.

———. *Biblical Theology of the Old and New Testaments: Theological Reflection on the Christian Bible.* Minneapolis: Fortress, 1992.

———. *Introduction to the Old Testament as Scripture.* Philadelphia: Fortress, 1979.

———. *The New Testament as Canon: An Introduction.* Valley Forge, PA: Trinity Press International, 1994.

———. *Old Testament Theology in a Canonical Context.* Philadelphia: Fortress, 1985.

Christensen, Duane L., ed. *A Song of Power and the Power of Song: Essays on the Book of Deuteronomy.* SBTS 3. Winona Lake, IN: Eisenbrauns, 1993.

Christensen, Michael J., and Jeffery A. Wittung. *Partakers of the Divine Nature: The His-*

tory and Development of Deification in the Christian Traditions. Grand Rapids: Baker Academic, 2007.

Claassens, L. Juliana. *The God Who Provides: Biblical Images of Divine Nourishment*. Nashville: Abingdon, 2004.

Clines, David J. A. "Humanity as the Image of God." Pages 292–93 in *On the Way to the Postmodern: Old Testament Essays, 1967–1998*. JSOTSup 268. Sheffield: Sheffield Academic Press, 1998.

———. *Job 1–20*. WBC 17. Dallas: Word, 1989.

———. "The Significance of the 'Sons of God' Episode (Genesis 6:1–4) in the Context of the 'Primeval History' (Genesis 1–11)." *JSOT* 4 (1979): 33–46.

Coe, Jonathan. *The Rotters' Club*. New York: Vintage, 2001.

Cogan, Mordechai, Barry L. Eichler, and Jeffrey H. Tigay, eds. *Tehillah le-Moshe: Biblical and Judaic Studies in Honor of Moshe Greenberg*. Winona Lake, IN: Eisenbrauns, 1997.

Cogan, Mordechai, and Hayim Tadmor. *II Kings: A New Translation with Introduction and Commentary*. AB 11. New York: Doubleday, 1988.

Cohn, Robert L. *2 Kings*. Berit Olam. Collegeville, MN: Liturgical Press, 2000.

Collins, Adela Yarbro. *Is Mark's Gospel a Life of Jesus? The Question of Genre*. Milwaukee: Marquette University Press, 1990.

Collins, John J. *Does the Bible Justify Violence?* Minneapolis: Fortress, 2004.

———. "The Exodus and Biblical Theology." *BTB* 25 (1995): 152–60.

Conti, Marco, with Gianluca Pilara, eds. *1–2 Kings, 1–2 Chronicles, Ezra, Nehemiah, Esther*. ACCS 5. Downers Grove, IL: InterVarsity, 2008.

Cooper, Jerrold S. *The Curse of Agade*. JHNES. Baltimore and London: Johns Hopkins University Press, 1983.

Corbon, Jean. *Path to Freedom: Christian Experiences and the Bible*. Cincinnati: St. Anthony Messenger, 2004.

Couey, J. Blake. *Reading the Poetry of First Isaiah: The Most Perfect Model of the Prophetic Poetry*. Oxford: Oxford University Press, 2015.

Cowles, C. S. "The Case for Radical Discontinuity." Pages 11–44 in *Show Them No Mercy: 4 Views on God and Canaanite Genocide*. Edited by Stanley N. Gundry. Grand Rapids: Zondervan, 2003.

Cox, James W. *Preaching: A Comprehensive Approach to the Design and Delivery of Sermons*. San Francisco: Harper & Row, 1985.

Coxe, A. Cleaveland. *Latin Christianity: Its Founder, Tertullian*. ANF 3. Grand Rapids: Eerdmans, 1993.

Craddock, Fred B. *Preaching*. Nashville: Abingdon, 1985.

Creach, Jerome F. D. *Violence in Scripture*. Interpretation. Louisville: Westminster John Knox, 2013.

Cross, F. L., and E. A. Livingstone, eds. *The Oxford Dictionary of the Christian Church.* 3rd ed. Oxford: Oxford University Press, 1997.

Cross, Frank Moore. *Canaanite Myth and Hebrew Epic: Essays in the History of the Religion of Israel.* Cambridge: Harvard University Press, 1973.

Crouch, C. L. "Genesis 1:26–27 as a Statement of Humanity's Divine Parentage." *JTS* 61 (2010): 1–15.

———. "Made in the Image of God: The Creation of אָדָם, the Commissioning of the King and the *Chaoskampf* of YHWH." *JANER* 16 (2016): 1–21.

Cuddon, J. A., and C. E. Preston. *The Penguin Dictionary of Literary Terms and Literary Theory.* 4th ed. London: Penguin, 1998.

Culler, Jonathan. "Lyric, History, and Genre." Pages 63–77 in *The Lyric Theory Reader: A Critical Anthology.* Edited by Virginia Jackson and Yopie Prins. Baltimore: Johns Hopkins University Press, 2014.

Cullmann, Oscar. *The Christology of the New Testament.* Rev. ed. Philadelphia: Westminster, 1963.

Cunningham, David S. *These Three Are One: The Practice of Trinitarian Theology.* Challenges in Contemporary Theology. London: Blackwell, 1998.

Curry, Patrick. *Defending Middle-earth: Tolkien, Myth and Modernity.* New York: Houghton Mifflin Harcourt, 2004.

Cushing, Steven. "'Air Cal Three Thirty Six, Go Around Three Thirty Six, Go Around': Linguistic Repetition in Air-Ground Communication." Pages 2:53–65 in Johnstone, *Repetition in Discourse.*

Daly, Mary. *Beyond God the Father: Toward a Philosophy of Women's Liberation.* Boston: Beacon, 1985.

Damasio, Antonio R. *Descartes' Error: Emotion, Reason, and the Human Brain.* New York: Quill, 1994.

———. *The Feeling of What Happens: Body and Emotion in the Making of Consciousness.* San Diego: Harcourt, 1999.

Davie, Donald. *Purity of Diction in English Verse.* London: Routledge & Kegan Paul, 1952.

Davis, Ellen F. "'And Pharaoh Will Change His Mind . . .' (Ezekiel 32:31): Dismantling Mythical Discourse." Pages 224–39 in Seitz and Greene-McCreight, *Theological Exegesis.*

———. *Getting Involved with God: Rediscovering the Old Testament.* Cambridge, MA: Cowley, 2001.

———. *Opening Israel's Scriptures.* New York: Oxford University Press, 2019.

———. *Wondrous Depth: Preaching the Old Testament.* Louisville: Westminster John Knox, 2005.

Davis, Stephen T., Daniel Kendall, and Gerald O'Collins, eds. *The Trinity: An Interdisciplinary Symposium on the Trinity.* Oxford: Oxford University Press, 1999.

Daube, David. *Studies in Biblical Law*. Cambridge: Cambridge University Press, 1947.

Dawkins, Richard. *The God Delusion*. Boston: Houghton Mifflin, 2006.

Dawson, John David. *Christian Figural Reading and the Fashioning of Identity*. Berkeley: University of California, 2002.

Day, David. *Tolkien: A Dictionary*. San Diego: Thunder Bay, 2013.

Dean, Kenda Creasy. *Almost Christian: What the Faith of Our Teenagers Is Telling the American Church*. Oxford: Oxford University Press, 2010.

DeClaissé-Walford, Nancy L. "The Theology of the Imprecatory Psalms." Pages 77–92 in Jacobson, *Soundings in the Theology of Psalms*.

Delatte, Paul. *Commentaire sur la Règle de Saint Benoît*. Paris: Librairie Plon, 1948.

Delbanco, Andrew. *The Death of Satan: How Americans Have Lost the Sense of Evil*. New York: Farrar, Straus and Giroux, 1995.

Deneffe, A. "Perichoresis, *circumincessio, circuminsessio*: eine terminologische Untersuchung." *ZKT* 47 (1923): 497–523.

Dever, William G. *Does God Have a Wife? Archaeology and Folk Religion in Ancient Israel*. Grand Rapids: Eerdmans, 2005.

Dever, William G., and Seymour Gitin, eds. *Symbiosis, Symbolism, and the Power of the Past: Canaan, Ancient Israel, and Their Neighbors from the Late Bronze Age through Roman Palaestina: Proceedings of the Centennial Symposium W. F. Albright Institute of Archaeological Research and American Schools of Oriental Research, Jerusalem, May 29–31, 2000*. Winona Lake, IN: Eisenbrauns, 2003.

Dick, Michael B., ed. *Born in Heaven, Made on Earth: The Making of the Cult Image in the Ancient Near East*. Winona Lake, IN: Eisenbrauns, 1999.

Dickie, Jane R., Amy K. Eshleman, Dawn M. Merasco, Amy Shepard, Michael Vander Wilt, and Melissa Johnson. "Parent-Child Relationships and Children's Images of God." *Journal for the Scientific Study of Religion* 36 (1997): 25–43.

Dickinson, Emily. "Tell all the Truth but tell it slant (1129)." Pages 506–7 in *The Complete Poems of Emily Dickinson*. Edited by Thomas H. Johnson. Boston: Back Bay, 1976.

Dobbs-Allsopp, F. W. *On Biblical Poetry*. Oxford: Oxford University Press, 2015.

———. "Rethinking Historical Criticism." *BibInt* 7 (1999): 235–71.

Dozeman, Thomas B. *Exodus*. ECC. Grand Rapids: Eerdmans, 2009.

———. *God on the Mountain: A Study of Redaction, Theology and Canon in Exodus 19–24*. SBLMS 37. Atlanta: Scholars Press, 1989.

———. "Inner-biblical Interpretation of Yahweh's Gracious and Compassionate Character." *JBL* 108 (1989): 207–23.

Driver, S. R. *A Critical and Exegetical Commentary on Deuteronomy*. ICC. 3rd ed. Edinburgh: T&T Clark, 1902.

———. *An Introduction to the Literature of the Old Testament*. New York: Meridian Books, 1960.

Duncan, Julie A. "Considerations of 4QDtʲ in Light of the 'All Souls Deuteronomy' and Cave 4 Phylactery Texts." Pages 1:199–215 in *The Madrid Qumran Congress: Proceedings of the International Congress on the Dead Sea Scrolls, Madrid 18–21 March, 1991*. Edited by Julio Trebolle Barrera and Luis Vegas Montaner. STDJ 11. 2 vols. Leiden: Brill, 1992.

———. "Excerpted Texts of Deuteronomy at Qumran." *RevQ* 18 (1997): 43–62.

Durham, John I. *Exodus*. WBC 3. Waco, TX: Word, 1987.

Eagleton, Terry. *How to Read a Poem*. Malden, MA: Blackwell, 2007.

Earl, Douglas S. *Reading Joshua as Christian Scripture*. JTISup 2. Winona Lake, IN: Eisenbrauns, 2010.

Eco, Umberto. *Inventing the Enemy: And Other Occasional Writings*. Translated by Richard Dixon. Boston: Houghton Mifflin Harcourt, 2012.

Edelman, Diana V., ed. *You Shall Not Abhor an Edomite for He Is Your Brother: Edom and Seir in History and Tradition*. ABS 3. Atlanta: Scholars Press, 1995.

Ehler, Bernhard. *Die Herrschaft des Gekreuzigten: Ernst Käsemanns Frage nach der Mitte der Schrift*. Berlin: de Gruyter, 1986.

Ehrman, Bart D. *The New Testament: A Historical Introduction to the Early Christian Writings*. 2nd ed. New York: Oxford University Press, 2000.

Eichrodt, Walther. *Ezekiel: A Commentary*. OTL. Philadelphia: Westminster, 1970.

———. *Theology of the Old Testament*. OTL. 2 vols. Philadelphia: Westminster, 1967.

Eitan, Israel. "An Identification of *tiškaḥ yĕmīnī*, Ps 137:5." *JBL* 47 (1928): 193–95.

———. "La répétition de la racine en Hébreu." *JPOS* 1 (1921): 171–86.

Eliade, Mircea. *The Myth of the Eternal Return*. Translated by Willard R. Trask. Princeton: Princeton University Press, 1965.

Eslinger, Lyle. "The Enigmatic Plurals Like 'One of Us' (Genesis I 26, III 22, and XI 7) in Hyperchronic Perspective." *VT* 56 (2006): 171–84.

Farber, Walter. "Die Vergöttlichung Naram-Sins." *Or* 52 (1983): 67–72.

Fensham, F. Charles. "Father and Son as Terminology for Treaty and Covenant." Pages 121–35 in Goedicke, *Near Eastern Studies in Honor of William Foxwell Albright*.

Ferguson, Christopher J. "No, Orcs Aren't Racist." *Psychology Today*. April 29, 2020. https://www.psychologytoday.com/us/blog/checkpoints/202004/no-orcs-arent-racist.

Ferguson, Everett. "God's Infinity and Man's Mutability: Perpetual Progress according to Gregory of Nyssa." *Greek Orthodox Theological Review* 18 (1973): 59–78.

Feuer, Avrohom Chaim. *Tehillim: A New Translation with a Commentary, Anthologized from Talmudic, Midrashic and Rabbinic Sources*. 2 vols. New York: Mesorah, 2013.

Fewell, Danna Nolan. *The Children of Israel: Reading the Bible for the Sake of Our Children*. Nashville: Abingdon, 2003.

Firth, David G. "Passing On the Faith in Deuteronomy." Pages 157–76 in *Interpreting*

Deuteronomy: Issues and Approaches. Edited by David G. Firth and Philip S. Johnston. Downers Grove, IL: IVP Academic, 2012.

Fitz, Erika J. "A Significant Other: Moab as Symbol in Biblical Literature." PhD diss., Emory University, 2012.

Fleming, Daniel E. "The Amorites." Pages 1–30 in *The World around the Old Testament: The People and Places of the Ancient Near East.* Edited by Bill T. Arnold and Brent A. Strawn. Grand Rapids: Baker Academic, 2016.

Fohrer, Georg. *History of Israelite Religion.* Translated by David E. Green. Nashville: Abingdon, 1972.

Fokkelman, J. P. *85 Psalms and Job 4–14.* Vol. 2 of *Major Poems of the Hebrew Bible at the Interface of Prosody and Structural Analysis.* Assen: Van Gorcum, 2000.

———. *The Psalms in Form: The Hebrew Psalter in Its Poetic Shape.* Leiden: Deo, 2002.

———. *Reading Biblical Narrative: An Introductory Guide.* Louisville: Westminster John Knox, 1999.

Ford, William. "The Challenge of the Canaanites." *TynBul* 68 (2017): 161–84.

Forster, E. M. *Aspects of the Novel.* San Diego: Harcourt, 1955.

Foster, Benjamin R. *Before the Muses: An Anthology of Akkadian Literature.* Bethesda: CDL, 2005.

Foster, Robert. *The Complete Guide to Middle-earth: From the Hobbit through the Lord of the Rings and Beyond.* Rev. ed. New York: Random House, 2001.

Fowl, Stephen. "Texts Don't Have Ideologies." *BibInt* 3 (1995): 15–34.

Fowler, Jeaneane D. *Theophoric Personal Names in Ancient Hebrew: A Comparative Study.* JSOTSup 49. Sheffield: JSOT Press, 1988.

Frechette, Christopher G. "Destroying the Internalized Perpetrator: A Healing Function of the Violent Language against Enemies in the Psalms." Pages 71–84 in *Trauma and Traumatization in Individual and Collective Dimensions: Insights from Biblical Studies and Beyond.* Edited by Eve-Marie Becker, Jan Dochhorn, and Else Kragelund Holt. SANT 2. Göttingen: Vandenhoeck & Ruprecht, 2014.

Freedman, David Noel. "The Structure of Psalm 137." Pages 187–205 in Goedecke, *Near Eastern Studies in Honor of William Foxwell Albright.*

Fretheim, Terence E. *Exodus.* Interpretation. Louisville: John Knox, 1991.

———. *First and Second Kings.* Westminster Bible Companion. Louisville: Westminster John Knox, 1999.

———. *God and World in the Old Testament: A Relational Theology of Creation.* Nashville: Abingdon, 2005.

———. "'God Was with the Boy' (Genesis 21:20): Children in the Book of Genesis." Pages 3–23 in Bunge, Fretheim, and Gaventa, *The Child in the Bible.*

———. "Issues of Agency in Exodus." Pages 591–609 in *The Book of Exodus: Compo-*

sition, Reception, and Interpretation. Edited by Thomas B. Dozeman, Craig A. Evans, and Joel N. Lohr. VTSup 164. Leiden: Brill, 2014.

———. "'I Was Only a Little Angry': Divine Violence in the Prophets." *Int* 58 (2004): 365–75.

———. *The Suffering of God: An Old Testament Perspective.* OBT. Philadelphia: Fortress, 1984.

Freud, Sigmund. *Beyond the Pleasure Principle.* Translated and edited by James Strachey. New York: Norton, 1961.

———. "Further Recommendations in the Technique of Psycho-Analysis: Recollection, Repetition and Working Through." Pages 2:366–76 in *Collected Papers.* Translated by Joan Riviere. 5 vols. New York: Basic Books, 1959.

———. *The Interpretation of Dreams.* Translated by James Strachey. New York: Basic, 2010.

———. *Moses and Monotheism.* Translated by Katherine Jones. New York: Vintage, 1939.

———. *Totem and Taboo: Some Points of Agreement between the Mental Lives of Savages and Neurotics.* Translated and edited by James Strachey. New York: Norton, 1950.

Friedman, Richard Elliott. *The Disappearance of God: A Divine Mystery.* Boston: Little, Brown, 1995.

Friedrich, Johannes, Wolfgang Pöhlmann, and Peter Stuhlmacher, eds. *Festschrift für Ernst Käsemann zum 70. Geburtstag.* Tübingen: Mohr Siebeck, 1976.

Fritz, Volkmar. *1 & 2 Kings: A Continental Commentary.* Translated by Anselm Hagedorn. Minneapolis: Augsburg Fortress, 2003.

Fromm, Erich. *You Shall Be as Gods: A Radical Interpretation of the Old Testament and Its Tradition.* New York: Henry Holt, 1991.

Frye, Northrop. "Expanding Eyes." *Critical Inquiry* 2 (1975): 199–216.

Frymer-Kensky, Tikva. *In the Wake of the Goddesses: Women, Culture, and the Biblical Transformation of Pagan Myth.* New York: Free Press, 1992.

Frymer-Kensky, Tikva, et al., eds. *Christianity in Jewish Terms.* Boulder: Westview, 2000.

Funk, Robert W., Roy W. Hoover, and the Jesus Seminar. *The Five Gospels: The Search for the Authentic Words of Jesus.* San Francisco: HarperSanFrancisco, 1993.

Gaiser, Frederick J. "'I Will Carry and Will Save': The Carrying God of Isaiah 40–66." Pages 94–102 in *"And God Saw That It Was Good": Essays on Creation and God in Honor of Terence E. Fretheim.* Edited by Frederick J. Gaiser and Mark A. Throntveit. Word and World Supplement 5. Saint Paul: Luther Seminary, 2006.

Garr, W. Randall. "'Image' and 'Likeness' in the Inscription from Tell Fakhariyeh." *IEJ* 50 (2000): 227–34.

———. *In His Own Image and Likeness: Humanity, Divinity, and Monotheism.* CHANE 15. Leiden: Brill, 2003.

Garrett, Duane A. *A Commentary on Exodus*. Grand Rapids: Kregel Academic, 2014.

Gault, Rebecca S. "Education by the Use of Ghosts: Strategies of Repetition in Effi Briest." Pages 1:139–51 in Johnstone, *Repetition in Discourse*.

Gaventa, Beverly Roberts. *The Acts of the Apostles*. ANTC. Nashville: Abingdon, 2003.

———. "Finding a Place for Children in the Letters of Paul." Pages 233–48 in Bunge, Fretheim, and Gaventa, *The Child in the Bible*.

———. "Our Mother St. Paul: Toward the Recovery of a Neglected Theme." *PSB* 17 (1996): 29–44.

Geller, Stephen A. "Fiery Wisdom: The Deuteronomic Tradition." Pages 30–61 in *Sacred Enigmas: Literary Religion in the Hebrew Bible*. London: Routledge, 1996.

George, A. R. *The Babylonian Gilgamesh Epic: Introduction, Critical Edition and Cuneiform Texts*. 2 vols. Oxford: Oxford University Press, 2003.

Gerhardsson, Birger. *Memory and Manuscript: Oral Tradition and Written Transmission in Rabbinic Judaism and Early Christianity with Tradition and Transmission in Early Christianity*. Grand Rapids: Eerdmans and Livonia: Dove, 1998.

Gillingham, Susan. "The Reception of Psalm 137 in Jewish and Christian Tradition." Pages 64–82 in Gillingham, *Jewish and Christian Approaches to the Psalms*.

———, ed. *Jewish and Christian Approaches to the Psalms: Conflict and Convergence*. Edited by Susan Gillingham. Oxford: Oxford University Press, 2013.

Gisel, Pierre. *Vérité et histoire: La théologie dans la modernité: Ernst Käsemann*. Théologie Historique 41. Paris: Éditions beauchesne, 1977.

Glassick, Charles E., Mary Taylor Huber, and Gene I. Maeroff. *Scholarship Assessed: Evaluation of the Professoriate*. San Francisco: Jossey-Bass, 1997.

Glazov, Gregory. "Theōsis, Judaism, and Old Testament Anthropology." Pages 16–31 in *Theōsis: Deification in Christian Theology*. Edited by Stephen Finlan and Vladimir Kharlamov. PTMS 52. Eugene, OR: Pickwick, 2006.

Glück, Louise. *Proofs and Theories: Essays on Poetry*. Hopewell: Ecco, 1994.

Gnuse, Robert K. *The Old Testament and Process Theology*. St. Louis: Chalice, 2000.

Goedicke, Hans, ed. *Near Eastern Studies in Honor of William Foxwell Albright*. Baltimore: Johns Hopkins University Press, 1971.

Goldhagen, Daniel Jonah. *Hitler's Willing Executioners: Ordinary Germans and the Holocaust*. New York: Vintage Books, 1997.

Goldingay, John. *Approaches to Old Testament Interpretation*. Rev. ed. Downers Grove, IL: InterVarsity, 1990.

———. *Psalms 90–150*. Vol. 3 of *Psalms*. BCOTWP. Grand Rapids: Baker Academic, 2008.

Goldsworthy, Graeme. *Preaching the Whole Bible as Christian Scripture: The Application of Biblical Theology to Expository Preaching*. Grand Rapids: Eerdmans, 2000.

Gould, Stephen Jay. *The Mismeasure of Man*. Rev. ed. New York: Norton, 1996.

Gowan, Donald E. *Theology in Exodus: Biblical Theology in the Form of a Commentary.* Louisville: Westminster John Knox, 1994.

———. *Theology of the Prophetic Books: The Death and Resurrection of Israel.* Louisville: Westminster John Knox, 1998.

———. *When Man Becomes God: Humanism and Hybris in the Old Testament.* PTMS 6. Eugene, OR: Pickwick, 1975.

Grabbe, Lester L. "'Canaanite': Some Methodological Observations in Relation to Biblical Study." Pages 113–32 in *Ugarit and the Bible: Proceedings of the International Symposium on Ugarit and the Bible.* Edited by George J. Brooke, Adrian H. W. Curtis, and John F. Healey. UBL 11. Münster: Ugarit-Verlag, 1994.

Grassi, Joseph A. "Child, Children." *ABD* 1:905.

Graves, Mike. *The Sermon as Symphony: Preaching the Literary Forms of the New Testament.* Valley Forge, PA: Judson Press, 1997.

Gray, John. *I & II Kings: A Commentary.* 2nd rev. ed. OTL. Philadelphia: Westminster, 1970.

Green, Clifford, ed. *Karl Barth: Theologian of Freedom.* The Making of Modern Theology. Minneapolis: Fortress, 1991.

Green, Joel B. "The (Re-)Turn to Theology." *JTI* 1 (2007): 1–3.

Greenspahn, Frederick E. *When Brothers Dwell Together: The Preeminence of Younger Siblings in the Hebrew Bible.* New York: Oxford University Press, 1994.

Greenstein, Edward L. "How Does Parallelism Mean?" Pages 41–70 in *A Sense of Text: The Art of Language in the Study of Biblical Literature.* Edited by L. Nemoy. Winona Lake, IN: Eisenbrauns, 1983.

Greidanus, Sidney. *Preaching Christ from the Old Testament: A Contemporary Hermeneutical Method.* Grand Rapids: Eerdmans, 1999.

Gross, Jules. *The Divinization of the Christian according to the Greek Fathers.* Translated by Paul A. Onica. Anaheim, CA: A & C, 2002.

Grossman, Dave. *On Killing: The Psychological Cost of Learning to Kill in War and Society.* Rev. ed. New York: Back Bay, 2009.

Gruber, Mayer I. *The Motherhood of God and Other Studies.* SFSHJ 57. Atlanta: Scholars Press, 1992.

Gunkel, Hermann. "Was haben wir am Alten Testament?" *Deutsche Rundschau* 161 (1914): 215–41.

———. *Water for a Thirsty Land: Israelite Literature and Religion.* Edited by K. C. Hanson. Fortress Classics in Biblical Studies. Minneapolis: Fortress, 2001.

———. *What Remains of the Old Testament and Other Essays.* Translated by A. K. Dallas. New York: Macmillan, 1928.

———. "Why Engage the Old Testament?" Pages 1–30 in *What Remains of the Old Testament and Other Essays.* Translated by A. K. Dallas. New York: Macmillan, 1928.

Gunn, David M., and Danna Nolan Fewell. *Narrative in the Hebrew Bible*. Oxford Bible Series Oxford: Oxford University Press, 1993.

Gunton, Colin. "The God of Jesus Christ." *ThTo* 54 (1997): 325–34.

Habachi, Labib. *Features of the Deification of Ramesses II*. ADAIK 5. Glückstadt: J. J. Augustin, 1969.

Habel, N. "The Form and Significance of the Call Narratives." *ZAW* 77 (1965): 297–323.

Hafiz. "Tired of Speaking Sweetly." Pages 187–88 in *The Gift: Poems by Hafiz the Great Sufi Master*. Translated by Daniel Ladinsky. New York: Penguin Compass, 1999.

Hammond, George C. *It Has Not Yet Appeared What We Shall Be: A Reconsideration of the Imago Dei in Light of Those with Severe Cognitive Disabilities*. Phillipsburg, NJ: P & R, 2017.

Hammond, Wayne G., and Christina Scull. *The Lord of the Rings: A Reader's Companion*. Boston: Houghton Mifflin Company, 2005.

Hamori, Esther J. *When Gods Were Men: The Embodied God in Biblical and Ancient Near Eastern Literature*. BZAW 384. Berlin: de Gruyter, 2008.

Hankle, Dominick D. "The Therapeutic Implications of the Imprecatory Psalms in the Christian Counseling Setting." *Journal of Psychology and Theology* 38 (2010): 275–80.

Haran, Menahem. "Midrashic and Literal Exegesis and the Critical Method in Biblical Research." Pages 19–48 in *Studies in Bible*. Edited by Sara Japhet. SH 31. Jerusalem: Magnes, 1986.

———. "The Shining of Moses' Face: A Case Study in Biblical and Ancient Near Eastern Iconography." Pages 159–73 in *In the Shelter of Elyon: Essays on Ancient Palestinian Life and Literature in Honor of G. W. Ahlström*. Edited by W. Boyd Barrick and John R. Spencer. JSOTSup 31. Sheffield: Sheffield Academic, 1984.

Hargroves, Jennifer G. "Law." Pages 347–48 in *J. R. R. Tolkien Encyclopedia: Scholarship and Critical Assessment*. Edited by Michael D. C. Drout. New York: Routledge, 2007.

Harrelson, Walter J. *The Ten Commandments and Human Rights*. Macon, GA: Mercer University Press, 1997.

Harrington, Daniel J. *Invitation to the Apocrypha*. Grand Rapids: Eerdmans, 1999.

Harrisville, Roy A., and Walter Sundberg. *The Bible in Modern Culture: Baruch Spinoza to Brevard Childs*. 2nd ed. Grand Rapids: Eerdmans, 2002.

Harvey, Van A. *A Handbook of Theological Terms*. New York: Collier, 1964.

Hasel, Gerhard F. *Old Testament Theology: Basic Issues in the Current Debate*. 4th ed. Grand Rapids: Eerdmans, 1991.

Hays, Richard B. *The Conversion of the Imagination: Paul as Interpreter of Israel's Scripture*. Grand Rapids: Eerdmans, 2005.

———. *Echoes of Scripture in the Letters of Paul*. New Haven: Yale University Press, 1989.

Heim, Knut Martin. *Poetic Imagination in Proverbs: Variant Repetitions and the Nature of Poetry*. BBRSup 4. Winona Lake, IN: Eisenbrauns, 2013.

Heffelfinger, Katie M. *I Am Large, I Contain Multitudes: Lyric Cohesion and Conflict in Second Isaiah*. BIS 105. Leiden: Brill, 2011.

Hens-Piazza, Gina. *1–2 Kings*. AOTC. Nashville: Abingdon, 2006.

Herrmann, Johannes. "Die Zahl zweiundvierzig im AT." *OLZ* 13 (1910): 150–52.

Herrmann, Judith. *Trauma and Recovery*. New York: Basic, 1997.

Herrmann, Siegfried. "Die Naturlehre des Schöpfungsberichtes: Erwägungen zur Vorgeschichte von Genesis 1." *TLZ* 86 (1961): 413–24.

Hess, Richard S. *Israelite Religions: An Archaeological and Biblical Survey*. Grand Rapids: Baker Academic, 2007.

———. "The Onomastics of Ugarit." Pages 499–528 in *Handbook of Ugaritic Studies*. Edited by Wilfred G. E. Watson and Nicolas Wyatt. HdO 1.39. Leiden: Brill, 1999.

Hitchens, Christopher. *God Is Not Great: How Religion Poisons Everything*. New York: Twelve, 2007.

Hofreiter, Christian. *Making Sense of Old Testament Genocide: Christian Interpretations of Herem Passages*. Oxford: Oxford University Press, 2018.

Holladay, William L. *Jeremiah 1: A Commentary on the Book of the Prophet Jeremiah Chapters 1–25*. Edited by Paul D. Hanson. Hermeneia. Philadelphia: Fortress, 1986.

Holmgren, Fredrick C. *The Old Testament and the Significance of Jesus: Embracing Change—Maintaining Christian Identity: The Emerging Center in Biblical Scholarship*. Grand Rapids: Eerdmans, 1999.

Hornung, Erik. *Conceptions of God in Ancient Egypt: The One and the Many*. Translated by John Baines. Ithaca, NY: Cornell University Press, 1982.

Horowitz, Maryanne Cline. "The Image of God in Man—Is Woman Included?" *HTR* 72 (1979): 175–206.

Hossfeld, Frank-Lothar, and Erich Zenger. *Psalms 3: A Commentary on Psalms 101–150*. Edited by Klaus Baltzer, translated by Linda M. Maloney. Hermeneia. Minneapolis: Fortress, 2011.

Hulster, Izaak J. de, and Brent A. Strawn. "Figuring YHWH in Unusual Ways: Deuteronomy 32 and Other Mixed Metaphors for God in the Old Testament." Pages 117–33 in de Hulster, Strawn, and Bonfiglio, *Iconographic Exegesis of the Hebrew Bible/Old Testament*.

Hulster, Izaak J. de, Brent A. Strawn, and Ryan P. Bonfiglio, eds. *Iconographic Exegesis of the Hebrew Bible/Old Testament: An Introduction to Its Method and Practice*. Göttingen: Vandenhoeck & Ruprecht, 2015.

Humphreys, W. Lee. *The Character of God in the Book of Genesis: A Narrative Appraisal*. Louisville: Westminster John Knox, 2001.

Hunsinger, George. *How to Read Karl Barth: The Shape of His Theology*. New York: Oxford University Press, 1991.

Hur, Shin Wook. "The Rhetoric of the Deuteronomic Code: Its Structures and Devices." PhD diss., Emory University, 2013.

Hurowitz, Victor Avigdor. "The Divinity of Humankind in the Bible and the Ancient Near East: A New Mesopotamian Parallel." Pages 263–74 in *Mishneh Todah: Studies in Deuteronomy and Its Cultural Environment in Honor of Jeffrey H. Tigay*. Edited by Nili Sacher Fox, David A. Glatt-Gilad, and Michael J. Williams. Winona Lake, IN: Eisenbrauns, 2009.

Hurtado, L. W. "Gospel (Genre)." Pages 276–82 in *Dictionary of Jesus and the Gospels*. Edited by Joel B. Green, Scot McKnight, and I. Howard Marshall. Downers Grove, IL: InterVarsity, 1992.

Hwang, Jerry. *The Rhetoric of Remembrance: An Investigation of the "Fathers" in Deuteronomy*. Siphrut 8. Winona Lake, IN: Eisenbrauns, 2012.

Iser, Wolfgang. *The Act of Reading: A Theory of Aesthetic Response*. Baltimore: Johns Hopkins University Press, 1978.

Jackson, Bernard S. *Essays in Jewish and Comparative Legal History*. SJLA 10. Leiden: Brill, 1975.

Jacob, Benno. *The First Book of the Bible, Genesis: Augmented Edition*. Translated and edited by Ernest I. Jacob and Walter Jacob. Brooklyn: Ktav, 2007.

———. *The Second Book of the Bible: Exodus*. Translated by W. Jacob. Hoboken, NJ: Ktav, 1992.

Jacobsen, Thorkild. "*Inuma Ilu awīlum*." Pages 113–17 in *Essays on the Ancient Near East in Memory of Jacob Joel Finkelstein*. Edited by Maria de Jong Ellis. Hamden, CT: Archon Books, 1977.

———. "Mesopotamia." Pages 125–219 in *The Intellectual Adventure of Ancient Man: An Essay on Speculative Thought in the Ancient Near East*. Edited by Henri and H. A. Frankfort. Chicago: University of Chicago Press, 1977.

———. *The Treasures of Darkness: A History of Mesopotamian Religion*. New Haven: Yale University Press, 1976.

Jacobson, Rolf A., ed. *Soundings in the Theology of Psalms: Perspectives and Methods in Contemporary Scholarship*. Minneapolis: Fortress, 2011.

Janzen, J. Gerald. "The Place of the Book of Job in the History of Israel's Religion." Pages 523–37 in *Ancient Israelite Religion: Essays in Honor of Frank Moore Cross*. Edited by Patrick D. Miller, Paul D. Hanson, and S. Dean McBride. Minneapolis: Fortress, 1987.

———. "Solidarity and Solitariness in Ancient Israel: The Case of Jeremiah." Pages 211–17 in *When Prayer Takes Place: Forays into a Biblical World*. Edited by Brent A. Strawn and Patrick D. Miller. Eugene, OR: Cascade, 2012.

———. *When Prayer Takes Place: Forays into a Biblical World*. Edited by Brent A. Strawn and Patrick D. Miller. Eugene, OR: Cascade, 2012.

Jenson, Robert W. *Systematic Theology*. 2 vols. New York: Oxford University Press, 1997–2001.

Jobling, David, Tina Pippin, and Ronald Scheifer. *The Postmodern Bible Reader*. Oxford: Blackwell, 2001.

Johnson, Elizabeth A. "Trinity: To Let the Symbol Sing Again." *ThTo* 54 (1997): 299–311.

Johnson, Luke Timothy. *The Creed: What Christians Believe and Why It Matters*. New York: Doubleday, 2003.

———. *Religious Experience in Earliest Christianity*. Minneapolis: Fortress, 1998.

———. *The Writings of the New Testament: An Interpretation*. Rev. ed. Minneapolis: Fortress, 1999.

Johnstone, Barbara. "An Introduction." *Text* 7 (1987): 205–14.

———, ed., *Repetition in Discourse: Interdisciplinary Perspectives*. Advances in Discourse Processes 47–48. 2 vols. Norwood, NJ: Ablex, 1994.

Johnstone, Barbara, et al. "Repetition in Discourse: A Dialogue." Pages 1–20 in Johnstone, *Repetition in Discourse*.

Johnstone, William. *Exodus 20–40*. SHBC. Macon, GA: Smyth & Helwys, 2014.

Jónsson, Gunnlaugur A. *The Image of God: Genesis 1:26–28 in a Century of Old Testament Research*. ConBOT 26. Stockholm: Almqvist & Wiksell, 1988.

Juel, Donald. *Messianic Exegesis: Christological Interpretation of the Old Testament in Early Christianity*. Philadelphia: Fortress, 1992.

———. "The Trinity and the New Testament." *ThTo* 54 (1997): 312–24.

Kaminsky, Joel S. *Corporate Responsibility in the Hebrew Bible*. JSOTSup 196. Sheffield: Sheffield Academic, 1995.

Kantorowicz, Ernst H. *The King's Two Bodies: A Study in Medieval Political Theology*. Princeton: Princeton University Press, 1997.

Käsemann, Ernst. "Blind Alleys in the 'Jesus of History' Controversy." Pages 23–65 in Käsemann, *New Testament Questions of Today*.

———. *Commentary on Romans*. Grand Rapids: Eerdmans, 1980.

———. *Essays on New Testament Themes*. Translated by W. J. Montague. Philadelphia: Fortress, 1964.

———. *The Future of Our Religious Past: Essays in Honour of Rudolf Bultmann*. Edited by J. M. Robinson. New York: Harper, 1971.

———. *Jesus Means Freedom*. Philadelphia: Fortress, 1974.

———. "Justification and Salvation History in the Epistle to the Romans." Pages 60–78 in Käsemann, *Perspectives on Paul*.

———. *New Testament Questions of Today*. Translated by W. J. Montague. Philadelphia: Fortress, 1969.

———. "On Paul's Anthropology." Pages 1–31 in Käsemann, *Perspectives on Paul.*

———. *Perspectives on Paul.* Philadelphia: Fortress, 1971.

———. "The Problem of a New Testament Theology." *NTS* 19 (1973): 235–45.

———. "The Problem of the Historical Jesus." Pages 15–47 in *Essays on New Testament Themes.* Translated by W. J. Montague. Philadelphia: Fortress, 1964.

———. "'The Righteousness of God' in Paul." Pages 168–82 in Käsemann, *New Testament Questions of Today.*

———. "The Saving Significance of the Death of Jesus in Paul." Pages 32–59 in Käsemann, *Perspectives on Paul.* Philadelphia: Fortress, 1971.

———. "Some Thoughts on the Theme 'The Doctrine of Reconciliation in the New Testament.'" Pages 49–64 in *The Future of Our Religious Past: Essays in Honour of Rudolf Bultmann.* Edited by J. M. Robinson. New York: Harper, 1971.

———. *The Testament of Jesus: A Study of the Gospel of John in the Light of Chapter 17.* Philadelphia: Fortress, 1978.

———. "Vom theologischen Recht historisch-kritischer Exegese." *ZTK* 64 (1967): 259–81.

———. *The Wandering People of God: An Investigation of the Letter to the Hebrews.* Minneapolis: Augsburg, 1984.

———. "What I Have Unlearned in 50 Years as a German Theologian." *CurTM* 15 (1988): 335.

———. "Worship and Everyday Life: A Note on Romans 12." Pages 188–95 in Käsemann, *New Testament Questions of Today.*

Kass, Leon R. *The Beginning of Wisdom: Reading Genesis.* Chicago: University of Chicago Press, 2003.

Kaufman, Stephen A. "The Structure of the Deuteronomic Law." *Maarav* 1/2 (1978–1979): 105–58.

Kawin, Bruce F. *Telling It Again and Again: Repetition in Literature and Film.* Boulder: University Press of Colorado, 1989.

Kay, James F. *Christus Praesens: A Reconsideration of Rudolf Bultmann's Christology.* Grand Rapids: Eerdmans, 1994.

Keel, Othmar, and Christoph Uehlinger. *Gods, Goddesses, and Images of God in Ancient Israel.* Translated by Thomas H. Trapp. Minneapolis: Fortress, 1998.

Keifert, Patrick R. "The Bible and Theological Education: A Report and Reflections on a Journey." Pages 165–82 in *The Ending of Mark and the Ends of God: Essays in Memory of Donald Harrisville Juel.* Edited by Beverly Roberts Gaventa and Patrick D. Miller. Louisville: Westminster John Knox, 2005.

Keillor, Garrison. *Good Poems.* New York: Penguin, 2002.

Kendi, Ibram X. *How to Be an Antiracist.* New York: One World, 2019.

Kierkegaard, Søren. *Fear and Trembling: Repetition.* Translated and edited by Howard V. Hong and Edna H. Hong. Kierkegaard's Writings 6. Princeton: Princeton University Press, 1983.

King, Philip J., and Lawrence E. Stager, *Life in Biblical Israel*. LAI. Louisville: Westminster John Knox, 2001.

Kinzie, Mary. *A Poet's Guide to Poetry*. Chicago: University of Chicago Press, 1999.

Kissling, Paul J. *Reliable Characters in the Primary History: Profiles of Moses, Joshua, Elijah, and Elisha*. JSOTSup 224. Sheffield: Sheffield Academic, 1996.

Kitchen, Kenneth A., and Paul J. N. Lawrence. "No. 93 Esarhaddon of Assyria and Baal, King of Tyre." Pages 1:957–62 in *Treaty, Law and Covenant in the Ancient Near East*. 3 vols. Wiesbaden: Harrassowitz, 2012.

Kitz, Anne Marie. *Cursed Are You! The Phenomenology of Cursing in Cuneiform and Hebrew Texts*. Winona Lake, IN: Eisenbrauns, 2014.

Klein, Jacob. "Sumerian Kingship and the Gods." Pages 115–31 in Beckman and Lewis, *Text, Artifact, and Image*.

Knierim, Rolf P. *The Task of Old Testament Theology: Method and Cases*. Grand Rapids: Eerdmans, 1995.

Knowles, Melody D. "A Woman at Prayer: A Critical Note on Psalm 131:2b." *JBL* 125 (2006): 385–89.

Koester, Craig R. *Revelation: A New Translation with Introduction and Commentary*. AYBC 38A. New Haven: Yale University Press, 2014.

Koester, Helmut. *Introduction to the New Testament*. 2 vols. Philadelphia: Fortress, 1982.

Köhler, Ludwig. *Hebrew Man*. Translated by P. R. Ackroyd. Nashville: Abingdon, 1956.

Kok, Jacobus (Kobus), and John Anthony Dunne. "Participation in Christ and Missional Dynamics in Galatians." Pages 59–85 in *Participation, Justification, and Conversion: Eastern Orthodox Interpretation of Paul and the Debate between "Old and New Perspectives on Paul."* Edited by Athanasios Despotis. WUNT 2.442. Tübingen: Mohr Siebeck, 2017.

Kolakowski, Lesek. *Religion*. New York: Oxford University Press, 1992.

Konrath, S. H., E. H. O'Brien, and C. Hsing. "Changes in Dispositional Empathy in American College Students over Time: A Meta-analysis." *Personality and Social Psychology Review* 15 (2011): 180–98.

Korpel, Marjo Christina Annette. *A Rift in the Clouds: Ugaritic and Hebrew Descriptions of the Divine*. UBL 8. Münster: Ugarit-Verlag, 1990.

Kraus, Hans-Joachim. *Psalms 60–150: A Continental Commentary*. Translated by Hilton C. Oswald. Minneapolis: Fortress, 1993.

Kugel, James L. *The Great Poems of the Bible: A Reader's Companion with New Translations*. New York: Free, 1999.

———. *The Idea of Biblical Poetry: Parallelism and Its History*. New Haven: Yale University Press, 1981.

———. *In Potiphar's House: The Interpretive Life of Biblical Texts*. 2nd ed. Cambridge: Harvard University Press, 1994.

Kynes, Bill, and Will Kynes, *Wrestling with Job: Defiant Faith in the Face of Suffering*. Downers Grove, IL: IVP Academic, 2022.

Labuschagne, C. J. *The Incomparability of Yahweh in the Old Testament*. POS 5. Leiden: Brill, 1966.

LaCugna, Catherine Mowry. *God for Us: The Trinity and Christian Life*. San Francisco: HarperSanFrancisco, 1991.

Lafont, Ghislain. "La pertinence théologique de l'histoire." *RSPT* 63 (1979): 161–202.

Lakoff, George, and Mark Johnson. *Metaphors We Live By*. Chicago: University of Chicago Press, 2003.

Lambert, W. G., and A. R. Millard. *Atra-Ḫasis: The Babylonian Story of the Flood*. Repr. Winona Lake, IN: Eisenbrauns, 1999.

Lampe, G. W. H. *A Patristic Greek Lexicon*. Oxford: Clarendon, 1961.

Lange, Armin, and Matthias Weigold. *Biblical Quotations and Allusions in Second Temple Jewish Literature*. JAJSup 5. Göttingen: Vandenhoeck & Ruprecht, 2011.

Lanham, Richard A. *A Handlist of Rhetorical Terms: A Guide for Students of English Literature*. Berkeley: University of California Press, 1969.

Lapsley, Jacqueline E. "Feeling Our Way: Love for God in Deuteronomy." *CBQ* 65 (2003): 350–69.

———. "'Look! The Children and I Are as Signs and Portents in Israel': Children in Isaiah." Pages 82–102 in Bunge, Fretheim, and Gaventa, *The Child in the Bible*.

Lasserre, Guy. *Synopse des lois du Pentateuque*. VTSup 59. Leiden: Brill, 1994.

Laurence, Trevor. "Cursing with God: The Imprecatory Psalms and the Ethics of Christian Prayer." PhD diss., Exeter University, 2020.

Lawrence, Brother. *The Practice of the Presence of God*. Pittsburgh: Whitaker House, 1982.

———. *The Practice of the Presence of God: Contemporary English Version*. Edited by Hal M. Helms. Brewster, MA: Paraclete Press, 2010.

Layton, Bentley. *The Gnostic Scriptures*. ABRL. New York: Doubleday, 1995.

Le Boulluec, Alain. *La notion d'hérésie dans la littérature grecque, IIe–IIIe siècles*. 2 vols. Paris: Etudes augustiniennes, 1985.

Legaspi, Michael C. *The Death of Scripture and the Rise of Biblical Studies*. Oxford: Oxford University Press, 2010.

LeMon, Joel. "The Power of Parallelism in KTU² 1.119: Another 'Trial Cut.'" *UF* 37 (2005): 375–94.

———. "Rereading a Difficult Text: Violence against Children and Girls in the Reception History of Psalm 137." Pages 75–93 in *Reading for Faith and Learning: Essays on Scripture, Community, and Libraries in Honor of M. Patrick Graham*.

Edited by John B. Weaver and Douglas L. Gragg. Abilene: Abilene Christian University Press, 2017.

———. "Saying Amen to Violent Psalms: Patterns of Prayer, Belief, and Action in the Psalter." Pages 93–111 in Jacobson, *Soundings in the Theology of Psalms*.

Lemos, T. M. "Dispossessing Nations: Population Growth, Scarcity, and Genocide in Ancient Israel and Twentieth-century Rwanda." Pages 27–66 in *Ritual Violence in the Hebrew Bible: New Perspectives*. Edited by Saul M. Olyan. New York: Oxford University Press, 2015.

———. "Neither Mice nor Men: Dehumanization and Extermination in Mesopotamian Sources, Ḥērem Texts, and the War Scroll." Pages 249–66 in *With the Loyal You Show Yourself Loyal: Essays on Relationships in the Hebrew Bible in Honor of Saul M. Olyan*. Edited by T. M. Lemos et al. Ancient Israel and Its Literature 42. Atlanta: Society of Biblical Literature, 2021.

Lenchak, Timothy A. *"Choose Life!": A Rhetorical-Critical Investigation of Deuteronomy 28,69–30,20*. AnBib 129. Rome: Pontifical Biblical Institute, 1993.

Leonard, Jeffrey M. *Creation Rediscovered: Finding New Meaning in an Ancient Story*. Peabody, MA: Hendrickson, 2020.

Leslie, Elmer. *Old Testament Religion*. Nashville: Abingdon, 1936.

Levenson, Jon D. *Creation and the Persistence of Evil: The Jewish Drama of Divine Omnipotence*. Rev. ed. Princeton: Princeton University Press, 1994.

———. *The Death and Resurrection of the Beloved Son: The Transformation of Child Sacrifice in Judaism and Christianity*. New Haven: Yale University Press, 1993.

———. "The Eighth Principle of Judaism and the Literary Simultaneity of Scripture." Pages 62–81 in Levenson, *The Hebrew Bible, the Old Testament, and Historical Criticism*.

———. "The Exodus and Biblical Theology: A Rejoinder to John J. Collins." *BTB* 26 (1996): 4–10.

———. "The Horrifying Closing of Psalm 137, or, The Limitations of Ethical Reading." Pages 18–40 in *Opportunity for No Little Instruction: Biblical Essays in Honor of Daniel J. Harrington, SJ, and Richard J. Clifford, SJ*. Edited by Christopher G. Frechette, Christopher R. Matthews, and Thomas D. Stegman, SJ. New York: Paulist, 2014.

———. *The Hebrew Bible, the Old Testament, and Historical Criticism: Jews and Christians in Biblical Studies*. Louisville: Westminster John Knox, 1993.

———. "Why Jews Are Not Interested in Biblical Theology." Pages 33–61 in Levenson, *The Hebrew Bible, the Old Testament, and Historical Criticism*.

Levine, Amy-Jill, and Marc Zvi Brettler. *The Bible with and without Jesus: How Jews and Christians Read the Same Stories Differently*. New York: HarperOne, 2020.

Levinson, Bernard. *Deuteronomy and the Hermeneutics of Legal Innovation*. New York: Oxford University Press, 1997.

Lewis, C. S. *The Great Divorce: A Dream*. New York: Macmillian, 1946.

———. *Perelandra: A Novel*. New York: Scribner, 1944.

Lieber, Laura S. "The Rhetoric of Participation: Experiential Elements of Early Hebrew Liturgical Poetry." *JR* 90 (2010): 119–47.

Lienhard, Joseph T., ed. *Exodus, Leviticus, Numbers, Deuteronomy*. ACCS 3. Downers Grove, IL: InterVarsity, 2001.

Lim, Bo H., and Daniel Castelo. *Hosea*. Two Horizons Commentary. Grand Rapids: Eerdmans, 2015.

Lind, Millard. *Yahweh Is a Warrior: The Theology of Warfare in Ancient Israel*. Scottsdale, PA: Herald, 1980.

Liverani, Mario. *Assyria: The Imperial Mission*. Translated by Andrea Trameri and Jonathan Valk. MC 21. Winona Lake, IN: Eisenbrauns, 2017.

Lodahl, Michael E. *Shekhinah/Spirit: Divine Presence in Jewish and Christian Religion*. Studies in Judaism and Christianity. New York: Paulist, 1992.

Loewenstamm, Samuel. *Comparative Studies in Biblical and Ancient Oriental Literatures*. AOAT 204. Neukirchen-Vluyn: Neukirchener, 1980.

Lohfink, Norbert. *Das Hauptgebot: Eine Untersuchung literarischer Einleitungsfragen zu Dtn 5–11*. AnBib 20. Rome: Pontifical Biblical Institute, 1963.

———. *Die Väter Israels im Deuteronomium*. OBO 111. Göttingen: Vandenhoeck & Ruprecht, 1991.

———. "Reading Deuteronomy 5 as Narrative." Pages 261–81 in Strawn and Bowen, *A God So Near*.

Long, Burke O. *2 Kings*. FOTL 10. Grand Rapids: Eerdmans, 1991.

Long, Thomas G. *Preaching and the Literary Forms of the Bible*. Philadelphia: Fortress, 1989.

———. *The Witness of Preaching*. 2nd ed. Louisville: Westminster John Knox, 2005.

Long, V. Philips. *The Art of Biblical History*. FCI 5. Grand Rapids: Zondervan, 1994.

Longenbach, James. *The Resistance to Poetry*. Chicago: University of Chicago Press, 2004.

Loretz, Oswald, and Ingo Kottsieper. *Colometry in Ugaritic and Biblical Poetry: Introduction, Illustrations and Topical Bibliography*. UBL 5. Altenberge: CIS-Verlag, 1987.

Lovering, E. H., Jr., and J. L. Sumney, eds. *Theology and Ethics in Paul and His Interpreters: Essays in Honor of Victor Paul Furnish*. Nashville: Abingdon, 1996.

Lundbom, Jack R. *Biblical Rhetoric and Rhetorical Criticism*. HBM 45. Sheffield: Sheffield Phoenix, 2013.

———. *Deuteronomy: A Commentary*. Grand Rapids: Eerdmans, 2013.

————. *Jeremiah: A Study in Ancient Hebrew Rhetoric.* 2nd ed. Winona Lake, IN: Eisenbrauns, 1997.

MacDonald, Margaret Y. "A Place of Belonging: Perspectives on Children from Colossians and Ephesians." Pages 278–304 in Bunge, Fretheim, and Gaventa, *The Child in the Bible.*

Machinist, Peter. "Kingship and Divinity in Imperial Assyria." Pages 152–88 in Beckman and Lewis, *Text, Artifact, and Image.*

Mackey, James P. "The Preacher, the Theologian, and the Trinity." *ThTo* 54 (1997): 347–66.

MacLeish, Archibald J. B. *A Play in Verse.* Boston: Houghton Mifflin, 1986.

Magonet, Jonathan. "Psalm 137: Unlikely Liturgy or Partisan Poem? A Response to Sue Gillingham." Pages 83–88 in Gillingham, *Jewish and Christian Approaches to the Psalms.*

Magrassi, Mariano. *Praying the Bible: An Introduction to* Lectio Divina. Collegeville, MN: Liturgical Press, 1998.

Malherbe, Abraham J., and Everett Ferguson, eds. *Gregory of Nyssa: The Life of Moses.* CWS. New York: Paulist, 1978.

Marcus, David. *From Balaam to Jonah: Anti-prophetic Satire in the Hebrew Bible.* BJS 301. Atlanta: Scholars, 1995.

Marno, David. "Tone." Pages 1141–42 in *The Princeton Encyclopedia of Poetry and Poetics.* 4th ed. Edited by Roland Greene et al. Princeton: Princeton University Press, 2012.

Martin, R. P. "Käsemann, Ernst (1906–1998)." Page 602 in *Dictionary of Major Biblical Interpreters.* Edited by Donald K. McKim. Downers Grove, IL: IVP Academic, 2007.

Martyn, J. Louis. "Epistemology at the Turn of the Ages: 2 Corinthians 5:16." Pages 269–87 in *Christian History and Interpretation: Studies Presented to John Knox.* Edited by W. R. Farmer, C. F. D. Moule, and R. R. Niebuhr. Cambridge: Cambridge University Press, 1967.

Mathews, Danny. *Royal Motifs in the Pentateuchal Portrayal of Moses.* LHBOTS 571. New York: T&T Clark, 2012.

Mayes, A. D. H. *Deuteronomy.* NCB. Grand Rapids: Eerdmans, 1981.

McBride, S. Dean, Jr. "Deuteronomy." Pages 255–309 in *The HarperCollins Study Bible.* Rev. ed. Edited by Harold W. Attridge et al. San Francisco: HarperSanFrancisco, 2006.

————. "The Yoke of the Kingdom: An Exposition of Deuteronomy 6:4–5." *Int* 27 (1973): 273–306.

McCarthy, Carmel. *Biblia Hebraica Quinta: Deuteronomy.* Stuttgart: Deutsche Bibelgesellschaft, 2007.

McCarthy, Dennis J. "Notes on the Love of God in Deuteronomy and the Father-Son Relationship Between Yahweh and Israel." *CBQ* 27 (1965): 144–47.

McColman, Carl. *The Big Book of Christian Mysticism: The Essential Guide to Contemplative Spirituality*. Charlottesville, VA: Hampton Roads, 2010.

McConnell, Frank. "Foreword." Pages ix–xviii in Kawin, *Telling It Again and Again*.

McConville, J. Gordon. *Being Human in God's World: An Old Testament Theology of Humanity*. Grand Rapids: Baker Academic, 2016.

———. "Time, Place and the Deuteronomic Altar-Law." Pages 89–139 in McConville and Millar, *Time and Place in Deuteronomy*.

McConville J. G., and J. G. Millar, *Time and Place in Deuteronomy*. JSOTSup 179. Sheffield: Sheffield Academic, 1994.

McCormack, Bruce L. "Participation with God, Yes; Deification, No: Two Modern Protestant Responses to an Ancient Question." Pages 235–60 in *Orthodox and Modern: Studies in the Theology of Karl Barth*. Grand Rapids: Baker Academic, 2008.

McDowell, Catherine L. *The Image of God in the Garden of Eden: The Creation of Humankind in Genesis 2:5–3:24 in Light of the* mīs pî pīt pî *and* wpt-r *Rituals of Mesopotamia and Ancient Egypt*. Siphrut 15. Winona Lake, IN: Eisenbrauns, 2015.

McFarland, Ian A. *The Divine Image: Envisioning the Invisible God*. Minneapolis: Fortress, 2005.

———. "The Ecstatic God: The Holy Spirit and the Constitution of the Trinity." *ThTo* 54 (1997): 335–46.

McGinnis, Claire R. Mathews. "Exodus as a 'Text of Terror' for Children." Pages 24–44 in Bunge, Fretheim, and Gaventa, *The Child in the Bible*.

McNeile, Alan Hugh. *The Book of Exodus*. Westminster Commentaries. London: Methuen, 1908.

———. *The Gospel According to St. Matthew: The Greek Text with Introduction, Notes, and Indices*. London: Macmillan, 1915.

Mead, James K. "'Elisha Will Kill'? The Deuteronomistic Rhetoric of Life and Death in the Theology of the Elisha Narratives." PhD diss., Princeton Theological Seminary, 1999.

Meadowcroft, Tim. "Daniel's Visionary Participation in the Divine Life: Dynamics of Participation in Daniel 8–12." *JTI* 11 (2017): 217–37.

———. "'One Like a Son of Man' in the Court of the Foreign King: Daniel 7 as Pointer to Wise Participation in the Divine Life." *JTI* 10 (2016): 245–63.

Meier, John P. *A Marginal Jew: Rethinking the Historical Jesus*. ABRL. 3 vols. New York: Doubleday, 1991–2001.

Melnyk, Janet L. R. "When Israel Was a Child: Ancient Near Eastern Adoption Formulas and the Relationship between God and Israel." Pages 245–59 in *History and Interpretation: Essays in Honour of John H. Hayes*. Edited by M. Patrick Graham, William P. Brown, and Jeffrey K. Kuan. JSOTSup 173. Sheffield: Sheffield Academic, 1993.

Meyers, Carol. *Exodus*. NCBC. New York: Cambridge University Press, 2005.

———. "The Family in Early Israel." Pages 1–47 in Perdue et al., *Families in Ancient Israel*.

Michener, James A. *The Source: A Novel*. New York: Random House, 1965.

Middleton, Richard. *The Liberating Image: The Imago Dei in Genesis 1*. Grand Rapids: Brazos, 2005.

Miles, Carol A. "Proclaiming the Gospel of God: The Promise of a Literary-Theological Hermeneutical Approach to Christian Preaching of the Old Testament." PhD diss., Princeton Theological Seminary, 2000.

———. "'Singing the Songs of Zion' and Other Sermons from the Margins of the Canon." *Koinonia* 6 (1994): 151–73.

Miles, Jack. *God: A Biography*. New York: Alfred A. Knopf, 1995.

Milgrom, Jacob. *Leviticus*. AB 3–3B. 3 vols. New York: Doubleday, 1991–2001.

Millar, J. G. "Living at the Place of Decision: Time and Place in the Framework of Deuteronomy." Pages 15–88 in McConville and Millar, *Time and Place in Deuteronomy*.

Millard, A. R. "The Canaanites." Pages 29–52 in *Peoples of Old Testament Times*. Edited by D. J. Wiseman. Oxford: Clarendon, 1973.

Miller, Alice. *The Body Never Lies: The Lingering Effects of Cruel Parenting*. Translated by Andrew Jenkins. New York: Norton, 2005.

———. *For Your Own Good: Hidden Cruelty in Child-Rearing and the Roots of Violence*. Translated by Hildegarde and Hunter Hannum. New York: Farrar, Straux, Giroux, 1990.

———. *Prisoners of Childhood*. Translated by Ruth Ward. New York: Basic, 1981.

———. *Thou Shalt Not Be Aware: Society's Betrayal of the Child*. Translated by Hildegarde Hannum and Hunter Hannum. New York: Farrar, Straus and Giroux, 1998.

Miller, Geoffrey Parsons. "Property." Pages 175–82 in vol. 2 of *The Oxford Encyclopedia of the Bible and Law*. Edited by Brent A. Strawn et al. New York: Oxford University Press, 2015.

Miller, J. Hillis. *Fiction and Repetition: Seven English Novels*. Cambridge: Harvard University Press, 1982.

Miller, John W. *Calling God "Father": Essays on the Bible, Fatherhood and Culture*. 2nd ed. New York: Paulist, 1999.

———. "God as Father in the Bible and the Father Image in Several Contemporary Ancient Near Eastern Myths: A Comparison." *SR* 14 (1985): 347–54.

Miller, Patrick D. *Deuteronomy*. Interpretation. Louisville: John Knox, 1990.

———. *Genesis 1–11: Studies in Structure and Theme*. JSOTSup 8. Sheffield: University of Sheffield, 1978.

———. "God's Other Stories: On the Margins of Deuteronomic Theology." Pages 592–602 in *Israelite Religion and Biblical Theology: Collected Essays*. JSOTSup 267. Sheffield: Sheffield Academic, 2000.

———. "The Hermeneutics of Imprecation." Pages 193–202 in *The Way of the Lord: Essays in Old Testament Theology*. FAT 39. Tübingen: Mohr Siebeck, 2004.

———. *The Lord of the Psalms*. Louisville: Westminster John Knox, 2013.

———. "'Moses My Servant': The Deuteronomic Portrait of Moses." Pages 301–12 in Christensen, *A Song of Power and the Power of Song*.

———. "The Most Important Word: The Yoke of the Kingdom." *IliffRev* 41 (1984): 17–29.

———. *The Religion of Ancient Israel*. LAI. Louisville: Westminster John Knox, 2000.

———. *Sin and Judgment in the Prophets: A Stylistic and Theological Analysis*. SBLMS 27. Chico, CA: Scholars, 1982.

———. "A Strange Kind of Monotheism." *ThTo* 54 (1997): 293–98.

———. "That the Children May Know: Children in Deuteronomy." Pages 45–62 in Bunge, Fretheim, and Gaventa, *The Child in the Bible*.

———. *They Cried to the Lord: The Form and Theology of Biblical Prayer*. Minneapolis: Fortress, 1995.

Mitchell, Stephen A., and Margaret J. Black. *Freud and Beyond: A History of Modern Psychoanalytic Thought*. New York: Basic, 1995.

Moberly, R. W. L. *The Bible in a Disenchanted Age: The Enduring Possibility of Christian Faith*. Grand Rapids: Baker Academic, 2018.

———. *The Bible, Theology, and Faith: A Study of Abraham and Jesus*. Cambridge Studies in Christian Doctrine. Cambridge: Cambridge University Press, 2000.

———. *Old Testament Theology: Reading the Hebrew Bible as Christian Scripture*. Grand Rapids: Baker Academic, 2013.

———. *The Theology of the Book of Genesis*. OTT. Cambridge: Cambridge University Press, 2009.

Mohr, Melissa. *Holy Sh*t: A Brief History of Swearing*. New York: Oxford University Press, 2013.

Mol, Jurrien. *Collective and Individual Responsibility: A Description of Corporate Personality in Ezekiel 18 and 20*. SSN 53. Leiden: Brill, 2009.

Moltmann, Jürgen. *The Source of Life: The Holy Spirit and the Theology of Life*. Minneapolis: Fortress, 1997.

———. *The Spirit of Life: A Universal Affirmation*. Minneapolis: Fortress, 1992.

———. *The Trinity and the Kingdom*. San Francisco: Harper & Row, 1981.

Montgomery, James A. *A Critical and Exegetical Commentary on the Books of Kings*. Edited by Henry Snyder Gehman. ICC. Edinburgh: T&T Clark, 1951.

Moran, William L. "The Ancient Near Eastern Background of the Love of God in Deuteronomy." *CBQ* 25 (1963): 77–87. Reprinted on pages 103–15 in *Essential Papers on Israel and the Ancient Near East*. Edited by Frederick E. Greenspahn. New York: New York University Press, 1991. And reprinted on pages 182–200 in *The Most Magic Word: Essays on Babylonian and Biblical Literature*. Edited by Ronald S. Hendel. CBQMS 35. Washington, DC: Catholic Biblical Association, 2002.

———. "The Babylonian Job." Pages 182–200 in *The Most Magic Word: Essays on Babylonian and Biblical Literature*. Edited by Ronald S. Hendel. CBQMS 35. Washington, DC: Catholic Biblical Association, 2002.

Morenz, Siegfried. *Egyptian Religion*. Translated by Ann E. Keep. Ithaca, NY: Cornell University Press, 1996.

Morgan, Robert. *The Nature of New Testament Theology*. SBT 25. London: SCM, 1973.

Morse, Christopher. *Not Every Spirit: A Dogmatics of Christian Disbelief*. 2nd ed. New York: Continuum, 2009.

Mosser, Carl. "The Earliest Patristic Interpretations of Psalm 82, Jewish Antecedents, and the Origin of Christian Deification." *JTS* 56 (2005): 30–74.

Mowbray, Thomas L. "The Function in Ministry of Psalms Dealing with Anger: The Angry Psalmist." *Journal of Pastoral Counseling* 21 (1986): 34–39.

Muffs, Yochanan. *The Personhood of God: Biblical Theology, Human Faith and the Divine Image*. Woodstock, VT: Jewish Lights, 2005.

Muilenburg, James. "The Form and Structure of the Covenantal Formulations." *VT* 9 (1959): 347–65.

———. "A Study in Hebrew Rhetoric: Repetition and Style." Pages 97–111 in *Congress Volume: Copenhagen, 1953*. Edited by George W. Anderson. VTSup 1. Leiden: Brill, 1953.

Mullen, E. Theodore, Jr. *Narrative History and Ethnic Boundaries: The Deuteronomistic Historian and the Creation of Israelite National Identity*. SemeiaST. Atlanta: Scholars, 1993.

Musurillo, Herbert, ed. *Gregorii Nysseni: De Vita Moysis*. Gregorii Nysseni Opera 7.1. Edited by Werner Jaeger and Hermann Langerbeck. Leiden: Brill, 1964.

Neale, J. M., and R. F. Littledale. *A Commentary on the Psalms from Primitive and Mediaeval Writers*. 4 vols. 2nd ed. London: Joseph Masters, 1883.

Nehrbass, Daniel Michael. *Praying Curses: The Therapeutic and Preaching Value of the Imprecatory Psalms*. Eugene, OR: Pickwick, 2013.

Nelson, Richard D. *First and Second Kings*. Interpretation. Louisville: Westminster John Knox, 1987.

Newsom, Carol A. "Woman and the Discourse of Patriarchal Wisdom: A Study of Proverbs 1–9." Pages 142–60 in *Gender and Difference in Ancient Israel*. Edited by Peggy L. Day. Minneapolis: Fortress, 1989.

Niditch, Susan. *"My Brother Esau Is a Hairy Man": Hair and Identity in Ancient Israel.* Oxford: Oxford University Press, 2008.

———. *Oral World and Written Word: Ancient Israelite Literature.* LAI. Louisville: Westminster John Knox, 1996.

Niskanen, Paul. "The Poetics of Adam: The Creation of אדם in the Image of אלהים." *JBL* 128 (2009): 417–36.

———. "Yhwh as Father, Redeemer, and Potter in Isaiah 63:7–64:11." *CBQ* 68 (2006): 397–407.

Noel, Ruth S. *The Languages of Tolkien's Middle-earth.* Boston: Houghton Mifflin, 1980.

Norin, Stig. *Personennamen und Religion im alten Israel untersucht mit besonderer Berücksichtigung der Namen auf El und Ba'al.* ConBOT 60. Winona Lake, IN: Eisenbrauns, 2013.

Norrick, Neal R. "Functions of Repetition in Conversation." *Text* 7 (1987): 245–64.

Noth, Martin. *The Deuteronomistic History.* 2nd ed. JSOTSup 15. Sheffield: JSOT Press, 1991.

Nussbaum, Martha C. *Poetic Justice: The Literary Imagination and Public Life.* Boston: Beacon, 1995.

O'Collins, Gerald. "The Holy Trinity: The State of the Question." Pages 1–27 in Davis, Kendall, and O'Collins, *The Trinity: An Interdisciplinary Symposium on the Trinity.*

O'Connor, David B., and David P. Silverman, eds. *Ancient Egyptian Kingship.* PdÄ 9. Leiden: Brill, 1995.

Oldenburg, Ulf. *The Conflict between El and Ba'al in Canaanite Religion.* Leiden: Brill, 1969.

Ollenburger, Ben C, ed. *Old Testament Theology: Flowering and Future.* SBTS 1. Winona Lake, IN: Eisenbrauns, 2004.

Olson, Dennis T. *The Death of the Old and the Birth of the New: The Framework of the Book of Numbers and the Pentateuch.* BJS 71. Chico, CA: Scholars Press, 1985.

———. *Deuteronomy and the Death of Moses: A Theological Reading.* OBT. Minneapolis: Fortress, 1994.

———. "How Does Deuteronomy Do Theology? Literary Juxtaposition and Paradox in the New Moab Covenant in Deuteronomy 29–32." Pages 201–13 in Strawn and Bowen, *A God So Near.*

———. "Violence for the Sake of Social Justice? Narrative, Ethics and Indeterminacy in Moses' Slaying of the Egyptian (Exodus 2:11–15)." Pages 138–48 in *The Meanings We Choose: Hermeneutical Ethics, Indeterminacy and the Conflict of Interpretations.* Edited by Charles H. Cosgrove. JSOTSup 511. London: T&T Clark, 2004.

Olyan, Saul M. "The Biblical Prohibition of the Mourning Rites of Shaving and Laceration: Several Proposals." Pages 181–89 in *"A Wise and Discerning Mind": Essays in Honor of Burke O. Long.* Edited by Saul M. Olyan and Robert C. Culley. BJS 325. Providence, RI: Brown Judaic Studies, 2000.

Ong, Walter J. *Orality and Literacy: The Technologizing of the Word.* London: Routledge, 1982.

Oppenheim, A. Leo. "Akkadian *pul(u)ḫ(t)u* and *melammu.*" *JAOS* 63 (1943): 31–34.

———. *Ancient Mesopotamia: Portrait of a Dead Civilization.* Rev. ed. Chicago: University of Chicago Press, 1977.

Orwell, George. *Nineteen Eighty-Four: A Novel.* New York: Harcourt, Brace and World, 1949.

Osborn, E. F. "Käsemann, Ernst." *DBI* 2:15.

Overbeck, Franz. *Über dei Anfänge der patristischen Literatur.* Darmstadt: Wissenschaftliche Buchgesellschaft, 1954.

Paddison, Angus. "Scripture, Participation and Universities." Pages 122–44 in *Scripture: A Very Theological Proposal.* London: T&T Clark, 2009.

Pals, Daniel L. *Eight Theories of Religion.* 2nd ed. New York: Oxford University Press, 2015.

Pannenberg, Wolfhart. "Problems in a Theology of (Only) the Old Testament." Pages 275–80 in *Problems in Biblical Theology: Essays in Honor of Rolf Knierim.* Edited by Henry T. C. Sun and Keith L. Eades. Grand Rapids: Eerdmans, 1997.

Pardee, Dennis. *Ugaritic and Hebrew Poetic Parallelism: A Trial Cut ('nt I and Proverbs 2).* VTSup39. Leiden: Brill, 1988.

Parker, Simon B. "Aqhat." Pages 49–80 in *Ugaritic Narrative Poetry.* Edited by Simon B. Parker. WAW 9. Atlanta: Scholars Press, 1997.

Parpola, Simo, and Kazuko Watanabe. *Neo-Assyrian Treaties and Loyalty Oaths.* SAA 2. Repr. ed. Winona Lake, IN: Eisenbrauns, 2014.

Patrick, Dale. *The Rhetoric of Revelation in the Hebrew Bible.* OBT. Minneapolis: Fortress, 1999.

Patrides, C. A. "The Salvation of Satan." *Journal of the History of Ideas* 28 (1967): 467–78.

Patton, Kimberley C. *The Religion of the Gods: Ritual, Paradox, and Reflexivity.* Oxford: Oxford University Press, 2009.

Paulsell, Stephanie. "Spiritual Formation and Intellectual Work in Theological Education." *ThTo* 55 (1998): 229–34.

Pennebaker, James W. *Opening Up: The Healing Power of Confiding in Others.* New York: William Morrow, 1990.

Perdue, Leo G. "The Household, Old Testament Theology, and Contemporary Hermeneutics." Pages 223–58 in Perdue et al., *Families in Ancient Israel.*

———. "The Israelite and Early Jewish Family: Summary and Conclusions." Pages 163–222 in Perdue et al., *Families in Ancient Israel.*

————. *The Sword and the Stylus: An Introduction to Wisdom in the Age of Empires.* Grand Rapids: Eerdmans, 2008.

Perdue, Leo G., Joseph Blenkinsopp, John J. Collins, and Carol Meyers. *Families in Ancient Israel.* The Family Religion and Culture. Louisville: Westminster John Knox, 1997.

Perelman, Chaïm, and L. Olbrechts-Tyteca. *The New Rhetoric: A Treatise on Argumentation.* Translated by John Wilkinson and Purcell Weaver. Notre Dame: University of Notre Dame Press, 1969.

Perrin, Norman. *Rediscovering the Teaching of Jesus.* New York: Harper, 1976.

Petersen, Ryan S. *The Imago Dei as Human Identity: A Theological Interpretation.* JTISup 14. Winona Lake, IN: Eisenbrauns, 2016.

Peterson, Eugene H. *Eat This Book: A Conversation in the Art of Spiritual Reading.* Grand Rapids: Eerdmans, 2006.

————. "Spiritual Reading (*Lectio Divina*)." Pages 768–69 in *Dictionary of Christian Spirituality.* Edited by Glen G. Scorgie et al. Grand Rapids: Zondervan, 2011.

Philo. *The Works of Philo: Complete and Unabridged, New Updated Edition.* Translated by C. D. Yonge. Repr. ed. Peabody, MA: Hendrickson, 1993.

Pixley, George V. *On Exodus: A Liberation Perspective.* Translated by R. R. Barr. Maryknoll, NY: Orbis, 1987.

Polzin, Robert. "Deuteronomy." Pages 92–101 in *The Literary Guide to the Bible.* Edited by Robert Alter and Frank Kermode. Cambridge: Belknap, 1987.

————. *Moses and the Deuteronomist: Deuteronomy, Joshua, Judges.* ISBL. Bloomington: Indiana University Press, 1993.

Porter, James E., and Patricia A. Sullivan. "Repetition and the Rhetoric of Visual Design." Pages 1:114–29 in Johnstone, *Repetition in Discourse.*

Powell, Samuel M. *Participating in God: Creation and Trinity.* Theology and the Sciences. Minneapolis: Fortress, 2003.

Prestige, G. L. *God in Patristic Thought.* London: SPCK, 1956.

————. "ΠΕΡΙΧΩΡΕΩ [*perichōreō*] and ΠΕΡΙΧΩΡΗΣΙΣ [*perichōrēsis*] in the Fathers." *JTS* 29 (1928): 242–52.

Propp, William H. C. "Did Moses Have Horns?" *BR* 4 (1988): 30–37, 44.

————. *Exodus 1–18: A New Translation with Introduction and Commentary.* AB 2. New York: Doubleday, 1999.

————. *Exodus 19–40: A New Translation with Introduction and Commentary.* AB 2A. New York: Doubleday, 2006.

————. "The Skin of Moses' Face—Transfigured or Disfigured?" *CBQ* 49 (1987): 375–86.

Puig I Tàrrech, Armand, ed. *Image de Déu.* Scripta Biblica 7. Catalonia: Associació Bíblica de Catalunya, 2006.

Racker, Heinrich. *Transference and Counter-Transference*. New York: International Universities Press, 1968.

Rad, Gerhard von. *Biblical Interpretations in Preaching*. Translated by John E. Steely. Nashville: Abingdon, 1977.

———. *Deuteronomy: A Commentary*. Translated by Dorothea Barton. OTL. Philadelphia: Westminster, 1966.

———. *Genesis: A Commentary*. Translated by John H. Marks. OTL. Philadelphia: Westminster, 1982.

———. "How to Read the Old Testament." Pages 9–18 in *God at Work in Israel*. Translated by John H. Marks. Nashville: Abingdon, 1980.

———. *Old Testament Theology*. Translated by D. M. G. Stalker. 2 vols. San Francisco: Harper & Row, 1962.

———. *Studies in Deuteronomy*. Translated by David Stalker. SBT. London: SCM, 1953.

———. *The Theology of Israel's Prophetic Traditions*. Vol. 2 of *Old Testament Theology*. Translated by D. M. G. Stalker. San Francisco: Harper & Row, 1965.

Radner, Ephraim. "The Absence of the Comforter: Scripture and the Divided Church." Pages 355–94 in Seitz and Greene-McCreight, *Theological Exegesis*.

———. *Time and the Word: Figural Reading of the Christian Scriptures*. Grand Rapids: Eerdmans, 2016.

Rae, Murray A. *History and Hermeneutics*. London: T&T Clark, 2005.

———. "Texts in Context: Scripture and the Divine Economy." *JTI* 1 (2007): 1–21.

Räisänen, Heikki. *Beyond New Testament Theology: A Story and a Programme*. Philadelphia: Trinity Press International, 1990.

Raitt, Thomas M. *A Theology of Exile: Judgment/Deliverance in Jeremiah and Ezekiel*. Philadelphia: Fortress, 1977.

Rearick, Anderson, III. "Why Is the Only Good Orc a Dead Orc? The Dark Face of Racism Examined in Tolkien's World." *Modern Fiction Studies* 50 (2004): 861–74.

Regt, L. J. de. *A Parametric Model for Syntactic Studies of a Textual Corpus, Demonstrated on the Hebrew of Deuteronomy 1–30*. SSN 24. Assen: Van Gorcum, 1988.

Rendsburg, Gary A. "Moses as Equal to Pharaoh." Pages 201–19 in Beckman and Lewis, *Text, Artifact, and Image*.

Rendsburg, Gary A., and Susan Rendsburg. "Physiological and Philological Notes to Psalm 137." *JQR* 83 (1993): 385–99.

Reventlow, Henning Graf. *Problems of Old Testament Theology in the Twentieth Century*. Philadelphia: Fortress, 1985.

Riches, John K. *A Century of New Testament Study*. Valley Forge, PA: Trinity Press International, 1993.

Ricoeur, Paul. *The Rule of Metaphor: Multi-Disciplinary Studies of the Creation of Mean-*

ing in Language. Translated by Robert Czerny, Kathleen McLaughlin, and John Costello. Toronto: University of Toronto Press, 1977.

Riemann, Paul A. "Am I My Brother's Keeper?" *Int* 24 (1970): 482–91.

Ringgren, Helmer. *Israelite Religion*. Translated by David E. Green. Philadelphia: Fortress, 1966.

Risse, Siegfried. "'Wohl dem, der deine kleinen Kinder packt und sie am Felsen zerschmettert: zur Augslegungsgeschichte von Ps 137,9." *BibInt* 14 (2006): 364–84.

Robertson, Amy H. C. "'He Kept the Measurements in His Memory as a Treasure': The Role of the Tabernacle Text in Religious Experience." PhD diss., Emory University, 2010.

Robinson, H. Wheeler. *Corporate Personality in Ancient Israel*. Philadelphia: Fortress, 1964.

Rendtorff, Rolf. *Canon and Theology: Overtures to an Old Testament Theology*. OBT. Minneapolis: Fortress, 1993.

———. *The Old Testament: An Introduction*. Translated by John Bowden. Philadelphia: Fortress, 1986.

Roberts, J. J. M. *The Bible and the Ancient Near East: Collected Essays*. Winona Lake, IN: Eisenbrauns, 2002.

———. "Divine Freedom and Cultic Manipulation in Israel and Mesopotamia." Pages 72–82 in Roberts, *The Bible and the Ancient Near East*.

———. "Job and the Israelite Religious Tradition." *ZAW* 89 (1977): 107–14. Reprinted on pages 110–16 in Roberts, *The Bible and the Ancient Near East*.

———. "The Old Testament's Contribution to Messianic Expectations." Pages 39–51 in *The Messiah: Developments in Earliest Judaism and Christianity*. Edited by James H. Charlesworth et al. Minneapolis: Fortress, 1992.

Rodd, Cyril S. *Glimpses of a Strange Land: Studies in Old Testament Ethics*. Edinburgh: T&T Clark, 2001.

Rogers, Steven A. "The Parent-Child Relationship as an Archetype for the Relationship Between God and Humanity in Genesis." *Pastoral Psychology* 50 (202): 377–85.

Rogerson, John W. *A Theology of the Old Testament: Cultural Memory, Communication, and Being Human*. Minneapolis: Fortress, 2010.

Römer, Thomas. *Israels Väter: Untersuchungen zur Väterthematik im Deuteronomium und in der deuteronomistischen Tradition*. OBO 99. Göttingen: Vandenhoeck & Ruprecht, 1990.

Rorem, Paul. "Empathy and Evaluation in Medieval Church History and Pastoral Ministry: A Lutheran Reading of Pseudo-Dionysius." *PSB* 19 (1998): 99–115.

Ross, Raymond S. *Understanding Persuasion*. 3rd ed. Englewood Cliffs, NJ: Prentice Hall, 1990.

Routledge, Carolyn. "Parallelism in Popular and Official Religion in Ancient Egypt." Pages 223–38 in Beckman and Lewis, *Text, Artifact, and Image.*

Rusch, William G. *The Trinitarian Controversy.* Sources of Early Christian Thought. Philadelphia: Fortress, 1980.

Russell, Norman. *The Doctrine of Deification in the Greek Patristic Tradition.* Oxford: Oxford University Press, 2004.

Rutledge, Fleming. *The Battle for Middle-earth: Tolkien's Divine Design in the Lord of the Rings.* Grand Rapids: Eerdmans, 2004.

Sadler, Rodney S., Jr. "Singing a Subversive Song: Psalm 137 and 'Colored Pompey.'" Pages 447–58 in *The Oxford Handbook of the Psalms.* Edited by William P. Brown. Oxford: Oxford University Press, 2014.

Salo, David. *A Gateway to Sindarin: A Grammar of an Elvish Language from J. R. R. Tolkien's Lord of the Rings.* Salt Lake City: University of Utah Press, 2004.

Sampley, J. Paul. "Reasoning from the Horizons of Paul's Thought World: A Comparison of Galatians and Philippians." Pages 114–31 in Lovering and Sumney, *Theology and Ethics in Paul and His Interpreters.*

Sarna, Nahum M. *Exodus* שמות: *The Traditional Hebrew Text with the New JPS Translation.* Philadelphia: Jewish Publication Society, 1991.

———. *Exploring Exodus: The Origins of Biblical Israel.* New York: Schocken, 1996.

———. *Genesis.* JPS Torah Commentary. Philadelphia: Jewish Publication Society, 1989.

Scalise, Pamela J. "'I Have Produced a Man with the LORD': God as Provider of Offspring in Old Testament Theology." *RevExp* 91 (1994): 577–89.

Scarry, Elaine. *On Beauty and Being Just.* Princeton: Princeton University Press, 1999.

Schaeffer, Konrad. *Psalms.* Berit Olam. Collegeville, MN: Liturgical Press, 2001.

Schillebeeckx, Edward. *Jesus: An Experiment in Christology.* New York: Seabury, 1979.

Schlimm, Matthew Richard. *From Fratricide to Forgiveness: The Language and Ethics of Anger in Genesis.* Siphrut 7. Winona Lake, IN: Eisenbrauns, 2011.

Schloen, J. David. *The House of the Father as Fact and Symbol: Patrimonialism in Ugarit and the Ancient Near East.* Studies in the Archaeology and History of the Levant 2. Winona Lake, IN: Eisenbrauns, 2001.

Schlosser, Jacques. "Le débat de Käsemann et de Bultmann à propos du Jésus de l'histoire." *RSR* 87 (1999): 373–95.

Schmid, Konrad. *A Historical Theology of the Hebrew Bible.* Translated by Peter Altmann. Grand Rapids: Eerdmans, 2019.

Schmidt, Werner H. *The Faith of the Old Testament: A History.* Translated by John Sturdy. Philadelphia: Westminster, 1983.

Schnackenburg, Rudolf. *The Gospel According to St. John.* 3 vols. New York: Crossroad, 1982.

Schneider, Tammi J. *An Introduction to Ancient Mesopotamian Religion*. Grand Rapids: Eerdmans, 2011.

Schneiders, Sandra M. *The Revelatory Text: Interpreting the New Testament as Sacred Scripture*. 2nd ed. Collegeville, MN: Liturgical Press, 1999.

Schnelle, Udo. *Antidocetic Christology in the Gospel of John: An Investigation of the Place of the Fourth Gospel in the Johannine School*. Minneapolis: Fortress, 1992.

———. *The History and Theology of the New Testament Writings*. Minneapolis: Fortress, 1998.

Schniedewind, William M. "Orality and Literacy in Ancient Israel." *RelSRev* 26 (2000): 327–32.

Schüle, Andreas. *Theology from the Beginning: Essays on the Primeval History and Its Canonical Context*. FAT 113. Tübingen: Mohr Siebeck, 2017.

Schweizer, Eduard. *A Theological Introduction to the New Testament*. Nashville: Abingdon, 1991.

Scoralick, Ruth. *Gottes Güte und Gottes Zorn: Die Gottesprädikationen in Exodus 34,6f und ihre intertextuellen Beziehungen zum Zwölfprophetenbuch*. HBS 33. Freiburg: Herder, 2002.

Scroggs, Robin. "Ernst Käsemann: The Divine Agent *Provocateur*." *RelSRev* 1 (1985): 260–63.

Scull, Christina, and Wayne G. Hammond. *The J. R. R. Tolkien Companion and Guide: Reader's Guide*. Revised and expanded ed. 2 vols. London: HarperCollins, 2017.

Segal, Alan F. "'Two Powers in Heaven' and Early Christian Trinitarian Thinking." Pages 73–98 in Davis, Kendall, and O'Collins, *The Trinity: An Interdisciplinary Symposium on the Trinity*.

Seitz, Christopher. "Christological Interpretations of Texts and Trinitarian Claims to Truth." *SJT* 52 (1999): 209–26.

———. *Figured Out: Typology and Providence in Christian Scripture*. Louisville: Westminster John Knox, 2001.

Seitz, Christopher, and Kathryn Greene-McCreight, eds. *Theological Exegesis: Essays in Honor of Brevard S. Childs*. Grand Rapids: Eerdmans, 1999.

Sellin, Ernst, and Georg Fohrer. *Introduction to the Old Testament*. Translated by David E. Green. Nashville: Abingdon, 1968.

Selms, A. van. *Marriage and Family Life in Ugaritic Literature*. London: Luzac, 1954.

Seow, C. L. *Ecclesiastes: A New Translation with Introduction and Commentary*. AB 18C. New York: Doubleday, 1997.

———. "The First and Second Books of Kings: Introduction, Commentary, and Reflections." Pages 1–295 in *NIB*. Edited by Leander E. Keck et al. Nashville: Abingdon, 1999.

———. *Job 1–21: Interpretation and Commentary*. Illuminations. Grand Rapids: Eerdmans, 2013.

Sexton, Jason S. "The Imago Dei Once Again: Stanley Grenz's Journey toward a Theological Interpretation of Genesis 1:26–27." *JTI* 4 (2010): 187–206.

Shalomi-Hen, Racheli. *The Writing of Gods: The Evolution of Divine Classifiers in the Old Kingdom*. Göttinger Orientforschungen IV/Reihe Ägypten 38. Wiesbaden: Harrassowitz, 2006.

Shapiro, David. "Gold and Cardboard." *Poetry* 196/5 (2010): 423.

Sharp, Carolyn J. *Joshua*. SHBC. Macon, GA: Smyth & Helwys, 2019.

Shippey, Tom. *The Road to Middle-earth*. 2nd ed. London: Grafton, 1992.

Shuler, P. L. *A Genre for the Gospels*. Philadelphia: Fortress, 1982.

Simpson, JoEllen M. "Regularized Intonation in Conversational Repetition." Pages 2:41–49 in Johnstone, *Repetition in Discourse*.

Ska, Jean-Louis. *A Basic Guide to the Old Testament*. New York: Paulist, 2019.

Smith, Christian, with Melinda Lundquist Denton. *Soul Searching: The Religious and Spiritual Lives of American Teenagers*. Oxford: Oxford University Press, 2005.

Smith, Jonathan Z. *On Teaching Religion: Essays by Jonathan Z. Smith*. Edited by Christopher I. Lehrich. Oxford: Oxford University Press, 2013.

———. "Religion, Religions, Religious." Pages 269–84 in *Critical Terms for Religious Studies*. Edited by Mark C. Taylor. Chicago: University of Chicago Press, 1998.

Smith, Mark S. *The Genesis of Good and Evil: The Fall(out) and Original Sin in the Bible*. Louisville: Westminster John Knox, 2019.

———. *The Origins of Biblical Monotheism: Israel's Polytheistic Background and the Ugaritic Texts*. New York: Oxford University Press, 2001.

———. "Recent Study of Israelite Religion in Light of the Ugaritic Texts." Pages 1–25 in *Ugarit at Seventy-Five*. Edited by K. Lawson Younger. Winona Lake, IN: Eisenbrauns, 2007.

———. "'Seeing God' in the Psalms: The Background to the Beatific Vision in the Hebrew Bible." *CBQ* 50 (1988): 171–83.

Smith, Morton. *Palestinian Parties and Politics That Shaped the Old Testament*. 2nd ed. London: SCM, 1987.

Smith, W. Robertson. *The Religion of the Semites: The Fundamental Institutions*. New York: Schocken, 1972.

Snodgrass, Klyne. "The Gospel of Participation." Pages 413–30 in *Earliest Christianity within the Boundaries of Judaism: Essays in Honor of Bruce Chilton*. Edited by Alan J. Avery-Peck, Craig A. Evans, and Jacob Neusner. BRLJ 49. Leiden: Brill, 2016.

Sommer, Benjamin D. *The Bodies of God and the World of Ancient Israel*. Cambridge: Cambridge University Press, 2009.

Sonnet, Jean-Pierre. *The Book within the Book: Writing in Deuteronomy.* BIS 14. Leiden: Brill, 1997.

———. "Le Deutéronome et la modernité du livre." *NRTh* 118 (1996): 481–96.

Sonsino, Rifat. *Motive Clauses in Hebrew Law: Biblical Forms and Near Eastern Parallels.* SBLDS 45. Chico, CA: Scholars Press, 1980.

Soulen, R. Kendall. *The God of Israel and Christian Theology.* Minneapolis: Fortress, 1998.

Sparks, Kenton L. *Ancient Texts for the Study of the Hebrew Bible: A Guide to the Background Literature.* Peabody, MA: Hendrickson, 2005.

———. *Ethnicity and Identity in Ancient Israel: Prolegomena to the Study of Ethnic Sentiments and Their Expression in the Hebrew Bible.* Winona Lake, IN: Eisenbrauns, 1998.

Spurgeon, Charles H. *The Treasury of David: Spurgeon's Classic Work on the Psalms.* Grand Rapids: Kregel, 2004.

Stavrakopoulou, Francesca, and John Barton, eds. *Religious Diversity in Ancient Israel and Judah.* London: T&T Clark, 2010.

Stec, David M. *The Targum of Psalms: Translated with Critical Introduction, Apparatus, and Notes.* Aramaic Bible 16. Collegeville, MN: Liturgical Press, 2004.

Steiner, George. *Language and Silence: Essays on Language, Literature, and the Inhuman.* New Haven: Yale University Press, 1998.

Steinmetz, David C. "The Superiority of Pre-Critical Exegesis." Pages 26–38 in *The Theological Interpretation of Scripture: Classic and Contemporary Readings.* Edited by Stephen E. Fowl. Malden, MA: Blackwell, 1997.

Stendahl, Krister. *Paul among Jews and Gentiles.* Philadelphia: Fortress, 1976.

Sternberg, Meir. *The Poetics of Biblical Narrative: Ideological Literature and the Drama of Reading.* Bloomington: Indiana University Press, 1987.

Stone, Lawson G. "Ethical and Apologetic Tendencies in the Redaction of the Book of Joshua." *CBQ* 52 (1991): 25–36.

Stowe, David W. *Song of Exile: The Enduring Mystery of Psalm 137.* Oxford: Oxford University Press, 2016.

Strawn, Brad D., and Brent A. Strawn. "From Petition to Praise: An Intrapsychic Phenomenon?" Paper presented at the annual meeting of the Society of Biblical Literature. Denver, Colorado, 2001.

Strawn, Brent A. "Bonhoeffer on Enemies and Imprecation in the Psalms: A Biblical-Theological Commentary." *TJT* 37 (2021): 156–67.

———. "Canaan and Canaanites." Pages 1:104–111 in *The Oxford Encyclopedia of the Bible and Theology.* Edited by Samuel E. Balentine et al. 2 vols. Oxford: Oxford University Press, 2015.

———. "Comparative Approaches: History, Theory, and the Image of God." Pages

117–42 in *Method Matters: Essays on the Interpretation of the Hebrew Bible in Honor of David L. Petersen*. Edited by Joel M. LeMon and Kent Harold Richards. SBLRBS 56. Atlanta: Society of Biblical Literature, 2009.

———. "David as One of the 'Perfect of (the) Way': On the Provenience of *David's Compositions* (and *11QPs*^a as a Whole?)." *RevQ* 24/96 (2010): 607–26.

———. "Deuteronomy." Pages 63–76 in *Theological Bible Commentary*. Edited by Gail R. O'Day and David L. Petersen. Louisville: Westminster John Knox, 2009.

———. "Deuteronomy." Pages 226–29 in *The Wesley Study Bible: NRSV*. Nashville: Abingdon, 2009.

———. "Docetism, Käsemann, and Christology: Can Historical Criticism Help Christological Orthodoxy (and Other Theology) After All?" *JTI* 2 (2008): 161–80.

———. "Excerpted Manuscripts at Qumran: Their Significance for the Textual History of the Hebrew Bible and the Socio-Religious History of the Qumran Community and Its Literature." Pages 107–67 in *The Bible and the Dead Sea Scrolls*. Vol. 2 of *The Dead Sea Scrolls and the Qumran Community*. Edited by James H. Charlesworth. Waco, TX: Baylor University Press, 2006.

———. "Exodus." Pages 33–34 in *The New Interpreter's Bible One Volume Commentary*. Edited by Beverly Roberts Gaventa and David L. Petersen et al. Nashville: Abingdon, 2010.

———. "Focus on Jonah: Jonah and Genre." Oxford Biblical Studies Online. https://global.oup.com/obso/focus/focus_on_jonah/.

———. "Herodotus' *Histories* 2.141 and the Deliverance of Jerusalem: On Parallels, Sources, and Histories of Ancient Israel." Pages 210–38 in I*srael's Prophets and Israel's Past: Essays on the Relationship of Prophetic Texts and Israelite History in Honor of John H. Hayes*, ed. Brad E. Kelle and Megan B. Moore. LHBOTS 466. London and New York: T&T Clark, 2006.

———. "The History of Israelite Religion." Pages 86–107 in *The Cambridge Companion to the Old Testament/Hebrew Bible*. Edited by Stephen B. Chapman and Marvin A. Sweeney. Cambridge: Cambridge University Press, 2016.

———. *Honest to God Preaching: Talking Sin, Suffering, and Violence*. Working Preacher Books 7. Minneapolis: Fortress, 2021.

———. "The Iconography of Fear: *Yir'at Yhwh* (יראת יהוה) in Artistic Perspective." Pages 91–134 in *Image, Text, Exegesis: Iconographic Interpretation and the Hebrew Bible*. Edited by Izaak J. de Hulster and Joel M. LeMon. LHBOTS. Edinburgh: T&T Clark, 2014.

———. "The Image of God: Comparing the Old Testament with Other Ancient Near Eastern Cultures." Pages 63–75 in de Hulster, Strawn, and Bonfiglio, *Iconographic Exegesis of the Hebrew Bible/Old Testament*.

———. "Imagery." Page 312 in *Dictionary of the Old Testament: Wisdom, Poetry and*

Writings. Edited by Tremper Longman III and Peter Enns. Downers Grove, IL: IVP Academic, 2008.

——. "Imprecation." Pages 314–20 in *Dictionary of the Old Testament: Wisdom, Poetry and Writings*. Edited by Tremper Longman III and Peter Enns. Downers Grove, IL: IVP Academic, 2008.

——. "'Israel, My Child': The Ethics of a Biblical Metaphor." Pages 103–40 in Bunge, Fretheim, and Gaventa, *The Child in the Bible*.

——. "Jeremiah's In/Effective Plea: Another Look at נער in Jeremiah I 6." *VT* 55 (2005): 366–77.

——. "*kwšrwt* in Psalm 68:7, Again: A (Small) Test Case in Relating Ugarit to the Hebrew Bible." *UF* 41 (2009): 631–48.

——. "Lion Hunting in the Psalms: Iconography and Images for God, the Self, and the Enemy." Pages 245–62 in de Hulster, Strawn, and Bonfiglio, *Iconographic Exegesis of the Hebrew Bible/Old Testament*.

——. "Luke 1:26–38." Pages 286–90 in *The Lectionary Commentary: Theological Exegesis for Sunday's Texts, The Third Readings: The Gospels*. Edited by Roger E. Van Harn. Grand Rapids: Eerdmans, 2001.

——. "Lyric Poetry." Pages 437–46 in *Dictionary of the Old Testament: Wisdom, Poetry and Writings*. Edited by Tremper Longman III and Peter Enns. Downers Grove, IL: IVP Academic, 2008.

——. "'Mischmetaphors': (Re-)Presenting God in Unusual and Sophisticated Ways." Pages 19–54 in *Image as Theology: The Power of Art in Shaping Christian Thought, Devotion, and Imagination*. Edited by Mark McInroy, C. A. Strine, and Alexis Torrance. Arts and the Sacred 6. Turnhout: Brepols, 2021.

——. "Must Animals Die? Genesis 3:21, *Enūma Eliš* IV, and the Power of Divine Utterance." *VT* 72 (2022): 122–50.

——. *The Old Testament: A Concise Introduction*. London: Routledge, 2019.

——. *The Old Testament Is Dying: A Diagnosis and Recommended Treatment*. Theological Explorations for the Church Catholic. Grand Rapids: Baker Academic, 2017.

——. "On (Not) Bashing Babies." *JP* 43 (2020): 34–38.

——. "On Walter Brueggemann: (A Personal) Testimony, (Three) Dispute(s), (and On) Advocacy." Pages 9–47 in *Imagination, Ideology, and Inspiration: Walter Brueggemann and Biblical Studies*. Edited by Jonathan Kaplan and Robert Williamson Jr. Hebrew Bible Monographs. Sheffield: Sheffield Academic, 2015.

——. "Pharaoh." Pages 631–36 in *Dictionary of the Old Testament: Pentateuch*. Edited by T. Desmond Alexander and David W. Baker. Downers Grove, IL: InterVarsity, 2003.

——. "Projecting on Joshua: You Can't Worship Both God and Glock." Pages 13–38 in *God and Guns: The Bible against American Gun Culture*. Edited by Christopher B. Hays and C. L. Crouch. Louisville: Westminster John Knox, 2021.

———. "Sanctified and Commercially Successful Curses: On Gangsta Rap and the Canonization of the Imprecatory Psalms." *ThTo* 69 (2013): 403–17.

———. "To See/Not See God: A Biblical-Theological Cutting on the Knowability of God." *Koinonia* 7 (1995): 157–80.

———. *The Visible Word: Essays in Iconography, the Hebrew Bible, and the History of Israelite Religion*. FAT 1. Tübingen: Mohr Siebeck, in press.

———. "*wĕnil'ā(h)*, 'O Victorious One,' in Ps 68,10." *UF* 34 (2002): 785–98.

———. "What Is Cush Doing in Amos 9:7? The Poetics of Exodus in the Plural." *VT* 63 (2013): 99–123.

———. *What Is Stronger Than a Lion? Leonine Image and Metaphor in the Hebrew Bible and the Ancient Near East*. OBO 212. Fribourg: Academic, 2005.

———. "Whence Leonine Yahweh? Iconography and the History of Israelite Religion." Pages 51–85 in *Images and Prophecy in the Ancient Eastern Mediterranean*. Edited by Martti Nissinen and Charles A. Carter. FRLANT 233. Göttingen: Vandenhoeck & Ruprecht, 2009.

———. "Who's Afraid of the Old Testament? Tough Texts for Rough Times." Pages 539–55 in *The Oxford Handbook of the Bible in Orthodox Christianity*. Edited by Eugen J. Pentiuc. Oxford: Oxford University Press, 2022.

———. "'With a Strong Hand and an Outstretched Arm': On the Meaning(s) of the Exodus Tradition(s)." Pages 103–16 in de Hulster, Strawn, and Bonfiglio, *Iconographic Exegesis of the Hebrew Bible/Old Testament*.

———. "Yahweh's Outstretched Arm Revisited Iconographically." Pages 163–211 in *Iconography and Biblical Studies: Proceedings of the Iconography Sessions at the Joint EABS/SBL Conference, 22–26 July 2007, Vienna, Austria*. Edited by Izaak J. de Hulster and Rüdiger Schmitt. AOAT 361. Münster: Ugarit-Verlag, 2009.

———. "YHWH, Chemosh, and the Rule of Faith." Pages 138–58 in *Divine Doppelgängers: YHWH's Ancient Look-alikes*. Edited by Collin Cornell. University Park: Eisenbrauns/Penn State University Press, 2020.

Strawn, Brent A., and Nancy R. Bowen, eds. *A God So Near: Essays on Old Testament Theology in Honor of Patrick D. Miller*. Winona Lake, IN: Eisenbrauns, 2003.

Strecker, Georg. *History of New Testament Literature*. Harrisburg: Trinity Press International, 1997.

———. *The Johannine Letters: A Commentary on 1, 2, and 3 John*. Hermeneia. Minneapolis: Fortress, 1996.

Strong, John T. "Shattering the Image of God: A Response to Theodore Hiebert's Interpretation of the Story of the Tower of Babel." *JBL* 127 (2008): 625–34.

Struble, Eudora, and Virginia Rimmer Herrmann. "An Eternal Feast at Sam'al: The New Iron Age Mortuary Stele from Zincirli in Context." *BASOR* 356 (2009): 15–49.

Studer, B. "Docetism." Page 1:244 in *Encyclopedia of the Early Church*. Edited by A. Di Berardino. 2 vols. New York: Oxford University Press, 1992.

Sweeney, Marvin A. *I & II Kings: A Commentary*. OTL. Louisville: Westminster John Knox, 2007.

Sylva, Dennis. *Psalms and the Transformation of Stress: Poetic-Communal Interpretation and the Family*. Louvain Theological and Pastoral Monographs 16. Louvain: Peeters and Grand Rapids: Eerdmans, 1994.

Tal, Abraham. בראשית Genesis. *BHQ* 1. Stuttgart: Deutsche Bibelgesellschaft, 2015.

Talbert, Charles. *What Is a Gospel? The Genre of the Canonical Gospels*. Philadelphia: Fortress, 1977.

Talmon, Shemaryahu. "The Textual Study of the Bible—A New Outlook." Pages 321–400 in *Qumran and the History of the Biblical Text*. Edited by Frank Moore Cross and Shemaryahu Talmon. Cambridge: Harvard University Press, 1975.

Tannen, Deborah. "Repetition in Conversation as Spontaneous Formulaicity." *Text* 7 (1987): 215–43.

———. "Repetition in Conversation: Toward a Poetics of Talk." *Language* 63 (1987): 574–605.

Tasker, David R. *Ancient Near Eastern Literature and the Hebrew Scriptures about the Fatherhood of God*. StBibLit 69. New York: Peter Lang, 2004.

Thompson, John L. *Reading the Bible with the Dead: What You Can Learn from the History of Exegesis That You Can't Learn from Exegesis Alone*. Grand Rapids: Eerdmans, 2007.

Thompson, Marianne Meye. "Children in the Gospel of John." Pages 195–214 in Bunge, Fretheim, and Gaventa, *The Child in the Bible*.

———. *The Promise of the Father: Jesus and God in the New Testament*. Louisville: Westminster John Knox, 2000.

Thompson, Trevor. "Punishment and Restitution." Pages 2:183–93 in *The Oxford Encyclopedia of the Bible and Law*. Edited by Brent A. Strawn et al. 2 vols. Oxford: Oxford University Press, 2015.

Tigay, Jeffrey H. *Deuteronomy*. JPS Torah Commentary. Philadelphia: Jewish Publication Society, 1996.

———. "'He Begot a Son in His Likeness after His Image' (Genesis 5:3)." Pages 139–47 in Cogan, Eichler, and Tigay, *Tehillah le-Moshe*.

———. "The Image of God and the Flood: Some New Developments." Pages 169–82 in ללמד וללמד: *Studies in Jewish Education and Judaica in Honor of Louis Newman*. Edited by Alexander M. Shapiro and Burton I. Cohen. New York: Ktav, 1984.

———. *You Shall Have No Other Gods: Israelite Religion in the Light of Hebrew Inscriptions*. HSS 31. Atlanta: Scholars Press, 1986.

Tillich, Paul. *The Eternal Now*. New York: Scribner's, 1963.

Tolkien, J. R. R. *The Hobbit or There and Back Again*. Boston: Houghton Mifflin, 1966.

———. *The Lord of the Rings*. Boston: Houghton Mifflin, 2004.

———. *Morgoth's Ring: The Later Silmarillion*, Part One: *The Legends of Aman*. Edited by Christopher Tolkien. The History of Middle-earth 10. Boston: Houghton Mifflin Harcourt, 1993.

———. *The Nature of Middle-earth: Late Writings on the Lands, Inhabitants, and Metaphysics of Middle-earth*. Edited by Carl F. Hostetter. Boston: Houghton Mifflin Harcourt, 2021.

———. "On Fairy-Stories." Pages 108–61 in *The Monsters and the Critics and Other Essays*. Edited by Christopher Tolkien. London: HarperCollinsPublishers, 2006.

———. *The Peoples of Middle-earth*. Edited by Christopher Tolkien. The History of Middle-Earth 12. Boston: Houghton Mifflin, 1996.

———. *The Silmarillion*. Edited by Christopher Tolkien. 2nd ed. Boston: Houghton Mifflin, 2001.

Tomlin, Russell S. "Repetition in Second Language Acquisition." Pages 1:172–94 in Johnstone, *Repetition in Discourse*.

Toorn, Karel van der. "The Ancient Near Eastern Literary Dialogue as a Vehicle of Critical Reflection." Pages 59–75 in *Dispute Poems and Dialogues in the Ancient and Mediaeval Near East*. Edited by G. J. Reinink and H. L. J. Vanstiphout. OLA 42. Leuven: Peeters, 1991.

———. *Family Religion in Babylonia, Syria and Israel: Continuity and Change in the Forms of Religious Life*. SHCANE 7. Leiden: Brill, 1996.

———. *From Her Cradle to Her Grave: The Role of Religion in the Life of the Israelite and Babylonian Woman*. Translated by Sara J. Denning-Bolle. BibSem 23. Sheffield: JSOT, 1994.

———. "Nine Months among the Peasants in the Palestinian Highlands: An Anthropological Perspective on Local Religion in the Early Iron Age." Pages 393–410 in Dever and Gitin, *Symbiosis, Symbolism, and the Power of the Past*.

———. *Scribal Culture and the Making of the Hebrew Bible*. Cambridge: Harvard University Press, 2007.

———. "Scribes and Scribalism." Pages 2:278–85 in *The Oxford Encyclopedia of the Bible and Law*. 2 vols. Edited by Brent A. Strawn. Oxford: Oxford University Press, 2015.

———. *Sin and Sanction in Israel and Mesopotamia: A Comparative Study*. SSN 22. Assen/Maastricht: Van Gorcum, 1985.

———. "Sources in Heaven: Revelation as a Scholarly Construct in Second Temple

Judaism." Pages 265–77 in *Kein Land für sich allein: Studien zum Kulturkontakt in Kanaan, Israel/Palästina und Ebirnâri für Manfred Weippert zum 65. Geburtstag.* Edited by U. Hübner and E. A. Knauf. OBO 186. Freiburg: Universitätsverlag, 2002.

Tov, Emanuel. "*Deut.* 12 and *11QTemple* LII–LIII: A Contrastive Analysis." *RevQ* 15 (1991): 169–73.

———. *Textual Criticism of the Hebrew Bible.* 3rd ed. Minneapolis: Fortress, 2012.

Tracy, David. "Traditions of Spiritual Practice and the Practice of Theology." *ThTo* 55 (1998): 235–41.

Trible, Phyllis. *God and the Rhetoric of Sexuality.* OBT. Philadelphia: Fortress, 1978.

Troutner, Timothy. "Bring Back the Imprecatory Psalms." *Church Life Journal.* August 11, 2021. https://churchlifejournal.nd.edu/articles/a-church-in-crisis-needs-the-imprecatory-psalms/.

Turkle, S. *Reclaiming Conversation: The Power of Talk in a Digital Age.* New York: Penguin, 2015.

Urban, Greg. "Repetition and Cultural Replication: Three Examples from Shokleng." Pages 2:145–61 in Johnstone, *Repetition in Discourse.*

Urbano López de Meneses, Pedro. *Theosis: La Doctrina de la Divinización en las Tradiciones Cristianas: Fundamentos para una Teología Ecuménica de la Gracia.* Pamplona: Ediciones Universidad de Navarra, 2001.

Van De Mieroop, Marc. *A History of the Ancient Near East, ca. 3000–323 BC.* 3rd ed. Malden, MA: Wiley Blackwell, 2016.

VanGemeren, Willem A. "'*Abbā*' in the Old Testament?" *JETS* 31 (1988): 385–98.

Vanhoozer, Kevin J., et al., eds., *Dictionary for Theological Interpretation of the Bible.* Grand Rapids: Baker Academic, 2005.

Van Seters, John. *The Edited Bible: The Curious History of the "Editor" in Biblical Criticism.* Winona Lake, IN: Eisenbrauns, 2006.

Vaux, Roland de. *Ancient Israel: Its Life and Institutions.* New York: McGraw-Hill, 1961.

Vendler, Helen. *Poets Thinking: Pope, Whitman, Dickinson, Yeats.* Cambridge: Harvard University Press, 2004.

Vines, Michael E. *The Problem of Markan Genre: The Gospel of Mark and the Jewish Novel.* Atlanta: Society of Biblical Literature, 2002.

Vink, Renée. "'Jewish' Dwarves: Tolkien and Anti-Semitic Stereotyping." *Tolkien Studies* 10 (2013): 123–45.

Vischer, Wilhelm. *The Witness of the Old Testament to Christ.* Translated by A. B. Crabtree. London: Lutterworth, 1949.

Vita, Juan-Pablo. "The Society of Ugarit." Pages 455–98 in *Handbook of Ugaritic Studies.* Edited by Wilfred G. E. Watson and Nicolas Wyatt. HdO 1.39. Leiden: Brill, 1999.

Volf, Miroslav. *After Our Likeness: The Church as the Image of the Trinity.* Sacra Doctrina. Grand Rapids: Eerdmans, 1998.

———. *Exclusion and Embrace: A Theological Exploration of Identity, Otherness, and Reconciliation.* Rev. ed. Nashville: Abingdon, 2019.

Vorster, Willem S. "Gospel Genre." *ABD* 2:1077.

Votaw, C. W. *The Gospels and Contemporary Biographies in the Greco-Roman World.* Philadelphia: Fortress, 1970.

Wagner, Andreas. *God's Body: The Anthropomorphic God in the Old Testament.* Translated by Marion Salzmann. London: T&T Clark, 2019.

Wagner, J. Ross. *Heralds of the Good News: Isaiah and Paul "In Concert" in the Letter to the Romans.* NTSup 101. Leiden: Brill, 2002.

Wainwright, Geoffrey. *Doxology: A Systematic Theology.* New York: Oxford University Press, 1980.

Waite, Linda J., and William J. Doherty, "Marriage and Responsible Fatherhood: The Social Science Case and Thoughts about a Theological Case." Pages 143–67 in *Family Transformed: Religion, Values, and Society in American Life.* Edited by Steven M. Tipton and John Witte Jr. Washington, DC: Georgetown University Press, 2005.

Walton, John H., and J. Harvey Walton. *The Lost World of the Israelite Conquest: Covenant, Retribution, and the Fate of the Canaanites.* Downers Grove, IL: IVP Academic, 2017.

Warrior, Robert Allen. "Canaanites, Cowboys, and Indians: Deliverance, Conquest, and Liberation Theology Today." *Christianity and Crisis* 49, no. 12 (September 11, 1989): 261–65. PDF available at: https://www.rmselca.org/sites/rmselca.org/files/media/canaanites_cowboys_and_indians.pdf. Pages 21–26.

Watson, Francis. "The Old Testament as Christian Scripture: A Response to Professor Seitz." *SJT* 52 (1999): 227–32.

———. *Text and Truth: Redefining Biblical Theology.* Grand Rapids: Eerdmans, 1997.

Watson, Wilfred G. E. *Classical Hebrew Poetry: A Guide to Its Techniques.* 2nd ed. JSOTSup 26. Sheffield: Sheffield Academic, 2001.

Watts, James W. *Psalm and Story: Inset Hymns in Hebrew Narrative.* JSOTSup 139. Sheffield: JSOT Press, 1992.

———. *Reading Law: The Rhetorical Shaping of the Pentateuch.* BibSem 5. Sheffield: Sheffield Academic Press, 1999.

Way, David V. *The Lordship of Christ: Ernst Käsemann's Interpretation of Paul's Theology.* New York: Oxford University Press, 1991.

Weems, Renita J. *Battered Love: Marriage, Sex, and Violence in the Hebrew Prophets.* OBT. Minneapolis: Fortress, 1995.

Weil, Simone. "Reflections on the Right Use of School Studies with a View to the Love of God." Pages 105–16 in *Waiting for God.* Translated by Emma Craufurd. New York: Harper & Row, 1951.

Weinfeld, Moshe. *Deuteronomy 1–11.* AB 5. New York: Doubleday, 1991.

———. *Deuteronomy and the Deuteronomic School*. Winona Lake, IN: Eisenbrauns, 1992.

———. *Social Justice in Ancient Israel and in the Ancient Near East*. Minneapolis: Fortress, 1995.

Weitzman, Steven. *Song and Story in Biblical Narrative: The History of a Literary Convention in Ancient Israel*. Bloomington: Indiana University Press, 1997.

Welker, Michael. *God the Spirit*. Minneapolis: Fortress, 1994.

Wendland, Ernest R. *Lovely, Lively Lyrics: Selected Studies in Biblical Hebrew Verse*. Dallas: SIL International, 2013.

Wenham, Gordon J. *Genesis 1–15*. WBC 1. Waco, TX: Word, 1987.

Wesley, John. "Free Grace." *The Works of John Wesley*. London: Wesleyan Conference Office, 1872.

———. *The Works of John Wesley*, Volume 1: *Sermons 1: 1–33*. Edited by Albert C. Outler. Nashville: Abingdon, 1984.

Wesselschmidt, Quentin F. *Psalms 51–150*. ACCSOT 8. Downers Grove, IL: InterVarsity, 2007.

Westermann, Claus. *Genesis 1–11: A Continental Commentary*. Translated by John J. Scullion. Minneapolis: Fortress, 1994.

———. *Genesis 37–50: A Continental Commentary*. Translated by John J. Scullion. Minneapolis: Fortress, 2002.

Wevers, John William. *Text History of the Greek Deuteronomy*. MSU 13. Göttingen: Vandenhoeck and Ruprecht, 1978.

White, Hayden. *The Content of the Form: Narrative Discourse and Historical Representation*. Baltimore: Johns Hopkins University Press, 1987.

Whitehead, Alfred North. *Religion in the Making*. New York: World, 1969.

Wilcoxen, Jay A. "Some Anthropocentric Aspects of Israel's Sacred History." *JR* 48 (1968): 333–50.

Wilken, Robert Louis. *The Spirit of Early Christian Thought*. New Haven: Yale University Press, 2003.

Williams, Ronald J., and John C. Beckman, *Williams' Hebrew Syntax*. 3rd ed. Toronto: University of Toronto Press, 2007.

Willitts, Joel. *Matthew's Messianic Shepherd-King: In Search of "the Lost Sheep of the House of Israel."* BZNW 147. Berlin: de Gruyter, 2007.

Wills, Lawrence M. *The Quest of the Historical Gospel: Mark, John, and the Origins of the Gospel Genre*. New York: Routledge, 1997.

Wilson, Edmund. "Oo, Those Awful Orcs!" *The Nation* 182 (April 14, 1956): 15.

Wilson, J. V. Kinnier. *The Legend of Etana: A New Edition*. Warminster: Aris & Phillips and Chicago: Bolchazy-Carducci, 1985.

Wink, Walter. *Engaging the Powers*. Minneapolis: Fortress, 1992.

Winnicott, D. W. *The Maturational Processes and the Facilitating Environment: Studies in the Theory of Emotional Development*. Madison, CT: International Universities, 1965.

———. "The Use of an Object and Relating through Identifications." Pages 115–27 in *Playing and Reality*. London: Routledge, 2005.

Winter, Irene J. *On Art in the Ancient Near East*. CHANE 34.1–2. 2 vols. Leiden: Brill, 2010.

Wolf, Maryanne. *Reader, Come Home: The Reading Brain in a Digital World*. New York: Harper, 2018.

Wolff, Hans Walter. *Anthropology of the Old Testament*. Translated by Margaret Kohl. Mifflintown, PA: Sigler, 1996.

Wolterstorff, Nicholas. "Comments on 'What about the Canaanites?'" Pages 283–88 in Bergmann, Murray, and Rea, *Divine Evil?*

———. "Reading Joshua." Pages 236–56 in Bergmann, Murray, and Rea, *Divine Evil?*

———. "Reply to Antony." Pages 263–64 in Bergmann, Murray, and Rea, *Divine Evil?*

Wood, Ralph C. *The Gospel according to Tolkien: Visions of the Kingdom in Middle-earth*. Louisville: Westminster John Knox, 2003.

Wray Beal, Lissa M. *1 & 2 Kings*. Apollos Old Testament Commentary 9. Downers Grove, IL: InterVarsity, 2014.

Wright, David P. *Ritual in Narrative: The Dynamics of Feasting, Mourning, and Retaliation Rites in the Ugaritic Tale of Aqhat*. Winona Lake, IN: Eisenbrauns, 2001.

———. "Syro-Canaanite Religions." Pages 129–50 in *The Cambridge History of Religions in the Ancient World*. Vol. 1: *From the Bronze Age to the Hellenistic Age*. Edited by Michele Renee Salzman and Marvin A. Sweeney. Cambridge: Cambridge University Press, 2013.

Wright, John W. "Toward a Holiness Hermeneutic: The Old Testament against Israelite Religion." *Wesleyan Theological Journal* 30 (1995): 68–90.

Wright, N. T. *The New Testament and the People of God*. Christian Origins and the Question of God 1. Minneapolis: Fortress, 1992.

Würthwein, Ernst. *The Text of the Old Testament: An Introduction to the Biblia Hebraica*. 3rd ed. Revised and expanded by Alexander Achilles Fischer. Grand Rapids: Eerdmans, 2014.

Wyschogrod, Michael. "The Impact of Dialogue with Christianity on the My Self-Understanding as a Jew." Pages 725–36 in *Die Hebräische Bibel und ihr zweifache Nachgeschichte: Festschrift für Rolf Rendtorff zum 65. Geburtstag*. Edited by Erhard Blum, Christian Macholz, and Ekkehard W. Stegemann. Neukirchen-Vluyn: Neukirchener, 1990.

Yancey, Philip. *The Bible Jesus Read*. Grand Rapids: Zondervan, 1999.

Yatt, John. "Wraiths and Race." *Guardian*. December 2, 2002. https://www.theguardian.com/books/2002/dec/02/jrrtolkien.lordoftherings.

Young, Helen. *Race and Popular Fantasy Literature: Habits of Whiteness*. New York and London: Routledge, 2016.

Younger, K. Lawson, Jr. *Ancient Conquest Accounts: A Study in Ancient Near Eastern and Biblical History Writing*. JSOTSup 98. Sheffield: JSOT Press, 1990.

Zadok, Ran. *The Pre-Hellenistic Israelite Anthroponymy and Prosopography*. OLA 28. Leuven: Peeters, 1988.

Zaleski, Philip, and Carol Zaleski. *The Fellowship: The Literary Lives of the Inklings*. New York: Farrar, Straus and Giroux, 2015.

Zenger, Erich. *A God of Vengeance? Understanding the Psalms of Divine Wrath*. Louisville: Westminster John Knox, 1996.

Zevit, Ziony. "False Dichotomies in Descriptions of Israelite Religion: A Problem, Its Origin, and a Proposed Solution." Pages 223–35 in Dever and Gitin, *Symbiosis, Symbolism, and the Power of the Past*.

——. *The Religions of Ancient Israel: A Synthesis of Parallactic Approaches*. London: Continuum, 2001.

Zilboorg, Gregory. Introduction to *Beyond the Pleasure Principle*, by Sigmund Freud. Translated and edited by James Stachey. New York: Norton, 1961.

Index of Authors

Index of Subjects

Index of Scripture and Other Ancient Sources